A
HISTORY OF THE SIKHS

A HISTORY OF THE SIKHS

FROM

THE ORIGIN OF THE NATION

TO

THE BATTLES OF THE SUTLEJ

BY

JOSEPH DAVEY CUNNINGHAM

EDITED BY

H. L. O. GARRETT, M. A., I. E. S.

GYAN

Published by

Gyan Publishing House
5, Ansari Road
Daryaganj, New Delhi-110002
Phone: 011-47034999, 9811692060
E-mail: books@gyanbooks.com

Distribution Network
gyanbooks.com
India, USA, Canada, UK, Australia, France

ISBN: 978-81-212-8290-1 (PB)
First Published, 1849

2nd Impression 2023

Printed at: Gyan Press, Delhi.

A HISTORY OF THE SIKHS
Author: JOSEPH DAVEY CUNNINGHAM

A HISTORY OF THE SIKHS

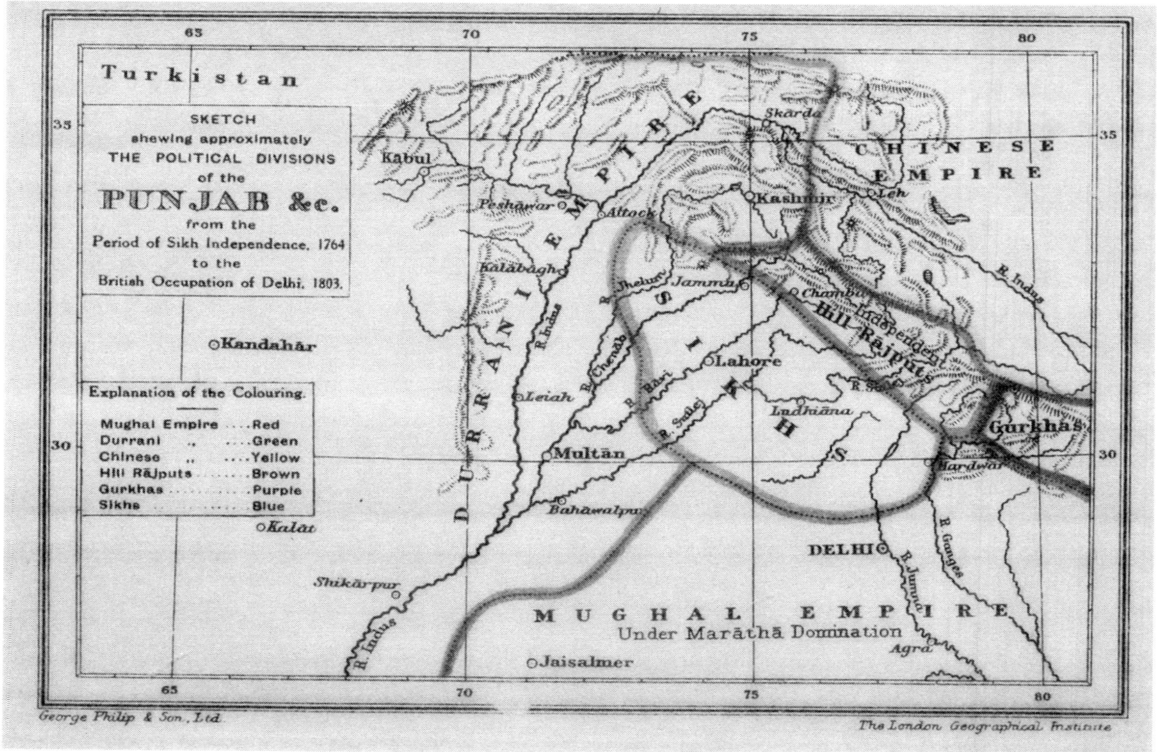
Turkistan
SKETCH
shewing approximately
THE POLITICAL DIVISIONS
of the
PUNJAB &c.
from the
Period of Sikh Independence, 1764
to the
British Occupation of Delhi, 1803.
Explanation of the Colouring.
Mughal Empire ....Red
Durrani ,, ...Green
Chinese ,, ...Yellow
Hill Rājputs ....Brown
Gurkhas ....Purple
Sikhs ....Blue
Kabul
Peshāwar
Attock
Kālābāgh
DURRANI EMPIRE
Kandahār
Kalāt
Shikārpur
Leiah
Multān
Bahāwalpur
Jaisalmer
R. Indus
R. Jhelum
R. Chenāb
R. Rāvi
R. Satlej
Jammu
Lahore
Ludhiāna
SIKHS
Skardo
Kashmir
Leh
CHINESE EMPIRE
Chamba
Independent Hill Rājputs
Gurkhas
Hardwār
DELHI
R. Jumna
R. Ganges
Agra
MUGHAL EMPIRE
Under Marāthā Domination
George Philip & Son, Ltd.
The London Geographical Institute

A HISTORY OF THE SIKHS

FROM

THE ORIGIN OF THE NATION

TO

THE BATTLES OF THE SUTLEJ

BY

JOSEPH DAVEY CUNNINGHAM

LIEUTENANT OF ENGINEERS, AND CAPTAIN IN THE ARMY OF INDIA

EDITED BY

H. L. O. GARRETT, M.A., I.E.S.

PROFESSOR OF HISTORY, GOVERNMENT COLLEGE, LAHORE

NEW AND REVISED EDITION
WITH TWO MAPS

HUMPHREY MILFORD
OXFORD UNIVERSITY PRESS
LONDON EDINBURGH GLASGOW NEW YORK
TORONTO MELBOURNE CAPE TOWN BOMBAY
1918

EDITOR'S NOTE

The author's original spelling of Indian names is archaic and almost intolerable to the modern reader. I have therefore adopted the modern accepted spelling, and for the arduous work of transliteration I am indebted to L. Tej Ram, M.A., Professor of Mathematics at the Randhīr College, Kapūrthala.

The author's text and notes have remained unaltered, but where necessary I have added additional notes, which will be found in brackets.

By permission of the Government of the Punjab, I am enabled to reproduce some of the results obtained by the recent examination of the manuscript records of the Sikh days, which have long been lying in the archives of the Civil Secretariat. In this connexion I have been greatly assisted by L. Sita Ram Kohly, M.A., the research student in charge of the work. Apart from this, he has been of great help in preparing the entire volume and, in particular, in the drawing up of the Bibliography. Finally, I tender my very grateful thanks to the Hon. Mr. J. P. Thompson, I.C.S., Chief Secretary to the Government of the Punjab, who has kindly looked through the manuscript and to whom I am indebted for many valuable hints and suggestions.

H. L. O. GARRETT.

LAHORE,
November 1915.

INTRODUCTORY

THE original edition of Capt. Cunningham's book appeared in 1849. A second edition was finished in 1851, but, as is explained in the second preface by his brother, this edition did not make its appearance till 1853, after the death of the author. The second edition did not differ materially from the first beyond certain re-arrangements and certain additions to the notes, with the exception of Chapter IX. This chapter, which deals with the events leading up to, and the progress and result of, the first Sikh War, was considerably modified in the second edition. Even in this form the chapter contains many statements of an injudicious nature. Indeed, as the result of certain strictures upon the policy of the Government of India in dealing with Gulāb Singh of Jammu, the author was dismissed from his employment in the Political Department by the Honourable East India Company and sent back to regimental duty. These strictures, together with a note upon the subsequent punishment meted out to the author, will be found in their proper place in Chapter IX.

To turn to the volume as a whole. The author, as he tells us in his own prefatory note, spent eight years of his service (from 1838 to 1846) in close contact with the Sikhs, and that too during a very important period of their history. His experiences began with the interview between Lord Auckland and Ranjīt Singh in 1838 and lasted down to the close of the first Sikh War, when he became resident in Bhopāl. The result of his eight years' residence was to give him a great insight into the history of the Sikhs and to inspire in him a partiality which is only too clearly visible in his handling of the events leading up to the outbreak of hostilities with the British. The whole book bears evidence of most meticulous care, and the voluminous footnotes show the breadth and variety of the author's study.

Chapter I deals with the country and its people. There

is a detailed description of the industries of the Punjab and its dependencies, much of which has been rendered archaic by the natural march of events. The ethnological part of this chapter has been carefully done, though this again is in need of supplementation in the light of modern research. It seems hardly necessary to guide the modern reader in this direction when so many excellent gazetteers are now available, but for a very lucid summary of the Hill States of the Punjab and their peoples, a subject in which the author is a little difficult to follow, reference may well be made to an article (in vol. iii of *The Journal of the Punjab Historical Society*) by Messrs. Hutchison and Vogel, which is admirably explicit and is supplemented by a short bibliography on the subject.

Chapter II is concerned with the old religions of India. Here again knowledge has moved forward and much of the author's information is archaic. His conception of the lingam and its significance, for example, is not in consonance with modern theory. Unfortunately, too, he lived before the days when the labours of the Archaeological Department had thrown a flood of light upon the teaching of Buddha and the prevalence of his religion in India. Indeed, his only reference to the British in this connexion is an accusation of iconoclasm which reads strangely to a modern generation. His account of 'modern reforms' naturally stops at an early point, and he seems to have been led into the somewhat erroneous conclusion that the whole Indian world—Hindu and Muhammadan—at the time that he wrote, was moving in the direction of a new revelation. As I have pointed out in a supplementary note, the tendency is rather, in the case of both creeds, towards a reversion to ancient purity and the removal of accretions and corruptions. The chapter concludes with an account of Gurū Nānak and his teaching.

Chapter III is concerned with the lives and teaching of the Gurūs. The gradual spread of the Sikh religion in the Punjab led to the establishment of a sort of *imperium in imperio*. This development caused the Mughal emperors to follow a line of policy much like that adopted by the Roman emperors when confronted by the rising organization of the Christian Church. This policy—one of repression and persecution—caused a profound modification of the whole Sikh system. The simple altruism of the early days was laid aside and, under Gobind Singh, the tenth and last Gurū, the Sikhs became a definite fighting force. At first the armies of the Khālsa met with little success, and the death of Gobind Singh in 1708, followed by that of Banda, his successor in the command of the armies, in 1716, seemed to sound the knell of Sikh hopes and ambitions. But the fervour of their belief rose triumphant over persecution, and the Sikhs found their opportunity in the years of disorder which followed the death of the Emperor Bahādur Shāh in 1712.

Chapter IV relates the gradual establishment of Sikh independence down to 1764. Northern India was a wild welter of confusion. The Mughal Empire was falling rapidly to pieces under the repeated blows of invaders from north and south. First Nādir Shāh and his Persian hosts, and then the Afghān Ahmad Shāh Durrāni, swept down upon the imperial capital. Like Rome of old, Delhi felt again and again the hand of the spoiler, and its glories became a thing of the past. The advent of the Marāthās upon the scene seemed at first the prelude to the establishment of Hindu supremacy in the north of India. But the battle of Pānīpat (1761) proved fatal to their ambitions and left the stage open for the development of a new power in the Punjab.

Amid all this confusion the Sikhs gradually achieved their independence. At first they were mere bands of plunderers, but gradually these bands became united into a formidable fighting force. In 1748 the army of the Khālsa became a recognized organization under Jassa Singh, and though it frequently suffered defeat, it never lost its definite character after that date. The Sikhs sustained their greatest disaster at the hands of the Afghāns at Ludhiāna in 1762, but the waves of Afghān invasion had spent their strength. In 1763, at Sirhind, the Sikhs avenged their defeat of the previous year and permanently occupied the province of Sirhind. In the following year, which witnessed the last Afghān invasion, they became masters of Lahore, and in the same year, at a meeting at Amritsar, organized themselves into a ruling political system, described by the author as a 'theocratic confederate feudalism'. The condition of the Punjab during these years of bloodshed and disorder was miserable in the extreme. To find any parallel in European history one would have to go back to the days of King Stephen in England or to some of the worst episodes of the Thirty Years' War. Wāris Shāh, the author of the story of *Hīr and Rānjhā*, who flourished during this period, gives, in the epilogue of this poem, a vivid account of the state of the country :

Fools and sinners give counsel to the world,
The words of the wise are set at naught.
No man tells the truth or cares for justice,
Telling what is untrue has become the practice in the world.

With violence men commit flagrant iniquity,
In the hands of tyrants there is a sharp sword.
There is no Governor, Ruler, or Emperor.
The country and all the people in it have been made desolate.

Great confusion has fallen on the country,
There is a sword in every man's hand.
The purdah of shame and modesty has been lifted
And all the world goes naked in the open bazaar.

Thieves have become leaders of men.
Harlots have become mistresses of the household.
The company of devils has multiplied exceedingly.
The state of the noble is pitiable.
Men of menial birth flourish and the peasants are in great prosperity.

The Jāts have become masters of our country,
Everywhere there is a new Government.[1]

The Sikhs had become a nation and, in theory, a united nation, but in actual fact such was far from being the case. The new State was composed of a number—twelve is the usually recognized total—of leagues or 'Misals'. Instead of uniting and forming a solid State, these 'Misals' were almost constantly engaged in civil war, grouping and regrouping in the struggle for pre-eminence. It needed a strong hand to check these internecine disputes, and, fortunately for the

[1] [I am indebted to Mr. C. F. Usborne, C.S., for the above translation.]

Punjab, Ranjīt Singh appeared on the scene. The career of the one-eyed Lion of the Punjab is fully described in the text and needs but little reference at this point. The Mahārājā's real career commences with his acquisition of Lahore in 1799. From that date he steadily extended his sway over the whole Punjab. Many books have been written on the career of this remarkable man and upon the system of comparatively orderly government which he introduced. There exist in the Secretariat at Lahore a number of manuscript records (accounts, muster rolls, pay sheets, &c.) of his government. These are now under examination, and it is hoped that a great deal of additional light will be thrown upon his system of government as a result. The papers that have been examined up to the present time (1915) show how actively Ranjīt Singh interested himself in the details of his administration. As regards his character, he was not altogether without faults. Temperance and chastity were not his conspicuous virtues. But with all his shortcomings, he was a strong and able ruler admirably suited to the conditions of the time. The Mahārājā's territorial expansion brought him into contact with the Cis-Sutlej States, which were under English protection, and so into contact with the English. The result of this was the Treaty of 1809, which Ranjīt Singh loyally observed down to his death in 1839, although at times he showed symptoms of irritation at the rising power of the English.

The death of Ranjīt Singh in 1839 was the signal for the outbreak of a series of palace revolutions, in which the army of the Khālsa played a part hardly dissimilar from that of the Praetorian Guards at their very worst. This period of the story is fully dealt with by the author in Chapter VIII. The disorder culminated in the crossing of the Sutlej by the Sikh forces and the consequent outbreak of the first Sikh War. From this point of the story the partiality of the author causes many of his statements to be viewed with suspicion. In his eyes the war represents a national tide of self-preservation rising against the ever-encroaching power of England. Such was far from being the case, and very different motives actuated the corrupt administration of Lahore. Terrified of the power of the army, that administration flung its legions across the Sutlej in the hope that they would be either annihilated or so seriously crippled as to cease to be a danger in the future. At the same time the outbreak of hostilities would divert attention from the shortcomings of the central government—a political manœuvre strongly reminiscent of some of the actions of Napoleon III. The author gives a somewhat turgid description of the battles of the war—indeed, the language in the account of the battle of Sobraon reminds one of the story of the battle in the poems of Mr. Robert Montgomery—and he concludes his narrative by some general remarks upon English policy in India. From the latter I have removed some passages which are not only injudicious but which have been stultified by the march of events.

Beyond a bare reference the author does not touch on the second Sikh War and the resultant annexation at all ; but, as he was transferred to Bhopāl at the conclusion of the first war, he probably lost touch with Punjab politics.

It is not possible in a short introduction of this nature to follow the history of the Sikhs in detail since the Punjab came under British control. That the Sikhs settled down peacefully and loyally under the new régime is sufficiently borne out by the records of the Mutiny, when the newly raised Sikh regiments—many of them composed of the disbanded regiments of the Khālsa army—did excellent service. The Sikhs have displayed their warlike aptitude in other fields since 1857 and are to be found to-day taking their share in the great European War.

In 1911 the Sikh population of the Punjab numbered a little over two millions out of a total population of some twenty-three and a half millions. As regards modern conversions to Sikhism and the relation of that religion to Hinduism, Mr. Candler has the following interesting remarks in an article which appeared in *Blackwood's Magazine* in September 1909 : ' The truth is that the Sikhs have only partially rid themselves of caste. They were able to suppress the instinct so long as it endangered their existence, but when they became paramount in the Punjab and the Khālsa was sufficient for its own needs, the old exclusive Brāhmanical spirit returned. The influence of Ranjīt Singh's Court increased this retrogressive tendency, and in spite of the Gurū's teaching it is not always easy for a low-caste Hindu to become a Sikh to-day. Still, it is not always impossible. The acceptance or rejection of a convert is likely to depend on whether the majority in the district Singh Sabhā or Sikh Council is conservative or progressive. The so-called Conservative Party is naturally exclusive, while the so-called Progressive Party are really purists who would revert to the injunctions of Nānak and Gobind. They are ready to receive all converts whom they believe to be genuine, of whatever caste. The Sikhs now number a little over two millions, and in the last ten years the numbers have only risen in proportion to the general increase in the Punjab. The lack of converts is due as much to apathy as to obstacles placed in the way by the priests.'

H. L. O. GARRETT.

ADDENDUM

Page xii, ll. 12-14. The passages referred to, with the exception of a single note (see p. 325), have now been restored, and the original text is given unaltered, as stated in the Editor's Note.

BIOGRAPHICAL NOTE

ON THE CUNNINGHAM FAMILY

Allan Cunningham, the father of the author of this volume, was born in the parish of Keir, Dumfriesshire, in 1784. Although apprenticed to his elder brother, then a stonemason, he soon showed a literary bent. At the age of eighteen he made the acquaintance of Hogg, the Ettrick shepherd, and the acquaintance ripened into a warm friendship. Early in the nineteenth century he commenced his career as an author, and his poems began to appear in various periodicals. When R. H. Cromek, the engraver, was travelling in Scotland in 1809, collecting Scottish songs, he met Cunningham, who showed him some of his work. Upon Cromek's advice Cunningham then went up to London to try his fortune at literature. For some years he worked both as a mason and as a literary man, producing a number of poems in the *Day* and the *Literary Gazette*. In 1814, Chantrey, the sculptor, to whom he had been introduced by Cromek, engaged him as his superintendent of works, and this connexion lasted down to Chantrey's death, in 1841. During this period he produced a quantity of literary work of a varied nature. He had become acquainted with Sir Walter Scott, when the latter was sitting for Chantrey, and in 1820 submitted to him a drama, *Sir Marmaduke Maxwell*. It was considered unsuitable to the stage, but Scott was favourably impressed with the style. In 1825 appeared *The Songs of Scotland, Ancient and Modern*, which contained the well-known sea song, 'A Wet Sheet and a Flowing Sea.' His connexion with Chantrey gave him an intimate knowledge of the artistic world, which he turned to account in his *Lives of the Most Eminent British Painters, Sculptors, and Architects*, which he published from 1829–33. His last important work was an edition of Burns, which appeared in 1834. Late in life he made the acquaintance of Carlyle, who had a warm regard for him. Cunningham died in 1842, leaving five sons and a daughter.

Joseph Davey Cunningham, the eldest son and the author of the present volume, was born in 1812. At an early age he showed such aptitude for mathematics that his father was advised to send him to Cambridge. But as he was keenly desirous of becoming a soldier a cadetship in the East India Company's service was procured for him, through the good offices of Sir Walter Scott. After a brilliant career at Addiscombe he sailed for India in 1834, and was at first employed on the staff of the chief engineer of the Bengal Presidency. In 1837 he was appointed assistant to Colonel (afterwards Sir Claude) Wade, the political agent on the Sikh frontier. For the next eight years he held various appointments under Colonel Wade and his successors, and at the time of the outbreak of the first Sikh War was political agent in the State of Bahāwalpur. Upon the commencement of hostilities he was attached first to the staff of Sir Charles Napier and then to that of Sir Hugh Gough. He was present, as political officer, with the division of Sir Harry Smith at the battles of Buddawal and Alīwāl. At Sobraon he served as an additional aide-de-camp to the Governor-General, Sir Henry Hardinge. His services earned him a brevet and the appointment of political agent to the State of Bhopāl. In 1849 appeared his *History of the Sikhs.* As has been noted elsewhere in this edition, the views taken by the author were anything but pleasing to his superiors. As a punishment, he was removed from his political appointment and sent back to regimental duty. The disgrace undoubtedly hastened his death, and soon after his appointment to the Meerut Division of Public Works he died suddenly at Ambāla, in 1851.

Like Joseph Davey Cunningham, his younger brothers inherited their father's literary abilities. Alexander, the second brother, had a distinguished career in India. He, too, obtained his cadetship through the influence of Sir Walter Scott, and arrived in India in 1833. Lord Auckland appointed him one of his aides-de-camp, and while on the Governor-General's staff he visited Kashmīr, then almost an unknown country. He served with distinction in the

Gwalior campaign of 1843 and acted as executive engineer of Gwalior until the outbreak of the first Sikh War. In this war and also in the second Sikh War he did good service, and then returned to Gwalior. In 1856 he was appointed chief engineer in Burma (after a brief period of service in Multān, where he designed the Vans Agnew and Anderson monument), and remained there till 1858. He was transferred to the North-Western Provinces in 1858, and remained there till his retirement in 1861 with the rank of major-general.

It was at this stage that he commenced his archaeological career. The Government of India decided to appoint an archaeological surveyor, and Cunningham, who during his whole career in India had displayed the greatest activity in this direction, was appointed to the post. This he held (with an interval from 1865 to 1870) down to his final retirement in 1885. His work in this capacity is too well known to need detailed treatment in a note of this nature. He continued his interest in Indian archaeology after his retirement, and the collection of coins in the British Museum bears testimony to his generosity. He died in 1893 as Sir Alexander Cunningham, having been created a K.C.I.E. in 1887.

Peter Cunningham, the third brother, under whose editorship the second edition of this book appeared in 1853, was a well-known antiquary. He held an appointment in the Audit Office, which he obtained through Sir Robert Peel in 1834. His chief work was the *Handbook of London*, which first appeared in 1849 and is still regarded as a standard authority. He also edited a large number of books—the collected letters of Horace Walpole (1857) and the works of Oliver Goldsmith (1854) being well-known examples of his work. He retired from the public service in 1860 and died in 1869.

Francis Cunningham, the youngest brother, also served in India. He joined the Madras army in 1838 and won distinction at the siege of Jalālābād. He retired from the army in 1861, and after his retirement devoted himself to literature, for which he displayed the family aptitude. He published editions of Marlowe (1870), Massinger (1871), and Ben Jonson (1871). His death took place in 1875.

BIBLIOGRAPHY

SECTION A. PRINTED BOOKS

(1) English

Archer, J. H. Laurence. *Commentaries on the Punjab Campaign* (1848–9). London, 1878.

Baird, J. G. A. *Private Letters of the Marquess of Dalhousie.* Blackwood, 1910.

Broadfoot, Major. *Career of Major George Broadfoot, C.B., in Afghanistan and the Punjab.* London, 1888.

Burnes, Sir A. *Travels into Bokhara.* London, 1834.

Burton, Lt.-Col. R. G. *The First and Second Sikh Wars.* Simla, 1911.

Coley, J. *Journal of the Sutlej Campaign* (1845–6). London, 1856.

Cotton, J. J. *Life of General Avitabile.* Calcutta, 1906.

Despatches of Lords Hardinge and Gough and General Sir Harry Smith, &c., relative to the Engagements of Moodkee, Ferozeshah, &c. (2nd edition.) London, 1846. (Olivier, Pall Mall.)

Dunlop, J. *Multan, during and after the Siege.* London, 1849.

Edwardes, Sir H. B. (vol. i), and H. Merivale (vol. ii). *Life of Sir H. Laurence.* London, 1872.

Fane, H. E. *Five Years in India,* 1835–39. (Author was aide-de-camp to Lord Auckland.) London, 1842.

Foster, G. *A Journey from Bengal to England through North India, Kashmir, Afghanistan, and Persia, into Russia* (1783–4). London, 1798.

Gardner, A. *Memoirs of Col. A. Gardner.* London (re-edited), 1898.

Gazetteer of the Punjab. Provincial Series of the *Imperial Gazetteer of India.* Oxford, 1908.

Gough, Sir C., and A. D. Innes. *The Sikhs and the Sikh Wars.* London, 1897.

Gough, Lord. *Despatches of Lord Gough* (Parliamentary Papers, 1846).

Griffin, L. H. *Ranjit Singh* ('Rulers of India' Series). Oxford, 1892.

Hardinge, Lord. *Despatches of Lord Hardinge* (Parliamentary Papers, 1846).

Honigberger, J. M. *Thirty-Five Years in the East.* (The author was court physician at Lahore for some time.) London, 1852.

Huegel, C. von. *Travels in Kashmir and the Country of the Sikhs.* Written in German, translated by T. B. Jervis. London, 1845.

Humbly, W. W. W. *Journal of a Cavalry Officer* (*Sikh Campaign,* 1845–6). London, 1854.

Irvine, W. *The Later Moguls.* *Journal of the Asiatic Society of Bengal,* vols. lxiii (1894), lxv (1896), lxvii (1898).

Jacquemont, V. *Letters from India* (translated). London, 1835.

Kaye, Sir J. W. *Life and Correspondence of Lord Metcalfe.* London, 1854.
Khazan Singh. *History and Philosophy of the Sikh Religion.* Lahore, 1914.
Latif, M. *A History of the Punjab.* Calcutta, 1891.
Laurence, J. *The Sikhs and their Country. Journal of the Asiatic Society of Bengal,* vol. iii.
Laurence, Major W. M. *Some Passages of the Life of an Adventurer in the Punjab.* Delhi, 1842.
Macauliffe, M. A. *The Sikh Religion, its Gurus, Sacred Writings, and Authors.* 6 vols. Oxford, 1909.
Macgregor, W. L. *The History of the Sikhs.* London, 1846.
Malcolm, J. *A Sketch of the Sikhs.* London and Bombay, 1812.
Marshman, J. C. *Memoirs of Sir H. Havelock.* London, 1860.
Masson, C. *Narrative of Various Journeys in Balochistan, Afghanistan, and the Punjab* (1826–38). 3 vols. London, 1842.
Massy, C. F., and Griffin, L. H. *The Chiefs and Families of Note in the Punjab,* 1909. Revised ed., 1907.
Mohana Lāla. *Travels in the Punjab, Afghanistan, Turkistan.* London, 1846.
Moorcroft and Trebeck. *Travels in the HimalayanProvinces* (1819–25), edited by H. H. Wilson. London, 1841.
Osborne, W. G. *Court and Camp of Runjeet Sing.* (Author was military secretary to Lord Auckland.) London, 1840.
Prinsep, H. T. *The Origin of the Sikh Power in the Punjab.* Calcutta, 1834.
Rait, R. S. *Life of Hugh, Viscount Gough.* Constable, London, 1903.
Smyth, G. *History of the Reigning Family of Lahore.* Calcutta, 1847.
Steinbach, Lt.-Col. H. *The Punjab.* (Author was employed in Ranjīt Singh's army for about eight years.) London, 1845.
Thackwell, E. J. *Narrative of the Second Sikh War.* London, 1851.
Thorburn, S. S. *The Punjab in Peace and War.* Blackwood, London, 1904.
Wade, C. *Our Relations with the Punjab.* London, 1823.

(2) Persian

Kanhya Lāl. *Ranjit Namā.* Lahore, 1876.
Khafi Khān. *Muntakhab ul lubāb.* (Translation in *History of India as told by its own Historians.* Elliot and Dowson. Vol. vii. 1877.)
Mōhsin Fāni. *Dabistān.* (Translation by D. Shea and A. Troyer. London, 1843.) (Author was a contemporary of Gurūs Har Gobind and Har Rai, VIth and VIIth Gurūs.)
Sohan Lāl. *Diary of Ranjit Singh or Umdat-ul-Tawarikh.* 1885. The MS. copy of this book in Bankipur Oriental Public Library closes at 1831. The published copy goes down to 1849. (Sohan Lāl was Ranjīt Singh's Court vakil and historian. A very faithful narrative of Ranjīt Singh's life.)

SECTION B. DOCUMENTS, UNPUBLISHED MSS.

1. Sarūp Lāl. *Tarikh-Sikhān.* (MSS. undated.)
2. *State Records.* MSS. Civil Secretariat, Punjab, 1812–49.
   Official documents of Ranjīt Singh's government. Papers of various descriptions. Civil and military departments. Written in the Persian language, and now under examination by a research student.
3. *Records of Ludhiana, Ambala, and Delhi agencies.* MSS. Civil Secretariat, Punjab, 1804–49.
   Dispatches and communications between the Sikh Government and the East India Company and their Agents. Written in English.
4. *In the Library of the India Office.*
   M. Ali ud din. *Ibrat Nama.* M. Khya Bux. *Sher Singh Nama. Tarikh Mulk-i-Hazara.*

ADVERTISEMENT TO THE SECOND EDITION, 1853

THE sheets of this Edition were seen and corrected by their Author, and were ready for publication several months previous to his death, in February, 1851. The reasons—of a painful, though temporary character—for the delay in the appearance of the work will be found in a Memoir already written and to be published hereafter, when regard for the living will no longer interfere with the truth of History.

The author fell a victim to the truth related in this book. He wrote History in advance of his time, and suffered for it; but posterity will, I feel assured, do justice to his memory.

My brother's anxiety to be correct was evinced in the unceasing labour he took to obtain the most minute information. Wherever he has been proved to be wrong—and this has been in very few instances—he has, with ready frankness, admitted and corrected his error. In matters of opinion he made no change—not from obstinacy, but from a firm conviction that he was right.

The new notes to this Edition contain some information of moment, contributed by Lord Gough, Sir Charles Napier, and others, and all received my brother's sanction.

The printed materials for the recent History of India are not of that character on which historians can rely. State Papers, presented to the people by 'both Houses of Parliament', have been altered to suit the temporary views of political warfare, or abridged out of mistaken regard to the tender feelings of survivors.[1] In matters of private life,

[1] The character and career of Alexander Burnes have both been misrepresented in those collections of State Papers which are supposed to furnish the best materials of history, but which are often only one-sided compilations of garbled documents,—counterfeits, which the

some tenderness may be shown to individual sensitiveness, but History, to be of any value, should be written by one superior to the influences of private or personal feelings. What Gibbon calls 'truth, naked, unblushing truth, the first virtue of more serious history', should alone direct the pen of the historian; and truth alone influenced the mind and guided the pen of the Author of this book.

PETER CUNNINGHAM.

KENSINGTON,
18th January, 1853.

ministerial stamp forces into currency, defrauding a present generation, and handing down to posterity a chain of dangerous lies.—KAYE, *Affghanistan*, ii. 13.

AUTHOR'S PREFACE TO THE SECOND EDITION

In this Second Edition the author has made some alterations in the text of the last chapter, where it seemed that his readers had inferred more than was meant; but the sense and spirit of what was originally written have been carefully preserved, notwithstanding the modifications of expression now introduced. Throughout the grammatical imperfections detected on reperusal have been removed; but no other changes have been made in the text of the first eight chapters. Some notes, however, altogether new, have been added, while others have been extended; and such as by their length crowded a series of pages, and from their subject admitted of separate treatment, have been formed into Appendices.

The author's principal object in writing this history has not always been understood, and he therefore thinks it right to say that his main endeavour was to give Sikhism its place in the general history of humanity, by showing its connexion with the different creeds of India, by exhibiting it as a natural and important result of the Muhammadan Conquest, and by impressing upon the people of England the great necessity of attending to the mental changes now in progress amongst their subject millions in the East, who are erroneously thought to be sunk in superstitious apathy, or to be held spell-bound in ignorance by a dark and designing priesthood. A secondary object of the author's was to give some account of the connexion of the English with the Sikhs, and in part with the Afghāns, from the time they began to take a direct interest in the affairs of these races, and to involve them in the web of their policy for opening the navigation of the Indus, and for bringing Turkestān and Khorasan within their commercial influence.

It has also been remarked by some public critics and private friends, that the author leans unduly towards the

Sikhs, and that an officer in the Indian army should appear to say he sees aught unwise or objectionable in the acts of the East India Company and its delegates is at the least strange. The author has, indeed, constantly endeavoured to keep his readers alive to that undercurrent of feeling or principle which moves the Sikh people collectively, and which will usually rise superior to the crimes or follies of individuals. It was the history of *Sikhs*, a new and peculiar nation, which he wished to make known to strangers ; and he saw no reason for continually recurring to the duty or destiny of the English in India, because he was addressing himself to his own countrymen who know the merits and motives of their supremacy in the East, and who can themselves commonly decide whether the particular acts of a viceroy are in accordance with the general policy of his government. The Sikhs, moreover, are so inferior to the English in resources and knowledge that there is no equality of comparison between them.

The glory to England is indeed great of her Eastern Dominion, and she may justly feel proud of the increasing excellence of her sway over subject nations; but this general expression of the sense and desire of the English people does not show that every proceeding of her delegates is necessarily fitting and far-seeing. The wisdom of England is not to be measured by the views and acts of any one of her sons, but is rather to be deduced from the characters of many. In India it is to be gathered in part from the high, but not always scrupulous, qualities which distinguished Clive, Hastings, and Wellesley, who acquired and secured the Empire; in part from the generous, but not always discerning, sympathies of Burke, Cornwallis, and Bentinck, who gave to English rule the stamp of moderation and humanity; and also in part from the ignorant well-meaning of the people at large, who justly deprecating ambition in the abstract vainly strive to check the progress of conquest before its necessary limits have been attained, and before the aspiring energies of the conquerors themselves have become exhausted. By conquest, I would be understood to imply the extension of supremacy, and not the extinction of dynasties, for such imperial form of domination should be the aim and scope of English sway in the East. England should reign over kings rather than rule over subjects.

The Sikhs and the English are each irresistibly urged forward in their different ways and degrees towards remote and perhaps diverse ends: the Sikhs, as the leaders of a congenial mental change; the English, as the promoters of rational law and material wealth; and individual chiefs and rulers can merely play their parts in the great social movements with more or less of effect and intelligence. Of the deeds and opinions of these conspicuous men, the Author has not hesitated to speak plainly but soberly, whether in praise or dispraise, and he trusts he may do both, without either idly flattering or malignantly traducing his country, and also without compromising his own character as a faithful and obedient servant of the State; for the soldiers of India are no longer mere sentinels over bales of goods, nor is the East India Company any longer a private association of traffickers which can with reason object to its mercantile transactions being subjected to open comment by one of its confidential factors. The merits of the administration of the East India Company are many and undoubted; but its constitution is political, its authority is derivative, and every Englishman has a direct interest in the proceedings of his Government; while it is likewise his country's boast that her children can at fitting times express in calm and considerate language their views of her career, and it is *her* duty to see that those to whom she entrusts power rightly understand both their own position and *her* functions.

25th October, 1849.

PREFACE TO THE FIRST EDITION[1]

One who possesses no claims to systematic scholarship, and who nevertheless asks the public to approve of his labours in a field of some difficulty, is bound to show to his readers that he has at least had fair means of obtaining accurate information and of coming to just conclusions.

Towards the end of the year 1837, the author received, through the unsolicited favour of Lord Auckland, the appointment of assistant to Colonel Wade, the political agent at Ludhiāna, and the officer in charge of the British relations with the Punjab and the chiefs of Afghānistān. He was at the same time required as an engineer officer, to render Ferozepore a defensible post, that little place having been declared a feudal escheat, and its position being regarded as one of military importance. His plans for effecting the object in view met the approval of Sir Henry Fane, the Commander-in-Chief; but it was not eventually thought proper to do more than cover the town with a slight parapet, and the scheme for reseating Shāh Shujā on his throne seemed at the time to make the English and Sikh Governments so wholly one, that the matter dropped, and Ferozepore was allowed to become a cantonment with scarcely the means at hand of saving its ammunition from a few predatory horse.

The author was also present at the interview which took place in 1838, between Ranjīt Singh and Lord Auckland. In 1839 he accompanied Shāhzāda Taimūr and Colonel Wade to Peshāwar, and he was with them when they forced the Pass of Khaibar, and laid open the road to Kābul. In 1840 he was placed in administrative charge of the district of Ludhiāna; and towards the end of the same year, he was deputed by the new frontier agent, Mr. Clerk, to accompany Colonel Shelton and his relieving brigade to Peshāwar, whence he returned with the troops

[1] Published in 1 vol. 8vo 19th March, 1849.

escorting Dost Muhammad Khān under Colonel Wheeler. During part of 1841 he was in magisterial charge of the Ferozepore district, and towards the close of that year, he was appointed—on the recommendation again of Mr. Clerk—to proceed to Tibet to see that the ambitious Rājās of Jammu surrendered certain territories which they had seized from the Chinese of Lassa, and that the British trade with Ladākh, &c., was restored to its old footing. He returned at the end of a year, and was present at the interviews between Lord Ellenborough and Dost Muhammad at Ludhiāna, and between his lordship and the Sikh chiefs at Ferozepore in December 1842. During part of 1843 he was in civil charge of Ambāla ; but from the middle of that year till towards the close of 1844, he held the post of personal assistant to Colonel Richmond, the successor of Mr. Clerk. After Major Broadfoot's nomination to the same office, and during the greater part of 1845, the author was employed in the Bahāwalpur territory in connexion with refugee Sindhians, and with boundary disputes between the Daudputras and the Rājpūts of Bīkaner and Jaisalmer. When war with the Sikhs broke out, the author was required by Sir Charles Napier to join his army of co-operation ; but after the battle of Ferozeshāh, he was summoned to Lord Gough's head-quarters. He was subsequently directed to accompany Sir Harry Smith, when a diversion was made towards Ludhiāna, and he was thus present at the skirmish of Badowal and at the battle of Alīwāl. He had likewise the fortune to be a participator in the victory of Sobraon, and the further advantage of acting on that important day as an aide-de-camp to the Governor-General. He was then attached to the head quarters of the Commander-in-Chief, until the army broke up at Lahore, when he accompanied Lord Hardinge's camp to the Simla Hills, preparatory to setting out for Bhopāl, the political agency in which state and its surrounding districts, his lordship had unexpectedly been pleased to bestow upon him.

The author was thus living among the Sikh people for a period of eight years, and during a very important portion of their history. He had intercourse, under every variety of circumstances, with all classes of men, and he had at the same time free access to all the public records bearing on the affairs of the frontier. It was after being required in 1844, to draw up reports on the British connexion generally with the states on the Sutlej, and especially on the military resources of the Punjab, that he conceived the idea, and felt he had the means, of writing the history which he now offers to the public.

The author's residence in Mālwā has been beneficial to him in many ways personally; and it has also been of advantage in the composition of this work, as he has had the opportunity of becoming acquainted with the ideas and modes of life of the military colonies of Sikhs scattered through Central India.

SEHORE, BHOPĀL,
December 9, 1848.

NOTE

In the references, and also in the text, from Chap. V to the end of the volume, the names of military officers and civil functionaries are quoted without any nice regard to the rank they may have held at the particular time, or to the titles by which they may have been subsequently distinguished. But as there is one person only of each name to be referred to, no doubt or inconvenience can arise from this laxity. Thus the youthful, but discreet Mr. Metcalfe of the treaty with Ranjīt Singh, and the Sir Charles Metcalfe so honourably connected with the history of India, is the Lord Metcalfe of riper years and approved services in another hemisphere. Lieutenant-Colonel, or more briefly Colonel, Pottinger, is now a Major-General and a Grand Cross of the Bath; while Mr. Clerk has been made a knight of the same Order, and Lieutenant-Colonel Lawrence has been raised to an equal title. Captain, or Lieutenant-Colonel, or Sir Claude Wade, mean one and the same person: and similarly the late Sir Alexander Burnes sometimes appears as a simple lieutenant, or as a captain, or as a lieutenant-colonel. On the other hand, Sir David Ochterlony is referred to solely under that title, although, when he marched to the Sutlej in 1809, he held the rank of lieutenant-colonel only.

CONTENTS

CHAPTER I

THE COUNTRY AND PEOPLE

CHAPTER II

OLD INDIAN CREEDS, MODERN REFORMS, AND THE TEACHING OF NĀNAK

UP TO A. D. 1539

CHAPTER III

THE SIKH GURŪS OR TEACHERS, AND THE MODIFICATION OF SIKHISM UNDER GOBIND

A. D. 1539–1716

CHAPTER IV

THE ESTABLISHMENT OF SIKH INDEPENDENCE

A. D. 1716–64

CHAPTER V

FROM THE INDEPENDENCE OF THE SIKHS TO THE ASCENDANCY OF RANJĪT SINGH AND THE ALLIANCE WITH THE ENGLISH

1765—1808-9

CHAPTER VI

FROM THE SUPREMACY OF RANJĪT SINGH TO THE REDUCTION OF MULTĀN, KASHMIR, AND PESHĀWAR

1809—1823-4

CHAPTER VII

FROM THE ACQUISITION OF MULTĀN, KASHMĪR, AND PESHĀWAR TO THE DEATH OF RANJĪT SINGH

1824–39

CHAPTER VIII

FROM THE DEATH OF MAHĀRĀJĀ RANJĪT SINGH TO THE DEATH OF WAZĪR JAWĀHIR SINGH

1839–45

CHAPTER IX

THE WAR WITH THE ENGLISH

1845–6

APPENDIXES

MAPS

A HISTORY OF THE SIKHS

CHAPTER I

THE COUNTRY AND PEOPLE

Geographical Limits of Sikh Occupation or Influence—Climate, Productions, &c. of the Sikh Dominions—Inhabitants, Races, Tribes—Religions of the People—Characteristics and Effects of Race and Religion—Partial Migrations of Tribes—Religious Proselytism.

Geographical limits.

DURING the sixteenth and seventeenth centuries of the Christian era, Nānak and Gobind, of the Kshattriya race, obtained a few converts to their doctrines of religious reform and social emancipation among the Jāt peasants of Lahore and the southern banks of the Sutlej. The 'Sikhs', or 'Disciples', have now become a nation; and they occupy, or have extended their influence, from Delhi to Peshāwar, and from the plains of Sind to the Karakoram mountains. The dominions acquired by the Sikhs are thus included between the 28th and 36th parallels of north latitude, and between the 71st and 77th meridians of east longitude; and if a base of four hundred and fifty miles be drawn from Pānīpat to the Khaibar Pass, two triangles, almost equilateral, may be described upon it, which shall include the conquests of Ranjīt Singh and the fixed colonies of the Sikh people.

Climate, productions, &c.

The country of the Sikhs, being thus situated in a medium degree of latitude, corresponding nearly with that of northern Africa and the American States, and consisting either of broad plains not much above the sea level, or of mountain ranges which rise two and three miles into the air, possesses every variety of climate and every description of natural produce. The winter of Ladākh is long and rigorous, snow covers the ground for half the year, the loneliness of

Grain, and shawl wool of Ladākh.

its vast solitudes appals the heart, and naught living meets the eye; yet the shawl-wool goat gives a value to the rocky wastes of that elevated region, and its scanty acres yield unequalled crops of wheat and barley, where the stars can be discerned at midday and the thin air scarcely bears the sound of thunder to the ear.[1] The heat and the dust storms of Multān are perhaps more oppressive than the cold and the drifting snows of Tibet; but the favourable position of the city, and the several overflowing streams in its neighbourhood, give an importance, the one to its manufactures of silks and carpets, and the other to the wheat, the indigo, and the cotton of its fields.[2] The southern slopes of the

Silks, indigo, and cotton of Multān.

[1] Shawl wool is produced most abundantly, and of the finest quality, in the steppes between the Shayuk and the main branch of the Indus. About 100,000 rupees, or £10,000 worth may be carried down the valley of the Sutlej to Ludhiāna and Delhi. (*Journal Asiatic Society of Bengal*, 1844, p. 210.) The importation into Kashmīr alone is estimated by Moorcroft (*Travels*, ii. 165) at about £75,000, and thus the Sutlej trade may represent less than a tenth of the whole.

Moorcroft speaks highly of the cultivation of wheat and barley in Tibet, and he once saw a field of the latter grain in that country such as he had never before beheld, and which, he says, an English farmer would have ridden many miles to have looked at. (*Travels*, i. 269, 280.)

The gravel of the northern steppes of Tibet yields gold in grains, but the value of the crude borax of the lakes surpasses, as an article of trade, that of the precious metal.

In Yarkand an intoxicating drug named *churrus*, much used in India, is grown of a superior quality, and while opium could be taken across the Himālayas, the Hindus and Chinese carried on a brisk traffic of exchange in the two deleterious commodities.

The trade in tea through Tibet to Kashmīr and Kābul is of local importance. The blocks weigh about eight pounds, and sell for 12*s.* and 16*s.* up to 36*s.* and 48*s.* each, according to the quality. (Cf. Moorcroft, *Travels*, i. 350, 351.)

[2] The wheat of Multān is beardless, and its grain is long and heavy. It is exported in large quantities to Rājputāna, and also, since the British occupation, to Sind to an increased extent. The value of the carpets manufactured in Multān does not perhaps exceed 50,000 rupees annually. The silk manufacture may be worth five times that sum, or, including that of Bahāwalpur, 400,000 rupees in all; but the demand for such fabrics has markedly declined since the expulsion of a native dynasty from Sind. The raw silk of Bokhara is used in preference to that of Bengal, as being stronger and more glossy.

English piece-goods, or (more largely) cotton twists to be woven

Himālayas are periodically deluged with rain, which is almost unknown beyond the snow, and is but little felt in Multān or along the Indus. The central Punjab is mostly a bushy jungle or a pastoral waste; its rivers alone have rescued it from the desert, but its dryness keeps it free from savage beasts, and its herds of cattle are of staple value to the country; while the plains which immediately bound the hills, or are influenced by the Indus and its tributaries, are not surpassed in fertility by any in India. The many populous towns of these tracts are filled with busy weavers of cotton and silk and wool, and with skilful workers in leather and wood and iron. Water is found near the surface, and the Persian wheel is in general use for purposes of irrigation. Sugar is produced in abundance, and the markets of Sind and Kābul are in part supplied with that valuable article by the traders of Amritsar, the commercial emporium of Northern India.[1] The artisans of Kashmīr, the varied

Black cattle of the central Punjab.

The Persian wheel used for irrigation.

Sugar of the upper plains.

into cloth, have been introduced everywhere in India; but those well-to-do in the world can alone buy foreign articles, and thus while about eighteen tons of cotton twist are used by the weavers of Bahāwalpur, about 300 tons of (cleaned) cotton are grown in the district, and wrought up by the villagers or exported to Rājputāna.

The Lower Punjab and Bahāwalpu yield respectively about 750 and 150 tons of indigo. It is worth on the spot from 9*d.* to 1*s.* 6*d.* the pound. The principal market is Khorasan; but the trade has declined of late, perhaps owing to the quantities which may be introduced into that country by way of the Persian Gulf from India. The fondness of the Sikhs, and of the poorer Muhammadans of the Indus, for blue clothing, will always maintain a fair trade in indigo. [It seems hardly necessary to state that the prosperity of the Western Punjab to-day depends principally upon its grain, and that cultivation has received a great stimulus from the canal system.

As regards the second paragraph of the note the statement about the consumption of foreign cotton, &c., reads strangely to a modern generation.—ED.]

[1] In 1844 the customs and excise duties of the Punjab amounted to £240,000 or £250,000, or to one-thirteenth of the whole revenue of Ranjīt Singh, estimated at £3,250,000. ['Under the present system of decentralization in finance, the Imperial Government delegates to the Punjab Government the control of expenditure on the ordinary administrative services, together with the whole or a certain proportion of certain heads of revenue sufficient to meet those charges. Of the various heads of revenue, post office, telegraphs, railways, opium, and salt are entirely Imperial. Land revenue, stamps, excise, income

The saffron and the shawls of Kashmīr. productions of that famous valley, its harvests of saffron, and its important manufacture of shawls, are well known and need only be alluded to.[1] The plains of Attock and

Rice and wheat of Peshāwar. Peshāwar no longer shelter the rhinoceros which Bābar delighted to hunt, but are covered with rich crops of rice, of wheat, and of barley. The mountains themselves pro-

Drugs, dyes, and metals of the hills. duce drugs and dyes and fruits; their precipitous sides support forests of gigantic pines, and veins of copper, or extensive deposits of rock salt and of iron ore are contained within their vast outline. The many fertile vales lying between the Indus and Kashmīr are perhaps unsurpassed in the East for salubrity and loveliness: the seasons are European, and the violent 'monsoon' of India is replaced by the genial spring rains of temperate climates.

Inhabitants. The people comprised within the limits of the Sikh rule or influence, are various in their origin, their language, and their faith. The plains of Upper India, in which the Brāhmans and Kshattriya had developed a peculiar civilization, have been overrun by Persian or Scythic tribes, from the age of Darius and Alexander to that of Bābar and Nādir Shāh. Particular traces of the successive conquerors may yet perhaps be found, but the main features are: (1) the

Immigration of the Jāts, and introduction of Muhammadanism. introduction of the Muhammadan creed; and (2) the long antecedent emigration of hordes of Jāts from the plains of Upper Asia. It is not necessary to enter into the antiquities of Grecian 'Getae' and Chinese 'Yuechi', to discuss the asserted identity of a peasant Jāt and a moon-descended Yadu, or to try to trace the blood of Kadphises in the veins

tax, and major irrigation works are divided between the Imperial and Provincial Governments in the proportion of one-half to each. Minor irrigation works and some minor heads are divided in varying proportions, while the revenue from forests, registration, courts of law, jails, police, and education are wholly provincial, as well as the income of district boards and municipalities. The Budget for 1914–15 shows a total revenue (including opening balance) of Rs. 6,44,50,000 and a total expenditure of Rs. 5,00,29,000, leaving a closing balance of Rs. 1,44,21,000.'—*Indian Year Book*, 1915.]

[1] Mr. Moorcroft (*Travels*, ii. 194) estimates the annual value of the Kashmīr manufacture of shawls at £300,000, but this seems a small estimate if the raw material be worth £75,000 alone (*Travels*, ii. 165, &c.), that is, 1,000 horse loads of 300 pounds, each pound being worth 5*s*.

of Ranjīt Singh. It is sufficient to observe that the vigorous Hindu civilization of the first ages of Christianity soon absorbed its barbarous invaders, and that in the lapse of centuries the Jāts became essentially Brāhmanical in language and belief. Along the southern Indus they soon yielded their conscience to the guidance of Islām ; those of the north longer retained their idolatrous faith, but they have lately had a new life breathed into them ; they now preach the unity of God and the equality of man, and, after obeying Hindu and Muhammadan rulers, they have themselves once more succeeded to sovereign power.[1] The Musalmān occupation forms the next grand epoch in general Indian history after the extinction of the Buddhist religion ; the common speech of the people has been partially changed, and the tenets of Muhammad are gradually revolutionizing the whole fabric of Indian society ; but the difference of race, or the savage manners of the conquerors, struck the vanquished even more forcibly than their creed, and to this day Jāts and others talk of 'Turks' as synonymous with oppressors, and the proud Rājpūts not only bowed before the Musalmāns, but have perpetuated the remembrance of their servitude by adopting 'Turkhāna', or Turk money, into their language as the equivalent of tribute.

The Tartars of Tibet.

In the valley of the Upper Indus, that is, in Ladākh and Little Tibet, the prevailing caste is the Bhoti subdivision of the great Tartar variety of the human race. Lower down that classical stream, or in Gilgit and Chulass, the remains of the old and secluded races of Dardus and Dūngars are still to be found, but both in Iskārdo and in Gilgit itself, there is some mixture of Turkomān tribes from the wilds of Pamer and Kashkār. The people of Kashmīr have from time to time been mixed with races from the north, the south, and the west ; and while their language is Hindu and their faith Muhammadan, the manners of the primitive Kash or Katch tribes, have been influenced by their proximity to the Tartars. The hills westward from Kashmīr to the Indus are inhabited by Kūkas and Bambās, of whom little is known, but towards the river itself the Yūsufzais

The ancient Dardus.

Turkomāns of Gilgit.

The Kashmīrīs

and their western neighbours,

[1] See Appendix I.

Kūkas, Bambās, Gūjars, &c.

and other Afghān tribes prevail; while there are many secluded valleys peopled by the widely spread Gūjars, whose history has yet to be ascertained, and who are the vassals of Arabian 'saiyids', or of Afghān and Turkomān lords.

The Gakhars and the Janjūas.

In the hills south of Kashmīr, and west of the Jhelum to Attock and Kālābāgh on the Indus, are found Gakhars, Gūjars, Khattars, Awāns, Janjūas, and others, all of whom may be considered to have from time to time merged into the Hindu stock in language and feelings. Of these, some, as the Janjūas and especially the Gakhars, have a local reputation. Peshāwar and the hills which surround it, are peopled by various races of Afghāns, as Yūsufzais and Mohmands in the north and west, Khalīls and others in the centre, and Afrīdis, Khattaks, and others in the south and east. The hills south of Kohāt, and the districts of Tāṇk and Bannu, are likewise peopled by genuine Afghāns, as the pastoral Wazīris and others, or by agricultural tribes claiming such a descent; and, indeed, throughout the mountains on either side of the Indus, every valley has its separate tribe or family, always opposed in interest, and sometimes differing in speech and manners. Generally it may be observed, that on the north, the Afghāns on one side, and the Turkomāns on the other, are gradually pressing upon the old but less energetic Dardus, who have been already mentioned.

The Yūsufzais, Afrīdis, &c.

Wazīris, and other Afghāns.

Baluchīs, Jāts, and Rains, of the Middle Indus.

In the districts on either side of the Indus south of Kālābāgh, and likewise around Multān, the population is partly Baluch and partly Jāt, intermixed, however, with other tribes, as Aroras and Rains, and towards the mountains of Suleimān some Afghān tribes are likewise to be found located. In the waste tracts between the Indus and Sutlej are found Juns, Bhutis, Siāls, Kurruls, Kāthīs, and other tribes, who are both pastoral and predatory, and who, with the Chibs and Buhows south of Kashmīr, between the Jhelum and Chenāb, may be the first inhabitants of the country, but little reclaimed in manners by Hindu or Muhammadan conquerors; or one or more of them, as the Bhutis, who boast of their lunar descent, may represent a tribe of ancient invaders or colonizers who have yielded

Juns, Bhutis, and Kāthīs, of the central plains.

Chibs and Buhows of the lower hills.

to others more powerful than themselves. Indeed, there seems little doubt of the former supremacy of the Bhuti or Bhati race in North-Western India : the tribe is extensively diffused, but the only sovereignty which remains to it is over the sands of Jaisalmer.[1] The tracts along the Sutlej, about Pākpattan, are occupied by Wattus and Johiya Rājpūts,[2] while lower down are found some of the Langah tribe, who were once the masters of Uch and Multān.

The Johiyas and Langahs of the south.

The hills between Kashmīr and the Sutlej are possessed by Rājpūt families, and the Muhammadan invasion seems to have thrust the more warlike Indians, on one side into the sands of Rājputāna and the hills of Bundelkhand, and on the other into the recesses of the Himālayas. But the mass of the population is a mixed race called Dogrās about Jammu, and Kanets to the eastward, even as far as the Jumna and Ganges, and which boasts of some Rājpūt blood. There are, however, some other tribes intermixed, as the Gaddīs, who claim to be Kshattriya, and as the Kohlīs, who may be the aborigines, and who resemble in manners and habits, and perhaps in language, the forest tribes of Central India. Towards the snowy limits there is some mixture of Bhutis, and towards Kashmīr and in the towns there is a similar mixture of the people of that valley.

The Dogrās and Kanets of the Himālayas.

The Kohlīs of the Himālayas.

The Jāts of the central plains

The central tract in the plains stretching from the Jhelum to Hānsi, Hissār, and Pānīpat, and lying to the north of Khushāb and the ancient Dīpālpur, is inhabited chiefly by Jāts ; and the particular country of the Sikh people may be said to lie around Lahore, Amritsar, and even Gujrāt to the north of the Sutlej, and around Bhatinda and Sunām

[1] The little chiefship of Karauli, between Jaipur and Gwalior, may also be added. The Rājā is admitted by the genealogists to be of the Yadu or Lunar race, but people sometimes say that his being an *Ahir* or *Cowherd* forms his only relationship to Krishna, the pastoral Apollo of the Indians.

[2] Tod (*Rājasthān*, i. 118) regards the Johiyas as extinct ; but they still flourish as peasants on either bank of the Sutlej, between Kasūr and Bahāwalpur : they are now Muhammadans. The Dahia of Tod (i. 118) are likewise to be found as cultivators and as Muhammadans on the Lower Sutlej, under the name of Deheh, or Dāhur and Dūhur ; and they and many other tribes seem to have yielded on one side to Rahtor Rājpūts, and on the other to Baluchīs.

to the south of that river. The one tract is pre-eminently called Mānjha or the middle land, and the other is known as Mālwā, from, it is said, some fancied resemblance in greenness and fertility to the Central Indian province of that name. Many other people are, however, intermixed, as Bhutis and Dogrās, mostly to the south and west, and Rains, Rurs, and others, mostly in the east. Gūjars are everywhere numerous, as are also other Rājpūts besides Bhutis, while Pathāns are found in scattered villages and towns. Among the Pathāns those of Kasūr have long been numerous and powerful, and the Rājpūts of Rāhon have a local reputation. Of the gross agricultural population of this central tract, perhaps somewhat more than four-tenths may be Jāt, and somewhat more than one-tenth Gūjar, while nearly two-tenths may be Rājpūts more or less pure, and less than a tenth claim to be Muhammadans of foreign origin, although it is highly probable that about a third of the whole people profess the Musalmān faith.[1]

mixed with Gūjars, Rājpūts, Pathāns, and others.

Relative proportions of some principal races.

In every town and city there are, moreover, tribes of religionists, or soldiers, or traders, or handicraftsmen, and thus whole divisions of a provincial capital may be peopled by holy Brāhmans[2] or as holy Saiyids, by Afghān or Bundelā soldiers, by Kshattriyas, Aroras, and Baniās engaged in trade, by Kashmīrī weavers, and by mechanics and dealers of the many degraded or inferior races of Hindustan. None of these are, however, so powerful, so united, or so numerous as to affect the surrounding rural population, although, after the Jāts, the Kshattriyas are perhaps the most influential and enterprising race in the country.[3]

Kshattriyas and Aroras of the cities.

Of the wandering houseless races, the Changars are the most numerous and the best known, and they seem to deserve notice as being probably the same as the Chinganehs

The wandering Changars.

[1] See Appendix II.

[2] In the Punjab, and along the Ganges, Brāhmans have usually the appellation of Missar or Mitter (i. e. Mithra) given to them, if not distinguished as Pandits (i. e. as doctors or men of learning). The title seems, according to tradition, or to the surmise of well-informed native Indians, to have been introduced by the first Muhammadan invaders, and it may perhaps show that the Brāhmans were held to be worshippers of the sun by the Unitarian iconoclasts.

[3] See Appendix III.

of Turkey, the Russian Tzigans, the German Zigueners, the Italian Zingaros, the Spanish Gitanos, and the English Gypsies. About Delhi the race is called Kanjar, a word which, in the Punjab, properly implies a courtezan dancing girl.[1]

The religions of the Sikh country.

The Lamaic Buddhists of Ladākh.

The Shiāh Muhammadans of Bultee.

The Sunni Muhammadans of Kashmīr, Peshāwar, and Multān.

The Brāhmanist hill tribes.

The Sikhs of the central plains mixed with Brāhmanists and Muhammadans.

The limits of Race and Religion are not the same, otherwise the two subjects might have been considered together with advantage. In Ladākh the people and the dependent rulers profess Lamaic Buddhism, which is so widely diffused throughout Central Asia, but the Tibetans of Iskārdo, the Dardus of Gilgit, and the Kūkas and Bambās of the rugged mountains, are Muhammadans of the Shiāh persuasion. The people of Kashmīr, of Kishtwār, of Bhimbar, of Pakhli, and of the hills south and west to the salt range and the Indus, are mostly Sunni Muhammadans,[2] as are likewise the tribes of Peshāwar and of the valley of the Indus southward, and also the inhabitants of Multān, and of the plains northward as far as Pind-Dādan-Khān, Chiniot, and Dīpālpur. The people of the Himālayas, eastward of Kishtwār and Bhimbar, are Hindus of the Brāhmanical faith, with some Buddhist colonies to the north, and some Muhammadan families to the south-west. The Jāts of 'Mānjha' and 'Mālwā' are mostly Sikhs, but perhaps not one-third of the whole population between the Jhelum and Jumna has yet embraced the tenets of Nānak and Gobind, the other two-thirds being still equally divided between Islām and Brāhmanism.

Hindu shopkeepers of Muhammadan cities.

In every town, excepting perhaps Leh, and in most of the villages of the Muhammadan districts of Peshāwar and Kashmīr, and of the Sikh districts of Mānjha and Mālwā, there are always to be found Hindu traders and shopkeepers. The Kshattriya prevail in the northern towns, and the Aroras are numerous in the province of Multān. The Kashmīrī Brāhmans emulate in intelligence and usefulness the

[[1] For the whole question of Indian gipsies the reader is referred to an article on 'The Indian Origin of the Gipsies in Europe', by Mr. A. C. Woolner, which appears in vol. ii of the *Journal of the Punjab Historical Society*.]

[2] The author learns from his brother, Major A. Cunningham who has twice visited Kashmīr, that the Muhammadans of that valley are nearly all Shiāh, instead of Sunni, as stated in the text.—J. D. C.

Marāthā Pandits and the Babus of Bengal; they are a good deal employed in official business, although the Kshattriya and the Aroras are the ordinary accountants and farmers of revenue. In 'Mālwā' alone, that is, about Bhatinda and Sunām, can the Sikh population be found unmixed, and there it has passed into a saying, that the priest, the soldier, the mechanic, the shopkeeper, and the ploughman are all equally Sikh.

Village population about Bhatinda purely Sikh.

The debased and secluded races, worshippers of local gods and oracular divinities.

There are, moreover, in the Punjab, as throughout India, several poor and contemned races, to whom Brāhmans will not administer the consolations of religion, and who have not been sought as converts by the Muhammadans. These worship village or forest gods, or family progenitors, or they invoke a stone as typical of the great mother of mankind; or some have become acquainted with the writings of the later Hindu reformers, and regard themselves as inferior members of the Sikh community. In the remote Himālayas, again, where neither Mulla, nor Lāma, nor Brāhman, has yet cared to establish himself, the people are equally without instructed priests and a determinate faith; they worship the Spirit of each lofty peak, they erect temples to the limitary god of each snow-clad summit, and believe that from time to time the attendant servitor is inspired to utter the divine will in oracular sentences, or that when the image of the Daitya or Titan is borne in solemn procession on their shoulders, a pressure to the right or left denotes good or evil fortune.[1]

Characteristics of race and religion.

The characteristics of race and religion are everywhere of greater importance than the accidents of position or the achievements of contemporary genius; but the influences of descent and manners, of origin and worship, need not

[1] In the Lower Himālayas of the Punjab there are many shrines to Gūgā or Goga, and the poorer classes of the plains likewise reverence the memory of the ancient hero. His birth or appearance is variously related. One account makes him the chief of Ghazni, and causes him to war with his brothers Arjūn and Surjan. He was slain by them, but behold! a rock opened and Gūgā again sprang forth armed and mounted. Another account makes him the lord of Durd-Durehra, in the wastes of Rajwāra, and this corresponds in some degree with what Tod (*Rājasthān*, ii. 447) says of the same champion, who died fighting against the armies of Mahmūd.

be dwelt upon in all their ramifications. The systems of Buddha, of Brāhma, and of Muhammad are extensively diffused in the Eastern world, and they intimately affect the daily conduct of millions of men. But, for the most part, these creeds no longer inspire their votaries with enthusiasm; the faith of the people is no longer a living principle, but a social custom,—a rooted, an almost instinctive deference to what has been the practice of centuries. The Tibetan, who unhesitatingly believes the Deity to dwell incarnate in the world, and who grossly thinks he perpetuates a prayer by the motion of a wheel, and the Hindu, who piously considers his partial gods to delight in forms of stone or clay, would indeed still resist the uncongenial innovations of strangers; but the spirit which erected temples to Sākya the Seer from the torrid to the frigid zone, or which raised the Brāhmans high above all other Indian races, and which led them to triumph in poetry and philosophy, is no longer to be found in its ancient simplicity and vigour. The Buddhist and the reverer of the Vedas, is indeed each satisfied with his own chance of a happy immortality, but he is indifferent about the general reception of truth, and, while he will not himself be despotically interfered with, he cares not what may be the fate of others, or what becomes of those who differ from him. Even the Muhammadan, whose imagination must not be assisted by any visible similitude, is prone to invest the dead with the powers of intercessors, and to make pilgrimages to the graves of departed mortals;[1] and we should now look in vain for any general expression of that feeling which animated the simple Arabian disciple,

Brāhmanism and Buddhism rather forms than feelings;

yet strong to resist innovation.

Muhammadanism, although corrupted, has more of vitality.

[[1] Such a phenomenon is not confined to Islām alone. It would seem to be a characteristic development in many religions. When once what one may call the 'human touch' weakens, and when the gulf separating the worshipper and the founder of his creed seems sharply defined, there is a tendency to interpose some form of mediation to bridge such an imaginary gulf. To such a feeling Catholic Europe owes the introduction of the worship of the Blessed Virgin and the invocation of countless saints. To such a feeling, also, Buddhism owes the introduction of the Bodhisattva or Pusas—the mediators for lost souls. And it will further be found that in course of time such mediating forces tend to lose their general character and to become localized tutelary powers.—ED.]

or the hardy Turkomān convert, to plant thrones across the fairest portion of the ancient hemisphere. It is true that, in the Muhammadan world, there are still many zealous individuals, and many mountain and pastoral tribes, who will take up arms, as well as become passive martyrs, for their faith, and few will deny that Turk, and Persian, and Pathān would more readily unite for conscience's sake under the banner of Muhammad, than Russian, and Swede, and Spaniard are ever likely to march under one common 'Labarum'. The Musalmān feels proudly secure of his path to salvation ; he will resent the exhortations of those whom he pities or contemns as wanderers, and, unlike the Hindu and the Buddhist, he is still actively desirous of acquiring merit by adding to the number of true believers. But Buddhist, and Brāhmanist, and Muhammadan have each an instructed body of ministers, and each confides in an authoritative ritual, or in a revealed law. Their reason and their hopes are both satisfied, and hence the difficulty of converting them to the Christian faith by the methods of the civilized moderns. Our missionaries, earnest and devoted men, must be content with the cold arguments of science and criticism ; they must not rouse the feelings, or appeal to the imagination ; they cannot promise aught which their hearers were not sure of before ; they cannot go into the desert to fast, nor retire to the mountain-tops to pray ; they cannot declare the fulfilment of any fondly cherished hope of the people, nor, in announcing a great principle, can they point to the success of the sword and the visible favour of the Divinity. No austerity of sanctitude convinces the multitude, and the Pandit and the Mulla can each oppose dialectics to dialectics, morality to morality, and revelation to revelation. Our zealous preachers may create sects among ourselves, half Quietist and half Epicurean, they may persevere in their laudable resolution of bringing up the orphans of heathen parents, and they may gain some converts among intelligent inquirers as well as among the ignorant and the indigent, but it seems hopeless that they should ever Christianize the Indian and Muhammadan worlds.[1]

All are satisfied with their own faith,

and cannot be reasoned into Christianity.

[1] The masses can only be convinced by means repudiated by reason

The observers of the ancient creeds quietly pursue the even tenor of their way, self satisfied and almost indifferent about others ; but the Sikhs are converts to a new religion, the seal of the double dispensation of Brāhma and Muhammad : *their* enthusiasm is still fresh, and *their* faith is still an active and a living principle. *They* are persuaded that God himself is present with them, that He supports them in all their endeavours, and that sooner or later He will confound *their* enemies for His own glory. This feeling of the Sikh people deserves the attention of the English, both as a civilized nation and as a paramount government. Those who have heard a follower of Gurū Gobind declaim on the destinies of his race, his eye wild with enthusiasm and every muscle quivering with excitement, can understand *that* spirit which impelled the naked Arab against the mail-clad troops of Rome and Persia, and which led our own chivalrous and believing forefathers through Europe to battle for the cross on the shores of Asia. The Sikhs do not form a numerous sect, yet their strength is not to be estimated by tens of thousands, but by the unity and energy of religious fervour and warlike temperament. They will dare much, and they will endure much, for the mystic 'Khālsa' or commonwealth ; they are not discouraged by defeat, and they ardently look forward to the day when Indians and Arabs and Persians and Turks shall all acknowledge the double mission of Nānak and Gobind Singh.

Sikhism an active and pervading principle.

The characteristics of race are perhaps more deep-seated and enduring than those of religion ; but, in considering any people, the results of birth and breeding, of descent

and the instructed intellect of man, and the futility of endeavouring to convince the learned by argument is exemplified in Martyn's Persian Controversies, translated by Dr. Lee, in the discussion carried on between the Christian missionaries at Allahābād and the Muhammadan Mullas at Lucknow, in Rām Mohan Roy's work on Deism and the Vedas, and in the published correspondence of the Tatubodhni Subha of Calcutta. For an instance of the satisfaction of the Hindus with *their* creed, see Moorcroft, *Travels*, i. 118, where some Udasis commend *him* for believing, like them, in a God ! [Col. Kennedy (*Res. Hind. Mythol.*, p. 141) states that the Brāhmans think little of the Christian missionaries (as propagandists), although the English have held authority in India for several generations.—J. D. C.]

The Jāts industrious and high-spirited.

and instruction, must be held jointly in view. The Jāts are known in the north and west of India as industrious and successful tillers of the soil, and as hardy yeomen equally ready to take up arms and to follow the plough. They form, perhaps, the finest rural population in India. On the Jumna their general superiority is apparent, and Bhartpur bears witness to their merits, while on the Sutlej religious reformation and political ascendancy have each served to give spirit to their industry, and activity and purpose to their courage.[1] The Rains, the Mālīs, and some others, are not inferior to the Jāts in laboriousness and sobriety, although they are so in enterprise and resolution. The Rājpūts are always brave men, and they form, too, a desirable peasantry. The Gūjars everywhere prefer pasturage to the plough, whether of the Hindu or Muhammadan faith. The Baluchīs do not become careful cultivators even when long settled in the plains, and the tribes adjoining the hills are of a disposition turbulent and predatory. They mostly devote themselves to the rearing of camels, and they traverse Upper India in charge of herds of that useful animal. The Afghāns are good husbandmen when they have been accustomed to peace in the plains of India, or when they feel secure in their own valleys, but they are even of a more turbulent character than the Baluchīs, and they are everywhere to be met with as mercenary soldiers. Both races are, in truth, in their own country little better than freebooters, and the Muhammadan faith has mainly helped them to justify their excesses against unbelievers, and to

The Rains and some others scarcely inferior as tillers of the ground.

The peasant Rājpūts.

The Gūjars a pastoral people.

The Baluchīs pastoral and predatory.

The Afghāns industrious, but turbulent.

[1] Under the English system of selling the proprietary right in villages when the old freeholder or former purchaser may be unable to pay the land tax, the Jāts of Upper India are gradually becoming the possessors of the greater portion of the soil, a fact which the author first heard on the high authority of Mr. Thomason, the Lieutenant-Governor of the North-Western Provinces. It is a common saying that if a Jāt has fifty rupees, he will rather dig a well or buy a pair of bullocks with the money than spend it on the idle rejoicings of a marriage. [' Socially the landed classes stand high, and of these the Jāts, numbering nearly five millions, are the most important. Roughly speaking, one-half of the Jāts are Mahomedan, one-third Sikh, and one-sixth Hindu. In distribution they are ubiquitous and are equally divided over the five divisions of the province.'—*Indian Year Book*, 1915.]

keep them together under a common banner for purposes of defence or aggression. The Kshattriya and Aroras of the cities and towns are enterprising as merchants and frugal as tradesmen. They are the principal financiers and accountants of the country; but the ancient military spirit frequently reappears amongst the once royal 'Kshattriya', and they become able governors of provinces and skilful leaders of armies.[1] The industry and mechanical skill of the stout-limbed prolific Kashmīrīs are as well known as their poverty, their tameness of spirit, and their loose morality. The people of the hills south and east of Kashmīr are not marked by any peculiar and well-determined character, excepting that the few unmixed Rājpūts possess the personal courage and the pride of race which distinguish them elsewhere, and that the Gakhars still cherish the remembrance of the times when they resisted Bābar and aided Humāyūn. The Tibetans, while they are careful cultivators of their diminutive fields rising tier upon tier, are utterly debased in spirit, and at present they seem incapable of independence and even of resistance to gross oppression. The system of polyandry obtains among them, not as a perverse law, but as a necessary institution. Every spot of ground within the hills which can be cultivated has been under the plough for ages; the number of mouths

The Kshattriyas and Aroras enterprising but frugal.

The Kashmīrīs skilful, but tame and spiritless.

The unmixed Rājpūts.

The Tibetans plodding and debased.

The custom of polyandry one of necessity.

[1] Harī Singh, a Sikh, and the most enterprising of Ranjīt Singh's generals, was a Kshattriya; and the best of his governors, Mohkam Chand and Sāwan Mal, were of the same race. The learning of Bolu Mal, a Khanna Kshattriya, and a follower of the Sikh chief of Ahluwalia, excites some little jealousy among the Brāhmans of Lahore and of the Jullundur Doāb; and Chandū Lāl, who so long managed the affairs of the Nizam of Hyderābād, was a Khattrī of Northern India, and greatly encouraged the Sikh mercenaries in that principality, in opposition to the Arabs and Afghāns. The declension of the Kshattriya from soldiers and sovereigns into traders and shopkeepers, has a parallel in the history of the Jews. Men of active minds will always find employment for themselves, and thus we know what Greeks became under the victorious Romans, and what they are under the ruling Turks. We likewise know that the vanquished Moors were the most industrious of the subjects of mediaeval Spain; that the Mughals of British India are gradually applying themselves to the business of exchange, and it is plain that the traffickers as well as the priests of Saxon England, Frankish Gaul, and Gothic Italy must have been chiefly of Roman descent.

must remain adapted to the number of acres, and the proportion is preserved by limiting each proprietary family to one giver of children. The introduction of Muhammadanism in the west, by enlarging the views of the people and promoting emigration, has tended to modify this rule, and even among the Lamaic Tibetans any casual influx of wealth, as from trade or other sources, immediately leads to the formation of separate establishments by the several members of a house.[1] The wild tribes of Chibs and Buhows in the hills, the Juns and Kāthīs, and the Dogrās and Bhutis of the plains, need not be particularly described; the idle and predatory habits of some, and the quiet pastoral occupations of others, are equally the result of position as of character. The Juns and Kāthīs, tall, comely, and long-lived races, feed vast herds of camels and black cattle, which furnish the towns with the prepared butter of the east, and provide the people themselves with their loved libations of milk.[2]

The Juns and Kāthīs pastoral and peaceful.

Partial migrations of tribes, and proselytism in religion.

Causes of migrations.

The limits of creeds and races which have been described must not be regarded as permanent. Throughout India there are constant petty migrations of the agricultural population taking place. Political oppression, or droughts, or floods cause the inhabitants of a village, or of a district, to seek more favoured tracts, and there are always chiefs and rulers who are ready to welcome industrious emigrants

[1] Regarding the polyandry of Ladākh, Moorcroft (*Travels*, ii. 321, 322) may be referred to, and also the *Journal of the Asiatic Society of Bengal* for 1844, p. 202, &c. The effects of the system on bastardy seem marked, and thus out of 760 people in the little district of Hungrung, around the junction of the Sutlej and Pittee (or Spiti) rivers, there were found to be twenty-six bastards, which gives a proportion of about one in twenty-nine; and as few grown-up people admitted themselves to be illegitimate, the number may even be greater. In 1835 the population of England and Wales was about 14,750,000 and the number of bastards affiliated (before the new poor law came into operation) was 65,475, or 1 in about 226 (Wade's *British History*, pp. 1041–55); and even should the number so born double those affiliated, the proportion would still speak against polyandry as it affects female purity.

[2] On milk sustained, and blest with length of days,
The Hippomolgi, peaceful, just, and wise.
Iliad, xiii. COWPER'S TRANSLATION.

and to assign them lands on easy terms. This causes some fluctuation in the distribution of races, and as in India the tendency is to a distinction or separation of families, the number of clans or tribes has become almost infinite. Within the Sikh dominions the migrations of the Baluchīs up the Indus are not of remote occurrence, while the occupation by the Sindhian Daudputras of the Lower Sutlej took place within the last hundred years. The migration of the Dogrās from Delhi to Ferozepore, and of the Johiyas from Mārwār to Pākpattan, also on the Sutlej, are historical rather than traditional, while the hard-working Hindu Mehtums are still moving, family by family and village by village, eastward, away from the Rāvi and Chenāb, and are insinuating themselves among less industrious but more warlike tribes.

Recent migration of the Baluchīs up the Indus, and of the Daudputras up the Sutlej. Migrations of the Dogrās, Johiyas, and Mehtums.

Although religious wars scarcely take place among the Buddhists, Brāhmanists, and Muhammadans of the present day, and although religious fervour has almost disappeared from among the professors at least of the two former faiths, proselytism is not unknown to any of the three creeds, and Muhammadanism, as possessing still a strong vitality within it, will long continue to find converts among the ignorant and the barbarous. Islāmism is extending up the Indus from Iskārdo towards Leh, and is thus encroaching upon the more worn-out Buddhism; while the limits of the idolatrous 'Kāfirs', almost bordering on Peshāwar, are daily becoming narrower. To the south and eastward of Kashmīr, Muhammadanism has also had recent triumphs, and in every large city and in every Musalmān principality in India there is reason to believe that the religion of the Arabian prophet is gradually gaining ground. In the Himālayas to the eastward of Kishtwār, the Rājpūt conquerors have not carried Brāhmanism beyond the lower valleys; and into the wilder glens, occupied by the ignorant worshippers of local divinities, the Buddhists have recently begun to advance, and Lāmas of the red or yellow sects are now found where none had set foot a generation ago. Among the forest tribes of India the influence of the Brāhmans continues to increase, and every Bhīl, or Gond, or Kohlī who acquires power or money, desires to be thought

Islāmism extending in Tibet;

and generally perhaps in towns and cities.

Lamaic Buddhism progressive in some parts of the Himālayas.

Brāhmanism likewise extending in the

wilder parts of the plains. But the peasantry and mechanics generally are becoming seceders from Brāhmanism.

a Hindu rather than a 'Mlechha'; [1] but, on the other hand, the Indian laity has, during the last few hundred years, largely assumed to itself the functions of the priesthood, and although Hinduism may lose no votaries, Gusains and secular Sādhs usurp the authority of Brāhmans in the direction of the conscience.[2] The Sikhs continue to make converts, but chiefly within the limits of their dependent sway, for the colossal power of the English has arrested the progress of their arms to the eastward, and has left the Jāts of the Jumna and Ganges to their old idolatry.

[1] Half of the principality of Bhopāl, in Central India, was founded on usurpations from the Gonds, who appear to have migrated in force towards the west about the middle of the seventeenth century, and to have made themselves supreme in the valley of the Narbadā about Hoshangābād, in spite of the exertions of Aurangzeb, until an Afghān adventurer attacked them on the decline of the empire, and completely subdued them. The Afghān converted some of the vanquished to his own faith, partly by force and partly by conferring Jagirs, partly to acquire merit and partly to soothe his conscience, and there are now several families of Muhammadan Gonds in the possession of little fiefs on either side of the Narbadā. These men have more fully got over the gross superstition of their race, than the Gonds who have adopted Hinduism.

[[2] The recent spread of the 'Mārwāri' traders over the centre, and to the south and east of India, may also be noticed, for the greater number of them are Jains. These traffickers of Rājputāna seem to have received a strong mercantile impulse about a hundred years ago, and their spirit of enterprise gives them at the same time a social and a religious influence, so that many families of Vaishnava or Brāhmanical traders either incline to Jainism or openly embrace that faith. Jainism is thus extending in India, and conversion is rendered the more easy by the similarity of origin and occupation of these various traders, and by the Quietism and other characteristics common to the Jains and Vaishnavas.—J. D. C.]

CHAPTER II

OLD INDIAN CREEDS, MODERN REFORMS, AND THE TEACHING OF NĀNAK, UP TO 1539 A.D.

The Buddhists—The Brāhmans and Kshattriyas—Reaction of Buddhism on victorious Brāhmanism—Latitude of orthodoxy—Shankar Achārj and Saivism—Monastic orders—Rāmānuj and Vaishnavism—The Doctrine of 'Maya'—The Muhammadan conquest—The reciprocal action of Brāhmanism and Muhammadanism—The successive innovations of Rāmānand, Gorakhnath, Kabīr, Chaitan, and Vallabh—The reformation of Nānak.

India and its successive masters.

THE condition of India from remote ages to the present time, is an episode in the history of the world inferior only to the fall of Rome and the establishment of Christianity. At an early period the Asiatic peninsula, from the southern 'Ghāts' to the Himālayan mountains, would seem to have been colonized by a warlike subdivision of the Caucasian race, which spoke a language similar to the ancient Medic and Persian, and which here and there, near the greater rivers and the shores of the ocean, formed orderly communities professing a religion resembling the worship of Babylon and Egypt—a creed which, under varying types, is still the solace of a large portion of mankind. 'Aryavarta', the land of good men or believers, comprised Delhi and Lahore, Gujrāt and Bengal; but it was on the banks of the Upper Ganges that the latent energies of the people first received an impulse, which produced the peculiar civilization of the Brāhmans, and made a few heroic families supreme from Arachosia to the Golden Chersonese. India illustrates the power of Darius and the greatness of Alexander, the philosophy of Greece and the religion of China; and while Rome was contending with Germans and Cimbri, and yielding to Goths and Huns, the Hindus absorbed, almost without an effort, swarms of Scythic

The Buddhists.

The Brāhmans and Kshattriyas.

The Muhammadans.

The Christians.

barbarians : they dispersed Sacae,[1] they enrolled Getae among their most famous tribes,[2] and they made others serve as their valiant defenders.[3] India afterwards checked the victorious career of Islām, but she could not wholly resist the fierce enthusiasm of the Turkomān hordes ; she became one of the most splendid of Muhammadan empires, and the character of the Hindu mind has been permanently altered by the genius of the Arabian prophet. The well-being of India's industrious millions is now linked with the fate of the foremost nation of the West, and the representatives of Judaean faith and Roman polity will long wage a war of principles with the speculative Brāhman, the authoritative Mulla, and the hardy believing Sikh.

Brāhmanism struggling with Buddhism becomes elaborated.

The Brāhmans and their valiant Kshattriyas had a long and arduous contest with that ancient faith of India, which, as successively modified, became famous as Buddhism.[4] When Manu wrote, perhaps nine centuries before

[1] Vikramājīt derived his title of Sakari from his exploits against the Sacae (Sakae). The race is still perhaps preserved pure in the wilds of Tartary, between Yarkand and the Mansarawar Lake, where the *Sokpos* called Kelmāks (Calmucs) by the Muhammadans, continue to be dreaded by the people of Tibet. [A dread effectually removed by the systematic conquest of Eastern Turkestan by the Chinese during the nineteenth century.—ED.]

[2] The Getae are referred to as the same with the ancient Chinese Yuechi and the modern Jāts, but their identity is as yet, perhaps, rather a reasonable conclusion than a logical or critical deduction.

[3] The four Agnikula tribes of Kshattriyas or Rājpūts are here alluded to, viz. the Chohāns, Solunkees, Powārs (or Prumārs), and the Purihārs. The unnamed progenitors of these races seem clearly to have been invaders who sided with the Brāhmans in their warfare, partly with the old Kshattriyas, partly with increasing schismatics, and partly with invading Graeco-Bactrians, and whose warlike merit, as well as timely aid and subsequent conformity, got them enrolled as 'fireborn', in contradistinction to the solar and lunar families. The Agnikulas are now mainly found in the tract of country extending from Ujjain to Rewah near Benares, and Mount Abu is asserted to be the place of their miraculous birth or appearance. Vikramājīt, the champion of Brāhmanism, was a Powār according to the common accounts.

[4] The relative priority of Brāhmanism and Buddhism continues to be argued and disputed among the learned. The wide diffusion at one period of Buddhism in India is as certain as the later predominance of Brāhmanism, but the truth seems to be that they are of independent origin, and that they existed for a long time contemporaneously ;

Its achievements and characteristics.

Christ, when Alexander conquered, and even seven hundred years afterwards, when the obscure Fāhian travelled and

the former chiefly in the south-west, and the latter about Oudh and Tirhut. It is not, however, necessary to suppose, with M. Burnouf, that Buddhism is purely and originally Indian (*Introduction à l'Histoire du Buddhisme Indien*, Avertissement i), notwithstanding the probable derivation of the name from the Sanskrit 'Buddhi', intelligence; or from the 'bō' or 'bōdee', i. e. the *ficus religiosa* or peepul tree. The Brāhmanical genius gradually received a development which rendered the Hindus proper supreme throughout the land; but their superior learning became of help to their antagonists, and Gautama, himself a Brāhman or a Kshattriya, would appear to have taken advantage of the knowledge of the hierarchy to give a purer and more scientific form to Buddhism, and thus to become its great apostle in succeeding times. [The whole subject, however, is complicated in the extreme; and it is rendered the more so by the probability that the same Gautama is the author of the popular 'Nyaya' system of Philosophy, and that Buddha himself is one form of the favourite divinity Vishnu; although the orthodox explain *that* circumstance by saying the Preserving Power assumed an heretical character to delude Deodas, king of Benares, who by his virtues and authority endangered the supremacy of the Gods. (Cf. Kennedy, *Res. Hind. Mythol.*, p. 248, &c.)—J. D. C.] Of the modern faiths, Saivism perhaps most correctly represents the original Vedic worship. (Cf. Wilson, *As. Res.*, xvii. 171, &c., and *Vishnu Purān*, preface, lxiv.) *Jainism* and *Vaishnavism* are the resultants of the two beliefs in a Buddhist and Brāhmanical dress respectively, while *Saktism* still vividly illustrates the old superstition of the masses of the people, whose ignorant minds quailed before the dread goddess of famine, pestilence, and death. The most important monument of Buddhism now remaining is perhaps the 'tope' or hemisphere, near Bhīlsa in Central India, which it is a disgrace to the English that they partially destroyed a generation ago in search of imaginary chambers or vessels containing relics, and are only now about to have delineated, and so made available to the learned. The numerous *bas-reliefs* of its singular stone enclosure still vividly represent the manners as well as the belief of the India of Asoka, and show that the Tree, the Sun, and the Stūpa (or 'tope') itself—apparently the type of Meru or the Central Mount of the World—were, along with the impersonated Buddha, the principal objects of adoration at that period, and that the country was then partly peopled by a race of men wearing high caps and short tunics, so different from the ordinary dress of Hindus. [It is now usually accepted that by about 600 B. C. Brāhmanism was generally the chief religion of India, and the probable date of the birth of Gautama (567 B.C.) makes Buddhism the younger of the two religions. It seems hardly necessary to add that, since the author wrote the above note, our knowledge of Buddhism in India has been enormously increased by the careful researches of the Archaeological Department.

studied, there were kingdoms ruled by others than 'Aryas'; and ceremonial Buddhism, with its indistinct apprehensions of a divinity, had more votaries than the monotheism of the Vedas, which admitted no similitude more gross than fire, or air, or the burning sun.[1] During this period the genius of Hinduism became fully developed, and the Brāhmans rivalled the Greeks in the greatness and the variety of their triumphs. Epic poems show high imaginative and descriptive powers, and the Rāmāyana and Mahābhārata [2] still move the feelings and affect the character of the

These have resulted in the discovery of a very large number of Buddhist remains which—in great contrast to the iconoclastic vandalism mentioned by the author—have been carefully preserved. Collections of such remains may be seen in many museums in India—there is one typical collection in the Central Museum in Lahore—and to such collections and the various descriptive works on the subject the reader is referred.—ED.]

[1] 'There seem to have been no images and no visible types of the objects of worship,' says Mr. Elphinstone, in his most useful and judicious *History* (i. 73), quoting Professor Wilson, *Oxford Lectures*, and the *Vishnu Purān*; while, with regard to fire, it is to be remembered that in the Old Testament, and even in the New, it is the principal symbol of the Holy Spirit. (Strauss, *Life of Jesus*, 361.) The Vedas, however, allude to personified energies and attributes, but the monotheism of the system is not more affected by the introduction of the creating Brāhma, the destroying Siva, and other minor powers, than the omnipotence of Jehovah is interfered with by the hierarchies of the Jewish heaven. Yet, in truth, much has to be learnt with regard to the Vedas and Vedantism, notwithstanding the invaluable labours of Colebrooke and others, and the useful commentary or interpretation of Rām Mohan Roy. (*Asiatic Researches*, viii; *Transactions Royal Asiatic Society*, i and ii; and Rām Mohan Roy on the Vedas.) The translation of the *Vedānt Sār* in Ward's *Hindoos* (ii. 175), and the improved version of Dr. Roer (*Journal Asiatic Society of Bengal*, February 1845, No. 108), may be consulted with advantage. If translators would repeat the Sanskrit terms with expanded meanings in English, instead of using terms of the scholastic or modern systems which seem to them to be equivalent, they would materially help students to understand the real doctrine of the original speculators.

[[2] These epics are rarely read *in extenso* by a modern generation, owing to a lack of knowledge of Sanskrit and also to their enormous length and the numerous later interpolations. A literal translation in English of the Mahābhārata was made by Mr. P. C. Roy in 1894. But it is intolerably lengthy and, for a simple summary of this Indian epic, the reader is referred to *The Great War of India*, by Thakur Rejendra Singh, published in Allahābād in 1915.—ED.]

people. Mathematical science was so perfect, and astronomical observation so complete, that the paths of the sun and moon were accurately measured.[1] The philosophy of the learned few was, perhaps, for the first time, firmly allied with the theology of the believing many, and Brāhmanism laid down as articles of faith, the unity of God, the creation of the world, the immortality of the soul, and the responsibility of man. The remote dwellers upon the Ganges distinctly made known that future life about which Moses is silent or obscure,[2] and that unity and omnipotence of the Creator which were unknown to the polytheism of the Greek and Roman multitude,[3] and to the dualism of the

[1] The so-called solar year in common use in India takes no account of the precession of the equinoxes, but, as a sidereal year, it is almost exact. The revolution of the points of intersection of the ecliptic and equator nevertheless appears to have been long known to the Hindus, and some of their epochs were obviously based on the calculated period of the phenomenon. (Cf. Mr. Davis's paper in the *As. Res.*, vol. ii, and Bentley's *Astronomy of the Hindoos*, pp. 2–6, 88.)

[2] One is almost more willing to admit that, in effect, the Jews generally held Jehovah to be *their* God only, or a limitary divinity, than that the wise and instructed Moses (whom Strabo held to be an Egyptian priest and a Pantheist, as quoted in *Volney's Ruins*, chap. xxii, § 9 note) could believe in the perishable nature of the soul; but the critical Sadducees nevertheless so interpreted their prophet, although the Egyptians his masters were held by Herodotus (*Euterpe*, cxxiii) to be the first who *defended* the undying nature of the spirit of man. Socrates and Plato, with all their longings, could only feel assured that the soul had more of immortality than aught else. (*Phaedo*, Sydenham and Taylor's translation, iv. 324.)

[3] The unknown God of the Athenians, Fate, the avenging Nemesis, and other powers independent of Zeus or Jupiter, show the dissatisfaction of the ancient mind with the ordinary mythology [yet the unity of the Godhead was the doctrine of the obscure Orpheus, of Plato the transcendentalist, and of such practical men as Cicero and Socrates.—J. D. C.]; and unless modern criticism has detected interpolations, perhaps both Bishop Thirlwall (*History of Greece*, i. 192, &c.) and Mr. Grote (*History of Greece*, i. 3 and chap. xvi, part i generally) have too much disregarded the sense which the pious and admiring Cowper gave to Homer's occasional mode of using 'theos'. (*Odyssey*, xiv with Cowper's note, p. 48, vol. ii, edition of 1802.) [Cf. also the care of the Greek or the Roman in addressing a deity, and in particular Zeus or Jupiter, in his particular 'capacity' most suited to the occasion.—Ed.]

Mithraic legislators; while Vyāsa perhaps surpassed Plato in keeping the people tremblingly alive to the punishment which awaited evil deeds.[1] The immortality of the soul was indeed encumbered with the doctrine of transmigration,[2] the active virtues were perhaps deemed less meritorious than bodily austerities and mental abstraction,[3] and the Brāhman polity was soon fatally clogged with the dogma

[1] Ritter (*Ancient Philosophy*, ii. 387) labours to excuse Plato for his '*inattention*' to the subject of duty or obligation, on the plea that the Socratic system did not admit of necessity or of a compulsory principle. [Nevertheless, Socrates, *as represented by Xenophon*, may be considered to have held *Worship* of the Gods to be a *Duty* of Man. (See the *Memorabilia*, b. iv, c. iii, iv, vi, and vii.)—J. D. C.] Bacon lies open in an inferior degree to the same objection as Plato, of underrating the importance of moral philosophy (cf. Hallam's *Literature of Europe*, iii. 191, and Macaulay, *Edinburgh Review*, July 1837, p. 84); and yet a strong sense of duty towards God is essential to the well-being of society, if not to systems of transcendental or material philosophy. In the East, however, philosophy has always been more closely allied to theology than in civilized Greece or modern Europe. Plato, indeed, arraigns the dead and torments the souls of the wicked (see for instance *Gorgias*, Sydenham and Taylor's translation, iv. 451), and practically among men the doctrine may be effective or sufficient; but with the Greek piety is simply justice towards the gods, and a matter of choice or pleasure on the part of the imperishable human spirit. (Cf. Schleiermacher's *Introductions to Plato's Dialogues*, p. 181, &c., and Ritter's *Ancient Philosophy*, ii. 374.) Nor can it be distinctly said that Vyāsa taught the principle of grateful righteousness as now understood to be binding on men, and to constitute their duty and obligation; and probably the Indian may merely have the advantage of being a theological teacher instead of an ontological speculator.

[2] The more zealous Christian writers on Hindu theology seize upon the doctrine of transmigration as limiting the freedom of the will and the degree of isolation of the soul, when thus successively manifested in the world clouded with the imperfection of previous appearances. A man, it is said, thus becomes subject to the Fate of the Greeks and Romans. (Cf. Ward on *The Hindoos*, ii; Introductory Remarks, xxviii, &c.) But the soul so weighed down with the sins of a former existence does not seem to differ in an ethical point of view, and as regards our conduct in the present life, from the soul encumbered with the sin of Adam. Philosophically, the notions seem equally but modes of accounting for the existence of evil, or for its sway over men. [See also note 3, p. 44.—J. D. C.] [Socrates, who inculcated every *active* virtue, nevertheless admitted, 'that he who wanted least was nearest to the Divinity; for to need nothing was the attribute of God.' (*Memorabilia*, b. l, c. vi, s. 10.) J. D. C.]

of inequality among men, and with the institution of a body of hereditary guardians of religion.[1]

The Brāhmans succeeded in expelling the Buddhist faith from the Indian peninsula, and when Shankar Achārj journeyed and disputed nine hundred years after Christ, a few learned men, and the inoffensive half-conforming Jains,[2] alone remained to represent the 'Mlechhas', the barbarians or 'gentiles' of Hinduism. The Kshattriyas had acquired kingdoms, heathen princes had been subdued or converted, and the Brāhmans, who ever denounced as prophets rather than preached as missionaries, were powerless in foreign countries if no royal inquirer welcomed them, or if no ambitious warrior followed them. Hinduism had attained its limits, and the victory brought with it the seeds of decay. The mixture with strangers led to a partial adoption of their usages, and man's desire for sympathy ever prompted him to seek an object of worship more

Brāhmanism victorious over Buddhism.

Loses its unity and vigour.

[1] See Appendix IV, on 'Caste'.

[2] The modern Jains frankly admit the connexion of their faith with that of the Buddhists, and the Jaini traders of Eastern Mālwā claim the ancient 'tope' near Bhīlsa, as virtually a temple of their own creed. The date of the general recognition of the Jains as a sect is doubtful, but it is curious that the 'Kōsh', or vocabulary of Amar Singh, does not contain the word Jain, although the word 'Jin' is enumerated among the names of Mayadevi, the regent goddess of the material universe, and the mother of Gautama, the Buddhist patriarch or prophet. In the Bhagavad, again, Baudh is represented as the son of Jin, and as about to appear in Kikat Dēs, or Bihār. (See Colonel Kennedy, *Res. Hind. Mythol.*, pp. 243–50.) Amar Singh, the author of the Sanskrit 'Kosa', or vocabulary, was himself a Buddhist; and he is differently stated to have flourished in the first century before, or in the fifth after, Christ (Colonel Kennedy, as above, pp. 127, 128), but in Mālwā he is traditionally said to have been confuted in argument by Shankar Achārj, which would place him in the eighth or ninth century of our era.—J. D. C.] ['Jainism is professed by a comparatively small sect, and it tends to shade off into ordinary Hinduism. Many Jains employ Brāhmans in their domestic worship, venerate the cow, and often worship in Hindu temples. Jainism and Buddhism have much in common, and up to recent years Jainism was believed to be an offshoot of Buddhism. It is now known that it originated independently of, though at the same time as, Buddhism; that is, in the sixth century before Christ.'—Holderness, *Peoples and Problems of India.* (See Stevenson, *The Heart of Jainism.* Oxford University Press, 1915.)—Ed.]

nearly allied to himself in nature than the invisible and passionless divinity.[1] The concession of a simple black stone as a mark of direction to the senses,[2] no longer satisfied the hearts or understandings of the people, and Shankar Achārj, who could silence the Buddha materialist, and confute the infidel Chārvāk,[3] was compelled to admit

[1] Mr. Elphinstone (*History of India*, i. 189) observes that Rāma and Krishna, with their human feelings and congenial acts, attracted more votaries than the gloomy Siva; and I have somewhere noticed, I think in the *Edinburgh Review*, the truth well enlarged upon, viz. that the sufferings of Jesus materially aided the growth of Christianity by enlisting the sympathies of the multitude in favour of a crucified God. The bitter remark of Xenophanes, that if oxen became religious their gods would be bovine in form, is indeed most true as expressive of a general desire among men to make their divinities anthropomorphous. (Grote, *History of Greece*, iv. 523, and Thirlwall, *History*, ii. 136.)

[2] Hindu Saivism, or the worship of the Lingam, seems to represent the compromise which the learned Brāhmans made when they endeavoured to exalt and purify the superstition of the multitude, who throughout India continue to this day to see the mark of the near presence of the Divinity in everything. The Brāhmans may thus have taught the mere fetichist, that when regarding a simple black stone, they should think of the invisible ruler of the universe; and they may have wished to leave the Buddhist image worshippers some point of direction for the senses. That the Lingam is typical of reproductive energy seems wholly a notion of later times, and to be confined to the few who ingeniously or perversely see recondite meanings in ordinary similitudes. (Cf. Wilson, *Vishnu Purān*, preface, lxiv [and Colonel Kennedy (*Res. Hind. Mythol.*, pp. 284, 308), who distinctly says the Lingam and Youi are not held to be typical of the destructive and reproductive powers; and that there is nothing in the Purāns to sanction such an opinion.—J. D. C.].) [The latter part of the author's note, which begs the whole question of phallic worship, is hardly in agreement with modern theory.—Ed.]

[3] Professor Wilson (*Asiatic Researches*, xvi. 18) derives the title of the Chārvāk school from a Muni or seer of that name; but the Brāhmans, at least of Mālwā, derive the distinctive name, both of the teacher and of the system, from *Charu*, persuasive, excellent, and *Vāk*, speech—thus making the school simply the logical or dialectic, or perhaps sophistical, as it has become in fact. The Chārvākites are wholly materialist, and in deriving consciousness from a particular aggregation or condition of the elements of the body, they seem to have anticipated the physiologist, Dr. Lawrence, who makes the brain to secrete thought as the liver secretes bile. The system is also styled the Vārhusputya, and the name of Vrihaspati, the orthodox Regent of the planet Jupiter, became connected with Atheism, say the Hindus, owing to the jealousy with which the

the worship of Virtues and Powers, and to allow images, as well as formless types, to be enshrined in temples. The 'self-existent' needed no longer to be addressed direct, and the orthodox could pay his devotions to the Preserving Vishnu, to the Destroying Siva, to the Regent of the Sun, to Ganesh, the helper of men, or to the reproductive energy of nature personified as woman, with every assurance that his prayers would be heard, and his offerings accepted, by the Supreme Being.[1]

Shankar Achārj methodizes polytheism, A. D. 800–1000.

The old Brāhman worship had been domestic or solitary, and that of the Buddhists public or congregational; the Brāhman ascetic separated himself from his fellows, but the Buddhist hermit became a coenobite, the member of a community of devotees; the Brāhman reared a family before he became an anchorite, but the Buddhist vowed celibacy and renounced most of the pleasures of sense. These customs of the vanquished had their effect upon the conquerors, and Shankar Achārj, in his endeavour to strengthen orthodoxy, enacted the double part of St. Basil and Pope Honorius.[2] He established a monastery of Brāh-

Reaction of Buddhism on Brāhmanism.

Shankar Achārj establishes ascetic orders, and gives pre-eminence to Saivism.

secondary or delegated powers of Heaven saw the degree of virtue to which man was attaining by upright living and a contemplation of the Divinity; wherefore Vrihaspati descended to confound the human understanding by diffusing error. (Cf. Wilson, *As. Res.*, xvii. 308, and Troyer's *Dabistān*, ii. 198, note.)

[1] The five sects enumerated are still held to represent the most orthodox varieties of Hinduism, [and of the eighteen Purāns, five only give supremacy to one form of Divinity over others. (Colonel Kennedy, *Res. Hind. Mythol.*, pp. 203, 204.)—J. D. C.]

[2] All scholars and inquirers are deeply indebted to Professor Wilson for the account he has given of the Hindu sects in the sixteenth and seventeenth volumes of the *Asiatic Researches*. The works, indeed, which are abstracted, are in the hands of many people in India, particularly the Bhagat Mala (or History of the Saints) and its epitomes; but the advantage is great of being able to study the subject with the aid of the notes of a deep scholar personally acquainted with the country. It is only to be regretted that Professor Wilson has not attempted to trace the progress of opinion or reform among sectaries; but neither does such a project appear to have occurred to Mr. Ward, in his elaborate and valuable but piecemeal volumes on the Hindus. Muhsin Fāni, who wrote the *Dabistān*, has even less of sequence or of argument, but the observations and views of an intelligent, although garrulous and somewhat credulous, Muhammadan, who flourished nearly two centuries ago, have nevertheless a peculiar value; and

man ascetics; he converted the solitary 'Dandi', with his staff and waterpot, into one of an order, a monk or friar, at once coenobitic and mendicant, who lived upon alms and who practised chastity.[1] The *order* was rendered still further distinct by the choice of Siva as the truest type of God, an example which was soon followed; and, during the eleventh century, Rāmānuj established a fraternity of Brāhmans, named after himself, who adopted some refined rules of conduct, who saw the Deity in Vishnu, and who degraded the Supreme Being by attributing to him form and qualities.[2] A consequence of the institution of an order or fraternity is the necessity of attention to its rules,

Rāmānuj establishes other orders, with Vishnu as a tutelary god, A. D. 1000–1200.

Capt. Troyer's careful translation has now rendered the book accessible to the English public. [Colonel Kennedy, in his valuable *Researches*, takes no notice of the modern reformers: and he even says that the Hindu religion has remained unchanged for three thousand years (p. 192, &c.); meaning, however, it would seem, that the Unity of the Godhead is still the doctrine of Philosophy, and that Brāhma, Vishnu, and Siva are still the principal divinities of Polytheism.—J. D. C.]

[1] Shankar Achārj was a Brāhman of the south of India, and according to Professor Wilson (*As. Res.*, xvii. 180), he flourished during the eighth or ninth century: but his date is doubtful, and if, as is commonly said, Rāmānuj was his disciple and sister's son, he perhaps lived a century or a century and a half later. He is believed to have established four muths, or monasteries, or denominations, headed by the four out of his ten instructed disciples, who faithfully adhered to his views. The adherents of these four are specially regarded as 'Dandis', or, including the representatives of the six heretical schools, the whole are called 'Dasnames'. (Cf. Wilson, *As. Res.*, xvii. 169, &c.)

[2] Rāmānuj is variously stated to have lived some time between the beginning of the eleventh and the end of the twelfth century. (Wilson, *As. Res.*, xvi. 28, note.) In Central India he is understood to have told his uncle that the path which he, Shankar Achārj, had chosen, was not the right one; and the nephew accordingly seceded and established the first four 'sumprdaees', or congregations, in opposition to the four muths or orders of his teacher, and at the same time chose Vishnu as the most suitable type of God. Rāmānuj styled his congregation that of Sri, or Lakshmī. The other three were successively founded by, first, Mādhav; secondly, by Vishnu Swāmi and his better-known follower Vallabh; and thirdly, by Nimbharak or Nimbhaditya. These, although all Vaishnavis, called their assemblies or schools respectively after Brāhma, and Siva, and Sannakādik, a son of Brāhma. (Cf. Wilson, *As. Res.*, xvi. 27, &c.)

or to the injunctions of the spiritual superior. The person of a Brāhman had always been held sacred. It was believed that a pious Buddhist could disengage his soul or attain to divinity even in this world; and when Shankar Achārj rejected some of his chosen disciples for nonconformity or disobedience, he contributed to centre the growing feelings of reverence for the teacher solely upon a mortal man; and, in a short time, it was considered that all things were to be abandoned for the sake of the 'Gurū', and that to him were to be surrendered 'Tan, Man, Dhan', or body, mind, and worldly wealth.[1] Absolute submission to the spiritual master readily becomes a lively impression of the divinity of his mission; the inward evidences of grace are too subtle for the understanding of the barbaric convert; fixed observances take the place of sentiment, and he justifies his change of opinion by some material act of devotion.[2] But faith is the usual test of sincerity and pledge of favour among the sectarians of peaceful and instructed communities, and the reformers of India soon began to require such a declaration of mystic belief and reliance from the seekers of salvation.

Spiritual teachers or heads of orders arrogate infallibility.

Philosophic speculation had kept pace in diversity with religious usage: learning and wealth, and an extended intercourse with men, produced the ordinary tendency towards scepticism, and six orthodox schools opposed six heretical systems, and made devious attempts to acquire a knowledge of God by logical deductions from the phenomena of nature or of the human mind.[3] They disputed about the reality and the eternity of matter; about consciousness and understanding; and about life and the soul,

Scepticism and heresy increase.

[1] Cf. Wilson, *As Res.*, xvi. 90.

[2] The reader will remember the fervent exclamation of Clovis when, listening after a victory to the story of the passion and death of Christ, he became a convert to the faith of his wife, and a disciple of the ancient pastor of Rheims: 'Had I been present at the head of my valiant Franks, I would have revenged his injuries.' (Gibbon, *Decline and Fall of the Roman Empire*, vi. 302.) The Muhammadans tell precisely the same story of Taimūr and Husain the son of Alī: 'I would have hurried', said the conquering Tartar, 'from remotest India, to have prevented or avenged the death of the martyred Imām.'

[3] See Appendix V.

as separate from, or as identical with one another and with God. The results were, the atheism of some, the belief of others in a limitary deity, and the more general reception of the doctrine of 'Māyā' or illusion, which allows sensation to be a true guide on this side of the grave, but sees nothing certain or enduring in the constitution of the material world; a doctrine eagerly adopted by the subsequent reformers, who gave it a moral or religious application.[1]

The dogma of 'Māyā' receives a moral application.

General decline of Brāhmanism.

Such was the state of the Hindu faith or polity a thousand years after Christ. The fitness of the original system for general adoption had been materially impaired by the gradual recognition of a distinction of race; the Brāhmans had isolated themselves from the soldiers and the peasants, and they destroyed their own unanimity by admitting a virtual plurality of gods, and by giving assemblies of ascetics a pre-eminence over communities of pious householders. In a short time the gods were regarded as rivals, and their worshippers as antagonists. The rude Kshattriya warrior became a politic chief, with objects of his own, and ready to prefer one hierarchy or one divinity to another; while the very latitude of the orthodox worship led the multitude to doubt the sincerity and the merits of a body of ministers who no longer harmonized among themselves.

Early Arab incursions into India but little felt.

A new people now entered the country, and a new element hastened the decline of corrupted Hinduism. India had but little felt the earlier incursions of the Arabs during the first and second centuries of the 'Hijri'; and when the Abbasides became caliphs, they were more anxious to consolidate their vast empire, already weakened by the separation of Spain, than to waste their means on distant conquests which rebellion might soon dismember. The Arab, moreover, was no longer a single-minded enthusiastic soldier, but a selfish and turbulent viceroy; the original impulse given by the prophet to his countrymen had achieved its limit of conquest, and Muhammadanism required a new infusion of faith and hardihood to enable it to triumph over the heathens of Delhi and the Christians

[1] See Appendix VI.

Muhammadanism receives a fresh impulse on the conversion of the Turkomāns.

of Constantinople. This awakening spirit was acquired partly from the mountain Kūrds, but chiefly from the pastoral Turkomāns, who, from causes imperfectly understood, were once more impelled upon the fertile and wealthy south. During the ninth century, these warlike shepherds began to establish themselves from the Indus to the Black Sea, and they oppressed and protected the empire of Muhammad, as Goths and Vandals and their own progenitors had before entered and defended and absorbed the dominions of Augustus and Trajan. Tughril Beg and Saladin are the counterparts of Stilicho and Theodoric, and the Mullas and Saiyids of Bagdad were as anxious for the conversion of unbelievers as the bishops and deacons of the Greek and Latin Churches. The migratory barbarians who fell upon Europe became Christians, and those who plundered Asia adopted, with perhaps greater ease and ardour, the more congenial creed of Islām. Their vague unstable notions yielded to the authority of learning and civilization, and to the majesty of one omnipotent God, and thus armed with religion as a motive, and empire as an object, the Turks precipitated themselves upon India and upon the diminished provinces of the Byzantine Caesars.

Muhammad invades India, A. D. 1001.

Muhammad crossed the Indus in the year 1001, not long after Shankar Achārj had vainly endeavoured to arrest the progress of heresy, and to give limits to the diversity of faith which perplexed his countrymen. The Punjab was permanently occupied, and before the sultan's death, Kanauj and Gujrāt had been overrun. The Ghaznivides were expelled by the Ghorīs about 1183. Bengal was conquered by these usurpers, and when the Ibak Turks supplanted them in 1206, Hindustān became a separate portion of the Muhammadan world. During the next hundred and fifty years the whole of India was subdued; a continued influx of Mughals in the thirteenth, and of Afghāns in the fifteenth century, added to their successive authority as rulers, gradually changed the language and the thoughts of the vanquished. The Khiljīs and Tughlaks and Lodīs were too rude to be inquisitorial bigots; they had a lawful option in tribute, and taxation was more profitable, if less meritorious, than conversion. They adopted as their own

Hindustān becomes a separate portion of the Muhammadan world under the Ibaks, A. D. 1206.

the country which they had conquered. Numerous mosques attest their piety and munificence, and the introduction of the solar instead of the intractable lunar year, proves their attention to ordinary business and the wants of agriculture.[1]

And the conquerors become Indianized.

The Muhammadans became Indianized; and in the sixteenth century the great Akbar conceived the design of establishing a national government or monarchy which should unite the elements of the two systems: but political obedience does not always denote social amalgamation, and the reaction upon the Muslim mind perhaps increased that intolerance of Aurangzeb which hastened the ruin of the dynasty.

Action and reaction of Muhammadanism and Brāhmanism.

The influence of a new people, who equalled or surpassed Kshattriyas in valour, who despised the sanctity of Brāhmans, and who authoritatively proclaimed the unity of God and his abhorrence of images, began gradually to operate on the minds of the multitudes of India, and recalled even the learned to the simple tenets of the Vedas, which Shankar Achārj had disregarded. The operation was necessarily slow, for the imposing system of powers and emanations had been adapted with much industry to the local or peculiar divinities of tribes and races, and in the lapse of ages the legislation of Manu had become closely interwoven with the thoughts and habits of the people. Nor did the proud distinctions of caste and the reverence shown to Brāhmans fail to attract the notice and the admiration of the barbarous

[1] The solar, i. e. really sidereal year, called the 'Shabur San', or vulgarly the 'Sūr San', that is, the year of (Arabic) months, was apparently introduced into the Deccan by Tughlak Shāh towards the middle of the fourteenth century of Christ, or between 1341 and 1344, and it is still used by the Marāthās in all their more important documents, the dates being inserted in Arabic words written in Hīndī (Marāthī) characters. (Cf. Prinsep's *Useful Tables*, ii. 30, who refers to a Report by Lieut.-Colonel Jervis, on Weights and Measures.) The other 'Fasli', or 'harvest' years of other parts of India, were not introduced until the reigns of Akbar and Shah Jahān, and they mostly continue to this day to be used, even by the English, in revenue accounts. The commencement of each might, without much violence, be adapted to the 1st of July of any year of the Christian era, and the Muhammadans and Hindus could at the same time retain, the former the Hijri, and the latter the Shak (Sāka) and Sambat names of the months respectively. No greater degree of uniformity or simplicity is required, and the general predominance of the English would render a measure so obviously advantageous of easy introduction.

victors. Shaikhs and Saiyids had an innate holiness assigned to them, and Mughals and Pathāns copied the exclusiveness of Rājpūts. New superstition also emulated old credulity. ' Pīrs ' and ' Shahīds ', saints and martyrs, equalled Krishna and Bhairon in the number of their miracles, and the Muhammadans almost forgot the unity of God in the multitude of intercessors whose aid they implored. Thus custom jarred with custom, and opinion with opinion, and while the few always fell back with confidence upon their revelations, the Korān and Vedas, the public mind became agitated, and found no sure resting-place with Brāhmans or Mullas, with Mahādev or Muhammad.[1]

The popular belief unsettled.

[1] Gibbon has shown (*History*, ii. 356) how the scepticism of learned Greeks and Romans proved favourable to the growth of Christianity, and a writer in the *Quarterly Review* (for June 1846, p. 116) makes some just observations on the same subject. The cause of the scepticism is not perhaps sufficiently attributed to the mixture of the Eastern and Western superstitions, which took place after the conquests of Alexander, and during the supremacy of Rome.

Similarly, the influence of Muhammadan learning and civilization in moulding the European mind seems to be underrated in the present day, although Hallam (*Literature of Europe*, i. 90, 91, 149, 150, 157, 158, 189, 190) admits our obligations in physical, and even in mental *science*; and a representative of Oxford, the critical yet fanciful William Gray (*Sketch of English Prose Literature*, pp. 22, 37), not only admires the *fictions* of the East, but confesses their beneficial effect on the Gothic genius. The Arabs, indeed, were the preservers and diffusers of that science or knowledge which was brought forth in Egypt or India, which was reduced to order in Greece and Rome, and which has been so greatly extended in particular directions by the moderns of the West. The pre-eminence of the Muhammadan over the Christian mind was long conspicuous in the metaphysics of the schoolmen, and it is still apparent in the administrative system of Spain, in the common terms of astronomical and medicinal science, and in the popular songs of feudal Europe, which ever refer to the Arabian prophet and to Turks and Saracens, or expatiate on the actions of the Cid, a Christian hero with a Musalmān title.

Whewell (*History of Inductive Sciences*, i. 22, 276), in demonstrating that the Arabs did very little, if aught, to *advance* exact science, physical or metaphysical, and in likening them to the servant who had the talent but put it not to use, might yet have excused them on the plea that the genius of the people was directed to the propagation of religious truth—to subjecting the Evil Principle to the Good in Persia, to restoring Monotheism in India, and to the subversion of gross idolatry in regions of Africa still untrodden by Europeans. With this view of the English Professor may be contrasted the opinion

Rāmānand establishes a comprehensive sect at Benares, about A. D. 1400;

The first result of the conflict was the institution, about the end of the fourteenth century, of a comprehensive sect by Rāmānand of Benares, a follower of the tenets of Rāmānuj. Unity of faith or of worship had already been destroyed, and the conquest of the country by foreigners diminished unity of action among the ministers of religion. Learning had likewise declined, and poetic fancy and family tradition were allowed to modify the ancient legends of the 'Purāns' or chronicles, and to usurp the authority of the Vedas.[1] The heroic Rāma was made the object of devotion to this new sect of the Middle Ganges, and as the doctrine of the innate superiority of Brāhmans and Kshattriyas had been rudely shaken by the Muhammadan ascendancy, Rāmānand seized upon the idea of man's equality before God. He instituted no nice distinctive observances, he admitted all classes of people as his disciples, and he declared that the true votary was raised above mere social forms, and became free or liberated.[2] During the same century the learned

and introduces hero-worship; but maintains the equality of true believers before God.

of Humboldt, who emphatically says that the Arabs are to be regarded as the proper founders of the *physical sciences*, in the sense which we are now accustomed to attach to the term. (*Kosmos*, Sabine's trans., ii. 212.)

[1] Modern criticism is not disposed to allow an ancient date to the Purāns, and doubtless the interpolations are both numerous and recent, just as the ordinary copies of the rhapsodies of the Rājpūt Bhāt, or Bard, Chand, contain allusions to dynasties and events subsequent to Pirthī Rāj and Mahmūd. The difficulty lies in separating the old from the new, and perhaps also objectors have too much lost sight of the circumstance that the criticized and less corrupted Rāmāyana and Mahābhārata are only the chief of the Purāns. They seem needlessly inclined to reject entirely the authority or authenticity of the conventional Eighteen Chronicles, merely because eulogiums on modern families have been introduced by successive flatterers. Nevertheless, the Purāns must rather be held to illustrate modes of thought, than to describe historical events with accuracy. [Colonel Kennedy (*Res. Hind. Mythol.*, pp. 130, 153, &c.) regards them mainly as complementary to the Vedas, explaining religious and moral doctrines, and containing disquisitions concerning the illusive nature of the universe, and not as in any way intended to be historical.—J. D. C.]

[2] Cf. *Dabistān*, ii. 179, and Wilson, *As. Res.*, xvi. 36, &c. Professor Wilson remarks (ibid., p. 44, and also xvii. 183), that the sects of Shankar Achārj and Rāmānuj included Brāhmans only, and indeed chiefly men of learning of that race. The followers of Rāmānand,

enthusiast Gorakhnath gave popularity, especially in the Punjab, to the doctrine of the 'Yōg', which belonged more properly as a theory or practice to the Buddhist faith, but which was equally adopted as a philosophic dogma by the followers of Vyāsa and of Sākya. It was, however, held that in this 'Kalyug', or iron age, fallen man was unequal to so great a penance, or to the attainment of complete beatitude; but Gorakh taught that intense mental abstraction would etherialize the body of the most lowly, and gradually unite his spirit with the all-pervading soul of the world. He chose Siva as the deity who would thus bless the austere perseverance of his votaries of whatever caste; and, not content with the ordinary frontal marks of sects and persuasions, he distinguished his disciples by boring their ears, whence they are familiarly known as the 'Kanphata', or ear-torn Jogis.[1]

Gorakhnath establishes a sect in the Punjab,

and maintains the equalizing effect of religious penance;

but causes further diversity by adopting Siva as the type of God.

or the Vaishnavas, were long violently opposed to the Saivic denominations; so much so, according to tradition, that they would not, on any account, cross the Narbadā river, which is held to be peculiarly sacred to Mahādev or Mahesh, but would rather, in performing a journey, go round by its sources.

Among the people of Central India there is a general persuasion that the Narbadā will one day take the place of the Ganges as the most holy of streams; but the origin of the feeling is not clear, as neither is the fact of the consecration of the river to Siva. At Maheshwar, indeed, there is a whirlpool, which, by rounding and polishing fallen stones, rudely shapes them into resemblances of a Lingam, and which are as fertile a source of profit to the resident priests as are the Vaishnava fossil ammonites of a particular part of the Himālayas. The labours of the whirlpool likewise diffuse a sanctitude over all the stones of the rocky channel, as expressed in the vernacular sentence, 'Rehwa ke kunkur sub sunkur sumān,' i. e. each stone of the Narbadā (Rehwa) is divine, or equal to Siva.

Maheshwar was the seat of Sahsar Bahu, or of the hundred-handed Kshattriya king, who was slain by Paras Rām, of the not very far distant town of Nimāwar, opposite Hindia; a probable occurrence, which was soon made the type, or the cause, of the destruction of the ancient warrior race by the Brāhmans. The same is declared by the Siva Purān. (Colonel Kennedy, *Res. Hind. Mythol.*, p. 309, note.)—J. D. C.]

[1] Cf. Wilson (*As. Res.*, xvii. 183, &c.) and the *Dabistān* (Troyer's translation, i. 123, &c.). In the latter, Muhsin Fāni shows some points of conformity between the Jogis and the Muhammadans. With regard to Yōg, in a scientific point of view, it may be observed that it corresponds with the state of abstraction or self-consciousness

The Vedas and Korān assailed by Kabīr, a disciple of Rāmā-nand, about A. D. 1450;

and the mother tongue of the people used as an instrument.

But asceticism still upheld.

A step was thus made, and faith and abandonment of the pleasures of life were held to abrogate the distinctions of race which had taken so firm a hold on the pride and vanity of the rich and powerful. In the next generation, or about the year 1450, the mysterious weaver Kabīr, a disciple of Rāmānand, assailed at once the worship of idols, the authority of the Korān and Shastras, and the exclusive use of a learned language. He addressed Muhammadans as well as Hindus, he urged them to call upon him, the invisible Kabīr, and to strive continually after inward purity. He personified creation or the world as 'Māyā', or as woman, prolific of deceit and illusion, and thus denounced man's weakness or his proneness to evil. Practically Kabīr admitted outward conformity, and leant towards Rāma or Vishnu as the most perfect type of God. Like his predecessors, he erringly gave shape and attributes to the divinity, and he further limited the application of his doctrines of reform, by declaring retirement from the world to be desirable, and the 'Sādh', or pure or perfect man, the passive or inoffensive votary, to be the living resemblance of the

which raised the soul above mortality or chance, and enabled it to apprehend the 'true' and to grasp Plato's 'idea', or archical form of the world, and that neither Indians nor Greeks considered man capable, in his present imperfect condition, of attaining to such a degree of 'union with God' or 'knowledge of the true'. (Cf. Ritter, *Ancient Philosophy*, Morrison's translation, ii. 207, 334–6, and Wilson, *As. Res.*, xvii. 185.) Were it necessary to pursue the correspondence further, it would be found that Plato's whole system is almost identical, in its rudimental characteristics, with the schemes of Kapil and Patanjal jointly: thus, God and matter are in both eternal; Mahat, or intelligence, or the informing spirit of the world, is the same with *nous* or *logos*, and so on. With both God, that is 'Poorsh' in the one and the Supreme God in the other, would seem to be separate from the world as appreciable by man. It may further be observed that the Sānkhya system is divided into two schools, independent of that of Patanjal, the first of which regards 'Poorsh' simply as life, depending for activity upon 'adrisht', chance or fate, while the second holds the term to denote an active and provident ruler, and gives to vitality a distinct existence. The school of Patanjal differs from this latter, principally in its terminology and in the mode (Yōg) laid down for attaining bliss—one of the four subdivisions of which mode, viz. that of stopping the breath, is allowed to be the doctrine of Gorakh, but is declared to have been followed of old by Mārkand, in a manner more agreeable to the Vedas, than the practice of the recent Reformer.

Almighty. The views, however, of Kabīr are not very distinctly laid down or clearly understood; but the latitude of usage which he sanctioned, and his employment of a spoken dialect, have rendered his writings extensively popular among the lower orders of India.[1]

Chaitan preaches religious reform in Bengal, A. D. 1500 1550.

In the beginning of the sixteenth century the reforms of Rāmānand were introduced into Bengal by Chaitan, a Brāhman of Nadiā. He converted some Muhammadans, and admitted all classes as members of his sect. He insisted upon 'Bhakti', or faith, as chastening the most impure; he allowed marriage and secular occupations; but his followers abused the usual injunction of reverence for the teacher, and some of them held that the Gurū was to be invoked before God.[2] About the same period Vallabh Swami, a Brāhman of Telingāna, gave a further impulse to the reformation in progress, and he taught that married teachers were not only admissible as directors of the conscience, but that the householder was to be preferred, and that the world was to be enjoyed by both master and

Insists upon the efficacy of faith, and admits of secular occupations.

Vallabh extends the reformation to the south,

[1] Cf. the *Dabistān*, ii. 184, &c., Wilson, *As. Res.*, xvi. 53, and Ward's *Hindoos*, iii. 406. Kabīr is an Arabic word, meaning the greatest, and Professor Wilson doubts whether any such person ever existed, and considers the Kabīr of Muhsin Fāni to be the personification of an idea, or that the title was assumed by a Hindu free-thinker as a disguise. The name, however, although significant, is now at least not uncommon, and perhaps the ordinary story that Kabīr was a foundling, reared by a weaver, and subsequently admitted as a disciple by Rāmānand, is sufficiently probable to justify his identity. His body is stated to have been claimed both by the Hindus and Muhammadans, and Muhsin Fāni observes that many Muhammadans became Bairāgis, i. e. ascetics of the modern Vaishnava sect, of which the followers of Rāmānand and Kabīr form the principal subdivisions. (*Dabistān*, ii. 193.) As a further instance of the fusion of feeling then, and now, going forward, the reply of the Hindu deist, Akāmnāth, to the keepers of the Kaba at Mecca may be quoted. He first scandalized them by asking where was the master of the house; and he then inquired why the idols had been thrown out. He was told that the works of men were not to be worshipped; whereupon he inquired whether the temple itself was not reared with hands, and therefore undeserving of respect (*Dabistān*, ii. 117).

[2] For an account of Chaitan and his followers, cf. Wilson, *Asiatic Researches*, xvi. 109, &c., and Ward, on *The Hindoos*, iii. 467, &c.; and for some apposite remarks on Bhakti or faith, see Wilson, *As Res.*, xvii. 312.

and further discountenances celibacy, about A. D. 1550.

disciple. This principle was readily adopted by the peaceful mercantile classes, and 'Gusains', as the conductors of family worship, have acquired a commanding influence over the industrious Quietists of the country; but they have at the same time added to the diversity of the prevailing idolatry by giving pre-eminence to Bala Gopāl, the *infant* Krishna, as the very God of the Universe.[1]

Recapitulation.

Thus, in the beginning of the sixteenth century, the Hindu mind was no longer stagnant or retrogressive; it had been leavened with Muhammadanism, and changed and quickened for a new development. Rāmānand and Gorakh had preached religious equality, and Chaitan had repeated that faith levelled caste. Kabīr had denounced images, and appealed to the people in their own tongue, and Vallabh had taught that effectual devotion was compatible with the ordinary duties of the world. But these good and able men appear to have been so impressed with the nothingness of this life, that they deemed the amelioration of man's social condition to be unworthy of a thought. They aimed chiefly at emancipation from priestcraft, or

The reforms partial, and leading to sectarianism only.

from the grossness of idolatry and polytheism. They formed pious associations of contented Quietists, or they gave themselves up to the contemplation of futurity in the hope of approaching bliss, rather than called upon their fellow creatures to throw aside every social as well as religious trammel, and to arise a new people freed from the debasing corruption of ages. They perfected forms of dissent rather than planted the germs of nations, and their *sects* remain

Nānak's views more comprehensive and profound.

to this day as they left them. It was reserved for *Nānak* to perceive the true principles of reform, and to lay those broad foundations which enabled his successor *Gobind* to fire the minds of his countrymen with a new nationality, and to give practical effect to the doctrine that the lowest is equal with the highest, in race as in creed, in political rights as in religious hopes.

[1] See Wilson, *Asiatic Researches*, xvi. 85, &c.; and for an account of the corresponding Vaishnava sect of Mādhav, which has, however, a leaning to Saivism, see also Wilson, *As. Res.*, xvi. 100. (See also Appendix VII for some remarks on the Metaphysics of Indian Reformers.)

1469–1539.

Nānak's birth and early life, A. D. 1469.

Nānak was born in the year 1469, in the neighbourhood of Lahore.[1] His father, Kālu, was a Hindu of the Bedī subdivision of the once warlike Kshattriyas, and he was, perhaps, like most of his race, a petty trader in his native village.[2] Nānak appears to have been naturally of a pious disposition and of a reflecting mind, and there is reason to believe that in his youth he made himself familiar with the popular creeds both of the Muhammadans and Hindus, and that he gained a general knowledge of the Korān and of the Brāhmanical Shastras.[3] His good sense and fervid

[1] Nānak is generally said to have been born in Talwandi, a village on the Rāvi above Lahore, which was held by one Rai Bhua of the Bhutti tribe. (Cf. Malcolm, *Sketch of the Sikhs*, p. 78, and Forster, *Travels*, i. 292–3.) But one manuscript account states that, although the father of Nānak was of Talwandi, the teacher himself was born in Kanakātch, about fifteen miles southerly from Lahore, in the house of his mother's parents. It is indeed not uncommon in the Punjab for women to choose their own parents' home as the place of their confinement, especially of their first child, and the children thus born are frequently called Nānak (or Nanki, in the feminine), from *Nanke*, one's mother's parents. Nānak is thus a name of usual occurrence, both among Hindus and Muhammadans, of the poor or industrious classes. The accounts agree as to the *year* of Nānak's birth, but differ, while they affect precision, with regard to the *day of the month* on which he was born. Thus one narrative gives the 13th, and another the 18th, of the month Kartik, of the year 1526 of Vikramājīt, which corresponds with the latter end of 1469 of Christ.

[2] In the *Siar ul Mutākharin* (Brigg's translation, i. 110) it is stated that Nānak's father was a grain merchant, and in the *Dabistān* (ii. 247) that Nānak himself was a grain factor. The Sikh accounts are mostly silent about the occupation of the father, but they represent the sister of Nānak to have been married to a corn factor, and state that he was himself placed with his brother-in-law to learn, or to give aid, in carrying on the business.

[3] A manuscript compilation in Persian mentions that Nānak's first teacher was a Muhammadan. The *Siar ul Mutākharin* (i. 110) states that Nānak was carefully educated by one Saiyid Hasan, a neighbour of his father's, who conceived a regard for him, and who was wealthy but childless. Nānak is further said, in the same book, to have studied the most approved writings of the Muhammadans. According to Malcolm (*Sketch*, p. 14), Nānak is reported, by the Muhammadans, to have learnt all earthly sciences from Khizar, i. e. the prophet Elias. The ordinary Muhammadan accounts also represent Nānak, when a child, to have astonished his teacher by asking him the hidden import of the first letter of the alphabet, which is almost a straight stroke in Persian and Arabic, and which is held

1469–1539. temper left him displeased with the corruptions of the vulgar faith, and dissatisfied with the indifference of the learned, or with the refuge which they sought in the specious abstractions of philosophy; nor is it improbable that the homilies of Kabīr and Gorakh had fallen upon his susceptible mind with a powerful and enduring effect.[1] In a moment of enthusiasm the ardent inquirer abandoned his home, and strove to attain wisdom by penitent meditation, by study, and by an enlarged intercourse with mankind.[2] He travelled, perhaps, beyond the limits of India, he prayed in solitude, he reflected on the Vedas and on the mission of Muhammad, and he questioned with equal anxiety the learned priest and the simple devotee about the will of God and the path to happiness.[3] Plato and Bacon, Des

The mental struggles of Nānak.

even vulgarly to denote the unity of God. The reader will remember that the apocryphal gospels state how Christ, before he was twelve years old, perplexed his instructors, and explained to them the mystical significance of the alphabetical characters. (Strauss, *Life of Jesus*, i. 272.)

[1] Extracts or selections from the writings of Kabīr appear in the *Adi-Granth*, and Kabīr is often, and Gorakh sometimes, quoted or referred to.

[2] A chance meeting with some Fakīrs (Malcolm, *Sketch*, pp. 8, 13) and the more methodical instructions of a Dervish (*Dabistān*, ii. 247) are each referred to as having subdued the mind of Nānak, or as having given him the impulse which determined the future course of his life. In Malcolm may be seen those stories which please the multitude, to the effect that although Nānak, when the spirit of God was upon him, bestowed all the grain in his brother-in-law's stores in charity, they were nevertheless always found replenished; or that Daulat Khān Lodī, the employer of Nānak's brother-in-law, although aware that much had really been given away, nevertheless found everything correct on balancing the accounts of receipts and expenditure.

The Sikh accounts represent Nānak to have met the Emperor Bābar, and to have greatly edified the adventurous sovereign by his demeanour and conversation, while he perplexed him by saying that both were kings and were about to found dynasties of ten. I have traced but two allusions to Bābar by name, and one by obvious inference, in the *Adi-Granth*, viz. in the Asa Rag and Tailang portions, and these bear reference simply to the destruction of a village, and to his incursions as a conqueror. Muhsin Fāni (*Dabistān*, ii. 249) preserves an idle report that Nānak, being dissatisfied with the Afghāns, called the Mughals into India.

[3] Nānak is generally said to have travelled over the whole of India,

Cartes and Alghazāli, examined the current philosophic systems of the world, without finding a sure basis of truth for the operations of the intellect; and, similarly, the heart of the pious Nānak sought hopelessly for a resting-place amid the conflicting creeds and practices of men. All was error, he said; he had read Korāns and Purāns, but God he had nowhere found.[1] He returned to his native land, he threw aside the habit of an ascetic, he became again the father of his family, and he passed the remainder of his long life in calling upon men to worship the One Invisible God, to live virtuously, and to be tolerant of the failings of others. The mild demeanour, the earnest piety, and persuasive eloquence of Nānak, are ever the themes of praise, and he died at the age of seventy, leaving behind him many zealous and admiring disciples.[2]

1469–1539.

He becomes a teacher.

Dies, aged seventy, A.D. 1539.

to have gone through Persia, and to have visited Mecca (cf. Malcolm, *Sketch*, p. 16, and Forster, *Travels*, i. 295–6), but the number of years he employed in wandering, and the date of his final return to his native province, are alike uncertain. He had several companions, among whom Mardāna, the rababi or harper (or rather a chanter, and player upon a stringed instrument like a guitar), Lahna, who was his successor, Bala, a Sindhu Jāt, and Rām Dās, styled Buddha or the Ancient, are the most frequently referred to. In pictorial representations Mardāna always accompanies Nānak. When at Mecca, a story is related that Nānak was found sleeping with his feet towards the temple, that he was angrily asked how he dared to dishonour the house of the Lord, and that he replied, 'Could he turn his feet where the house of God was not?' (Malcolm, *Sketch of the Sikhs*, p. 159.) Nānak adopted, sometimes at least, the garb of a Muhammadan Dervish, and at Multān he visited an assembly of Musalmān devotees, saying he was but as the stream of the Ganges entering the ocean of holiness. (Cf. Malcolm, *Sketch*, p. 21, and the *Siar ul Mutākharin*, i. 311.)

[1] There is current a verse imputed to Nānak, to the effect that—

'Several scriptures and books had he read,
But one (God) he had not found:
Several Korāns and Purāns had he read,
But faith he could not put in any.'

The *Adi-Granth* abounds with passages of a similar tenor, and in the supplemental portion, called the Ratan Mala, Nānak says, 'Man may read Vedas and Korāns, and reach to a temporary bliss, but without God salvation is unattainable.'

[2] The accounts mostly agree as to the date of Nānak's death, and they place it in 1596 of Vikramājīt, or 1539 of Christ. A Gurmukhī abstract states precisely that he was a teacher for seven years, five

1469–1539. The excellences of Nānak's doctrine.

Nānak combined the excellences of preceding reformers, and he avoided the more grave errors into which they had fallen. Instead of the circumscribed divinity, the anthropomorphous God of Rāmānand and Kabīr, he loftily invokes the Lord as the one, the sole, the timeless being; the creator, the self-existent, the incomprehensible, and the everlasting. He likens the Deity to Truth, which was before the world began, which is, and which shall endure for ever, as the ultimate idea or cause of all we know or behold.[1]

The godhead.

months, and seven days, and that he died on the 10th of the Hindu month Asauj. Forster (*Travels*, i. 295) represents that he travelled for fifteen years. Nānak died at Kartārpur, on the Rāvi, about forty miles above Lahore, where there is a place of worship sacred to him. He left two sons, Sri Chand, an ascetic, whose name lives as the founder of the Hindu sect of Udasis, and Lachmī Das, who devoted himself to pleasure, and of whom nothing particular is known. The Nānakputras, or descendants of Nānak, called also Sahibzadas, or sons of the master, are everywhere reverenced among Sikhs, and if traders, some privileges are conceded to them by the chiefs of their country. Muhsin Fāni observes (*Dabistān*, ii. 253) that the representatives of Nānak were known as Kartāris, meaning, perhaps, rather that they were held to be holy or devoted to the service of God, than that they were simply residents of Kartārpur.

[1] See the *Adi-Granth* in, for instance, the portion called *Gowree Rag*, and the prefatory *Jup*, or prayer of admonition and remembrance. Cf. also Wilkins, *Asiatic Researches*, i. 289, &c.

'Akalpurik', or the Timeless Being, is the ordinary Sikh appellation of God, corresponding idiomatically with the 'Almighty', in English. Yet Gobind, in the second *Granth* (Hazāra Shabd portion), apostrophizes Time itself as the only true God, for God was the first and the last, the being without end, &c.

Milton assigns to time a casual or limited use only, and Shakespeare makes it finite:

'For time, though in eternity applied
To motion, measures all things durable
By present, past, and future.'

Paradise Lost, v.

'But thought's the slave of life, and life, time's fool;
And time, that takes survey of all the world,
Must have a stop.'

1 Henry IV, v. iv.

Three of the modern philosophizing schools of India, viz. a division of the Sānkhyas, the Purāniks, and the Saivas, make Kāl, or time, one of the twenty-seven, or thirty, or thirty-six component essences or phenomena of the universe of matter and mind, and thus give it distinct functions, or a separate existence.

1469-1539.

He addresses equally the Mulla and the Pandit, the Dervish and the Sannyāsī, and tells them to remember *that* Lord of Lords who has seen come and go numberless Muhammads, and Vishnus, and Sivas.[1] He tells them that virtues and charities, heroic acts and gathered wisdom, are nought of themselves, that the only knowledge which availeth is the knowledge of God;[2] and then, as if to rebuke those vain men who saw eternal life in their own act of faith, he declares that they only can find the Lord on whom the Lord looks with favour.[3] Yet the extension of grace is linked with the exercise of our will and the beneficent use of our faculties. God, said Nānak, places salvation in good works and uprightness of conduct: the Lord will ask of man, 'What has he done?'[4]—and the teacher further required timely repentance of men, saying, 'If not until the day of reckoning the sinner abaseth himself, punishment shall overtake him'.[5]

Muhammadans and Hindus equally called on to worship God in truth.

Faith, grace, and good works all necessary.

Nānak adopted the philosophical system of his countrymen, and regarded bliss as the dwelling of the soul with God after its punitory transmigrations should have ceased. Life, he says, is as the shadow of the passing bird, but the soul of man is, as the potter's wheel, ever circling on its pivot.[6] He makes the same uses of the current language or notions of the time on other subjects, and thus says, he who remains bright amid darkness (Anjan), unmoved amid deceit (Māyā), that is, perfect amid temptation, should

Nānak adopts the Brāhmanical philosophy; but in a popular sense, or by way of illustration only.

[1] A passage of Nānak's in the supplement to the *Adi-Granth*, after saying that there have been multitudes of prophets, teachers, and holy men, concludes thus:

The Lord of Lords is the One God, the Almighty God himself;
Oh Nānak! his qualities are beyond comprehension.'

[2] See the *Adi-Granth*, towards the end of the portion called *Asa*.

[3] See the *Adi-Granth*, end of the *Asa Rag*, and in the supplementary portion called the *Ratan Mala*.

[4] The *Adi-Granth*, *Parbhātī Ragni*. Cf. Malcolm (*Sketch*, p. 161) and Wilkins (*As. Res.*, i. 289, &c.).

[5] See the Nasihat Nama, or admonition of Nānak to Karon, a fabulous monarch, which, however, is not admitted into the *Granth*, perhaps because its personal or particular application is not in keeping with the abstract and general nature of that book. Neither, indeed, is it certainly known to be Nānak's composition, although it embodies many of his notions.

[6] *Adi-Granth*, end of the *Asa Rag*.

1469–1539. attain happiness.[1] But it would be idle to suppose that he speculated upon being, or upon the material world, after the manner of Plato or Vyāsa ; [2] and it would be unreasonable to condemn him because he preferred the doctrine of a succession of habiliments, and the possible purification of the most sinful soul, to the resurrection of the same body, and the pains of everlasting fire.[3] Nānak also referred to the Arabian prophet, and to the Hindu incarnations, not as impostors and the diffusers of evil, but as having truly been sent by God to instruct mankind, and he lamented that sin should nevertheless prevail. He asserted no special divinity, although he may possibly have considered himself, as he came to be considered by others, the successor of these inspired teachers of his belief, sent to reclaim fallen mortals of all creeds and countries within the limits of his knowledge. He rendered his mission applicable to all times and places, yet he declared himself to be but the slave, the humble messenger of the Almighty, making use of universal truth as his sole instrument.[4] He did not claim for his

Nānak admits the mission of Muhammad as well as the Hindu incarnations.

[1] *Adi-Granth*, in the *Suhi* and *Ramkali* portions.

[2] See Appendix VIII.

[3] The usual objection of the Muhammadans to the Hindu doctrine of transmigration is, that the wicked soul of this present world has no remembrance of its past condition and bygone punishments, and does not, therefore, bring with it any inherent incentive to holiness. The Muhammadans, however, do not show that a knowledge of the sin of Adam, and *consequent* corruption of his posterity, is instinctive to a follower of Christ or to a disciple of their own prophet; and, metaphysically, an impartial thinker will perhaps prefer the Brāhman doctrine of a soul finally separated from the changeable matter of our senses, to the Egyptian scheme of the resurrection of the corruptible body,—a notion which seems to have impressed itself on the Israelites, notwithstanding the silence of Moses, and which resisted for centuries the action of other systems, and which was at length revived with increased force in connexion with the popular belief in miracles. See also note 2, p. 24 *ante*.

[4] The whole scope of Nānak's teaching is that God is all in all, and that purity of mind is the first of objects. He urges all men to practise devotion, and he refers to past prophets and dispensations as being now of no avail, but he nowhere attributes to himself any superiority over others. He was a man among men, calling upon his fellow creatures to live a holy life. (Cf. the *Dabistān*, ii. 249, 250, 253 ; and see Wilson, *As. Res.*, xvii. 234, for the expression 'Nānak thy slave is a freewill offering unto thee'.)

writings, replete as they were with wisdom and devotion,[1] the merit of a direct transcription of the words of God; nor did he say that his own preaching required or would be sanctioned by miracles.[2] 'Fight with no weapon,' said he, 'save the word of God; a holy teacher hath no means save the purity of his doctrine.'[3] He taught that asceticism or abandonment of the world was unnecessary, the pious hermit and the devout householder being equal in the eyes of the Almighty; but he did not, like his contemporary Vallabh, express any invidious preference for married teachers, although his own example showed that he considered every one should fulfil the functions of his nature.[4] In treating the two prominent external observances of Hindus and Muhammadans, veneration for the cow and abhorrence of the hog, he was equally wise and conciliatory, yielding perhaps something to the prejudices of his education as well as to the gentleness of his disposition. 'The rights of strangers,' said he, 'are the one the ox, and the other the swine, but "Pīrs" and "Gurūs" will praise those who partake not of that which hath enjoyed life.'[5]

1469–1539.

Disclaims miraculous powers.

Discourages asceticism.

Conciliatory between Muhammadans and Hindus.

[1] The Muhammadan writers are loud in their praises of Nānak's writings. (Cf. the *Siar ul Mutākharin*, i. 110, 111, and the *Dabistān*, ii. 251, 252.)

With these sober views of the Orientals may be contrasted the opinion of the European Baron Hügel, who says (*Travels*, p. 283) that the *Granth* is 'a compound of mystical absurdities'. He admits, however, that the Sikhs worship one God, abhor images, and reject caste, at least in theory.

[2] See particularly the *Sri Rag* chapter of the *Adi-Granth*. In the Maj Vār portion Nānak says to a pretender to miracles, 'Dwell thou in flame uninjured, remain unharmed amid eternal ice, make blocks of stone thy food, spurn the solid earth before thee with thy foot, weigh the heavens in a balance, and then ask thou that Nānak perform wonders!'

Strauss (*Life of Jesus*, ii. 237) points out that Christ censured the seeking for miracles (John iv. 48), and observes that the apostles in their letters do not mention miracles at all.

[3] Malcolm, *Sketch*, pp. 20, 21, 165.

[4] *Adi-Granth*, particularly the *Asa Ragni* and *Ramkali Ragni*. (Cf. the *Dabistān*, ii. 271.)

[5] *Adi-Granth*, *Maj* chapter. Cf. Malcolm (*Sketch*, p. 36, note, and p. 137), where it is said Nānak prohibited swine's flesh; but, indeed, the flesh of the *tame* hog had always been forbidden to Hindus. (Manu's *Institutes*, v. 19.) The *Dabistān* (ii, 248) states that Nānak

1469–1539.

Nānak fully extricates his followers from error.

But his reformation necessarily religious and moral only.

Nānak left his Sikhs or disciples without new social laws as a separate people.

Thus Nānak extricated his followers from the accumulated errors of ages, and enjoined upon them devotion of thought and excellence of conduct as the first of duties. He left them, erect and free, unbiassed in mind and unfettered by rules, to become an increasing body of truthful worshippers. His reform was in its immediate effect religious and moral only; believers were regarded as 'Sikhs' or disciples, not as subjects; and it is neither probable, nor is it necessary to suppose, that he possessed any clear and sagacious views of social amelioration or of political advancement. He left the progress of his people to the operation of time; for his congregation was too limited, and the state of society too artificial, to render it either requisite or possible for him to become a municipal lawgiver, to subvert the legislation of Manu, or to change the immemorial usages of tribes or races.[1] His care was rather

prohibited wine and pork, and himself abstained from all flesh: but, in truth, contradictory passages about food may be quoted, and thus Ward (*The Hindoos*, iii. 466) shows that Nānak defended those who eat flesh, and declared that the infant which drew nurture from its mother lived virtually upon flesh. The author of the *Gur Ratnāvalī* pursues the idea, in a somewhat trivial manner indeed, by asking whether man does not take woman to wife, and whether the holiest of books are not bound with the skins of animals!

The general injunctions of Nānak have sometimes been misinterpreted by sectarian followers and learned strangers, to mean 'great chariness of animal life', almost in a mere ceremonial sense. (Wilson, *As. Res.*, xvii. 233.) But the Sikhs have no such feeling, although the Jains and others carry a pious regard for worms and flies to a ludicrous extent—a practice which has reacted upon at least some families of Roman Catholic Christians in India. Those in Bhopāl reject, during Lent, the use of unrefined sugar, an article of daily consumption, because, in its manufacture, the lives of many insects are necessarily sacrificed! [It is curious that the Greeks and Romans believed the life of the ox to have been held sacred during the golden age; and Cicero quotes Aratus, to show that it was only during the *iron age* the flesh of cattle began to be eaten. (*On the Nature of the Gods*, Francklin's translation, p. 154.)—J. D. C.]

[1] Malcolm (*Sketch*, pp. 44, 147) says Nānak made little or no alteration in the civil institutions of the Hindus, and Ward (*The Hindoos*, iii. 463) says, the Sikhs have no written civil or criminal laws. Similar observations of dispraise or applause might be made with regard to the code of the early Christians, and we know the difficulties under which the apostles laboured, owing to the want of a new declaratory law, or owing to the scruples and prejudices of their disciples. (Acts

1469–1539.

to prevent his followers contracting into a sect, and his comprehensive principles narrowing into monastic distinctions. This he effected by excluding his son, a meditative and perhaps bigoted ascetic, from the ministry when he should himself be no more; and, as his end approached, he is stated to have made a trial of the obedience or merits of his chosen disciples, and to have preferred the simple and sincere Lahna. As they journeyed along, the body of a man was seen lying by the wayside. Nānak said, 'Ye who trust in me, eat of this food.' All hesitated save Lahna; he knelt and uncovered the dead, and touched without tasting the flesh of man; but, behold! the corpse had disappeared and Nānak was in its place. The Gurū embraced his faithful follower, saying he was as himself, and that his spirit would dwell within him.[1] The name of Lahna was changed to Angi-Khud, or Angad, or own body,[2] and whatever may be the foundation of the story or the truth of the etymology, it is certain that the Sikhs fully believe the spirit of Nānak to have been incarnate in each succeeding Gurū.[3] Angad was acknowledged as the teacher

But guarded against their narrowing into a sect.

Nānak declares Angad to be his successor as a teacher of men.

xv. 20, 28, 29, and other passages.) The seventh of the articles of the Church of England, and the nineteenth chapter of the Scottish Confession of Faith, show the existing perplexity of modern divines, and, doubtless, it will long continue to be disputed how far Christians are amenable to some portions of the Jewish law, and whether Sikhs should wholly reject the institutions of Manu and the usages of race. There were Judaizing Christians and there are Brāhmanizing Sikhs; the swine was a difficulty with one, the cow is a difficulty with the other; and yet the greatest obstacle, perhaps, to a complete obliteration of caste, is the rooted feeling that marriages should properly take place only between people of the same origin or nation, without much reference to faith. (Cf. Ward on *The Hindoos*, iii. 459; Malcolm, *Sketch*, p. 157 note; and Forster's *Travels*, i. 293, 295, 308.)

[1] This story is related by various Punjabī compilers, and it is given with one of the variations by Dr. Macgregor, in his *History of the Sikhs* (i. 48). In the *Dabistān* (ii. 268, 269) there is a story of a similar kind about the successive sacrifice in the four ages of a cow, a horse, an elephant, and a man. The pious partakers of the flesh of the last offering were declared to be saved, and the victim himself again appeared in his bodily shape.

[2] Cf. Malcolm, *Sketch of the Sikhs*, p. 24 note. [Angad, however, is an old Hindu name, and the ambassador of Rāma to Ravan was so called. (Kennedy, *Res. Hind. Mythol.*, p. 438.)—J. D. C.]

[3] This belief is an article of faith with the Sikhs. Cf. the *Dabistān*

1469-1539. of the Sikhs, and Sri Chand, the son of Nānak, justified his father's fears, and became the founder of the Hindu sect of 'Udasis', a community indifferent to the concerns of this world.[1]

(ii. 253, 281). The Gurū Har Gobind signed himself 'Nānak' in a letter to Muhsin Fāni, the author of that work.

[1] For some account of the Udasis, see Wilson, *Asiatic Researches*, xvii. 232. The sect is widely diffused; its members are proud of their connexion with the Sikhs, and all reverence, and most possess and use, the *Granth* of Nānak.

NOTE.—For many stories regarding Nānak himself, which it has not been thought necessary to introduce into the text or notes, the curious reader may refer with profit to Malcolm's *Sketch*, to the second volume of the *Dabistān*, and to the first volume of Dr. Macgregor's recently published *History*.

CHAPTER III

THE SIKH GURŪS OR TEACHERS, AND THE MODIFICATION OF SIKHISM UNDER GOBIND
1539–1716

Gurū Angad—Gurū Amar Dās and the Udasi Sect—Gurū Rām Dās—Gurū Arjūn—The First Granth and Civil Organization of the Sikhs—Gurū Har Gobind and the Military Ordering of the Sikhs—Gurū Har Rai—Gurū Har Kishan—Gurū Tegh Bahādur—Gurū Gobind, and the Political Establishment of the Sikhs—Banda Bairāgi the Temporal Successor of Gobind—The Dispersion of the Sikhs.

1539–52.

Angad upholds the broad principles of Nānak.

Dies 1552.

NĀNAK died in 1539, and he was succeeded by the Angad of his choice, a Kshattriya of the Tihan subdivision of the race, who himself died in 1552, at Kadūr, near Goïndwal, on the Beās river. Little is related of his ministry, except that he committed to writing much of what he had heard about Nānak from the Gurū's ancient companion, Bala Sindhu, as well as some devotional observations of his own, which were afterwards incorporated in the *Granth*. But Angad was true to the principles of his great teacher, and, not deeming either of his own sons worthy to succeed him, he bestowed his apostolic blessing upon Amar Dās, an assiduous follower.[1]

Amar Dās succeeds.

Amar Dās was likewise a Kshattriya, but of the Bhalla subdivision. He was active in preaching, and successful in obtaining converts, and it is said that he found an attentive listener in the tolerant Akbar. The immediate followers of

[1] Angad was born, according to most accounts, in 1561 Sambat, or A. D. 1504, but according to others in 1567 (or A. D. 1510). His death is usually placed in 1609 Sambat (A. D. 1552), but sometimes it is dated a year earlier, and the Sikh accounts affect a precision as to days and months which can never gain credence. Forster (*Travels*, i. 296) gives 1542, perhaps a misprint for 1552, as the period of his death.

1552–74.

Separates the Sikhs from the Udasis.

Sri Chand, the son of Nānak, had hitherto been regarded as almost equally the disciples of the first teacher with the direct adherents of Angad; but Amar Dās declared passive and recluse 'Udasis' to be wholly separate from active and domestic 'Sikhs', and thus finally preserved the infant church or state from disappearing as one of many sects.[1] In the spirit of Nānak he likewise pronounced that the 'true Satī was she whom grief and not flame consumed, and that the afflicted should seek consolation with the Lord'; thus mildly discountenancing a perverse custom, and leading the way to amendment by persuasion rather than by positive enactment.[2] Amar Dās died in 1574, after a ministration of about twenty-two years and a half.[3] He had a son and a daughter, and it is said that his delight with the uniform filial love and obedience of the latter led him to prefer her husband before other disciples, and to bestow upon him his 'Barkat' or apostolic virtue. The fond mother, or ambitious woman, is further stated to have obtained an assurance from the Gurū that the succession should remain with her posterity.

His views with regard to 'Satī'.

Dies 1574.

Rām Dās succeeds and establishes himself at Amritsar.

Rām Dās, the son-in-law of Amar Dās, was a Kshattriya of the Sodhī subdivision, and he was worthy of his master's choice and of his wife's affection. He is said to have been held in esteem by Akbar, and to have received from him a piece of land, within the limits of which he dug a reservoir, since well known as Amritsar, or the pool of immortality; but the temples and surrounding huts were at first named

[1] Malcolm (*Sketch*, p. 27) says distinctly that Amar Dās made this separation. The *Dabistān* (ii. 271) states generally that the Gurūs had effected it, and in the present day some educated Sikhs think that Arjūn first authoritatively laid down the difference between an Udasi and a genuine follower of Nānak.

[2] The *Adi-Granth*, in that part of the *Suhi* chapter which is by Amar Dās. Forster (*Travels*, i. 309) considers that Nānak prohibited Satī, and allowed widows to marry; but Nānak did not make positive laws of the kind, and perhaps self-sacrifice was not authoritatively interfered with until first Akbar and Jahāngīr (*Memoirs of Jahāngīr*, p. 28), and afterwards the English, endeavoured to put an end to it.

[3] The accounts agree as to the date of Amar Dās's birth, placing it in 1566 Sambat, or A. D. 1509. The period of his death, 1631 Sambat, or A. D. 1574, seems likewise certain, although one places it as late as A. D. 1580.

Rāmdāspur, from the founder.[1] Rām Dās is among the most revered of the Gurūs, but no precepts of wide application, or rules of great practical value or force, are attributed to him. His own ministry did not extend beyond seven years, and the slow progress of the faith of Nānak seems apparent from the statement that at the end of forty-two years his successor had not more than double that number of disciples or instructed followers.[2]

1574–81.

Dies 1581.

Arjūn succeeded his father in 1581, and the wishes of his mother, the daughter of Amar Dās, were thus accomplished.[3] Arjūn was perhaps the first who clearly understood the wide import of the teachings of Nānak, or who perceived how applicable they were to every state of life and to every condition of society. He made Amritsar the proper seat of his followers, the centre which should attract their worldly longings for a material bond of union; and the obscure hamlet, with its little pool, has become a populous city and the great place of pilgrimage of the Sikh people.[4] Arjūn next arranged the various writings of his

Arjūn succeeds and fairly grasps the idea of Nānak.

Makes Amritsar the 'Holy City' of the Sikhs.

[1] Malcolm, *Sketch*, p. 29; Forster, *Travels*, i. 297; the *Dabistān*, ii. 275. The Sikh accounts state that the possession of Akbar's gift was disputed by a Bairāgi, who claimed the land as the site of an ancient pool dedicated to Rām Chandra, the tutelary deity of his order; but the Sikh Gurū said haughtily he was himself the truer representative of the hero. The Bairāgi could produce no proof; but Rām Dās dug deep into the earth, and displayed to numerous admirers the ancient steps of the demi-god's reservoir!

[2] Such seems to be the meaning of the expression, 'He held holy converse with eighty-four Sikhs,' used by Bhai Kanh Singh in a manuscript compilation of the beginning of this century.

Rām Dās's birth is placed in 1581 Sambat, or A. D. 1524, his marriage in A. D. 1542, the founding of Amritsar in A. D. 1577, and his death in A. D. 1581.

[3] It seems doubtful whether Rām Dās had two or three sons, Pirthī Chand (or Bharut Mal or Dhi Mal), Arjūn, and Mahadev, and also whether Arjūn was older or younger than Pirthī Chand. It is more certain, however, that Pirthī Chand claimed the succession on the death of his brother, if not on the death of his father, and he was also indeed accused of endeavouring to poison Arjūn. (Cf. Malcolm, *Sketch*, p. 30, and the *Dabistān*, ii. 273.) The descendants of Pirthī Chand are still to be found in the neighbourhood of the Sutlej, especially at Kot Har Sahai, south of Ferozepore.

[4] The ordinary Sikh accounts represent Arjūn to have taken up his residence at Amritsar; but he lived for some time at least at

1581–1606.

Compiles the *Adi-Granth.*

predecessors;[1] he added to them the best known, or the most suitable, compositions of some other religious reformers of the few preceding centuries, and completing the whole with a prayer and some exhortations of his own, he declared the compilation to be pre-eminently the '*Granth*' or Book; and he gave to his followers their fixed rule of religious and moral conduct, with an assurance that multitudes even of divine Brāhmans had wearied themselves with reading the Vedas, and had found not the value of an oil-seed within them.[2] The Gurū next reduced to a systematic tax the customary offerings of his converts or adherents, who, under his ascendancy, were to be found in every city and province. The Sikhs were bound by social usage, and disposed from reverential feelings, to make such presents to their spiritual guide; but the agents of Arjūn were spread over the country to demand and receive the contributions of the faithful, which they proceeded to deliver to the Gurū in person at an annual assembly. Thus the Sikhs, says the almost contemporary Muhsin Fāni, became accustomed to a regular government.[3] Nor was Arjūn heedless of other means of acquiring wealth and influence; he dispatched his followers into foreign countries to be as keen in traffic as they were zealous in belief, and it is probable that his transactions as a merchant were extensive, although confined to the purchase of horses in Turkestan.[4]

Reduces customary offerings to a systematic tax or tithe;

and engages in traffic.

Arjūn became famous among pious devotees, and his biographers dwell on the number of saints and holy men who were edified by his instructions. Nor was he unheeded

Taran Taran, which lies between that city and the junction of the Beās and Sutlej. (Cf. the *Dabistān*, ii. 275.)

[1] Malcolm, *Sketch*, p. 30. General tradition and most writers attribute the arrangement of the First Granth to Arjūn; but Angad is understood to have preserved many observations of Nānak, and Forster (*Travels*, i. 297) states that Rām Dās compiled the histories and precepts of his predecessors, and annexed a commentary to the work. The same author, indeed (*Travels*, i. 296 note), also contradictorily assigns the compilation to Angad.

[2] *Adi-Granth*, in that portion of the *Suhi* chapter written by Arjūn. For some account of the Adi, or First Granth, see Appendix I.

[3] The *Dabistān*, ii. 270, &c. Cf. Malcolm, *Sketch*, p. 30.

[4] The ordinary Sikh accounts are to this effect. Cf. the *Dabistān*, ii. 271.

by those in high station, for he is said to have refused to betroth his son to the daughter of Chandū Shāh, the finance administrator of the Lahore province;[1] and he further appears to have been sought as a political partisan, and to have offered up prayers for Khusrū, the son of Jahāngīr, when in rebellion and in temporary possession of the Punjab. The Gurū was summoned to the emperor's presence, and fined and imprisoned at the instigation chiefly, it is said, of Chandū Shāh, whose alliance he had rejected, and who represented him as a man of a dangerous ambition.[2] Arjūn died in 1606, and his death is believed to have been hastened by the rigours of his confinement; but his followers piously assert that, having obtained leave to bathe in the river Rāvi, he vanished in the shallow stream, to the fear and wonder of those guarding him.[3]

1581–1606

Arjūn provokes the enmity of Chandū Shāh.

Becomes a partisan of Prince Khusrū in rebellion.

Imprisonment and death of Arjūn, 1606.

[1] Cf. Forster, *Travels*, i. 298. The Sikh accounts represent that the son of Arjūn was mentioned to Chandū as a suitable match for his daughter, and that Chandū slightingly objected, saying, Arjūn, although a man of name and wealth, was still a beggar, or one who received alms. This was reported to Arjūn; he resented the taunt, and would not be reconciled to the match, notwithstanding the personal endeavours of Chandū to appease him and bring about the union.

Shāh is a corrupted suffix to names, extensively adopted in India. It is a Persian word signifying a king, but applied to Muhammadan Fakīrs as Mahārāja is used by or towards Hindu devotees. It is also used to denote a principal merchant, or as a corruption of Sahu or Sahukār, and it is further used as a name or title, as a corruption of Sah or Sahai. The Gōnd converts to Muhammadanism on the Narbadā all add the word Shāh to their names.

[2] *Dabistān*, ii. 272, 273. The Sikh accounts correspond sufficiently as to the fact of the Gurū's arraignment, while they are silent about his treason. They declare the emperor to have been satisfied of his sanctity and innocence (generally), and attribute his continued imprisonment to Chandū's malignity and disobedience of orders. (Cf. Malcolm, *Sketch*, p. 32.) Muhsin Fāni also states that a Muhammadan saint of Thānesar was banished by Jahāngīr for aiding Khusrū with his prayers. (*Dabistān*, ii. 273.) The emperor himself simply states (*Memoirs*, p. 88) that at Lahore he impaled seven hundred of the rebels, and on his way to that city he appears (*Memoirs*, p. 81) to have bestowed a present on Shaikh Nizām of Thānesar; but he may have subsequently become aware of his hostility.

[3] Cf. Malcolm, *Sketch*, p. 33; the *Dabistān*, ii. 272–3; and Forster, *Travels*, i. 298.

A. D. 1553 seems the most probable date of Arjūn's birth, although

1581–1606.

Diffusion of Sikhism. The writings of Gur Dās Bhulleh.

During the ministry of Arjūn the principles of Nānak took a firm hold on the minds of his followers,[1] and a disciple named Gur Dās gives a lofty and imaginative view of the mission of that teacher. He regards him as the successor of Vyāsa and Muhammad, and as the destined restorer of purity and sanctity; the regenerator of a world afflicted with the increasing wickedness of men, and with the savage contentions of numerous sects. He declaims against the bigotry of the Muhammadans and their ready resort to violence; he denounces the asceticism of the Hindus, and he urges all men to abandon their evil ways, to live peacefully and virtuously, and to call upon the name of the one true God to whom Nānak had borne witness. Arjūn is commonly said to have refused to give these writings of his stern but fervid disciple a place in the *Granth*, perhaps as unsuited to the tenor of Nānak's exhortations, which scarcely condemn or threaten others. The writings of Gur Dās are, indeed, rather figurative descriptions of actual affairs than simple hymns in praise of God; but they deserve attention as expounding Nānak's object of a gradual fusion of Muhammadans and Hindus into common observers of a new and a better creed, and as an almost contemporary instance of the conversion of the noble but obscure idea of an individual into the active principle of a multitude, and of the gradual investiture of a simple fact with the gorgeous mythism of memory and imagination. The unpretending Nānak, the deplorer of human frailty and the lover of his fellow men, becomes, in the mind of Gur Dās and of the Sikh people, the first of heavenly powers and emanations, and the proclaimed instrument of God for the redemption of the world; and every hope and feeling of the Indian races is appealed to in proof or in illustration of the reality and the splendour of his mission.[2]

The conceptions of Nānak become the moving impulses of a people; and his real history a mythical narrative.

one account places it as late as A. D. 1565. Similarly 1663 Sambat, or 1015 Hijri, or A. D. 1606, seems the most certain date of his death.

[1] Muhsin Fāni observes (*Dabistān*, ii. 270) that in the time of Arjūn Sikhs were to be found everywhere throughout the country.

[2] The work of Bhai Gur Dās Bhulleh, simply known as such, or as the Gyan Ratnavalī (Malcolm, *Sketch*, p. 30, note), is much read by the Sikhs. It consists of forty chapters, and is written in different kinds of verse. Some extracts may be seen in Appendix XIX, and

On the death of Arjūn, his brother Pirthī Chand made some attempts to be recognized as Gurū, for the only son of the deceased teacher was young, and ecclesiastical usage has everywhere admitted a latitude of succession. But some suspicion of treachery towards Arjūn appears to have attached to him, and his nephew soon became the acknowledged leader of the Sikhs, although Pirthī Chand himself continued to retain a few followers, and thus sowed the first fertile seeds of dissent, or elements of dispute or of change, which ever increase with the growth of a sect or a system.[1] Har Gobind was not, perhaps, more than eleven years of age at his father's death, but he was moved by his followers to resent the enmity of Chandū Shāh, and he is represented either to have procured his condemnation by the emperor, or to have slain him by open force without reference to authority.[2] Whatever may be the truth about the death of Chandū and the first years of Har Gobind's ministry, it is certain that, in a short time, he became a military leader as well as a spiritual teacher. Nānak had sanctioned or enjoined secular occupations, Arjūn carried the injunction into practice, and the impulse thus given speedily extended and became general. The temper and the circumstances of Har Gobind both prompted him to

1606–45.

Har Gobind becomes Gurū after a disputed succession.

Chandū Shāh slain or put to death.

Har Gobind arms the Sikhs and becomes a military leader.

in Malcolm, *Sketch*, p. 152, &c. Gur Dās was the scribe of Arjūn, but his pride and haughtiness are said to have displeased his master, and his compositions were refused a place in the sacred book. Time and reflection—and the Sikhs add a miracle—made him sensible of his failings and inferiority, and Arjūn perceiving his contrition, said he would include his writings in the *Granth*. But the final meekness of Gur Dās was such, that he himself declared them to be unworthy of such association; whereupon Arjūn enjoined that all Sikhs should nevertheless read them. He describes Arjūn (Malcolm, *Sketch*, p. 30, note) to have become Gurū without any formal investiture or consecration by his father, which may further mark the commanding character of that teacher.

Malcolm (*Sketch*, p. 32) appears to confound Chandū Shāh (or Dhani Chand) with Gur Dās.

[1] Malcolm, *Sketch*, p. 30, and *Dabistān*, ii. 273. These sectaries were called *Mina*, a term commonly used in the Punjab, and which is expressive of contempt or opprobrium, as stated by Muhsin Fāni. The proneness to sectarianism among the first Christians was noticed and deprecated by Paul (1 Cor. i. 10–13).

[2] Cf. Forster, *Travels*, i. 298.

1606–45. innovation; he had his father's death to move his feelings, and in surpassing the example of his parent, even the jealous dogma of the Hindu law, which allows the most lowly to arm in self-defence, may not have been without its influence on a mind acquainted with the precepts of Manu.[1] Arjūn trafficked as a merchant, and played his part as a priest in affairs of policy; but Har Gobind grasped a sword, and marched with his devoted followers among the troops of the empire, or boldly led them to oppose and overcome provincial governors or personal enemies. Nānak had himself abstained from animal food, and the prudent Arjūn endeavoured to add to his saintly merit or influence by a similar moderation; but the adventurous Har Gobind became a hunter and an eater of flesh, and his disciples imitated him in these robust practices.[2] The genial disposition of the martial apostle led him to rejoice in the companionship of a camp, in the dangers of war, and in the excitements of the chase, nor is it improbable that the policy of a temporal chief mingled with the feelings of an injured son and with the duties of a religious guide, so as to shape his acts to the ends of his ambition, although *that* may not have aimed at more than a partial independence under the mild supremacy of the son of Akbar. Har Gobind appears to have admitted criminals and fugitives among his followers, and where a principle of antagonism had already arisen, they may have served him zealously without greatly reforming the practice of their lives; and, indeed, they are stated to have believed that the faithful Sikh would pass unquestioned into heaven.[3] He had a stable of eight hundred horses; three hundred mounted followers were constantly in attendance upon him, and a guard of sixty matchlock-men secured the safety of his person, had he ever feared or thought of assassination.[4] The impulse which he gave to the Sikhs was such as to

The gradual modification of Sikhism;

[1] For this last supposition, see Malcolm, *Sketch*, pp. 44, 189. There is perhaps some straining after nicety of reason in the notion, as Manu's injunction had long become obsolete in such matters, especially under the Muhammadan supremacy.

[2] The *Dabistān*, ii. 248, and Malcolm, *Sketch*, p. 36.

[3] The *Dabistān*, ii. 284, 286.

[4] The *Dabistān*, ii. 277.

separate them a long way from all Hindu sects, and after the time of Har Gobind the 'disciples' were in little danger of relapsing into the limited merit or utility of monks and mendicants.[1] 1606-45.

and complete separation of the Sikhs from Hindu dissenters.

Har Gobind became a follower of the Emperor Jahāngīr, and to the end of his life his conduct partook as much of the military adventurer as of the enthusiastic zealot. He accompanied the imperial camp to Kashmīr, and he is at one time represented as in holy colloquy with the religious guide of the Mughal, and at another as involved in difficulties with the emperor about retaining for himself that money which he should have disbursed to his troops. He had, too, a multitude of followers, and his passion for the chase, and fancied independence as a teacher of men, may have led him to offend against the sylvan laws of the court. The emperor was displeased, the fine imposed on Arjūn had never been paid, and Har Gobind was placed as a prisoner on scanty food in the fort of Gwalior. But the faithful Sikhs continued to revere the mysterious virtues or the real merits of their leader. They flocked to Gwalior, and bowed themselves before the walls which restrained their persecuted Gurū, till at last the prince, moved, perhaps, as much by superstition as by pity, released him from confinement.[2]

HarGobind falls under the displeasure of Jahāngīr; is imprisoned, and released.

On the death of Jahāngīr in 1628, Har Gobind continued in the employ of the Muhammadan Government, but he appears soon to have been led into a course of armed resistance to the imperial officers in the Punjab. A disciple brought some valuable horses from Turkestān; they were seized, as was said, for the emperor, and one was conferred as a gift on the Kāzī or Judge of Lahore. The Gurū

Jahāngīr dies 1628, and Har Gobind engages in a petty warfare.

[1] See Appendix IX.

[2] Cf. the *Dabistān*, ii. 273, 274, and Forster, *Travels*, i. 298, 299. But the journey to Kashmīr, and the controversy with Muhammadan saints or Mullas, are given on the authority of the native chronicles. Muhsin Fāni represents Har Gobind to have been imprisoned for twelve years, and Forster attributes his release to the intervention of a Muhammadan leader, who had originally induced him to submit to the emperor.

The Emperor Jahāngīr, in his *Memoirs*, gives more than one instance of his credulity and superstitious reverence for reputed saints and magicians. See particularly his *Memoirs*, p. 120, &c., where his visit to a worker of wonders is narrated.

1606–45. recovered this one animal by pretending to purchase it; the judge was deceived, and his anger was further roused by the abduction of, the Sikhs say his daughter, the Muhammadans his favourite concubine, who had become enamoured of the Gurū. Other things may have rendered Har Gobind obnoxious, and it was resolved to seize him and to disperse his followers. He was assailed by one Mukhlis Khān, but he defeated the imperial troops near Amritsar, fighting, it is idly said, with five thousand men against seven thousand. Afterwards a Sikh, a converted robber, stole two of the emperor's prime horses from Lahore, and the Gurū was again attacked by the provincial levies, but the detachment was routed and its leaders slain. Har Gobind now deemed it prudent to retire for a time to the wastes of Bhatinda, south of the Sutlej, where it might be useless or dangerous to follow him; but he watched his opportunity and speedily returned to the Punjab, only, however, to become engaged in fresh contentions. The mother of one Painda Khān, who had subsequently risen to some local eminence, had been the nurse of Har Gobind, and the Gurū had ever been liberal to his foster brother. Painda Khān was moved to keep to himself a valuable hawk, belonging to the Gurū's eldest son, which had flown to his house by chance: he was taxed with the detention of the bird; he equivocated before the Gurū, and became soon after his avowed enemy. The presence of Har Gobind seems ever to have raised a commotion, and Painda Khān was fixed upon as a suitable leader to coerce him. He was attacked; but the warlike apostle slew the friend of his youth with his own hand, and proved again a victor. In this action a soldier rushed furiously upon the Gurū; but he warded the blow and laid the man dead at his feet, exclaiming, 'Not so, but thus, is the sword used'; an observation from which the author of the *Dabistān* draws the inference 'that Har Gobind struck not in anger, but deliberately and to give instruction; for the function of a Gurū is to teach'.[1]

Har Gobind retires to the wastes of Hariāna.

Returns to the Punjab.

Slays in fight one Painda Khān, his friend.

[1] See the *Dabistān*, ii. 275; but native accounts, Sikh and Muhammadan, have been mainly followed in narrating the sequence of events. Compare, however, the *Dabistān*, ii. 284, for the seizure of horses belonging to a disciple of the Gurū.

Har Gobind appears to have had other difficulties and adventures of a similar kind, and occasionally to have been reduced to great straits; but the Sikhs always rallied round him, his religious reputation increased daily, and immediately before his death he was visited by a famous saint of the ancient Persian faith.[1] He died in peace in 1645, at Kīratpur on the Sutlej, a place bestowed upon him by the hill chief of Kahlūr, and the veneration of his followers took the terrible form of self-sacrifice. A Rājpūt convert threw himself amid the flames of the funeral pyre, and walked several paces till he died at the feet of his master. A Jāt disciple did the same, and others, wrought upon by these examples, were ready to follow, when Har Rai, the succeeding Gurū, interfered and forbade them.[2]

1606–45.

Death of Har Gobind A.D. 1645.

Self-sacrifice of disciples on his pyre.

During the ministry of Har Gobind, the Sikhs increased greatly in numbers, and the fiscal policy of Arjūn, and the armed system of his son, had already formed them into a kind of separate state within the empire. The Gurū was, perhaps, not unconscious of his latent influence, when he played with the credulity or rebuked the vanity of his Muhammadan friend. 'A Rājā of the north', said he, 'has sent an ambassador to ask about a place called Delhi, and the name and parentage of its king. I was astonished that he had not heard of the commander of the faithful, the lord of the ascendant, Jahāngīr.'[3] But during his busy life he

The body of Sikhs forms a separate establishment within the empire.

Some anecdotes of Har Gobind.

[1] The *Dabistān*, ii. 280.

[2] This is related on the authority of the *Dabistān*, ii. 280, 281. Har Gobind's death is also given agreeably to the text of the *Dabistān* as having occurred on the 3rd Mohurrum, 1055 Hijrī, or on the 19th Feb., A. D. 1645. Malcolm, *Sketch*, p. 37, and Forster, *Travels*, i. 299, give A. D. 1644 as the exact or probable date, obviously from regarding 1701 Sambat (which Malcolm also quotes) as identical throughout, instead of for about the first nine months only, with A. D. 1644, an error which may similarly apply to several conversions of dates in this history. The manuscript accounts consulted place the Gurū's death variously in A. D. 1637, 1638, and 1639; but they lean to the middle term. All, however, must be too early, as Muhsin Fāni (*Dabistān*, ii. 281) says he saw Har Gobind in A. D. 1643. Har Gobind's birth is placed by the native accounts in the early part of 1652 Sambat, corresponding with the middle of A. D. 1595.

[3] See the *Dabistān*, ii. 276, 277. The friend being Muhsin Fāni himself. The story perhaps shows that the Sikh truly considered the Muhammadan to be a gossiping and somewhat credulous person.

1606–45. never forgot his genuine character, and always styled himself 'Nānak', in deference to the firm belief of the Sikhs, that the soul of their great teacher animated each of his successors.[1] So far as Har Gobind knew or thought of philosophy as a science, he fell into the prevailing views of the period: God, he said, is one, and the world is an illusion, an appearance without a reality; or he would adopt the more Pantheistic notion, and regard the universe as composing the one Being. But such reflections did not occupy his mind or engage his heart, and the rebuke of a Brāhman that if the world was the same as God, he, the Gurū, was one with the ass grazing hard by, provoked a laugh only from the tolerant Har Gobind.[2] That he thought conscience and understanding our only divine guides, may probably be inferred from his reply to one who declared the marriage of a brother with a sister to be forbidden by the Almighty. Had God prohibited it, said he, it would be impossible for man to accomplish it.[3] His contempt for idolatry, and his occasional wide departure from the mild and conciliatory ways of Nānak, may be judged from the following anecdote: One of his followers smote the nose off an image; the several neighbouring chiefs complained to the Gurū, who summoned the Sikh to his presence; the culprit denied the act, but said ironically, that if the god bore witness against him, he would die willingly. 'Oh, fool!' said the Rājās, 'how should the god speak?' 'It is plain', answered the Sikh, 'who is the fool; if the god cannot save his own head, how will he avail you?'[4]

His philosophical views.

Har Rai succeeds as Gurū, 1645.

Gurdit, the eldest son of Har Gobind, had acquired a high reputation, but he died before his father, leaving

The dates would rather point to Shāh Jahān as the emperor alluded to than Jahāngīr, as given parenthetically in the translated text of the *Dabistān*. Jahāngīr died in A. D. 1628, and Muhsin Fāni's acquaintance with Har Gobind appears not to have taken place till towards the last years of the Gurū's life, or till after A. D. 1640.

[1] Cf. the *Dabistān*, ii. 281. [2] Cf. the *Dabistān*, ii. 277, 279, 280.

[3] The *Dabistān*, ii. 280. [Cicero seems to have almost as high an opinion of the functions of conscience. It points out to us, he says, without Divine assistance, the difference between virtue and vice. (*Nature of the Gods*, Francklin's translation, p. 213.)—J. D. C.]

[4] The *Dabistān*, ii. 276.

two sons, one of whom succeeded to the apostleship.[1] Har Rai, the new Gurū, remained at Kīratpur for a time, until the march of troops to reduce the Kahlūr Rājā to obedience induced him to remove eastward into the district of Sarmor.[2] There he also remained in peace until he was induced, in 1658–9, to take part, of a nature not distinctly laid down, with Dārā Shikoh, in the struggle between him and his brothers for the empire of India. Dārā failed, his adherents became rebels, and Har Rai had to surrender his elder son as a hostage. The youth was treated with distinction and soon released, and the favour of the politic Aurangzeb is believed to have roused the jealousy of the father.[3] But the end of Har Rai was at hand, and he died at Kīratpur in the year 1661.[4] His ministry was mild, yet such as won

1645–61.

Becomes a political partisan.

Dies A.D. 1661.

[1] For some allusions to Gurdit or Gurditta, see the *Dabistān*, ii. 281, 282. His memory is yet fondly preserved, and many anecdotes are current of his personal strength and dexterity. His tomb is at Kīratpur, on the Sutlej, and it has now become a place of pilgrimage. In connexion with his death, a story is told, which at least serves to mark the aversion of the Sikh teachers to claim the obedience of the multitude by an assumption of miraculous powers. Gurditta had raised a slaughtered cow to life, on the prayer, some say, of a poor man the owner, and his father was displeased that he should so endeavour to glorify himself. Gurditta said that as a life was required by God, and as he had withheld one, he would yield his own ; whereupon he lay down and gave up his spirit. A similar story is told of Atal Rai, the youngest son of Har Gobind, who had raised the child of a sorrowing widow to life. His father reproved him, saying, Gurūs should display their powers in purity of doctrine and holiness of living. The youth, or child as some say, replied as Gurditta had done, and died. His tomb is in Amritsar, and is likewise a place deemed sacred.

Gurditta's younger son was named Dhirmal, and his descendants are still to be found at Kartārpur, in the Jullundur Doāb.

[2] See the *Dabistān*, ii. 282. The place meant seems to be Taksāl or Tangsāl, near the present British station of Kasaulī to the northward of Ambāla.

The important work of Muhsin Fāni brings down the history of the Sikhs to this point only.

[3] The Gurū's leaning towards Dārā is given on the authority of native accounts only, but it is highly probable in itself, considering Dārā's personal character and religious principles.

[4] The authorities mostly agree as to the date of Har Rai's death, but one account places it in A. D. 1662. The Gurū's birth is differently placed in 1628 and 1629.

1661–74. for him general respect; and many of the 'Bhais', or brethren, the descendants of the chosen companions of a Gurū, trace their descent to one disciple or other distinguished by Har Rai.[1] Some sects also of Sikhs, who affect more than ordinary precision, had their origin during the peaceful supremacy of this Gurū.[2]

Har Kishan succeeds, 1661.

Har Rai left two sons, Rām Rai, about fifteen, and Har Kishan, about six years of age; but the elder was the offspring of a handmaiden, and not of a wife of equal degree, and Har Rai is further said to have declared the younger his successor. The disputes between the partisans of the two brothers ran high, and the decision was at last referred to the emperor. Aurangzeb may have been willing to allow the Sikhs to choose their own Gurū, as some accounts have it, but the more cherished tradition relates that, being struck with the child's instant recognition of the empress among a number of ladies similarly arrayed, he declared the right of Har Kishan to be indisputable, and he was accordingly recognized as head of the Sikhs: but before the infant apostle could leave Delhi, he was attacked with

Dies 1664. small-pox, and died, in 1664, at that place.[3]

[1] Of these Bhai Bhagtu, the founder of the Kaithal family, useful partisans of Lord Lake, but now reduced to comparative insignificance under the operation of the British system of escheat, was one of the best known. Dharam Singh, the ancestor of the respectable Bhais of Bagrian, a place between the Sutlej and Jumna, was likewise a follower of Har Rai.

Nowadays the title of Bhai is in practice frequently given to any Sikh of eminent sanctity, whether his ancestor were the companion of a Gurū or not. The Bedīs and Sodhīs, however, confine themselves to the distinctive names of their tribes, or the Bedīs call themselves Bāba or father, and the Sodhīs sometimes arrogate to themselves the title of Gurū, as the representatives of Gobind and Rām Dās.

[2] Of these sects the Suthris or the Suthra-Shahis are the best known. Their founder was one Sūcha, a Brāhman, and they have a *st'hān* or *dera*, or place under the walls of the citadel of Lahore. (Cf. Wilson, *As. Res.*, xvii. 236.) The name, or designation, means simply the pure. Another follower of Har Rai was a Khattrī trader, named Fattu, who got the title, or adopted the name of Bhai P'hiru, and who, according to the belief of some people, became the real founder of the Udasis.

[3] Cf. Malcolm, *Sketch*, p. 38, and Forster, *Travels*, i. 299. One native account places Har Kishan's death in A. D. 1666, but 1664 seems the preferable date. His birth took place in A. D. 1656.

When Har Kishan was about to expire, he is stated to have signified that his successor would be found in the village of Bakala, near Goïndwal, on the Beās river. In this village there were many of Har Gobind's relatives, and his son, Tegh Bahādur, after many wanderings and a long sojourn at Patna, on the Ganges, had taken up his residence at the same place. Rām Rai continued to assert his claims, but he never formed a large party, and Tegh Bahādur was generally acknowledged as the leader of the Sikhs. The son of Har Gobind was rejoiced, but he said he was unworthy to wear his father's sword, and in a short time his supremacy and his life were both endangered by the machinations of Rām Rai, and perhaps by his own suspicious proceedings.[1] He was summoned to Delhi as a pretender to power and as a disturber of the peace, but he had found a listener in the chief of Jaipur; the Rājpūt advocated his cause, saying such holy men rather went on pilgrimages than aspired to sovereignty, and he would take him with him on his approaching march to Bengal.[2] Tegh

1664–75.

Tegh Bahādur succeeds as ninth Gurū, 1664.

Rām Rai disputes his claims.

[1] Cf., generally, Malcolm, *Sketch*, p. 38; Forster, *Travels*, i. 299; and Browne's *India Tracts*, ii. 3, 4. Tegh Bahādur's refusal to wear the sword of his father is given, however, on the authority of manuscript native accounts, which likewise furnish a story, showing the particular act which led to his recognition as Gurū. A follower of the sect, named Makhan Sah (or Shāh), who was passing through Bakala, wished to make an offering to the Gurū of his faith, but he was perplexed by the number of claimants. His offering was to be 525 rupees in all, but the amount was known to him alone, and he silently resolved to give a rupee to each, and to hail him as Gurū who should (from intuition) claim the remainder. Tegh Bahādur demanded the balance, and so on.

[2] Forster and Malcolm, who follow native Indian accounts, both give Jai Singh as the name of the prince who countenanced Tegh Bahādur, and who went to Bengal on an expedition; but one manuscript account refers to Bīr Singh as the friendly chief. Tod (*Rājasthān*, ii. 355) says Rām Singh, the son of the first Jai Singh, went to Assam, but he is silent about his actions. It is not unusual in India to talk of eminent men as living, although long since dead, as a Sikh will now say he is Ranjīt Singh's soldier; and it is probable that Rām Singh was nominally forgotten, owing to the fame of his father, the 'Mirza Rājā', and even that the Sikh chroniclers of the early part of the last century confounded the first with the second of the name, their contemporary Sawai Jai Singh, the noted astronomer and patron of the learned. Malcolm (*Sketch*, p. 39), who, perhaps, copies Forster (*Travels*, i. 299, 300), says Tegh Bahādur was, at this time, imprisoned for two years.

1664–75.

Tegh Bahādur retires for a time to Bengal.

Bahādur accompanied the Rājā to the eastward. He again resided for a time at Patna, but afterwards joined the army, to bring success, says the chronicler, to the expedition against the chiefs of Assam. He meditated on the banks of the Brahmaputra, and he is stated to have convinced the heart of the Rājā of Kāmrūp, and to have made him a believer in his mission.[1]

Tegh Bahādur returns to the Punjab.

After a time Tegh Bahādur returned to the Punjab, and bought a piece of ground, now known as Makhowāl, on the banks of the Sutlej, and close to Kīratpur, the chosen residence of his father. But the hostility and the influence of Rām Rai still pursued him, and the ordinary Sikh accounts represent him, a pious and innocent instructor of men, as once more arraigned at Delhi in the character of a criminal; but the truth seems to be that Tegh Bahādur followed the example of his father with unequal footsteps, and that, choosing for his haunts the wastes between Hānsi and the Sutlej, he subsisted himself and his disciples by plunder, in a way, indeed, that rendered him not unpopular with the peasantry. He is further credibly represented to have leagued with a Muhammadan zealot, named Adam Hāfiz, and to have levied contributions upon rich Hindus, while his confederate did the same upon wealthy Musalmāns. They gave a ready asylum to all fugitives, and their power interfered with the prosperity of the country; the imperial troops marched against them, and they were at last defeated and made prisoners. The Muhammadan saint was banished, but Aurangzeb determined that the Sikh should be put to death.[2]

Leads a life of violence; and is constrained to appear at Delhi.

When Tegh Bahādur was on his way to Delhi, he sent for his youthful son, and girding upon him the sword of Har Gobind, he hailed him as the Gurū of the Sikhs. He told him he was himself being led to death, he counselled him not to leave his body a prey to dogs, and he enjoined

[1] These last two clauses are almost wholly on the authority of a manuscript Gurmukhī summary of Tegh Bahādur's life.

[2] The author of the *Siar ul Mutākharin* (i. 112, 113) mentions these predatory or insurrectionary proceedings of Tegh Bahādur, and the ordinary manuscript compilations admit that such charges were made, but deprecate a belief in them. For Makhowāl the Gurū is said to have paid 500 rupees to the Rājā of Kahlūr.

upon him the necessity and the merit of revenge. At Delhi, the story continues, he was summoned before the emperor, and half-insultingly, half-credulously, told to exhibit miracles in proof of the alleged divinity of his mission. Tegh Bahādur answered that the duty of man was to pray to the Lord ; yet he would do one thing, he would write a charm, and the sword should fall harmless on the neck around which it was hung. He placed it around his own neck and inclined his head to the executioner : a blow severed it, to the surprise of a court tinged with superstition, and upon the paper was found written, 'Sir dia, Sirr na dia,'—he had given his head but not his secret ; his life was gone, but his inspiration or apostolic virtue still remained in the world. Such is the narrative of a rude and wonder-loving people ; yet it is more certain that Tegh Bahādur was put to death as a rebel in 1675, and that the stern and bigoted Aurangzeb had the body of the unbeliever publicly exposed in the streets of Delhi.[1]

1664–75.

Tegh Bahādur put to death, 1675.

Tegh Bahādur's character and influence.

Tegh Bahādur seems to have been of a character hard and moody, and to have wanted both the genial temper of his father and the lofty mind of his son. Yet his own example powerfully aided in making the disciples of Nānak a martial as well as a devotional people. His reverence for the sword of his father, and his repeated injunction that his disciples should obey the bearer of his arrows, show more of the kingly than of the priestly spirit ; and, indeed,

[1] All the accounts agree that Tegh Bahādur was ignominiously put to death. The end of the year A. D. 1675—as Maugsar is sometimes given as the month—seems the most certain date of his execution. His birth is differently placed in A. D. 1612 and 1621. [It was on this occasion that the famous prophecy on the ultimate sovereignty of the white race in Delhi is said to have been uttered (though some modern critics consider it a later invention). 'I see', he said dauntlessly to the emperor, 'a power rising in the West which will sweep your empire into the dust.' His body was quartered and hung before the city gates ; but the Sikhs never forgot his prophetic words. They have accounted largely for Sikh loyalty to British rule ; and they were on the lips of the gallant Punjab regiments before Delhi in 1857 when at last they avenged in blood the martyrdom of their leader (Rawlinson, *Indian Historical Studies*, p. 177, and Macauliffe, vol. i, Preface, pp. xiii–xviii and vol. iv, 381). The story is related by two Sikh authors.—ED.]

1675-1708. about this time the Sikh Gurūs came to talk of themselves, and to be regarded by their followers as 'Sachcha Pādshahs', or as 'veritable kings', meaning, perhaps, that they governed by just influence and not by the force of arms, or that they guided men to salvation, while others controlled their worldly actions. But the expression could be adapted to any circumstances, and its mystic application seems to have preyed upon and perplexed the minds of the Mughal princes, while it illustrates the assertion of an intelligent Muhammadan writer, that Tegh Bahādur, being at the head of many thousand men, aspired to sovereign power.[1]

The title 'True king' applied to the Gurūs.

Gobind succeeds to the apostleship, 1675.

When Tegh Bahādur was put to death, his only son was in his fifteenth year. The violent end and the last injunction of the martyr Gurū made a deep impression on the mind of Gobind, and in brooding over his own loss and the fallen condition of his country, he became the irreconcilable foe of the Muhammadan name, and conceived the noble idea of moulding the vanquished Hindus into a new and aspiring people. But Gobind was yet young, the government was suspicious of his followers, and among the Sikhs themselves there were parties inimical to the son of Tegh Bahādur. His friends were therefore satisfied that the mutilated body of the departed Gurū was recovered by the zeal and dexterity of some humble disciples,[2] and that the son himself performed the funeral rites so essential to the welfare of the living and the peace of the dead. Gobind was placed in

[1] Saiyid Ghulām Husain, the author of the *Siar ul Mutākharin* (i. 112), is the writer referred to.

Browne, in his *India Tracts* (ii. 2, 3), and who uses a compilation, attributes Aurangzeb's resolution to put Tegh Bahādur to death, to his assumption of the character of a 'true king', and to his use of the title of 'Bahādur', expressive of valour, birth, and dignity. The Gurū, in the narrative referred to, disavows all claim to miraculous powers. For some remarks on the term 'Sachcha Pādshah', see Appendix XIII.

Tegh Bahādur's objections to wear his father's sword, and his injunction to reverence his arrows, that is, to heed what the bearer of them should say, are given on native authority.

[2] Certain men of the unclean and despised caste of Sweepers were dispatched to Delhi to bring away the dispersed limbs of Tegh Bahādur, and it is said they partly owed their success to the exertions of that Makhan Shāh, who had been the first to hail the deceased as Gurū.

retirement amid the lower hills on either side of the Jumna, and for a series of years he occupied himself in hunting the tiger and wild boar, in acquiring a knowledge of the Persian language, and in storing his mind with those ancient legends which describe the mythic glories of his race.[1]

1675–1708.

But lives in retirement for several years.

In this obscurity Gobind remained perhaps twenty years;[2] but his youthful promise gathered round him the disciples of Nānak, he was acknowledged as the head of the Sikhs, the adherents of Rām Rai declined into a sect of dissenters, and the neighbouring chiefs became impressed with a high sense of the Gurū's superiority and a vague dread of his ambition. But Gobind ever dwelt upon the fate of his father, and the oppressive bigotry of Aurangzeb; study and reflection had enlarged his mind, experience of the world had matured his judgement, and, under the mixed impulse of avenging his own and his country's wrongs, he resolved upon awakening his followers to a new life, and upon giving precision and aim to the broad and general institutions of Nānak. In the heart of a powerful empire he set himself to the task of subverting it, and from the midst of social degradation and religious corruption, he called up simplicity of manners, singleness of purpose, and enthusiasm of desire.[3]

Gobind's character becomes developed.

He resolves on modifying the system of Nānak, and on combating the Muhammadan faith and power.

Gobind's views and motives;

[1] The accounts mostly agree as to this seclusion and occupation of Gobind during his early manhood; but Forster (*Travels*, i. 301) and also some Gurmukhī accounts, state that he was taken to Patna in the first instance, and that he lived there for some time before he retired to the Srīnagar hills.

[2] The period is nowhere definitely given by English or Indian writers; but from a comparison of dates and circumstances, it seems probable that Gobind did not take upon himself a new and special character as a teacher of men until about the thirty-fifth year, or until the year 1695 of Christ. A Sikh author, indeed, quoted by Malcolm (*Sketch*, p. 186, note) makes Gobind's reforms date from A. D. 1696; but contradictorily one or more of Gobind's sayings or writings are made to date about the same period from the south of India, whither he proceeded only just before his death.

[3] The ordinary accounts represent Gobind, as they represent his grandfather, to have been mainly moved to wage war against Muhammadans by a desire of avenging the death of his parent. It would be unreasonable to deny to Gobind the merit of other motives likewise; but, doubtless, the fierce feeling in question strongly impelled him

1675–1708. Gobind was equally bold, systematic, and sanguine; but it is not necessary to suppose him either an unscrupulous impostor or a self-deluded enthusiast. He thought that the minds of men might be wrought upon to great purposes, he deplored the corruption of the world, he resented the tyranny which endangered his own life, and he believed the time had come for another teacher to arouse the latent energies of the human will. His memory was filled with the deeds of primaeval seers and heroes; his imagination dwelt on successive dispensations for the instruction of the world, and his mind was not perhaps untinged with a superstitious belief in his own earthly destiny.[1] In an extant and authentic composition,[2] he traces his mortal descent to ancient kings, and he extols the piety of his immediate parents which rendered them acceptable to God. But his own unembodied soul, he says, reposed in bliss, wrapt in meditation, and it murmured that it should appear on earth even as the chosen messenger of the Lord—the inheritor of the spirit of Nānak, trans-

and mode of presenting his mission.

in the prosecution of his lofty and comprehensive design. The sentiment is indeed common to all times and places: it is as common in the present Indian as it was in the ancient European world; and even the 'most Christian of poets' has used it without rebuke to justify the anger of a shade in Hades, and his own sympathy as a mortal man yet dwelling in the world:

'Oh guide beloved!
His violent death yet unavenged, said I,
By any who are partners in his shame
Made him contemptuous; therefore, as I think,
He passed me speechless by, and doing so
Hath made me more compassionate his fate.'

Dante, *Hell*, xxix. Cary's translation.

[1] The persuasion of being moved by something more than the mere human will and reason, does not necessarily imply delusion or insanity in the ordinary sense of the term, and the belief is everywhere traceable as one of the phenomena of 'mind', both in the creation of the poet and in the recorded experience of actual life. Thus the reader will remember the 'unaccustomed spirit' of Romeo, and the 'rebuked genius' of Macbeth, as well as the 'star' of Napoleon; and he will call to mind the 'martial transports' of Ajax infused by Neptune, as well as the 'daemon' of Socrates and the 'inspiration' of the holy men of Israel.

[2] The *Vichitr Natak*, or Wondrous Tale, which forms a portion of the *Daswin Padshah ka Granth*, or Book of the Tenth King.

mitted to him as one lamp imparts its flame to another.[1] He describes how the 'Daityas' had been vainly sent to reprove the wickedness of man, and how the succeeding 'Devtas' procured worship for themselves as Siva and Brāhma and Vishnu. How the Siddhs had established divers sects, how Gorakhnath and Rāmānand introduced other modes, and how Muhammad had required men to repeat his own name when beseeching the Almighty. Each perversely, continues Gobind, established ways of his own and misled the world, but he himself had come to declare a perfect faith, to extend virtue, and to destroy evil. Thus, he said, had he been manifested, but *he* was only as other men, the servant of the supreme, a beholder of the wonders of creation, and whosoever worshipped *him* as the Lord should assuredly burn in everlasting flame. The practices of Muhammadans and Hindus he declared to be of no avail, the reading of Korāns and Purāns was all in vain, and the votaries of idols and the worshippers of the dead could never attain to bliss. God, he said, was not to be found in texts or in modes, but in humility and sincerity.[2]

1675–1708

The religions of the world held to be corrupt, and a new dispensation to have been vouchsafed.

The legend regarding Gobind's reformation of the sect of Nānak.

Such is Gobind's mode of presenting his mission ; but his followers have extended the allegory, and have variously given an earthly close to his celestial vision. He is stated to have performed the most austere devotions at the fane of the goddess-mother of mankind on the summit of the hill named Naina, and to have asked how in the olden times

[1] The reader will contrast what Virgil says of the shade of Rome's 'great emperor', with the devoted Quietism of the Indian reformer :

> 'There mighty Caesar waits his vital hour,
> Impatient for the world, and grasps his promised power.'
>
> *Aeneid*, vi.

He will also call to mind the sentiment of Milton, which the more ardent Gobind has greatly heightened.

> 'He asked, but all the heavenly quire stood mute,
> And silence was in heaven : on man's behalf,
> Patron or intercessor none appeared.'

Until Christ himself said—

> 'Account me man, I for his sake will leave
> Thy bosom, and this glory next to thee
> Freely put off.'—*Paradise Lost*, iii.

[2] Cf. the extracts given by Malcolm from the *Vichitr Natak* (*Sketch*, p. 173, &c.).

1675–1708. the heroic Arjūn transpierced multitudes with an arrow. He was told that by prayer and sacrifice the power had been attained. He invited from Benares a Brāhman of great fame for piety and for power over the unseen world. He himself carefully consulted the Vedas, and he called upon his numerous disciples to aid in the awful ceremony he was about to perform. Before all he makes successful trial of the virtue of the magician, and an ample altar is laboriously prepared for the *Hôm*, or burnt offering. He is told that the goddess will appear to him, an armed shade, and that, undaunted, he should hail her and ask for fortune. The Gurū, terror-struck, could but advance his sword, as if in salutation to the dread appearance. The goddess touched it in token of acceptance, and a divine weapon, an axe of iron, was seen amid the flames. The sign was declared to be propitious, but fear had rendered the sacrifice incomplete, and Gobind must die himself, or devote to death one dear to him, to ensure the triumph of his faith. The Gurū smiled sadly ; he said *he* had yet much to accomplish in this world, and that his father's spirit was still unappeased. He looked towards his children, but maternal affection withdrew them : twenty-five disciples then sprang forward and declared their readiness to perish ; one was gladdened by being chosen, and the fates were satisfied.[1]

The principles inculcated by Gobind. The 'Khālsa'. Old forms useless. God is one.

Gobind is next represented to have again assembled his followers, and made known to them the great objects of his mission. A new faith had been declared, and henceforth the 'Khālsa', the saved or liberated,[2] should alone prevail. God must be worshipped in truthfulness and sincerity, but no material resemblance must degrade the Omnipotent ; the Lord could only be beheld by the eye

[1] This legend is given with several variations, and one may be seen in Malcolm (*Sketch*, p. 53, note) and another in Macgregor's *History of the Sikhs* (i. 71). Perhaps the true origin of the myth is to be found in Gobind's reputed vision during sleep of the great goddess. (Malcolm, p. 187.) The occurrence is placed in the year A. D. 1696. (Malcolm, *Sketch*, p. 86.)

[2] Khālsa, or Khālisa, is of Arabic derivation, and has such original or secondary meanings as pure, special, free, &c. It is commonly used in India to denote the immediate territories of any chief or state

1675–1708.

All men are equal. Idolatry to be contemned, and Muhammadanism destroyed.

of faith in the general body of the Khālsa.[1] All, he said, must become as one; the lowest were equal with the highest; caste must be forgotten; they must accept the 'Pāhul' or initiation from him,[2] and the four races must eat as one out of one vessel. The Turks must be destroyed, and the graves of those called saints neglected. The ways of the Hindus must be abandoned, their temples viewed as holy and their rivers looked upon as sacred; the Brāhman's thread must be broken; by means of the Khālsa alone could salvation be attained. They must surrender themselves wholly to their faith and to him their guide. Their words must be 'Kritnash, Kulnash, Dharmnash, Karmnash,' the forsaking of occupation and family, of belief and ceremonies. 'Do thus,' said Gobind, 'and the world is yours.'[3] Many Brāhman and Kshattriya followers murmured, but the contemned races rejoiced; they reminded Gobind of their devotion and services, and asked that *they* also should be allowed to bathe in the sacred pool, and offer up prayers in the temple of Amritsar. The murmurings of the twice-born increased, and many took their departure, but Gobind exclaimed that the lowly should be raised, and that hereafter the despised should dwell next to himself.[4] Gobind then poured water into a vessel and

as distinguished from the lands of tributaries and feudal followers. Khālsa can thus be held either to denote the kingdom of Gobind, or that the Sikhs are the chosen people.

[1] This assurance is given in the Rehet Nameh, or Rule of Life of Gobind, which, however, is not included in the *Granth*. In the same composition he says, or is held to have said, that the believer who wishes to see the Gurū shall behold him in the Khālsā.

Those who object to such similitudes, or to such struggles of the mind after precision, should remember that Abelard likened the Trinity to a syllogism with its three terms; and that Wallis, with admitted orthodoxy, compared the Godhead to a mathematical cube with its three dimensions. (Bayle's *Dictionary*, art. 'Abelard'.)

[2] Pāhul (pronounced nearly as *Powl*), means literally a gate, a door, and thence initiation. The word may have the same origin as the Greek πύλη.

[3] The text gives the substance and usually the very words of the numerous accounts to the same purport. (Cf. also Malcolm, *Sketch*, pp. 148, 151.)

[4] Churhas, or men of the Sweeper caste, brought away the remains of Tegh Bahādur from Delhi, as has been mentioned (*ante*, p. 66, note). Many of that despised, but not oppressed race, have adopted the

1675–1708. stirred it with the sacrificial axe, or with the sword rendered divine by the touch of the goddess. His wife passed by, as it were by chance, bearing confections of five kinds: he hailed the omen as propitious, for the coming of woman denoted an offspring to the Khālsa numerous as the leaves of the forest. He mingled the sugars with the water, and then sprinkled a portion of it upon five faithful disciples, a Brāhman, a Kshattriya, and three Sūdras. He hailed them as 'Singhs', and declared them to be the Khālsa. He himself received from them the 'Pāhul' of his faith, and became Gobind Singh, saying, that hereafter, when-

The Pāhul or initiation of the sect of Singhs.

Sikh faith in the Punjab, and they are commonly known as Ranghrheta Sikhs. *Rangghar* is a term applied to the Rājpūts about Delhi who have become Muhammadans; but in Mālwā the predatory Hindu Rājpūts are similarly styled, perhaps from *Rank*, a poor man, in opposition to *Rana*, one of high degree. Ranghrheta seems thus rather a diminutive of Rangghar than a derivative of *rang* (colour) as commonly understood. The Ranghrheta Sikhs are sometimes styled *Mazhabi*, or of the (Muhammadan) faith, from the circumstance that the converts from Islām are so called, and that many Sweepers throughout India have become Muhammadans.

[These Mazhabis in the past have proved themselves, and are at the present time, extremely good soldiers. The Pioneer regiments—23rd, 32nd, 34th—into which they are recruited have a proud record of service in many campaigns. Mr. Candler, in an article in *Blackwood's Magazine*, September 1909, observes: 'The general reluctance of the low-caste Hindu to elevate himself by becoming a Sikh may perhaps be explained by the historical exception of the Mazhabis. These Sikhs, the descendants of converts from the despised Sweeper caste, were welcomed by the Khālsa at a time when they were engaged in a desperate struggle with the forces of Islām. But when the Sikhs dominated the Punjab they found that the equality their religion promised them existed in theory rather than in fact. They occupied much the same position among the Jāt and Khālsa descended Sikhs as their ancestors, the Sweepers, enjoyed among Hindus. They were debarred from all privileges and were, at one time, excluded from the army.'

According to the Census Report of 1912 the Mazhabi population now numbers 21,691. 'They have taken to husbandry and have been declared as a separate agricultural tribe in the districts of Gujranwala and Lyallpur.' (*Census Report*, 1912.)—Ed.]

In allusion to the design of inspiring the Hindus with a new life, Gobind is reported to have said that he 'would teach the sparrow to strike the eagle'. (See Malcolm, *Sketch*, p. 74, where it is used with reference to Aurangzeb, but the saying is attributed to Gobind under various circumstances by different authors.)

ever five Sikhs should be assembled together, there he also would be present.[1] 1675–1708.

The visible distinctions of Sikhs or Singhs.

Gobind thus abolished social distinctions,[2] and took away from his followers each ancient solace of superstition; but he felt that he must engage the heart as well as satisfy the reason, and that he must give the Sikhs some common bonds of union which should remind the weak of their new life, and add fervour to the devotion of the sincere. They should have one form of initiation, he said, the sprinkling of water by five of the faithful;[3] they should worship the One Invisible God; they should honour the memory of Nānak and of his transanimate successors;[4] their watchword should be, Hail Gurū![5] but they should revere and bow to nought visible save the *Granth*, the book of their belief.[6]

Lustration by water. Reverence for Nānak.

The exclamation, Hail Gurū!

[1] The Brāhman novitiate is stated to have been an inhabitant of the Deccan, and the Kshattriya of the Punjab; one Sūdra, a Jhīnwar (Kahār), was of Jaganāth, the second, a Jāt, was of Hastināpur, and the third, a Chhīmbā or cloth printer, was of Dwārka in Gujrāt.

For the declaration about five Sikhs forming a congregation, or about the assembly of five men ensuring the presence or the grace of the Gurū, cf. Malcolm, *Sketch*, p. 186. [Five is also the number of the necessary attributes of the true follower of Gobind Singh, viz. Kes, Khanda, Kangha, Kara, Kach—long hair, dagger, comb, bangle, breeches.—ED.]

Gobind had originally the cognomen, or titular name, of 'Rai', one in common use among Hindus, and largely adopted under the variation of 'Rao' by the military Marāthās; but on declaring the comprehensive nature of his reform, the Gurū adopted for himself and followers the distinctive appellation of 'Singh', meaning literally a lion, and metaphorically a champion or warrior. It is the most common of the distinctive names in use among Rājpūts, and it is now the invariable termination of every proper name among the disciples of Gobind. It is sometimes used alone, as Khān is used among the Muhammadans, to denote pre-eminence. Thus Sikh chiefs would talk of Ranjīt Singh, as ordinary Sikhs will talk of their own immediate leaders, as the 'Singh Sahib', almost equivalent to 'Sir King', or 'Sir Knight', in English. Strangers likewise often address any Sikh respectfully as 'Singhji'.

[2] See Appendix X. [3] See Appendix XI.

[4] The use of the word 'transanimate' may perhaps be allowed. The Sikh belief in the descent of the individual spirit of Nānak upon each of his successors, is compared by Gobind in the *Vichitr Natak* to the imparting of flame from one lamp to another.

[5] See Appendix XII.

[6] Obeisance to the *Granth* alone is inculcated in the Rahat Nama

1675–1708.

Unshorn locks; the title of Singh; and devotion to arms.

They should bathe, from time to time, in the pool of Amritsar; their locks should remain unshorn; they should all name themselves 'Singhs', or soldiers, and of material things they should devote their finite energies to steel alone.[1] Arms should dignify their person; they should be ever waging war, and great would be his merit who fought in the van, who slew an enemy, and who despaired not although overcome. He cut off the three sects of dissenters from all intercourse: the Dhirmalis, who had laboured to destroy Arjūn; the Rām Rais, who had compassed the death of his father; and the Masandis, who had resisted his own authority. He denounced the 'shaven', meaning, perhaps, all Muhammadans and Hindus; and for no reason which bears clearly on the worldly scope of his mission, he held up to reprobation those slaves of a perverse custom, who impiously take the lives of their infant daughters.[2]

The character and condition of the Mughal empire when Gobind resolved to assail it.

Gobind had achieved one victory, he had made himself master of the imagination of his followers; but a more laborious task remained, the destruction of the empire of unbelieving oppressors. He had established the Khālsa, the theocracy of Singhs, in the midst of Hindu delusion and Muhammadan error; he had confounded Pīrs and Mullas, Sādhs and Pandits, but he had yet to vanquish the armies of a great emperor, and to subdue the multitudes whose faith he impugned. The design of Gobind may seem wild and senseless to those accustomed to consider the firm sway and regular policy of ancient Rome, and who daily witness the power and resources of the well-ordered governments of modern Europe. But the extensive empires of the East, as of semi-barbarism in the West, have never been based on the sober convictions of a numerous people; they have been mere dynasties of single tribes, rendered triumphant by the rapid development of warlike energy, and by the comprehensive genius of eminent leaders. Race has succeeded race in dominion, and what Cyrus did with his Persians and Charlemagne with his Franks, Bābar began

or Rule of Life of Gobind, and he endeavoured to guard against being himself made an object of future idolatry, by denouncing (in the *Vichitr Natak*) all who should regard him as a god.

[1] See Appendix XIII. [2] See Appendix XIV.

and Akbar completed with a few Tartars their personal followers. The Mughals had even a less firm hold of empire than the Achaemenides or the Carlovingians; the devoted clansmen of Bābar were not numerous, his son was driven from his throne, and Akbar became the master of India as much by political sagacity, and the generous sympathy of his nature, as by military enterprise and the courage of his partisans. He perceived the want of the times, and his commanding genius enabled him to reconcile the conflicting interests and prejudices of Muhammadans and Hindus, of Rājpūts, Turks, and Pathāns. At the end of fifty years he left his heir a broad and well-regulated dominion; yet one son of Jahāngīr contested the empire with his father, and Shāh Jahān first saw his children waging war with one another for the possession of the crown which he himself still wore, and at length became the prisoner of the ablest and most successful of the combatants. Aurangzeb ever feared the influence of his own example: his temper was cold; his policy towards Muhammadans was one of suspicion, while his bigotry and persecutions rendered him hateful to his Hindu subjects. In his old age his wearied spirit could find no solace; no tribe of brave and confiding men gathered round him: yet his vigorous intellect kept *him* an emperor to the last, and the hollowness of his sway was not apparent to the careless observer until he was laid in his grave. The empire of the Mughals wanted political fusion, and its fair degree of administrative order and subordination was vitiated by the doubt which hung about the succession.[1] It comprised a number of petty states which rendered an unwilling obedience to the sovereign power; it was also studded over with feudal retainers, and all these hereditary princes and mercenary 'Jagīrdārs' were

1675–1708.

Akbar.

Aurangzeb.

[1] Notwithstanding this defect, the English themselves have yet to do much before they can establish a system which shall last so long and work so well as Akbar's organization of Pargana Chaudris and Qanungos, who may be likened to hereditary county sheriffs, and registers of landed property and holdings. The objectionable hereditary law was modified in practice by the adoption of the most able or the most upright as the representative of the family. [A somewhat pessimistic statement viewing the way in which modern administrators have dealt with the land question.—ED.]

1675–1708. ever ready to resist, or to pervert, the measures of the central government. They considered then, as they do now, that a monarch exercised sway for his own interests only, without reference to the general welfare of the country; no public opinion of an intelligent people systematically governed controlled them, and applause always awaited the successful aspirant to power. Akbar did something to remove this antagonism between the rulers and the ruled, but his successors were less wise than himself, and religious discontent was soon added to the love of political independence. The southern portions of India, too, were at this time recent conquests, and Aurangzeb had been long absent,[1] hopelessly endeavouring to consolidate his sway in that distant quarter. The Himālayas had scarcely been penetrated by the Mughals, except in the direction of Kashmīr, and rebellion might rear its head almost unheeded amid their wild recesses. Lastly, during this period, Sivājī had roused the slumbering spirit of the Marāthā tribes. He had converted rude herdsmen into successful soldiers, and had become a territorial chief in the very neighbourhood of the emperor. Gobind added religious fervour to warlike temper, and his design of founding a kingdom of Jāts upon the waning glories of Aurangzeb's dominion does not appear to have been idly conceived or rashly undertaken.

Sivājī the Marāthā.

Gurū Gobind.

Gobind's plans of active opposition, (about) 1695.

Yet it is not easy to place the actions of Gobind in due order, or to understand the particular object of each of his proceedings. He is stated by a credible Muhammadan author to have organized his followers into troops and bands, and to have placed them under the command of trustworthy disciples.[2] He appears to have entertained a body of Pathāns, who are everywhere the soldiers of fortune,[3] and it is certain that he established two or three forts along

[[1] A reference to the conquest by Aurangzeb of the kingdom of Bijapur (1686) and Golconda (1687). From 1681 to his death in 1707 the Emperor was almost incessantly engaged in a series of campaigns against these kingdoms and the rising power of the Marāthās.—Ed.]

[2] *Siar ul Mutākharin*, i. 113.

[3] The Marāthā histories show that Sivājī likewise hired bands of Pathāns, who had lost service in the declining kingdom of Bijapur. (Grant Duff, *Hist. of the Marāthās*, i. 165.)

1675–1708.

His military posts; and leagues with the chiefs of the Lower Himālayas.

the skirts of the hills between the Sutlej and Jumna. He had a post at Paunta in the Kirda vale near Nāhan, a place long afterwards the scene of a severe struggle between the Gurkhas and the English. He had likewise a retreat at Anandpur-Makhowāl, which had been established by his father,[1] and a third at Chamkaur, fairly in the plains and lower down the Sutlej than the chosen haunt of Tegh Bahādur. He had thus got strongholds which secured him against any attempts of his hill neighbours, and he would next seem to have endeavoured to mix himself up with the affairs of these half-independent chiefs, and to obtain a commanding influence over them, so as by degrees to establish a virtual principality amid mountain fastnesses to serve as the basis of his operations against the Mughal government. As a religious teacher he drew contributions and procured followers from all parts of India, but as a leader he perceived the necessity of a military pivot, and as a rebel he was not insensible to the value of a secure retreat.

His influence as a religious teacher.

Gobind quarrels with the Rājās of Nāhan and Nālāgarh.

Gobind has himself described the several actions in which he was engaged, either as a principal or as an ally.[2] His pictures are animated ; they are of some value as historical records, and their sequence seems more probable than that of any other narrative. His first contest was with his old friend the chief of Nāhan, aided by the Rājā of Hindūr, to whom he had given offence, and by the mercenary Pathāns in his own service, who claimed arrears of pay, and who may have hoped to satisfy all demands by the destruction of Gobind and the plunder of his establishments. But the Gurū was victorious, some of the Pathān leaders fell, and Gobind slew the young warrior, Harī Chand of Nālāgarh,

[1] Anandpur is situated close to Makhowāl. The first name was given by Gobind to his own particular residence at Makhowāl, as distinguished from the abode of his father, and it signified the place of happiness. A knoll, with a seat upon it, is here pointed out, whence it is said Gobind was wont to discharge an arrow a coss and a quarter —about a mile and two-thirds English, the Punjabi coss being small.

[2] Namely, in the *Vichitr Natak*, already quoted as a portion of the Second *Granth*. The *Gurū Bilas*, by Sukha Singh, corroborates Gobind's account, and adds many details. Malcolm (*Sketch*, p. 58,&c.) may be referred to for translations of some portions of the *Vichitr Natak* bearing on the period, but Malcolm's own general narrative of the events is obviously contradictory and inaccurate.

1675–1708.

Aids the Rājā of Kuhlur and other chiefs against the imperial forces.

with his own hand. The Gurū nevertheless deemed it prudent to move to the Sutlej; he strengthened Anandpur, and became the ally of Bhīm Chand of Kuhlur, who was in resistance to the imperial authorities of Kot Kangra. The Muhammadan commander was joined by various hill chiefs, but in the end he was routed, and Bhīm Chand's rebellion seemed justified by success. A period of rest ensued, during which, says Gobind, he punished such of his followers as were lukewarm or disorderly. But the aid which he rendered to the chief of Kuhlur was not forgotten, and a body of Muhammadan troops made an unsuccessful attack upon his position. Again an imperial commander took the field, partly to coerce Gobind, and partly to reduce the hill rājās, who, profiting by the example of Bhīm Chand, had refused to pay their usual tribute. A desultory warfare ensued; some attempts at accommodation were made by the hill chiefs, but these were broken off, and the expedition ended in the rout of the Muhammadans.

Gobind's proceedings excite the suspicions of the hill chiefs, and cause the emperor some anxiety, (about) 1701.

The success of Gobind, for all was attributed to him, caused the Muhammadans some anxiety, and his designs appear likewise to have alarmed the hill chiefs, for they loudly claimed the imperial aid against one who announced himself as the True King. Aurangzeb directed the governors of Lahore and Sirhind to march against the Gurū, and it was rumoured that the emperor's son, Bahādur Shāh, would himself take the field in their support.[1] Gobind was surrounded at Anandpur by the forces of the empire. His own resolution was equal to any emergency, but numbers of his followers deserted him. He cursed them in this world and in the world to come, and others who wavered he caused to renounce their faith, and then dismissed them with igno-

Gobind reduced to straits at Anandpur.

[1] Malcolm (*Sketch*, p. 60, note) says that this allusion would place the warfare in A. D. 1701, as Bahādur Shāh was at that time sent from the Deccan towards Kābul. Some Sikh traditions, indeed, represent Gobind as having gained the goodwill of, or as they put it, as having shown favour to, Bahādur Shāh; and Gobind himself, in the *Vichitr Natak*, says that a son of the emperor came to suppress the disturbances, but no name is given. Neither does Mr. Elphinstone (*History*, ii. 545) specify Bahādur Shāh; and, indeed, he merely seems to conjecture that a prince of the blood, who was sent to put down disturbances near Multān, was really employed against the Sikhs near Sirhind.

miny. But his difficulties increased, desertions continued to take place, and at last he found himself at the head of no more than forty devoted followers. His mother, his wives, and his two youngest children effected their escape to Sirhind, but the boys were there betrayed to the Muhammadans and put to death.[1] The faithful forty said they were ready to die with their priest and king, and they prayed him to recall his curse upon their weaker-hearted brethren, and to restore to them the hope of salvation. Gobind said that his wrath would not endure. But he still clung to temporal success; the fort of Chamkaur remained in his possession, and he fled during the night and reached the place in safety.

1675–1708.

His children escape; but are subsequently put to death.

He himself flies to Chamkaur.

At Chamkaur Gobind was again besieged.[2] He was called upon to surrender his person and to renounce his faith, but Ajīt Singh, his son, indignantly silenced the bearer of the message. The troops pressed upon the Sikhs; the Gurū was himself everywhere present, but his two surviving sons fell before his eyes, and his little band was nearly destroyed. He at last resolved upon escape, and taking advantage of a dark night, he threaded his way to the outskirts of the camp, but there he was recognized and stopped by two Pathāns. These men, it is said, had in former times received kindness at the hands of the Gurū, and they now assisted him in reaching the town of Bahlolpur, where he trusted his person to a third follower of Islām, one Pīr Muhammad, with whom it is further said the Gurū had once studied the Korān. Here he ate food from Muhammadans, and declared that such might be done by Sikhs under pressing circumstances. He further disguised himself in the blue dress of a Musalmān Dervish, and speedily reached the wastes of Bhatinda. His disciples again rallied round him, and he succeeded in repulsing his pursuers at a place since called

Gobind escapes from Chamkaur, 1705–6.

Successfully resists his pursuers at Muktsar;

[1] The most detailed account of this murder of Gobind's children is given in Browne's *India Tracts*, ii. 6, 7.

[2] At Chamkaur, in one of the towers of the small brick fort, is still shown the tomb of a distinguished warrior, a Sikh of the Sweeper caste, named Jīwan Singh, who fell during the siege. The bastion itself is known as that of the Martyr. A temple now stands where Ajīt Singh and Jujhār Singh, the eldest sons of Gobind, are reputed to have fallen.

Gobind's defeat and flight are placed by the Sikhs in A.D. 1705–6.

1675–1708.

'Muktsar', or the Pool of Salvation. He continued his flight to Dam-Dama, or the Breathing Place, half way between Hānsi and Ferozepore; the imperial authorities thought his strength sufficiently broken, and they did not follow him further into a parched and barren country.

and rests at Dam-Dama, near Bhatinda.

At Dam-Dama Gobind remained for some time, and he occupied himself in composing the supplemental *Granth*, 'the Book of the Tenth King', to rouse the energies and sustain the hopes of the faithful. This comprises the *Vichitr Natak*, or 'Wondrous Tale', the only historical portion of either *Granth*, and which he concludes by a hymn in praise of God, who had ever assisted him. He would, he says, make known in another book the things which he had himself accomplished, the glories of the Lord which he had witnessed, and his recollections or visions of his antecedent existence. All he had done, he said, had been done with the aid of the Almighty; and to 'Loh', or the mysterious virtue of iron, he attributed his preservation. While thus living in retirement, messengers arrived to summon him to the emperor's presence; but Gobind replied to Aurangzeb in a series of parables admonitory of kings, partly in which, and partly in a letter which accompanied them, he remonstrates rather than humbles himself. He denounces the wrath of God upon the monarch, rather than deprecates the imperial anger against himself; he tells the emperor that he puts no trust in him, and that the 'Khālsā' will avenge him. He refers to Nānak's religious reform, and he briefly alludes to the death of Arjūn and of Tegh Bahādur. He describes his own wrongs and his childless condition. He was, as one without earthly link, patiently awaiting death, and fearing none but the sole Emperor, the King of Kings. Nor, said he, are the prayers of the poor ineffectual; and on the day of reckoning it would be seen how the emperor would justify his manifold cruelties and oppressions. The Gurū was again desired to repair to Aurangzeb's presence, and he really appears to have proceeded to the south some time before the aged monarch was removed by death.[1]

Gobind composes the Vichitr Natak.

Summoned by Aurangzeb to his presence.

Replies to the emperor in a denunciatory strain.

[1] In this narrative of Gobind's warlike actions, reference has been mainly had to the *Vichitr Natak* of the Gurū, to the *Gurū Bilas* of Sukha Singh, and to the ordinary modern compilations in Persian and

1675–1708.

Aurangzeb dies, and Bahādur Shāh succeeds, A. D. 1707.

Gobind proceeds to the south of India.

Enters the imperial service.

Aurangzeb died in the beginning of 1707, and his eldest son, Bahādur Shāh, hastened from Kābul to secure the succession. He vanquished and slew one brother near Agra, and, marching to the south, he defeated a second, Kāmbakhsh, who died of his wounds. While engaged in this last campaign, Bahādur Shāh summoned Gobind to his camp. The Gurū went; he was treated with respect, and he received a military command in the valley of the Godāvari. The emperor perhaps thought that the leader of insurrectionary Jāts might be usefully employed in opposing rebellious Marāthās, and Gobind perhaps saw in the imperial service a ready way of disarming suspicion and of reorganizing his followers.[1] At Dam-Dama he had again denounced evil upon all who should thenceforward desert him; in the south he selected the daring Banda as an instrument, and the Sikhs speedily reappeared in overwhelming force upon the banks of the Sutlej. But Gobind's race was run, and he was not himself fated to achieve aught more in person. He had engaged the services of an Afghān, half-adventurer, half-merchant, and he had procured from him a considerable number of horses.[2] The merchant, or servant, pleaded his own necessities, and urged the payment

Gurmukhī; transcripts, imperfect apparently, of some of which latter have been put into English by Dr. Macgregor (*History of the Sikhs*, pp. 79–99).

[1] The Sikh writers seem unanimous in giving to their great teacher a military command in the Deccan, while some recent Muhammadan compilers assert that he died at Patna. But the liberal conduct of Bahādur Shāh is confirmed by the contemporary historian, Khafi Khān, who states that he received rank in the Mughal army (see Elphinstone, *Hist. of India*, ii. 566 note), and it is in a degree corroborated by the undoubted fact of the Gurū's death on the banks of the Godāvari. The traditions preserved at Nadēr give Kartik, 1765 (Sambat), or towards the end of A. D. 1703, as the date of Gobind's arrival at that place.

[2] It would be curious to trace how far India was colonized in the intervals of great invasions by petty Afghān and Turkomān leaders, who defrayed their first or occasional expenses by the sale of horses. Tradition represents that both the destroyer of Mānikiāla in the Punjab, and the founder of Bhatnair in Hariāna, were emigrants so circumstanced; and Amīr Khān, the recent Indian adventurer, was similarly reduced to sell his steeds for food. (*Memoirs of Amīr Khān*, p. 16.)

1675–1708. of large sums due to him. Impatient with delay, he used an angry gesture, and his mutterings of violence provoked Gobind to strike him dead. The body of the slain Pathān was removed and buried, and his family seemed reconciled to the fate of its head. But his sons nursed their revenge, and awaited an opportunity of fulfilling it. They succeeded in stealing upon the Gurū's retirement, and stabbed him mortally when asleep or unguarded. Gobind sprang up and the assassins were seized; but a sardonic smile played upon their features, and they justified their act of retribution. The Gurū heard: he remembered the fate of their father, and he perhaps called to mind his own unavenged parent. He said to the youths that they had done well, and he directed that they should be released uninjured.[1] The expiring Gurū was childless, and the assembled disciples asked in sorrow who should inspire them with truth and lead them to victory when he was no more. Gobind bade them be of good cheer; the appointed Ten had indeed fulfilled their mission, but he was about to deliver the Khālsa to God, the never-dying. 'He who wishes to behold the Gurū, let him search the *Granth* of Nānak. The Gurū will dwell with the Khālsa; be firm and be faithful: wherever five Sikhs are gathered together there will I also be present.'[2]

Gobind wounded by assassins,

and dies, A.D. 1708, declaring his mission to be fulfilled, and the Khālsa to be committed to God.

[1] All the common accounts narrate the death of Gobind as given in the text, but with slight differences of detail, while some add that the widow of the slain Pathān continually urged her sons to seek revenge. Many accounts, and especially those by Muhammadans, likewise represent Gobind to have become deranged in his mind, and a story told by some Sikh writers gives a degree of countenance to such a belief. They say that the heart of the Gurū inclined towards the youths whose father he had slain, that he was wont to play simple games of skill with them, and that he took opportunities of inculcating upon them the merit of revenge, as if he was himself weary of life, and wished to fall by their hands. The *Siar ul Mutākharin* (i. 114) simply says that Gobind died of grief on account of the loss of his children. (Cf. Malcolm, *Sketch*, p. 70, &c.; and Elphinstone, *History*, ii. 564.) The accounts now furnished by the priests of the temple at Nadēr, represent the *one* assassin of the Gurū to have been the grandson of the Painda Khān, slain by Har Gobind, and they do not give him any further cause of quarrel with Gobind himself.

[2] Such is the usual account given of the Gurū's dying injunctions; and the belief that Gobind consummated the mission or dispensation of Nānaks eems to have been agreeable to the feelings of the times,

1675–1708.

Gobind's end untimely, but labours not fruitless.

Gobind was killed in 1708, at Nadēr, on the banks of the Godāvari.[1] He was in his forty-eighth year, and if it be thought by any that his obscure end belied the promise of his whole life, it should be remembered that—

'The hand of man
Is but a tardy servant of the brain,
And follows, with its leaden diligence,
The fiery steps of fancy';[2]

that when Muhammad was a fugitive from Mecca, 'the lance of an Arab might have changed the history of the world';[3] and that the Achilles of poetry, the reflexion of truth, left Troy untaken. The lord of the Myrmidons, destined to a short life and immortal glory, met an end almost as base as that which he dreaded when struggling with Simois and Scamander; and the heroic Richard, of eastern and western fame, whose whole soul was bent upon the deliverance of Jerusalem, veiled his face in shame and

while it now forms a main article of faith. The mother, and one wife of Gobind, are represented to have survived him some years; but each, when dying, declared the Gurūship to rest in the general body of the Khālsa, and not in any one mortal; and hence the Sikhs do not give such a designation even to the most revered of their holy men, their highest religious title being 'Bhai', literally 'brother', but corresponding in significance with the English term 'elder'.

[1] Gobind is stated to have been born in the month of Poh, 1718 (Sambat), which may be the end of A. D. 1661 or beginning of 1662, and all accounts agree in placing his death about the middle of 1765 (Sambat), or towards the end of A. D. 1708.

At Nadēr there is a large religious establishment, partly supported by the produce of landed estates, partly by voluntary contributions, and partly by sums levied annually, agreeably to the mode organized by Arjūn. The principal of the establishment dispatches a person to show his requisition to the faithful, and all give according to their means. Thus the common horsemen in the employ of Bhopāl give a rupee and a quarter each a year, besides offerings on occasions of pilgrimage.

Ranjīt Singh sent considerable sums to Nadēr, but the buildings commenced with the means which he provided have not been completed.

Nadēr is also called Apchalanagar, and in Southern and Central India it is termed pre-eminently 'the Gurūdwara', that is, 'the house of the Gurūs'.

[2] *Sir Marmaduke Maxwell*, a dramatic poem, Act iv, scene 6.

[3] Gibbon, *Decline and Fall of the Roman Empire*, ix. 285.

1708–16.

sorrow that God's holy city should be left in the possession of infidels: he would not behold that which he could not redeem, and he descended from the Mount to retire to captivity and a premature grave.[1] Success is thus not always the measure of greatness. The last apostle of the Sikhs did not live to see his own ends accomplished, but he effectually roused the dormant energies of a vanquished people, and filled them with a lofty although fitful longing for social freedom and national ascendancy, the proper adjuncts of that purity of worship which had been preached by Nānak. Gobind saw what was yet vital, and he relumed it with Promethean fire. A living spirit possesses the whole Sikh people, and the impress of Gobind has not only elevated and altered the constitution of their minds, but has operated materially and given amplitude to their physical frames. The features and external form of a whole people have been modified, and a Sikh chief is not more distinguishable by his stately person and free and manly bearing, than a minister of his faith is by a lofty thoughtfulness of look, which marks the fervour of his soul, and his persuasion of the near presence of the Divinity.[2] Notwithstanding these changes it has been usual to regard the Sikhs as essentially Hindu, and they doubtless are so in language and everyday customs, for Gobind did not fetter his

A new character impressed upon the reformed Hindus;

[1] For this story of the lion-like king, see Gibbon (*Decline and Fall*, xi. 143). See also Turner's comparison of the characters of Achilles and Richard (*History of England*, p. 300), and Hallam's assent to its superior justness relatively to his own parallel of the Cid and the English hero (*Middle Ages*, iii. 482).

[2] This physical change has been noticed by Sir Alexander Burnes (*Travels*, i. 285, and ii. 39), by Elphinstone (*History of India*, ii. 564), and it also slightly struck Malcolm (*Sketch*, p. 129). Similarly a change of aspect, as well as of dress, &c., may be observed in the descendants of such members of Hindu families as became Muhammadans one or two centuries ago, and whose personal appearance may yet be readily compared with that of their undoubted Brāhmanical cousins in many parts of Mālwā and Upper India. That Prichard (*Physical History of Mankind*, i. 183 and i. 191) notices no such change in the features, although he does in the characters, of the Hottentots and Esquimaux who have been converted to Christianity, may either show that the attention of our observers and inquirers has not been directed to the subject, or that the savages in question have embraced a new faith with little of living ardour and absorbing enthusiasm.

disciples with political systems or codes of municipal laws; yet, in religious faith and worldly aspirations, they are wholly different from other Indians, and they are bound together by a community of inward sentiment and of outward object unknown elsewhere. But the misapprehension need not surprise the public nor condemn our scholars,[1] when it is remembered that the learned of Greece and Rome misunderstood the spirit of those humble men who obtained a new life by baptism. Tacitus and Suetonius regarded the early Christians as a mere Jewish sect, they failed to perceive the fundamental difference, and to appreciate the latent energy and real excellence, of that doctrine, which has added dignity and purity to modern civilization.[2]

1708–16.

although not fully apparent to strangers, if so to Indians.

[1] The author alludes chiefly to Professor H. H. Wilson, whose learning and industry are doing so much for Indian history. (See *Asiatic Researches*, xvii. 237, 238; and continuation of Mill's *History*, vii. 101, 102.) Malcolm holds similar views in one place (*Sketch*, pp. 144, 148, 150), but somewhat contradicts himself in another (*Sketch*, p. 43). With these opinions, however, may be compared the more correct views of Elphinstone (*History of India*, ii. 562, 564) and Sir Alexander Burnes (*Travels*, i. 284, 285), and also Major Browne's observation (*India Tracts*, ii. 4) that the Sikh doctrine bore the same relation to the Hindu as the Protestant does to the Romish.

[2] See the *Annals of Tacitus*, Murphy's translation (book xv, sect. 44, note 15). Tacitus calls Christianity a dangerous superstition, and regards its professors as moved by 'a sullen hatred of the whole human race'—the Judaic characteristic of the period. Suetonius talks of the *Jews* raising disturbances in the reign of Claudius, at the instigation of 'one Chrestus', thus evidently mistaking the whole of the facts, and further making a Latin name, genuine indeed, but misapplied, of the Greek term for anointed.

Again, the obscure historian, Vopiscus, preserves a letter, written by the Emperor Hadrian, in which the Christians are confounded with the adorers of Serapis, and in which the *bishops* are said to be especially devoted to the worship of that strange god, who was introduced into Egypt by the Ptolemies (Waddington, *History of the Church*, p. 37); and even Eusebius himself did not properly distinguish between Christians and the Essenic Therapeutae (Strauss, *Life of Jesus*, i. 294), although the latter formed essentially a mere sect, or order, affecting asceticism and mystery.

It is proper to add that Mr. Newman quotes the descriptions of Tacitus and others as referring really to Christians and not to Jews (*On the Development of Christian Doctrine*, p. 205, &c.). He may be right, but the grounds of his dissent from the views of preceding scholars are not given.

1708–16.

Banda succeeds Gobind as a temporal leader.

Banda, the chosen disciple of Gobind, was a native of the south of India, and an ascetic of the Bairāgi order;[1] and the extent of the deceased Gurū's preparations and means will be best understood from the narrative of the career of his followers, when his own commanding spirit was no more.

Proceeds to the north, and captures Sirhind, 1709–10.

The Sikhs gathered in numbers round Banda when he reached the north-west, bearing with him the arrows of Gobind as the pledge of victory. Banda put to flight the Mughal authorities in the neighbourhood of Sirhind, and then attacked, defeated, and slew the governor of the province. Sirhind was plundered, and the Hindu betrayer and Musalmān destroyer of Gobind's children were themselves put to death by the avenging Sikhs.[2] Banda next established a stronghold below the hills of Sirmūr,[3] he occupied the country between the Sutlej and Jumna, and he laid waste the district of Sahāranpur.[4]

The emperor marches towards Lahore.

Bahādur Shāh, the emperor, had subdued his rebellious brother Kāmbakhsh, he had come to terms with the Marāthās, and he was desirous of reducing the princes of Rājputāna to their old dependence, when he heard of the defeat of his troops and the sack of his city by the hitherto unknown Banda.[5] He hastened towards the Punjab, and

[1] Some accounts represent Banda to have been a native of Northern India, and the writer, followed by Major Browne (*India Tracts*, ii. 9), says he was born in the Jullundur Doāb.

'Banda' signifies *the slave*, and Sarūp Chand, the author of the *Gur-Ratnāvalī*, states that the Bairāgi took the name or title when he met Gobind in the south, and found that the powers of his tutelary god Vishnu were ineffectual in the presence of the Gurū. Thenceforward, he said, he would be the slave of Gobind.

[2] For several particulars, true or fanciful, relating to the capture of Sirhind, see Browne, *India Tracts*, ii. 9, 10. See also Elphinstone, *History of India*, ii. 565, 566. Wazīr Khān was clearly the name of the governor, and not Faujdār Khān, as mentioned by Malcolm (*Sketch*, pp. 77, 78). Wazīr Khān was indeed the 'Faujdār', or military commander in the province, and the word is as often used as a proper name as to denote an office.

[3] This was at Mukhlispur, near Sadowra, which lies north-east from Ambāla, and it appears to be the 'Lohgarh', that is, the iron or strong fort, of the *Siar ul Mutākharin* (i. 115).

[4] Forster, *Travels*, i. 304.

[5] Cf. Elphinstone, *History of India*, ii. 561, and Forster, *Travels*, i. 304. This was in A. D. 1709–10.

1708–16.

he did not pause to enter his capital after his southern successes; but in the meantime his generals had defeated a body of Sikhs near Pānīpat, and Banda was surrounded in his new stronghold. A zealous convert, disguised like his leader, allowed himself to be captured during a sally of the besieged, and Banda withdrew with all his followers.[1] After some successful skirmishes he established himself near Jammu in the hills north of Lahore, and laid the fairest part of the Punjab under contribution. Bahādur Shāh had by this time advanced to Lahore in person, and he died there in the month of February, 1712.[2]

But Banda is in the meantime driven towards Jammu.

Bahādur Shāh dies at Lahore, 1712.

The death of the emperor brought on another contest for the throne. His eldest son, Jahāndār Shāh, retained power for a year, but in February 1713 he was defeated and put to death by his nephew Farrukhsīyar. These commotions were favourable to the Sikhs; they again became united and formidable, and they built for themselves a considerable fort, named Gurdāspur, between the Beās and Rāvi.[3] The viceroy of Lahore marched against Banda, but he was defeated in a pitched battle, and the Sikhs sent forward a party towards Sirhind, the governor of which, Bāyazīd Khān, advanced to oppose them. A fanatic crept under his tent and mortally wounded him; the Muhammadans dispersed, but the city does not seem to have fallen a second time a prey to the exulting Sikhs.[4] The emperor now ordered Abdus Samad Khān, the governor of Kashmīr, a Tūrāni noble and a skilful general, to assume the command in the Punjab, and he sent to his aid some chosen troops from the eastward. Abdus Samad Khān brought with him some thousands of his own warlike countrymen, and as soon as he was in

Jahāndār Shāh slain by Farrukhsīyar, who becomes emperor, 1713.

The Sikhs reappear under Banda, and the province of Sirhind is plundered.

[1] Cf. Elphinstone, *History*, ii. 566, and Forster, *Travels*, i. 305. The zeal of the devotee was applauded without being pardoned by the emperor.

[2] Cf. the *Siar ul Mutākharin*, i. 109, 112.

[3] Gurdāspur is near Kalānaur, where Akbar was saluted as emperor, and it appears to be the Lohgarh of the ordinary accounts followed by Forster, Malcolm, and others. It now contains a monastery of Sārsut Brāhmans, who have adopted many of the Sikh modes and tenets.

[4] Some accounts nevertheless represent Banda to have again possessed himself of Sirhind.

1708–16. possession of a train of artillery he left Lahore, and falling upon the Sikh army he defeated it, after a fierce resistance on the part of Banda. The success was followed up, and Banda retreated from post to post, fighting valiantly and inflicting heavy losses on his victors; but he was at length compelled to shelter himself in the fort of Gurdāspur. He was closely besieged; nothing could be conveyed to him from without; and after consuming all his provisions, and eating horses, asses, and even the forbidden ox, he was reduced to submit.[1] Some of the Sikhs were put to death, and their heads were borne on pikes before Banda and others as they were marched to Delhi with all the signs of ignominy usual with bigots, and common among barbarous or half-civilized conquerors.[2] A hundred Sikhs were put to death daily, contending among themselves for priority of martyrdom, and on the eighth day Banda himself was arraigned before his judges. A Muhammadan noble asked the ascetic from conviction, how one of his knowledge and understanding could commit crimes which would dash him into hell; but Banda answered that he had been as a mere scourge in the hands of God for the chastisement of the wicked, and that he was now receiving the meed of his own crimes against the Almighty. His son was placed upon his knees, a knife was put into his hands, and he was required to take the life of his child. He did so, silent and unmoved; his own flesh was then torn with red-hot pincers, and amid these torments he expired, his dark soul, say the Muhammadans, winging its way to the regions of the damned.[3]

Banda eventually reduced and taken prisoner, A.D. 1716;

and put to death at Delhi.

[1] Cf. Malcolm, *Sketch*, pp. 79, 80; Forster, *Travels*, i. 306 and note; and the *Siar ul Mutākharin*, i. 116, 117. The ordinary accounts make the Sikh army amount to 35,000 men (Forster says 20,000); they also detain Abdus Samad a year at Lahore before he undertook anything, and they bring down all the hill chiefs to his aid, both of which circumstances are probable enough.

[2] *Siar ul Mutākharin*, i. 118, 120. Elphinstone (*History*, ii. 574, 575), quoting the contemporary Khafi Khān, says the prisoners amounted to 740. The *Siar ul Mutākharin* relates how the old mother of Bāyazīd Khān killed the assassin of her son, by letting fall a stone on his head, as he and the other prisoners were being led through the streets of Lahore.

[3] Malcolm (*Sketch*, p. 82), who quotes the *Siar ul Mutākharin*. The defeat and death of Banda are placed by the *Siar ul Mutākharin*

1708–16.

The views of Banda confined and his memory not revered.

The memory of Banda is not held in much esteem by the Sikhs; he appears to have been of a gloomy disposition, and he was obeyed as an energetic and daring leader, without being able to engage the personal sympathies of his followers. He did not perhaps comprehend the general nature of Nānak's and Gobind's reforms; the spirit of sectarianism possessed him, and he endeavoured to introduce changes into the modes and practices enjoined by these teachers, which should be more in accordance with his own ascetic and Hindu notions. These unwise innovations and restrictions were resisted by the more zealous Sikhs, and they may have caused the memory of an able and enterprising leader to be generally neglected.[1]

The Sikhs generally much depressed after the death of Banda.

After the death of Banda an active persecution was kept up against the Sikhs, whose losses in battle had been great and depressing. All who could be seized had to suffer death, or to renounce their faith. A price, indeed, was put upon their heads, and so vigorously were the measures of prudence, or of vengeance, followed up, that many conformed to Hinduism; others abandoned the outward signs of their belief, and the more sincere had to seek a refuge among the recesses of the hills, or in the woods to the south of the Sutlej. The Sikhs were scarcely again heard of in history for the period of a generation.[2]

Recapitulation.

Nānak.

Thus, at the end of two centuries, had the Sikh faith become established as a prevailing sentiment and guiding principle to work its way in the world. Nānak disengaged his little society of worshippers from Hindu idolatry and

(i. 109), by Orme (*History*, ii. 22), and apparently by Elphinstone (*History*, ii. 564), in the year A. D. 1716; but Forster (*Travels*, i. 306 note) has the date 1714.

[1] Cf. Malcolm, *Sketch*, pp. 83, 84. But Banda is sometimes styled Gurū by Indians, as in the *Siar ul Mutākharin* (i. 114), and there is still an order of half-conformist Sikhs which regards him as its founder. Banda, it is reported, wished to establish a sect of his own, saying that of Gobind could not endure; and he is further declared to have wished to change the exclamation or salutation, 'Wah Gurū ke Fateh!' which had been used or ordained by Gobind, into 'Fateh Dharam!' and 'Fateh Darsan!' (Victory to faith! Victory to the sect!). Cf. Malcolm, *Sketch*, pp. 83, 84.

[2] Cf. Forster (*Travels*, i. 312, 313), and Browne (*India Tracts*, ii. 13), and also Malcolm (*Sketch*, pp. 85, 86).

1708–1716. Muhammadan superstition, and placed them free on a broad basis of religious and moral purity; Amar Dās preserved the infant community from declining into a sect of quietists or ascetics , Arjūn gave his increasing followers a written rule of conduct and a civil organization ; Har Gobind added the use of arms and a military system ; and Gobind Singh bestowed upon them a distinct political existence, and inspired them with the desire of being socially free and nationally independent. No further legislation was required ; a firm persuasion had been elaborated, and a vague feeling had acquired consistence as an active principle. The operation of this faith become a fact, is only now in progress, and the fruit it may yet bear cannot be foreseen. Sikhism arose where fallen and corrupt Brāhmanical doctrines were most strongly acted on by the vital and spreading Muhammadan belief. It has now come into contact with the civilization and Christianity of Europe, and the result can only be known to a distant posterity.[1]

Amar Dās.

Arjūn.

Har Gobind.

Gobind Singh.

[1] There are also elements of change within Sikhism itself, and dissent is everywhere a source of weakness and decay, although sometimes it denotes a temporary increase of strength and energy. Sikh sects, at least of quietists, are already numerous, although the great development of the tenets of Gurū Gobind has thrown other denominations into the shade. Thus the prominent division into ‘ Khulāsa ’, meaning ‘ of Nānak ’, and ‘ Khālsa ’, meaning ‘ of Gobind ’, which is noticed by Forster (*Travels*, i. 309), is no longer in force. The former term, Khulāsa, is almost indeed unknown in the present day, while all claim membership with the Khālsa. Nevertheless, the peaceful Sikhs of the first teacher are still to be everywhere met with in the cities of India, although the warlike Singhs of the tenth king have become predominant in the Punjab, and have scattered themselves as soldiers from Kābul to the south of India.

NOTE.—The reader is referred to Appendices I, II, III, and IV for some account of the *Granths* of the Sikhs, for some illustrations of principles and practices taken from the writings of the Gurūs, and for abstracts of certain letters attributed to Nānak and Gobind, and which are descriptive of some views and modes of the Sikh people. Appendix V may also be referred to for a list of some Sikh sects or denominations.

CHAPTER IV

THE ESTABLISHMENT OF SIKH INDEPENDENCE

1716–64

Decline of the Mughal Empire—Gradual reappearance of the Sikhs—The Sikhs coerced by Mīr Mannu, and persecuted by Taimūr the son of Ahmad Shāh—The Army of the 'Khālsa' and the State of the 'Khālsa' proclaimed to be substantive Powers—Adīna Beg Khān and the Marāthās under Raghuba—Ahmad Shāh's incursions and victories—The provinces of Sirhind and Lahore possessed in sovereignty by the Sikhs—The political organization of the Sikhs as a feudal confederacy—The Order of Akālis.

1716–38.

The Mughal empire rapidly declines. Nādir Shāh, the Marāthās, &c.

AURANGZEB was the last of the race of Taimūr who possessed a genius for command, and in governing a large empire of incoherent parts and conflicting principles, his weak successors had to lean upon the doubtful loyalty of selfish and jealous ministers, and to prolong a nominal rule by opposing insurrectionary subjects to rebellious dependents. Within a generation Muhammadan adventurers had established separate dominations in Bengal, Lucknow, and Hyderābād; the Marāthā Peshwā had startled the Muslims of India by suddenly appearing in arms before the imperial city,[1] and the stern usurping Nādir had scornfully hailed the long descended Muhammad Shāh as a brother Turk in the heart of his blood-stained capital.[2] The Afghān colonists of Rohilkhand and the Hindu Jāts of Bhartpur had raised themselves to importance as substantive powers,[3] and when

[1] This was in A. D. 1737, when Bājī Rao, the Peshwā, made an incursion from Agra towards Delhi. (See Elphinstone, *History*, ii. 609, and Grant Duff, *History of the Mahrattas*, i. 533, 534.)

[2] See Nādir Shāh's letter to his son, relating his successful invasion of India. (*Asiatic Researches*, x. 545, 546.)

[3] A valuable account of the Rohillas may be found in Forster's *Travels* (i. 115, &c.), and the public is indebted to the Oriental Translation Committee of London for the memoirs of Hāfiz Rahmat Khān, one of the most eminent of their leaders.

The Jāts of Bhartpur and Dholpur, and of Hāthras and other minor places, deserve a separate history.

1716–38. the Persian conqueror departed with the spoils of Delhi,[1] the government was weaker, and society was more disorganized, than when the fugitive Bābar entered India in search of a throne worthy of his lineage and his personal merits.

The weakness of the Muhammadan government favourable to the Sikhs, 1716–38.

These commotions were favourable to the reappearance of a depressed sect; but the delegated rule of Abdus Samad in Lahore was vigorous, and, both under him and his weaker successor,[2] the Sikhs comported themselves as peaceful subjects in their villages, or lurked in woods and valleys to obtain a precarious livelihood as robbers.[3] The tenets of Nānak and Gobind had nevertheless taken root in the hearts of the people; the peasant and the mechanic nursed their faith in secret, and the more ardent clung to the hope of ample revenge and speedy victory. The departed Gurū had declared himself the last of the prophets; the believers were without a temporal guide, and rude untutored men, accustomed to defer to their teacher as divine, were left to work their way to greatness, without an ordained method, and without any other bond of union than the sincerity of their common faith. The progress of the new religion, and the ascendancy of its votaries, had thus been trusted to the pregnancy of the truths announced, and to the fitness of the Indian mind for their reception. The general acknowledgement of the most simple and comprehensive principle is sometimes uncertain, and is usually slow and irregular, and this fact should be held in view in considering the history of the Sikhs from the death of Gobind to the present time.

The Sikhs kept together by the fervour of their belief.

The Sikhs form bands of plunderers, 1738–9.

During the invasion of Nādir Shāh, the Sikhs collected in small bands, and plundered both the stragglers of the Persian army and the wealthy inhabitants who fled towards the hills on the first appearance of the conqueror, or when the massacre at Delhi became generally known.[4] The

[1] [These included the famous peacock throne of Shāh Jahān and the celebrated Koh-i-Nur. The subsequent history of the latter is too well known to need repetition.—Ed.]

[2] He was likewise the son of the conqueror of Banda. His name was Zakariya Khān, and his title Khān Bahādur.

[3] Cf. Forster's *Travels*, i. 313, and Browne's *India Tracts*, ii. 13.

[4] Browne, *India Tracts*, ii. 13, 14. Nādir acquired from the Mughal

1738–46.

impunity which attended these efforts encouraged them to bolder attempts, and they began to visit Amritsar openly instead of in secrecy and disguise. The Sikh horseman, says a Muhammadan author, might be seen riding at full gallop to pay his devotions at that holy shrine. Some might be slain, and some might be captured, but none were ever known to abjure their creed, when thus taken on their way to that sacred place.[1] Some Sikhs next succeeded in establishing a small fort at Dalhwāl on the Rāvi, and they were unknown or disregarded, until considerable numbers assembled and proceeded to levy contributions around Eminabād, which lies to the north of Lahore. The marauders were attacked, but the detachment of troops was repulsed and its leader slain. A larger force pursued and defeated them; many prisoners were brought to Lahore, and the scene of their execution is now known as 'Shahīd Ganj', or the place of martyrs.[2] It is further marked by the tomb of Bhai Taru Singh, who was required to cut his hair and to renounce his faith; but the old companion of Gurū Gobind would yield neither his conscience nor the symbol of his conviction, and his real or pretended answer is preserved to the present day. The hair, the scalp, and the skull, said he, have a mutual connexion; the head of man is linked with life, and *he* was prepared to yield his breath with cheerfulness.

Establish a fort at Dalhwāl on the Rāvi;

but are at last dispersed, (about) 1745–6.

The viceroyalty of Lahore was about this time contested between the two sons of Zakariya Khān, the successor of Abdus Samad, who defeated Banda. The younger, Shāh Nawāz Khān, displaced the elder, and to strengthen himself

Ahmad Shāh's first invasion of India, 1747–8.

emperor the provinces of Sindh and Kābul, and four districts of the province of Lahore, lying near the Jhelum river.

Zakariya Khān, son of Abdul Samad, was viceroy of Lahore at the time.

The defeat of the Delhi sovereign, and Nādir's entry into the capital, took place on the 13th of February and early in March, 1739, respectively, but were not known in London until the 1st of October, so slow were the communications, and of so little importance was Delhi to Englishmen, three generations ago. (Wade's *Chronological British History*, p. 417.)

[1] The author is quoted, but not named by Malcolm, *Sketch*, p. 88.

[2] Cf. Browne, *India Tracts*, ii. 13; Malcolm, *Sketch*, p. 86; and Murray's *Ranjīt Singh*, by Prinsep, p. 4. Yahya Khān, the elder son of Zakariya Khān, was governor of the Punjab at the time.

1747–8.

in his usurpation, he opened a correspondence with Ahmad Shāh Abdāli, who became master of Afghānistān on the assassination of Nādir Shāh, in June 1747. The Durrāni king soon collected round his standard numbers of the hardy tribes of Central Asia, who delight in distant inroads and successful rapine. He necessarily looked to India as the most productive field of conquest or incursion, and he could cloak his ambition under the double pretext of the tendered allegiance of the governor of Lahore, and of the favourable reception at Delhi of *his* enemy, Nādir Shāh's fugitive governor of Kābul.[1] Ahmad Shāh crossed the Indus: but the usurping viceroy of Lahore had been taunted with his treason; generosity prevailed over policy, and he resolved upon opposing the advance of the Afghāns. He was defeated, and the Abdāli became master of the Punjab. The Shāh pursued his march to Sirhind, where he was met by the

Retires from Sirhind, and is harassed by the Sikhs, March 1748.

Wazīr of the declining empire. Some desultory skirmishing and one more decisive action took place, but the result of the whole was so unfavourable to the invader that he precipitately recrossed the Punjab, and gave an opportunity to the watchful Sikhs of harassing his rear and of gaining confidence in their own prowess. The minister of Delhi was killed by a cannon ball during the short campaign, but the

Mīr Mannu governor of the Punjab.

gallantry and the services of his son, Mīr Mannu, had been conspicuous, and he became the viceroy of Lahore and Multān, under the title of Muīn-ul-mulk.[2]

Mīr Mannu rules vigorously, and employs Kaura Mal and Adīna Beg Khān, 1748.

The new governor was a man of vigour and ability, but his object was rather to advance his own interests than to serve the emperor; and in the administration of his provinces he could trust to no feelings save those which he personally inspired. He judiciously retained the services of two experienced men, Kaura Mal and Adīna Beg Khān, the one as his immediate deputy, and the other as the manager of the Jullundur Doāb. Both had dealt skilfully

[1] Cf. Murray's *Ranjīt Singh*, by Prinsep, p. 9, and Browne, *India Tracts*, ii. 15. Nasir Khān, the governor, hesitated about marrying his daughter to Ahmad Shāh, one of another race, as well as about rendering obedience to him as sovereign. Cf., however, Elphinstone (*Account of Kābul*, ii. 285), who makes no mention of these particulars.

[2] Cf. Elphinstone, *Kābul*, ii. 285, 286, and Murray's *Ranjīt Singh*, pp. 6–8.

for the times with the insurrectionary Sikhs, who continued to press themselves more and more on the attention of their unloyal governors.[1] During the invasion of Ahmad Shāh they had thrown up a fort close to Amritsar, called the Rām Rauni, and one of their most able leaders had arisen, Jassa Singh Kalāl, a brewer or distiller, who boldly proclaimed the birth of a new power in the state—the 'Dal' of the 'Khālsa', or army of the theocracy of 'Singhs'.[2] As soon as Mīr Mannu had established his authority, he marched against the insurgents, captured their fort, dispersed their troops, and took measures for the general preservation of good order.[3] His plans were interrupted by the rumoured approach of a second Afghān invasion; he marched to the Chenāb to repel the danger, and he dispatched agents to the Durrāni camp to avert it by promises and concessions. Ahmad Shāh's own rule was scarcely consolidated, he respected the ability of the youth who had checked him at Sirhind, and he retired across the Indus on the stipulation that the revenues of four fruitful districts should be paid to him as they had been paid to Nādir Shāh, from whom he pretended to derive his title.[4]

1748.

But the Sikhs reappear, and Jassa Singh Kalāl proclaims the existence of the 'Dal' or army of the Khālsa.

Mannu disperses the Sikhs, and comes to terms with Ahmad Shāh, who had again crossed the Indus, end of 1748.

Mīr Mannu gained applause at Delhi for the success of his measures, but his ambition was justly dreaded by the Wazīr Safdar Jang, who knew his own designs on Oudh, and felt that the example would not be lost on the son of his pre-

Mīr Mannu breaks with Delhi by resisting his supercession in Multān;

[1] Kaura Mal was himself a follower of Nānak, without having adopted the tenets of Gobind. (Forster, *Travels*, i. 314.) Adīna Beg Khān was appointed manager of the Jullundur Doāb by Zakariya Khān, with orders to coerce the Sikhs after Nādir Shāh's retirement. (Browne, *India Tracts*, ii. 14.)

[2] Cf. Browne, *India Tracts*, ii. 16, who gives Charsa Singh, Tuka Singh, and Kirwar Singh, as the confederates of Jassa Kalāl.

[3] Both Kaura Mal and Adīna Beg, but especially the former, the one from predilection, and the other from policy, are understood to have dissuaded Mīr Mannu from proceeding to extremities against the Sikhs. Cf. Browne, *Tracts*, ii. 16, and Forster, *Travels*, i. 314, 315, 327, 328, which latter, however, justly observes, that Mannu had objects in view of greater moment to himself than the suppression of an infant sect.

[4] The Afghāns state that Mīr Mannu also became the Shāh's tributary for the whole of the Punjab, and, doubtless, he *promised* anything to get the invader away and to be left alone. (Cf. Elphinstone, *Kābul*, ii. 286, and Murray, *Ranjīt Singh*, pp. 9, 10.)

1749–52. decessor. It was proposed to reduce his power by conferring the province of Multān on Shāh Nawaz Khān, whom Mīr Mannu himself had supplanted in Lahore;[1] but Mannu had an accurate knowledge of the imperial power and of his own resources, and he sent his deputy, Kaura Mal, to resist the new governor. Shāh Nawaz Khān was defeated and slain, and the elated viceroy conferred the title of Mahārājā on his successful follower.[2] This virtual independence of Delhi, and the suppression of Sikh disturbances, emboldened Mannu to persevere in his probably original design, and to withhold the promised tribute from Ahmad Shāh. A pretence of demanding it was made, and the payment of all arrears was offered, but neither party felt that the other could be trusted, and the Afghān king marched towards Lahore. Mannu made a show of meeting him on the frontier, but finally he took up an entrenched position under the walls of the city. Had he remained on the defensive the Abdāli might probably have been foiled, but, after a four months' beleaguer, he was tempted to risk an action. Kaura Mal was killed; Adīna Beg scarcely exerted himself; Mannu saw that a prolonged contest would be ruinous, and he prudently retired to the citadel and gave in his adhesion to the conqueror. The Shāh was satisfied with the surrender of a considerable treasure and with the annexation of Lahore and Multān to his dominions. He expressed his admiration of Mannu's spirit as a leader, and efficiency as a manager, and he continued him as his own delegate in the new acquisitions. The Shāh took measures to bring Kashmīr also under his sway, and then retired towards his native country.[3]

and withholds tribute from Ahmad Shāh, who crosses the Indus for the third time, 1749–51. Abdāli reaches Lahore, 1752, and defeats Mannu; but retains him as governor of the Punjab, April 1752.

The Sikhs gradually increase in strength;

This second capture of Lahore by strangers necessarily weakened the administration of the province, and the Sikhs, ever ready to rise, again became troublesome; but Adīna Beg found it advisable at the time to do away with the

[1] Hayātulla Khān, the younger son of Zakariya Khān, is stated in local Multān chronicles to have held that province when Nādir Shāh entered Sind, in 1739–40, to fairly settle and subdue it, and to have then tendered his allegiance to the Persian conqueror, from whom he received the title of Shāh Nawaz Khān.

[2] Cf. Murray's *Ranjīt Singh*, p. 10.

[3] Cf. Elphinstone, *Kābul*, ii. 288, and Murray's *Ranjīt Singh*, pp. 10, 13.

1752–6.

suspicions which attached to his inaction at Lahore, and to the belief that he temporized with insurgent peasantry for purposes of his own. He was required to bring the Sikhs to order, for they had virtually possessed themselves of the country lying between Amritsar and the hills. He fell suddenly upon them during a day of festival at Makhowāl, and gave them a total defeat. But his object was still to be thought their friend, and he came to an understanding with them that their payment of their own rents should be nominal or limited, and their exactions from others moderate or systematic. He took also many of them into his pay; one of the number being Jassa Singh, a carpenter, who afterwards became a chief of consideration.[1]

but are defeated by Adīna Beg, who nevertheless gives them favourable terms, A.D. 1752.

Jassa the carpenter.

Mīr Mannu died a few months after the re-establishment of his authority as the deputy of a new master.[2] His widow succeeded in procuring the acknowledgement of his infant son as viceroy under her own guardianship, and she endeavoured to stand equally well with the court of Delhi and with the Durrāni king. She professed submission to both, and she betrothed her daughter to Ghāzi-ud-dīn, the grandson of the first Nizam of the Deccan, who had supplanted the viceroy of Oudh as the minister of the enfeebled empire of India.[3] But the Wazīr wished to recover a province for his sovereign, as well as to obtain a bride for himself. He proceeded to Lahore and removed his enraged mother-in-law; and the Punjab remained for a time under the nominal rule of Adīna Beg Khān, until Ahmad Shāh again marched and made it his own. The Durrāni king passed through Lahore in the winter of 1755–6, leaving his son Taimūr under the tutelage of a chief, named Jahān Khān, as governor. The Shāh likewise annexed Sirhind to his territories, and although he extended his pardon to Ghāzi-ud-dīn personally, he did not return to Kandahar until he had plundered Delhi

Mīr Mannu dies, and Lahore is reannexed to Delhi, end of 1752.

Ahmad Shāh's fourth invasion. Prince Taimūr, governor of the Punjab, and Najīb ud-daula placed at

[1] Cf. Browne, *India Tracts*, ii. 17, and Malcolm, *Sketch*, p. 82.

[2] Forster (*Travels*, i. 315) and Malcolm (*Sketch*, p. 92), say 1752. Browne (*Tracts*, ii. 18) gives the Hijri year, 1165, which corresponds with A. D. 1751, 1752. Murray (*Ranjīt Singh*, p. 13) simply says Mannu did not long survive his submission, but Elphinstone (*Kābul*, ii. 288) gives 1756 as the date of the viceroy's death.

[3] The original name of Ghāzi-ud-dīn was Shahab-ud-dīn, corrupted into Sahoodeen and Shaodeen by the Marāthās.

1756–8.

and Mathurā, and placed Najīb-ud-daula, a Rohilla leader, near the person of the Wazīr's puppet king, as the titular commander of the forces of the Delhi empire, and as the efficient representative of Abdāli interests.[1]

the head of the Delhi army, 1755–6.

Taimūr expels the Sikhs from Amritsar.

Prince Taimūr's first object was to thoroughly disperse the insurgent Sikhs, and to punish Adīna Beg for the support which he had given to the Delhi minister in recovering Lahore. Jassa, the carpenter, had restored the Rām Rauni of Amritsar; that place was accordingly attacked, the fort was levelled, the buildings were demolished, and the sacred reservoir was filled with the ruins. Adīna Beg would not trust the prince, and retired to the hills, secretly aiding and encouraging the Sikhs in their desire for revenge. They assembled in great numbers, for the faith of Gobind was the living conviction of hardy single-minded villagers, rather than the ceremonial belief of busy citizens, with thoughts diverted by the opposing interests and conventional usages of artificial society. The country around Lahore swarmed with horsemen; the prince and his guardian were wearied with their cumbrous efforts to scatter them, and they found it prudent to retire towards the Chenāb. Lahore was temporarily occupied by the triumphant Sikhs, and the same Jassa Singh, who had proclaimed the 'Khālsa' to be a state and to possess an army, now gave it another symbol of substantive power. He used the mint of the Mughals to strike a rupee bearing the inscription, 'Coined by the grace of the "Khālsa" in the country of Ahmad, conquered by Jassa the Kalāl.'[2]

But the Afghāns eventually retire, and the Sikhs occupy Lahore and coin money, 1756–8.

[1] Cf. Forster, *Travels*, i. 316, 317; Browne, *Tracts*, ii. 48; Malcolm, *Sketch*, pp. 92, 94; Elphinstone, *Kābul*, ii. 288, 289; and Murray, *Ranjīt Singh*, pp. 14, 15.

During the nominal viceroyalty of Mīr Mannu's widow, one Bikari Khān played a conspicuous part as her deputy. He was finally put to death by the lady as one who designed to supplant her authority; but he was, nevertheless, supposed to have been her paramour. (Cf. Browne, ii. 18, and Murray, p. 14.) The gilt mosque at Lahore was built by this Bikari Khān.

[2] Cf. Browne, *Tracts*, ii. 19; Malcolm, *Sketch*, p. 93, &c.; Elphinstone, *Kābul*, ii. 289; and Murray, *Ranjīt Singh*, p. 15.

Elphinstone, using Afghān accounts, says Adīna Beg defeated a body of Taimūr troops; and Murray, using apparently the accounts of Punjab Muhammadans, omits the occupation of Lahore by the Sikhs.

1758–61.

The Delhi minister had about this time called in the Marāthās to enable him to expel Najīb-ud-daula, who, by his own address and power, and as the agent of Ahmad Shāh Abdāli, had become paramount in the imperial councils. Ghāzi-ud-dīn easily induced Raghuba, the Peshwā's brother, to advance; Delhi was occupied by the Marāthās, and Najīb-ud-daula escaped with difficulty. Adīna Beg found the Sikhs less willing to defer to him than he had hoped; they were, moreover, not powerful enough to enable him to govern the Punjab unaided, and he accordingly invited the Marāthās to extend their arms to the Indus. He had also a body of Sikh followers, and he marched from the Jumna in company with Raghuba. Ahmad Shāh's governor of Sirhind was expelled, but Adīna Beg's Sikh allies incensed the Marāthās by anticipating them in the plunder of the town, which, after two generations of rapine, they considered as peculiarly their right. The Sikhs evacuated Lahore, and the several Afghān garrisons retired and left the Marāthās masters of Multān and of Attock, as well as of the capital itself. Adīna Beg became the governor of the Punjab, but his vision of complete independence was arrested by death, and a few months after he had established his authority he was laid in his grave.[1] The Marāthās seemed to see all India at their feet, and they concerted with Ghāzi-ud-dīn a scheme pleasing to both, the reduction of Oudh and the expulsion of the Rohillas.[2] But the loss of the Punjab brought Ahmad Shāh a second time to the banks of the Jumna, and dissipated for ever the Marāthā dreams of supremacy.[3]

The Marāthās at Delhi, 1758.

Marātha aid against the Afghāns sought by Adīna Beg Khān.

Raghuba enters Lahore, and appoints Adīna Beg viceroy of the Punjab, May 1758. Adīna Beg dies, end of 1758.

The Durrāni king marched from Baluchistān up the Indus to Peshāwar, and thence across the Punjab. His presence caused Multān and Lahore to be evacuated by the Marāthās, and his approach induced the Wazīr Ghāzi-ud-dīn to take the life of the emperor, while the young prince,

Ahmad Shāh's fifth expedition, 1759–61.

[1] Cf. Browne, *India Tracts*, ii. 19, 20; Forster, *Travels*, i. 317, 318; Elphinstone, *Kābul*, ii. 290; and Grant Duff, *History of the Marāthās*, ii. 132. Adīna Beg appears to have died before the end of 1758.

[2] Cf. Elphinstone, *History of India*, ii. 669, 670.

[3] Najīb-ud-daula, and the Rohillas likewise, urged Ahmad to return, when they saw their villages set on flames by the Marāthās. (Elphinstone, *India*, ii. 670, and Browne, *Tracts*, ii. 20.)

1760–1.

afterwards Shāh Alam, was absent endeavouring to gain strength by an alliance with the English, the new masters of Bengal. The Marāthā commanders, Sindhia and Holkar, were separately overpowered; the Afghān king occupied Delhi, and then advanced towards the Ganges to engage Shujā-ud-daula, of Oudh, in the general confederacy against the southern Hindus, who were about to make an effort for the final extinction of the Muhammadan rule. A new commander, untried in the northern wars, but accompanied by the Peshwā's heir and by all the Marāthā chiefs of name, was advancing from Poona, confident in his fortune and in his superior numbers. Sedasheo Rao easily expelled the Afghān detachment from Delhi, while the main body was occupied in the Doāb, and he vainly talked of proclaiming young Wiswas Rao to be the paramount of India. But Ahmad Shāh gained his great victory of Pānīpat in the beginning of 1761, and both the influence of the Peshwā among his own people, and the power of the Marāthās in Hindustān, received a blow, from which neither fully recovered, and which, indirectly, aided the accomplishment of *their* desires by almost unheeded foreigners.[1]

Delhi occupied by the Afghāns, but afterwards taken by the Marāthās, 1760.

The Marāthās signally defeated at Pānīpat, and expelled temporarily from Upper India, 7th Jan., 1761.

The Afghān king returned to Kābul immediately after the battle, leaving deputies in Sirhind and Lahore,[2] and the Sikhs only appeared, during this campaign, as predatory bands hovering round the Durrāni army; but the absence of all regular government gave them additional strength, and they became not only masters of their own villages, but began to erect forts for the purpose of keeping stranger communities in check. Among others Charat Singh, the grandfather of Ranjīt Singh, established a stronghold of the kind in his wife's village of Gujrnauli (or Gujrānwāla), to the northward of Lahore. The Durrāni governor, or his deputy, Khwāja Obed, went to reduce it in the beginning

The Sikhs unrestrained in the open country.

[1] Browne, *India Tracts*, ii. 20, 21; Elphinstone, *History of India*, ii. 670, &c.; and Murray, *Ranjīt Singh*, pp. 17, 20.

Elphinstone says the Marāthā leader only delayed to proclaim Wiswas the paramount of Hindustān until the Durrānis should be driven across the Indus. See also Grant Duff, *History of the Marāthās*, ii. 142 and note.

[2] Baland Khān in Lahore, and Zain Khān in Sirhind, according to Browne, *India Tracts*, ii. 21, 23.

1761-2.

Gujrānwāla successfully defended by Charat Singh, and the Durrānis confined to Lahore, 1761-2.

of 1762,[1] and the Sikhs assembled for its relief. The Afghān was repulsed, he left his baggage to be plundered, and fled to shut himself up within the walls of Lahore.[2] The governor of Sirhind held his ground better, for he was assisted by an active Muhammadan leader of the country, Hinghan Khān of Māler Kotla ; but the Sikhs resented this hostility of an Indian Pathān as they did the treason of a Hindu religionist of Jīndiāla, who wore a sword like themselves, and yet adhered to Ahmad Shāh. The 'army of the Khālsa' assembled at Amritsar, the faithful performed their ablutions in the restored pool, and perhaps the first regular 'Gurūmatta', or diet for conclave, was held on this occasion. The possessions of Hinghan Khān were ravaged, and Jīndiāla was invested, preparatory to attempts of greater moment.[3]

The Sikhs assemble at Amritsar, and ravage the country on either side of the Sutlej.

Ahmad Shāh's sixth invasion, 1762.

But the restless Ahmad Shāh was again at hand. This prince, the very ideal of the Afghān genius, hardy and enterprising, fitted for conquest, yet incapable of empire, seemed but to exist for the sake of losing and recovering provinces. He reached Lahore towards the end of 1762, and the Sikhs retired to the south of the Sutlej, perhaps with some design of joining their brethren who were watching Sirhind, and of overpowering Zain Khān the governor, before they should be engaged with Ahmad Shāh himself; but in two long and rapid marches from Lahore, by way of Ludhiāna, the king came up with the Sikhs when they were about to enter into action with his lieutenant. He gave them a total defeat, and the Muhammadans were as active in the pursuit as they had been ardent in the attack. The Sikhs are variously reported to have lost from twelve to twenty-five thousand men, and the rout is still familiarly

The 'Ghulu Ghāra', or great defeat of the Sikhs near Ludhiāna, Feb. 1762.

[1] Murray (*Ranjīt Singh*, p. 21) makes Khwāja Obed the governor, and he may have succeeded or represented Baland Khān, whom other accounts show to have occasionally resided at Rohtās. Gujrānwāla is the more common, if less ancient, form of the name of the village attacked. It was also the place of Ranjīt Singh's birth, and is now a fair-sized and thriving town. (Cf. Munshi Shahamat Ali's *Sikhs and Afghāns*, p. 51.)

[2] Murray, *Ranjīt Singh*, pp. 22, 23.

[3] Cf. Browne, *India Tracts*, ii. 22, 23 ; and Murray, *Ranjīt Singh*, p. 23.

1762–3.

Alhā Singh of Patiāla.

known as the 'Ghulu Ghāra', or great disaster.[1] Alhā Singh, the founder of the present family of Patiāla, was among the prisoners, but his manly deportment pleased the warlike king, and the conqueror may not have been insensible to the policy of widening the difference between a *Mālwā* and a *Mānjha* Singh. He was declared a rājā of the state and dismissed with honour. The Shāh had an interview at Sirhind with his ally or dependent, Najīb-ud-daula; he made a Hindu, named Kābuli Mal, his governor of Lahore, and then hastened towards Kandahār to suppress an insurrection in that distant quarter; but he first gratified his own resentment, and indulged the savage bigotry of his followers, by destroying the renewed temples of Amritsar, by polluting the pool with slaughtered cows, by encasing numerous pyramids with the heads of decapitated Sikhs, and by cleansing the walls of desecrated mosques with the blood of his infidel enemies.[2]

Kābuli Mal governor of Lahore.

Ahmad Shāh retires after committing various excesses, end of 1762.

The Sikhs continue to increase in strength.

The Sikhs were not cast down; they received daily accessions to their numbers; a vague feeling that they were a people had arisen among them; all were bent on revenge, and their leaders were ambitious of dominion and of fame. Their first efforts were directed against the Pathān colony of Kasūr, which place they took and plundered, and they then fell upon and slew their old enemy Hinghan Khān of Malēr Kotla. They next marched towards Sirhind, and the court of Delhi was incapable of raising an arm in support of Muhammadanism. Zain Khān, the Afghān governor, gave battle to the true or probable number of 40,000 Sikhs in the month of December 1763, but he was defeated and slain, and the plains of Sirhind, from the Sutlej to the Jumna, were occupied by the victors without further opposition. Tradition still describes how the Sikhs dispersed as soon as the battle was won, and how, riding day and night, each horseman would throw his belt and scabbard, his articles of dress and accoutrement, until he was almost

Kasūr plundered.

The Afghāns defeated, Dec. 1763.

[1] The scene of the fight lay between Gujerwal and Bernala, perhaps twenty miles south from Ludhiāna. Hinghan Khān, of Malēr Kotla, seems to have guided the Shāh. Cf. Browne, *Tracts*, ii. 23; Forster, *Travels*, i. 319; and Murray, *Ranjīt Singh*, pp. 23, 25. The action appears to have been fought in February 1762.

[2] Cf. Forster, *Travels*, i. 320; and Murray, *Ranjīt Singh*, p. 25.

naked, into successive villages, to mark them as his. Sirhind itself was totally destroyed, and the feeling still lingers which makes it meritorious to carry away a brick from the place which witnessed the death of the mother and children of Gobind Singh. The impulse of victory swept the Sikhs across the Jumna, and their presence in Sahāranpur recalled Najīb-ud-daula from his contests with the Jāts, under Sūraj Mal, to protect his own principality, and he found it prudent to use negotiation as well as force, to induce the invaders to retire.[1]

1763–4.

Sirhind taken and destroyed, and the province permanently occupied by the Sikhs.

Najīb-ud-daula was successful against the Jāts, and Sūraj Mal was killed in fight; but the wazīr, or regent, was himself besieged in Delhi, in 1764, by the son of the deceased chief, and the heir of Bhartpur was aided by a large body of Sikhs, as well as of Marāthās more accustomed to defy the imperial power.[2] The loss of Sirhind had brought Ahmad Shāh a seventh time across the Indus, and the danger of Najīb-ud-daula led him onwards to the neighbourhood of the Jumna; but the siege of Delhi being raised—partly through the mediation or the defection of the Marāthā chief, Holkar, and the Shāh having perhaps rebellions to suppress in his native provinces, hastened back without making any effective attempt to recover Sirhind. He was content with acknowledging Alhā Singh of Patiāla as governor of the province on his part, that chief having opportunely procured the town itself in exchange from the descendant of an old companion of the Gurū's, to whom the confederates had assigned it. The Sikh accounts do not allow that the Shāh retired unmolested, but describe a long and arduous contest in the vicinity of Amritsar, which ended without either party being able to claim a victory, although it precipitated the already hurried retirement of the Afghāns. The Sikhs found little difficulty in ejecting Kābuli Mal, the governor of Lahore, and the whole country, from the Jhelum to the Sutlej, was partitioned among chiefs and

The Sikhs aid the Jāts of Bhartpur in besieging Delhi, 1764.

Ahmad Shāh's seventh expedition and speedy retirement.

The Sikhs become masters of Lahore.

[1] Cf. Browne, *India Tracts*, ii. 24, and Murray, *Ranjīt Singh*, pp. 26, 27. Some accounts represent the Sikhs to have also become temporarily possessed of Lahore at this period.

[2] Cf. Browne, *Tracts*, ii. 24. Sikh tradition still preserves the names of the chiefs who plundered the vegetable market at Delhi on this occasion.

1764. their followers, as the plains of Sirhind had been divided in the year previous. Numerous mosques were demolished, and Afghāns in chains were made to wash the foundations with the blood of hogs. The chiefs then assembled at Amritsar, and proclaimed their own sway and the prevalence of their faith, by striking a coin with an inscription to the effect that Gurū Gobind had received from Nānak 'Dēg, Tēgh, and Fath', or Grace, Power, and Rapid Victory.[1]

A general assembly held at Amritsar, and the sect established as a ruling people.

The Sikhs form or fall into a political system,

The Sikhs were not interfered with for two years, and the short interval was employed in ascertaining their actual possessions, and in determining their mutual relations in their unaccustomed condition of liberty and power. Every Sikh was free, and each was a substantive member of the commonwealth; but their means, their abilities, and their opportunities were various and unequal, and it was soon found that all could not lead, and that there were even then masters as well as servants. Their system naturally resolved itself into a theocratic confederate feudalism, with all the confusion and uncertainty attendant upon a triple alliance of the kind in a society half-barbarous. God was their helper and only judge, community of faith or object was their moving principle, and warlike array, the devotion to steel of Gobind, was their material instrument. Year by year the 'Sarbat Khālsa', or whole Sikh people, met once at least at Amritsar, on the occasion of the festival of the

which may be termed a theocratic confederate feudalism.

1 Cf. Browne, *India Tracts*, ii. 25, 27; Forster, *Travels*, i. 321, 323; Elphinstone, *Kābul*, ii. 296, 297; and Murray, *Ranjīt Singh*, pp. 26, 27.

The rupees struck were called 'Gobindshāhi', and the use of the emperor's name was rejected (Browne, *Tracts*, ii. 28), although existing coins show that it was afterwards occasionally inserted by petty chiefs. On most coins struck by Ranjīt Singh is the inscription,

'Dēg, tēgh, wa fath, wa nasrat bē darang
Yāft az Nānak Gurū Gobind Singh',

that is, literally, 'Grace, power, and victory, victory without pause, Gurū Gobind Singh obtained from Nānak.' For some observations on the words Dēg, and Tēgh, and Fath, see Appendices IX and XII. Browne (*Tracts*, ii. Introd. vii) gives no typical import to 'Dēg', and therefore leaves it meaningless; but he is perhaps more prudent than Col. Sleeman, who writes of 'the sword, the *pot* victory, and conquest being quickly found', &c. &c. (See *Rambles of an Indian Official*, ii. 233, note.)

mythological Rāma, when the cessation of the periodical rains rendered military operations practicable. It was perhaps hoped that the performance of religious duties, and the awe inspired by so holy a place, might cause selfishness to yield to a regard for the general welfare, and the assembly of chiefs was termed a 'Gurūmatta', to denote that, in conformity with Gobind's injunction, they sought wisdom and unanimity of counsel from their teacher and the book of his word.[1] The leaders who thus piously met, owned no subjection to one another, and they were imperfectly obeyed by the majority of their followers; but the obvious feudal, or military notion of a chain of dependence, was acknowledged as the law, and the federate chiefs partitioned their joint conquests equally among themselves, and divided their respective shares in the same manner among their own leaders of bands, while these again subdivided their portions among their own dependents, agreeably to the general custom of subinfeudation.[2] This positive or understood rule was not, however, always applicable to actual conditions, for the Sikhs were in part of their possessions 'earth-

1764.

Their Gurūmattas, or diets.

[1] 'Mat' means understanding, and 'Matta' counsel or wisdom. Hence Gurūmatta becomes, literally, 'the advice of the Gurū.'

Malcolm (*Sketch*, p. 52) considers, and Browne (*Tracts*, ii. vii) leaves it to be implied, that Gobind directed the assemblage of Gurūmatta; but there is no authority for believing that he ordained any formal or particular institution, although, doubtless, the general scope of his injunctions, and the peculiar political circumstances of the times, gave additional force to the practice of holding diets or conclaves—a practice common to mankind everywhere, and systematized in India from time immemorial. Cf. Forster, *Travels*, i. 328, &c., for some observations on the transient Sikh government of the time, and on the more enduring characteristics of the people. See also Malcolm, *Sketch*, p. 120, for the ceremonial forms of a Gurūmatta.

[2] Cf. Murray, *Ranjīt Singh*, pp. 33–7. From tracts of country which the Sikhs subdued but did not occupy, 'Rakhī' (literally, protection money) was regularly levied. The Rakhī varied in amount from perhaps a fifth to a half of the rental or government share of the produce. It corresponded with the Marāthā 'Chowt', or fourth, and both terms meant 'blackmail', or, in a higher sense, tribute. Cf. Browne, *India Tracts*, ii. viii, and Murray, *Ranjīt Singh*, p. 32. The subdivisions of property were sometimes so minute that two, or three, or ten Sikhs might become co-partners in the rental of one village, or in the house tax of one street of a town, while the fact that jurisdiction accompanied such right increased the confusion.

1764.

born', or many held lands in which the mere withdrawal of a central authority had left them wholly independent of control. In theory such men were neither the subjects nor the retainers of any feudal chief, and they could transfer their services to whom they pleased, or they could themselves become leaders, and acquire new lands for their own use in the name of the Khālsa or commonwealth.[1] It would be idle to call an everchanging state of alliance and dependence by the name of a constitution, and we must look for the existence of the faint outline of a system, among the emancipated Sikhs, rather in the dictates of our common nature, than in the enactments of assemblies, or in the injunctions of their religious guides. It was soon apparent that the strong were ever ready to make themselves obeyed, and ever anxious to appropriate all within their power, and that unity of creed or of race nowhere deters men from preying upon one another. A full persuasion of God's grace was nevertheless present to the mind of a Sikh, and every member of that faith continues to defer to the mystic Khālsa; but it requires the touch of genius, or the operation of peculiar circumstances, to give direction and complete effect to the enthusiastic belief of a multitude.

The system not devised, or knowingly adopted, and therefore incomplete and temporary.

The confederacies called Misals.

The confederacies into which the Sikhs resolved themselves have been usually recorded as twelve in number, and the term used to denote such a union was the Arabic word 'Misal', alike or equal.[2] Each Misal obeyed or followed a 'Sirdār', that is, simply, a chief or leader; but so general a title was as applicable to the head of a small band as to the commander of a large host of the free and equal 'Singhs' of the system. The confederacies did not all exist in their full strength at the same time, but one 'Misal' gave birth to another; for the federative principle necessarily pervaded the union, and an aspiring chief could

[1] Hallam shows that the Anglo-Saxon freeholder had a similar latitude of choice with regard to a lord or superior. (*Middle Ages*, Supplemental Notes, p. 210.)

[2] Notwithstanding this usual derivation of the term, it may be remembered that the Arabic term 'Musluhut' (spelt with another *s* than that in 'misal') means armed men and warlike people. 'Misal', moreover, means, in India, a file of papers, or indeed anything serried or placed in ranks.

separate himself from his immediate party, to form, perhaps, a greater one of his own. The Misals were again distinguished by titles derived from the name, the village, the district, or the progenitor of the first or most eminent chief, or from some peculiarity of custom or of leadership. Thus, of the twelve: (1) the *Bhangīs* were so called from the real or fancied fondness of its members for the use of an intoxicating drug;[1] (2) the *Nishānias* followed the standard bearers of the united army; (3) the *Shahīds* and *Nihangs* were headed by the descendants of honoured martyrs and zealots; (4) the *Rāmgarhias* took their name from the Rām Rauni, or Fortalice of God, at Amritsar, enlarged into Rāmgarh, or Fort of the Lord, by Jassa the Carpenter; (5) the *Nakkais* arose in a tract of country to the south of Lahore so-called; (6) the *Ahluwalias* derived their title from the village in which Jassa, who first proclaimed the existence of the army of the new theocracy, had helped his father to distil spirits; (7) the *Ghanais* or *Kanhayās*; (8) the *Feizulapurias* or *Singhpurias*; (9) the *Sukerchukias*, and (10), perhaps, the *Dallehwalas*, were similarly so denominated from the villages of their chiefs; (11) the *Krora Singhias* took the name of their third leader, but they were sometimes called *Punjgurhias*, from the village of their first chief; and (12) the *Phūlkiās* went back to the common ancestor of Alhā Singh and other Sirdārs of his family.[2]

1764.

Their names and particular origin.

[1] Bhang is a product of the hemp plant, and it is to the Sikhs what opium is to Rājpūts, and strong liquor to Europeans. Its qualities are abused to an extent prejudicial to the health and understanding.

[2] Capt. Murray (*Ranjīt Singh*, pp. 29, &c.) seems to have been the first who perceived and pointed out the Sikh system of 'Misals'. Neither the organization nor the term is mentioned specifically by Forster, or Browne, or Malcolm, and at first Sir David Ochterlony considered and acted as if 'misal' meant tribe or race, instead of party or confederacy. (Sir D. Ochterlony to the Government of India, December 30, 1809.) The succession to the leadership of the Krora Singhia confederacy may be mentioned as an instance of the uncertainty and irregularity natural to the system of 'Misals', and indeed to all powers in process of change or development. The founder was succeeded by his nephew, but that nephew left his authority to Krora Singh, a petty personal follower, who again bequeathed the command to Baghēl Singh, his own menial servant. The reader will remember the parallel instance of Alfteghin and Sebekteghin, and it is curious that Mr. Macaulay notices a similar kind of descent among

1764.

The relative pre-eminence of the Misals or confederacies.

Of the Misals, all save that of Phūlkiā arose in the Punjab or to the north of the Sutlej, and they were termed *Mānjha* Singhs, from the name of the country around Lahore, and in contradistinction to the *Mālwā* Singhs, so called from the general appellation of the districts lying between Sirhind and Sirsa. The Feizulapurias, the Ahluwalias, and the Rāmgarhias, were the first who arose to distinction in Mānjha, but the Bhangīs soon became so predominant as almost to be supreme ; they were succeeded to some extent in this pre-eminence by the Ghanais, an offshoot of the Feizulapurias, until all fell before Ranjīt Singh and the Sukerchukias. In Mālwā the Phūlkiās always admitted the superior merit of the Patiāla branch ; this dignity was confirmed by Ahmad Shāh's bestowal of a title on Alhā Singh, and the real strength of the confederacy made it perhaps inferior to the Bhangīs alone. The Nishānias and Shahīds scarcely formed Misals in the conventional meaning of the term, but complementary bodies set apart and honoured by all for particular reasons.[1] The Nakkais never achieved a high power or name, and the Dallchwalas and Krora Singhias, an offshoot of the Feizulapurias, acquired nearly all their possessions by the capture of Sirhind ; and although the last obtained a great reputation, it never became predominant over others.

The original and acquired possessions of the Misals.

The native possessions of the Bhangīs extended north, from their cities of Lahore and Amritsar to the Jhelum, and then down that river. The Ghanais dwelt between Amritsar and the hills. The Sukerchukias lived south of the Bhangīs, between the Chenāb and Rāvi. The Nakkais held along the Rāvi, south-west of Lahore. The Feizulapurias possessed tracts along the right bank of the Beās and of the Sutlej, below its junction. The Ahluwalias similarly occupied the

the English admirals of the seventeenth century, viz. from chief to cabin-boy, in the cases of Myngs, Narborough, and Shovel (*History of England*, i. 306).

[1] Perhaps Capt. Murray is scarcely warranted in making the Nishānias and Shahīds regular Misals. Other bodies, especially to the westward of the Jhelum, might, with equal reason, have been held to represent separate confederacies. Capt. Murray, indeed, in such matters of detail, merely expresses the local opinions of the neighbourhood of the Sutlej.

left bank of the former river. The Dallehwalas possessed themselves of the right bank of the Upper Sutlej, and the Rāmgarhias lay in between these last two, but towards the hills. The Krora Singhias also held lands in the Jullundur Doāb. The Phūlkiās were native to the country about Sunām and Bhatinda, to the south of the Sutlej, and the Shahīds and Nishānias do not seem to have possessed any villages which they did not hold by conquest; and thus these two Misals, along with those of Mānjha, who captured Sirhind, viz. the Bhangīs, the Ahluwalias, the Dallehwalas, the Rāmgarhias, and the Krora Singhias, divided among themselves the plains lying south of the Sutlej and under the hills from Ferozepore to Karnāl, leaving to their allies, the Phūlkiās, the lands between Sirhind and Delhi, which adjoined their own possessions in Mālwā.[1] 1764.

The gross forces of the Sikhs, and the relative strength of the Misals.

The number of horsemen which the Sikhs could muster have been variously estimated from seventy thousand to four times that amount, and the relative strength of each confederacy is equally a subject of doubt.[2] All that is certain is the great superiority of the Bhangīs, and the low position of the Nakkais and Sukerchukias. The first could perhaps assemble 20,000 men, in its widely scattered possessions, and the last about a tenth of that number; and the most moderate estimate of the total force of the nation may likewise be assumed to be the truest. All the Sikhs were horsemen, and among a half-barbarous people dwelling on plains, or in action with undisciplined forces, cavalry must ever be the most formidable arm. The Sikhs speedily became famous for the effective use of the matchlock when mounted, and this skill is said to have descended to them

[1] Dr. Macgregor, in his *History of the Sikhs* (i. 28, &c.), gives an abstract of some of the ordinary accounts of a few of the Misals.

[2] Forster, in 1783 (*Travels*, i. 333), said the Sikh forces were estimated at 300,000, but might be taken at 200,000. Browne (*Tracts*, Illustrative Map) about the same period enumerates 73,000 horsemen and 25,000 foot. Twenty years afterwards Col. Francklin said, in one work (*Life of Shāh Alam*, note, p. 75), that the Sikhs mustered 248,000 cavalry, and in another book (*Life of George Thomas*, p. 68 note) that they could not lead into action more than 64,000. George Thomas himself estimated their strength at 60,000 horse and 5,000 foot. (*Life*, by Francklin, p. 274.)

1764. from their ancestors, in whose hands the bow was a fatal weapon. Infantry were almost solely used to garrison forts, or a man followed a misal on foot, until plunder gave him a horse or the means of buying one. Cannon was not used by the early Sikhs, and its introduction was very gradual, for its possession implies wealth, or an organization both civil and military.[1]

Besides the regular confederacies, with their moderate degree of subordination, there was a body of men who threw off all subjection to earthly governors, and who peculiarly represented the religious element of Sikhism. These were the 'Akālis', the immortals, or rather the soldiers of God, who, with their blue dress and bracelets of steel, claimed for themselves a direct institution by Gobind Singh. The Gurū had called upon men to sacrifice everything for their faith, to leave their homes and to follow the profession of arms; but he and all his predecessors had likewise denounced the inert asceticism of the Hindu sects, and thus the fanatical feeling of a Sikh took a destructive turn. The Akālis formed themselves in their struggle to reconcile warlike activity with the relinquishment of the world. The meek and humble were satisfied with the assiduous performance of menial offices in temples, but the fierce enthusiasm of others prompted them to act from time to time as the armed guardians of Amritsar, or suddenly to go where blind impulse might lead them, and to win their daily bread, even single-handed, at the point of the sword.[2]

The order of Akālis.

Their origin and principles of action.

[1] George Thomas, giving the supposed status of A.D. 1800, says the Sikhs had 40 pieces of field artillery. (*Life*, by Francklin, p. 274.)

[2] Cf. Malcolm (*Sketch*, p. 116), who repeats, and apparently acquiesces in, the opinion, that the Akālis were instituted as an order by Gurū Gobind. There is not, however, any writing of Gobind's on record, which shows that he wished the Sikh faith to be represented by mere zealots, and it seems clear that the class of men arose as stated in the text.

So strong is the feeling that a Sikh should work, or have an occupation, that one who abandons the world, and is not of a warlike turn, will still employ himself in some way for the benefit of the community. Thus the author once found an Akāli repairing, or rather making, a road, among precipitous ravines, from the plain of the Sutlej to the petty town of Kīratpur. He avoided intercourse with the world generally. He was highly esteemed by the people, who left food and

They also took upon themselves something of the authority 1764.
of censors, and, although no leader appears to have fallen by their hands for defection to the Khālsa, they inspired awe as well as respect, and would sometimes plunder those who had offended them or had injured the commonwealth. The passions of the Akālis had full play until Ranjīt Singh became supreme, and it cost that able and resolute chief much time and trouble, at once to suppress them, and to preserve his own reputation with the people.

clothing at particular places for him, and his earnest persevering character had made an evident impression on a Hindu shepherd boy, who had adopted part of the Akāli dress, and spoke with awe of the devotee.

CHAPTER V

FROM THE INDEPENDENCE OF THE SIKHS TO THE ASCENDANCY OF RANJĪT SINGH AND THE ALLIANCE WITH THE ENGLISH

1765—1808-9

Ahmad Shāh's last Invasion of India—The Pre-eminence of the Bhangī Confederacy among the Sikhs—Taimūr Shāh's Expeditions—The Phūlkiā Sikhs in Hariāna—Zābita Khān—The Kanhayā Confederacy paramount among the Sikhs—Mahān Singh Sukerchukia becomes conspicuous—Shāh Zamān's Invasions and Ranjīt Singh's rise—The Marāthās under Sindhia Predominant in Northern India—General Perron and George Thomas—Alliances of the Marāthās and Sikhs—Intercourse of the English with the Sikhs—Lord Lake's Campaigns against Sindhia and Holkar—First Treaty of the English with the Sikhs—Preparations against a French Invasion of India—Treaty of Alliance with Ranjīt Singh, and of Protection with Cis-Sutlej Sikh Chiefs.

1767

The Sikhs hurried into activity by Ahmad Shāh's final descent, A.D. 1767.

THE Sikhs had mastered the upper plains from Karnāl and Hānsi to the banks of the Jhelum. The necessity of union was no longer paramount, and rude untaught men are ever prone to give the rein to their passions, and to prefer their own interests to the welfare of the community. Some dwelt on real or fancied injuries, and thought the time had come for ample vengeance; others were moved by local associations to grasp at neighbouring towns and districts; and the truer Sikh alone at once resolved to extend his faith, and to add to the general domain of the Khālsa, by complete conquest or by the imposition of tribute. When thus about to arise, after their short repose, refreshed and variously inclined, they were again awed into unanimity by the final descent of Ahmad Shāh. That monarch, whose activity and power declined with increase of years and the progress of disease, made yet another attempt to recover the Punjab, the most fertile of his

1767–8.

provinces. He crossed the Indus in 1767, but he avoided Lahore and advanced no farther than the Sutlej. He endeavoured to conciliate when he could no longer overcome, and he bestowed the title of Mahārājā, and the office of military commander in Sirhind, upon the warlike Amar Singh, who had succeeded his grandfather as chief of Patiāla, or of the Mālwā Sikhs. He likewise saw a promising ally in the Rājpūt chief of Katōtch, and he made him his deputy in the Jullundur Doāb and adjoining hills. His measures were interrupted by the defection of his own troops; twelve thousand men marched back towards Kābul, and the Shāh found it prudent to follow them. He was harassed in his retreat, and he had scarcely crossed the Indus before Sher Shāh's mountain stronghold of Rohtās was blockaded by the Sukerchukias, under the grandfather of Ranjīt Singh, aided by a detachment of the neighbouring Bhangī confederacy. The place fell in 1768, and the Bhangīs almost immediately afterwards occupied the country as far as Rāwalpindi and the vale of Khānpur, the Gakhars showing but little of that ancient hardihood which distinguished them in their contests with invading Mughals.[1]

Amar Singh of Patiāla, and the Rājpūt chief of Katōtch, appointed to command under the Abdāli.

Ahmad Shāh retires.

Rohtās taken by the Sikhs, 1768.

The Bhangīs, under Harī Singh, next marched towards Multān, but they were met by the Muhammadan Daudputras, who had migrated from Sind on learning Nādir Shāh's intention of transplanting them to Ghazni, and had established the principality now known as Bhawalpur.[2] The

The Sikhs ravage the Lower Punjab;

[1] Forster, *Travels*, i. 323; Elphinstone, *Kābul*, ii. 297; Murray, *Ranjīt Singh*, p. 27; Moorcroft, *Travels*, i. 127; and manuscript accounts consulted by the author.

[2] When Nādir Shāh proceeded to establish his authority in Sindh, he found the ancestor of the Bhawalpur family a man of reputation in his native district of Shikārpur. The Shāh made him the deputy of the upper third of the province; but, becoming suspicious of the whole clan, he resolved on removing it to Ghazni. The tribe then migrated up the Sutlej, and seized lands by force. The Daudputras are so called from Daud (David), the first of the family who acquired a name. They fabulously trace their origin to the Caliph Abbās; but they may be regarded as Sindian Baluchīs, or as Baluchīs changed by a long residence in Sind. In establishing themselves on the Sutlej, they reduced the remains of the ancient Langahs and Johiyas to further insignificance; but they introduced the Sindian system of canals of irrigation, and both banks of the river below Pākpattan bear witness to their original industry and love of agriculture.

1770. chief, Mobārik Khān, after a parley with Harī Singh, arranged that the neutral town of Pākpattan, held by a Musalmān saint of eminence, should be the common boundary. Harī Singh then swept towards Dera Ghāzi Khān and the Indus, and while thus employed, his feudatory of Gujrāt, who had recently taken Rāwalpindi, made an attempt to penetrate into Kashmīr by the ordinary road, but was repulsed with loss. On the Jumna, and in the great Doāb, the old Najīb-ud-daula was so hard pressed by Rai Singh Bhangī, who emulated him as a paternal governor in his neighbouring town and district of Jagādhri, and by Baghēl Singh Krora Singhia, that he proposed to the Marāthās a joint expedition against these new lords. His death, in 1770, put an end to the plan, for his succeeding son had other views, and encouraged the Sikhs as useful allies upon an emergency.[1]

and enter into terms with Bhawalpur; threaten Kashmīr, and press Najīb-ud-daula on the Jumna and Ganges, 1770.

Harī Singh Bhangī died, and he was succeeded by Jhanda Singh, who carried the power of the Misal to its height. He rendered Jammu tributary, and the place was then of considerable importance, for the repeated Afghān invasions, and the continued insurrections of the Sikhs, had driven the transit trade of the plains to the circuitous but safe route of the hills; and the character of the Rājpūt chief, Ranjīt Deo, was such as gave confidence to traders, and induced them to flock to his capital for protection. The Pathāns of Kasūr were next rendered tributary, and Jhanda Singh then deputed his lieutenant, Mujja Singh, against Multān; but that leader was repulsed and slain by the united forces of the joint Afghān governors and of the Bhawalpur chief. Next year, or in 1772, these joint managers quarrelled, and as one of them asked the assistance of Jhanda Singh, that unscrupulous leader was enabled to possess himself of the citadel. On his return to the northward, he found that a rival claimant of the Jammu chiefship had obtained the aid of Charat Singh Sukerchukia, and of Jai Singh, the rising leader of the Kanhayā Misal. Charat Singh was killed by the bursting of his own matchlock, and Jai Singh was then so base as to procure the assassination of Jhanda Singh.

Jhanda Singh of the Bhangī Misal preeminent, 1770. Jammu rendered tributary. Kasūr reduced to submission, and Multān occupied, 1772. Jhanda Singh assassinated

[1] The memoirs of the Bhawalpur family, and manuscript Sikh histories. Cf. also Forster, *Travels*, i. 148.

Being satisfied with the removal of this powerful chief, the Kanhayā left the Jammu claimant to prosecute his cause alone, and entered into a league with the old Jassa Singh Ahluwalia, for the expulsion of the other Jassa Singh the Carpenter, who had rendered Ahmad Shāh's nominal deputy, Ghamand Chand of Katōtch, and other Rājpūts of the hills, his tributaries. The Rāmgarhia Jassa Singh was at last beaten, and he retired to the wastes of Hariāna to live by plunder. At this time, or about 1774, died the Muhammadan governor of Kāngra. He had contrived to maintain himself in independence, or in reserved subjection to Delhi or Kābul, although the rising chief of Katōtch had long desired to possess so famous a stronghold. Jai Singh Kanhayā was prevailed on to assist him, and the place fell; but the Sikh chose to keep it to himself, and the possession of the imperial fort aided him in his usurpation of Jassa Singh's authority over the surrounding Rājās and Thākurs.[1]

1772–4.

by Jai Singh Kanhayā, 1774.

Jai Singh Kanhayā and Jassa Singh Kalāl expel Jassa the Carpenter.

Kāngra falls to the Kanhayā Misal about 1774.

In the south of the Punjab the Bhangī Sikhs continued predominant; they seem to have possessed the strong fort of Mankerā as well as Multān, and to have levied exactions from Kālābāgh downwards. They made an attempt to carry Shujābād, a place built by the Afghāns on losing Multān, but seem to have failed. Taimūr Shāh, who succeeded his father in 1773, was at last induced or enabled to cross the Indus, but his views were directed towards Sind, Bhawalpur, and the Lower Punjab, and he seems to have had no thought of a reconquest of Lahore. In the course of 1777–8, two detachments of the Kābul army unsuccessfully endeavoured to dislodge the Sikhs from Multān, but in the season of 1778–9 the Shāh marched in person against the place. Ghanda Singh, the new leader of the Bhangīs, was embroiled with other Sikh chiefs, and his lieutenant surrendered the citadel after a show of resistance. Taimūr Shāh

Taimūr Shāh of Kābul recovers Multān, 1779.

Taimūr Shāh dies, leaving the Sikhs masters of

[1] The memoirs of the Bhawalpur chief and manuscript Sikh accounts. Cf. Murray, *Ranjīt Singh*, p. 38, &c.; and Forster, *Travels*, i. 283, 286, 336.

Ranjīt Deo, of Jammu, died in A. D. 1770.

Charat Singh was killed accidentally, and Jhanda Singh was assassinated, in 1774.

Harī Singh Bhangī appears to have been killed in battle with Amar Singh of Patiāla, about 1770.

The Sikhs occupy the Upper Punjab as far as Attock, 1793.

reigned until 1793, but he was fully occupied with Sindian, Kashmīrī, and Uzbeg rebellions; the Sikhs were even unmolested in their possession of Rāwalpindi, and their predatory horse traversed the plains of Chach up to the walls of Attock.[1]

The Phūlkiās master Hariāna, 1768–78.

In the direction of Hariāna and Delhi, the young Amar Singh Phūlkiā began systematically to extend and consolidate his authority. He acquired Sirsa and Fatehābād, his territories marched with those of Bīkaner and Bhawalpur, and his feudatories of Jīnd and Kaithal possessed the open country around Hānsi and Rohtak. He was recalled to his capital of Patiāla by a final effort of the Delhi court to re-establish its authority in the province of Sirhind.

An expedition sent from Delhi against the Mālwā Sikhs, 1779–80.

An army, headed by the minister of the day, and by Farkhunda Bukht, one of the imperial family, marched in the season 1779–80. Karnāl was recovered; some payments were promised; and the eminent Krora-Singhia leader, Baghēl Singh, tendered his submission. Dehsu Singh, of Kaithal, was seized and heavily mulcted, and the army approached Patiāla. Amar Singh promised fealty and tribute, and Baghēl Singh seemed sincere in his mediation; but suddenly it was learnt that a large body of Sikhs had marched from Lahore, and the Mughal troops retired with precipitation to Pānīpat, not without a suspicion that the cupidity of the minister had been gratified with Sikh gold, and had induced him to betray his master's interests.

Succeeds in part only.

Amar Singh of Patiāla dies, 1781.

Amar Singh died in 1781, leaving a minor son of imbecile mind. Two years afterwards a famine desolated Hariāna; the people perished or sought other homes; Sirsa was deserted, and a large tract of country passed at the time from under regular sway, and could not afterwards be recovered by the Sikhs.[2]

Zābita Khān, son of Najīb-ud-daula, aided in his

In the Doāb of the Ganges and Jumna, the Sikhs rather subsidized Zābita Khān, the son of Najīb-ud-daula, than

[1] Memoirs of the Bhawalpur chief, and other manuscript histories. Cf. Browne, *India Tracts*, ii. 28, and Forster, *Travels*, i. 324; Elphinstone (*Kābul*, ii. 303) makes 1781, and not 1779, the date of the recovery of Multān from the Sikhs.

[2] Manuscript histories, and Mr. Ross Bell's report of 1836, on the Bhattiana boundary. Cf. Francklin, *Shāh Alam*, pp. 86, 90, and Shāh Nawāz Khān's Epitome of Indian History, called *Mirrit-i-Aftāb Numa*.

became his deferential allies. That chief had designs, perhaps, upon the titular ministry of the empire, and having obtained a partial success over the imperial troops, he proceeded, in 1776, towards Delhi, with the intention of laying siege to the city. But when the time for action arrived he mistrusted his power; the emperor, on his part, did not care to provoke him too far; a compromise was effected, and he was confirmed in his possession of Sahāranpur. On this occasion Zābita Khān was accompanied by a body of Sikhs, and he was so desirous of conciliating them, that he is credibly said to have adopted their dress, to have received the Pāhul, or initiatory rite, and to have taken the new name of Dharam Singh.[1]

1781-5.

designs on the ministry by the Sikhs, 1776.

Jassa Singh Rāmgarhia, when compelled to fly to the Punjab by the Kanhayā and Ahluwalia confederacies, was aided by Amar Singh Phūlkiā in establishing himself in the country near Hissār, whence he proceeded to levy exactions up to the walls of Delhi. In 1781 a body of Phūlkiā and other Sikhs marched down the Doāb, but they were successfully attacked under the walls of Meerut by the imperial commander Mirza Shafi Beg, and Gajpat Singh of Jīnd was taken prisoner. Nevertheless, in 1783, Baghēl Singh and other commanders were strong enough to propose crossing the Ganges, but they were deterred by the watchfulness of the Oudh troops on the opposite bank. The destructive famine already alluded to seems to have compelled Jassa Singh to move into the Doāb, and, in 1785, Rohilkhand was entered by the confederates and plundered as far as Chandosi, which is within forty miles of Bareilly. At this period Zābita Khān was almost confined to the walls of his fort of Ghausgarh, and the hill rājā of Garhwāl, whose ancestor had received Dārā as a refugee in defiance of Aurangzeb, had been rendered tributary, equally with all his brother Rājpūts, in the lower hills westward to the Chenāb. The Sikhs were predominant from the frontiers of Oudh to the Indus, and the traveller Forster amusingly describes the alarm caused to a little chief and his people by the appearance of *two* Sikh horsemen under the walls of their fort, and the assiduous

The ravages of the Sikhs in the Doāb and Rohilkhand under Baghēl Singh Krora Singhia, 1781-5.

The Sikhs defeated at Meerut, 1783.

A.D. 1785.

The Rājpūts of the Lower Himālayas rendered tributary.

[1] Cf. Forster, *Travels*, i. 325; Browne, *India Tracts*, ii. 29; and Francklin, *Shāh Alam*, p. 72.

1784–92. services and respectful attention which the like number of troopers met with from the local authorities of Garhwāl, and from the assembled wayfarers at a place of public reception.[1]

Jai Singh Kanhayā pre-eminent, 1784–5.

Rise of Mahān Singh Sukerchukiā.

In the Punjab itself Jai Singh Kanhayā continued to retain a paramount influence. He had taken Mahān Singh, the son of Charat Singh Sukerchukia, under his protection, and he aided the young chief in capturing Russulnaggar on the Chenāb, from a Muhammadan family. Mahān Singh's reputation continued to increase, and, about 1784–5, he so far threw off his dependence upon Jai Singh as to interfere in the affairs of Jammu on his own account. His interference is understood to have ended in the plunder of the place; but the wealth he had obtained and the independence he had shown both roused the anger of Jai Singh, who rudely repelled Mahān Singh's apologies and offers of atonement, and the spirit of the young chief being fired, he went away resolved to appeal to arms. He sent to Jassa Singh Rāmgarhia, and that leader was glad of an opportunity of recovering his lost possessions. He joined Mahān Singh, and easily procured the aid of Sansār Chand, the grandson of Ghamand Chand of Katōtch. The Kanhayās were attacked and defeated; Gurbakhsh Singh, the eldest son of Jai Singh, was killed, and the spirit of the old man was effectually humbled by this double sorrow. Jassa Singh was restored to his territories, and Sansār Chand obtained the fort of Kāngra, which his father and grandfather had been so desirous of possessing. Mahān Singh now became the most influential chief in the Punjab, and he gladly assented to the proposition of Sudda Kōur, the widow of Jai Singh's son, that the alliance of the two families should be cemented by the union of her infant daughter with Ranjīt Singh, the only son of Mahān Singh, and who was born to him about 1780. Mahān Singh next proceeded to attack Gujrāt, the old Bhangī chief of which, Gūjar Singh, his father's confederate, died in 1791; but he was himself taken ill during the siege, and expired in the beginning of the following year at the early age of twenty-seven.[2]

The Kanhayās reduced, 1785–6.

Jassa the Carpenter restored, and Kāngra made over to Sansār Chand of Katōtch.

Mahān Singh pre-eminent among the Sikhs, 1785–92.

Mahān Singh dies, 1792.

[1] Forster, *Travels*, i. 228, 229, 262, 326 and note. Cf. also Francklin, *Shāh Alam*, pp. 93, 94, and the Persian epitome *Mirrit-i-Aftāb Numa*.

[2] Manuscript histories and chronicles. Cf. Forster, *Travels*, i. 288;

1793–7.

Shāh Zamān succeeded to the throne of Kābul in the year 1793, and his mind seems always to have been filled with idle hopes of an Indian empire. In the end of 1795 he moved to Hassan Abdāl, and sent forward a party which is said to have recovered the fort of Rohtās; but the exposed state of his western dominions induced him to return to Kābul. The rumours of another Durrāni invasion do not seem to have been unheeded by the princes of Upper India, then pressed by the Marāthās and the English. Ghulām Muhammad, the defeated usurper of Rohilkhand, crossed the Punjab in 1795–6, with the view of inducing Shāh Zamān to prosecute his designs, and he was followed by agents on the part of Asaf-ud-daula of Oudh, partly to counteract, perhaps, the presumed machinations of his enemy, but mainly to urge upon his majesty that all Muhammadans would gladly hail him as a deliverer. The Shāh reached Lahore, in the beginning of 1797, with thirty thousand men, and he endeavoured to conciliate the Sikhs and to render his visionary supremacy an agreeable burden. Several chiefs joined him, but the proceedings of his brother Mahmūd recalled him before he had time to make any progress in settling the country, even had the Sikhs been disposed to submit without a struggle; but the Sikhs were perhaps less dismayed than the beaten Marāthās and the ill-informed English. The latter lamented, with the Wazīr of Oudh, the danger to which his dominions were exposed; they prudently cantoned a force at Anūpshahr in the Doāb, and their apprehensions led them to depute a mission to Teheran, with the view of instigating the Shāh of Persia to invade the Afghān territories. Shāh Zamān renewed his invasion in 1798; a body of five thousand men, sent far in advance, was attacked and dispersed on the Jhelum, but he entered Lahore without opposition, and renewed his measures of mixed conciliation and threat. He found an

Shāh Zamān succeeds to the throne of Kābul, 1793.

Invited to enter India by the Rohillas and the Wazīr of Oudh, 1795–6.

Shāh Zamān at Lahore, 1797.

The Shāh's second march to Lahore, 1798–9.

Murray, *Ranjīt Singh*, pp. 42, 48; and Moorcroft, *Travels*, i. 127. The date of 1785–6, for the reduction of the Kanhayās and the restoration of Jassa Singh, &c., is preferred to 1782, which is given by Murray, partly because the expedition to Rohilkhand took place in 1785, as related by Forster (*Travels*, i. 326 note), and Jassa Singh is generally admitted to have been engaged in it, being then in banishment.

1798–9. able leader, but doubtful partisan, in Nizām-ud-dīn Khān, a Pathān of Kasūr, who had acquired a high local reputation, and he was employed to coerce such of the Sikhs, including the youthful Ranjīt Singh, as pertinaciously kept aloof. *They* distrusted the Shāh's honour; but Nizām-ud-dīn distrusted the permanence of his power, and he prudently forbore to proceed to extremities against neighbours to whom he might soon be left a prey. Some resultless skirmishing took place, but the designs of Mahmūd, who had obtained the support of Persia, again withdrew the ill-fated king to the west, and he quitted Lahore in the beginning of 1799. During this second invasion the character of Ranjīt Singh seems to have impressed itself, not only on other Sikh leaders, but on the Durrāni Shāh. He coveted Lahore, which was associated in the minds of men with the possession of power, and, as the king was unable to cross his heavy artillery over the flooded Jhelum, he made it known to the aspiring chief that their transmission would be an acceptable service. As many pieces of cannon as could be readily extricated were sent after the Shāh, and Ranjīt Singh procured what he wanted, a royal investiture of the capital of the Punjab. Thenceforward the history of the Sikhs gradually centres in their great Mahārājā; but the revival of the Marāthā power in Upper India, and the appearance of the English on the scene, require that the narrative of his achievements should be somewhat interrupted.[1]

Ranjīt Singh rises to eminence, and obtains a cession of Lahore from the Afghān king, 1799.

1785–8. The power of the Marāthās under

The abilities of Madhagi Sindhia restored the power of the Marāthās in Northern India, and the discipline of his regular brigades seemed to place his administration on a

[1] Elphinstone (*Kābul*, ii. 308) states that Shāh Zamān was exhorted to undertake his expedition of 1795 by a refugee prince of Delhi, and encouraged in it by Tipū Sultān. The journey of Ghulām Muhammad, the defeated Rohilla chief, and the mission of the Wazīr of Oudh, are given on the authority of the Bhawalpur family annals, and from the same source may be added an interchange of deputations on the part of Shāh Zamān and Sindhia, the envoys, as in the other instance, having passed through Bhawalpur town. A suspicion of the complicity of Asaf-ud-daula, of Lucknow, does not seem to have occurred to the English historians, who rather dilate on the exertions made by their government to protect their pledged ally from the northern invaders. Nevertheless, the statements of the Bhawalpur chronicles on the subject seem in every way credible.

1785-97.

firm and lasting basis. He mastered Agra in 1785, and was made deputy vicegerent of the empire by the titular emperor, Shāh Alam. He entered at the same time into an engagement with the confederate Sikh chiefs, to the effect that of all their joint conquests on either side of the Jumna, he should have two-thirds and the 'Khālsa' the remainder.[1] This alliance was considered to clearly point at the kingdom of Oudh, which the English were bound to defend, and perhaps to affect the authority of Delhi, which they wished to see strong; but the schemes of the Marāthā were for a time interrupted by the Rohilla Ghulām Kādir. This chief succeeded his father, Zābita Khān, in 1785, and had contrived, by an adventurous step, to become the master of the emperor's person a little more than a year afterwards. He was led on from one excess to another, till at last, in 1788, he put out the eyes of his unfortunate sovereign, plundered the palace in search of imaginary treasures, and declared an unheeded youth to be the successor of Akbar and Aurangzeb. These proceedings facilitated Sindhia's views, nor was his supremacy unwelcome in Delhi after the atrocities of Ghulām Kādir and the savage Afghāns. His regular administration soon curbed the predatory Sikhs, and instead of being received as allies they found that they would merely be tolerated as dependants or as servants. Rai Singh, the patriarchal chief of Jagādhri, was retained for the time as farmer of considerable districts in the Doāb, and, during ten years, three expeditions of exaction were directed against Patiāla and other states in the province of Sirhind. Patiāla was managed with some degree of prudence by Nānu Mal, the Hindu Dīwān of the deceased Amar Singh; but he seems to have trusted for military support to Baghēl Singh, the leader of the Krora Singhias, who contrived to maintain a large body of horse, partly as a judicious mediator, and partly by helping Patiāla in levying contributions on weaker brethren, in aid of the Mughal and Marāthā demands, which could neither be readily met nor prudently resisted.[2]

Sindhia in Upper India, 1785.

Sindhia's alliance with the Sikhs.

Ghulām Kādir blinds Shāh Alam, 1788.

Sindhia masters Delhi and curbs the Sikhs, 1788.

General Perron succeeded his countryman, De Boigne, in

[1] Browne, *India Tracts*, ii. 29.

[2] Manuscript accounts. Cf. Francklin, *Shāh Alam*, pp. 179-85.

1787-97.

General Perron appointed Sindhia's deputy in Northern India, 1797.

Sindhia's and Perron's views crossed by Holkar and George Thomas,

1787-97.

George Thomas establishes

the command of Daulat Rāo Sindhia's largest regular force, in the year 1797, and he was soon after appointed the Mahārājā's deputy in Northern India. His ambition surpassed his powers; but his plans were nevertheless systematic, and he might have temporarily extended his own, or the Marāthā, authority to Lahore, had not Sindhia's influence been endangered by Holkar, and had not Perron's own purposes been crossed by the hostility and success of the adventurer George Thomas.[1] This Englishman was bred to the sea, but an eccentricity of character, or a restless love of change, caused him to desert from a vessel of war at Madras in 1781–2, and to take military service with the petty chiefs of that presidency. He wandered to the north of India, and in 1787 he was employed by the well-known Begum Samru,[2] and soon rose high in favour with that lady. In six years he became dissatisfied, and entered the service of Appa Khande Rāo, one of Sindhia's principal officers, and under whom De Boigne had formed his first regiments. While in the Marāthā employ, Thomas defeated a party of Sikhs at Karnāl, and he performed various other services; but seeing the distracted state of the country, he formed the not impracticable scheme of establishing a separate authority of his own. He repaired the crumbling walls of the once important Hānsi, he assembled soldiers about him, cast guns,

[1] [For an excellent sketch of the life of this adventurer see the article 'A Free Lance from Tipperary' in *Strangers within the Gates*, by G. Festing. Edinburgh and London, 1914.—Ed.]

[2] [This remarkable woman, whose origin is wrapped in mystery, was said to have been a dancing-girl in Delhi. She subsequently married 'Somru', a European adventurer, who had entered the service of the Emperor and had received the Jagir of Sardhana, a few miles from Delhi. 'Somru'—whose real name was Reinhard—was a man of the foulest antecedents, and among his other exploits he had been principally concerned in the murder of the English prisoners at Patna in 1763. Upon her husband's death the Begum succeeded to his estate and to the leadership of the disreputable band of cutthroats who formed his army. After the battle of Assaye she submitted to the English, embraced Christianity about 1781, and was publicly embraced by Lord Lake, to the great horror of the spectators. She ended her days in great sanctity, and was buried in the Roman Catholic Cathedral at Sardhana which she herself had built. See also Sleeman, *Rambles and Recollections*, ed. V. A. Smith, chap. 75. Oxford University Press, 1915.—Ed.]

and deliberately proceeded to acquire territory. Perron was apprehensive of his power—the more so, perhaps, as Thomas was encouraged by Holkar, and supported by Lakwa Dādā and other Marāthās, who entertained a great jealousy of the French commandant.[1]

1798–1800. himself at Hānsi, 1798,

In 1799 Thomas invested the town of Jīnd, belonging to Bhāg Singh, of the Phūlkīa confederacy. The old chief, Baghēl Singh Krora Singhia, and the Amazonian sister of the imbecile Rājā of Patiāla, relieved the place, but they were repulsed when they attacked Thomas on his retreat to Hānsi. In 1800 Thomas took Fatehābād, which had been deserted during the famine of 1783, and subsequently occupied by the predatory Bhattis of Hariāna, then rising into local repute, notwithstanding the efforts of the Patiāla chief, who, however, affected to consider them as his subjects, and gave them some aid against Thomas. Patiāla was the next object of Thomas's ambition, and he was encouraged by the temporary secession of the sister of the chief; but the aged Tāra Singh, of the Dallehwala confederacy, interfered, and Thomas had to act with caution. He obtained, nevertheless, a partial success over Tāra Singh, he received the submission of the Pathāns of Malēr Kotla, and he was welcomed as a deliverer by the converted Muhammadans of Raikot, who had held Ludhiāna for some time, and all of whom were equally jealous of the Sikhs. At this time Sāhib Singh, a Bedī of the race of Nānak, pretended to religious inspiration, and, having collected a large force, he invested Ludhiāna, took the town of Malēr Kotla, and called on the English adventurer to obey him as the true representative of the Sikh prophet. But Sāhib Singh could not long impose even on his countrymen, and he had to retire across the Sutlej. Thomas's situation was not greatly improved by the absence of the Bedī, for the combination against him was general, and he retired from the neighbourhood of Ludhiāna towards his stronghold of Hānsi. He again took the field, and attacked Safidon, an old town belonging to the chief of Jīnd. He was repulsed, but the

and engages in hostilities with the Sikhs, 1799.

Thomas marches towards Ludhiāna, 1800.

Opposed by Sāhib Singh Bedī.

Retires to Hānsi, but afterwards masters Safidon, near Delhi.

[1] Francklin, *Life of George Thomas*, pp. 1, 79, 107, &c., and Major Smith, *Account of Regular Corps in the Service of Indian Princes*, p. 118, &c.

1801–3.

place not appearing tenable, it was evacuated, and he obtained possession of it. At this time he is said to have had ten battalions and sixty guns, and to have possessed a territory yielding about 450,000 rupees, two-thirds of which he held by right of seizure, and one-third as a Marāthā feudatory; but he had rejected all Perron's overtures with suspicion, and Perron was resolved to crush him. Thomas was thus forced to come to terms with the Sikhs, and he wished it to appear that he had engaged them on his side against Perron; but they were really desirous of getting rid of one who plainly designed their ruin, or at least their subjection, and the alacrity of Patiāla in the Marāthā service induced a promise, on the part of the French commander, of the restitution of the conquests of Amar Singh in Hariāna. After twice beating back Perron's troops at points sixty miles distant, Thomas was compelled to surrender in the beginning of 1802, and he retired into the British provinces, where he died in the course of the same year.[1]

Thomas rejects Perron's overtures and resorts to arms, 1801.

Surrenders to Perron, 1802.

The Marāthās under Perron paramount among the Sikhs of Sirhind, 1802–3.

Perron had thus far succeeded. His lieutenant, by name Bourquin, made a progress through the Cis-Sutlej states to levy contributions, and the commander himself dreamt of a dominion reaching to the Afghān hills, and of becoming as independent of Sindhia as that chief was of the Peshwā.[2] He formed an engagement with Ranjīt Singh for a joint expedition to the Indus, and for a partition of the country south of Lahore;[3] but Holkar had given a rude shock to Sindhia's power, and Perron had long evaded a compliance with the Mahārājā's urgent calls for troops to aid him where support was most essential. Sindhia became involved with the English, and the interested hesitation of Perron was

Perron forms an alliance with Ranjit Singh.

Is distrusted by Sindhia.

[1] See generally Francklin, *Life of George Thomas*, and Major Smith, *Account of Regular Corps in Indian States*, p. 21, &c. The Sikh accounts attribute many exploits to the sister of the Rājā of Patiāla, and among them an expedition into the hill territory of Nāhan, the state from which Patiāla wrested the vale of Pinjaur, with its hanging gardens, not, however, without the aid of Bourquin, the deputy of Perron.

[2] Malcolm (*Sketch*, p. 106) considers that Perron could easily have reduced the Sikhs, and mastered the Punjab.

[3] This alliance is given on the authority of a representation made to the Resident at Delhi, agreeably to his letter to Sir David Ochterlony of July 5, 1814.

punished by his supersession. He was not able, or he did not try, to recover his authority by vigorous military operations; he knew he had committed himself, and he effected his escape from the suspicious Marāthās to the safety and repose of the British territories, which were then about to be extended by the victories of Delhi and Laswāri, of Assaye and Argaon.[1] 1803.

Flees to the English, then at war with the Marāthās, 1803.

In the beginning of the eighteenth century the agents of the infant company of English merchants were vexatiously detained at the imperial court by the insurrection of the Sikhs under Banda, and the discreet 'factors', who were petitioning for some trading privileges, perhaps witnessed the heroic death of the national *Singhs*, the soldiers of the 'Khālsa', without comprehending the spirit evoked by the genius of Gobind, and without dreaming of the broad fabric of empire about to be reared on their own patient labours.[2] Forty years afterwards, the merchant Omichand

First intercourse of the English with the Sikhs.

The mission to Farrukhsīyar detained by the campaign against Banda, 1715–17.

[1] Cf. Major Smith, *Account of Regular Corps in Indian States*, p. 31, &c.

[2] See Orme, *History*, ii. 22, &c., and Mill, Wilson's edition, iii. 34, &c. The mission was two years at Delhi, during 1715, 1716, 1717, and the genuine patriotism of Mr. Hamilton, the surgeon of the deputation, mainly contributed to procure the cession of thirty-seven villages near Calcutta, and the exemption from duty of goods protected by English passes. This latter privilege was a turning-point in the history of the English in India, for it gave an impulse to trade, which vastly increased the importance of British subjects, if it added little to the profits of the associated merchants. [It may be added that a dispute about the issue of those passes brought about an open rupture between the East India Company and Mīr Kāsim, Nawāb of Bengal, in 1763. The latter was utterly defeated at the Battle of Bunar in 1764 and, as one of the terms of peace in the following year—the year of Clive's return to India—the Dīwāni (fiscal administration) of Bengal, Bihār and Orissa was granted by the Emperor Shāh Alam to the Company, in return for a yearly payment of 26 lakhs, while the Nawāb, the successor of Mīr Kāsim, was deprived of all power and pensioned.—Ed.]

In the *Granth* of Gurū Gobind there are at least four allusions to Europeans, the last referring specially to an Englishman. First, in the *Akāl Stut*, Europeans are enumerated among the tribes inhabiting India; second and third, in the *Kalki* chapters of the 24 *Autārs*, apparently in praise of the systematic modes of Europeans; and fourth, in the Persian *Hikayats*, where both a European and an Englishman appear as champions for the hand of a royal damsel, to be vanquished, of course, by the hero of the tale.

1757–88.

Clive and Omichand, 1757.

played a conspicuous part in the revolution which was crowned by the battle of Plassey; but the sectarian *Sikh*, the worldly votary of Nānak, who used religion as a garb of outward decorum, was outwitted by the audacious falsehood of Clive; he quailed before the stern scorn of the English conqueror, and he perished the victim of his own base avarice.[1] In 1784 the progress of the genuine Sikhs attracted the notice of Hastings, and he seems to have thought that the presence of a British agent at the court of Delhi might help to deter them from molesting the Wazīr of Oudh.[2] But the Sikhs had learnt to dread others as well as to be a cause of fear, and shortly afterwards they asked the British Resident to enter into a defensive alliance against the Marāthās, and to accept the services of thirty thousand horsemen, who had posted themselves near Delhi to watch the motions of Sindhia.[3] The English had then a slight knowledge of a new and distant people, and an estimate, two generations old, may provoke a smile from the protectors of Lahore. 'The Sikhs', says Col. Francklin, 'are in their persons tall, . . . their aspect is ferocious, and their eyes piercing; . . . they resemble the Arabs of the Euphrates, but they speak the language of the Afghāns; . . . their collected army amounts to 250,000 men, a terrific force, yet from want of union not much to be dreaded.'[4] The judicious and observing Forster put some confidence in similar statements of their vast array, but he estimated more surely than any other early writer the real character of the Sikhs, and the remark of 1783, that an able chief would probably attain to absolute power on the ruins of the rude commonwealth, and become the terror of his neighbours, has been amply borne out by the career of Ranjīt Singh.[5]

Warren Hastings tries to guard Oudh against the Sikhs, 1784.

The Sikhs ask English aid against the Marāthās, 1788.

Early English estimates of the Sikhs.

Col. Francklin.

The traveller Forster.

[1] That Omichand was a Sikh is given on the authority of Forster, *Travels*, i. 337. That he died of a broken heart is doubted by Professor Wilson. (Mill, *India*, iii 192 note, ed. 1840.)

[2] Browne, *India Tracts*, ii. 29, 30; and Francklin, *Shāh Alam*, pp. 115, 116.

[3] Auber, *Rise and Progress of the British Power in India*, ii. 26, 27. The chief who made the overtures was Dulcha Singh of Rudaur on the Jumna, who afterwards entered Sindhia's service. Cf. Francklin, *Shāh Alam*, p. 78 note.

[4] Francklin, *Shāh Alam*, pp. 75, 77, 78.

[5] Forster's *Travels*, ii. 340. See also p. 324, where he says the Sikhs

1803-5.

The battle of Delhi [1] was fought on the 11th September, 1803, and five thousand Sikhs swelled an army which the speedy capture of Alīgarh had taken by surprise.[2] The Marāthās were overthrown, and the Sikhs dispersed; but the latter soon afterwards tendered their allegiance to the British commander. Among the more important chiefs whose alliance or whose occasional services were accepted were Bhai Lāl Singh of Kaithal, who had witnessed the success of Lord Lake, Bhāg Singh, the patriarchal chief of Jīnd, and, after a time, Bhanga Singh the savage master of Thānesar.[3] The victory of Laswāri was won within two months, and the Marāthā power seemed to be annihilated in Northern India. The old blind emperor Shāh Alam was again flattered with the semblance of kingly power, his pride was soothed by the demeanour of the conqueror, and, as the Mughal name was still imposing, the feelings of the free but loyal soldier were doubtless gratified by the bestowal of a title which declared an English nobleman to be 'the sword of the state' of the great Tamerlane.[4]

Sikhs opposed to Lord Lake at Delhi, 1803.

The Sikhs of Sirhind tender their allegiance to the English.

The chiefs of Jīnd and Kaithal.

Shāh Alam freed from Marāthā thraldom.

The enterprising Jaswant Rao Holkar had by this time determined on the invasion of Upper India, and the retreat of Col. Monson [5] buoyed him up with hopes of victory

The English wars with Holkar, 1804-5.

had raised in the Punjab a solid structure of religion. The remark of the historian Robertson may also be quoted as apposite, and with the greater reason as prominence has lately been given to it in the House of Commons on the occasion of thanking the army for its services during the Sikh campaign of 1848-9. He says that the enterprising commercial spirit of the English, and the martial ardour of the Sikhs, who possess the energy natural to men in the earlier stages of society, can hardly fail to lead sooner or later to open hostility. (*Disquisition Concerning Ancient India*, note iv, sect. 1, written in 1789-90.)

[1] [For an interesting discussion as to the exact site of this battle, the result of which was the occupation of Delhi by the English and the placing of the Emperor Shāh Alam under their protection, the reader is referred to an article by Sir Edward Maclagan, in the *Journal of the Punjab Historical Society*, vol. iii.—ED.]

[2] Major Smith, *Account of Regular Corps in Indian States*, p. 34.

[3] Manuscript memoranda of personal inquiries.

[4] Mill, *History of British India*, Wilson's ed., vi. 510.

[5] [He had made a rash advance into Holkar's territory in July 1804, to unite with another English force under Col. Murray. Lack of supplies caused him to retreat, and he only reached Agra at the end of August, after losing the major part of his army. However, he took his revenge at Dīg, as that victory was mainly his work.—ED.]

1805.

and dominion. Delhi was invested, and the Doāb was filled with troops; but the successful defence of the capital by Sir David Ochterlony, and the reverse of Dīg, drove the great marauder back into Rājputāna. During these operations a British detachment, under Col. Burn, was hard pressed at Shāmlī, near Sahāranpur, and the opportune assistance of Lāl Singh of Kaithal and Bhāg Singh of Jīnd contributed to its ultimate relief.[1] The same Sikh chiefs deserved and received the thanks of Lord Lake for attacking and killing one Ika Rao, a Marāthā commander who had taken up a position between Delhi and Pānīpat; but others were disposed to adhere to their sometime allies, and Sher Singh of Būriya fell in action with Col. Burn, and the conduct of Gurdit Singh of Lādwa induced the British general to deprive him of his villages in the Doāb, and of the town of Karnāl.[2]

The Sikhs mostly side with the English and render good service.

Holkar retires towards the Sutlej, 1805.

In 1805 Holkar and Amīr Khān again moved northward, and proclaimed that they would be joined by the Sikhs, and even by the Afghāns; but the rapid movements of Lord Lake converted their advance into a retreat or a flight. They delayed some time at Patiāla, and they did not fail to make a pecuniary profit out of the differences then existing between the imbecile Rājā and his wife;[3] but when the English army reached the neighbourhood of Karnāl, Holkar continued his retreat towards the north, levying contributions where he could, but without being joined by any of the Sikh chiefs of the Cis-Sutlej states. In the Punjab itself he is represented to have induced some to adopt his cause, but Ranjīt Singh long kept aloof, and when at last he met Holkar at Amritsar, the astute young chief wanted

Delays at Patiāla.

Halts at Amritsar, but fails in gaining over Ranjīt Singh.

1 Manuscript memoranda. Both this aid in 1804, and the opposition of the Sikhs at Delhi, in 1803, seem to have escaped the notice of English observers, or to have been thought undeserving of record by English historians. (Mill, *History*, vi. 503, 592, ed. 1840.)

2 Manuscript memoranda of written documents and of personal inquiries.

3 Amīr Khān, in his *Memoirs* (p. 276), says characteristically, that Holkar remarked to him, on observing the silly differences between the Rājā and the Rānī, 'God has assuredly sent us these two pigeons to pluck; do you espouse the cause of the one, while I take up with the other.'

1803-8.

aid in reducing the Pathāns of Kasūr before he would give the Marāthās any assistance against the English. Amīr Khān would wish it to be believed, that *he* was unwilling to be a party to an attack upon good Muhammadans, and it is certain that the perplexed Jaswant Rao talked of hurrying on to Peshāwar; but Lord Lake was in force on the banks of the Beās, the political demands of the British commander were moderate, and, on the 24th December, 1805, an arrangement was come to, which allowed Holkar to return quietly to Central India.[1]

Holkar comes to terms with the English and marches to the south, 1805-6.

Lord Lake was joined on his advance by the two chiefs, Lāl Singh and Bhāg Singh, whose services have already been mentioned, and at Patiāla he was welcomed by the weak and inoffensive Sāhib Singh, who presented the keys of his citadel, and expatiated on his devotion to the British Government. Bhāg Singh was the maternal uncle of Ranjīt Singh, and his services were not unimportant in determining that calculating leader to avoid an encounter with disciplined battalions and a trained artillery. Ranjīt Singh is believed to have visited the British camp in disguise, that he might himself witness the military array of a leader who had successively vanquished both Sindhia and Holkar,[2] and he was, moreover, too acute to see any permanent advantage in linking his fortunes with those of men reduced to the condition of fugitives. Fateh Singh Ahluwalia, the grand-nephew of Jassa Singh Kalāl, and the chosen companion of the future Mahārājā, was the medium of intercourse, and an arrangement was soon entered into with 'Sardārs' Ranjīt Singh and Fateh Singh jointly, which provided that Holkar should be compelled to retire from Amritsar, and that so long as the two chiefs conducted themselves as friends the English Government would never form any plans for the seizure of their territories.[3] Lord Lake entered into a friendly correspondence with Sansār Chand, of Katōtch, who was imitating Ranjīt Singh by bringing the petty hill chiefs under subjection; but no

Friendly relations of the English with the Sikhs of Sirhind, 1803-8.

Formal engagement entered into with Ranjīt Singh and Fateh Singh Ahluwalia, 1806.

The English correspond with Sansār

[1] Cf. Amīr Khān, *Memoirs*, pp. 275, 285; and Murray, *Ranjīt Singh*, p. 57, &c.

[2] See Moorcroft, *Travels*, i. 102.

[3] See the treaty itself, Appendix XXIII.

1804. Chand of Katōtch.

engagement was entered into, and the British commander returned to the provinces by the road of Ambāla and Karnāl.[1]

The Sikhs of Sirhind regarded as virtually dependants of the English by Lord Lake.

The connexion of Lord Lake with many of the Sikh chiefs of Sirhind had been intimate, and the services of some had been opportune and valuable. Immediately after the battle of Delhi, Bhāg Singh of Jīnd was upheld in a jāgīr which he possessed near that city, and in 1804 another estate was conferred jointly on him and his friend Lāl Singh of Kaithal. In 1806 these leaders were further rewarded with life grants, yielding about £11,000 a year, and Lord Lake was understood to be willing to give them the districts of Hānsi and Hissār on the same terms; but these almost desert tracts were objected to as unprofitable. Other petty chiefs received rewards corresponding with their services, and all were assured that they should continue to enjoy the territorial possessions which they held at the time of British interference without being liable to the payment of tribute.

But the connexion not regularly declared, or made binding in form.

These declarations or arrangements were made when the policy of Lord Wellesley was suffering under condemnation; the reign of the English was to be limited by the Jumna, a formal treaty with Jaipur was abrogated, the relations of the Indian Government with Bhartpur were left doubtful, and, although nothing was made known to the Sikh chiefs of Sirhind, their connexion with the English came virtually to an end, so far as regarded the reciprocal benefits of alliance.[2]

Retrospect with reference to Ranjīt Singh's rise.

It is now necessary to return to Ranjīt Singh, whose authority had gradually become predominant among the Sikh people. His first object was to master Lahore from the incapable chiefs of the Bhangī confederacy who possessed

[1] The public records show that a newswriter was maintained for some time in Katōtch, and the correspondence about Sansār Chand leaves the impression that Ranjīt Singh could never wholly forget the Rājā's original superiority, nor the English divest themselves of a feeling that he was independent of Lahore.

[2] The original grants to Jīnd, Kaithal, and others, and also similar papers of assurance, are carefully preserved by the several families; and the various English documents show that Bhāg Singh, of Jīnd, was always regarded with much kindliness by Lord Lake, Sir John Malcolm, and Sir David Ochterlony.

it, and before Shāh Zamān had been many months gone, effect was given to his grant by a dexterous mixture of force and artifice. Ranjīt Singh made Lahore his capital, and, with the aid of the Kanhayās (or Ghani) confederacy, he easily reduced the whole of the Bhangīs to submission, although they were aided by Nizām-ud-dīn Khān of Kasūr. In 1801–2 the Pathān had to repent his rashness; his strongholds were difficult of capture, but he found it prudent to become a feudatory, and to send his best men to follow a new master. After this success Ranjīt Singh went to bathe in the holy pool of Taran Tāran, and, meeting with Fateh Singh Ahluwalia, he conceived a friendship for him, as has been mentioned, and went through a formal exchange of turbans, symbolical of brotherhood. During 1802 the allies took Amritsar from the widow of the last Bhangī leader of note, and, of their joint spoil, it fell to the share of the master of the other capital of the Sikh country. In 1803 Sansār Chand, of Katōtch, in prosecution of his schemes of aggrandizement, made two attempts to occupy portions of the fertile Doāb of Jullundur, but he was repulsed by Ranjīt Singh and his confederate. In 1804 Sansār Chand again quitted his hills, and captured Hoshiārpur and Bajwāra; but Ranjīt Singh's approach once more compelled him to retreat, and he soon afterwards became involved with the Gurkhas, a new people in search of an empire which should comprise the whole range of Himālayas.[1]

1799–1804.

Ranjīt Singh masters Lahore, 1799.

Reduces the Bhangī Misal and the Pathāns of Kasūr, 1801–2.

Allies himself with Fateh Singh Ahluwalia.

Ranjīt Singh acquires Amritsar, 1802;

and confines Sansār Chand to the hills, 1803–4, who becomes involved with the Gurkhas.

[1] Cf. Murray, *Ranjīt Singh*, pp. 51, 55.

Capt. Murray, the political agent at Ambāla, and Capt. Wade, the political agent at Ludhiāna, each wrote a narrative of the life of Ranjīt Singh, and that of the former was printed in 1834, with a few corrections and additions, and some notes, by Mr. Thoby Prinsep, secretary to the Indian Government. The author has not seen Capt. Wade's report, or narrative, but he believes that it, even in a greater degree than Capt. Murray's, was founded on personal recollections and on oral report, rather than on contemporary English documents, which reflected the opinions of the times, and which existed in sufficient abundance after 1803 especially. The two narratives in question were, indeed, mainly prepared from accounts drawn up by intelligent Indians, at the requisition of the English functionaries, and of these the chronicles of Buta Shāh, a Muhammadan, and Sohan Lāl, a Hindu, are the best known, and may be had for purchase The inquiries of Capt. Wade, in especial, were extensive, and to both

1803–5.

Shāh Zamān deposed by Shāh Mahmūd and the Durrāni empire weakened;

In little more than a year after Shāh Zamān quitted the Punjab, he was deposed and blinded by his brother Mahmūd, who was in his turn supplanted by a third brother, Shāh Shujā, in the year 1803. These revolutions hastened the fall of the exotic empire of Ahmad Shāh, and Ranjīt Singh was not slow to try his arms against the weakened Durrāni governors of districts and provinces. In 1804–5 he marched to the westward; he received homage and presents from the Muhammadans of Jhang and Sāhiwāl, and Muzaffar Khān of Multān, successfully deprecated an attack by rich offerings. Ranjīt Singh had felt his way and was satisfied; he returned to Lahore, celebrated the festival of the Holi in his capital, and then went to bathe in the Ganges at Hardwār, or to observe personally the aspect of affairs to the eastward of the Punjab. Towards the close of 1805 he made another western inroad, and added weight to the fetters already imposed on the proprietor of Jhang; but the approach of Holkar and Amīr Khān recalled, first Fateh Singh, and afterwards himself, to the proper city of the whole Sikh people. The danger seemed imminent, for a famed leader of the dominant Marāthās was desirous of bringing down an Afghān host, and the English army, exact in discipline, and representing a power of unknown views and resources, had reached the neighbourhood of Amritsar.[1]

wherefore Ranjīt Singh proceeds to the south-west of the Punjab, 1805.

Returns to the north on Holkar's approach, 1805.

A Sikh Gurū-matta, or national council, held;

A formal council was held by the Sikhs, but a portion only of their leaders were present. The singleness of purpose, the confident belief in the aid of God, which had animated mechanics and shepherds to resent persecution, and to triumph over Ahmad Shāh, no longer possessed the minds of their descendants, born to comparative power and affluence, and who, like rude and ignorant men broken loose from all law, gave the rein to their grosser passions.

officers the public is indebted for the preservation of a continuous narrative of Ranjīt Singh's actions.

The latter portion of the present chapter, and also chapters VI and VII, follow very closely the author's narratives of the British connexion with the Sikhs, drawn up for Government, a [*literary*] use which he trusts may be made, without any impropriety, of an unprinted paper of his own writing.

[1] See Elphinstone, *Kābul*, ii. 325; and Murray, *Ranjīt Singh*, pp. 56, 57.

Their ambition was personal and their desire was for worldly enjoyment. The genuine spirit of Sikhism had again sought the dwelling of the peasant to reproduce itself in another form; the rude system of mixed independence and confederacy was unsuited to an extended dominion; it had served its ends of immediate agglomeration, and the 'Misals' were in effect dissolved. The mass of the people remained satisfied with their village freedom, to which taxation and inquisition were unknown; but the petty chiefs and their paid followers, to whom their faith was the mere expression of a conventional custom, were anxious for predatory licence, and for additions to their temporal power. Some were willing to join the English, others were ready to link their fortunes with the Marāthās, and all had become jealous of Ranjīt Singh, who alone was desirous of excluding the stranger invaders, as the great obstacles to his own ambition of founding a military monarchy which should ensure to the people the congenial occupation of conquest. In truth, Ranjīt Singh laboured, with more or less of intelligent design, to give unity and coherence to diverse atoms and scattered elements; to mould the increasing Sikh nation into a well-ordered state or commonwealth, as Gobind had developed a sect into a people, and had given application and purpose to the general institutions of Nānak.[1]

1805.

but the confederate system found decayed and lifeless,

and a single temporal authority virtually admitted in the person of Ranjīt Singh.

Holkar retired, and Ranjīt Singh, as has been mentioned, entered into a vague but friendly alliance with the British Government. Towards the close of the same year he was invited to interfere in a quarrel between the chief of Nābha and the Rājā of Patiāla, and it would be curious to trace whether the English authorities had first refused to mediate in the dispute in consequence of the repeated instructions to avoid all connexion with powers beyond the Jumna. Ranjīt Singh crossed the Sutlej, and took Ludhiāna from the declining Muhammadan family which had sought the protection of the adventurer George Thomas. The place was bestowed upon his uncle, Bhāg Singh of Jīnd, and as

Ranjīt Singh interferes in the affairs of the Sikhs of Sirhind 1806.

Takes Ludhiāna, 1806;

[1] Malcolm (*Sketch*, pp. 106, 107) remarks on the want of unanimity among the Sikhs at the time of Lord Lake's expedition. Cf. Murray, *Ranjīt Singh*, pp. 57, 58.

1806.

both Jaswant Singh of Nābha, whom he had gone to aid, and Sāhib Singh of Patiāla, whom he had gone to coerce, were glad to be rid of his destructive arbitration, he retired with the present of a piece of artillery and some treasure, and went towards the hills of Kāngra, partly that he might pay his superstitious devotions at the natural flames of Juāla Mukhi.[1]

and receives offerings from Patiāla.

Sansār Chand and the Gurkhas, 1805.

At this time the unscrupulous ambition of Sansār Chand of Katōtch had brought him into fatal collision with the Gurkhas. That able chief might have given life to a confederacy against the common enemies of all the old mountain principalities, who were already levying tribute in Garhwāl: but Sansār Chand in his desire for supremacy had reduced the chief of Kahlūr, or Belaspur, to the desperate expedient of throwing himself on the support of the Nepāl commander. Amar Singh Thappa gladly advanced, and, notwithstanding the gallant resistance offered by the young chief of Nālāgarh, Sansār Chand's coadjutor in his own aggressions, the Gurkha authority was introduced between the Sutlej and Jumna before the end of 1805, during which year Amar Singh crossed the former river and laid siege to Kāngra. At the period of Ranjīt Singh's visit to Juāla Mukhi, Sansār Chand was willing to obtain his aid; but, as the fort was strong and the sacrifices required considerable, he was induced to trust to his own resources, and no arrangement was then come to for the expulsion of the new enemy.[2]

Sansār Chand and his confederate of Nālāgarh driven to the north of the Sutlej, 1805;

and the Gurkhas invest Kāngra.

[1] See Murray, *Ranjīt Singh*, pp. 59, 60. The letter of Sir Charles Metcalfe to Government, of June 17, 1809, shows that Ranjīt Singh was not strong enough at the time in question, 1806, to interfere, by open force, in the affairs of the Mālwā Sikhs, and the letters of Sir David Ochterlony, of February 14, March 7, 1809 and July 30, 1811, show that the English engagements of 1805, with the Patiāla and other chiefs, were virtually at an end, so far as regarded the reciprocal benefits of alliance.

[2] Cf. Murray, *Ranjīt Singh*, p. 60; and Moorcroft, *Travels*, i. 127, &c. Sansār Chand attributed his overthrow by the Gurkhas to his dismissal of his old Rājpūt troops and employment of Afghāns, at the instigation of the fugitive Rohilla chief, Ghulām Muhammad, who had sought an asylum with him.

The Gurkhas crossed the Jumna to aid the chief of Nāhan against his subjects, and they crossed the Sutlej to aid one Rājpūt prince against another—paths always open to new and united races. Refe-

In 1807 Ranjīt Singh first directed his attention to Kasūr, which was again rebellious, and the relative independence of which caused him disquietude, although its able chief, Nizām-ud-dīn, had been dead for some time; nor was he, perhaps, without a feeling that the reduction of a large colony of Pathāns, and the annexation of the mythological rival of Lahore, would add to his own merit and importance. The place was invested by Ranjīt Singh, and by Jodh Singh Rāmgarhia, the son of his father's old ally, Jassa the Carpenter. Want of unity weakened the resistance of the then chief, Kutb-ud-dīn, and at the end of a month he surrendered at discretion, and received a tract of land on the opposite side of the Sutlej for his maintenance. Ranjīt Singh afterwards proceeded towards Multān, and succeeded in capturing the walled town; but the citadel resisted such efforts as he was able to make, and he was perhaps glad that the payment of a sum of money enabled him to retire with credit; he was, nevertheless, unwilling to admit his failure, and, in the communications which he then held with the Nawāb of Bahāwalpur, the ready improver of opportunities endeavoured to impress that chief with the belief that a regard for him alone had caused the Afghān governor to be left in possession of his stronghold.[1]

1807.

Ranjīt Singh expels the Pathān chief of Kasūr, 1807;

and partially succeeds against Multān.

During the same year, 1807, Ranjīt Singh took into his employ a Kshattriya, named Mohkam Chand, an able man, who fully justified the confidence reposed in him. With this new servant in his train he proceeded to interfere in the dissensions between the Rājā of Patiāla and his intriguing wife, which were as lucrative to the master of Lahore as they had before been to Holkar and Amīr Khān. The Rānī wished to force from the weak husband a large assignment for the support of her infant son, and she tempted Ranjīt Singh, by the offer of a necklace of diamonds and a piece of brass ordnance, to espouse her cause. He crossed the Sutlej, and decreed to the boy a maintenance of 50,000 rupees per annum. He then attacked Naraingarh, between Ambāla

Ranjīt Singh employs Mohkam Chand, 1807.

Crosses the Sutlej for the second time;

rences in public records show that the latter river was crossed in A. D. 1805.

[1] Murray, *Ranjīt Singh*, pp. 60, 61, and the manuscript memoirs of the Bahāwalpur family.

1808–9.

and the hills, and held by a family of Rājpūts, but he only secured it after a repulse and a heavy loss. Tāra Singh, the old chief of the Dallehwala confederacy, who was with the Lahore force on this occasion, died before Naraingarh, and Ranjīt Singh hastened back to secure his possessions in the Jullundur Doāb. The widow of the aged leader equalled the sister of the Rājā of Patiāla in spirit, and she is described to have girded up her garments, and to have fought, sword in hand, on the battered walls of the fort of Rāhon.[1]

and returns to seize the territories of the deceased Dallewala chief.

The Sikhs of Sirhind become apprehensive of Ranjīt Singh.

In the beginning of 1808 various places in the Upper Punjab were taken from their independent Sikh proprietors, and brought under the direct management of the new kingdom of Lahore, and Mohkam Chand was at the same time employed in effecting a settlement of the territories which had been seized on the left bank of the Sutlej. But Ranjīt Singh's systematic aggressions had begun to excite fear in the minds of the Sikhs of Sirhind, and a formal deputation, consisting of the chiefs of Jīnd and Kaithal, and the Dīwān, or minister, of Patiāla, proceeded to Delhi, in March 1808, to ask for British protection. The communications of the English Government with the chiefs of the Cis-Sutlej states had not been altogether broken off, and the Governor-General had at this time assured the Muhammadan Khān of Kunjpura, near Karnāl,[2] that he need be under no apprehensions with regard to his hereditary possessions, while the petty Sikh chief of Sikri had performed some services which were deemed worthy of a pension.[3] But the deputies of the collective states could obtain no positive assurances from the British authorities at Delhi, although they were led to hope that, in the hour of need, they would not be deserted. This was scarcely sufficient to save them from loss, and perhaps from ruin; and, as Ranjīt Singh had sent messengers to calm their apprehensions, and to urge them to join his camp, they left Delhi for the purpose

British protection asked, 1808;

but not distinctly acceded.

Whereupon the chiefs repair to Ranjīt Singh.

[1] Cf. Murray, *Ranjīt Singh*, pp. 61, 63. The gun obtained by Ranjīt Singh from Patiāla on this occasion was named Karri Khān, and was captured by the English during the campaign of 1845–6.

[2] In a document dated 18th January, 1808.

[3] Mr. Clerk of Ambāla to the agent at Delhi, 19th May, 1837.

of making their own terms with the acknowledged Rājā of Lahore.[1] 1808–9.

The Governor-General of 1805,[2] who dissolved or deprecated treaties with princes beyond the Jumna, and declared that river to be the limit of British dominion, had no personal knowledge of the hopes and fears with which the invasions of Shāh Zamān agitated the minds of men for the period of three or four years; and had the Sikhs of Sirhind sought protection from Lord Cornwallis, they would doubtless have received a decisive answer in the negative. But the reply of encouragement given in the beginning of 1808 was prompted by renewed danger; and the belief that the French, the Turkish, and the Persian emperors meditated the subjugation of India led another new Governor-General to seek alliances, not only beyond the Jumna, but beyond the Indus.[3] The designs or the desires of Napoleon appeared to render a defensive alliance with the Afghāns and with the Sikhs imperative; Mr. Elphinstone was deputed to the court of Shāh Shujā, and in September 1808 Mr. Metcalfe was sent on a mission to Ranjīt Singh for the purpose of bringing about the desired confederation.[4] The chiefs of Patiāla, Jīnd, and Kaithal were also verbally assured that they had become dependent princes of the British Government; for the progress of Ranjīt Singh seemed to render the interposition of some friendly states, between his military domination and the peaceful sway of the English, a measure of prudence and foresight.[5]

The understood designs of the French on India modify the policy of the English towards the Sikhs, 1808–9.

The chiefs of Sirhind taken under protection, and a close alliance sought with Ranjīt Singh.

[1] See Murray, *Ranjīt Singh*, pp. 64, 65.

[2] [Lord Cornwallis had been sent out in 1805 with strict orders to pursue a pacific and economizing policy, as the Directors were alarmed at the expense of the wars waged by his predecessor—Lord Wellesley. But Cornwallis died two months after his arrival, and was temporarily succeeded by Sir G. Barlow.—Ed.]

[3] Mr. Auber (*Rise and Progress of the British Power in India*, ii. 461), notices the *triple* alliance which threatened Hindustān. [Lord Minto had arrived as Governor-General in 1807.—Ed.]

[4] [Col. Malcolm was dispatched on a similar mission to Persia at the same time, and concluded a treaty (1809) which did away with the possibility of French interference in that quarter.—Ed.]

[5] Government to Sir David Ochterlony, 14th Nov., 1808. Cf. Murray, *Ranjīt Singh*, pp. 65, 66.

1808-9.

Mr. Metcalfe sent as envoy to Lahore, 1808-9.

Mr. Metcalfe was received by Ranjīt Singh at his newly conquered town of Kasūr, but the chief affected to consider himself as the head of the whole Sikh people, and to regard the possession of Lahore as giving him an additional claim to supremacy over Sirhind. He did not, perhaps, see that a French invasion would be ruinous to *his* interests; he rather feared the colossal power on his borders, and he resented the intention of confining him to the Sutlej.[1] He suddenly broke off negotiations, and made his third inroad to the south of the Sutlej. He seized Farīdkot and Ambāla, levied exactions in Māler Kotla and Thānesar, and entered into a symbolical brotherhood or alliance with the Rājā of Patiāla. The British envoy remonstrated against these virtual acts of hostility, and he remained on the banks of the Sutlej until Ranjīt Singh recrossed that river.[2]

Aversion of Ranjīt Singh to a restrictive treaty, and his third expedition across the Sutlej.

British troops moved to the Sutlej, 1809.

The proceedings of the ruler of Lahore determined the Governor-General, if doubtful before, to advance a detachment of troops to the Sutlej, to support Mr. Metcalfe in his negotiations, and to effectually confine Ranjīt Singh to the northward of that river.[3] Provision would also be thus made, it was said, for possible warlike operations of a more extensive character, and the British frontier would be covered by a confederacy of friendly chiefs, instead of threatened by a hostile military government. A body of troops was accordingly moved across the Jumna in January 1809, under the command of Sir David Ochterlony. The General advanced, by way of Būriya and Patiāla, towards Ludhiāna; he was welcomed by all the Sirhind chiefs, save Jodh Singh Kalsia, the nominal head of the Krora-Singhia confederacy: but during his march he was not without apprehensions that Ranjīt Singh might openly break with his government. and, after an interview with certain agents whom that chief had sent to him with the view of opening a double negotiation, he made a détour and

[1] Moorcroft ascertained (*Travels*, i. 94) that Ranjīt Singh had serious thoughts of appealing to the sword, so unpalatable was English interference. The well-known Fakīr Uziz-ud-dīn was one of the two persons who dissuaded him from war.

[2] Murray, *Ranjīt Singh*, p. 66.

[3] Government to Sir David Ochterlony, 14th Nov. and 29th Dec., 1808.

a halt, in order to be near his supplies should hostilities take place.[1] 1809.

The views of the English become somewhat modified; but Ranjīt Singh still required to keep to the north of the Sutlej.

Ranjīt Singh was somewhat discomposed by the near presence of a British force but he continued to evade compliance with the propositions of the envoy, and he complained that Mr. Metcalfe was needlessly reserved about his acquisitions on the south banks of the Sutlej, with regard to which the Government had only declared that the restoration of his last conquests, and the absolute withdrawal of his troops to the northward of the river, must form the indispensable basis of further negotiations.[2] Affairs were in this way when intelligence from Europe induced the Governor-General to believe that Napoleon must abandon his designs upon India, or at least so far suspend them as to render defensive precautions unnecessary.[3] It was therefore made known that the object of the English Government had become limited to the security of the country south of the Sutlej from the encroachments of Ranjīt Singh; for that, independent of the possible approach of a European enemy, it was considered advisable on other grounds to afford protection to the southern Sikhs. Ranjīt Singh must still, nevertheless, withdraw his troops to the right bank of the Sutlej, his last usurpations must also be restored, but the

[1] Sir David Ochterlony to Government, 20th Jan., and 4th, 9th, and 14th Feb., 1809, with Government to Sir David Ochterlony, of 13th March, 1809. Government by no means approved of what Sir David Ochterlony had done, and he, feeling aggrieved, virtually tendered his resignation of his command. (Sir David Ochterlony to Government, 19th April, 1809.)

[2] Sir David Ochterlony to Government, 14th Feb., 1809, and Government to Sir David Ochterlony, 30th July, 1809. Lieut.-Col. Lawrence (*Adventures in the Punjab*, p. 131, note *g*) makes Sir Charles Metcalfe sufficiently communicative on this occasion with regard to other territories, for he is declared to have told the Mahārājā that by a compliance with the then demands of the English, he would ensure their neutrality with respect to encroachments elsewhere.

[3] Government to Sir David Ochterlony, 30th Jan., 1809. [Probably the altered relations between Napoleon and Turkey were the main cause of this. The Franco-Turkish alliance of 1807 had come to an end with the deposition of Mustapha IV and accession of Mahmud II—July 1808—and the improved relations of England and Turkey led to the signature by the latter powers of the Treaty of the Dardanelles (January 1809).—Ed.]

1809.

restitution of his first conquests would not be insisted on; while, to remove all cause of suspicion, the detachment under Sir David Ochterlony could fall back from Ludhiāna to Karnāl, and take up its permanent position at the latter place.[1] But the British commander represented the advantage of keeping the force where it was; his Government assented to its detention, at least for a time, and Ludhiāna thus continued uninterruptedly to form a station for British troops.[2]

Ranjīt Singh yields;

In the beginning of February 1809, Sir David Ochterlony had issued a proclamation declaring the Cis-Sutlej states to be under British protection, and that any aggressions of the Chief of Lahore would be resisted with arms.[3] Ranjīt Singh then perceived that the British authorities were in earnest, and the fear struck him that the still independent leaders of the Punjab might likewise tender their allegiance and have it accepted. All chance of empire would thus be lost, and he prudently made up his mind without further delay. He withdrew his troops as required, he relinquished his last acquisitions, and at Amritsar, on the 25th April, 1809, the now single Chief of Lahore signed a treaty which left him the master of the tracts he had originally occupied to the south of the Sutlej, but confined his ambition for the future to the north and westward of that river.[4]

and enters into a formal treaty, 25th April, 1809.

The terms of Sikh dependence and of English supremacy in Sirhind.

The Sikh, and the few included Hindu and Muhammadan chiefs, between the Sutlej and Jumna, having been taken under British protection, it became necessary to define the terms on which they were secured from foreign danger. Sir David Ochterlony observed,[5] that when the chiefs first sought protection, their jealousy of the English would have yielded to their fears of Ranjīt Singh, and they would have agreed to any conditions proposed, including a regular tribute. But their first overtures had been rejected, and

[1] Government to Sir David Ochterlony, 30th Jan., 6th Feb., and 13th March, 1809.

[2] Sir David Ochterlony to Government, 6th May, 1809, and Government to Sir David Ochterlony, 13th June, 1809.

[3] See Appendix XXIV.

[4] See the treaty itself, Appendix XXV. Cf. Murray, *Ranjīt Singh*, pp. 67, 68.

[5] Sir David Ochterlony to Government, 17th March, 1809.

1809.

Sir David Ochterlony shows that the English regarded themselves alone in offering protection.

the mission to Lahore had taught them to regard *their* defence as a secondary object, and to think that *English* apprehensions of remote foreigners had saved *them* from the arbiter of the Punjab. Protection, indeed, had become no longer a matter of choice; they must have accepted it, or they would have been treated as enemies.[1] Wherefore, continued Sir David, the chiefs expected that the protection would be gratuitous. The Government, on its part, was inclined to be liberal to its new dependants, and finally a proclamation was issued on the 3rd May, 1809, guaranteeing the chiefs of 'Sirhind and Mālwā' against the power of Ranjīt Singh, leaving them absolute in their own territories exempting them from tribute, but requiring assistance in time of war, and making some minor provisions which need not be recapitulated.[2]

The relations of the protected chiefs among themselves.

No sooner were the chiefs relieved of their fears of Ranjīt Singh, than the more turbulent began to prey upon one another, or upon their weaker neighbours; and, although the Governor-General had not wished them to consider themselves as in absolute subjection to the British power,[3] Mr. Metcalfe pointed out[4] that it was necessary to declare the chiefs to be protected singly against one another, as well as collectively against Ranjīt Singh; for, if such a degree of security were not guaranteed, the oppressed would necessarily have recourse to the only other person who could use coercion with effect, viz. to the Rājā of Lahore The justness of these views was admitted, and, on the 22nd August, 1811, a second proclamation was issued, warning the chiefs against attempts at usurpation, and reassuring them of independence and of protection against Ranjīt Singh.[5] Nevertheless, encroachments did not at

[1] See also Government to Resident at Delhi, 26th Dec., 1808. Baron Hügel (*Travels*, p. 279) likewise attributes the interference of the English, in part at least, to selfishness, but with him the motive was the petty desire of benefiting by escheats, which the dissipated character of the chiefs was likely to render speedy and numerous! This appetite for morsels of territory, however, really arose at a subsequent date, and did not move the English in 1809.

[2] See Appendix XXVI.

[3] Government to Sir David Ochterlony, 10th April, 1809.

[4] Mr. Metcalfe to Government, 17th June, 1809.

[5] See the proclamation, Appendix XXVII.

1809–18. once cease, and the Jodh Singh Kalsia, who avoided giving in his adhesion to the British Government on the advance of Sir David Ochterlony, required to have troops sent against him in 1818 to compel the surrender of tracts which he had forcibly seized.[1]

Perplexities of British authorities regarding the rights of supremacy, and the operation of international laws.

The history of the southern or Mālwā Sikhs need not be continued, although it presents many points of interest to the general reader, as well as to the student and to those concerned in the administration of India. The British functionaries soon became involved in intricate questions about interference between equal chiefs, and between chiefs and their confederates or dependants; they laboured to reconcile the Hindu laws of inheritance with the varied customs of different races, and with the alleged family usages of peasants suddenly become princes. They had to decide on questions of escheat, and being strongly impressed with the superiority of British municipal rule, and with the undoubted claim of the paramount to some benefit in return for the protection it afforded, they strove to prove that collateral heirs had a limited right only, and that exemption from tribute necessarily implied an enlarged liability to confiscation. They had to define the common boundary of the Sikh states and of British rule, and they were prone to show, after the manner of Ranjīt Singh, that the present possession of a principal town gave a right to all the villages which had ever been attached to it as the seat of a local authority, and that all waste lands belonged to the supreme power, although the dependant might have last possessed them in sovereignty and intermediately brought them under the plough. They had to exercise a paramount municipal control, and in the surrender of criminals, and in the demand

[1] Resident at Delhi to Agent at Ambāla, 27th Oct., 1818, mulcting the chief in the military expenses incurred, 65,000 rupees. The head of the family, Jodh Singh, had recently returned with Ranjīt Singh's army from the capture of Multān, and he was always treated with consideration by the Mahārājā; and, bearing in mind the different views taken by dependent Sikhs and governing English, of rights of succession, he had fair grounds of dissatisfaction. He claimed to be the head of the 'Krora Singhia' Misal, and to be the heir of all childless feudatories. The British Government, however, made itself the valid or efficient head of the confederacy.

1809–18.

for compensation for property stolen from British subjects, the original arbitrary nature of the decisions enforced has not yet been entirely replaced by rules of reciprocity. But the government of a large empire will always be open to obloquy, and liable to misconception, from the acts of officious and ill-judging servants, who think that they best serve the complicated interests of their own rulers by lessening the material power of others, and that any advantage they may seem to have gained for the state they obey will surely promote their own objects. Nor, in such matters, are servants alone to blame, and the whole system of internal government in India requires to be remodelled and made the subject of a legislation at once wise, considerate, and comprehensive. In the Sikh states ignorance has been the main cause of mistakes and heart-burnings, and in 1818 Sir David Ochterlony frankly owned to the Marquis of Hastings[1] that his proclamation of 1809 had been based on an erroneous idea. He thought that a few great chiefs only existed between the Sutlej and Jumna, and that on them would devolve the maintenance of order; whereas he found that the dissolution of the 'Misals', faulty as was their formation, had almost thrown the Sikhs back upon the individual independence of the times of Ahmad Shāh. Both in considering the relation of the chiefs to one another, and their relation collectively to the British Government, too little regard was perhaps had to the peculiar circumstances of the Sikh people. They were in a state of progression among races as barbarous as themselves, when suddenly the colossal power of England arrested them, and required the exercise of political moderation and the practice of a just morality from men ignorant alike of despotic control and of regulated freedom.[2]

Sir David Ochterlony's frank admission of the false basis of his original policy.

[1] In a private communication, dated 17th May, 1818.

[2] In the Sikh States on either side of the Sutlej, the British Government was long fortunate in being represented by such men as Capt Murray and Mr. Clerk, Sir David Ochterlony, and Lieut.-Col. Wade—so different from one another, and yet so useful to one common purpose of good for the English power. These men, by their personal character or influence, added to the general reputation of their countrymen, and they gave adaptation and flexibility to the rigid unsympathizing nature of a foreign and civilized supremacy. Sir

1809–18. David Ochterlony will long live in the memory of the people of Northern India as one of the greatest of the conquering English chiefs; and he was among the very last of the British leaders who endeared himself both to the army which followed him and to the princes who bowed before the colossal power of his race.

Nevertheless, the best of subordinate authorities, immersed in details and occupied with local affairs, are liable to be biassed by views which promise immediate and special advantage. They can seldom be more than upright or dexterous administrators, and they can still more rarely be men whose minds have been enlarged by study and reflexion as well as by actual experience of the world. Thus the ablest but too often resemble merely the practical man of the moment; while the supreme authority, especially when absent from his councillors and intent upon some great undertaking, is of necessity dependent mainly upon the local representatives of the Government, whose notions must inevitably be partial or one-sided, for good, indeed, as well as for evil. The author has thus, even during his short service, seen many reasons to be thankful that there is a remote deliberative or corrective body, which can survey things through an atmosphere cleared of mists, and which can judge of measures with reference both to the universal principles of justice and statesmanship, and to their particular bearing on the English supremacy in India, which should be characterized by certainty and consistency of operation, and tempered by a spirit of forbearance and adaptation.

CHAPTER VI

FROM THE SUPREMACY OF RANJĪT SINGH TO THE REDUCTION OF MULTĀN, KASHMĪR, AND PESHĀWAR

1809—1823-4

Mutual distrust of Ranjīt Singh and the English gradually removed—Ranjīt Singh and the Gurkhas—Ranjīt Singh and the ex-kings of Kābul—Ranjīt Singh and Fateh Khān, the Kābul Wazīr—Ranjīt Singh and Shāh Shujā each fail against Kashmīr—Fateh Khān put to death—Ranjīt Singh captures Multān, overruns Peshāwar, occupies Kashmīr, and annexes the 'Derajāt' of the Indus to his dominions—The Afghāns defeated, and Peshāwar brought regularly under tribute—Death of Muhammad Azīm Khān of Kābul, and of Sansār Chand of Katōtch—Ranjīt Singh's power consolidated—Shāh Shujā's expedition of 1818–21—Appa Sāhib of Nagpur—The traveller Moorcroft—Ranjīt Singh's Government—The Sikh Army—The Sikhs and other military tribes—French officers—Ranjīt Singh's family—Ranjīt Singh's failings and Sikh vices—Ranjīt Singh's personal favourites and trusted servants.

1809.

The English suspicious of Ranjīt Singh, notwithstanding their joint treaty;

A TREATY of peace and friendship was thus formed between Ranjīt Singh and the English Government; but confidence is a plant of slow growth, and doubt and suspicion are not always removed by formal protestations. While arrangements were pending with the Mahārājā, the British authorities were assured that he had made propositions to Sindhia;[1] agents from Gwalior, from Holkar, and from Amīr Khān,[2] continued to show themselves for years at Lahore, and their masters long dwelt on the hope that the tribes of the Punjab and of the Deccan might yet be united against the stranger conquerors. It was further believed by the English rulers that Ranjīt Singh was anxiously trying to induce the Sikhs of Sirhind to throw off their allegiance,

[1] Resident at Delhi to Sir David Ochterlony, 28th June, 1809.

[2] Sir D. Ochterlony to Government, 15th Oct., 1809; 5th, 6th, and 7th Dec, 1809; and 5th and 30th Jan., and 22nd Aug., 1810.

1809–11.

and to join him and Holkar against their protectors.[1] Other special instances might also be quoted, and Sir David Ochterlony even thought it prudent to lay in supplies and to throw up defensive lines at Ludhiāna.[2] Ranjīt Singh had likewise *his* suspicions, but they were necessarily expressed in ambiguous terms, and were rather to be deduced from his acts and correspondence, and from a consideration of his position, than to be looked for in overt statements or remonstrances. By degrees the apprehensions of the two governments mutually vanished, and, while Ranjīt Singh felt he could freely exercise his ambition beyond the Sutlej, the English were persuaded he would not embroil himself with its restless allies in the south, so long as he had occupation elsewhere. In 1811 presents were exchanged between the Governor-General and the Mahārājā,[3] and during the following year Sir David Ochterlony became his guest at the marriage of his son, Kharak Singh,[4] and from that period until within a year of the late war, the rumours of a Sikh invasion served to amuse the idle and to alarm the credulous, without causing uneasiness to the British viceroy.

and Ranjīt Singh equally doubtful on his part: but distrust gradually vanishes on either side.

Ranjīt Singh acquires Kāngra, and confines the Gurkhas to the left of the Sutlej, 1809.

On the departure of Mr. Metcalfe, the first care of Ranjīt Singh was to strengthen both his frontier post of Phillaur opposite Ludhiāna, and Gobindgarh the citadel of Amritsar, which he had begun to build as soon as he got possession of the religious capital of his people.[5] He was invited, almost at the same time, by Sansār Chand of Katōtch, to aid in resisting the Gurkhas, who were still pressing their long-continued siege of Kāngra, and who had effectually dispelled the Rājpūt prince's dreams of a supremacy reaching from the Jumna to the Jhelum. The stronghold was offered to the Sikh ruler as the price of his assistance, but Sansār Chand hoped, in the meantime, to gain admittance himself, by

[1] Sir D. Ochterlony to Government, 5th Jan., 1810.

[2] Sir D. Ochterlony to Government, 31st Dec., 1809, and 7th Sept., 1810.

[3] A carriage was at this time sent to Lahore. See, further, Resident of Delhi to Sir D. Ochterlony, 25th Feb., 1811, and Sir D. Ochterlony to Government, 15th Nov., 1811.

[4] Sir D. Ochterlony to Government, 18th July, 1811, and 23rd Jan., 1812.

[5] Cf. Murray, *Ranjīt Singh*, p. 76.

showing to the Gurkhas the futility of resisting Ranjīt Singh, and by promising to surrender the fort to the Nepāl commander, if allowed to withdraw his family. The Mahārājā saw through the schemes of Sansār Chand, and he made the son of his ally a prisoner, while he dexterously cajoled the Khātmāndū general, Amar Singh Thappa, who proposed a joint warfare against the Rājpūt mountaineers, and to take, or receive, in the meantime, the fort of Kāngra as part of the *Gurkha* share of the general spoil. The Sikhs got possession of the place by suddenly demanding admittance as the expected relief. Sansār Chand was foiled, and Amar Singh retreated across the Sutlej, loudly exclaiming that he had been grossly duped.[1] The active Nepālese commander soon put down some disorders which had arisen in his rear, but the disgrace of his failure before Kāngra rankled in his mind, and he made preparations for another expedition against it. He proposed to Sir David Ochterlony a joint march to the Indus, and a separate appropriation of the plains and the hills;[2] and Ranjīt Singh, ignorant alike of English moderation and of international law, became apprehensive lest the allies of Nepāl should be glad of a pretext for coercing one who had so unwillingly acceded to their limitation of his ambition. He made known that *he* was desirous of meeting Amar Singh Thappa on his own ground; and the reply of the Governor-General that he might not only himself cross the Sutlej to chastise the invading Gurkhas in the hills, but that, if they descended into the plains of Sirhind, he would receive English assistance, gave him another proof that the river of the treaty was really to be an impassable barrier. He had got the assurance he wanted, and he talked no more of carrying his horsemen into mountain recesses.[3] But Amar Singh long brooded over his reverse, and tried in various ways to induce the British authorities to join him in assailing

1809.

The Gurkhas urge the English to effect a joint conquest of the Punjab, 1809.

But Ranjīt Singh told he may cross the Sutlej to resist the Nepāl leader, 1811.

Amar Singh Thappa again presses an alliance against the Sikhs, 1813.

[1] Murray, *Ranjīt Singh*, pp. 76, 77. The Mahārājā told Capt. Wade that the Gurkhas wanted to share Kashmīr with him, but that he thought it best to keep them out of the Punjab altogether. (Capt. Wade to Government, 25th May, 1831.)

[2] Sir D. Ochterlony to Government, 16th and 30th Dec., 1809.

[3] Sir D. Ochterlony to Government, 12th Sept., 1811, and Government to Sir D. Ochterlony, 4th Oct. and 22nd Nov., 1811.

1811–15. the Punjab. The treaty with Nepāl, he would say, made all strangers the mutual friends or enemies of the two governments, and Ranjīt Singh had wantonly attacked the Gurkha possessions in Katōtch. Besides, he would argue, to advance is the safest policy, and what could have brought the English to the Sutlej but the intention of going beyond it ?[1] The Nepāl war of 1814 followed, and the English became the neighbours of the Sikhs in the hills as well as in the plains, and the Gurkhas, instead of grasping Kashmīr, trembled for their homes in Khātmāndū. Ranjīt Singh was not then asked to give his assistance, but Sansār Chand was directly called upon by the English representative to attack the Gurkhas and their allies,—a hasty requisition, which produced a remonstrance from the Mahārājā, and an admission, on the part of Sir David Ochterlony, that his supremacy was not questioned; while the experienced Hindu chief had forborne to commit himself with either state, by promising much and doing little.[2]

War between the English and Gurkhas, 1814–15.

Sansār Chand of Katōtch, Ranjīt Singh and the English.

Shāh Shujā expelled from Afghānistān, 1809–10.

Ranjīt Singh felt secure on the Upper Sutlej, but a new danger assailed him in the beginning of 1810, and again set him to work to dive to the bottom of British counsels. Mr. Elphinstone had scarcely concluded a treaty with Shāh Shujā against the Persians and French, before that prince was driven out of his kingdom by the brother whom he had himself supplanted, and who had placed his affairs in the hands of the able minister, Fateh Khān. The Mahārājā was

[1] Sir D. Ochterlony to Government, 20th December, 1813.

[2] Government to Sir D. Ochterlony, 1st and 20th Oct., 1814. Resident at Delhi to Sir D. Ochterlony, 11th Oct., 1814, and Sir David's letter to Ranjīt Singh, dated 29th Nov., 1814.

During the war of 1814 Sir David Ochterlony sometimes almost despaired of success; and, amid his vexations, he once at least recorded his opinion that the Sepoys of the Indian army were unequal to such mountain warfare as was being waged. (Sir D. Ochterlony to Government, 22nd Dec., 1814.) The most active and useful ally of the English during the war was Rājā Rām Saran of Hindūr (or Nālāgarh), the descendant of the Harī Chand slain by Gurū Gobind, and who was himself the ready coadjutor of Sansār Chand in many aggressions upon others, as well as in resistance to the Gurkhas. The venerable chief was still alive in 1846, and he continued to talk with admiration of Sir David Ochterlony and his 'eighteen pounders', and to expatiate upon the aid he himself rendered in dragging them up the steeps of the Himālayas.

1809–10.

at Wazīrābād, sequestering that place from the family of a deceased Sikh chief, when he heard of Shāh Shujā's progress to the eastward with vague hopes of procuring assistance from one friendly power or another. Ranjīt Singh remembered the use he had himself made of Shāh Zamān's grant of Lahore, he feared the whole Punjab might similarly be surrendered to the English in return for a few battalions, and he desired to keep a representative of imperial power within his own grasp.[1] He amused the ex-king with the offer of co-operation in the recovery of Multān and Kashmīr, and he said he would himself proceed to meet the Shāh to save him further journeying towards Hindustān.[2] They saw one another at Sāhiwāl, but no determinate arrangement was come to, for some prospects of success dawned upon the Shāh, and he felt reason to distrust Ranjīt Singh's sincerity.[3] The conferences were broken off; but the Mahārājā hastened, while there was yet an appearance of union, to demand the surrender of Multān for himself in the name of the king. The great gun called 'Zamzam',[4] or the 'Bhangī Top', was brought from Lahore to batter the walls of the citadel; but all his efforts were in vain, and he retired, foiled, in the month of April, with no more than 180,000 rupees to soothe his mortified vanity. The Governor, Muzaffar Khān, was by this time in correspondence with the British viceroy in Calcutta, and Ranjīt Singh feared that a tender of allegiance might not only be made but accepted.[5] He therefore proposed to Sir David Ochterlony that the two 'allied powers' should march against Multān and divide the conquest equally.[6] It was surmised that he

Ranjīt Singh's suspicions and plans.

The Mahārājā meets the Shāh, but no arrangement come to, 1810.

Ranjīt Singh attempts Multān, but fails, Feb.–April, 1810;

and proposes to the English a joint expedition against it.

[1] Sir D. Ochterlony to Government, 10th and 30th Dec., 1809.

[2] Sir D. Ochterlony to Government, 7th, 10th, 17th, and 30th Dec., 1809, and 30th Jan., 1810.

[3] Shāh Shujā's 'Autobiography', chap. xxii, published in the *Calcutta Monthly Journal* for 1839. The original was undoubtedly revised, if not really written, by the Shāh.

[4] [Known to all the world as 'Kim's' gun, it now reposes in its last resting-place outside the Central Museum in Lahore.—ED.]

[5] Sir D. Ochterlony to Government, 29th March and 23rd May, 1810. In the latter it is stated that 250,000 rupees were paid, and the sum of 180,000 is given on Capt. Murray's authority. (*Life of Ranjīt Singh*, p. 81.)

[6] Sir D. Ochterlony to Government, 23rd July and 13th Aug., 1810.

1810–12. wanted the siege train of the English, but he may likewise have wished to know whether the Sutlej was to be as good a boundary in the south as in the north. He was told reprovingly that the English committed aggressions upon no one, but otherwise the tenor of the correspondence was such as to lead him to believe that he would not be interfered with in his designs upon Multān.[1]

Shāh Shujā's Peshāwar and Multān campaign, and subsequent imprisonment in Kashmīr, 1810–12.

Shāh Shujā proceeded towards Attock after his interview with Ranjīt Singh, and having procured some aid from the rebellious brother of the Governor of Kashmīr, he crossed the Indus, and, in March 1810, made himself master of Peshāwar. He retained possession of the place for about six months, when he was compelled to retreat southward by the Wazīr's brother, Muhammad Azīm Khān. He made an attempt to gain over the Governor of Multān, but he was refused admittance within its walls, and was barely treated with courtesy, even when he encamped a few miles distant. He again moved northward, and, as the enemies of Mahmūd were numerous, he succeeded in mastering Peshāwar a second time, after two actions, one a reverse and the other a victory. But those who had aided him became suspicious that he was in secret league with Fateh Khān the Wazīr, or, like Ranjīt Singh, they wished to possess his person; and, in the course of 1812, he was seized in Peshāwar by Jahān Dād Khān, Governor of Attock. and removed, first to that fort, and afterwards to Kashmīr, where he remained as a prisoner for more than twelve months.[2]

After the failure before Multān, Ranjīt Singh and his minister, Mohkam Chand, were employed in bringing more fully under subjection various Sikh and Muhammadan chiefs in the plains, and also the hill Rājās of Bhimbar,

[1] Sir D. Ochterlony to Government, 29th March and 17th Sept., 1810, and Government to Sir D. Ochterlony, 25th Sept., 1840. (Cf. Murray, *Ranjīt Singh*, pp. 80, 81.)

[2] Sir D. Ochterlony to Government, 10th Jan. and 26th Feb., 1810, and 27th April, 1812. Shāh Shujā's 'Autobiography', chaps. xxiii–xxv, in the *Calcutta Monthly Journal* for 1839, and Murray, *Ranjīt Singh*, pp. 79, 87, 92.

Shāh Shujā's second appearance before Multān in 1810–11 is given mainly on Capt. Murray's authority, and the attempt is not mentioned in the Shāh's memoirs, although it is admitted that he went into the Derajāt of the Indus, i.e. to Dera Ismail Khān, &c.

1811–12.

Rajaori, and other places. In the month of February 1811, the Mahārājā had reached the salt mines between the Jhelum and Indus, and hearing that Shāh Mahmūd had crossed the latter river, he moved in force to Rāwalpindi, and sent to ascertain his intentions. The Shāh had already deputed agents to state that his object was to punish or overawe the Governor of Kashmīr, who had sided with his brother, Shāh Shujā, then in the neighbourhood of Multān; and the two princes being satisfied, they had a meeting of ceremony before the Mahārājā returned to Lahore, to renew his confiscation of lands held by the many petty chiefs who had achieved independence or sovereignty while the country was without a general controlling power, but who now fell unresistingly before the systematic activity of the young Mahārājā.[1]

Ranjīt Singh meets Shāh Mahmūd, 1811.

In the year 1811, the blind Shāh Zamān crossed the Punjab, and was visited by Ranjīt Singh. He took up his residence in Lahore for a time, and deputed his son Eunus to Ludhiāna, where he was received with attention by Sir David Ochterlony; but as the prince perceived that he was not a welcome guest, his father quitted Ranjīt Singh's city, and became a wanderer for a time in Central Asia.[2] In the following year the families of the two ex-kings took up their abode at Lahore, and as the Mahārājā was preparing to bring the hill chiefs south of Kashmīr under his power, with a view to the reduction of the valley itself, and as he always endeavoured to make success more complete or more easy by appearing to labour in the cause of others, he pro-

The blind Shāh Zamān repairs for a time to Lahore, 1811.

The family of Shāh Shujā repairs to Lahore, 1812.

[1] Murray, *Ranjīt Singh*, p. 83, &c. The principal of the chiefs whose territories were usurped was Būdh Singh, of the Singhpuria or Feizulapuria Misal. See also Sir D. Ochterlony to Government, 15th Oct., 1811.

[2] Murray, *Ranjīt Singh*, p. 87. The visit of the prince was considered very embarrassing with reference to Ranjīt Singh; for Shāh Shujā might follow, and he was one who claimed British aid under the treaty of 1809. It was regretted that the 'obligations of political necessity should supersede the dictates of compassion'; it was argued that the treaty referred to defence against the French, and not against a brother; and the loyal-hearted Sir David Ochterlony was chidden for the reception he gave to the distressed Shāhzāda. (Government to Sir D. Ochterlony, 19th Jan., 1811, and the correspondence generally of Dec. 1810 and Jan. 1811.)

1812–13.

Ranjīt Singh uses the Shāh's name for purposes of his own.

fessed to the wife of Shāh Shujā that he would release her husband and replace Kashmīr under the Shāh's sway; but he hoped the gratitude of the distressed lady would make the great diamond, Koh-i-nur, the reward of his chivalrous labours when they should be crowned with success. His principal object was doubtless the possession of the Shāh's person, and when, after his preliminary successes against the hill chiefs, including the capture of Jammu by his newly married son, Kharak Singh, he heard, towards the end of 1812, that Fateh Khān the Kābul Wazīr had crossed the Indus with the design of marching against Kashmīr, he sought an interview with him, and said he would assist in bringing to punishment both the rebel, who detained the king's brother, and likewise the Governor of Multān, who had refused obedience to Mahmūd. Fateh Khān had been equally desirous of an interview, for he felt that he could not take Kashmīr if opposed by Ranjīt Singh, and he readily promised anything to facilitate his immediate object. The Mahārājā and the Wazīr each hoped to use the other as a tool, yet the success of neither was complete. Kashmīr was occupied in February 1813; but Fateh Khān outstripped the Sikhs under Mohkam Chand, and he maintained that as he alone had achieved the conquest, the Mahārājā could not share in the spoils. The only advantage which accrued to Ranjīt Singh was the possession of Shāh Shujā's person, for the ill-fated king was allowed by Fateh Khān to go whither he pleased, and he preferred joining the Sikh army, which he accompanied to Lahore, to becoming virtually a prisoner in Kābul.[1] But the Mahārājā's expedients did not entirely fail him, and as the rebel Governor of Attock was alarmed by the success of Shāh Mahmūd's party in Kashmīr, he was easily persuaded to yield the fort to Ranjīt Singh. This unlooked-for stroke incensed Fateh Khān, who accused the Mahārājā of barefaced treachery, and endeavoured further to intimidate him by pretending to make overtures to Shāh Shujā; but the Mahārājā felt confident of his strength, and a battle was fought on the 13th July,

Ranjīt Singh meets Fateh Khān, the Kābul Wazīr, 1812;

and a joint enterprise against Kashmīr resolved on.

Fateh Khān outstrips the Sikhs, and holds the valley for Mahmūd, 1813.

Shāh Shujā joins Ranjīt Singh, who acquires Attock;

while Mohkam Chand defeats the Kābul Wazīr in a pitched battle.

[1] Murray, *Ranjīt Singh*, pp. 92, 95; Sir D. Ochterlony to Government, 4th March, 1813; and Shāh Shujā's 'Autobiography', chap. xxv.

1813, near Attock, in which the Kābul Wazīr, and his brother Dost Muhammad Khān, were defeated by Mohkam Chand and the Sikhs.[1] 1813–14.

Ranjīt Singh obtains the Koh-i-nur diamond, 1813–14;

Ranjīt Singh was equally desirous of detaining Shāh Shujā in Lahore, and of securing the great diamond which had adorned the throne of the Mughals. The king evaded a compliance with all demands for a time, and rejected even the actual offer of moderate sums of money; but at last the Mahārājā visited the Shāh in person, mutual friendship was declared, an exchange of turbans took place, the diamond was surrendered,[2] and the king received the assignment of a jāgīr in the Punjab for his maintenance, and a promise of aid in recovering Kābul. Ranjīt Singh then moved towards the Indus to watch the proceedings of Fateh Khān, who was gradually consolidating the power of Mahmūd, and he required Shāh Shujā to join him, perhaps with some design of making an attempt on Kashmīr; but Fateh Khān was likewise watchful, the season was advanced, and the Mahārājā suddenly returned. Shāh Shujā followed slowly, and on the way he was plundered of many valuables, by ordinary robbers, as the Sikhs said, but by the Sikhs themselves, as the Shāh believed. The inferior agents of Ranjīt Singh may not have been very scrupulous, but the Shāh had traitors in his own household, and the high officer who had been sent to conduct Mr. Elphinstone to Peshāwar, embezzled much of the Shāh's property when misfortune overtook him. This Mīr Abdul Hassan had originally informed the Sikh chief of the safety of the Koh-i-nur and other valuables, he plotted when in Lahore to make it appear the king was in league with the Governor of Kashmīr, and he finally threw difficulties in the way of the escape of

and promises aid to Shāh Shujā.

Makes a movement towards the Indus.

Shāh Shujā's distresses.

[1] Murray, *Ranjīt Singh*, pp. 95, 100; Sir D. Ochterlony to Government, 1st July, 1813.

[2] Murray, *Ranjīt Singh*, p. 96, &c.; Shāh Shujā's 'Autobiography', chap. xxv; Sir D. Ochterlony to Government, 16th and 23rd April, 1813, and to the Resident at Delhi, 15th Oct., 1813. The Shah's own account of the methods practised to get possession of the diamond is more favourable than Capt. Murray's to Ranjīt Singh. The Shāh wanted a jāgīr of 100,000 rupees, and one of 50,000 was assigned to him; but effect to the assignment was never given, nor perhaps expected.

1814–16. his master's family from the Sikh capital. The flight of the Bēgums to Ludhiāna was at last effected in December 1814; for Shāh Shujā perceived the design of the Mahārājā to detain him a prisoner, and to make use of his name for purposes of his own. A few months afterwards the Shāh himself escaped to the hills; he was joined by some Sikhs discontented with Ranjīt Singh, and he was aided by the chief of Kishtwār in an attack upon Kashmīr. He penetrated into the valley, but he had to retreat, and, after residing for some time longer with his simple, but zealous, mountain host, he marched through Kulū, crossed the Sutlej, and joined his family at Ludhiāna in September 1816.[1] His presence on the frontier was regarded as embarrassing by the British Government, which desired that he should be urged to retire to Karnāl or Sahāranpur, and Sir David Ochterlony was further discretionally authorized to tell Ranjīt Singh that the ex-king of Kābul was not a welcome guest within the limits of Hindustān. Nevertheless the annual sum of 18,000 rupees, which had been assigned for the support of his family, was raised to 50,000 on his arrival, and personally he was treated with becoming respect and consideration.[2]

The flight of his family from Lahore to Ludhiāna, 1814; April, 1815; and his own escape to Kishtwār. Fails against Kashmīr, and retires to Ludhiāna, 1816.

Shāh Shujā thus slipped from the hands of the Mahārājā, and no use could be made of his name in further attempts upon Kashmīr; but Ranjīt Singh continued as anxious as ever to obtain possession of the valley, although the Governor had, in the meantime, put himself in communication with the English.[3] The chiefs south of the Pīr Panjāl range having been brought under subjection, military operations were commenced towards the middle of the year 1814. Sickness detained the experienced Mohkam Chand at the capital, but he warned the Mahārājā of the difficulties which would beset him as soon as the rains set in, and he almost

Ranjīt Singh attempts Kashmīr and is repulsed, 1814.

1 Murray, *Ranjīt Singh*, pp. 102, 103; Shāh Shujā's 'Autobiography', chaps. xxv, xxvi.

2 Government to Sir D. Ochterlony, 2nd and 20th Aug., 1815, and 14th, 21st, and 28th Sept., 1816. The Wafa Bēgam had before been told that the Shāh's family had no claims to British protection or intervention. (Government to Resident at Delhi, 19th Dec., 1812, and 1st July, 1813.)

3 Government to Sir D. Ochterlony, 29th Oct. and 23rd Nov., 1813.

urged the postponement of the expedition. But the necessary arrangements had been completed, and the approach was made in two columns. The more advanced division surmounted the lofty barrier, a detachment of the Afghān force was repulsed, and the town of Supain was attacked; but the assault failed, and the Sikhs retired to the mountain passes. Muhammad Azīm Khān, the Governor, then fell on the main body of Ranjīt Singh, which had been long in view on the skirts of the valley, and compelled the Mahārājā to retreat with precipitation. The rainy season had fairly set in, the army became disorganized, a brave chief, Mit'h Singh Behrānia, was slain, and Ranjīt Singh reached his capital almost alone about the middle of August. The advanced detachment was spared by Muhammad Azīm Khān, out of regard, he said, for Mohkam Chand, the grandfather of its commander; and as doubtless the aspiring brother of the Wazīr Fateh Khān had views of his own amid the struggles then going on for power, he may have thought it prudent to improve every opportunity to the advantage of his own reputation.[1] 1815–16.

Various chiefs in the hills, and various places towards the Indus, reduced, 1815–16.

The efforts made during the expedition to Kashmīr had been great, and the Mahārājā took some time to reorganize his means. Towards the middle of 1815 he sent detachments of troops to levy exactions around Multān, but he himself remained at Adīnānagar, busy with internal arrangements, and perhaps intent upon the war then in progress between the British and the Nepālese, which, for a period of six months, was scarcely worthy of the English name. The end of the same year was employed in again reducing the Muhammadan tribes south-east of Kashmīr, who had thrown off their allegiance during the retreat of the Sikhs. In the beginning of 1816 the refractory hill Rājā of Nūrpur sought poverty and an asylum in the British dominions, rather than resign his territories and accept a maintenance. The Muhammadan chiefship of Jhang was next finally confiscated, and Leiah, a dependency of Dera Ismail Khān, was laid under contribution. Uch on the Chenāb, the seat of

[1] Murray, *Ranjīt Singh*, pp. 104, 108, and Sir D. Ochterlony to Government, 13th Aug., 1814. Dīwān Mohkam Chand died soon after Ranjīt Singh's return.

1816–18. families of Saiyids, was temporarily occupied by Fateh Singh Ahluwalia, and the possessions of Jodh Singh Rāmgarhia, lately deceased, the son of Jassa the Carpenter (the confederate of the Mahārājā's father), were seized and annexed to the territories of the Lahore government. Sansār Chand was honoured and alarmed by a visit from his old ally, and the year 1816 terminated with the Mahārājā's triumphant return to Amritsar.[1]

Ranjīt Singh captures Multān, 1818.

The northern plains and lower hills of the Punjab had been fairly reduced to obedience and order, and Ranjīt Singh's territories were bounded on the south and west by the real or nominal dependencies of Kābul, but the Mahārājā's meditated attacks upon them were postponed for a year by impaired health. His first object was Multān, and early in 1818 an army marched to attack it, under the nominal command of his son, Kharak Singh, the titular reducer of Jammu. To ask what were the Mahārājā's reasons for attacking Multān would be futile ; he thought the Sikhs had as good a right as the Afghāns to take what they could, and the actual possessor of Multān had rather asserted his own independence than faithfully served the heirs of Ahmad Shah. A large sum of money was demanded and refused. In the course of February, the city was in possession of the Sikhs, but the fort held out until the beginning of June, and chance had then some share in its capture. An Akāli, named Sadhu Singh, went forth to do battle for the ' Khālsa ', and the very suddenness of the onset of his small band led to success The Sikhs, seeing the impression thus strangely made, arose together, carried the outwork, and found an easy entry through the breaches of a four months' batter. Muzaffar Khān, the governor, and two of his sons, were slain in the assault, and two others were made prisoners. A considerable booty fell to the share of the soldiery, but when the army reached Lahore, the Mahārājā directed that the plunder should be restored. He may have felt some pride that his commands were not altogether unheeded, but he complained that they were not so productive as he had expected.[2]

[1] Cf. Murray, *Ranjīt Singh*, pp. 108, 111.

[2] The place fell on the 2nd June, 1818. See Murray, *Ranjīt Singh*,

During the same year, 1818, Fateh Khān, the Kābul Wazīr, was put to death by Kāmrān, the son of Mahmūd, the nominal ruler. He had gone to Herāt to repel an attack of the Persians, and he was accompanied by his brother, Dost Muhammad, who again had among his followers a Sikh chief, Jai Singh Atāriwala, who had left the Punjab in displeasure. Fateh Khān was successful, and applause was freely bestowed upon his measures; but he wished to place Herāt, then held by a member of Ahmad Shāh's family, within his own grasp, and Dost Muhammad and his Sikh ally were employed to eject and despoil the prince-governor. Dost Muhammad effected his purposes somewhat rudely, the person of a royal lady was touched in the eagerness of the riflers to secure her jewels, and Kāmrān made this affront offered to a sister a pretext for getting rid of the man who from the stay had become the tyrant of his family. Fateh Khān was first blinded and then murdered; and the crime saved Herāt, indeed, to Ahmad Shāh's heirs, but deprived them for a time, and now perhaps for ever, of the rest of his possessions. Muhammad Azīm Khān hastened from Kashmīr, which he left in charge of Jabbār Khān, another of the many brothers. He at first thought of reinstating Shāh Shujā, but he at last proclaimed Shāh Ayūb as king, and in a few months he was master of Peshāwar and Ghazni, of Kābul and Kandahār. This change of rulers favoured, if it did not justify, the views of Ranjīt Singh, and towards the end of 1818 he crossed the Indus and entered Peshāwar, which was evacuated on his approach. But it did not suit his purposes, at the time, to endeavour to retain the district; he garrisoned Khairābād, which lies on the right bank of the river, so as to command the passage for the

1818.

Fateh Khān, Wazīr of Kābul, put to death, 1818.

Muhammad Azīm proclaims Shāh Ayūb.

Ranjīt Singh marches to Peshāwar,

p. 114, &c. The Mahārājā told Mr. Moorcroft that he had got very little of the booty he attempted to recover. (Moorcroft, *Travels*, i. 102.) Muhammad Muzaffar Khān, the governor, had held Multān from the time of the expulsion of the Sikhs of the Bhangī 'Misal', in 1779. In 1807 he went on a pilgrimage to Mecca, and, although he returned in two years, he left the nominal control of affairs with his son, Sarafrāz Khān. On the last approach of Ranjīt Singh, the old man refused, according to the Bahāwalpur annals, to send his family to the south of the Sutlej, as on other occasions of siege; but whether he did so in the confidence, or in the despair, of a successful resistance is not clear.

1818–19. future, and then retired, placing Jahān Dād Khān, his old ally of Attock, in possession of Peshāwar itself, to hold it as he could by his own means. The Bārakzai governor, Yār Muhammad Khān, returned as soon as Ranjīt Singh had gone, and the powerless Jahān Dād made no attempt to defend his gift.[1]

which he makes over to Jahān Dād Khān, 1818.

Ranjīt Singh intent upon Kashmīr.

Ranjīt Singh's thoughts were now directed towards the annexation of Kashmīr, the garrison of which had been reduced by the withdrawal of some good troops by Muhammad Azīm Khān; but the proceedings of Desā Singh Majīthīā and Sansār Chand for a moment changed his designs upon others into fears for himself. These chiefs were employed on an expedition in the hills to collect the tribute due to the Mahārājā; and the Rājā of Kahlūr, who held territories on both sides of the Sutlej, ventured to resist the demands made. Sansār Chand rejoiced in this opportunity of revenge upon the friend of the Gurkhas; the river was crossed, but the British authorities were prompt, and a detachment of troops stood ready to oppose force to force. Ranjīt Singh directed the immediate recall of his men, and he desired Sirdār Desā Singh to go in person, and offer his apologies to the English agent.[2] This alarm being over, the Mahārājā proceeded with his preparations against Kashmīr, the troops occupying which had, in the meantime, been reinforced by a detachment from Kābul. The Brāhman, Dīwān Chand, who had exercised the real command at Multān, was placed in advance, the Prince Kharak Singh headed a supporting column, and Ranjīt Singh himself remained behind with a reserve and for the purpose of expediting the transit of the various munitions of war. The choice of the Sikh cavalry marched on foot over the mountains along with the infantry soldiers, and they dragged with them a few light guns; the passes were scaled on the 5th July 1819, but Jabbār Khān

Delayed by a discussion with the English, March 1819.

But finally annexes the valley to

[1] Cf. Murray, *Ranjīt Singh*, pp. 117, 120; Shāh Shujā's 'Autobiography', chap. xxvii; and Munshi Mohan Lāl, *Life of Dost Muhammad*, i. 99, 104.

Capt. Murray (p. 131) places the defection of Jai Singh of Atāri in the year 1822; but cf. also Mr. Masson, *Travels*, iii. 21, 32, in support of the earlier date assigned.

[2] Cf. Murray, *Ranjīt Singh*, pp. 121, 122, and Moorcroft, *Travels*, 110, for the duration of the Mahārājā's displeasure with Desā Singh.

was found ready to receive them. The Afghāns repulsed the invaders, and mastered two guns; but they did not improve their success, and the rallied Sikhs again attacked them, and won an almost bloodless victory.[1] 1819–20. his dominions, 1819.

The Derajāt of the Indus annexed to Lahore, 1819–20.

A few months after Kashmīr had been added to the Lahore dominions, Ranjīt Singh moved in person to the south of the Punjab, and Dera Ghāzi Khān on the Indus, another dependency of Kābul, was seized by the victorious Sikhs. The Nawāb of Bahāwalpur, who held lands under Ranjīt Singh in the fork of the Indus and Chenāb, had two years before made a successful attack on the Durrāni chief of the place, and it was now transferred to him in form, although his Cis-Sutlej possessions had virtually, but not formally, been taken under British protection in the year 1815, and he had thus become, in a measure, independent of the Mahārājā's power.[2] During the year 1820 partial attempts were made to reduce the turbulent Muhammadan tribes to the south-west of Kashmīr, and, in 1821, Ranjīt Singh proceeded to complete his conquests on the Central Indus by the reduction of Dera Ismail Khān. The strong fort of Mankerā, situated between the two westernmost rivers of the Punjab, was held out for a time by Hāfiz Ahmad Khān, the father of the titular governor, who scarcely owned a nominal subjection to Kābul; but the promise of honourable terms induced him to surrender before the end of the year, and the country on the right bank of the Indus, including Dera Ismail Khān, was left to him as a feudatory of Lahore.[3]

Muhammad Azīm Khān desirous of securing Peshāwar, 1818–21;

Muhammad Azīm had succeeded to the power of his brother, Fateh Khān, and, being desirous of keeping Ranjīt Singh to the left bank of the Indus, he moved to Peshāwar in the year 1822, accompanied by Jai Singh, the fugitive

[1] Cf. Murray, *Ranjīt Singh*, pp. 122–4.

[2] Government to Superintendent Ambāla, 15th Jan., 1815, and Sir D. Ochterlony to Government, 23rd July, 1815. Cf. Murray, *Ranjīt Singh*, p. 124. The Bahāwalpur Memoirs state that Ranjīt Singh came down the Sutlej as far as Pākpattan, with the view of seizing Bahāwalpur, but that a show of resistance having been made, and some presents offered, the Mahārājā moved westward.

[3] Cf. Murray, *Ranjīt Singh*, pp. 129, 130, and Sir A. Burnes' *Kābul*, p. 92.

1822–3. Sikh chief, with the intention of attacking Khairābād opposite Attock. Other matters caused him hastily to retrace his steps, but his proceedings had brought the Mahārājā to the westward, who sent to Yār Muhammad Khān, the governor of Peshāwar, and demanded tribute. This leader, who apprehended the designs of his brother, Muhammad Azīm Khān, almost as much as he dreaded Ranjīt Singh, made an offering of some valuable horses.[1] The Mahārājā was satisfied and withdrew perhaps the more readily, as some differences had arisen with the British authorities regarding the right to a place named Whadni, to the south of the Sutlej, which had been transferred by Ranjīt Singh to his intriguing and ambitious mother-in-law, Sada Kaur, in the year 1808. The lady was regarded by the English agents as being the independent representative of the interests of the Kanhayā (or Ghani) confederacy of Sikhs on *their* side of the river, and therefore as having a right to their protection. But Ranjīt Singh had quarrelled with and imprisoned his mother-in-law, and had taken possession of the fort of Whadni. It was resolved to eject him by force, and a detachment of troops marched from Ludhiāna and restored the authority of the captive widow. Ranjīt Singh prudently made no attempt to resist the British agent, but he was not without apprehensions that his occupation of the place would be construed into a breach of the treaty, and he busied himself with defensive preparations. A friendly letter from the superior authorities at Delhi relieved him of his fears, and allowed him to prosecute his designs against Peshāwar without further interruption.[2]

from which Ranjīt Singh demands and receives tribute, 1822.

But the prosecution of his plans interfered with by a discussion with the English about his mother-in-law, and a place called Whadni, 1822.

[1] Cf. Murray, *Ranjīt Singh*, pp. 134–7.

[2] Cf. Murray, *Ranjīt Singh*, p. 134, where the proceedings are given very briefly, and scarcely with accuracy. Capt. Murray's and Capt. Ross's letters to the Resident at Delhi, from Feb. to Sept. 1822, give details, and other information is obtainable from the letters of Sir D. Ochterlony to Capt. Ross, dated 7th Nov., 1821, and of the Governor-General's Agent at Delhi to Capt. Murray, of 22nd June, and to Government of the 23rd Aug. 1822; and from those of Government to the Governor-General's Agent, 24th April, 13th July, and 18th Oct., 1822. On this occasion the Akāli Phūla Singh is reported by Capt. Murray to have offered to retake Whadni single-handed, and Ranjīt Singh to have commissioned him to embody a thousand of his brethren. Sir Claude Wade (*Narrative of Personal Services*, p. 10 note)

Muhammad Azīm Khān disapproved of the presentation of horses to Ranjīt Singh by Yār Muhammad Khān, and he repaired to Peshāwar in January 1823. Yār Muhammad fled into the Usufzaī hills rather than meet his brother, and the province seemed lost to one branch of the numerous family; but the chief of the Sikhs was at hand, resolved to assert his equality of right or his superiority of power. The Indus was forded on the 13th March, the guns being carried across on elephants. The territory of the Khattaks bordering the river was occupied, and at Akōra the Mahārājā received and pardoned the fugitive Jai Singh Atāriwala. A religious war had been preached, and twenty thousand men, of the Khattak and Usufzai tribes, had been assembled by their priests and devotees to fight for their faith against the unbelieving invaders. This body of men was posted on and around heights near Noshahra, but on the left bank of the Kābul river, while Muhammad Azīm Khān, distrustful of his influence over the independent militia, and of the fidelity of his brothers, occupied a position higher up on the right bank of the stream. Ranjīt Singh detached a force to keep the Wazīr in check, and crossed the river to attack the armed peasantry. The Sikh 'Akālis' at once rushed upon the Muhammadan 'Ghazis', but Phūla Singh, the wild leader of the fanatics of Amritsar, was slain, and his horsemen made no impression on masses of footmen advantageously posted. The Afghāns then exultingly advanced, and threw the drilled infantry of the Lahore ruler into confusion. They were checked by the fire of the rallying battalions, and by the play of the artillery drawn up on the opposite bank of the river, and at length Ranjīt Singh's personal exertions with his cavalry converted the check into a victory. The brave and believing mountaineers reassembled after their rout, and next day they were willing to renew the fight under their 'Pīrzada', Muhammad Akbar; but the Kābul Wazīr had fled with precipitation, and they were without countenance or support. Peshāwar was sacked, and the country plundered up to the Khaibar Pass; but

1823.

The Sikhs march against Peshāwar, 1823.

The battle of Noshahra, 14th March, 1823.

Peshāwar reduced, but left as

represents Sir Charles Metcalfe to have considered the proceedings of the English with regard to Whadni as unwarranted—for with the domestic concerns of the Mahārājā they had no political concern.

1823–4. the hostile spirit of the population rendered the province of difficult retention, and the prudent Mahārājā gladly accepted Yār Muhammad's tender of submission. Muhammad Azīm Khān died shortly afterwards, and with him expired all show of unanimity among the bands of brothers who possessed the three capitals of Peshāwar, Kābul, and Kandahār; while Shāh Mahmūd and his son Kāmrān exercised a precarious authority in Herāt, and Shāh Ayūb, who had been proclaimed titular monarch of Afghānistān, remained a cipher in his chief city.[1]

a dependency with Yār Muhammad Khān.

Death of Muhammad Azīm Khān, 1823.

Ranjīt Singh feels his way towards Sind, 1823–4.

Towards the end of the year 1823, Ranjīt Singh marched to the south-west corner of his territories, to reduce refractory Muhammadan Jāgīrdārs, and to create an impression of his power on the frontiers of Sind—to tribute from the Amīrs of which country he had already advanced some claims.[2] He likewise pretended to regard Shikārpur as a usurpation of the Tālpur dynasty; but his plans were not yet matured, and he returned to his capital to learn of the death of Sansār Chand. He gave his consent to the succes-

[1] Cf. Murray, *Ranjīt Singh*, p. 137, &c.; Moorcroft, *Travels*, ii. 333, 334; and Masson, *Journeys*, iii. 58–60. Ranjīt Singh told Capt. Wade that, of his disciplined troops, his Gurkhas alone stood firm under the assault of the Muhammadans. (Capt. Wade to Resident at Delhi, 3rd April, 1839.)

The fanatic, Phūla Singh, already referred to in the preceding note, was a man of some notoriety. In 1809 he attacked Sir Charles Metcalfe's camp, and afterwards the party of a British officer employed in surveying the Cis-Sutlej states. In 1814–15 he fortified himself in Abohar (between Ferozepore and Bhatnair), since construed into a British possession (Capt. Murray to Agent, Delhi, 15th May, 1823); and in 1820 he told Mr. Moorcroft that he was dissatisfied with Ranjīt Singh, that he was ready to join the English, and that, indeed, he would carry fire and sword wherever Mr. Moorcroft might desire. (*Travels*, i. 110.)

With regard to Dost Muhammad Khān, it is well known, and Mr. Masson (*Journeys*, iii. 59, 60) and Munshi Mohan Lāl (*Life of Dost Muhammad*, i. 127, 128) both show the extent to which he was an intriguer on this occasion. This circumstance was subsequently lost sight of by the British negotiators and the British public, and Sikh and Afghān leaders were regarded as essentially antagonistic, instead of as ready to coalesce for their selfish ends under any of several probable contingencies.

[2] Capt. Murray to the Governor-General's Agent, Delhi, 15th Dec. 1825, and Capt. Wade to the same, 7th Aug. 1823.

sion of the son of a chief whose power once surpassed his own, and the Prince Kharak Singh exchanged turbans, in token of brotherhood, with the heir of tributary Katōtch.[1]

1824.

Sansār Chand of Katōtch dies, end of 1824.

Ranjīt Singh had now brought under his sway the three Muhammadan provinces of Kashmīr, Multān, and Peshāwar: he was supreme in the hills and plains of the Punjab proper; the mass of his dominion had been acquired; and although his designs on Ladākh and Sind were obvious, a pause in the narrative of his actions may conveniently take place, for the purpose of relating other matters necessary to a right understanding of his character, and which intimately bear on the general history of the country.

Ranjīt Singh's power consolidated, and the mass of his dominion acquired.

Miscellaneous transactions. Shāh Shujā's expedition against Shikārpur and Peshāwar, 1818–21.

Shāh Shujā reached Ludhiāna, as has been mentioned, in the year 1816, and secured for himself an honoured repose: but his thoughts were intent on Kābul and Kandahār; he disliked the British notion that he had tamely sought an asylum, and he wished to be regarded as a prince in distress, seeking for aid to enable him to recover his crown. He had hopes held out to him by the Amīrs of Sind when hard pressed, perhaps, by Fateh Khān, and he conceived that an invasion of Afghānistān might be successfully prosecuted from the southward. He made offers of advantage to the English, but he was told that they had no concern with the affairs of strangers, and desired to live in peace with all their neighbours. He was thus casting about for means when Fateh Khān was murdered, and the tenders of allegiance which he received from Muhammad Azīm Khān at once induced him to quit Ludhiāna. He left that place in October 1818: with the aid of the Nawāb of Bahāwalpur, he mastered Dera Ghāzi Khān; he sent his son Timūr to occupy Shikārpur, and he proceeded in person towards Peshāwar, to become, as he believed, the king of the Durrānis. But Muhammad Azīm Khān had, in the meantime, seen fit to proclaim himself the Wazīr of Ayūb, and Shāh Shujā, hard pressed, sought safety among some friendly clans in the Khaibar hills. He was driven thence at the end of two months, and had scarcely entered Shikārpur when Muhammad

[1] Murray, *Ranjīt Singh*, p. 141. For an interesting account of Sansār Chand, his family, and his country, see Moorcroft, *Travels*, i. 126–46.

1821–2.

Azīm Khān's approach compelled him to retire. He went first to Khairpur, and afterwards to Hyderābād, and, having procured some money from the Sindians, he returned and recovered Shikārpur, where he resided for a year. But Muhammad Azīm Khān again approached, the Hyderābād chiefs pretended that the Shāh was plotting to bring in the English, and their money was this time paid for his expulsion.

The Shāh returns to Ludhiāna, 1821;

The ex-king, finding his position untenable, retired through Rājputāna to Delhi, and eventually took up his residence a second time at Ludhiāna, in June 1821.

and is followed by Shāh Zamān, who takes up his abode at the same place.

His brother, the blind Shāh Zamān, after visiting Persia, and perhaps Arabia, arrived at the same place about the same time and nearly by the same road. Shāh Shujā's stipend had all along been drawn by his family, represented by the able and faithful Wafa Begum, and an allowance, first of 18,000, and afterwards of 24,000 rupees a year, was assigned for the support of Shāh Zamān, when he also became a petitioner to the English Government.[1]

Appa Sāhib, ex-Rājā of Nāgpur, 1820–2.

In the year 1820, Appa Sāhib, the deposed Rājā of the Marāthā kingdom of Nāgpur, escaped from the custody of the British authorities and repaired to Amritsar. He would seem to have had the command of large sums of money, and he endeavoured to engage Ranjīt Singh in his cause; but the Mahārājā had been told the fugitive was the violent enemy of his English allies, and he ordered him to quit his territories. The chief took up his abode for a time in Sansār Chand's principality of Katōtch, and while there he would appear

His idle schemes with the son of Shāh Zamān.

to have entered into some idle schemes with Prince Haidar, a son of Shāh Zamān, for the subjugation of India south and east of the Sutlej. The Durrāni was to be monarch of the whole, from Delhi to Cape Comorin ; but the Marāthā was

[1] Cf. Shāh Shujā's 'Autobiography', chaps. xxvii, xxviii, xxix, in the *Calcutta Monthly Journal* for 1839, and the *Bahāwalpur Family Annals* (Manuscript). Capt. Murray (*History of Ranjīt Singh*, p. 103) merely states that Shāh Shujā made an unsuccessful attempt to recover his throne; but the following letters may be referred to in support of all that is included in the paragraph : Government to Resident, Delhi, 10th May and 7th June 1817; Capt. Murray to Resident, Delhi, 22nd Sept. and 10th Oct. 1818, and 1st April 1825; and Capt. Murray to Sir D. Ochterlony, 29th April, 30th June, and 27th Aug. 1821.

1822.

to be Wazīr of the empire, and to hold the Deccan as a dependent sovereign. The Punjab was not included; but it did not transpire that either Ranjīt Singh, or Sansār Chand, or the two ex-kings of Kābul, were privy to the design, and, as soon as the circumstance became known, Sansār Chand compelled his guest to proceed elsewhere. Appa Sāhib repaired, in 1822, to Mandī, which lies between Kāngra and the Sutlej; but he wandered to Amritsar about 1828, and only finally quitted the country during the following year, to find an asylum with the Rājā of Jodhpur. That state had become an English dependency, and the ex-Rājā's surrender was required; but the strong objections of the Rājpūt induced the Government to be satisfied with a promise of his safe custody, and he died almost forgotten in the year 1840.[1]

The petty ex-chief of Nūrpur causes Ranjīt Singh some anxiety owing to his resort to the English.

As has been mentioned, the Rājā Bīr Singh, of Nūrpur, in the hills, had been dispossessed of his chiefship in the year 1816. He sought refuge to the south of the Sutlej, and immediately made proposals to Shāh Shujā, who had just reached Ludhiāna, to enter into a combination against Ranjīt Singh. The Mahārājā had not altogether despised similar tenders of allegiance from various discontented chiefs, when the Shāh was his prisoner-guest in Lahore; he remembered the treaty between the Shāh and the English, and he knew how readily dethroned kings might be made use of by the ambitious. He wished to ascertain the views of the English authorities, but he veiled his suspicions of *them* in terms of apprehension of the Nūrpur Rājā. His troops, he said, were absent in the neighbourhood of Multān, and Bīr Singh might cross the Sutlej and raise disturbances. The reception of emissaries by Shāh Shujā was then discountenanced, and the residence of the exiled Rājā at Ludhiāna was discouraged; but Ranjīt Singh was told that his right to attempt the recovery of his chiefship was admitted, although he would not be allowed to organize the

[1] Cf. Murray, *Ranjīt Singh*, p. 126; Moorcroft, *Travels*, i. 109; and the quasi-official authority, the *Bengal and Agra Gazetteer* for 1841, 1842 (articles 'Nagpur' and 'Jodhpur'). See also Capt. Murray, letters to Resident at Delhi, 24th Nov. and 22nd Dec. 1821, the 13th Jan. 1822, and 16th June 1824; and likewise Capt. Wade to Resident at Delhi, 15th March 1828.

1819–20. means of doing so within the British limits. The Mahārājā seemed satisfied that Lahore would be safe while he was absent in the south or west, and he said no more.[1]

The traveller Moorcroft in the Punjab, 1820. In the year 1819 the able and adventurous traveller, Moorcroft, left the plains of India in the hope of reaching Yarkand and Bukhara. In the hills of the Punjab he experienced difficulties, and he was induced to repair to Lahore to wait upon Ranjīt Singh. He was honourably received, and any lurking suspicions of his own designs, or of the views of his Government, were soon dispelled. The Mahārājā conversed with frankness of the events of his life; he showed the traveller his bands of horsemen and battalions of infantry, and encouraged him to visit any part of the capital without hesitation, and at his own leisure. Mr. Moorcroft's medical skill and general knowledge, his candid manner and personal activity, produced an impression favourable to himself and advantageous to his countrymen; but his proposition that British merchandise should be admitted into the Punjab at a fixed scale of duties was received with evasion. The Mahārājā's revenues might be affected, it was said, and his principal officers, whose advice was necessary, were absent on distant expeditions. Every facility was afforded to Mr. Moorcroft in prosecuting his journey, and it was arranged that, if he could not reach Yarkand from Tibet, he might proceed through Kashmīr to Kābul and Bukhara, the route which it was eventually found necessary to pursue. Mr. Moorcroft reached Ladākh in safety, and in 1821 he became possessed of a letter from the Russian minister, Prince Nesselrode, recommending a merchant to the good offices of Ranjīt Singh, and assuring him that the traders of the Punjab would be well received in the Russian dominions—for the emperor was himself a benign ruler, he earnestly desired the prosperity of other countries, and he was especially the well-wisher of that

[1] The public correspondence generally of 1816–17 has here been eferred to, and especially the letter of Government to Resident at Delhi, dated 11th April 1817. In 1826 Bīr Singh made another attempt to recover his principality; but he was seized and imprisoned. (Murray, *Ranjīt Singh*, p. 145, and Capt. Murray to Resident at Delhi, 25th Feb. 1827.) He was subsequently released, and was alive, but unheeded, in 1844.

reigned over by the King of the Sikhs. The person recommended had died on his way southward from Russia; and it appeared that, six years previously, he had been the bearer of similar communications for the Mahārājā of Lahore, and the Rājā of Ladākh.[1] 1821.

Ranjīt Singh's general system of government, and view of his means and authority as leader of the Sikhs.

Ranjīt Singh now possessed a broad dominion, and an instructed intellect might have rejoiced in the opportunity afforded for wise legislation, and for consolidating aggregated provinces into one harmonious empire. But such a task neither suited the Mahārājā's genius nor that of the Sikh nation; nor is it, perhaps, agreeable to the constitution of any political society, that its limits shall be fixed, or that the pervading spirit of a people shall rest, until its expansive force is destroyed and becomes obnoxious to change and decay. Ranjīt Singh grasped the more obvious characteristics of the impulse given by Nānak and Gobind; he dexterously turned them to the purposes of his own material ambition, and he appeared to be an absolute monarch in the midst of willing and obedient subjects. But he knew that he merely directed into a particular channel a power which he could neither destroy nor control, and that, to prevent the Sikhs turning upon himself, or contending with one another, he must regularly engage them in conquest and remote warfare. The first political system of the emancipated Sikhs had crumbled to pieces, partly through its own defects, partly owing to its contact with a well-ordered and civilized government, and partly in consequence of the ascendancy of one superior mind. The 'Misals' had vanished, or were only represented by Ahluwalia and Patiāla (or Phūlkīa), the one depending on the personal friendship of Ranjīt Singh for its chief, and the other upheld in separate portions by the expediency of the English. But Ranjīt Singh never thought his own or the Sikh sway was to be confined to the Punjab, and his only wish was to lead armies as far as faith in the Khālsa and confidence in his skill would take brave and believing men. He troubled himself not at all with the theory or the practical niceties of administration, and he

[1] Moorcroft, *Travels*, i. 99, 103; and see also pp. 383, 387, with respect to a previous letter to Ranjīt Singh.

1821. would rather have added a province to his rule than have received the assurances of his English neighbours that he legislated with discrimination in commercial affairs and with a just regard for the amelioration of his ignorant and fanatical subjects of various persuasions. He took from the land as much as it could readily yield, and he took from merchants as much as they could profitably give; he put down open marauding; the Sikh peasantry enjoyed a light assessment; no local officer dared to oppress a member of the Khālsa; and if elsewhere the farmers of revenue were resisted in their tyrannical proceedings, they were more likely to be changed than to be supported by battalions. He did not ordinarily punish men who took redress into their own hands, for which, indeed, his subordinates were prepared, and which they guarded against as they could. The whole wealth and the whole energies of the people were devoted to war, and to the preparation of military means and equipment. The system is that common to all feudal governments, and it gives much scope to individual ambition, and tends to produce independence of character. It suited the mass of the Sikh population; they had ample employment, they loved contention, and they were pleased that city after city admitted the supremacy of the Khālsa and enabled them to enrich their families. But Ranjīt Singh never arrogated to himself the title or the powers of despot or tyrant. He was assiduous in his devotions; he honoured men of reputed sanctity, and enabled them to practise an enlarged charity; he attributed every success to the favour of God, and he styled himself and people collectively the 'Khālsa', or commonwealth of Gobind. Whether in walking barefooted to make his obeisance to a collateral representative of his prophets, or in rewarding a soldier distinguished by that symbol of his faith, a long and ample beard, or in restraining the excesses of the fanatical Akālis, or in beating an army and acquiring a province, his own name and his own motives were kept carefully concealed, and everything was done for the sake of the Gurū, for the advantage of the Khālsa, and in the name of the Lord.[1]

[1] Ranjīt Singh, in writing or in talking of his government, always used the term 'Khālsa'. On his seal he wrote, as any Sikh usually writes, his name, with the prefix 'Akāl Sahai', that is, for instance,

1822.

The Sikh army.

Arrival of French officers at Lahore, 1822.

In the year 1822 the French Generals, Ventura and Allard, reached Lahore by way of Persia and Afghānistān, and, after some little hesitation, they were employed and treated with distinction.[1] It has been usual to attribute the superiority of the Sikh army to the labours of these two officers, and of their subsequent coadjutors, the Generals Court and Avitabile; but, in truth, the Sikh owes his excellence as a soldier to his own hardihood of character, to that

'God the helper, Ranjīt Singh'—an inscription strongly resembling the 'God with us' of the Commonwealth of England. Professor Wilson (*Journal Royal Asiatic Society*, No. xvii, p. 51) thus seems scarcely justified in saying that Ranjīt Singh deposed Nānak and Gobind, and the supreme ruler of the universe, and held himself to be the impersonation of the Khālsa!

With respect to the abstract excellence or moderation, or the practical efficiency or suitableness of the Sikh government, opinions will always differ, as they will about all other governments. It is not simply an unmeaning truism to say that the Sikh government suited the Sikhs well, for such a degree of fitness is one of the ends of all governments of ruling classes, and the adaptation has thus a degree of positive merit. In judging of *individuals*, moreover, the extent and the peculiarities of the civilization of their times should be remembered, and the present condition of the Punjab shows a combination of the characteristics of rising mediaeval Europe and of the decaying Byzantine empire—semi-barbarous in either light, but possessed at once of a native youthful vigour, and of an extraneous knowledge of many of the arts which adorn life in the most advanced stages of society.

The fact, again, that a city like Amritsar is the creation of the Sikhs at once refutes many charges of oppression or misgovernment, and Col. Francklin only repeats the general opinion of the time when he says (*Life of Shāh Alam*, p. 77) that the lands under Sikh rule were cultivated with great assiduity. Mr. Masson could hear of no complaints in Multān (*Journeys*, i. 30, 398), and although Moorcroft notices the depressed condition of the Kashmīrīs (*Travels*, i. 123) he does not notice the circumstance of a grievous famine having occurred shortly before his visit, which drove thousands of the people to the plains of India, and he forgets that the valley had been under the sway of Afghān adventurers for many years, the severity of whose rule is noticed by Forster (*Travels*, ii. 26, &c.). The ancestors of the numerous families of Kashmīrī Brāhmans, now settled in Delhi, Lucknow, &c., were likewise refugees from Afghān oppression; and it is curious that the consolidation of Ranjīt Singh's power should have induced several of these families to repair to the Punjab, and even to return to their original country. This, notwithstanding the Hinduism of the Sikh faith, is still somewhat in favour of Sikh rule.

[1] Murray, *Ranjīt Singh*, p. 131, &c.

1822

Excellences of the Sikhs as soldiers. Characteristics of Rājpūts and Pathāns, of Marāthās, and of Gurkhas.

spirit of adaptation which distinguishes every new people, and to that feeling of a common interest and destiny implanted in him by his great teachers. The Rājpūts and Pathāns are valiant and high-minded warriors: but their pride and their courage are personal only, and concern them as men of ancient family and noble lineage; they will do nothing unworthy of their birth, but they are indifferent to the political advancement of their race. The efforts of the Marāthās, in emancipating themselves from a foreign yoke, were neither guided nor strengthened by any distinct hope or desire. They became free, but knew not how to remain independent, and they allowed a crafty Brāhman[1] to turn their aimless aspirations to his own profit, and to found a dynasty of 'Peshwās' on the achievements of unlettered Sūdras. Ambitious soldiers took a further advantage of the spirit called up by Sivājī, but as it was not sustained by any pervading religious principle of action, a few generations saw the race yield to the expiring efforts of Muhammadanism, and the Marāthās owe their present position, as rulers, to the intervention of European strangers. The genuine Marāthā can scarcely be said to exist, and the two hundred thousand spearmen of the last century are once more shepherds and tillers of the ground. Similar remarks apply to the Gurkhas, that other Indian people which has risen to greatness in latter times by its own innate power, unmingled with religious hope. They became masters, but no peculiar

[1] [The reference is to Nana Farnavis, who became Prime Minister of the Peshwa in 1775 and who died in 1800, having exercised an extraordinary influence over Marāthā politics during his years of ascendancy. 'He had consistently been opposed to the political progress of the English as subversive of Marāthā power, and he objected to the employment of foreign troops under any conditions; but he was faithful to his political engagements, and his devotion to the maintenance of the honour of his own nation is attested by the respect of all his contemporaries. The faithless materials with which he had to deal at the close of his life threw him into intrigues and combinations for his own preservation which would otherwise have been avoided and left him at liberty to continue the able administration he had conducted for twenty-five years' (Meadows Taylor). On the occasion of his death the English Resident at Poona wrote: 'With him has departed all the wisdom and moderation of the Marāthā Government.' See Grant Duff, *History of the Marāthās*, ed. 1826, p. 188.—Ed.]

institution formed the landmark of their thoughts, and the vitality of the original impulse seems fast waning before the superstition of an ignorant priesthood and the turbulence of a feudal nobility. The difference between these races and the fifth tribe of Indian warriors will be at once apparent. The Sikh looks before him only, the ductility of his youthful intellect readily receives the most useful impression, or takes the most advantageous form, and religious faith is ever present to sustain him under any adversity, and to assure him of an ultimate triumph. 1822.

Aversion of the older military tribes of India to regular discipline, with the exception of the Gurkhas, and partially of the Muhammadans.

The Rājpūt and Pathān will fight as Pirthī Raj and Jenghiz Khān waged war; they will ride on horses in tumultuous array, and they will wield a sword and spear with individual dexterity: but neither of these cavaliers will deign to stand in regular ranks and to handle the musket of the infantry soldier, although the Muhammadan has always been a brave and skilful server of heavy cannon. The Marāthā is equally averse to the European system of warfare, and the less stiffened Gurkha has only had the power or the opportunity of forming battalions of footmen, unsupported by an active cavalry and a trained artillery.

The Sikh forces originally composed of horsemen armed with matchlocks.

The early force of the Sikhs was composed of horsemen, but they seem intuitively to have adopted the new and formidable matchlock of recent times, instead of their ancestral bows, and the spear common to every nation.

Notices of the Sikh troops, by Forster, 1783; by Malcolm, 1805; and by Ochterlony, 1810.

Mr. Forster noticed this peculiarity in 1783, and the advantage it gave in desultory warfare.[1] In 1805, Sir John Malcolm did not think the Sikh was better mounted than the Marāthā;[2] but, in 1810, Sir David Ochterlony considered that, in the confidence of untried strength, his great native courage would show him more formidable than a follower of Sindhia or Holkar, and readily lead him to face a battery of well-served guns.[3]

Characteristic arms of different races, including th English.

The peculiar arm of the contending nations of the last century passed into a proverb, and the phrase, the Marāthā spear, the Afghān sword, the Sikh matchlock, and the English cannon, is still of common repetition; nor does it gratify the pride of the present masters of India to hear their success attributed rather to the number and excellence of

[1] Forster, *Travels*, i. 332. [2] Malcolm, *Sketch of the Sikhs*, pp. 150, 151.
[3] Sir D. Ochterlony to Government, 1st Dec. 1810.

1822.

The general importance given to artillery by the Indians, a consequence of the victories of the English.

their artillery, than to that dauntless courage and firm array which have enabled the humble footmen to win most of those distant victories which add glory to the English name. Nevertheless it has always been the object of rival powers to obtain a numerous artillery; the battalions of De Boigne would never separate themselves from their cannon, and the presence of that formidable arm is yet, perhaps, essential to the full confidence of the British Sepoy.[1]

Ranjīt Singh labours to introduce discipline;

Ranjīt Singh said that, in 1805, he went to see the order of Lord Lake's army,[2] and it is known that in 1809 he admired and praised the discipline of Mr. Metcalfe's small escort, which repulsed the sudden onset of a body of enraged Akālis.[3] He began, after that period, to give his attention to the formation of regular infantry, and in 1812 Sir David Ochterlony saw two regiments of Sikhs, besides several of Hindustānis, drilled by men who had resigned or

[1] This feeling is well known to all who have had any experience of Indian troops. A gunner is a prouder man than a musketeer: when battalions are mutinous, they will not allow strangers to approach their guns, and the best-dispositioned regiments will scarcely leave them in the rear to go into action unencumbered, an instance of which happened in Perron's warfare with George Thomas. (Major Smith, *Regular Corps in Indian Employ*, p. 24.)

The ranks of the British Army are indeed filled with Rājpūts and Pathāns so called, and also with Brāhmans; but nearly all are from the provinces of the Upper Ganges, the inhabitants of which have become greatly modified in character by complete conquest and mixture with strangers; and, while they retain some of the distinguishing marks of their races, they are, as soldiers, the merest mercenaries, and do not possess the ardent and restless feeling, or that spirit of clanship, which characterize the more genuine descendants of Kshattriyas and Afghāns. The remarks in the text thus refer especially to the Pathāns of Rohilkhand and Hariāna and similar scattered colonies, and to the yeomanry and little proprietors of Rājputāna. [Much of this is of course incorrect and refers to the pre-Mutiny conditions of the Army. With the exception of a few mountain batteries the artillery is now entirely in the hands of British troops. The Brāhman element in the Army has also been greatly reduced. At the present time 63 per cent. of the efficient fighting forces of the Indian Army came from the Punjab.—Ed.]

[2] Moorcroft, *Travels*, i. 102. [The fact of this visit having been made is also borne out by a passage in the Diary of L. Sohan Lāl. The latter was Court Vakil to Ranjīt Singh.—Ed.]

[3] Murray, *Ranjīt Singh*, p. 68.

deserted the British service.[1] The next year the Mahārājā talked of raising twenty-five battalions,[2] and his confidence in discipline was increased by the resistance which the Gurkhas offered to the British arms. He enlisted people of that nation, but his attention was chiefly given to the instruction of his own countrymen, and in 1820 Mr. Moorcroft noticed with approbation the appearance of the Sikh foot-soldier.[3] Ranjīt Singh had not got his people to resign their customary weapons and order of battle without some trouble. He encouraged them by good pay, by personal attention to their drill and equipment, and by himself wearing the strange dress, and going through the formal exercise.[4] The old chiefs disliked the innovation, and Desā Singh Majīthīā, the father of the present mechanic and disciplinarian Lahna Singh, assured the companions of Mr. Moorcroft that Multān and Peshāwar and Kashmīr had all been won by the free Khālsa cavalier.[5] By degrees the infantry service came to be preferred, and, before Ranjīt Singh died, he saw it regarded as the proper warlike array of his people. Nor did they give their heart to the musket alone, but were perhaps more readily brought to serve guns than to stand in even ranks as footmen. 1820.

and at length fully succeeds in making the Sikhs regular infantry and artillery soldiers.

Such was the state of change of the Sikh army, and such were the views of Ranjīt Singh, when Generals Allard and Ventura obtained service in the Punjab. They were fortu-

European discipline introduced into the

1 Sir D. Ochterlony to Government, 27th Feb. 1812.

2 Sir D. Ochterlony to Government, 4th March 1813.

3 Moorcroft, *Travels*, i. 98. There were at that time, as there are still, Gurkhas in the service of Lahore.

4 The author owes this anecdote to Munshi Shāhamat Alī, otherwise favourably known to the public by his book on the Sikhs and Afghāns.

5 Moorcroft, *Travels*, i. 98. Ranjīt Singh usually required his feudatories to provide for constant service, a horseman for every 500 rupees which they held in land, besides being ready with other fighting-men on an emergency. This proportion left the Jāgīrdār one-half only of his estate untaxed, as an efficient horseman cost about 250 rupees annually. The Turks (Ranke, *Ottoman Empire*, ed. 1843, Introd., p. 5) required a horseman for the first 3,000 *aspers*, or 50 dollars, or say 125 rupees, and an additional one for every other 5,000 aspers, or 208 rupees. In England, in the seventeenth century, a horseman was assessed on every five hundred pounds of income. (Macaulay, *History of England*, i, 291.)

1820.

Punjab before the arrival of French officers; whose services were yet of value to Ranjīt Singh, and honourable to themselves.

nate in having an excellent material to work with, and, like skilful officers, they made a good use of their means and opportunities. They gave a moderate degree of precision and completeness to a system already introduced; but their labours are more conspicuous in French words of command, in treble ranks, and in squares salient with guns, than in the ardent courage, the alert obedience, and the long endurance of fatigue, which distinguished the Sikh horsemen sixty years ago, and which pre-eminently characterize the Sikh footman of the present day among the other soldiers of India.[1] Neither did Generals Ventura and Allard, Court and Avitabile, ever assume to themselves the merit of having created the Sikh army, and perhaps their ability and independence of character added more to the general belief in European superiority, than all their instructions to the real efficiency of the Sikhs as soldiers.

Ranjīt Singh's marriages and family relations.

When a boy, Ranjīt Singh was betrothed, as has been related, to Mehtāb Kaur, the daughter of Gurbakhsh Singh, the young heir of the Kanhayā (or Ghani) chiefship, who

[1] For notices of this endurance of fatigue, see Forster, *Travels*, i. 332, 333; Malcolm, *Sketch*, p. 141; Mr. Masson, *Journeys*, i. 433; and Col. Steinbach, *Punjab*, pp. 63, 64.

The general constitution of a Sikh regiment was a commandant and adjutant, with subordinate officers to each company. The men were paid by deputies of the 'Bakshī', or paymaster; but the rolls were checked by 'Mutasaddis', or clerks, who daily noted down whether the men were absent or present. To each regiment at least one 'Granthi', or reader of the scriptures, was attached, who, when not paid by the government, was sure of being supported by the men. The Granth was usually deposited near the 'jhanda', or flag, which belonged to the regiment, and which represented its head-quarters. Light tents and beasts of burden were allowed in fixed proportions to each battalion, and the state also provided two cooks, or rather bakers, for each company, who baked the men's cakes after they had themselves kneaded them, or who, in some instances, provided unleavened loaves for those of their own or an inferior race. In cantonments the Sikh soldiers lived to some extent in barracks, and not each man in a separate hut, a custom which should be introduced into the British service. [The barrack system has been introduced. The whole organization of the Sikh army under Ranjīt Singh is of much interest. Quite recently some research has been initiated and is still in progress upon the Sikh records in the Secretariat at Lahore. The result of this, as far as it concerns the army, will be found in the Appendix, section XXXIX.—Ed.]

fell in battle with his father Mahān Singh. Sada Kaur, the mother of the girl, possessed a high spirit and was ambitious of power, and, on the death of the Kanhayā leader, Jai Singh, about 1793, her influence in the affairs of the confederacy became paramount. She encouraged her young son-in-law to set aside the authority of his own widow mother, and at the age of seventeen the future Mahārājā is not only said to have taken upon himself the management of his affairs, but to have had his mother put to death as an adultress. The support of Sada Kaur was of great use to Ranjīt Singh in the beginning of his career, and the co-operation of the Kanhayā Misal mainly enabled him to master Lahore and Amritsar. Her hope seems to have been that, as the grandmother of the chosen heir of Ranjīt Singh, and as a chieftainess in her own right, she would be able to exercise a commanding influence in the affairs of the Sikhs; but her daughter was childless, and Ranjīt Singh himself was equally able and wary. In 1807 it was understood that Mehtāb Kaur was pregnant, and it is believed that she was really delivered of a daughter; but, on Ranjīt Singh's return from an expedition, he was presented with two boys as his offspring. The Mahārājā doubted: and perhaps he always gave credence to the report that Sher Singh was the son of a carpenter, and Tāra Singh the child of a weaver, yet they continued to be brought up under the care of their reputed grandmother, as if their parentage had been admitted. But Sada Kaur perceived that she could obtain no power in the names of the children, and the disappointed woman addressed the English authorities in 1810, and denounced her son-in-law as having usurped her rights, and as resolved on war with his new allies. Her communications received some attention, but she was unable to organize an insurrection, and she became in a manner reconciled to her position. In 1820, Sher Singh was virtually adopted by the Mahārājā, with the apparent object of finally setting aside the power of his mother-in-law. She was required to assign half of the lands of the Kanhayā chiefship for the maintenance of the youth; but she refused, and she was in consequence seized and imprisoned, and her whole possessions confiscated. The little estate of Whadni, to the south

1807–20.

His wife, Mehtāb Kaur, and mother-in-law, Sada Kaur.

Sher Singh and Tāra Singh, the declared sons of Mehtāb Kaur, not fully recognized, 1807.

Sada Kaur's vexation of spirit and hostile views, 1810.

1802–21.

of the Sutlej, was however restored to her through British intervention, as has already been mentioned.[1]

Kharak Singh born to Ranjīt Singh by another wife, 1802.

Ranjīt Singh was also betrothed, when a boy, to the daughter of Khazān Singh, a chief of the Nakkais confederacy, and by her he had a son in the year 1802, who was named Kharak Singh, and brought up as his heir The youth was married, in the year 1812, to the daughter of a Kanhayā leader, and the nuptials were celebrated amid many rejoicings. In 1816 the Mahārājā placed the mother under some degree of restraint owing to her mismanagement of the estates assigned for the maintenance of the prince, and he endeavoured to rouse the spirit of his son to exertion and enterprise; but he was of a weak and indolent character, and the attempt was vain. In the year 1821 a son was born to Kharak Singh, and the child, Nau Nihāl Singh, soon came to be regarded as the heir of the Punjab.[2]

Nau Nihāl Singh born to Kharak Singh, 1821.

Ranjīt Singh's personal licentiousness and intemperance, in connexion with the vices vaguely attributed to the mass of the Sikh people.

Such were the domestic relations of Ranjīt Singh, but he shared largely in the opprobrium heaped upon his countrymen as the practisers of every immorality, and he is not only represented to have frequently indulged in strong drink, but to have occasionally outraged decency by appearing in public inebriated, and surrounded with courtesans.[3] In his earlier days one of these women, named Mohra, obtained a great ascendancy over him, and, in 1811, he caused coins or medals to be struck bearing her name; but it would be idle to regard Ranjīt Singh as an habitual drunkard or as one greatly devoted to sensual pleasures; and it would be equally unreasonable to believe the mass of the Sikh people as wholly lost to shame, and as revellers in every vice which disgraces humanity. Doubtless the sense of personal honour and of female purity is less high among the rude and ignorant of every age, than among the informed and the civilized; and when the whole peasantry of a country suddenly attain to power and wealth, and are freed from many of the restraints of society, an unusual proportion will necessarily

[1] Cf. Murray, *Ranjīt Singh*, pp. 46–51, 63, 127, 128, 134, 135. See also Sir D. Ochterlony to Government, 1st and 10th Dec. 1810, and p. 160 of this volume.

[2] Cf. Murray, *Ranjīt Singh*, pp. 48, 53, 90, 91, 112, 129.

[3] Cf. Murray, *Ranjīt Singh*, p. 85.

resign themselves to the seductions of pleasure, and freely give way to their most depraved appetites. But such excesses are nevertheless exceptional to the general usage, and those who vilify the Sikhs at one time, and describe their long and rapid marches at another, should remember the contradiction, and reflect that what common-sense and the better feelings of our nature have always condemned, can never be the ordinary practice of a nation. The armed defenders of a country cannot be kept under the same degree of moral restraint as ordinary citizens, with quiet habits, fixed abodes, and watchful pastors, and it is illogical to apply the character of a few dissolute chiefs and licentious soldiers to the thousands of hardy peasants and industrious mechanics, and even generally to that body of brave and banded men which furnishes the most obvious examples of degradation.[1] The husbandman of the Punjab, as of other provinces in Upper India, is confined to his cakes of millet or wheat and to a draught of water from the well; the soldier fares not much better, and neither indulge in strong liquors, except upon occasions of rejoicing. The indolent man of wealth or station, or the more idle religious fanatic, may seek excitement, or a refuge from the vacancy of his mind, in drugs and drink; but expensiveness of diet is rather a Muhammadan than an Indian characteristic, and the Europeans carry their potations and the pleasures of the table to an excess unknown to the Turk and Persian, and which greatly scandalize the frugal Hindu.[2]

1802-21.

[1] Col. Steinbach (*Punjab*, pp. 76, 77) admits general simplicity of diet, but he also makes some revolting practices universal. Capt. Murray (*Ranjīt Singh*, p. 85) and Mr. Masson (*Journeys*, i. 435) are likewise somewhat sweeping in their condemnations, and even Mr. Elphinstone (*History of India*, ii. 565) makes the charge of culpable devotion to sensual pleasures very comprehensive. The morals, or the manners, of a people, however, should not be deduced from a few examples of profligacy; but the Indians equally exaggerate with regard to Europeans, and, in pictorial or pantomimic pieces, they usually represent Englishmen drinking and swearing in the society of courtesans, and as equally prompt to use their weapons with or without a reason.

[2] Forster (*Travels*, i. 333) notices the temperance of the Sikhs, and their forbearance from many enervating sensual pleasures, and he quotes, he thinks, Col. Polier to a similar effect. Malcolm (*Sketch*,

1802–21.

Ranjīt Singh's favourites.

Yet Ranjīt Singh not only yielded more than was becoming to the promptings of his appetites, but, like all despots and solitary authorities, he laid himself open to the charge of extravagant partiality and favouritism. He had placed himself in some degree in opposition to the whole Sikh people; the free followers of Gobind could not be the observant slaves of an equal member of the Khālsa, and he sought for strangers whose applause would be more ready if less sincere, and in whom he could repose some confidence as the creatures of his favour. The first who thus rose to distinction was Khushal Singh, a Brāhman from near Sahāranpur, who enlisted in one of the first raised regiments, and next became a runner or footman on the Mahārājā's establishment. He attracted Ranjīt Singh's notice, and was made Jamadar of the Devni, or master of the entry, about the year 1811. His brother seemed likely to supplant him, but his refusal to become a Sikh favoured Khushal Singh's continuance in power, until both yielded to the Jammu Rājpūts in the year 1820. Gulāb Singh, the eldest of three sons, claimed that his grandfather was the brother of the well-known Ranjīt Deo; but the family was perhaps illegitimate, and had become impoverished, and Gulāb Singh took service as a horseman in a band commanded by Jamadar Khushal Singh. He sent for his second brother, Dhiān Singh, and then, again like the reigning favourite, they both became running footmen under Ranjīt Singh's eye. Their joint assiduity, and the graceful bearing of the younger man, again attracted the Mahārājā's notice, and Dhiān Singh speedily took the place of the Brāhman chamberlain, without, however, consigning him to neglect, for he retained his estates and his position as a noble. Gulāb Singh obtained a petty command and signalized himself by the seizure of the turbulent Muhammadan Chief of Rajauri. Jammu was then conferred in jāgīr or fief upon the family, and the youngest brother, Suchēt Singh, as well as the two elder, were one by one raised to the rank of Rājā, and rapidly obtained an engrossing and prejudicial influence

Khushal Singh, a Brāhman, 1811–20.

The Rājpūts of Jammu, 1820.

p. 141) likewise describes the Sikhs as hardy and simple; but, doubtless, as the power of the nation has increased since these times, luxuries and vicious pleasures have, in numerous instances, followed wealth and indolence.

in the counsels of the Mahārājā, excepting, perhaps, in connexion with his English relations, the importance of which required and obtained the exercise of his own unbiassed opinion. The smooth and crafty Gulāb Singh ordinarily remained in the hills, using Sikh means to extend his own authority over his brother Rājpūts, and eventually into Ladākh; the less able, but more polished, Dhiān Singh, remained continually in attendance upon the Mahārājā, ever on the watch, in order that he might anticipate his wishes; while the elegant Suchēt Singh fluttered as a gay courtier and gallant soldier, without grasping at power or creating enemies. The nominal fakīr or devotee, the Muhammadan Aziz-ud-dīn, never held the place of an ordinary favourite, but he attached himself at an early period to Ranjīt Singh's person, and was honoured and trusted as one equally prudent and faithful; and, during the ascendancy both of Khushal Singh and Dhiān Singh, he was always consulted, and invariably made the medium of communication with the British authorities. The above were the most conspicuous persons in the Lahore court; but the mind of Ranjīt Singh was never prostrate before that of others, and he conferred the government of Multān on the discreet Sāwan Mal, and rewarded the military talents and genuine Sikh feelings of Harī Singh Nalwa by giving him the command on the Peshāwar frontier; while his ancient companion, Fateh Singh Ahluwalia, remained, with increased wealth, the only representative of the original 'Misals', and Desā Singh Majīthīā enjoyed the Mahārājā's esteem and confidence as governor of Amritsar and of the Jullundur Doāb.[1]

1802–21.

Ranjīt Singh's chosen servants.

Fakīr Aziz-ud-dīn.

Dīwān Sāwan Mal.

Harī Singh Nalwa.

Fateh Singh Ahluwalia.

Desā Singh Majīthīā.

[1] Cf. Murray, *Ranjīt Singh*, pp. 84, 113, 125, 147; Munshi Shāhamat Ali's *Sikhs and Afghāns*, chaps. iv and vii; and, with regard to Aziz-ud-dīn and Desā Singh, see Moorcroft, *Travels*, i. 94, 98, 110, &c. Lieut.-Col. Lawrence's work, *The Adventurer in the Punjab*, and Capt. Osborne's *Court and Camp of Ranjīt Singh*, likewise contain some curious information about the Mahārājā's chiefs and favourites; and the author has had the further advantage of referring to a memorandum on the subject, drawn up by Mr. Clerk for Lord Ellenborough. Mohkam Chand has already been alluded to (see *ante*, p. 136), and the Brāhman Dīwān Chand may also be mentioned. He was the real commander when Multān was stormed, and he led the advance when Kashmīr was at last seized. Of genuine Sikhs, too, Mit'h Singh Behrānia was distinguished as a brave and generous soldier.

CHAPTER VII

FROM THE ACQUISITION OF MULTĀN, KASHMĪR, AND PESHĀWAR, TO THE DEATH OF RANJĪT SINGH

1824–39

Changed Relations of the English and Sikhs—Miscellaneous Transactions—Capt. Wade, the Political Agent for Sikh Affairs—The Jammū Rājās—Syed Ahmad Shāh's Insurrection at Peshāwar—The Fame of Ranjīt Singh—The Meeting at Rūpar with Lord William Bentinck—Ranjīt Singh's views on Sindh, and the English Scheme of Navigating the Indus—Shāh Shujā's Expedition of 1833–5, and Ranjīt Singh's Regular Occupation of Peshāwar—Ladākh reduced by Rājā Gulāb Singh—Ranjīt Singh's Claims on Shikārpur and designs on Sindh crossed by the Commercial Policy of the English—The connexion of the English with the Bārakzais of Afghānistān — Dost Muhammad retires before Ranjīt Singh—The Sikhs defeated by the Afghāns—The Marriage of Nau Nihāl Singh—Sir Henry Fane—The English, Dost Muhammad, and the Russians, and the Restoration of Shāh Shujā—Ranjīt Singh feels curbed by the English—The Death of Ranjīt Singh.

1823.

Change in the position of the Sikhs relatively to the English after the year 1823.

RANJĪT SINGH had brought Peshāwar under his sway, but the complete reduction of the province was yet to cost him an arduous warfare of many years. He had become master of the Punjab almost unheeded by the English ; but the position and views of that people had changed since they asked his aid against the armies of Napoleon. The Jumna and the sea-coast of Bombay were no longer the proclaimed limits of their empire ; the Narbadā had been crossed, the states of Rājputāna had been rendered tributary, and, with the laudable design of diffusing wealth and of linking remote provinces together in the strong and useful bonds of commerce, they were about to enter upon schemes of navigation and of trade, which caused them to deprecate the ambition of the king of the Sikhs, and led them, by sure yet unforeseen steps, to absorb his dominion in their own, and to grasp, perhaps inscrutably to chasten, with the cold unfeeling hand of worldly rule, the youthful spirit of social change and religious reformation evoked by the genius of Nānak and Gobind. 1824-5.

In the year 1824, the turbulent Muhammadan tribes on either side of the Indus above Attock arose in rebellion, and the Sikh General, Harī Singh, received a severe check. The Mahārājā hastened by forced marches to that quarter, and again forded the rapid, stony-bedded Indus; but the mountaineers dispersed at his approach, and his display of power was hardly rewarded by Yār Muhammad Khān's renewed protestations of allegiance.[1] In 1825 Ranjīt Singh's attention was amused with overtures from the Gurkhas, who forgot his former rivalry in the overwhelming greatness of the English; but the precise objeet of the Nepālese did not transpire, and the restless spirit of the Sikh chief soon led him to the Chenāb, with the design of seizing Shikārpur.[2] The occurrence of a scarcity in Sind, and perhaps the rumours of the hostile preparations of the English against Bharatpur,[3] induced him to return to his capital before the end of the year. The *Jāt* usurper of the Jumna asked his brother *Jat* of the Rāvi to aid him; but the Mahārājā affected to discredit the mission, and so satisfied the British authorities without compromising himself with the master of a fortress which had successfully resisted the disciplined troops and the dreaded artillery of his neighbours.[4] But about the same time Ranjīt Singh likewise found reason to distrust the possessors of strongholds; and Fateh Singh

Miscellaneous transactions, 1824-5.

Peshāwar.

Nepāl.

Sind.

Bharatpur

[1] Capt. Murray, *Ranjīt Singh*, pp. 141, 142.

[2] Agent at Delhi to Capt. Murray, 18th March 1825, and Capt. Murray in reply, 28th March. Cf. also Murray, *Ranjīt Singh*, p. 144.

[3] [This famous fortress was besieged by the English forces (20,000 men and 100 guns) on 10th Dec. 1825, and fell on 18th Jan. 1826. Its capture made a great impression, as it had been deemed impregnable. The operations were under the direction of Lord Combermere, the Commander-in-Chief who, as Sir Stapleton Cotton, had fought under Wellington in the Peninsula.—ED.]

[4] Capt. Murray to the Resident at Delhi, 1st and 3rd Oct. 1825, and Capt. Wade to Capt. Murray, 5th Oct. 1825. Capt. Wade, however, in the printed *Narrative of his Services*, p. 7, represents Ranjīt Singh as pausing to take advantage of any disasters which might befall the English.

1826. Ahluwalia was constrained by his old brother in arms to leave a masonry citadel unfinished, and was further induced by his own fears to fly to the south of the Sutlej. He was assured of English protection in his ancestral estates in the Sirhind province, but Ranjīt Singh, remembering perhaps the joint treaty with Lord Lake, earnestly endeavoured to allay the fears of the fugitive, and to recall a chief so dangerous in the hands of his allies. Fateh Singh returned to Lahore in 1827; he was received with marked honour, and he was confirmed in nearly all his possessions.[1]

Fateh Singh the Ahluwalia chief.

Ranjit Singh falls sick, and is attended by an English surgeon, 1826.

Towards the end of 1826, Ranjīt Singh was attacked with sickness, and he sought the aid of European skill. Dr. Murray, a surgeon in the British-Indian army, was sent to attend him, and he remained at Lahore for some time, although the Mahārājā was more disposed to trust to time and abstinence, or to the empirical remedies of his own physicians, than to the prescribers of unknown drugs and the practisers of new ways. Ranjīt Singh, nevertheless, liked to have his foreign medical adviser near him, as one from whom information could be gained, and whom it might be advantageous to please. He seemed anxious about the proposed visit of Lord Amherst, the Governor-General, to the northern provinces; he asked about the qualities of the Burmese troops,[2] and the amount of money demanded by the English victors at the end of the war with that people; he was inquisitive about the mutiny of a regiment of Sepoys

Anecdotes.

[1] Resident at Delhi to Capt. Murray, 13th Jan. 1826, and Capt. Murray, *Ranjīt Singh*, p. 144. The old chief had, as early as 1811, desired to be regarded as separately connected with the English, so fearful had he become of his 'turban-brother'. (Government to Sir D. Ochterlony, 4th Oct. 1811.)

The Cis-Sutlej Muhammadan Chief of Mamdot, formerly of Kasūr, fled and returned about the same time as Fateh Singh, for similar reasons, and after making similar endeavours to be recognized as an English dependant. (Government to Resident at Delhi, 28th April 1827, with correspondence to which it relates, and cf. Murray, *Ranjīt Singh*, p. 145.)

[2] [The Burmese War broke out on 24th Feb. 1824 as the result of disturbed relations going back as far as 1818. It lasted till 24th Feb. 1826, when, by the Treaty of Yandabu, the Burmese Government ceded the provinces of Tenasserim, Aracan, and Assam, and paid an indemnity of one million sterling.—Ed.]

at Barrackpore, and he wished to know whether native troops had been employed in quelling it.[1] On the arrival of Lord Amherst at Simla, in 1827, a further degree of intimacy became inevitable ; a mission of welcome and inquiry was sent to wait upon his lordship, and the compliment was returned by the deputation of Capt. Wade, the British frontier authority, to the Mahārājā's court.[2] During the following year the English Commander-in-Chief arrived at Ludhiāna, and Ranjīt Singh sent an agent to convey to him his good wishes ; but an expected invitation to visit the strongholds of the Punjab was not given to the captor of Bharatpur.[3]

1827.

Lord Amherst, the British Governor-General, 1827.

Lord Combermere, the British Commander-in-Chief.

The little business to be transacted between the British and Sikh governments was entrusted to the management of the Resident at Delhi, who gave his orders to Capt. Murray,

Capt. Wade made the immediate agent for the affairs of Lahore, 1827.

[1] Capt. Wade to the Resident at Delhi, 24th Sept. and 30th Nov. 1826, and 1st Jan. 1827. Cf. Murray, *Ranjīt Singh*, p. 145. [The mutiny at Barrackpore was the result of the disinclination of the troops to go on service in Burma. There were three native regiments at this station—26th, 47th, and 62nd—and all of them became disaffected. On 1st Nov. 1824, the 47th broke into open mutiny. English troops were sent to the station, and the 47th were dispersed by artillery and the regiment was struck off the army list. The other two regiments escaped without punishment.—ED.]

[2] Government to Capt. Wade, 2nd May, 1827.

[3] Murray, *Ranjīt Singh*, p. 147. About this time the journeyings and studies of the enthusiastic scholar Csoma de Koros, and the establishment of Simla as a British post, had made the Chinese of Tibet as curious about the English in one way as Ranjīt Singh was in another. Thus the authorities at Gāro appear to have addressed the authorities of Bissēhir, an English dependency, saying, 'that in ancient times there was no mention of the "Filingha" (i. e. Faranghis or Franks), a bad and small people, whereas now many visited the upper countries every year, and had caused the chief of Bissēhir to make preparations for their movements. The Great Lama was displeased, and armies had been ordered to be watchful. The English should be urged to keep within their own limits, or, if they wanted an alliance, they could go by sea to Pekin. The people of Bissēhir should not rely on the wealth and the expertness in warfaring of the English : the emperor was 30 *paktsat* (120 miles) higher than they ; he ruled over the four elements ; a war would involve the six nations of Asia in calamities ; the English should remain within their boundaries ;'—and so on, in a strain of deprecation and hyperbole. (Political Agent Sabāthu to Resident at Delhi, 26th March 1827.)

1827-8. the political agent at Ambāla, who again had under him an assistant, Capt. Wade, at Ludhiāna, mainly in connexion with the affairs of the garrison of that place. When Capt. Wade was at Lahore, the Mahārājā expressed a wish that, for the sake of dispatch in business, the agency for his Cis-Sutlej possessions should be vested in the officer at Ludhiāna subordinate to the resident at Delhi, but independent of the officer at Ambāla.[1] This wish was complied with;[2] but in attempting to define the extent of the territories in question, it was found that there were several doubtful points to be settled. Ranjīt Singh claimed supremacy over Chamkaur, and Anandpur Makhowāl, and other places belonging to the Sodhīs, or collateral representatives of Gurū Gobind. He also claimed Whadni, which, a few years before, had been wrested from him on the plea that it was his mother-in-law's; and he claimed Ferozepore, then held by a childless widow, and also all the Ahluwalia districts, besides others which need not be particularized.[3] The claims of the Mahārājā over Ferozepore and the ancestral possessions of Fateh Singh Ahluwalia were rejected; but the British title to supremacy over Whadni could no longer, it was found, be maintained. The claims of Lahore to Chamkaur and Anandpur Makhowāl were expediently admitted, for the British right did not seem worth maintaining, and the affairs of the priestly class of Sikhs could be best managed by a ruler of their own faith.[4] Ranjīt Singh disliked the loss of Ferozepore, which the English long continued to admire as a commanding position;[5] but the

Discussions about rights to districts south of the Sutlej, 1827-8. Anandpur, Whadni, Ferozepore, &c.

[1] Capt. Wade to Resident at Delhi, 20th June 1827.

[2] Government to Resident at Delhi, 4th Oct. 1827.

[3] Capt. Wade to the Resident at Delhi, 20th Jan. 1828, and Capt. Murray to the same, 19th Feb. 1828.

In the case of Ferozepore, Government subsequently decided (Government to Agent at Delhi, 24th Nov. 1838) that certain collateral heirs (who had put in a claim) could not succeed, as, according to Hindu law and Sikh usage, no right of descent existed after a division had taken place. So uncertain, however, is the practice of the English, that one or more precedents in favour of the Ferozepore claimants might readily be found within the range of cases connected with the Sikh states.

[4] Government to the Resident at Delhi, 14th Nov. 1828.

[5] In 1823 Capt. Murray talked of the 'strong and important

settlement generally was such as seemed to lessen the chances of future collision between the two governments. 1828.

Ranjīt Singh's connexion with the English thus became more and more close, and about the same time he began to resign himself in many instances to the views of his new favourites of Jammu. The Mahārājā had begun to notice the boyish promise of Hīra Singh, the son of Dhiān Singh, and he may have been equally pleased with the native simplicity, and with the tutored deference, of the child. He gave him the title of Rājā, and his father, true to the Indian feeling, was desirous of establishing the purity of his descent by marrying his son into a family of local power and of spotless genealogy. The betrothal of a daughter of the deceased Sansār Chand of Kāngra was demanded in the year 1828, and the reluctant consent of the new chief, Anrudh Chand, was obtained when he unwittingly had put himself wholly in the power of Dhiān Singh by visiting Lahore with his sisters for the purpose of joining in the nuptial ceremonies of the son of Fateh Singh Ahluwalia. The proposed degradation rendered the mother of the girls more indignant perhaps than the head of the family, and she contrived to escape with them to the south of the Sutlej. Anrudh Chand was required to bring them back, but he himself also fled, and his possessions were seized. The mother died of grief and vexation, and the son followed her to the grave, after idly attempting to induce the English to restore him by force of arms to his little principality. Sansār Chand had left several illegitimate children, and in 1829 the disappointed Mahārājā endeavoured to obtain some revenge by marrying two of the daughters himself, and by elevating a son to the rank of Rājā, and investing him with an estate out of his father's chiefship. The marriage of Hīra Singh to a maiden of his own degree was celebrated during the same year with much splendour, and the greatness

Gradual ascendancy of Dhiān Singh, his brothers, and his son, 1820–8.

Proposed marriage of Hīra Singh into the family of Sansār Chand, 1828.

Flight of Sansār Chand's widow and son.

Rājā Hīra Singh's marriage, 1829.

fortress' of Ferozepore having been recovered by Ranjīt Singh, for the widow proprietress from whom it had been seized by a claimant (Capt. Murray to the Agent at Delhi, 20th July 1823), and the supreme authorities similarly talked (Government to Agent at Delhi, 30th Jan. 1824) of the political and military advantages of Ferozepore over Ludhiāna.

1829.

of Ranjīt Singh's name induced even the chiefs living under British protection to offer their congratulations and their presents on the occasion.[1]

Insurrection at Peshāwar under Saiyid Ahmad Shāh Ghāzi, 1827.

History of the Saiyid.

In the meanwhile a formidable insurrection had been organized in the neighbourhood of Peshāwar, by an unheeded person and in an unlooked-for manner. One Ahmad Shāh, a Muhammadan of a family of Saiyids of Bareilly in Upper India, had been a follower of the great mercenary leader, Amīr Khān, but he lost his employment when the military force of his chief was broken up on the successful termination of the campaign against the joint Marāthā and Pindāri powers, and after Amīr Khān's own recognition by the English as a dependent prince. The Saiyid went to Delhi, and a preacher of that city, named Abdul Azīz, declared himself greatly edified by the superior sanctity of Ahmad, who denounced the corrupt forms of worship then prevalent, and endeavoured to enforce attention to the precepts of the Korān alone, without reference to the expositions of the early fathers. His reputation increased, and two Maulais, Ismail and Abdul Hai, of some learning, but doubtful views, attached themselves to the Saiyid as his humble disciples and devoted followers.[2]

His doctrines of religious reform.

[1] Murray, *Ranjīt Singh*, pp. 147, 148, and Resident at Delhi to Government, 28th Oct. 1828.

[2] A book was composed by Mauli Ismail, on the part of Saiyid Ahmad, in the Urdū, or vernacular language of Upper India, at once exhortative and justificatory of his views. It is called the *Takvia-ul-Imān*, or 'Basis of the Faith', and it was printed in Calcutta. It is divided into two portions, of which the first only is understood to be the work of Ismail, the second part being inferior, and the production of another person.

In the preface the writer deprecates the opinion 'that the wise and learned alone can comprehend God's word. God himself had said a prophet had been raised up among the rude and ignorant for their instruction, and that He, the Lord, had rendered obedience easy. There were two things essential: a belief in the unity of God, which was to know no other, and a knowledge of the Prophet, which was obedience to the law. Many held the sayings of the saints to be their guide; but the word of God was alone to be attended to, although the writings of the pious, which agreed with the Scriptures, might be read for edification.'

The first chapter treats of the unity of God, and in it the writer

A pilgrimage was preached as a suitable beginning for all undertakings, and Ahmad's journey to Calcutta in 1822, for the purpose of embarkation, was one of triumph, although his proceedings were little noticed until his presence in a large city gave him numerous congregations. He set sail for Mecca and Medina, and he is commonly believed, but without reason, to have visited Constantinople. After an absence of four years he returned to Delhi, and called upon the faithful to follow him in a war against infidels. He acted as if he meant by unbelievers the Sikhs alone, but his precise objects are imperfectly understood. He was careful not to offend the English; but the mere *supremacy* of a remote nation over a wide and populous country gave him ample opportunities for unheeded agitation. In 1826 he left Delhi with perhaps five hundred attendants, and it was arranged that other bands should follow in succession under appointed leaders. He made some stay at Tonk, the residence of his old master, Amīr Khān, and the son of the chief, the present Nawāb, was enrolled among the disciples of the new saint. He obtained considerable assistance, at least in money, from the youthful convert, and he proceeded through the desert to Khairpur in Sind, where he was well received by Mīr Rustam Khān, and where he awaited the junction of the 'Ghāzis', or fighters for the faith, who were following him. Ahmad

1822–6.

His pilgrimage.

His journey through Rājputāna and Sind, to Kandahār and Peshāwar.

deprecates the supplication of saints, angels, &c., as impious. He declares the reasons given for such worship to be futile, and to show an utter ignorance of God's word. 'The ancient idolaters had likewise said that they merely venerated powers and divinities, and did not regard them as the equal of the Almighty; but God himself had answered these heathens. Likewise the Christians had been admonished for giving to dead monks and friars the honour due to the Lord. God is alone, and companion he has none; prostration and adoration are due to him, and to no other.' The writer proceeds in a similar strain, but assumes some doubtful positions, as that Muhammad says God is one, and man learns from his parents that he was born; he believes his mother, and yet he distrusts the apostle: or that an evil-doer who has faith is a better man than the most pious idolater.

The printed Urdū Korāns are eagerly bought by all who can afford the money, and who know of their existence.

1827-9. marched to Kandahār, but his projects were mistrusted or misunderstood; he received no encouragement from the Bārakzai brothers in possession, and he proceeded northward through the Ghilzai country, and in the beginning of 1827 he crossed the Kābul river to Panjtār in the Usufzai hills, between Peshāwar and the Indus.[1]

Rouses the Usufzais to a religious war.

Saiyid Ahmad Shāh fails against the Sikhs at Akōra, 1827.

The Panjtār family is of some consequence among the warlike Usufzais, and as the tribe had become apprehensive of the designs of Yār Muhammad Khān, whose dependence on Ranjīt Singh secured him from danger on the side of Kābul, the Saiyid and his 'Ghāzis' were hailed as deliverers, and the authority or supremacy of Ahmad was generally admitted. He led his ill-equipped host to attack a detachment of Sikhs, which had been moved forward to Akōra, a few miles above Attock, under the command of Būdh Singh Sindhanwala, of the same family as the Mahārājā. The Sikh commander entrenched his position, and repulsed the tumultuous assault of the mountaineers with considerable loss, but as he could not follow up his success, the fame and the strength of the Saiyid continued to increase, and Yār Muhammad deemed it prudent to enter into an agreement obliging him to respect the territories of the Usufzais. The curbed governor of Peshāwar is accused of a base attempt to remove Ahmad by poison, and, in the year 1829, the fact or the report was made use of by the Saiyid as a reason for appealing to arms. Yār Muhammad

[1] Cf. Murray, *Ranjīt Singh*, pp. 145, 146. About Saiyid Ahmad, the author has learnt much from the 'Ghāzi's' brother-in-law, and from a respectable Mauli, who likewise followed his fortunes, and both of whom are now in honourable employ in the chiefship of Tonk. He has likewise learnt many particulars from Munshi Shāhamat Alī, and especially from Pīr Ibrahim Khān, a straightforward and intelligent Pathān of Kasūr, in the British service, who thinks Ahmad right, notwithstanding the holy neighbourhood of Pākpattan, Multān, and Utch! Indeed, most educated Muhammadans admit the reasonableness of his doctrines, and the able Regent-Begum of Bhopāl is not indisposed to emulate the strictness of the Chief of Tonk, as an abhorrer of vain ceremonies. Among humbler people the Saiyid likewise obtained many admirers, and it is said that his exhortations generally were so efficacious, that even the tailors of Delhi were moved to scrupulously return remnants of cloth to their employers!

was defeated and mortally wounded, and Peshāwar was perhaps saved to his brother, Sultān Muhammad, by the presence of a Sikh force under the Prince Sher Singh and General Ventura, which had been moved to that quarter under pretence of securing for the Mahārājā a long-promised horse of famous breed named Laila, the match of one of equal renown named Kahār, which Ranjīt Singh had already prided himself on obtaining from the Bārakzai brothers.[1]

1830.

But defeats Yār Muhammad, who dies of his wounds, 1829.

Saiyid Ahmad Shāh crosses the Indus, 1830.

The Sikh troops withdrew to the Indus, leaving Sultān Muhammad Khān and his brothers to guard their fief or dependency as they could, and it would even seem that Ranjīt Singh hoped the difficulties of their position, and the insecurity of the province, would justify its complete reduction.[2] But the influence of Saiyid Ahmad reached to Kashmīr, and the mountaineers between that valley and the Indus were unwilling subjects of Lahore. Ahmad crossed the river in June 1830, and planned an attack upon the Sikh force commanded by Harī Singh Nalwa and General Allard; but he was beaten off, and forced to retire to the west of the river. In a few months he was strong enough to attack Sultān Muhammad Khān; the Bārakzai was defeated, and Peshāwar was occupied by the Saiyid and his 'Ghāzis'. His elation kept pace with his success, and, according to tradition, already busy with his career, he proclaimed himself Khalīf, and struck a coin in the name of 'Ahmad the Just, the defender of the faith, the glitter of whose sword scattereth destruction among infidels'. The fall of Peshāwar caused some alarm in Lahore, and the force on the Indus was strengthened, and placed under the

He is compelled to retire, but falls upon and routs Sultān Muhammad Khān, and occupies Peshāwar, 1830.

[1] Cf. Murray, *Ranjīt Singh*, pp. 146, 149. The followers of Saiyid Ahmad believe that poison was administered, and describe the 'Ghāzi' as suffering much from its effects.

General Ventura at last succeeded in obtaining *a* Laila, but that the real horse, so named, was transferred, is doubtful, and at one time it was declared to be dead. (Capt. Wade to the Resident, Delhi, 17th May 1829.)

[2] Capt. Wade to the Resident, Delhi, 13th Sept. 1830. The Mahārājā also reserved a cause of quarrel with the Bārakzais, on account of their reduction of the Khattaks, a tribe which Ranjīt Singh said Fateh Khān, the Wazīr, had agreed to leave independent. (Capt. Wade to Government, 9th Dec. 1831.)

1830–1. The Saiyid's influence decreases.

command of Prince Sher Singh. The petty Muhammadan chiefs generally, with whom self-interest overcame faith, were averse to the domination of the Indian adventurer, and the imprudence of Saiyid Ahmad gave umbrage to his Usufzai adherents. He had levied from the peasants a tithe of their goods, and this measure caused little or no dissatisfaction, for it agreed with their notion of the rights of a religious teacher; but his decree that all the young women of marriageable age should be at once wedded, interfered with the profits of Afghān parents, proverbially avaricious, and who usually disposed of their daughters to the wealthiest bridegrooms. But when Saiyid Ahmad was accused, perhaps unjustly, of assigning the maidens one by one to his needy Indian followers, his motives were impugned, and the discontent was loud. Early in November 1830 he was constrained to relinquish Peshāwar to Sultān Muhammad at a fixed tribute, and he proceeded to the left bank of the Indus to give battle to the Sikhs. The Saiyid depended chiefly on the few 'Ghāzis' who had followed his fortunes throughout, and on the insurrectionary spirit of the Muzaffarābād and other chiefs, for his Usufzai adherents had greatly decreased. The hill 'khāns' were soon brought under subjection by the efforts of Sher Singh and the governor of Kashmīr; yet Ahmad continued active, and, in a desultory warfare amid rugged mountains, success for a time attended him; but, during a cessation of the frequent conflicts, he was surprised, early in May 1831, at a place called Balakot, and fallen upon and slain. The Usufzais at once expelled his deputies, the 'Ghāzis' dispersed in disguise, and the family of the Saiyid hastened to Hindustān to find an honourable asylum with their friend the Nawāb of Tonk.[1]

He relinquishes Peshāwar, 1830; and retires towards Kashmīr, and is surprised and slain, May 1831.

Ranjīt Singh courted by various parties.

The fame of Ranjīt Singh was now at its height, and his friendship was sought by distant sovereigns. In 1829, agents from Baluchistān brought horses to the Sikh ruler, and hoped that the frontier posts of Harrand and Dājal,

[1] Capt. Wade to Resident at Delhi, 21st March 1831, and other dates in that and the previous year. Cf. Murray, *Ranjīt Singh*, p. 150. The followers of the Saiyid strenuously deny his assumption of the title of Khalīf, his new coinage, and his bestowal of Usufzai maidens on his Indian followers.

westward of the Indus, which his feudatory of Bahāwalpur had usurped, would be restored to the Khān.[1] The Mahārājā was likewise in communication with Shāh Mahmūd of Herāt,[2] and in 1830 he was invited, by the Baiza Bai of Gwalior, to honour the nuptials of the young Sindhia with his presence.[3] The English were at the same time not without a suspicion that he had opened a correspondence with Russia,[4] and they were themselves about to flatter him as one necessary to the fulfilment of their expanding views of just influence and profitable commerce. 1831. The Baluchīs. Shāh Mahmūd. The Baiza Bai of Gwalior. The Russians and the English.

In the beginning of 1831, Lord William Bentinck, the Governor-General of India, arrived at Simla, and a Sikh deputation waited upon his Lordship to convey to him Ranjīt Singh's complimentary wishes for his own welfare and the prosperity of his Government. The increasing warmth of the season prevented the dispatch of a formal return mission, but Capt. Wade, the political agent at Ludhiāna, was made the bearer of a letter to the Mahārājā, thanking him for his attention. The principal duty of the agent was, however, to ascertain whether Ranjīt Singh wished, and would propose, to have an interview with Lord William Bentinck, for it was a matter in which it was thought the English Viceroy could not take the initiative.[5] The object of the Governor-General was mainly to give the world an impression of complete unanimity between the two states; but the Mahārājā wished to strengthen his own authority, and to lead the Sikh public to believe his Lord Bentinck, the Governor-General, at Simla, 1831. A meeting proposed with Ranjīt Singh, and desired by both parties for different reasons.

[1] Capt. Wade to the Resident at Delhi, 3rd May 1829, and 29th April 1830. Harrand was once a place of considerable repute. (See Munshi Mohan Lāl, *Journal*, under date 3rd March 1836.) The Bahāwalpur Memoirs show that the Nawāb was aided by the treachery of others in acquiring it. The place had to be retaken by General Ventura (as the author learnt from that officer), when Bahāwal Khān was deprived of his territories west of the Sutlej.

[2] Capt. Wade to Resident at Delhi, 21st Jan. 1829, and 3rd Dec. 1830.

[3] Capt. Wade to Resident at Delhi, 7th April 1830. The Mahārājā declined the invitation, saying Sindhia was not at Lahore when *his* son was married.

[4] Capt. Wade to Resident at Delhi, 24th August 1830.

[5] Government to Capt. Wade, 28th April 1831, and Murray, *Ranjīt Singh*, p. 162.

1831.

dynasty was acknowledged as the proper head of the 'Khālsa', by the predominant English rulers. The able chief, Harī Singh, was one of those most averse to the recognition of the right of the Prince Kharak Singh, and the heir apparent himself would seem to have been aware of the feelings of the Sikh people, for he had the year before opened a correspondence with the Governor of Bombay, as if to derive hope from the vague terms of a complimentary reply.[1] Ranjīt Singh thus readily proposed a meeting, and one took place at Rūpar, on the banks of the Sutlej, in the month of October (1831). A present of horses from the King of England had, in the meantime, reached Lahore, by the Indus and Rāvi rivers, under the escort of Lieut. Burnes, and during one of the several interviews with the Governor-General, Ranjīt Singh had sought for and obtained a written assurance of perpetual friendship.[2] The impression went abroad that his family would be supported by the English Government, and ostensibly Ranjīt Singh's objects seemed wholly, as they had been partly, gained. But his mind was not set at ease about Sind: vague accounts had reached him of some design with regard to that country; he plainly hinted his own schemes, and observed the Amīrs had no efficient troops, and that they could not be well disposed towards the English, as they had thrown difficulties in the way of Lieut. Burnes's progress.[3] But the Governor-General

The meeting at Rūpar, 17th July 1831.

31st Oct. 1831.

Ranjīt Singh's anxiety about Sind.

[1] With regard to this interchange of letters, see the Persian Secretary to the Political Secretary at Bombay, 6th July 1830.

That Ranjīt Singh was jealous, personally, of Harī Singh, or that the servant would have proved a traitor to the living master, is not probable: but Harī Singh was a zealous Sikh and an ambitious man, and Kharak Singh was always full of doubts and apprehensions with respect to his succession and even his safety. Ranjīt Singh's anxiety with regard to the meeting at Rūpar, exaggerated, perhaps, by M. Allard, may be learnt from Mr. Prinsep's account in Murray, *Ranjīt Singh*, p. 162. Col. Wade has informed the author that the whole of the Sikh chiefs were said by Ranjīt Singh himself to be averse to the meeting with the British Governor-General.

[2] Murray, *Ranjīt Singh*, p. 166.

[3] Murray, *Ranjīt Singh*, p. 167. This opinion of Ranjīt Singh about Sindian troops may not be pleasing to the victors of Dabo and Miāni, although the Mahārājā impugned not their courage, but their discipline and equipment. Shāh Shujā's expedition of 1834, nevertheless, served to show the fairness of Ranjīt Singh's conclusions.

would not divulge to his inquiring guest and ally the tenor of propositions already on their way to the chiefs of Sind, confessedly lest the Mahārājā should at once endeavour to counteract his peaceful and beneficial intentions.[1] Ranjīt Singh may or may not have felt that he was distrusted, but as he was to be a party to the opening of the navigation of the Indus, and as the project had been matured, it would have better suited the character and the position of the British Government had no concealment been attempted. 1831.

The scheme of opening the Indus to commerce.

The traveller Moorcroft had been impressed with the use which might be made of the Indus as a channel of British commerce,[2] and the scheme of navigating that river and its tributaries was eagerly adopted by the Indian Government, and by the advocates of material utilitarianism. One object of sending King William's presents for Ranjīt Singh by water was to ascertain, as if undesignedly, the trading value of the classical stream,[3] and the result of Lieut. Burnes's observations convinced Lord William Bentinck of its superiority over the Ganges. There seemed also, in his Lordship's opinion, good reason to believe that the great western valley had at one time been as populous as that of the east, and it was thought that the judicious exercise of the paramount influence of the British Government might remove those political obstacles which had banished commerce from the rivers of Alexander.[4] It was therefore resolved, in the current language of the day, to open the Indus to the navigation of the world.

Proposal made to the Sindians and the Sikhs.

Before the Governor-General met Ranjīt Singh, he had directed Col. Pottinger[5] to proceed to Hyderābād, to negotiate with the Amīrs of Sind the opening of the lower portion of the river to all boats on the payment of a fixed

[1] Murray, *Ranjīt Singh*, pp. 167, 168. The whole of the tenth chapter of Capt. Murray's book, which includes the meeting at Rūpar, may be regarded as the composition of Mr. Prinsep, the Secretary to Government, with the Governor-General.

[2] Moorcroft, *Travels*, ii. 338.

[3] Government to Col. Pottinger, 22nd Oct. 1831, and Murray, *Ranjīt Singh*, p. 153.

[4] Government to Col. Pottinger, 22nd Oct. 1831.

[5] [Afterwards Sir H. E. Pottinger, Bart., first Governor of Hong Kong.—ED.]

1831. toll;[1] and, two months afterwards, or towards the end of

19th Dec. 1831. 1831, he wrote to the Mahārājā that the desire he had formerly expressed to see a steamboat, was a proof of his enlightened understanding, and was likely to be gratified before long, as it was wished to draw closer the commercial relations of the two states. Capt. Wade was at the same time sent to explain, in person, the object of Col. Pottinger's mission to Sind, to propose the free navigation of the Sutlej in continuation of that of the Lower Indus, and to assure the Mahārājā that, by the extension of British commerce, was not meant the extension of the British power.[2] But

Ranjīt Singh's views and suspicions. Ranjīt Singh, also, had his views and his suspicions.[3] In the south of the Punjab he had wrought by indirect means, as long as it was necessary to do so among a newly conquered people. The Nawāb of Bahāwalpur, his manager of the country across to Dera Ghāzi Khān, was less regular in his payments than he should have been, and his expulsion from the Punjab Proper would be profitable, and unaccompanied with danger, if the English remained neutral. Again, Bahāwal Khān was virtually a chief protected by the British Government on the left bank of the Sutlej, and Lieut. Burnes was on his way up the Indus. The Mahārājā, ever mistrustful, conceived that the political status of that officer's observation would be referred to and upheld by his Government as the true and permanent one,[4] and hence the envoy found affairs in process of change when he left the main stream of the Indus, and previous to the interview

He repels the Daudputras from the Lower Punjab, 1831, at Rūpar, General Ventura had dispossessed Bahāwal Khān both of his Lahore farms and of his ancestral territories on the right bank of the Sutlej.[5] Further, Shikārpur formed no

[1] Murray, *Ranjīt Singh*, p. 168.

[2] Government to Capt. Wade, 19th Dec. 1831. It is admitted that the mission, or the schemes, had a political reference to Russia and her designs, but the Governor-General would not avow his motives. (Murray, *Ranjīt Singh*, p. 168.)

[3] Ranjīt Singh's attention was mainly directed to Sind, and a rumoured matrimonial alliance between one of the Amīrs, or the son of one of them, and a Persian princess, caused him some anxiety. (Capt. Wade to Government, 5th Aug. 1831.)

[4] This view appears to have subsequently occurred to Capt. Wade as having influenced the Mahārājā. See his letter to Government, 18th Oct. 1836.

[5] Capt. Wade to Government, 5th Nov. 1831.

1831–2.

part of the Sind of the Kalhoras or Tālpurs; it had only fallen to the latter usurpers after the death of Muhammad Azīm Khān, the wazīr of the titular king, Shāh Ayūb, and it continued to be held jointly by the three families of Khairpur, Mīrpur, and Hyderābād, as a fortuitous possession. Ranjīt Singh considered that he, as the paramount of the Bārakzais of the Indus, had a better right to the district than the Amīrs of south-eastern Sind, and he was bent upon annexing it to his dominions.[1]

and declares his superior right to Shikārpur.

Such was Ranjīt Singh's temper of mind when visited by Capt. Wade to negotiate the opening of the Sutlej to British traders. The Mahārājā avowed himself well pleased, but he had hoped that the English were about to force their way through Sind; he asked how many regiments Col. Pottinger had with him, and he urged his readiness to march and coerce the Amīrs.[2] It was further ascertained that he had made propositions to Mīr Alī Murād of Mīrpur, to farm Dera Ghāzi Khān, as if to sow dissensions among the Tālpurs, and to gain friends for Lahore, while Col. Pottinger was winning allies for the English.[3] But he perceived that the Governor-General had resolved upon his course, and he gave his assent to the common use of the Sutlej and Indus, and to the residence of a British officer at Mithankot to superintend the navigation.[4] He did not desire to appear as if in opposition to his allies of many years, but he did not seek to conceal from Capt. Wade his opinion that the commercial measures of the English had really abridged his political power, when he gave up for the time the intention of seizing Shikārpur.[5]

Ranjīt Singh yields to the English demands, 1832.

Declaring, however, that their commerce interfered with his policy.

[1] This argument was continually used by Ranjīt Singh. See, for instance, Capt. Wade to Government, 15th Jan. 1837.

[2] Capt. Wade to Government, 1st and 13th Feb. 1832.

[3] Capt. Wade to Government, 21st Dec. 1831; and Col. Pottinger to Government, 23rd Sept. 1837.

[4] See Appendices XXVIII and XXIX. A tariff on goods was at first talked of, but subsequently a toll on boats was preferred. From the Himālayas to the sea the whole toll was fixed at 570 rupees, of which the Lahore Government got Rs. 155, 4, 0 for territories on the right bank, and Rs. 39, 5, 1 for territories on the left bank of the Sutlej. (Government to Capt. Wade, 9th June 1834, and Capt. Wade to Government, 13th Dec. 1835.)

[5] Capt. Wade to Government, 13th Feb. 1832.

1833-5.

Shāh Shujā's second expedition to Afghānistān, 1833-5.

The connexion of the English with the nations of the Indus was about to be rendered more complicated by the revived hopes of Shāh Shujā. That ill-fated king had taken up his abode, as before related, at Ludhiāna, in the year 1821, and he brooded at his leisure over schemes for the reconquest of Khorasan. In 1826 he was in correspondence with Ranjīt Singh, who ever regretted that the Shāh was not his guest or his prisoner.[1] In 1827 he made propositions to the British Government, and he was told that he was welcome to recover his kingdom with the aid of Ranjīt Singh or of the Sindians, but that, if he failed, his present hosts might not again receive him.[2] In 1829 the Shāh was induced, by the strange state of affairs in Peshāwar consequent on Saiyid Ahmad's ascendancy, to suggest to Ranjīt Singh that, with Sikh aid, he could readily master it, and reign once more an independent sovereign. The Mahārājā amused him with vain hopes, but the English repeated their warning, and the ex-king's hopes soon fell.[3] In 1831 they again rose, for the Tālpur Amīrs disliked the approach of English envoys, and they gave encouragement to the tenders of their titular monarch.[4] Negotiations were reopened with Ranjīt Singh, who was likewise out of humour with the English about Sind, and he was not unwilling to aid the Shāh in the recovery of his rightful throne; but the views of the Sikh reached to the Persian frontier as well as to the shores of the ocean, and he suggested that it would be well if the slaughter of kine were prohibited throughout Afghānistān, and if the gates of Somnāth were restored to their original temple. The Shāh was not prepared for these concessions, and he evaded them by reminding the Mahārājā that his chosen allies, the English, freely took the lives of cows, and that a prophecy foreboded the downfall of the Sikh empire on the removal of the gates from Ghazni.[5]

The Shāh's overtures to the English, 1827.

His negotiations with the Sindians, 1831; and with Ranjīt Singh, 1831.

The gates of Somnāth and the slaughter of kine.

1 Capt. Wade to the Resident at Delhi, 25th July 1826.

2 Resident at Delhi to Capt. Wade, 25th July 1827.

3 Government to Resident at Delhi, 12th June 1829.

4 Capt. Wade to Government, 9th Sept. 1831.

5 Capt. Wade to Government, 21st Nov. 1831.—Considering the ridicule occasioned by the subsequent removal by the English of these traditional gates, it may gratify the approvers and originators

In 1832 a rumoured advance of the Persians against Herāt gave further encouragement to Shāh Shujā in his designs.[1] The perplexed Amīrs of Sind offered him assistance if he would relinquish his supremacy, and the Shāh promised acquiescence if he succeeded.[2] To Ranjīt Singh the Shāh offered to waive his right to Peshāwar and other districts beyond the Indus, and also to give an acquittance for the Koh-i-nur diamond, in return for assistance in men and money. The Mahārājā was doubtful what to do; he was willing to secure an additional title to Peshāwar, but he was apprehensive of the Shāh's designs, should the expedition be successful.[3] He wished, moreover, to know the precise views of the English, and he therefore proposed that they should be parties to any engagement entered into, for he had no confidence, he said, in Afghāns.[4] Each of the three parties had distinct and incompatible objects. Ranjīt Singh wished to get rid of the English *commercial* objections to disturbing the Amīrs of Sind, by offering to aid the rightful *political* paramount in its recovery. The ex-king thought the Mahārājā really wished to get him into his power, and the project of dividing Sind fell to the ground.[5] The Tālpur Amīrs, on their part, thought that they would save Shikārpur by playing into the Shāh's hands, and they therefore endeavoured to prevent a coalition between him and the Sikh ruler.[6]

1832.

Further negotiations with the Sikhs and Sindians, 1832.

The Shāh could not come to any satisfactory terms with Ranjīt Singh, but as his neutrality was essential, especially with regard to Shikārpur, a treaty of alliance was entered

The English indifferent about the Shāh's attempts;

of that measure to know that they *were* of some local importance. When the author was at Bahāwalpur in 1845, a number of Afghān merchants came to ask him whether their restoration could be brought about—for the repute of the fane (a tomb made a temple by superstition), and the income of its *pīr* or saint, had much declined. They would carefully convey them back, they said, and they added that they understood the Hindus did not want them, and that of course they could be of no value to the Christians!

1 Government to Capt. Wade, 19th Oct. 1832.

2 Capt. Wade to Government, 15th Sept. 1832.

3 Capt. Wade to Government, 13th Dec. 1832.

4 Capt. Wade to Government, 31st Dec. 1832.

5 Capt. Wade to Government, 9th April 1833.

6 Capt. Wade to Government, 27th March 1833.

1832. into by which the districts beyond the Indus, and in the possession of the Sikhs, were formally ceded to the Mahārājā.[1] The English had also become less averse to his attempt, and he was assured that his annual stipend would be continued to his family, and no warning was held out to him against returning, as had before been done.[2] A third of his yearly allowance was even advanced to him: but the political agent was at the same time desired to impress upon all people, that the British Government had no interest in the Shāh's proceedings, that its policy was one of complete neutrality, and it was added that Dost Muhammad could be so assured in reply to a letter received from him.[3] Dost Muhammad had mastered Kābul shortly after Muhammad Azīm Khān's death, and he soon learnt to become apprehensive of the English. In 1832 he cautioned the Amīrs of Sind against allowing them to establish a commercial factory in Shikārpur, as Shāh Shujā would certainly soon follow to guard it with an army,[4] and he next sought, in the usual way, to ascertain the views of the paramounts of India by entering into a correspondence with them.

but Dost Muhammad Khān is alarmed, and courts their friendship.

The Shāh sets out, Feb. 1833.

Shāh Shujā left Ludhiāna in the middle of February 1833. He had with him about 200,000 rupees in treasure, and nearly 3,000 armed followers.[5] He got a gun and some camels from Bahāwal Khān, he crossed the Indus towards

[1] This treaty, which became the foundation of the Tripartite Treaty of 1838, was drawn up in March 1833, and finally agreed to in August of that year. (Capt. Wade to Government, 17th June 1834.)

[2] Government to Capt. Wade, 19th Dec. 1832.

[3] Government to Capt. Faithful, Acting Political Agent, 13th Dec. 1832, and to Capt. Wade, 5th and 9th of March 1833.

[4] The Bahāwalpur Memoirs state that such a recommendation was pressed by Dost Muhammad on the Amīrs; the belief in the gradual conversion of 'Kothis', or residencies or commercial houses, into 'Chaonis', or military cantonments, having, it may be inferred, become notorious as far as Kābul. Dost Muhammad's main object, however, was to keep Shāh Shujā at a distance; and he always seems to have held that he was safe from the English themselves so long as Lahore remained unshaken. For another instance of the extent to which the English were thought to be identified with Shāh Shujā, see the *Asiatic Journal*, xix. 38, as quoted by Professor Wilson in Moorcroft's *Travels*, p. 340 *n.*, vol. ii.

[5] Capt. Wade to Government, 9th April 1833.

1833–5.

the middle of May, and he entered Shikārpur without opposition. The Sindians did not oppose him, but they rendered him no assistance, and they at last thought it better to break with him at once than to put *their* means into *his* hands for their own more assured destruction.[1] But they were signally defeated near Shikārpur on the 9th January 1834, and they willingly paid 500,000 rupees in cash, and gave a promise of tribute for Shikārpur, to get rid of the victor's presence.[2] The Shāh proceeded towards Kandahār, and he maintained himself in the neighbourhood of that city for a few months; but, on the 1st July, he was brought to action by Dost Muhammad Khān and his brothers, and fairly routed.[3] After many wanderings, and an appeal to Persia and to Shāh Kāmrān of Herāt, and also an attempt upon Shikārpur,[4] he returned to his old asylum at Ludhiāna in March 1835, bringing with him about 250,000 rupees in money and valuables.[5]

Defeats the Sindians, 9th Jan. 1834.

But is routed at Kandahār, 1st July 1834, and returns to Ludhiāna, 1835.

Ranjīt Singh, on his part, was apprehensive that Shāh Shujā might set aside their treaty of alliance, so he resolved to guard against the possible consequences of the ex-king's probable success, and to seize Peshāwar before his tributaries could tender their allegiance to Kābul.[6] A large force, under the nominal command of the Mahārājā's grandson, Nau Nihāl Singh, but really led by Sirdār Harī Singh, crossed the Indus, and an increased tribute of horses was demanded on the plea of the prince's presence, for the first time, at the head of an army. The demand would seem to have been complied with, but the citadel of Peshāwar was nevertheless assaulted and taken on the 6th May 1834.[7] The hollow negotiations with Sultān Muhammad Khān are understood to have been precipitated by the impetuous Harī Singh, who openly expressed his contempt for all Afghāns, and

Ranjīt Singh suspicious of Shāh Shujā. Strengthens himself by regularly annexing Peshāwar to his dominions, 1834.

[1] Capt. Wade to Government, 25th Aug. 1833, and the Memoirs of the Bahāwalpur Family.

[2] Capt. Wade to Government, 30th Jan. 1834.

[3] Capt. Wade to Government, 25th July 1834.

[4] Capt. Wade to Government, 21st Oct. and 29th Dec. 1834, and 6th Feb. 1845.

[5] Capt. Wade to Government, 19th March 1835.

[6] Capt. Wade to Government, 17th June 1834.

[7] Capt. Wade to Government, 19th May 1834.

1832–6.

did not conceal his design to carry the Sikh arms beyond Peshāwar.[1]

20th July 1832.

The Huzara and the Derajāt more completely reduced, 1832–6.

The Sikhs were, in the meantime, busy elsewhere as well as in Peshāwar itself. In 1832 Harī Singh had finally routed the Muhammadan tribes above Attock, and to better ensure their obedience, he built a fort on the right side of the Indus.[2] In 1834 a force was employed against the Afghāns of Tāk and Bannu, beyond Dera Ismail Khān; but a considerable detachment signally failed in an attack upon a mountain stronghold, and a chief of rank and upwards of 300 men were slain. The ill success vexed the Mahārājā, and he desired his agent to explain to the British authorities the several particulars; but lest they should still be disposed to reflect upon the quality of his troops, he reminded Capt. Wade that such things had happened before, that his rash officers did not wait until a breach had been effected, and that, indeed, the instance of General Gillespie and the Gurkhas at Kalanga afforded an exact illustration of what had taken place![3]

Sansār Chand's grandson returns, 1833.

In 1833 the grandson of Sansār Chand, of Katōtch, was induced to return to his country, and on his way through Ludhiāna he was received with considerable ceremony by the British authorities, for the fame of Sansār Chand gave to his posterity some semblance of power and regal dignity. A jāgīr or fief of 50,000 rupees was conferred upon the young chief, for the Mahārājā was not disposed from nature to be wantonly harsh, nor from policy to drive any one to desperation.[4]

Ranjīt Singh sends a mission to Calcutta, 1834–6.

During the same year Ranjīt Singh proposed to send a chief to Calcutta with presents for the King of England, and not improbably with the view of ascertaining the general opinion about his designs on Sind. The mission, under Gūjar Singh Majīthīā, finally

[1] These views of Harī Singh's were sufficiently notorious in the Punjab some years ago, when that chief was a person before the public.

[2] Capt. Wade to Government, 7th Aug. 1832.

[3] Capt. Wade to Government, 10th May 1834. Dera Ismail Khān and the country about it was not fairly brought into order until two years afterwards. (Capt. Wade to Government, 7th and 13th July 1836.)

[4] Capt. Wade to Government, 9th Oct. 1833, and 3rd Jan. 1835.

took its departure in September 1834, and was absent a year and a half.[1] 1833–6.

Ranjīt Singh and Ladākh, 1821.

When Mr. Moorcroft was in Ladākh (in 1821, &c.), the fear of Ranjīt Singh was general in that country, and the Sikh governor of Kashmīr had already demanded the payment of tribute ;[2] but the weak and distant state was little molested until the new Rājās of Jammu had obtained the government of the hill principalities between the Rāvi and Jhelum, and felt that their influence with Ranjīt Singh was secure and commanding. In 1834 Zorāwar Singh, Rājā Gulāb Singh's commander in Kishtwār, took advantage of internal disorders in Leh, and declared that an estate, anciently held by the Kishtwār chief, must be restored. He crossed into the southern districts, but did not reach the capital until early in 1835. He sided with one of the contending parties, deposed the reigning Rājā, and set up his rebellious minister in his stead. He fixed a tribute of 30,000 rupees, he placed a garrison in the fort, he retained some districts along the northern slopes of the Himālayas, and reached Jammu with his spoils towards the close of 1835. The dispossessed Rājā complained to the Chinese authorities in Lassa ; but, as the tribute continued to be regularly paid by his successor, no notice was taken of the usurpation. The Governor of Kashmīr complained that Gulāb Singh's commercial regulations interfered with the regular supply of shawl wool, and that matter was at once adjusted ; yet the grasping ambition of the favourites nevertheless caused Ranjīt Singh some misgivings amid all their protestations of devotion and loyalty.[3]

Ladākh reduced by the Jammu Rājās, 1834–5.

Ranjīt Singh recurs to his claims on Shikārpur, and his designs on Sind, 1835–6.

But Ranjīt Singh's main apprehensions were on the side of Peshāwar, and his fondest hopes in the direction of Sind. The defeat which the Amīrs had sustained diminished their confidence in themselves, and when Shāh Shujā returned

[1] Capt. Wade to Government, 11th Sept. 1834, and 4th April 1836.

[2] Moorcroft, *Travels*, i. 420.

[3] Capt. Wade to Government, 27th Jan. 1835, and Mr. Vigne, *Travels in Kashmīr and Tibet*, ii. 352 ; their statements being corrected or amplified from the author's manuscript notes. The prince Kharak Singh became especially apprehensive of the designs of the Jammū family. (Capt. Wade to Government, 10th Aug. 1836.)

1835–6.

Negotiations.

beaten from Kandahār, Nur Muhammad of Hyderābād was understood to be willing to surrender Shikārpur to the Mahārājā, on condition of his guarantee against the attempts of the ex-king.[1] But this pretext would not get rid of the English objections ; and Ranjīt Singh, moreover, had little confidence in the Sindians. He kept, as a check over them, a representative of the expelled Kalhoras, as a pensioner on his bounty, in Rājanpur beyond the Indus ; [2] and, at once to overawe both them and the Bārakzais, he again opened a negotiation with Shāh Shujā as soon as he returned to Ludhiāna.[3] But his main difficulty was with his British allies ; and, to prove to them the reasonableness of his discontent, he would instance the secret aid which the Mazāri freebooters received from the Amīrs ; [4] he would again insist that Shikārpur was a dependency of the chiefs of Khorassan,[5] and he would hint that the river below Mithankot was not the Indus but the Sutlej, the river of the treaty,—the stream which had so long given freshness and beauty to the emblematic garden of their friendship, and which continued its fertilizing way to the ocean, separating, yet uniting, the realms of the two brotherly powers of the East ! [6]

Ranjīt Singh's ambition displeasing to the English.

But the English had formed a treaty of navigation with Sind, and the designs of Ranjīt Singh were displeasing to them. They said they could not view without regret and disapprobation the prosecution of plans of unprovoked

1 Capt. Wade to Government, 6th Feb. 1835.

2 Capt. Wade to Government, 17th June 1834. Sarafrāz Khān, otherwise called Ghulām Shāh, was the Kalhora expelled by the Tālpurs. He received Rājanpur in jāgīr from Kābul, and was maintained in it by Ranjīt Singh. The place was held to yield 100,000 rupees, including certain rents reserved by the state, but the district was not really worth 30,000 rupees.

3 Capt. Wade to Government, 17th April 1835, and other letters of the same year. The Mahārājā still urged that the English should guarantee, as it were, Shāh Shujā's moderation in success ; partly, perhaps, because the greatness of the elder dynasty of Ahmad Shāh still dwelt in the mind of the first paramount of the Sikhs, but partly also with the view of sounding his European allies as to *their* real intentions.

4 Capt. Wade to Government, 5th Oct. 1836.

5 Capt. Wade to Government, 15th Jan. 1837.

6 Capt. Wade to Government, 5th Oct. 1836.

hostility against states to which *they* were bound by ties of interest and goodwill.[1] They therefore wished to dissuade Ranjīt Singh against any attempt on Shikārpur; but they felt that this must be done discreetly, for their object was to remain on terms of friendship with every one, and to make their influence available for the preservation of the general peace.[2] Such were the sentiments of the English; but, in the meantime, the border disputes between the Sikhs and Sindians were fast tending to produce a rupture. In 1833 the predatory tribe of Mazāris, lying along the right bank of the Indus, below Mithankot, had been chastised by the Governor of Multān, who proposed to put a garrison in their stronghold of Rojhan, but was restrained by the Mahārājā from so doing.[3] In 1835 the Amīrs of Khairpur were believed to be instigating the Mazāris in their attacks on the Sikh posts; and as the tribe was regarded by the English as dependent on Sind, although possessed of such a degree of separate existence as to warrant its mention in the commercial arrangements as being entitled to a fixed portion of the whole toll, the Amīrs were informed that the English looked to them to restrain the Mazāris, so as to deprive Ranjīt Singh of all pretext for interference.[4] The aggressions nevertheless continued, or were alleged to be continued; and in August 1836, the Multān Governor took formal possession of Rojhan.[5] In the October following the Mazāris were brought to action and defeated, and the Sikhs occupied a fort called Ken, to the south of Rojhan, and beyond the proper limit of that tribe.[6]

1835–6.

The Mahārājā nevertheless keeps in view his plans of aggrandizement.

Thus was Ranjīt Singh gradually feeling his way by force; but the English had, in the meantime, resolved to go far beyond him in diplomacy. It had been determined that Capt. Burnes should proceed on a commercial mission to

The objects of the English become political as well as commercial, 1836;

[1] Government to Capt. Wade, 22nd Aug. 1836.—This plea will recall to mind the usual argument of the Romans for interference, viz. that *their* friends were not to be molested by strangers.

[2] Government to Capt. Wade, 22nd Aug. 1836.

[3] Capt. Wade to Government, 27th May 1835.

[4] Government to Capt. Wade, 27th May 1835, and 5th Sept. 1836; and Government to Col. Pottinger, 19th Sept. 1836.

[5] Capt. Wade to Government, 29th Aug. 1836.

[6] Capt. Wade to Government, 2nd Nov. 1836.

1836.

the countries bordering on the Indus, with the view of completing the reopening of that river to the traffic of the world.[1] But the Mahārājā, it was said, should understand that their objects were purely mercantile, and that, indeed, his aid was looked for in establishing somewhere a great entrepôt of trade, such as, it had once been hoped, might have been commenced at Mithankot.[2] Yet the views of the British authorities with regard to Sind were inevitably becoming political as well as commercial. The condition of that country, said the Governor-General, had been much thought about, and the result was a conviction that the connexion with it should be drawn closer.[3] The Amīrs, he continued, might desire the protection of the English against Ranjīt Singh, and previous negotiations, which their fears or their hostility had broken off, might be renewed with a view to giving them assistance; and, finally, it was determined that the English Government should mediate between Ranjīt Singh and the Sindians, and afterwards adjust the other external relations of the Amīrs when a Resident should be stationed at Hyderābād.

and they resolve on mediating between Ranjīt Singh and the Sindians.

The English desire to restrain Ranjīt Singh without threatening him.

With regard to Ranjīt Singh, the English rulers observed that they were bound by the strongest considerations of political interest to prevent the extension of the Sikh power along the course of the Indus, and that, although they would respect the acknowledged territories of the Mahārājā, they desired that his existing relations of peace should not be disturbed; for, if war took place, the Indus would never be opened to commerce. The political agent was directed to use every means short of menace to induce Ranjīt Singh to abandon his designs against Shikārpur; and Shāh Shujā, whose hopes were still great, and whose negotiations were still talked of, was to be told that if he left Ludhiāna he must not return, and that the maintenance for his family would be at once discontinued. With regard to the Mazāris, whose lands had been actually occupied by the Sikhs, it was said that their reduction had effected an object of general benefit, and that the question of their

[1] Government to Capt. Wade, 5th Sept. 1836.

[2] Government to Capt. Wade, 5th Sept. 1836.

[3] Government to Col. Pottinger, 26th Sept. 1836.

permanent control could be determined at a future period.[1] 1836.

The Sindians, on their part, complained that the fort of Ken had been occupied, and in reply to Ranjīt Singh's demand that their annual complimentary or prudential offerings should be increased, or that a large sum should be paid for the restoration of their captured fort, they avowed their determination to resort to arms.[2] Nor can there be any doubt that Sind would have been invaded by the Sikhs, had not Col. Pottinger's negotiations for their protection deterred the Mahārājā from an act which he apprehended the English might seize upon to declare *their* alliance at an end. The princes Kharak Singh and Nau Nihāl Singh were each on the Indus, at the head of considerable armies, and the remonstrances of the British political agent alone detained the Mahārājā himself at Lahore. Nevertheless, so evenly were peace and war balanced in Ranjīt Singh's mind, that Capt. Wade thought it advisable to proceed to his capital to explain to him in person the risks he would incur by acting in open opposition to the British Government. He listened, and at last yielded. His deference, he said, to the wishes of his allies took place of every other consideration; he would let his relations with the Amīrs of Sind remain on their old footing, he would destroy the fort of Ken, but he would continue to occupy Rojhan and the Mazāri territory.[3] Ranjīt Singh was urged by his chiefs not to yield to the demands of the English, for to their understanding it was not clear where such demands would stop; but he shook his head, and asked them what had become of the two hundred thousand spears of the Marāthās![4]—and,

The Sindians impatient, and ready to resort to arms.

Ranjīt Singh equally ready;

but yields to the representations of the English, Dec. 1836.

[1] Government to Capt. Wade, 26th Sept. 1836.

[2] Capt. Wade to Government, 2nd Nov. and 13th Dec. 1836.

[3] Capt. Wade to Government, 3rd Jan. 1837.

[4] Cf. Capt. Wade to Government, 11th Jan. 1837. Ranjīt Singh not unfrequently referred to the overthrow of the Marāthā power as a reason for remaining, under all and any circumstances, on good terms with his European allies. See also Col. Wade's *Narrative of Personal Services*, p. 44, note. [Though the Mahārājā kept loyally to his treaty of friendship with the English, he occasionally manifested some suspicion of their victorious advance in India. On one occasion he was shown a map of the country in which the English possessions were marked in red. The Mahārājā asked what the red portions

1836.

as if to show how completely he professed to forget or forgive the check imposed on him, he invited the Governor-General to be present at Lahore on the occasion of the marriage of the grandson whom he had hoped to hail as the conqueror of Sind.[1] Nevertheless he continued to entertain a hope that his objects might one day be attained; he avoided a distinct settlement of the boundary with the Amīrs, and of the question of supremacy over the Mazāris.[2] Neither was he disposed to relinquish Rojhan; the place remained a Sikh possession, and it may be regarded to have become formally such by the submission of the chief of the tribe in the year 1838.[3]

Yet continues to hold Rojhan with ulterior views.

Retrospect. The English and Bārakzais, 1829–36.

It is now necessary to go back for some years to trace the connexion of the English Government with the Bārakzai rulers of Afghānistān. Muhammad Azīm Khān died in 1823, as has been mentioned, immediately after Peshāwar became tributary to the Sikhs. His son Habīb-ullah nominally succeeded to the supremacy which Fateh Khān and Muhammad Azīm had both exercised; but it soon became evident that the mind of the youth was unsettled, and his violent proceedings enabled his crafty and unscrupulous uncle, Dost Muhammad Khān, to seize Kābul, Ghazni, and Jalālābād as his own, while a second set of his brothers held Kandahār in virtual independence, and a third governed Peshāwar as the tributaries of Ranjīt Singh.[4] In the year 1824 Mr. Moorcroft, the traveller, was upon the whole well satisfied with the treatment he received from the Bārakzais, although their patronage cost him money.[5] A few years afterwards Sultān Muhammad Khān of Peshāwar, who had most to fear from strangers, opened a communication with the political agent at Ludhiāna,[6] and in 1829 he

Sultān Muhammad Khān solicits the

indicated, and on being told tossed the map aside with the impatient remark, *Sab lāl hojāegā* (All will become red).—ED.]

[1] Capt. Wade to Government, 5th Jan. 1837.

[2] Capt. Wade to Government, 13th and 15th Feb., 8th July, and 10th Aug. 1837.

[3] Capt. Wade to Government, 9th Jan. 1838.

[4] Cf. Moorcroft, *Travels*, ii. 345, &c., and Munshi Mohan Lāl, *Life of Dost Muhammad Khān*, i. 130, 153, &c.

[5] Moorcroft, *Travels*, ii. 346, 347.

[6] Capt. Wade to the Resident at Delhi, 21st April 1828.

1829–32.

wished to negotiate as an independent chief with the British Government.[1] But the several brothers were jealous of one another, many desired separate principalities, Dost Muhammad aimed at supremacy, rumours of Persian designs alarmed them on the west, the aggressive policy of Ranjīt Singh gave them greater cause of fear on the east, and the chance presence of English travellers in Afghānistān again led them to hope that the foreign masters of India might be induced to give them stability between contending powers.[2] In 1832 Sultān Muhammad Khān again attempted to open a negotiation, if only for the release of his son, who was a hostage with Ranjīt Singh.[3] The Nawāb, Jabbār Khān of Kābul, likewise addressed letters to the British frontier authority, and in 1832 Dost Muhammad himself directly asked for the friendship of the English.[4] All these communications were politely acknowledged, but at the time it was held desirable to avoid all intimacy of connexion with rulers so remote.[5]

friendship or protection of the English against the Sikhs, 1829.

Dost Muhammad Khān does the same, 1832.

In 1834 new dangers threatened the usurping Bārakzais. Shāh Shujā had defeated the Sindians and had arrived in force at Kandahār, and the brothers once again endeavoured to bring themselves within the verge of British supremacy. They had heard of English arts as well as of English arms;

The Bārakzais, apprehensive of Shāh Shujā, again press for an alliance with the English;

[1] Capt. Wade to Government, 19th May 1832. The brothers had already (1823, 1824) made similar proposals through Mr. Moorcroft. (See *Travels*, ii. 340.)

[2] Mr. Fraser and Mr. Stirling, of the Bengal Civil Service, were in Afghānistān, the former in 1826, apparently, and the latter in 1828. Mr. Masson also entered the country by way of the Lower Punjab in 1827, and the American, Dr. Harlan, followed him in a year by the same route. Dr. Harlan came to Lahore in 1829, after leading the English authorities to believe that he desired to constitute himself an agent between their Government and Shāh Shujā, with reference doubtless to the ex-king's designs on Kābul. (Resident at Delhi to Capt. Wade, 3rd Feb. 1829.) The Rev. Mr. Wolff should be included among the travellers in Central Asia at the time in question.

[3] Capt. Wade to Government, 19th May and 3rd July 1832.

[4] Capt. Wade to Government, 9th July 1832, and 17th Jan. 1833. Col. Wade in the *Narrative of Personal Services*, p. 23, note, regards these overtures of Dost Muhammad, and also the increased interest of Russia and Persia in Afghān affairs, to Lieut. Burnes's Journey (to Bokhara, in 1832) and to Shāh Shujā's designs.

[5] Government to Capt. Wade, 28th Feb. 1833.

1834.

and Jabbār Khān sends his son to Ludhiāna, 6th May 1834.

they knew that all were accessible of flattery, and Jabbār Khān suddenly proposed to send his son to Ludhiāna, in order, he said, that his mind might be improved by European science and civilization.[1] But Jabbār Khān, while he appeared to adhere to Dost Muhammad rather than to others, had nevertheless an ambition of his own, and he was more than suspected of a wish to make his admiration of the amenities of English life the means of acquiring political power.[2] Thus, doubtful of all about him, Dost Muhammad left Kābul to oppose Shāh Shujā, but the Sikhs had, in the meantime, occupied Peshāwar, and the perplexed ruler grasped once more at British aid as his only sure resource.[3]

Dost Muhammad formally tenders his allegiance to the English, 1st July 1834;

but defeats Shāh Shujā and recovers confidence.

He tendered his submission as a dependent of Great Britain, and having thus endeavoured to put his dominions in trust, he gave Shāh Shujā battle. But the Shāh was defeated, and the rejoicing victor forgot his difficulties. He declared war against the Sikhs on account of their capture of Peshāwar, and he endeavoured to make it a religious contest by rousing the population generally to destroy infidel invaders.[4] He assumed the proud distinction of ‘ Ghāzi ’, or champion of the faith, and the vague title of ‘ Amīr ’, which he interpreted ‘ the noble ’, for he did not care to wholly offend his brothers, whose submission he desired, and whose assistance was necessary to him.[5]

Dost Muhammad attempts to recover Peshāwar.

Dost Muhammad Khān, amid all his exultation, was still willing to use the intervention of unbelievers as well as the arms of the faithful, and he asked the English masters of India to help him in recovering Peshāwar.[6] The youth who had been sent to Ludhiāna to become a student, was invested with the powers of a diplomatist, and the Amīr sought to prejudice the British authorities against the Sikhs, by urging that *his* nephew and *their* guest had been treated with suspicion, and had suffered restraint on his way across the Punjab. But the English had not yet thought of re-

[1] Capt. Wade to Government, 9th March 1834.

[2] Capt. Wade to Government, 17th May 1834. Cf. Masson, *Journeys*, iii. 218, 220.

[3] Capt. Wade to Government, 17th June 1834.

[4] Capt. Wade to Government, 25th Sept. 1834.

[5] Capt. Wade to Government, 27th Jan. 1835.

[6] Capt. Wade to Government, 4th Jan. and 13th Feb. 1835.

quiring him to be an ally for purposes of their own, and Dost Muhammad was simply assured that the son of Nawāb Jabbār Khān should be well taken care of on the eastern side of the Sutlej. A direct reply to his solicitation was avoided, by enlarging on the partial truth that the Afghāns were a commercial people equally with the English, and on the favourite scheme of the great traffickers of the world, the opening of the Indus to commerce. It was hoped, it was added, that the new impulse given to trade would better help the two governments to cultivate a profitable friendship, and the wondering Amīr, full of warlike schemes, was naïvely asked, whether he had any suggestions to offer about a direct route for merchandise between Kābul and the great boundary river of the Afghāns![1] The English rulers had also to reply to Ranjīt Singh, who was naturally suspicious of the increasing intimacy between his allies and his enemies, and who desired that the European lords might appear rather as his than as Dost Muhammad's supporters; but the Governor-General observed that any endeavours to mediate would lead to consequences seriously embarrassing, and that Dost Muhammad would seem to have interpreted general professions of amity into promises of assistance.[2]

1835.

The English decline interfering.

The two parties were thus left to their own means. Ranjīt Singh began by detaching Sultān Muhammad Khān from the Amīr, with whom he had sought a refuge on the occupation of Peshāwar by the Sikhs; and the ejected tributary listened the more readily to the Mahārājā's propositions, as he apprehended that Dost Muhammad would retain Peshāwar for himself, should Ranjīt Singh be beaten. Dost Muhammad came to the eastern entrance of the Khaibar Pass, and Ranjīt Singh amused him with proposals until he had concentrated his forces. On the 11th of May 1835, the Amīr was almost surrounded. He was to have been attacked on the 12th, but he thought it prudent to

Ranjīt Singh and Dost Muhammad in force at Peshāwar, 1835.

Dost Muhammad retires rather than risk a battle, 11th May 1835.

[1] Government to Capt. Wade, 19th April 1834, and 11th Feb. 1835. Abdul Ghias Khān, the son of Jabbār Khān, reached Ludhiāna in June 1834, and the original intention of sending him to study at Delhi was abandoned.

[2] Government to Capt. Wade, 20th April 1835.

1835-6. retreat, which he did with the loss of two guns and some baggage. He had designed to carry off the Sikh envoys, and to profit by their presence as hostages or as prisoners; but his brother, Sultān Muhammad Khān, to whom the execution of the project had been entrusted, had determined on joining Ranjīt Singh, and the rescue of the agents gave him a favourable introduction to the victor. Sultān Muhammad and his brothers had considerable jāgīrs conferred on them in the Peshāwar district, but the military control and civil management of the province was vested solely in an officer appointed from Lahore.[1]

Dost Muhammad looks towards Persia, but still prefers an English alliance, 1836.

Dost Muhammad suffered much in general estimation by withdrawing from an encounter with the Sikhs. His hopes in the English had not borne fruit, and he was disposed to court Persia; [2] but the connexion was of less political credit and utility than one with the English, and he tried once more to move the Governor-General in his favour. The Sikhs, he said, were faithless, and he was wholly devoted to the interests of the British Government.[3] The Kandahār brothers, also, being pressed by Shāh Kāmrān of Herāt, and unable to obtain aid from Dost Muhammad, made propositions to the English authorities; but Kāmrān's own apprehensions of Persia soon relieved them of their fears, and they did not press their solicitations for European aid.[4] Ranjīt Singh, on his part, disliked an English and Afghān alliance, and sought to draw Dost Muhammad within the vortex of his own influence. He gave the Amīr vague hopes of obtaining Peshāwar, and he asked him to send him some horses, which he had learnt was a sure way of leading others to believe they had won his favour. Dost Muhammad was

The Kandahār chiefs desirous of English aid. Ranjīt Singh endeavours to gain over Dost Muhammad.

[1] Capt. Wade to Government, 25th April, and 1st, 15th, and 19th May 1835. Cf. Masson, *Journeys*, iii. 342, &c.; Mohan Lal, *Life of Dost Muhammad*, i. 172, &c.; and also Dr. Harlan's *India and Afghānistān*, pp. 124, 158. Dr. Harlan himself was one of the envoys sent to Dost Muhammad on the occasion.

The Sikhs are commonly said to have had 80,000 men in the Peshāwar valley at this time.

[2] Capt. Wade to Government, 23rd Feb. 1836. Dost Muhammad's overtures to Persia seem to have commenced in Sept. 1835.

[3] Capt. Wade to Government, 19th July 1836.

[4] Capt. Wade to Government, 9th March 1836.

not unwilling to obtain a hold on Peshāwar, even as a tributary, but he felt that the presentation of horses would be declared by the Sikh to refer to Kābul and not to that province.[1] The disgrace of his retreat rankled in his mind, and he at last said that a battle must be fought at all risks.[2] He was the more inclined to resort to arms, as the Sikhs had sounded his brother, Jabbār Khān, and as Sirdār Harī Singh had occupied the entrance of the Khaibar Pass and entrenched a position at Jamrūd, as the basis of his scheme for getting through the formidable defile.[3] The Kābul troops marched and assembled on the eastern side of Khaibar, under the command of Muhammad Akbar Khān,[4] the most warlike of the Amīr's sons. An attack was made on the post at Jamrūd, on the 30th of April 1837; but the Afghāns could not carry it, although they threw the Sikhs into disorder. Harī Singh, by feigning a retreat, drew the enemy more fully into the plains; the brave leader was present everywhere amid his retiring and rallying masses, but he fell mortally wounded, and the opportune arrival of another portion of the Kābul forces converted the confusion of the Sikhs into a total defeat. But two guns only were lost; the Afghāns could not master Jamrūd or Peshāwar itself, and, after plundering the valley for a few days, they retreated rather than risk a second battle with the reinforced army of Lahore.[5]

1836–7.

But the Amīr prefers war, 1836–7.

Harī Singh's designs.

Battle of Jamrūd, 30th April 1837.

The Sikhs defeated, and Harī Singh killed; but the Afghāns retire.

[1] Capt. Wade to Government, 12th April 1837.

[2] Capt. Wade to Government, 1st May 1837.

[3] Capt. Wade to Government, 13th Jan. 1837.

[4] [Afterwards the murderer of Sir W. Macnaghten and the chief actor in the tragedy of the retreat from Kabul (1842).—ED.]

[5] Capt. Wade to Government, 13th and 23rd May and 5th July 1837. Cf. Masson, *Journeys*, iii. 382, 387, and Mohan Lal, *Life of Dost Muhammad*, i. 226, &c.

It seems that the Afghāns were at first routed or repulsed with the loss of some guns, but that the opportune arrival of Shams-ud-dīn Khān, a relation of the Amīr, with a considerable detachment, turned the battle in their favour. It is nevertheless believed that had not Harī Singh been killed, the Sikhs would have retrieved the day. The troops in the Peshāwar valley had been considerably reduced by the withdrawal of large parties to Lahore, to make a display on the occasion of Nau Nihāl Singh's marriage, and of the expected visit of the English Governor-General and Commander-in-Chief.

1837.

Ranjīt Singh's efforts to retrieve his affairs at Peshāwar.

The death of Harī Singh and the defeat of his army caused some anxiety in Lahore ; but the Mahārājā promptly roused his people to exertion, and all readily responded to his call. It is stated that field guns were dragged from Ramnagar, on the Chenāb, to Peshāwar in six days, a distance by road of more than two hundred miles.[1] Ranjīt Singh advanced in person to Rohtās, and the active Dhiān Singh hastened to the frontier, and set an example of devotion and labour by working with his own hands on the foundations of a regular fort at Jamrūd.[2] Dost Muhammad was buoyed up by his fruitless victory, and he became more than ever desirous of recovering a province so wholly Afghān ; but Ranjīt Singh contrived to amuse him, and the Mahārājā was found to be again in treaty with the Amīr, and again in treaty with Shāh Shujā, and with both at the same time.[3] But the commercial envoy of the English had gradually sailed high up the Indus of their imaginary commerce, and to his Government the time seemed to have come when political interference would no longer be embarrassing, but, on the contrary, highly advantageous to schemes of peaceful trade and beneficial intercourse. It was made known that the British rulers would be glad to be the means of negotiating a peace honourable to both parties, yet the scale was turned in favour of the Afghān, by the simultaneous admission that Peshāwar was a place to which Dost Muhammad could scarcely be expected to resign all claim.[4] Nevertheless, it was said, the wishes of Ranjīt Singh could be ascertained by Capt. Wade, and Capt. Burnes could similarly inquire about the views of the Amīr. The latter officer was formally invested with diplomatic powers,[5] and the idle designs, or restless intrigues, of Persians and Russians, soon caused the disputes of Sikhs and Afghāns to

His negotiations with Dost Muhammad and Shāh Shujā.

The English resolve on mediating between the Sikhs and Afghāns, 1837;

the more especially as they are apprehensive of Russia,

[1] Lieut.-Col. Steinbach (*Punjab*, pp. 64, 68) mentions that he had himself marched with his Sikh regiment 300 miles in twelve days, and that the distance had been performed by others in eleven.

[2] Mr. Clerk's Memorandum of 1842, regarding the Sikh chiefs, drawn up for Lord Ellenborough.

[3] Cf. Capt. Wade to Government, 3rd June 1837, and Government to Capt. Wade, 7th Aug. 1837.

[4] Government to Capt. Wade, 31st July 1837.

[5] Government to Capt. Wade, 11th Sept. 1837.

merge in the British scheme of reseating Shāh Shujā on the throne of Kābul. At the end of a generation the repose of the English masters of India was again disturbed by the rumoured march of European armies,[1] and their suspicions were further roused by the conduct of the French General, Allard. That officer, after a residence of several years in the Punjab, had been enabled to visit his native country, and he returned by way of Calcutta in the year 1836. While in France he had induced his Government to give him a document, accrediting him to Ranjīt Singh, in case his life should be endangered, or in case he should be refused permission to quit the Lahore dominions. It was understood by the English that the paper was only to be produced to the *Mahārājā* in an extremity of the kind mentioned; but General Allard himself considered that it was only to be so laid in form before the *English authorities*, in support of a demand for aid when he might chance to be straitened. He at once delivered his credentials to the Sikh ruler; it was rumoured that General Allard had become a French ambassador, and it was some time before the British authorities forgave the fancied deceit, or the vain effrontery of their guest.[2]

1837.

and are further dissatisfied with the proceedings of General Allard.

[1] The idea of Russian designs on India engaged the attention of the British viceroy in 1831 (see Murray, *Ranjīt Singh*, by Prinsep, p. 168), and it at the same time possessed the inquiring but sanguine mind of Capt. Burnes, who afterwards gave the notion so much notoriety. (See Capt. Wade to Government, 3rd Aug. 1831.)

[2] The author gives what the French officers held to be the intended use of the credentials, on the competent authority of General Ventura, with whom he formerly had conversations on the subject. The English view, however, is that which was taken by the British ambassador in Paris, as well as by the authorities in Calcutta, with whom General Allard was in personal communication. (Government to Capt. Wade, 16th Jan. and 3rd April 1837.)

Of the two views, that of the English is the less honourable, with reference to their duty towards Ranjīt Singh, who might have justly resented any attempt on the part of a servant to put himself beyond the power of his master, and any interference in that servant's behalf on the part of the British Government.

In the letter to Ranjīt Singh, Louis Philippe is styled, in French, 'Empereur' (Capt. Wade to Government, 15th Sept. 1837); a title which, at the time, may have pleased the vanity of the French, although it could not have informed the understandings of the Sikhs,

1837.

The marriage of Nau Nihāl Singh, 1837.

Ranjīt Singh had invited the Governor-General of India, the Governor of Agra (Sir Charles Metcalfe), and the Commander-in-Chief of the British forces to be present at the nuptials of his grandson, which he designed to celebrate with much splendour. The prince was wedded to a daughter of the Sikh chief, Shām Singh Atariwala, in the beginning of March 1837, but of the English authorities Sir Henry Fane alone was able to attend.

Sir Henry Fane at Lahore.

That able commander was ever a careful observer of military means and of soldierly qualities; he formed an estimate of the force which would be required for the complete subjugation of the Punjab, but at the same time he laid it down as a principle, that the Sutlej and the wastes of Rājputāna and Sind were the best boundaries which the English could have in the east.[1] The prospect of a war with the Sikhs was then remote, and hostile designs could not with honour be entertained by a guest. Sir Henry Fane, therefore, entered heartily into the marriage festivities of Lahore, and his active mind was amused with giving shape to a scheme, which the intuitive sagacity of Ranjīt Singh had acquiesced in as pleasing to the just pride or useful vanity of English soldiers.

The Sikh military Order of the Star.

The project of establishing an Order of merit similar to those dying exponents of warlike skill and chivalrous fraternity

as, agreeably to Persian and Indian practice, king or queen is always translated 'Pādshāh' equally with emperor. Sir Claude Wade seems to think that the real design of the French was to open a regular intercourse with Ranjīt Singh, and to obtain a political influence in the Punjab. The Mahārājā, however, after consulting the British Agent, decided on not taking any notice of the overtures. (Sir Claude Wade, *Narrative*, p. 38, note.) [A piece of diplomacy on the part of the French Government, typical of the chicanery of Louis Philippe and his advisers. The monarch who could perpetrate the sordid scandal of the Spanish marriage was equally capable of an underhand intrigue with Ranjīt Singh.—Ed.]

[1] These views of Sir Henry Fane's may not be on record, but they were well known to those about his Excellency. His estimate was, as I remember to have heard from Capt. Wade, 67,000 men, and he thought there might be a two years' active warfare.

This visit to Lahore was perhaps mainly useful in enabling Lieut.-Col. Garden, the indefatigable quarter-master-general of the Bengal Army, to compile a detailed map of that part of the country, and which formed the groundwork of all the maps used when hostilities did at last break out with the Sikhs.

among European nations, had been for some time entertained, and although such a system of distinction can be adapted to the genius of any people, the object of the Mahārājā was simply to gratify his English neighbours, and advantage was accordingly taken of Sir Henry Fane's presence to establish the 'Order of the auspicious Star of the Punjab' on a purely British model.[1] This method of pleasing, or occupying the attention of the English authorities, was not unusual with Ranjīt Singh, and he was always ready to inquire concerning matters which interested them, or which might be turned to account by himself. He would ask for specimens of, and for information about, the manufacture of Sāmbhar salt and Mālwā opium.[2] So early as 1812 he had made trial of the sincerity of his new allies, or had shown his admiration of their skill, by asking for five hundred muskets. These were at once furnished to him, but a subsequent request for a supply of fifty thousand such weapons excited a passing suspicion.[3] He readily entered into a scheme of freighting a number of boats with merchandise for Bombay, and he was praised for the interest he took in commerce, until it was known that he wished the return cargo to consist of arms for his infantry.[4] He would have his artillerymen learn gunnery at Ludhiāna,[5] and he would send shells of zinc to be inspected in the hope that he might receive some hints about the manufacture of iron shrapnels.[6] He would inquire about the details of European warfare, and he sought for copies of the pay regulations of the Indian

1837.

Ranjīt Singh's object the gratification of his guests and allies.

Anecdotes showing a similar purpose.

[1] Capt. Wade to Government, 7th April 1837. [On the occasion of this visit the Mahārājā displayed considerable interest in the great wars of Europe. He was particularly interested in the career of Napoleon. Col. Wallis, one of Sir Henry's staff, had fortunately been at Waterloo, and the Mahārājā asked him many questions concerning the battle.—ED.]

[2] Capt. Wade to the Resident at Delhi, 2nd Jan. 1831, and to Government, 25th Dec. 1835.

[3] Capt. Wade to Government, 22nd July 1836.

[4] Cf. Government to Capt. Wade, 11th Sept. 1837.

[5] Capt. Wade to Government, 7th Dec. 1831.

[6] When the restoration of Shāh Shujā was resolved on, Ranjit Singh sent shells to Ludhiāna to be looked at and commented on, as if, being engaged in one political cause, there should not be any reserve about military secrets!

1837.

army and of the English practice of courts martial, and bestowed dresses of honour on the translator of these complicated and inapplicable systems;[1] while, to further satisfy himself, he would ask what punishment had been found an efficient substitute for flogging.[2] He sent a lad, the relation of one of his chiefs, to learn English at the Ludhiāna school, in order, he said, that the youth might aid him in his correspondence with the British Government, which Lord William Bentinck had wished to carry on in the English tongue instead of in Persian;[3] and he sent a number of young men to learn something of medicine at the Ludhiāna dispensary, which had been set on foot by the political agent—but in order, the Mahārājā said, that they might be useful in his battalions.[4] In such ways, half-serious, half-idle, did Ranjīt Singh endeavour to ingratiate himself with the representatives of a power he could not withstand and never wholly trusted.

The British scheme of opening the Indus to commerce ends in the project of restoring Shāh Shujā.

Ranjīt Singh's rejoicings over the marriage and youthful promise of his grandson were rudely interrupted by the success of the Afghāns at Jamrūd, and the death of his able leader Harī Singh, as has been already related. The old man was moved to tears when he heard of the fate of the only genuine Sikh chief of his creation;[5] and he had scarcely vindicated his supremacy on the frontier, by filling the valley of Peshāwar with troops, when the English interfered to embitter the short remainder of his life, and to set bounds to

[1] Major Hough, who has added to the reputation of the Indian army by his useful publications, put the practice of courts martial into a Sikh dress for Ranjīt Singh. (Government to Capt. Wade, 21st November 1834.)

[2] Government to Capt. Wade, 18th May 1835, intimating that solitary confinement had been found a good substitute.

[3] Capt. Wade to Government, 11th April 1835. Some of the princes of India, all of whom are ever prone to suspicion, were not without a belief that, by writing in English, it was designed to keep them in ignorance of the real views and declarations of their paramount.

[4] Some of these young men were employed with the force raised at Peshāwar, in 1839, to enable Prince Taimūr to march through Khaibar.

[5] Capt. Wade to Government, 13th May 1837, quoting Dr. Wood, a surgeon in the British army, temporarily deputed to attend on Ranjīt Singh, and who was with his camp at Rohtās on this occasion.

his ambition on the west, as they had already done on the east and south. The commercial policy of the British people required that peace and industry should at once be introduced among the half-barbarous tribes of Sind, Khorasan, and the Punjab; and it was vainly sought to give fixed limits to newly-founded feudal governments, and to impress moderation of desire upon grasping military sovereigns. It was wished that Ranjīt Singh should be content with his past achievements; that the Amīrs of Sindh, and the chiefs of Herāt, Kandahār, and Kābul should feel themselves secure in what they held, but incapable of obtaining more; and that the restless Shāh Shujā should quietly abandon all hope of regaining the crown of his daily dreams.[1] These were the views which the English viceroy required his agents to impress on Tālpurs, Bārakzais, and Sikhs; and their impracticability might have quietly and harmlessly become apparent, had not Russia found reason and opportunity to push her intrigues, through Persia and Turkestān, to the banks of the Indus.[2] The desire of effecting a reconciliation between Ranjīt Singh and Dost Muhammad induced the British Government to offer its mediation;[3] the predilections of its frank and enterprising envoy led him to seize upon the admission that the Amīr could scarcely be expected to resign all pretensions to Peshāwar.[4] The crafty chief

1837.

Sir Alex. Burnes at Kābul, 1837–8.

[1] Cf. Government to Capt. Wade, 13th Nov. 1837, and to Capt. Burnes and Capt. Wade, both of the 20th January 1838. With regard to Sind, also, the views of Ranjīt Singh were not held to be pleasing, and the terms of his communication with the Amīrs were thought equivocal, or denotative of a reservation, or of the expression of a right he did not possess. (Government to Capt. Wade, 25th Sept. and 13th Nov. 1837.)

[2] Without reference to the settled policy of Russia, or to what she may always have thought of the virtual support which England gives to Persia and Turkey against her power, the presence of inquiring agents in Khorasan and Turkestān, and the progressive extension of the British Indian dominion, must have put her on the alert, if they did not fill her with reasonable suspicions.

[3] Government to Capt. Wade, 31st July 1837.

[4] These predilections of Sir Alex. Burnes, and the hopes founded on them by Dost Muhammad, were sufficiently notorious to those in personal communication with that valuable pioneer of the English; and his strong wish to recover Peshāwar, at least for Sultān Muhammad Khān, is distinctly stated in his own words, in Masson, *Journeys*,

1837–8.

made use of this partiality, and of the fact that his friendship was courted, to try and secure himself against the only power he really feared, viz. that of the Sikhs; and he renewed his overtures to Persia and welcomed a Russian emissary, with the view of intimidating the English into the surrender of Peshāwar, and into a guarantee against Ranjīt Singh. Friendly assurances to the Kandahār brothers, and a hint that the Sikhs were at liberty to march on Kābul, would have given Dost Muhammad a proper sense of his insignificance;[1] but the truth and the importance of his hostile designs were both believed or assumed by the British Government, while the rumours of a northern invasion were eagerly received and industriously spread by the vanquished princes of India, and the whole country vibrated with the hope that the uncongenial domination of the English was about to yield to the ascendancy of another and less dissimilar race.[2] The recall of Capt. Burnes from Kābul gave speciousness to the wildest statements; the advantage of striking some great blow became more and more obvious; for the sake of consistency it was necessary to maintain peace on the Indus, and it was wisely resolved to make a triumphant progress through Central Asia, and to leave Shāh Shujā as a dependent prince on his ancestral throne. The conception was bold and perfect; and had it been

Dost Muhammad eventually falls into the views of Persia and Russia.

The original policy of the English erroneous.

But, under the circumstances brought about, the expedition to Kābul wisely and boldly conceived.

iii. 423. The idea of taking the district from the Sikhs, either for Dost Muhammad or his brothers, is moreover apparent from Sir Alex. Burnes's published letters of 5th Oct. 1837, and 26th Jan. and 13th March 1838 (Parliamentary Papers, 1839), from the Government replies of remark and caution, dated 20th Jan., and especially of 27th April 1838, and from Mr. Masson's statement (*Journeys*, iii. 423, 448). Mr. Masson himself thought it would be but justice to restore the district to Sultān Muhammad Khān, while Munshi Mohan Lāl (*Life of Dost Muhammad*, i. 257, &c.) represents the Amīr to have thought that the surrender of Peshāwar to his brother would have been more prejudicial to his interests than its retention by the Sikhs.

[1] Such were Capt. Wade's views, and they are sketched in his letters of the 15th May and 28th Oct. 1837, with reference to commercial objects, although the line of policy may not have been steadily adhered to, or fully developed.

[2] The extent to which this feeling was prevalent is known to those who were observers of Indian affairs at the time, and it is dwelt upon in the Governor-General's minute of the 20th Aug. 1839.

steadily adhered to, the whole project would have eminently answered the ends intended, and would have been, in every way, worthy of the English name.[1] 1838.

Negotiations regarding the restoration of Shāh Shujā, May, July, 1838.

In the beginning of 1838 the Governor-General did not contemplate the restoration of Shāh Shujā ;[2] but in four months the scheme was adopted, and in May of that year Sir William Macnaghten was sent to Ranjīt Singh to unfold the views of the British Government.[3] The Mahārājā grasped at the first idea which presented itself, of making use of the Shāh at the head of *his* armies, with the proclaimed support of the paramount power in India ; but he disliked the complete view of the scheme, and the active co-operation of his old allies. It chafed him that he was to resign all hope of Shikārpur, and that he was to be enclosed within the iron arms of the English rule. He suddenly broke up

Ranjīt Singh dissatisfied ; but finally assents.

1 The Governor-General's minute of 12th May 1838, and his declaration of the 1st October of the same year, may be referred to as summing up the views which moved the British Government on the occasion. Both were published by order of Parliament in March 1839.

2 Government to Capt. Wade, 20th Jan. 1838.

3 The proximate cause of the resolution to restore Shāh Shujā was, of course, the preference given by Dost Muhammad to a Persian and Russian over a British alliance, and the immediate object of deputing Sir W. Macnaghten to Lahore was to make Ranjīt Singh as much as possible a party to the policy adopted. (See, among other letters, Government to Capt. Wade, 15th May 1838.) The deputation crossed into the Punjab at Rūpar on the 20th May. It remained some time at Dīnānagar, and afterwards went to Lahore. The first interview with Ranjīt Singh was on the 31st May, the last on the 13th July. Sir William Macnaghten recrossed the Sutlej at Ludhiāna on the 15th July, and on that and the following day he arranged with Shāh Shujā in person the terms of his restoration.

Two months before the deputation waited upon Ranjīt Singh, he had visited Jammu for apparently the first time in his life, and the same may be regarded as the last in which the worn-out prince tasted of unalloyed happiness. Gulāb Singh received his sovereign with every demonstration of loyalty, and, bowing to the Mahārājā's feet, he laid before him presents worth nearly forty thousand pounds, saying he was the humblest of his slaves, and the most grateful of those on whom he had heaped favours. Ranjīt Singh shed tears, but afterwards pertinently observed that, in Jammu, gold might be seen where formerly there was naught but stones. (Major Mackeson's letter to Capt. Wade of 31st March 1838.)

1838. his camp at Dīnānagar, leaving the British envoys to follow at their leisure, or to return, if they pleased, to Simla; and it was not until he was told the expedition would be undertaken whether he chose to share in it or not, that he assented to a modification of his own treaty with Shāh Shujā, and that the triple alliance was formed for the subversion of the power of the Bārakzais.[1] The English, on their part, insisted on a double invasion of Afghānistān: first, because the Amīrs of Sind disliked a proffered treaty of alliance or dependence, and they could conveniently be coerced as tributaries by Shāh Shujā on his way to Kandahār; and, secondly, because it was not deemed prudent to place the ex-king in the hands of Ranjīt Singh, who might be tempted to use him for Sikh rather than for British objects.[2] It was therefore arranged that the Shāh himself should march by way of Shikārpur and Quetta, while his son moved on Kābul by the road of Peshāwar, and at the head of a force provided by the Mahārājā of the Punjab. The British force assembled at Ferozepore towards the close of 1838, and further éclat was given to

[1] That Ranjīt Singh was told he would be left out if he did not choose to come in, does not appear on public record. It was, however, the only convincing argument used during the long discussions, and I think Major Mackeson was made the bearer of the message to that effect.

[2] Cf. the Governor-General's minute of 12th of May 1838, and his instructions to Sir William Macnaghten of the 15th of the same month. Ranjīt Singh was anxious to get something lasting and tangible as his share of the profit of the expedition, and he wanted Jalālābād, as there seemed to be a difficulty about Shikārpur. The Mahārājā got, indeed, a subsidy of two hundred thousand rupees a year from the Shāh for the use of his troops; a concession which did not altogether satisfy the Governor-General (see letter to Sir William Macnaghten, 2nd July, 1838), and the article became, in fact, a dead letter.

The idea of creating a friendly power in Afghānistān, by guiding Ranjīt Singh upon Kābul, seems to have been seriously entertained, and it was a scheme which promised many solid advantages. Cf. the Governor-General's minute, 12th May 1838, the author's abstract of which differs somewhat from the copy printed by order of Parliament in 1839, and Mr. Masson (*Journeys*, iii. 487, 488) who refers to a communication from Sir William Macnaghten on the subject. For the treaty about the restoration of Shāh Shujā, see Appendix XXX.

1838–9.

the opening of a memorable campaign, by an interchange of hospitalities between the English viceroy and the Sikh ruler.[1] Ostensibly Ranjīt Singh had reached the summit of his ambition; he was acknowledged to be an arbiter in the fate of that empire which had tyrannized over his peasant forefathers, and he was treated with the greatest distinction by the foreign paramounts of India: but his health had become seriously impaired; he felt that he was in truth fairly in collision with the English, and he became indifferent about the careful fulfilment of the engagements into which he had entered. Shāhzāda Taimūr marched from Lahore in January 1839, accompanied by Col. Wade as the British representative; but it was with difficulty the stipulated auxiliary force was got together at Peshāwar, and although a considerable army at last encamped in the valley, the commander, the Mahārājā's grandson, thwarted the negotiations of Prince Taimūr and the English agent, by endeavouring to gain friends for Lahore rather than for the proclaimed sovereign of the Afghāns.[2] Ranjīt Singh's health continued to decline. He heard of the fall of Kandahār in April, and the delay at that place may have served to cheer his vexed spirit with the hope that the English would yet be baffled; but he died on the 27th of June, at the age of fifty-nine, before the capture of Ghazni and the

Ranjīt Singh apparently at the height of greatness;

but chafed in mind, and enfeebled in health.

Death of Ranjīt Singh, 27th June 1839.

[1] At one of the several meetings which took place on this occasion, there was an interchange of compliments, which may be noticed. Ranjīt Singh likened the friendship of the two states to an apple, the red and yellow colours of which were, he said, so blended, that although the semblance was twofold the reality was one. Lord Auckland replied that the Mahārājā's simile was very happy, inasmuch as red and yellow were the national colours of the English and Sikhs respectively; to which Ranjīt Singh rejoined in the same strain that the comparison was indeed in every way appropriate, for the friendship of the two powers was, like the apple, fair and delicious. The translations were given in English and Urdū with elegance and emphasis by Sir William Macnaghten and Fakīr Azīz-ud-dīn, both of whom were masters, although in different ways, of language, whether written or spoken.

[2] See, among other letters, Capt. Wade to Government, 18th Aug. 1839. For some interesting details regarding Capt. Wade's military proceedings, see Lieut. Barr's published *Journal*; and for the diplomatic history, so to speak, of his mission, see Munshi Shāhamat Alī, *Sikhs and Afghāns*.

1839. occupation of Kābul, and the forcing of the Khaibar Pass with the aid of his own troops, placed the seal of success on a campaign in which he was an unwilling sharer.

The political condition of the Sikhs, as modified by the genius of Ranjīt Singh.

Ranjīt Singh found the Punjab a waning confederacy, a prey to the factions of its chiefs, pressed by the Afghāns and the Marāthās, and ready to submit to English supremacy. He consolidated the numerous petty states into a kingdom, he wrested from Kābul the fairest of its provinces, and he gave the potent English no cause for interference. He found the military array of his country a mass of horsemen, brave indeed, but ignorant of war as an art, and he left it mustering fifty thousand disciplined soldiers, fifty thousand well-armed yeomanry and militia, and more than three hundred pieces of cannon for the field. His rule was founded on the feelings of a people, but it involved the joint action of the necessary principles of military order and territorial extension; and when a limit had been set to Sikh dominion, and his own commanding genius was no more, the vital spirit of his race began to consume itself in domestic contentions.[1]

[1] In 1831, Capt. Murray estimated the Sikh revenue at little more than 2½ millions sterling, and the army at 82,000 men, including 15,000 regular infantry and 376 guns. (Murray, *Ranjīt Singh*, by Prinsep, pp. 185, 186.) In the same year Capt. Burnes (*Travels*, i. 289, 291) gives the revenue at 2½ millions, and the army at 75,000, including 25,000 regular infantry. Mr. Masson (*Journeys*, i. 430) gives the same revenue; but fixes the army at 70,000 men, of whom 20,000 were disciplined. This may be assumed as an estimate of 1838, when Mr. Masson returned from Kābul. In 1845, Lieut.-Col. Steinbach (*Punjab*, p. 58) states the army to have amounted to 110,000 men, of whom 70,000 were regulars. The returns procured for Government in 1844, and which cannot be far wrong, show that there were upwards of 40,000 regularly drilled infantry, and a force of about 125,000 men in all, maintained with about 375 guns or field carriages. Cf. the *Calcutta Review*, iii. 176; Dr. Macgregor, *Sikhs*, ii. 86, and Major Smith, *Reigning Family of Lahore*, appendices, p. xxxvii, for estimates, correct in some particulars, and moderate in others.

For a statement of the Lahore revenues, see Appendix XXXVIII; and for a list of the Lahore army, see Appendix XXXIX.

Many descriptions of Ranjīt Singh's person and manners have been written, of which the fullest is perhaps that in Prinsep's edition of Murray, *Life*, p. 187, &c.; while Capt. Osborne's *Court and Camp*, and Col. Lawrence's *Adventurer in the Punjab*, contain many illus-

When Ranjīt Singh was Lord Auckland's host at Lahore and Amritsar, his utterance was difficult, and the powers of his body feeble; he gradually lost the use of his speech, and of the faculties of his mind; and, before his death, the Rājās of Jammu had usurped to themselves the whole of the functions of government, which the absence of Nau Nihāl Singh enabled them to do with little difficulty. The army was assembled, and a litter, said to contain the dying Mahārājā, was carried along the extended line. Dhiān Singh was assiduous in his mournful attentions; he seemed to take orders as if from his departing sovereign, and from time to time, during the solemn procession, he made known that Ranjīt Singh declared the Prince Kharak Singh his successor, and himself, Dhiān Singh, the wazīr or minister of the kingdom.[1] The soldiery acquiesced in silence, and the British Government was perhaps more sincere than the Sikh people in the congratulations offered, agreeably to custom, to the new and unworthy master of the Punjab.

1839.

The artifices of Dhiān Singh to bringabout the quiet succession of Kharak Singh.

trative touches and anecdotes. The only good likeness of the Mahārājā which has been published is that taken by the Hon. Miss Eden; and it, especially in the original drawing, is true and expressive. Ranjīt Singh was of small stature. When young he was dexterous in all manly exercises, but in his old age he became weak and inclined to corpulency. He lost an eye when a child by the small-pox, and the most marked characteristic of his mental powers was a broad and massive forehead, which the ordinary portraits do not show.

1 Mr. Clerk's memorandum of 1842 for Lord Ellenborough.

CHAPTER VIII

FROM THE DEATH OF MAHĀRĀJĀ RANJĪT SINGH TO THE DEATH OF WAZĪR JAWĀHIR SINGH

1839–45

Kharak Singh's power usurped by his son Nau Nihāl Singh—Lieut.-Col. Wade and Mr. Clerk—Nau Nihāl Singh and the Rājās of Jammu—The death of Kharak Singh—The death of Nau Nihāl Singh—Sher Singh proclaimed Mahārājā, but the authority of sovereign assumed by the mother of Nau Nihāl Singh—Sher Singh gains over the troops and succeeds to power—The army assumes a voice in affairs, and becomes an organized political body—The English willing to interfere—The English undervalue the Sikhs—The Sikhs in Tibet:—opposed by the Chinese, and restrained by the English—The English in Kābul—General Pollock's campaign—The Sindhianwala and Jammu families—The death of Sher Singh—The death of Rājā Dhiān Singh—Dalīp Singh proclaimed Mahārājā with Hīra Singh as Wazīr—Unsuccessful insurrections—Pandit Jall's proceedings and views—Hīra Singh expelled and slain—Jawāhir Singh nominated Wazīr—Gulāb Singh submits—Pishaura Singh in rebellion—Jawāhir Singh put to death by the army.

1839.

Sher Singh claims the succession, June–July 1839; but Nau Nihāl Singh assumes all real power, and temporarily allies himself with the Jammu Rājās.

THE imbecile Kharak Singh was acknowledged as the master of the Punjab; but Sher Singh, the reputed son of the deceased king, at once urged *his* superior claims or merits on the attention of the British viceroy;[1] and Nau Nihāl Singh, the real offspring of the titular sovereign, hastened from Peshāwar to take upon himself the duties of ruler. The prince, a youth of eighteen, was in his heart opposed to the proclaimed minister and the Rājās of Jammu; but the ascendancy of one Chet Singh over the

[1] Government to Mr. Clerk, 12th July 1839. Mr. Clerk, who was acting for Col. Wade while absent at Peshāwar, seems to have detained Sher Singh's messenger, and to have sent his letter to the Governor-General somewhat in that ordinary spirit of Indian correspondence, which 'transmits' everything 'for information and for such orders as may seem necessary'. Lord Auckland hastily desired Sher Singh to be told Kharak Singh was his master.

1839.

weak mind of the Mahārājā, and Kharak Singh's own desire of resting upon the influence of the British agent, induced the two parties to coalesce, first for the destruction of the minion, and afterwards for the removal of Col. Wade. That officer had stood high with Ranjīt Singh as a liberal construer of Sikh rights, or as one who would carefully show how a collision with the English was to be avoided ; he had steadily refused to make Dhiān Singh the medium of his communications with the old Mahārājā ; he had offended the heir-apparent by unceremoniously accusing him of machinations with Afghān chiefs ; and in the eyes of the Sikhs he was pledged to Kharak Singh at all hazards, by the prominent part he had taken in the meeting at Rūpar before noticed. His presence was thus disliked, and his interference dreaded, by men not inclined to wholly yield themselves to English counsels, and yet accustomed to see the suggestions of the Governor-General regularly carried into effect by the sovereign of Lahore.

The favourite, Chet Singh, put to death, 8th Oct. 1839.

The privacy of the Mahārājā's household was rudely violated by the prince and minister at daybreak on the 8th of October 1839, and Chet Singh was awakened from his slumbers to be put to death, within a few paces of his terrified master.[1] The removal of Col. Wade was mixed up with the passage of British troops across the Punjab, and had to be effected in another manner.

Mr. Clerk succeeds Lieut.-Col. Wade as Agent, 1st April, 1840.

The Governor-General had designed that the Anglo-Indian army which accompanied Shāh Shujā should return by way of Peshāwar, instead of retracing its steps through the Bolān Pass ; and when his lordship visited Ranjīt Singh at Lahore, the proposition was verbally conceded, although

[1] Gulāb Singh was perhaps the most prominent and resolute actor in this tragedy, although his brother and Nau Nihāl Singh were both present. Col. Wade was desired to express to the Lahore Court the regret of the British Government that such a scene of violence should have occurred (Government to Col. Wade, 28th Oct. 1839) ; and similarly Mr. Clerk had been directed to explain to Kharak Singh the disapprobation with which the English viewed the practice of satī, with reference to what had taken place at his father's funeral. (Government to Mr. Clerk, 29th Aug. 1839.) [For a detailed account of this satī the reader is referred to Latif, *History of the Punjab*, pp. 492-6—ED.].

1840. not definitively settled by an interchange of letters.[1] In September 1839, Mr. Clerk was sent on a mission of condolence and congratulation to the new Mahārājā, and to finally arrange about the return of Lord Keane with the stormers of Ghazni.[2] The prince and minister were each conscious of their mutual enmity and secret design of grasping supremacy, but they were even more averse to the presence of a British army in the heart of the Punjab than to one hovering on a distant frontier. It might be used to take part with one or other claimant, or it might be turned against both in favour of the contemned Kharak Singh : but the passage of the troops could not be wholly refused, and they therefore urged a march by the difficult route of Dera Ismail Khān, and they succeeded in fixing upon a line which prudently avoided the capital, and also in obtaining a premature assurance that an English force should not again march through the Sikh country.[3] The chiefs were pleased with the new English negotiator, as all have ever been with that prompt and approved functionary. Something is always expected from a change, and when a return mission was deputed to Simla, it was whispered that Col. Wade had made himself personally objectionable to those who exercised sway at Lahore ; and the complaint was repeated to Lord Keane, when he quitted his army for a few days to visit the Mahārājā.[4] In the month of November (1839), Col. Wade was himself at the Sikh metropolis on his way from Kâbul, but Kharak Singh was kept at a distance on pretence of devotional observances, lest he should throw himself on the protection of one believed to

[1] Government to Mr. Clerk, 20th Aug. 1839.

[2] [Kandahar had been entered by the English and Shāh Shujā proclaimed Amīr on May 8th, 1839. Ghazni was stormed in July. Kābul was entered in August, and it was then arranged that the bulk of the army should return to India, leaving an army of occupation to maintain Shāh Shujā upon his throne.—Ed.]

[3] Mr. Clerk to Government, 14th Sept. 1839. The Governor-General was not satisfied that a kind of pledge had been given that British troops should not again cross the Punjab. (Government to Mr. Clerk, 14th Oct. 1839.)

[4] See, particularly, Government to Col. Wade, 29th Jan. 1840, and Col. Wade to Government, 1st April 1840.

be ill-disposed towards those who sought his life, or his virtual relinquishment of power.[1] 1840.

The relief of the British troops in Kābul.

A portion of the British army of invasion had eventually to be left in Afghānistān, as it was thought that Shāh Shujā could not maintain himself without support. The wants of regular forces are manifold, and a supply of stores and ammunition had to be collected for transmission to Kābul on Col. Wade's resumption of his duties at Ludhiāna, towards the end of 1839. It was desired to send a regiment of Sepoys as a guard with the convoy, but the Sikh minister and heir apparent urged that such could not be done under the terms of the agreement concluded a few months previously. Their aversion to their old English representative was mixed up with the general objection to making their country a common highway for foreign armies, and they thus ventured to offer obstructions to the speedy equipment of the isolated British forces, mainly with the view of discrediting Col. Wade. The Governor-General was justly impressed with the necessity of keeping open the straight road to Kābul, and he yielded to the wishes of the Lahore factions and removed his agent, but not before Dhiān Singh and the prince had despaired of effecting their object, and had allowed the convoy, bristling with bayonets, to proceed on its way.[2] In the beginning of April 1840, Mr. Clerk succeeded to the charge of the British relations with the Punjab; and, independent of his general qualifications, he was the person best suited to the requirements of the time; for the very reason which rendered the agency of

[1] Cf. Munshi Shāhamat Alī, *Sikhs and Afghāns*, p. 543, &c., and some remarks in a note, p. 545, about the English policy generally towards Kharak Singh, which note may safely be held to be Col. Wade's own. Doubtless had Col. Wade continued to enjoy the complete confidence or support of the Governor-General, the subsequent history of the Punjab would have been different from, if not better than, that which all have witnessed. So much may the British representative effect at an Indian court, without directly interfering, provided he is at once firm, judicious, and well-informed.

[2] The Governor-General was about to proceed to Calcutta, which made him the more desirous of having an agent on the frontier, at once approved of by himself and agreeable to the Sikhs, i. e. to the influential parties for the time being at Lahore. (Government to Col. Wade, 29th Jan. 1840.)

1840. Col. Wade invaluable when it was desired to preserve Sind and to invade Afghānistān, now rendered that of Mr. Clerk equally beneficial to the indeterminate policy of the English in India. Both officers had the confidence of the *de facto* Sikh rulers of the time, and all their recommendations were held to be given in a spirit of goodwill towards the Government of the Punjab, as well as in obedience to the dictates of British interests.

English negotiations about trade.

The Sikh prince and the English viceroy had thus each accomplished the objects of the moment. On the one hand, the Mahārājā was overawed by the vigour and success of his aspiring son, and, on the other, the Punjab was freely opened to the passage of British troops, in support of a policy which connected the west of Europe with the south of Asia by an unbroken chain of alliances. The attention of each party was next turned to other matters of near concern, and the English recurred to their favourite scheme of navigating the Indus, and of forming an entrepôt on that river, which should at once become the centre of a vast traffic.[1] The treaty of 1834 had placed a toll on boats which used the channels of the Indus and Sutlej, and in 1839 the Sikhs deferred to the changing views of their allies, and put the duty on the goods themselves, according to an assumed *ad valorem* scale, instead of on the containing vessels.[2] This scheme inevitably gave rise to a system of search and detention, and in June 1840 the tolls upon the *boats* were again reimposed, but at reduced rates, and with the omission of such as contained grain, wood, and limestone.[3] But in spite

[1] Government to Mr. Clerk, 4th May 1840. The establishment of a great entrepôt of trade was a main feature of the scheme for opening the navigation of the Indus. (Government to Capt. Wade, 5th Sept. 1836.)

[2] Mr. Clerk to Government, 19th May and 18th Sept. 1839, and Government to Mr. Clerk, 20th Aug. 1839. For the agreement itself, see Appendix XXXI.

[3] Mr. Clerk to Government, 5th May and 15th July 1840. For the agreement itself, see Appendix XXXII. Subsequently, idle discussions occasionally arose with local authorities, as to whether lime was included under limestone, whether bamboos were wood, and whether rice was comprehended under the technical term 'grain', which it is not in India. Similarly the limited meaning of 'corn' in England has, perhaps, given rise to the modern phrase 'bread-stuffs'.

1840.

of every government endeavour, and of the adventitious aid of large consuming armies, the expectation of creating an active and valuable commerce by the Indus has not yet been fulfilled; partly because Sind and Afghānistān are, in truth, unproductive countries on the whole, and are inhabited by half-savage races, with few wants and scanty means; and partly because a large capital has for ages been embarked in the land trade which connects the north of India with the south, which traverses the old principalities of Rājputāna and the fertile plains of Mālwā, and which gives a livelihood to the owners of numerous herds of camels and black cattle. To change the established economy of prudent merchants must be the work of time in a country long subject to political commotion, and the idea of forming an emporium by proclamation savours more of Eastern vanity than of English sense and soberness.[1]

Nau Nihāl Singh's schemes against the Rājās of Jammu.

Nau Nihāl Singh's great aim was to destroy, or to reduce to insignificance, the potent Rājās of Jammu, who wished to engross the whole power of the state, and who jointly held Ladākh and the hill principalities between the Rāvi and Jhelum in fief, besides numerous estates in various parts of the Punjab. He took advantage of the repeated dilatoriness of the Mandī and other Rājput chiefs around Kāngra in paying their stipulated tribute, to move a large force into the eastern hills, and the resistance his troops experienced amid mountain fastnesses seemed fully to justify the continuous dispatch of reinforcements. His design was, to place a considerable army immediately to the north-east of Jammu, to be ready to co-operate with the troops which could reach that place in a few marches from Lahore. The commanders chosen were the skilful General Ventura and the ardent young chief Ajīt Singh Sindhianwala, neither of whom bore goodwill towards Rājā Dhiān Singh.[2] The plans of the

[1] Nevertheless the experiment was repeated in 1846, on the annexation of the Jullundur Doāb, when it was hoped, but equally in vain, that Hoshiārpur might suddenly become a centre of exchange. Every part of India bears various marks of the unrealized hopes of sanguine individuals with reference to the expected benefits of English sway, which diffuses, indeed, some moral as well as material blessings, but which must effect its work by slow and laborious means

[2] Cf. Mr. Clerk to Government, 6th Sept. 1840.

1840.

Interrupted by discussions with the English about Afghānistān.

youthful prince thus seemed in every way well devised for placing the rājās in his grasp, but his attention was distracted by disputes with the English authorities about the limits of the expanding dominion of Lahore and of the restored empire of Kābul, and by a direct accusation not only of encouraging turbulent refugees from Shāh Shujā's power, but of giving friendly assurances to Dost Muhammad Khān, who was then preparing for that inroad which fluttered the English authorities in Khorasan, and yet paved the way for the surrender of their dreaded enemy. Shāh Shujā claimed all places not specified in the treaty, or not directly held by Lahore ; nor can it be denied that the English functionaries about the Shāh were disposed to consider old Durrāni claims as more valid than the new rights of Sikh conquerors ; and thus the *province* of Peshāwar, which the Punjab Government further maintained to have been ceded in form by the Shāh separately in 1834, as well as by the treaty of 1838, was proposed to be reduced to strips of land along the banks of its dividing river.[1] Intercepted papers were produced, bearing the seals of Nau Nihāl Singh, and promising pecuniary aid to Dost Muhammad ; but the charge of treachery was calmly repelled, the seals were alleged to be forgeries, and the British agent for the Punjab admitted that it was not the character of the free and confident Sikhs to resort to secret and traitorous correspondence.[2] The Bārakzai chief, Sultān Muhammad Khān, was, however, made to lead as prisoners to Ludhiāna the Ghilzai rebels who had sought an asylum in his fief of Kohāt, near Peshāwar, and whose near presence disturbed the antagonistic rule of the arbitrary Shāh and his moderate English allies.[3]

[1] See particularly Sir William Macnaghten to Government, 28th Feb. and 12th March 1840.

[2] Government to Mr. Clerk, 1st Oct. 1840, and Mr. Clerk to Government, 9th Dec. 1840. Cf., however, Col. Steinbach (*Punjab*, p. 23), who states that the prince was rousing Nepāl as well as Kābul to aid him in expelling the English ; forgetful that Nau Nihāl Singh's first object was to make himself master of the Punjab by destroying the Jammu Rājās.

[3] Government to Mr. Clerk, 12th Oct., and Mr. Clerk to Government, 14th May, 10th Sept., and 24th Oct. 1840.

1840.

Death of Mahārājā Kharak Singh, 5th Nov. 1840.

Nau Nihāl Singh thus seemed to have overcome the danger which threatened him on the side of England, and to be on the eve of reducing the overgrown power of his grandfather's favourites. At the same time the end of the Mahārājā's life was evidently approaching; and although his decline was credibly declared to have been hastened by drugs as well as by unfilial harshness, there were none who cared for a ruler so feeble and unworthy. Kharak Singh at last died on the 5th November 1840, prematurely old and care-worn, at the age of thirty-eight, and Nau Nihāl Singh became a king in name as well as in power; but the same day dazzled him with a crown and deprived him of life. He had performed the last rites at the funeral pyre of his father, and he was passing under a covered gateway with the eldest son of Gulāb Singh by his side, when a portion of the structure fell, and killed the minister's nephew on the spot, and so seriously injured the prince that he became senseless at the time, and expired during the night. It is not positively known that the Rājās of Jammu thus designed to remove Nau Nihāl Singh; but it is difficult to acquit them of the crime, and it is certain that they were capable of committing it. Self-defence is the only palliation, for it is equally certain that the prince was compassing their degradation, and, perhaps, their destruction.[1] Nau Nihāl Singh was killed in his twentieth year; he promised to be an able and vigorous ruler; and had his life been spared, and had not English policy partly forestalled him, he would have found an ample field for his ambition in Sind, in Afghānistān, and beyond the Hindu Kush; and he might, perhaps, at last have boasted that the inroads of Mahmud and of

Death of the Prince Nau Nihāl Singh, 5th Nov. 1840.

[1] Cf. Mr. Clerk to Government, 6th, 7th, and 10th Nov. 1840, who, further, in his memorandum of 1842, drawn up for Lord Ellenborough, mentions Gen. Ventura's opinion that the fall of the gateway was accidental. Lieut.-Col. Steinbach, *Punjab* (p. 24), and Major Smith, *Reigning Family of Lahore* (p. 35, &c.), may be quoted as giving some particulars, the latter on the authority of an eye-witness, a European adventurer, known as Capt. Gardner, who was present a part of the time, and whose testimony is unfavourable to Rājā Dhiān Singh. [The scene of this tragedy was the gateway in the fort at Lahore facing the Hazuri Bagh and the Badshāhi Musjid. It is now closed, but may be easily recognized by its prominent towers.—ED.]

1840. Taimūr had been fully avenged by the aroused peasants of India.

Sher Singh proclaimed sovereign;

The good-natured voluptuary, Sher Singh, was regarded by the Sikh minister and by the British agent as the only person who could succeed to the sovereignty of the Punjab; and as he was absent from Lahore when the Mahārājā died and his son was killed, Dhiān Singh concealed the latter circumstance as long as possible, to give Sher Singh time to collect his immediate friends; and the English representative urged him by message to maintain good order along the frontier, as men's minds were likely to be excited by what had taken place.[1] But Sher Singh's paternity was more than doubtful; he possessed no commanding and few popular qualities; the Rājās of Jammu were odious to the majority of the Sikh chiefs; and thus Chand Kaur, the widow of Kharak Singh, and the mother of the slain prince, assumed to herself the functions of regent or ruler, somewhat unexpectedly indeed, but still unopposed at the moment by those whom she had surprised. She was supported by several men of reputation, but mainly by the Sindhianwala family, which traced to a near and common ancestor with Ranjīt Singh. The lady herself talked of adding to the claims of the youthful Hīra Singh, by adopting him, as he had really, if not formally, been adopted by the old Mahārājā. She further distracted the factions by declaring that her daughter-in-law was pregnant; and one party tried to gain her over by suggesting a marriage with Sher Singh, an alliance which she spurned, and the other more reasonably proposed Atar Singh Sindhianwala as a suitable partner, for she might have taken an honoured station in his household agreeably to the latitude of village custom in the north-west of India. But the widow of the Mahārājā loudly asserted her own right to supreme power, and after a few weeks the government was stated to be composed, 1st, of the 'Mai', or 'Mother', pre-eminently as sovereign, or as regent for the expected offspring of Nau Nihāl Singh; 2nd, of Sher Singh as vicegerent, or as president of the council of state; and, 3rd, of Dhiān Singh as wazīr,

but Chand Kaur, the widow of Kharak Singh, assumes power, and Sher Singh retires.

[1] Cf. Mr. Clerk to Government, 7th Nov. 1840, and also Mr. Clerk's Memorandum of 1842.

1840.

or executive minister. The compromise was a mere temporary expedient, and Dhiān Singh and Sher Singh soon afterwards began to absent themselves for varying periods from Lahore: the one partly in the hope that the mass of business which had arisen with the English, and with which he was familiar, would show to all that his aid was essential to the government; and the other, or indeed both of them, to silently take measures for gaining over the army with promises of donatives and increased pay, so that force might be resorted to at a fitting time. But the scorn with which Sher Singh's hereditary claim was treated made the minister doubtful whether a more suitable instrument might not be necessary, and the English authorities were accordingly reminded of what perhaps they had never known, viz. that Rāni Jindan, a favourite wife or concubine of Ranjīt Singh, had borne to him a son named Dalīp, a few months before the conferences took place about reseating Shāh Shujā on the throne of Kābul.[1]

Dalīp Singh's birth and pretensions made known.

The British viceroy did not acknowledge Mai Chand Kaur as the undoubted successor of her husband and son, or as the sovereign of the country; but he treated her government as one *de facto*, so far as to carry on business as usual through the accredited agents of either power. The Governor-General's anxiety for the preservation of order in the Punjab was nevertheless considerable; and it was increased by the state of affairs in Afghānistān, for the attempts of Dost Muhammad and the resolution of meeting him with English means alone, rendered the dispatch of additional troops necessary, and before Kharak Singh's death three thousand men had reached Ferozepore on their way to Kābul.[2] The progress of this strong brigade was not delayed by the contentions at Lahore; it pursued its march without interruption, and on its arrival at Peshāwar it found Dost Muhammad a prisoner instead of a victor. The ex-Amīr journeyed

The English remain neutral at the time.

Dost Muhammad Khān attempts Kābul, but eventually surrenders to the English.

[1] Cf. Mr. Clerk to Government, of dates between the 10th Nov. 1840, and 2nd Jan. 1841, inclusive, particularly of the 11th and 24th Nov. and 11th Dec., besides those specified. It seems almost certain that the existence of the boy Dalīp was not before known to the British authorities.

[2] Government to Mr. Clerk, 1st and 2nd Nov. 1840, and other letters to and from that functionary.

1840.

through the Punjab escorted by a relieved brigade; and although Sher Singh was then laying siege to the citadel of Lahore, the original prudence of fixing a route for British troops clear of the Sikh capital, and the complete subjugation of the Muhammadan tribes, left the English commander unaware of the struggle going on, except from ordinary reports and news-writers.[1]

Sher Singh gains over the troops with Dhiān Singh's aid.

The English Government made, indeed, no declaration with regard to the Lahore succession; but it was believed by all that Sher Singh was looked upon as the proper representative of the kingdom, and the advisers of Mai Chand Kaur soon found that they could not withstand the specious claims of the prince, and the commanding influence of the British name, without throwing themselves wholly on the support of Rājā Dhiān Singh. That chief was at one time not unwilling to be the sole minister of the Mahārāni, and the more sagacious Gulāb Singh saw advantages to his family amid the complex modes necessary in a female rule, which might not attend the direct sway of a prince of average understanding, inclined to favouritism, and pledged to Sikh principles. But the Mai's councillors would not consent to be thrown wholly into the shade, and Dhiān Singh thus kept aloof, and secretly assured Sher Singh of his support at a fitting time. The prince, on his part, endeavoured to sound the English agent as to his eventual recognition, and he was satisfied with the reply, although he merely received an assurance that the allies of thirty-two years wished to see a strong government in the Punjab.[2]

Sher Singh attacks Lahore, 14th–18th Jan. 1841.

Sher Singh had, with the minister's aid, gained over some divisions of the army, and he believed that all would declare for him if he boldly put himself at their head. The eagerness of the prince, or of his immediate followers, somewhat precipitated measures; and when he suddenly appeared at Lahore, on the 14th January 1841, he found that Dhiān Singh had not arrived from Jammu, and that Gulāb Singh

[1] The returning brigade was commanded by the veteran Col. Wheeler [afterwards Sir Hugh Wheeler, the ill-fated commander of the garrison of Cawnpore—Ed.], whose name is familiar to the public in connexion both with Afghān and Sikh wars.

[2] See Mr. Clerk's letters to Government of Dec. 1840 and Jan. 1841, generally, particularly that of the 9th Jan.

would rather fight for the Mahārānī, the acknowledged head of the state, than tamely becom a party on compulsion to his ill-arranged schemes. But Sher Singh was no longer his own master, and the impetuous soldiery at once proceeded to breach the citadel. Gulāb Singh in vain urged some delay, or a suspension of hostilities; but on the 18th January Dhiān Singh and most of the principal chiefs had arrived and ranged themselves on one side or the other. A compromise took place; the Mai was outwardly treated with every honour, and large estates were conferred upon her; but Sher Singh was proclaimed Mahārājā of the Punjab, Dhiān Singh was declared once more to be wazīr of the state, and the pay of the soldiery was permanently raised by one rupee *per mensem*. The Sindhianwalas felt that they must be obnoxious to the new ruler; and Atar Singh and Ajīt Singh took early measures to effect their escape from the capital, and eventually into the British territories; but Lehna Singh, the other principal member, remained with the division of the army which he commanded in the hills of Kulū and Mandī.[1]

1841.

Chand Kaur yields, and Sher Singh proclaimed Mahārājā.

The Sindhianwala family.

Sher Singh had induced the troops of the state to make him a king, but he was unable to command them as soldiers, or to sway them as men, and they took advantage of his incapacity and of their own strength to wreak their vengeance upon various officers who had offended them, and upon various regimental accountants and muster-masters who may have defrauded them of their pay. Some houses were plundered, and several individuals were seized and slain. A few Europeans had likewise rendered themselves obnoxious; and General Court, a moderate and high-minded man, had to fly for his life, and a brave young Englishman named Foulkes was cruelly put to death. Nor was this spirit of violence confined to the troops at the capital, or to those in the eastern hills, but it spread to Kashmīr and Peshāwar; and in the former place Miān Singh, the governor, was killed by the soldiery; and in the latter, General Avitabile was so hard pressed that he was ready to abandon his post and to seek safety in Jalālābād.[2]

The army becomes uncontrollable.

[1] See Mr. Clerk's letters, of dates from 17th to 30th Jan. 1841.

[2] Cf. Mr. Clerk to Government, 26th Jan., 8th and 14th Feb., 28th April, and 30th May 1841.

1841.

It was believed at the time, that the army would not rest satisfied with avenging what it considered its own injuries; it was thought it might proceed to a general plunder or confiscation of property; the population of either side of the Sutlej was prepared for an extensive commotion, and the wealthy merchants of Amritsar prophesied the pillage of their warehouses, and were clamorous for British protection. Sher Singh shrank within himself appalled, and he seemed timorously to resort to the English agent for support against the fierce spirit he had roused and could not control; or he doubtfully endeavoured to learn whether such disorders would be held equally to end his reign and the British alliance. The English watched the confusion with much interest and some anxiety, and when cities seemed about to be plundered, and provinces ravaged, the question of the duty of a civilized and powerful neighbour naturally suggested itself, and was answered by a cry for interference; but the shapes which the wish took were various and contradictory. Nevertheless, the natural desire for aggrandizement, added to the apparently disorganized state of the army, contributed to strengthen a willing belief in the inferiority of the Sikhs as soldiers, and in the great excellence of the mountain levies of the chiefs of Jammu, who alone seemed to remain the masters of their own servants. To the apprehension of the English authorities, the Sikhs were mere upstart peasants of doubtful courage, except when maddened by religious persecution; but the ancient name of Rājput was sufficient to invest the motley followers of a few valiant chiefs with every warlike quality. This erroneous estimate of the Sikhs tainted British counsels until the day of P'heerooshuhur.[1]

Sher Singh alarmed.

The English anxious about the general tranquillity,

undervalue the Sikhs,

[1] This erroneous estimate of the troops of the Jammū Rājās and other hill chiefs of the Punjab relatively to the Sikhs, may be seen insisted on in Mr. Clerk's letters to Government of the 2nd Jan. and 13th April 1841, and especially in those of the 8th and 10th Dec. of that year, and of the 15th Jan., 10th Feb., and 23rd April, 1842. Mr. Clerk's expressions are very decided, such as that the Sikhs feared the hill-men, who were braver, and that Rājputs might hold Afghāns in check, which Sikhs could not do; but he seems to have forgotten that the ancient Rājputs had, during the century gone by, yielded on either side to the new and aspiring Gurkhas and Marathās,

The English seemed thus called upon to do something, and their agent in Kābul, who was committed to make Shāh Shujā a monarch in means as well as in rank, grasped at the death of Ranjīt Singh's last representative; he pronounced the treaties with Lahore to be at an end, and he wanted to annex Peshāwar to the Afghān sway. The British Government in Calcutta rebuked this hasty conclusion, but cheered itself with the prospect of eventually adding the Derajat of the Indus, as well as Peshāwar, to the unproductive Durrāni kingdom, without any breach of faith towards the Sikhs; for it was considered that their dominions might soon be rent in two by the Sindhianwala Sirdars and the Jammu Rājās.[1] The British agent on the Sutlej did not think the Lahore empire so near its dissolution in that mode, and confident in his own dexterity, in the superiority of his troops, and in the greatness of the English name, he proposed to march to the Sikh capital with 12,000 men, to beat and disperse a rebel army four times more numerous, to restore order, to strengthen the sovereignty of Sher Singh, and take the cis-Sutlej districts and forty lakhs of rupees in coin as the price of his aid.[2] This promptitude made the Mahārājā think himself in danger of his life at the hands of his subjects, and of his kingdom at the hands of his allies;[3] nor was the Governor-General prepared for a virtual invasion, although he was ready to use force if a large majority of the Sikhs as well as

1841.

and are ready to interfere by force of arms, Feb. 1841.

and even that the Sikhs themselves had laid the twice-born princes of the Himālayas under contribution from the Ganges to Kashmīr.

[1] See especially Government to Sir William Macnaghten, of 28th Dec. 1840, in reply to his proposals of the 26th Nov. The Governor-General justly observed that the treaty was not formed with an individual chief, but with the Sikh state, so long as it might last and fulfil the obligations of its alliance.

[2] Mr. Clerk to Government, of the 26th March 1841.

[3] When Sher Singh became aware of Mr. Clerk's propositions, he is said simply to have drawn his finger across his throat, meaning that the Sikhs would at once take his life if he assented to such measures. The readiness of the English to co-operate was first propounded to Fakīr Azīz-ud-dīn, and that wary negotiator said the matter could not be trusted to paper; he would himself go and tell Sher Singh of it. He went, but he did not return, his object being to keep clear of schemes so hazardous.

1841.

The military disorders subside, but the people become suspicious of the English.

the Mahārājā himself desired such intervention.[1] After this, the disorders in the army near Lahore gradually subsided ; but the opinion got abroad that overtures had been made to the eager English ; and so far were the Sikh soldiery from desiring foreign assistance, that Lehna Singh Sindhianwala was imprisoned by his own men, in the Mandī hills, on a charge of conspiracy with his refugee brother to introduce the supremacy of strangers.[2]

Major Broadfoot's passage across the Punjab.

The suspicions and hatred of the Sikhs were further roused by the proceedings of an officer, afterwards nominated to represent British friendship and moderation. Major Broadfoot had been appointed to recruit a corps of Sappers and Miners for the service of Shāh Shujā, and as the family of that sovereign, and also the blind Shāh Zamān with his wives and children, were about to proceed to Kābul, he was charged with the care of the large and motley convoy. He entered the Punjab in April 1841, when the mutinous spirit of the Sikh army was spreading from the capital to the provinces. A body of mixed or Muhammadan troops had been directed by the Lahore Government to accompany the royal families as an escort of protection, but Major Broadfoot became suspicious of the good faith of this detachment, and on the banks of the Rāvi he prepared to resist, with his newly recruited regiment, an attack on the part of those who had been sent to conduct him in safety. On his way to the Indus he was even more suspicious of other bodies of troops which he met or passed ; he believed them to be intent on plundering his camp, and he considered that he only avoided collisions by dexterous negotiations and by timely demonstrations of force. On crossing the river at Attock, his persuasion of the hostile designs of the battalions in that neighbourhood and towards Peshāwar was so strong, that he put his camp in a complete state of defence, broke up the bridge of boats, and called upon the Afghān population to rise and aid him against the troops of their government. But it does not appear that his apprehensions had

[1] Government to Mr. Clerk, 18th Feb. and 29th March 1841. The Governor-General truly remarked that Mr. Clerk, rather than the Mahārājā, had proposed an armed interference.

[2] Mr. Clerk to Government, 25th March 1841.

1841.

even a plausible foundation, until at this time he seized certain deputies from a mutinous regiment when on their way back from a conference with their commander, and who appear to have come within the limits of the British pickets. This proceeding alarmed both General Avitabile, the governor of Peshāwar, and the British agent at that place; and a brigade, already warned, was hurried from Jalālābād to overawe the Sikh forces encamped near the Indus. But the Shāh's families and their numerous followers had passed on unmolested before the auxiliary troops had cleared the Khaibar Pass, and the whole proceeding merely served to irritate and excite the distrust of the Sikhs generally, and to give Sher Singh an opportunity of pointing out to his tumultuous soldiers that the Punjab was surrounded by English armies, both ready and willing to make war upon them.[1]

The Sikhs further irritated against the English.

The changed relation of the Lahore army to the state.

Before the middle of 1841 the more violent proceedings of the Lahore troops had ceased, but the relation of the army to the state had become wholly altered; it was no longer the willing instrument of an arbitrary and genial government, but it looked upon itself, and was regarded by others, as the representative body of the Sikh people, as the 'Khālsa' itself assembled by tribes or centuries to take its part in public affairs. The efficiency of the army as a disciplined force was not much impaired, for a higher feeling possessed the men, and increased alacrity and resolution supplied the place of exact training. They were sensible of the advantages of systematic union, and they were proud of their armed array as the visible body of Gobind's commonwealth. As a general rule, the troops were obedient to their appointed officers, so far as concerned their ordinary military duties, but the position of a regiment, of a brigade, of a division, or of the whole army, relatively to the executive government of the country, was determined by a committee or assemblage of committees, termed a 'Panch' or 'Panchāyat', i.e. a jury or committee of five, composed of men selected from each battalion, or each company, in consideration of their general character as faithful *Sikh* soldiers, or from their particular influence in

Its military organization enables it to become the representative body of the Khālsa.

[1] Cf. Mr. Clerk to Government, 25th May and 10th June 1841.

1841. their native villages.[1] The system of Panchāyats is common throughout India, and every tribe, or section of a tribe, or trade, or calling, readily submits to the decisions of its elders or superiors seated together in consultation. In the Punjab the custom received a further development from the organization necessary to an army; and even in the crude form of representation thus achieved, the Sikh people were enabled to interfere with effect, and with some degree of consistency, in the nomination and in the removal of their rulers. But these large assemblies sometimes added military licence to popular tumult, and the corrupt spirit of mercenaries to the barbarous ignorance of ploughmen. Their resolutions were often unstable or unwise, and the representatives of different divisions might take opposite sides from sober conviction or self-willed prejudice, or they might be bribed and cajoled by such able and unscrupulous men as Rājā Gulāb Singh.[2]

Negotiations with the English about inland trade, 1841.

The partial repose in the autumn of 1841 was taken advantage of to recur to those mercantile objects, of which the British Government never lost sight. The facilities of navigating the Indus and Sutlej had been increased, and it was now sought to extend corresponding advantages to the land trade of the Punjab. Twenty years before, Mr. Moorcroft had, of his own instance, made proposals to Ranjīt Singh for the admission of British goods into the Lahore dominions at fixed rates of duty.[3] In 1832, Col. Wade again brought forward the subject of a general tariff for the Punjab, and the Mahārājā appeared to be not indisposed to meet the views of his allies; but he really disliked to make arrangements of which he did not fully see the scope and tendency, and he thus tried to evade even a settlement of the river tolls, by saying that the prosperity

[[1] One is strongly reminded of the organization of the Parliamentary army under Cromwell, with its regimental 'elders', &c.—Ed.]

[2] See Mr. Clerk's letter of the 14th March 1841, for Fakīr Azīz-ud-dīn's admission, that even then the army was united and ruled by its panchāyats. With reference to the Panchāyats of India, it may be observed that Hallam shows, chiefly from Palgrave, that English juries likewise were originally as much arbitrators as investigators of facts. (*Middle Ages*, Notes to Chap. VIII.)

[3] Moorcroft, *Travels*, i. 103.

of Amritsar would be affected, and by recurring to that ever ready objection, the slaughter of kine. Cows, he said, might be used as food by those who traversed the Punjab under a British guarantee.[1] In 1840, when Afghānistān was garrisoned by Indian troops, the Governor-General pressed the subject a second time on the notice of the Lahore authorities; and after a delay of more than a year, Sher Singh assented to a reduced scale and to a fixed rate of duty, and also to levy the whole sum at one place; but the charges still appeared excessive, and the British viceroy lamented the ignorance displayed by the Sikh Mahārājā, and the disregard which he evinced for the true interests of his subjects.[2]

1841.

Zorāwar Singh, the deputy of the Jammu Rājās, takes Iskārdo, 1840.

The Lahore Government was convulsed at its centre, but its spirit of progress and aggrandizement was active on the frontiers, where not hemmed in by British armies. The deputies in Kashmīr had always been jealous of the usurpations of Gulāb Singh in Tibet, but Mīān Singh, a rude soldier, the governor of the valley during the commotions at Lahore, was alarmed into concessions by the powerful and ambitious Rājās of Jammu, and he left Iskārdo, and the whole valley of the Upper Indus, a free field for the aggressions of their lieutenants.[3] Ahmad Shāh, the reigning chief of Balti, had differences with his family, and he proposed to pass over his eldest son in favour of a younger one, in fixing the succession. The natural heir would seem to have endeavoured to interest the Governor of Kashmīr,

[1] Cf. Col. Wade to Government, 7th Nov. and 5th Dec. 1832. These objections are often urged in India, not because they are felt to be reasonable in themselves, or applicable to the point at issue, but because religion is always a strong ground to stand on, and because it is the only thing which the English do not virtually profess a desire to change. Religion is thus brought in upon all occasions of apprehension or disinclination.

[2] Government to Mr. Clerk, 4th May 1840 and 11th Oct. 1841, and Mr. Clerk to Government of 20th Sept. 1841.

[3] Sir Claude Wade (*Narrative of Services*, p. 33, note) represents the Jammu family to have obtained from the British Government an assurance that the limitations put upon Sikh conquests to the west and south by the Tripartite Treaty of 1839 would not be held to apply to the north or Tibetan side, in which direction, it was said, the Sikhs were free to act as they might please.

1841.

and also Zorāwar Singh, the Jammu deputy in Ladākh, in his favour; and in 1840 he fled from his father and sought refuge and assistance in Leh. Gnodup Tanzin, the puppet king of Ladākh, had conceived the idea of throwing off the Jammu authority; he had been trying to engage Ahmad Shāh in the design; the absence of Zorāwar Singh was opportune, and he allowed a party of Iskārdo troops to march on Leh, and to carry off the son of their chief. Zorāwar Singh made this inroad a pretext for war; and before the middle of the year 1840 he was master of Little Tibet, but he left the chiefship in the family of Ahmad Shāh, on the payment of a petty yearly tribute of seven thousand rupees, so barren are the rocky principalities between Imaus and Emodus.[1] Zorāwar Singh was emboldened by his own success and by the dissensions at Lahore; he claimed fealty from Gilgit; he was understood to be desirous of quarrelling with the Chinese governor of Yarkand; and he renewed antiquated claims of Ladākh supremacy, and demanded the surrender of Rohtak, Gāro, and the lakes of Mānsarowar, from the priestly king of Lhasa.[2]

Zorāwar Singh seizes Gāro from the Chinese of Lassa, 1841.

Zorāwar Singh was desirous of acquiring territory, and he was also intent on monopolizing the trade in shawl-wool, a considerable branch of which followed the Sutlej and more eastern roads to Ludhiāna and Delhi, and added nothing to the treasury of Jammu.[3] In May and June 1841, he occupied the valleys of the Indus and Sutlej, to the sources of those rivers, and he fixed a garrison close to the frontiers of Nepāl, and on the opposite side of the snowy range from the British post of Almorā. The petty Rājpūt princes between the Kālī and Sutlej suffered in their revenues, and trembled for their territories; the Nepāl Government had renewed intrigues set on foot in 1838, and was in correspondence with the crafty minister of Lahore, and with the disaffected Sindhianwala chiefs;[4] and the English Government itself

[1] Cf. Mr. Clerk to Government, 26th April, 9th and 31st May, and 25th Aug. 1840.

[2] Cf. Mr. Clerk to Government, 25th Aug. and 8th Oct. 1840, and 2nd Jan. and 5th June 1841.

[3] Cf. Mr. Clerk to Government, 5th and 22nd June, 1841

[4] Cf. Mr. Clerk to Government, 16th Aug. and 23rd Nov. 1840, and 17th Jan. 1841; and Government to Mr. Clerk, 19th Oct. 1840.

was at war with China, at the distance of half the earth's circumference.[1] It was held that the trade of British Indian subjects must not be interfered with by Jammū conquests in Chinese Tibet; it was deemed unadvisable to allow the Lahore and Nepāl dominions to march with one another behind the Himālayas; and it was thought the Emperor of Pekin might confound independent Sikhs with the predominant English, and throw additional difficulties in the way of pending or probable negotiations.[2] It was, therefore, decided that Sher Singh should require his feudatories to evacuate the Lassa territories; a day, the 10th of December 1841, was fixed for the surrender of Gāro; and a British officer was sent to see that the Grand Lama's authority was fully re-established. The Mahārājā and his tributaries yielded, and Zorāwar Singh was recalled; but before the order could reach him, or be acted on, he was surrounded in the depth of winter, and at a height of

1841.

The English interfere.

The correspondence of Nepāl with the Sikhs, or rather with the Jammu faction, doubtless arose in part from the presence of Mātabar Singh, an eminent Gurkha, as a refugee in the Punjab. He crossed the Sutlej in 1838, and soon got a high command in the Lahore service, or rather, perhaps, a high position at the court. His success in this way, and his necessary correspondence with British functionaries, made the Nepāl Government apprehensive of him, and at last he became so important in the eyes of the English themselves, that in 1840, when differences with Kātmāndu seemed likely to lead to hostilities, overtures were virtually made to him, and he was kept in hand, as it were, to be supported as a claimant for power, or as a partisan leader, should active measures be necessary. He was thus induced to quit the Punjab, where his presence, indeed, was not otherwise satisfactory; but the differences with the Gurkhas were composed, and Mātabar Singh was cast aside with an allowance of a thousand rupees a month from the potent government which had demeaned itself by using him as a tool. (Cf. particularly Government to Mr. Clerk, 4th May and 26th Oct. 1840; and Mr. Clerk to Government, 22nd Oct. 1840.)

[[1] The first China or Opium War ended by the Treaty of Nankin (1842), which resulted in the cession of Hong Kong and the opening of the first five treaty ports.—Ed.]

[2] Cf. Government to Mr. Clerk, 16th Aug. and 6th and 20th Sept. 1841. The Sikhs, too, had their views with regard to China, and naïvely proposed co-operation with the English, or a diversion in *Tartary* in favour of the war then in progress on the *sea coast*! (Mr. Clerk to Government, 18th Aug. and 20th Oct. 1841.)

1841. twelve thousand feet or more above the sea, by a superior force from Lassa inured to frost and snow. The men of the Indian plains and southern Himālayas were straitened for fuel—as necessary as food in such a climate and at such a season; some even burnt the stocks of their muskets to warm their hands; and on the day of battle, in the middle of December, they were benumbed in their ranks during a fatal pause; their leader was slain, a few principal men were reserved as prisoners, but the mass was left to perish, huddled in heaps behind rocks, or at the bottoms of ravines. The neighbouring garrison on the Nepāl frontier fled on hearing of the defeat; the men were not pursued, but in passing over ranges sixteen thousand feet high, on their way to Almorā, the deadly cold reduced them to half their numbers, and left a moiety of the remainder maimed for life.[1]

The Sikhs defeated by a force from Lassa.

The Chinese recover Garo.

During the spring of 1842 the victorious Chinese advanced along the Indus, and not only recovered their own province, but occupied Ladākh and laid siege to the citadel of Leh. The Kalmaks and the ancient Sokpos, or Sacae, talked of another invasion of Kashmīr, and the Tartars of the Greater and Lesser Tibet were elate with the prospect of revenge and plunder: but troops were poured across the Himālayas; the swordsmen and cannoneers of the south were dreaded by the unwarlike Bhotiās; the siege of Leh was raised, and in the month of September (1842) Gulāb Singh's commander seized the Lassa Wazīr by treachery, and dislodged his troops by stratagem from a position between Leh and Rohtak, where they had proposed to await the return of winter. An arrangement was then come to between the Lassa and Lahore authorities, which placed matters on their old footing, agreeably to the desire of the English; and as

Peace between the Chinese and Sikhs.

[1] In this rapid sketch of Ladākh affairs, the author has necessarily depended for the most part on his own personal knowledge. After the battle on the Mānsarowar Lake, the western passes remained closed for five weeks, and the defeat of the Sikhs was thus made known in Calcutta and Peshāwar, through the reports of the fugitives to Almorā, before it was heard of in the neighbouring Gāro. From the observations of Lieut. H. Strachey it would appear that the height of the Mānsarowar Lake is 15,250 feet. (*Jour. As. Soc.*, Bengal, Aug. 1848, p. 155.)

the shawl-wool trade to the British provinces was also revived, no further intervention was considered necessary between the jealous Chinese and the restrained Sikhs.[1] 1841.

The ambitious views of the Jammu Rājās towards the Indus.

When, in April 1841, the troops in Kashmīr put their governor to death, Rājā Gulāb Singh was sent to restore order, and to place the authority of the new manager, Ghulām Muhī-ud-dīn, on a firm footing. The mutinous regiments were overpowered by numbers and punished with severity, and it was soon apparent that Gulāb Singh had made the governor whom he was aiding a creature of his own, and had become the virtual master of the valley.[2] Neither the minister nor his brother had ever been thought well pleased with English interference in the affairs of the Punjab; they were at the time in suspicious communication with Nepāl; and they were held to be bound to Sultān Muhammad Khān, whose real or presumed intrigues with the enemies of Shāh Shujā had occasioned his removal to Lahore a year previously.[3] General Avitabile had become more and more urgent to be relieved from his dangerous post at Peshāwar; the influence of Dhiān Singh was predominant in Sikh counsels; and the English opinion of the ability of the Jammu Rājās and of the excellence of their troops was well known, and induced a belief in partiality to be presumed.[4] It was therefore proposed by

[1] At Amritsar in March 1846, when Gulāb Singh was formally inaugurated as Mahārājā of Jammū, he exhibited the engagements with the Lama of Lassa, drawn out on his part in yellow, and on the part of the Chinese in red ink, and each impressed with the open hand of the negotiators dipped in either colour instead of a regular seal or written signature. The 'Panja', or *hand*, seems in general use in Asia as typical of a covenant, and it is, moreover, a common emblem on the standards of the eastern Afghāns.

[2] Cf. Mr. Clerk to Government, 13th May, 9th July, and 3rd Sept. 1840.

[3] For this presumed understanding between the Jammū Rājās and the Bārakzais of Peshāwar, Mr. Clerk's letter of the 8th Oct. 1840, may be referred to among others.

[4] Mr. Clerk leant upon and perhaps much overrated Dhiān Singh's capacity, 'his military talents, and aptitude for business.' (Mr. Clerk to Government, 7th Nov. 1840, and 13th May 1841.) General Ventura, for instance, considered the Rājā to possess a very slender understanding, and in such a matter he may be held to be a fair as well as a competent judge, although personally averse to the minister.

1841.

Clash with the policy of the English.

Sher Singh to bestow the Afghān province on the restorer of order in Kashmīr. But this arrangement would have placed the hills from the neighbourhood of Kāngra to the Kaibar Pass in the hands of men averse to the English and hostile to Shāh Shujā; and as their troublesome ambition had been checked in Tibet, so it was resolved that their more dangerous establishment on the Kābul river should be prevented. In the autumn of 1841, therefore, the veto of the English agent was put upon Rājā Gulāb Singh's nomination to Peshāwar.[1]

The insurrection at Kābul, Nov. 1841.

About two months afterwards, or on the 2nd November (1841), that insurrection broke out in Kābul which forms so painful a passage in British history. No valiant youth arose superior to the fatal influence of military subordination, to render illustrious the retreat of a handful of Englishmen, or, more illustrious still, the successful defence of their position.[2] The brave spirit of Sir William Macnaghten laboured perseveringly, but in vain, against the unworthy fear which possessed the highest officers of the army; and the dismay of the distant commanders imparted some of its poison to the supreme authorities in India, who were weary of the useless and burdensome occupation of Khorasan. The first generous impulse was awed into a desire of annulling the Durrāni alliance, and of collecting a force on the Indus, or even so far back as the Sutlej, there to fight for the empire of Hindustān with the torrents of exulting Afghāns which the startled imaginations of Englishmen readily conjured up.[3] No confidence was placed in the efficiency or the

[1] Government to Mr. Clerk, 2nd Aug., and Mr. Clerk to Government, 20th Aug. 1841.

[2] There was no want of gallant and capable men in the subordinate ranks of the army, and it is known that the lamented Major Pottinger recorded his disapprobation of the retreat so fatuously commenced and so fatally ended, although, to give validity to documents, or an appearance of unanimity to counsels, he unfortunately put his name to the orders requiring the surrender of Kandahār and Jalālābād.

[3] Cf. Government to the Commander-in-Chief, 2nd Dec. 1841, and 10th Feb. 1842; Government to Mr. Clerk, 10th Feb. 1842; and Government to General Pollock, 24th Feb. 1842. Of those who recorded their opinions about the policy to be followed at the moment, it may be mentioned that Mr. Robertson, the Lieutenant-Governor of Agra, and Sir Herbert Maddock, the Political Secretary, advised a

friendship of the Sikhs ;[1] and although their aid was always considered of importance, the mode in which it was asked and used only served to sink the Lahore army lower than before in British estimation.[2] 1841.

Four regiments of sepoys marched from Ferozepore without guns, and unsupported by cavalry, to vainly endeavour to force the Pass of Khaibar ; and the Sikh troops at Peshāwar were urged by the local British authorities in their praiseworthy ardour, rather than deliberately ordered by their own government at the instance of its ally, to co-operate in the attempt, or indeed to march alone to Jalālābād. The fact that the English had been beaten was notorious, and the belief in their alarm was welcome : the Sikh governor was obliged, in the absence of orders, to take the sense of the regimental 'punches' or committees ; and the hasty requisition to march was rejected, through fear alone, as the English said, but really with feelings in which contempt, distrust, and apprehension were all mixed. The district Governor-General, Avitabile, who fortunately still retained his province, freely gave what aid he could ; some pieces of artillery were furnished as well as abundance

The English distrustful of the Sikhs, but yet urgent upon them for aid.

stand at Peshāwar ; and that Mr. Prinsep, a member of council, and Mr. Colvin, the Governor-General's private secretary, recommended a withdrawal to the Sutlej. All, however, contemplated ulterior operations.

The Commander-in-Chief, it is well known, thought the means of the *English* for defending India itself somewhat scanty, and Mr. Clerk thought the *Sikhs* would be unable to check the invasion of mountaineers, which would assuredly take place were Jalālābād to fall. (Mr. Clerk to Government, 15th Jan. 1842.)

[1] Government to the Commander-in-Chief, 15th March 1842.

[2] Mr. Colvin, in the minute referred to in the preceding note, grounds his proposition for withdrawing to the Sutlej partly on Mr. Clerk's low estimate of the Sikhs, and their presumed inability to resist the Afghāns. Col. Wade seems to have had a somewhat similar opinion of the comparative prowess of the two races, on the fair presumption that the note (p. 535) of Munshi Shahāmat Alī's *Sikhs and Afghāns* is his. He says the Sikhs always dreaded the Khaibaris ; and, indeed, General Avitabile could also take up the notion with some reason, in one sense, as the magistrate of a district surrounded by marauding highlanders, and with sufficient adroitness in another when he did not desire to see Sikh regiments hurried into mountain defiles at the instance of the English authorities. (Cf. the *Calcutta Review*, No. III, p. 182.)

1841.

of ordinary supplies, and the British detachment effected the relief of Alī Masjid. But the unpardonable neglect of going to the fort without the food which had been provided, obliged the garrison to retreat after a few days, and the disinclination of the Sikhs to fight the battles of strangers communicated itself to the mercenary soldiers of the English, and thus added to the Governor-General's dislike of the Afghān connexion.[1]

An army of retribution assembled, 1842.

The necessity of at least relieving the garrison of Jalālābād was paramount, and in the spring of 1842 a well-equipped British force arrived at Peshāwar; but the active co-operation of the Sikhs was still desirable, and it was sought for under the terms of an obsolete article of the tripartite treaty with Shāh Shujā, which gave Lahore a subsidy of two lakhs of rupees in exchange for the services of 5,000 men.[2] Sher Singh was willing to assist beyond this limited degree; he greatly facilitated the purchase of grain and the hire of carriage cattle in the Punjab, and his auxiliaries could be made to outnumber the troops of his allies; but he felt uneasy about the proceedings of the Sindhianwala chiefs, one of whom had gone to Calcutta to urge his own claims, or those of Mai Chand Kaur, and all of whom retained influence in the Sikh ranks. He was assured that the refugees should not be allowed to disturb his reign, and there thus seemed to be no obstacle in the way of his full co-operation.[3] But the genuine Sikhs were held by the

[1] The statements in this paragraph are mainly taken from the author's notes of official and demi-official correspondence. The letter of Government to Mr. Clerk, of the 7th Feb. 1842, may also be referred to about the failure to hold Alī Musjid; and, further, it may be mentioned that Mr. Clerk, in his letter of the 10th February, pointed out, that although the Sikhs might not willingly co-operate in any sudden assault planned by the English, they would be found ready to give assistance during the campaign in the ways their experience taught them to be the most likely to lead to success.

[2] See Government to Mr. Clerk, 3rd May and 23rd July 1842. The English agents, however, rather tauntingly and imploringly reminded the Sikh authorities that they were bound to have such a force ready by agreement as well as by friendship, than formally revived the demand for its production under the stipulations of the treaty.

[3] Cf. Mr. Clerk to Government, 2nd Jan. and 31st March 1842, and Government to Mr. Clerk, 17th Jan. and 12th May 1842. With regard to assistance rendered by the Sikhs durin the Afghān War in

English to be both mutinous in disposition and inferior in warlike spirit; the soldiers of Jammu were preferred, and Gulāb Singh was required to proceed to Peshāwar to repress the insubordinate 'Khālsa', and to give General Pollock the assurance of efficient aid.[1] The Rājā was at the time completing the reduction of some insurgent tribes between Kashmīr and Attock, and his heart was in Tibet, where he had himself lost an army and a kingdom. He went, but he knew the temper of his own hill levies: he was naturally unwilling to run any risk by following the modes of strangers to which he was unused, and he failed in rendering the Sikh battalions as decorous and orderly as English regiments. His prudence and ill success were looked upon as collusion and insincerity, and he was thought to be in league with Akbar Khān for the destruction of the army of an obnoxious European power.[2] Still his aid was held to be essential, and the local British officers proposed to bribe him by the offer of Jalālābād, independent of his sovereign Sher Singh. The scheme was justly condemned by Mr. Clerk,[3] the Khaibar Pass was forced in the month of April, and the auxiliary Sikhs acquitted themselves to the satisfaction of the English general, without any promises having been made to the Rājā of Jammū, who gladly hurried to the Ladākh frontier to look after interests dearer to him than the success or the vengeance of foreigners. It was designed by General Pollock to leave the whole of the Sikh division at Jalālābād, to assist in holding that district, while the main English army went to Kābul; but the proper interposition of

1842.

Gulāb Singh sent to co-operate.

Kābul retaken.

furnishing escorts, grain, and carriage for the British troops, Mr. Clerk's letters of the 15th Jan., 18th May, and 14th June 1842 may be quoted. In the last it is stated that 17,381 camels had been procured through Sikh agency between 1839 and 1842.

[1] Cf. Mr. Clerk to Government, 15th Jan., 10th Feb., and 6th May, 1842. Government at first seemed indifferent whether Gulāb Singh went or not; and, indeed, Mr. Clerk himself rather suggested than required the Rājā's employment; but suggestions or wishes could not, under the circumstances, be misconstrued.

[2] Cf. Mr. Clerk to Government, 19th March 1842.

[3] Mr. Clerk to Government, 13th Feb. 1842. The officers referred to are Major Mackeson and Lieut.-Col. Sir Henry Lawrence, whose names are so intimately, and in so many ways honourably, identified with the career of the English in the north-west of India.

1842.

Col. Lawrence[1] enabled a portion of the Lahore troops to share in that retributive march, as they had before shared in the first invasion, and fully shown their fitness for meeting difficulties when left to do so in their own way.

Discussions regarding Jalālābād, and the limits of Sikh dominion.

The proposition of conferring Jalālābād on Gulāb Singh was taken up in a modified form by the new Governor-General, Lord Ellenborough. As his lordship's views became formed, he laid it down as a principle that neither the English nor the Sikh Government should hold dominion beyond the Himālayas and the 'Safed Koh' of Kābul; and as the Durrāni alliance seemed to be severed, there was little to apprehend from Jammū and Bārakzai intrigues. It was, therefore, urged that Gulāb Singh should be required by the Mahāṛājā to relinquish Ladākh, and to accept Jalālābād on equal terms of dependency on the Punjab.[2] The Sikhs were sufficiently desirous of adding to their dominion another Afghān district; but the terms did not satisfy Gulāb Singh, nor did Sher Singh see fit to come to any conclusion until he should know the final views of the English with regard to the recognition of a government in Kābul.[3] The death of Shāh Shujā and his suspicious proceedings were held to render the re-occupation of the country unnecessary, and the tripartite treaty was declared to be at an end;[4] but the policy of a march on the Afghān capital was strongly urged and wisely adopted.[5] There

[1] Lieut.-Col. Lawrence to Major Mackeson, 23rd Aug. 1842. Lieut.-Col. Lawrence's article in the *Calcutta Review* (No. III, p. 180) may also be advantageously referred to about the proceedings at Peshāwar under Col. Wild, Sir George Pollock, and Rājā Gulāb Singh.

[2] Government to Mr. Clerk, 27th April 1842.

[3] Mr. Clerk to Government, 18th May 1842.

[4] Government to Mr. Clerk, 27th May and 29th July 1842. In the treaty drafted by the Sikhs to take the place of the tripartite one, they put forward a claim of superiority over Sind, and somewhat evaded the question of being parties only, instead of principals, to the acknowledgement of a ruler in Kābul. The treaty, however, never took a definite shape.

[5] Even the Sikhs talked of the impolicy, or, at least, the disgrace, of suddenly and wholly withdrawing from Afghānistān in the manner proposed. (Mr. Clerk to Government, 19th July 1842.) Mr. Clerk himself was among the most prominent of those who at first modestly urged a march on Kābul, and afterwards manfully remonstrated

seemed to be a prospect of wintering in Kābul, and it was 1842.
not until the victorious troops were on their return to India that it was believed the English would ever forgo the possession of an empire. The Sikhs then consented to take Jalālābād, but before the order transferring it could reach General Pollock,[1] that commander had destroyed the fortifications, and nominally abandoned the place to the king whom he had expediently set up in the Bālā Hisār.[2] It is probable that Sher Singh was not unwilling to be relieved of the invidious gift, for his own sway in Lahore was distracted, and Dost Muhammad was about to be released under the pledge of a safe passage through the Punjab dominions; and it may have been thought prudent to conciliate the father of Akbar Khān, so famous for his successes against the English, by the surrender of a possession it was inconvenient to hold.[3]

against a hasty abandonment of the country. (See his letter above quoted, and also that of the 23rd April 1842.)

[1] The order was dated the 18th Oct. 1842. Lord Ellenborough himself was not without a suspicion that the victorious generals might frame excuses for wintering in Kābul, and the expedition of Sir John M'Caskill into the Kohistān was less pleasing to him on that account than it would otherwise have been.

[2] The *Calcutta Review* for June 1849 (p. 539) points out that the king, viz. Shāhpur, son of Shāh Shujā, was rather set up solely by the chiefs at Kābul than in any way by Sir George Pollock, who had no authority to recognize any sovereign in Afghānistān. My expression has, indeed, reference mainly to the prudent countenance afforded to a native prince by a foreign conqueror about to retrace his steps through a difficult country, inhabited by a warlike people; but as it may mislead as to Sir George Pollock's actual proceedings, I gladly insert this note.

[3] The Sikhs were not unwilling to acquire territory, but they wished to see their way clearly, and they were unable to do so until the English had determined on their own line of policy. The Sikhs knew, indeed, of the resolution of the Governor-General to sever all connexion with Afghānistān, but they also knew the sentiments of the majority of Englishmen about at least temporarily retaining it. They saw, moreover, that recruited armies were still in possession of every stronghold, and the policy was new to them of voluntarily relinquishing dominion. They therefore paused, and the subsequent release of Dost Muhammad again fettered them when the retirement of the troops seemed to leave them free to act, for they were bound to escort the Amīr safely across the Punjab, and could not therefore make terms with him. The Sikhs would have worked through Sultān

1842.

The Governor-General meets the Sikh minister and heir-apparent at Ferozepore, 1842.

The Governor-General had prudently resolved to assemble an army at Ferozepore, as a reserve in case of further disasters in Afghānistān, and to make known to the princes of India that their English masters had the ready means of beating any who might rebel.[1] Lord Ellenborough was also desirous of an interview with Sher Singh, and as gratitude was uppermost for the time, and added a grace even to success, it was proposed to thank the Mahārājā in person for the proofs which he had afforded of his continued friendship. To invest the scene with greater éclat, it was further determined, in the spirit of the moment, to give expression to British sincerity and moderation at the head of the two armies returning victorious from Kābul, with their numbers increased to nearly forty thousand men by the force assembled on the Sutlej. The native English portion of this array was considerable, and perhaps so many Europeans had never stood together under arms on Indian ground since Alexander and his Greeks made the Punjab a province of Macedon. The Sikhs generally were pleased with one cause of this assemblage, and they were glad to be relieved of the presence of the English on their western frontier; but Sher Singh himself did not look forward to his visit to Lord Ellenborough without some misgivings, although under other circumstances his vanity would have been gratified by the opportunity of displaying

Muhammad Khān and other chiefs until they were in a condition to use the frequent plea of the English, of being able to govern better than dependants. (Cf. Mr. Clerk to Government, 2nd Sept. 1842.)

[1] Lord Auckland had likewise thought that such a demonstration might be advisable. (Government to Mr. Clerk, 3rd Dec. 1841.) Of measures practically identified with Lord Ellenborough's administration, Lord Auckland may further claim the merit of giving the generals commanding in Afghānistān supreme authority (Resolution of Government, 6th Jan. 1842), and of directing Sir William Nott to act without reference to previous instructions, and as *he* might deem best for the safety of his troops and the honour of the British name. (Government to Sir William Nott, 10th Feb. 1842.) To Lord Auckland, however, is due the *doubtful* praise of suggesting the release of Dost Muhammad (Government to Mr. Clerk, 24th Feb. 1842); and he must certainly bear a share of the blame attached to the exaggerated estimate formed of the dangers which threatened the English after the retreat from Kābul, and to the timorous rather than prudent design of falling back on the Indus, or even on the Sutlej.

his power and magnificence. He felt his incapacity as a ruler, and he needlessly feared that he might be called to account for Sikh excesses and for a suspected intercourse with the hostile Amīrs of Sind then trembling for their fate, and even that the subjugation of the Punjab was to be made the stepping-stone to the complete reduction of Afghānistān. He had no confidence in himself; and he dreaded the vengeance of his followers, who believed him capable of sacrificing the Khālsa to his own interests. Nor was Dhiān Singh supposed to be willing that the Mahārājā should meet the Governor-General, and his suspicious temper made him apprehensive that his sovereign might induce the English viceroy to accede to his ruin, or to the reduction of his exotic influence. Thus both Sher Singh and his minister perhaps rejoiced that a misunderstanding which prevented the reception at Ludhiāna of Lahna Singh Majīthīā, was seized hold of by the English to render a meeting doubtful or impossible.[1] Lord Ellenborough justly took offence at a slight which, however unwittingly, had been really offered to him; he was not easily appeased; and when the personal apologies of the minister, accompanied by the young heir-apparent, had removed every ground of displeasure, tne appointed time, the beginning of January 1843, for the 1842.

[1] On several occasions Rājā Dhiān Singh expressed his apprehensions of an English invasion, as also did Mahārājā Sher Singh. (See, for instance, Mr. Clerk to Government, 2nd Jan. 1842.) The writer of the article in the *Calcutta Review* (No. II, p. 493), who is believed to be Lieut.-Col. Lawrence, admits Dhiān Singh's aversion to a meeting between his sovereign and the British Governor-General. The reviewer likewise describes Sher Singh's anxiety at the time, but considers him to have been desirous of throwing himself unreservedly on English protection, as doubtless he might have been, had he thought himself secure from assassination, and that Lord Ellenborough would have kept *him* seated on the throne of Lahore at all hazards.

About the suspected hostile intercourse with the Amīrs of Sind, see Thornton's *History of India*, vi. 447. The Sikhs, however, were never required to give any explanation of the charges.

The misunderstanding to which Sardār Lahna Singh was a party was simply as follows: The Sardār had been sent to wait upon the Governor-General on his arrival on the frontier, according to ordinary ceremonial. It was arranged that the Sardār should be received by his lordship at Ludhiāna, and the day and hour were fixed, and preparations duly made. Mr. Clerk went in person to meet the chief, and

1842. breaking-up of the large army had arrived, and the Governor-General did not care to detain his war-worn regiments any longer from their distant stations. No interview thus took place with Sher Singh; but the boy prince, Pertab Singh, was visited by Lord Ellenborough; and the rapidity with which a large escort of Sikh troops was crossed over the Sutlej when swollen with rain, and the alacrity and precision with which they manœuvred, deserved to have been well noted by the English captains, proud as they had reason to be of the numbers and achievements of their own troops. The prince likewise reviewed the Anglo-Indian forces, and the Sikh chiefs looked with interest upon the defenders of Jalālābād, and with unmixed admiration upon General Nott followed by his valiant and compact band. At last the armed host broke up; the plains of Ferozepore were no longer white with numerous camps; and the relieved Sher Singh hastened, or was hurried, to Amritsar to return thanks to God that a great danger had passed away. This being over, he received Dost Muhammad Khān with distinction at Lahore, and in February (1843) entered into a formal treaty of friendship with the released Amīr, which said nothing about the English gift of Jalālābād.[1]

Dost Muhammad returns to Kābul, 1843.

Anxieties of Sher Singh.

But Sher Singh principally feared his own chiefs and subjects, and although the designed or fortuitous murder of Mai Chand Kaur, in June 1842,[2] relieved him of some of his

conduct him to the Governor-General's presence, *his* understanding being that he was to go half the distance or so towards the Sikh encampment. The Sardār understood or held that Mr. Clerk should or would come to his tent, and thus he sat still while Mr. Clerk rested half-way for two hours or more. Lord Ellenborough thought the excuse of the Sardār frivolous, and that offence was wantonly given, and he accordingly required an explanation to be afforded. (Government to Mr. Clerk, 15th Dec. 1842.) There is some reason to believe that the Lahore Vakil, who was in the interest of Rājā Dhiān Singh, misled the obnoxious Lahna Singh about the arrangements for conducting him to the Governor-General's tents, with the view of discrediting him both with his own master and with the English.

[1] Government to Mr. Clerk, 15th Feb. and 17th Mar. 1843.

[2] Mr. Clerk to Government, 15th June 1842. The widow of Mahārājā Kharak Singh was so severely beaten, as was said by her female attendants, that she almost immediately expired. The only explanation offered, was that she had chidden the servants in question

apprehensions, he felt uneasy under the jealous domination of Dhiān Singh, and began to listen readily to the smooth suggestions of Bhai Gurmukh Singh, his priest so to speak, and who was himself of some religious reputation, as well as the son of a man of acknowledged sanctity and influence.[1] The English Government, in its well-meant but impracticable desire to unite all parties in the country, had urged the restoration to favour of the Sindhianwala chiefs, who kept its own agents on the alert, and the Mahārājā himself in a state of doubt or alarm.[2] Sher Singh, from his easiness of nature, was not averse to a reconciliation, and by degrees he even became not unwilling to have the family about him as some counterpoise to the Rājās of Jammu. Neither was Dhiān Singh opposed to their return, for he thought they might be made some use of since Mai Chand Kaur was no more, and thus Ajīt Singh and his uncles again took their accustomed places in the court of Lahore. Nevertheless, during the summer of 1843, Dhiān Singh perceived that his influence over the Mahārājā was fairly on the wane; and he had good reason to dread the machinations of Gurmukh Singh and the passions of the multitude when roused by a man of his character. The minister then again began to talk of the boy, Dalīp Singh, and to endeavour to possess the minds of the Sindhianwala chiefs with the belief that they had been inveigled to Lahore for their more assured destruction. Ajīt Singh had by this time become the boon companion of the Mahārājā; but he was himself ambitious

1843.

The Sindhianwala chiefs and the Jammu Rājās coalesce.

for some fault, and the public was naturally unwilling to believe Sher Singh, at least, guiltless of instigating the murder.

[1] In the beginning of his reign Sher Singh had leant much upon an active and ambitious follower, named Jawāla Singh, whose bravery was conspicuous during the attack on Lahore. This petty leader hoped to supplant both the Sindhianwala chiefs and the Jammu Rājās as leading courtiers, but he proceeded too hastily; he was seized and imprisoned by Dhiān Singh in May 1841, and died by foul means immediately afterwards. (Cf. Mr. Clerk to Government, 7th May and 10th June 1841.)

[2] Mr. Clerk to Government, 7th April 1842, and Government to Mr. Clerk, 12th May 1842; see also Lieut.-Col. Richmond to Government, 5th Sept. 1843. Mr. Clerk became Lieutenant-Governor of Agra in June 1843, and he was succeeded as Agent on the frontier by Lieut.-Col. Richmond, an officer of repute, who had recently distinguished himself under Sir George Pollock.

1843. of power, and he and his uncle Lahna Singh grasped at the idea of making the minister a party to their own designs. They appeared to fall wholly into his views; and they would, they said, take Sher Singh's life to save their own. On the 15th September (1843), Ajīt Singh induced the Mahārājā to inspect some levies he had newly raised; he approached, as if to make an offering of a choice carbine, and to receive the commendations usual on such occasions, but he raised the weapon and shot his sovereign dead. The remorseless Lahna Singh took the life of the boy Pertab Singh at the same time, and the kinsmen then joined Dhiān Singh, and proceeded with him to the citadel to proclaim a new king. The hitherto wary minister was now caught in his own toils, and he became the dupe of his accomplices. He was separated from his immediate attendants, as if for the sake of greater privacy, and shot by the same audacious chief who had just imbrued his hands in the blood of their common master.[1] The conspirators were thus far successful in their daring and in their crimes, but they neglected to slay or imprison the son of their last victim; and the minds of the soldiers do not seem to have been prepared for the death of Dhiān Singh, as they were for that of the Mahārājā. The youthful Hīra Singh was roused by his own danger and his filial duty; he could plausibly accuse the Sindhianwalas of being alone guilty of the treble murder which had taken place, and he largely promised rewards to the troops if they would avenge the death of *their* friend and *his* father. The army generally responded to his call, and the citadel was immediately assaulted; yet so strong was the feeling of aversion to Jammu ascendancy among the Sikh people, that could the feeble garrison have held out for three or four days, until the first impulse of anger and surprise had passed away, it is almost certain that Hīra Singh must have fled for his life. But the place was entered on the second evening; the wounded Lahna Singh was at once slain; and Ajīt Singh, in attempting to boldly escape over the lofty walls, fell and was also killed.[2] Dalīp Singh was then proclaimed Mahārājā, and Hīra Singh was raised

Sher Singh assassinated by Ajīt Singh, Sept. 15, 1843;

who likewise puts Dhiān Singh to death, Sept. 15, 1843.

Hīra Singh avenges his father.

[1] Lieut.-Col. Richmond to Government, 17th and 18th Sept. 1843.

[2] Lieut.-Col. Richmond to Government, 20th Sept. 1843.

1843.

Dalīp Singh proclaimed Mahārājā, Sept. 1843.

to the high and fatal office of Wazīr; but he was all-powerful for the moment; the Sindhianwala possessions were confiscated, and their dwellings razed to the ground: nor did the youthful avenger stay until he had found out and put to death Bhai Gurmukh Singh and Missar Belī Rām, the former of whom was believed to have connived at the death of his confiding master, and to have instigated the assassination of the minister; and the latter of whom had always stood high in the favour of the great Mahārājā, although strongly opposed to the aggrandizement of the Jammu family. Sardār Atar Singh Sindhianwala, who was hurrying to Lahore when he heard of the capture of the citadel, made a hasty attempt to rouse the village population in his favour through the influence of Bhai Bīr Singh, a devotee of great repute; but the 'Khālsa' was almost wholly represented by the army, and he crossed at once into the British territories to avoid the emissaries of Hīra Singh.[1]

The power of the army increases.

The new minister added two rupees and a half, or five shillings a month, to the pay of the common soldiers, and he also discharged some arrears due to them. The army felt that it had become the master of the state, and it endeavoured to procure donatives, or to place itself right in public estimation, by threatening to eject the Jammū faction, and to make the Bhai Bīr Singh, already mentioned, a king as well as a priest.[2] Jawāhir Singh, the maternal uncle of the boy Mahārājā, already grasped the highest post he could occupy; nor was the minister's family united within itself. Suchēt Singh's vanity was mortified by the ascendancy of his nephew, a stripling, unacquainted with war, and inexperienced in business; and he endeavoured to form a party which should place him in power.[3] The youthful Wazīr naturally turned to his other uncle, Gulāb Singh, for support, and that astute chief cared not who held titles so long as he was deferred to and left unrestrained; but the Sikhs were still averse to him personally, and jealous lest he should attempt to garrison every stronghold with his own followers. Gulāb Singh was, therefore, cautious in his pro-

[1] Lieut.-Col. Richmond's letters from 21st Sept. to 2nd Oct. 1843.
[2] Lieut.-Col. Richmond to Government, 26th Sept. 1843.
[3] Lieut.-Col. Richmond to Government, 16th and 22nd Oct. 1843.

1843.

Rājā Gulāb Singh.

Sardār Jawāhir Singh, Nov. 24, 1843.

ceedings, and before he reached Lahore, on the 10th of November, he had sought to ingratiate himself with all parties, save Jawāhir Singh, whom he may have despised as of no capacity.[1] Jawāhir Singh resented this conduct, and, taking advantage of the ready access to the Mahārājā's person which his relationship gave him, he went with the child in his arms, on the occasion of a review of some troops, and urged the assembled regiments to depose the Jammu Rājās, otherwise he would fly with his nephew, their acknowledged prince, into the British territories. But the design of procuring aid from the English was displeasing to the Sikhs, both as an independent people and as a licentious soldiery, and Jawāhir Singh was immediately made a prisoner, and thus received a lesson which influenced his conduct during the short remainder of his life.[2]

Fateh Khān Tiwānā.

Nevertheless, Hīra Singh continued to be beset with difficulties. There was one Fateh Khān Tiwānā, a personal follower of Dhiān Singh, who was supposed to have been privy to the intended assassination of his master, and to have designedly held back when Ajīt Singh took the Rājā to one side. This petty leader fled as soon as the army attacked the citadel, and endeavoured to raise an insurrection in his native province of Dera Ismail Khān, which caused the greater anxiety, as the attempt was supposed to be countenanced by the able and hostile Governor of Multān.[3] Scarcely had measures been adopted for reducing the petty rebellion, when Kashmīra Singh and Peshāwara Singh, sons born to, or adopted by, Ranjīt Singh at the period of his conquest of the two Afghān provinces from which they were named, started up as the rivals of the child Dalīp, and endeavoured to form a party by appearing in open opposition at Siālkot. Some regiments ordered to Peshāwar joined the two princes; the Muhammadan regiments at Lahore refused to march against them unless a pure Sikh force did the same; and it was with difficulty, and only with the aid of Rājā Gulāb Singh, that the siege of

The insurrection of Kashmīra Singh and Peshāwara Singh, 1843–4.

[1] Cf. Lieut.-Col. Richmond to Government, 26th Sept. and 16th Nov. 1843.

[2] Lieut.-Col. Richmond to Government, 28th Nov. 1843.

[3] Lieut.-Col. Richmond to Government, 12th Dec. 1843.

1844.

Siālkot was formed. The two young men soon showed themselves to be incapable of heading a party; Hīra Singh relaxed in his efforts against them; and towards the end of March he raised the siege, and allowed them to go at large.[1] The minister had, however, less reason to be satisfied with the success of Jawāhir Singh, who, about the same time, induced his guards to release him, and he was unwillingly allowed to assume his place in the court as the uncle of the child to whose sovereignty in the abstract all nominally deferred.[2]

Jawāhir Singh.

The attempt of Rājā Suchēt Singh, March 1844.

Rājā Suchēt Singh was believed to have been a secret party to the attempts of Kashmīra Singh, and the release of Jawāhir Singh was also probably effected with his cognizance. The Rājā believed himself to be popular with the army, and especially with the cavalry portion of it, which, having an inferior organization, began to show some jealousy of the systematic proceedings of the regular infantry and artillery. He had retired to the hills with great reluctance; he continued intent upon supplanting his nephew; and suddenly, on the evening of the 26th of March 1844, he appeared at Lahore with a few followers; but he appealed in vain to the mass of the troops, partly because Hīra Singh had been liberal in gifts and profuse in promises, and partly because the shrewd deputies who formed the Panchāyats of the regiments had a sense of their own importance, and were not to be won for purposes of mere faction, without diligent and judicious seeking. Hence, on the morning after the arrival of the sanguine and hasty Rājā, a large force marched against him without demur; but the chief was brave: he endeavoured to make a stand in a ruinous building, and he died fighting to the last, although his little band was almost destroyed by the fire of a numerous artillery before the assailants could reach the enclosure.[3]

The insurrection of Sardār Atar Singh and Bhai Bīr Singh, May 1844.

Within two months after this rash undertaking, Atar Singh Sindhianwala, who had been residing at Thānesar, made a similar ill-judged attempt to gain over the army,

[1] Lieut.-Col. Richmond to Government, 23rd and 27th March 1844.

[2] Lieut.-Col. Richmond to Government, 27th March 1844.

[3] Lieut.-Col. Richmond to Government, 29th March 1844.

1844. and to expel Hīra Singh. He crossed the Sutlej on the 2nd May, but instead of moving to a distance, so as to avoid premature collisions, and to enable him to appeal to the feelings of the Sikhs, he at once joined Bhai Bīr Singh, whose religious repute attracted numbers of the agricultural population, and took up a position almost opposite Ferozepore, and within forty miles of the capital. The disaffected Kashmīra Singh joined the chief, but Hīra Singh stood as a suppliant before the assembled Khālsa, and roused the feelings of the troops by reminding them that the Sindhianwalas looked to the English for support. A large force promptly marched from Lahore, but it was wished to detach Bhai Bīr Singh from the rebel, for to assail so holy a man was held to be sacrilege by the soldiers, and on the seventh of the month deputies were sent to induce the Bhai to retire. Some expressions moved the anger of Sardār Atar Singh, and he slew one of the deputies with his own hand. This act led to an immediate attack. Atar Singh and Kashmīra Singh were both killed, and it was found that a cannon-shot had likewise numbered Bhai Bīr Singh with the slain. The commander on this occasion was Labh Singh, a Rājput of Jammu, and the possession of the family of Kashmīra Singh seemed to render his success more complete; but the Sikh infantry refused to allow the women and children to be removed to Lahore; and Labh Singh, alarmed by this proceeding and by the lamentations over the death of Bīr Singh, hastened to the capital to ensure his own safety.[1]

The Governor of Multān submits.

Hīra Singh was thus successful against two main enemies of his rule, and as he had also come to an understanding with the Governor of Multān, the proceedings of Fateh Khan Tiwānā gave him little uneasiness.[2] The army itself was his great cause of anxiety, not lest the Sikh dominion should be contracted, but lest he should be rejected as its master; for the Panchāyats, although bent on retaining their own power, and on acquiring additional pay and privileges for their constituents the soldiers, were equally resolved on maintaining the integrity of the empire, and they arranged

[1] Lieut.-Col. Richmond to Government, 10th, 11th, and 12th May 1844.

[2] Cf. Lieut.-Col. Richmond to Government, 29th April 1844.

1844.

among themselves about the relief of the troops in the provinces. On the frontiers, indeed, the Sikhs continued to exhibit their innate vigour, and towards the end of 1843 the secluded principality of Gilgit was overrun and annexed to Kashmīr. The Panchāyats likewise felt that it was the design of the Rājā and his advisers to disperse the Sikh army over the country, and to raise additional corps of hill men, but the committees would not allow a single regiment to quit Lahore without satisfying themselves of the necessity of the measure; and thus Hīra Singh was induced to take advantage of a projected relief of the British troops in Sind, and the consequent march of several battalions towards the Sutlej, to heighten or give a colour to his own actual suspicions, and to hint that a near danger threatened the Sikhs on the side of the English. The 'Khālsa' was most willing to encounter *that* neighbour, and a brigade was induced to move to Kasūr, and others to shorter distances from the capital, under the plea, as avowed to the British authorities, of procuring forage and supplies with greater facility.[1] Such had indeed been Ranjīt Singh's occasional practice when no assemblage of British forces could add to his ever present fears;[2] but Hīra Singh's apprehensions of his own army and of his English allies were lessened by his rapid successes, and by the disgraceful spirit which then animated the regular regiments in the British service. The Sepoys refused to proceed to Sind, and the Sikhs watched the progress of the mutiny with a pleased surprise. It was new to them to see these renowned soldiers in opposition to their government; but any glimmering hopes of fatal embarrassment to the colossal power of the foreigners were dispelled by the march of European troops, by the good example of the irregular cavalry, and by the returning sense of obedience of the sepoys themselves. The British forces proceeded to Sind, and the Lahore detachment was withdrawn from Kasūr.[3]

Gilgit reduced, 1843.

Hīra Singh professes suspicions of the English.

The mutiny of the British Sepoys ordered to Sind.

[1] Cf. Lieut.-Col. Richmond to Government, 20th Dec. 1843, and 23rd March 1844.

[2] See, for instance, Sir David Ochterlony to Government, 16th Oct. 1812.

[3] Cf. Lieut.-Col. Richmond to Government, 29th April 1844.

1844.

Discussions with the English about the village Moran,

Nevertheless there were not wanting causes of real or alleged dissatisfaction with the British Government, which at last served the useful purpose of engaging the attention of the Lahore soldiery. The protected Sikh Rājā of Nābha had given a village, named Moran, to Ranjīt Singh at the Mahārājā's request, in order that it might be bestowed on Dhānna Singh, a Nābha subject, but who stood high in favour with the master of the Punjab. The village was so given in 1819, or after the introduction of the English supremacy, but without the knowledge of the English authorities, which circumstance rendered the alienation invalid, if it were argued that the village had become separated from the British sovereignty. The Rājā of Nābha became displeased with Dhānna Singh, and he resumed his gift in the year 1843; but in so doing his soldiers wantonly plundered the property of the feudatory, and thus gave the Lahore Government a ground of complaint, of which advantage was taken for party purposes.[1] But Hīra Singh and his advisers took greater exception still to the decision of the British Government with regard to a quantity of coin and bullion which Rājā Suchēt Singh had secretly deposited in Ferozepore, and which his servants were detected in endeavouring to remove after his death. The treasure was estimated at 1,500,000 rupees, and it was understood to have been sent to Ferozepore during the recent Afghān War, for the purpose of being offered as part of an ingratiatory loan to the English Government, which was borrowing money at the time from the protected Sikh chiefs. The Lahore minister claimed the treasure both as the escheated property of a feudatory without male heirs of his body, and as the confiscated property of a rebel killed in arms against his sovereign; but the British Government considered the right to the property to be unaffected by the owner's treason, and required that the title to it, according to the laws of Jammu or of the Punjab, should be regularly pleaded and proved in a British court. It was argued in favour of Lahore that no British subject or dependent claimed the treasure, and that it might be expediently made over to the ruler of the Punjab for surrender to the

and about treasure buried by Suchēt Singh.

[1] Lieut.-Col. Richmond to Government, 18th and 28th May 1844.

legal or customary owner; but the supreme British authorities would not relax further from the conventional law of Europe than to say that if the Mahārājā would write that the Rājās Gulāb Singh and Hīra Singh assented to the delivery of the treasure to the Sikh state for the purpose of being transferred to the rightful owners, it would no longer be detained. This proposal was not agreed to, partly because differences had in the meantime arisen between the uncle and nephew, and partly because the Lahore councillors considered their original grounds of claim to be irrefragable, according to Indian law and usage, and thus the money remained a source of dissatisfaction, until the English stood masters in Lahore, and accepted it as part of the price of Kashmīr, when the valley was alienated to Rājā Gulāb Singh.[1] 1844.

[1] For the discussions about the surrender or the detention of the treasure, see the letters of Lieut.-Col. Richmond to Government of the 7th April, 3rd and 27th May, 25th July, 10th Sept., and 5th and 25th Oct. 1844; and of Government to Lieut.-Col. Richmond of the 19th and 22nd April, 17th May, and 10th Aug. of the same year.

The principle laid down of deciding the claim to the treasure at a British tribunal, and according to the laws of Lahore or of Jammū, does not distinguish between public and individual right of heirship; or rather it decides the question with reference solely to the law in private cases. Throughout India, the practical rule has ever been that such property shall be administered agreeably to the customs of the tribe or province to which the deceased belonged; and very frequently, when the only litigants are subjects of one and the same foreign state, it is expediently made over to the sovereign of that state for adjudication, on the plea that the rights of the parties can be best ascertained on the spot, and that every ruler is a renderer of justice.

In the present instance the imperfection of the International Law of Europe may be more to blame than the Government of India and the legal authorities of Calcutta, for refusing to acknowledge the right of an allied and friendly state to the property of a childless rebel; to which property, moreover, no British subject or dependent preferred a claim. Vattel lays it down that a stranger's property remains a part of the aggregate wealth of his nation, and that the right to it is to be determined according to the laws of his own country (Book II, chap. viii, §§ 109 and 110); but in the section in question reference is solely had to cases in which subjects or private parties are litigants; although Mr. Chitty, in his note to § 103 (ed. 1834), shows that foreign sovereigns can in England sue, at least, British subjects.

The oriental customary law with regard to the estates and property

1844.

Hīra Singh guided by Pandit Jalla, his preceptor.

Hīra Singh had, in his acts and successes, surpassed the general expectation, and the manner in which affairs were carried on seemed to argue unlooked-for abilities of a high order; but the Rājā himself had little more than a noble presence and a conciliatory address to recommend him, and the person who directed every measure was a Brāhman Pandit, named Jalla, the family priest, so to speak, of the Jammu brothers, and the tutor of Dhiān Singh's sons. This crafty and ambitious man retained all the influence over the youthful minister which he had exercised over the boyish pupil on whom Ranjīt Singh lavished favours. Armies had marched, and chiefs had been vanquished, as if at the bidding of the preceptor become councillor. His views expanded, and he seems to have entertained the idea of founding a dynasty of 'Peshwās' among the rude Jāts of the Punjab, as had been done by one of his tribe among the equally rude Marāthās of the south. He fully perceived that the Sikh army must be conciliated, and also that it must be employed. He despised, and with some reason, the spirit and capacity of most of the titular chiefs of the country; and he felt that Rājā Gulāb Singh absorbed a large proportion of the revenues of the country, and seriously embarrassed the central government by his overgrown power and influence. It was primarily requisite to keep the army well and regularly paid, and hence the Pandit proceeded without scruple to sequester several of the fiefs of the sirdars, and gradually

of Jāgīrdārs (feudal beneficiaries) may be seen in Bernier's *Travels* (p. 181), and it almost seems identical with that anciently in force among the Anglo-Saxons with reference to 'nobles by service', the followers of a lord or king. (See Kemble's *Saxons in England*, i. 178, &c.) The right of the Government is full, and it is based on the feeling or principle that a beneficiary has only the use during life of estates or offices, and that all he may have accumulated, through parsimony or oppression, is the property of the state. It may be difficult to decide between a people and an expelled sovereign, about his guilt or his tyranny, but there can be none in deciding between an allied state and its subject about treason or rebellion. Neither refugee traitors nor patriots are allowed to abuse their asylum by plotting against the Government which has cast them out; and an extension of the principle would prevent desperate adventurers defrauding the state which has reared and heaped favours on them, by removing their property previous to engaging in rash and criminal enterprises.

to inspire the soldiery with the necessity of a march against Jammu. Nor was he without a pretext for denouncing Gulāb Singh, as that unscrupulous chief had lately taken possession of the estates of Rājā Suchet Singh, to which he regarded himself as the only heir.[1] 1844.

Pandit Jalla and Gulāb Singh.

Jalla showed vigour and capacity in all he did, but he proceeded too hastily in some matters, and he attempted too much at one time. He did not, perhaps, understand the Sikh character in all its depths and ramifications, and he probably undervalued the subtlety of Gulāb Singh. The Rājā, indeed, was induced to divide the Jāgīrs of Suchēt Singh with his nephew,[2] but Fateh Khān Tiwānā again excited an insurrection in the Derajāt;[3] Chattar Singh Atariwala took up arms near Rāwalpindi,[4] and the Muhammadan tribes south-west of Kashmīr were encouraged in rebellion by the dexterous and experienced chief whom Pandit Jalla sought to crush.[5] Peshāwara Singh again aspired to the sovereignty of the Punjab; he was supported by Gulāb Singh, and Jalla at last perceived the necessity of coming to terms with one so formidable.[6] A reconciliation was accordingly patched up, and the Rājā sent his son Sohan Singh to Lahore.[7] The hopes of Peshāwara Singh then vanished, and he fled for safety to the south of the Sutlej.[8]

Pandit Jalla irritates the Sikhs, and offends the Queen-mother.

Pandit Jalla made the additional mistake of forgetting that the Sikhs were not jealous of Gulāb Singh alone, but of all strangers to their faith and race; and in trying to crush the chiefs, he had forgotten that they were Sikhs

[1] Cf. Lieut.-Col. Richmond to Government, 13th Aug. and 10th Oct. 1844.

[2] Lieut.-Col. Richmond to Government, 30th Oct. 1844.

[3] Lieut.-Col. Richmond to Government, 14th June 1844.

[4] Lieut.-Col. Richmond to Government, 16th Oct. 1844.

[5] Major Broadfoot to Government, 24th Nov. 1844.

[6] Lieut.-Col. Richmond to Government, 16th Oct. 1844, and Major Broadfoot to Government, 24th Nov. 1844.

[7] Lieut.-Col. Richmond to Government, 30th Oct. 1844, and Major Broadfoot to Government, 13th Nov. and 16th Dec. 1844.

[8] Major Broadfoot to Government, 14th and 18th Nov. 1844. Major Broadfoot, who succeeded Lieut.-Col. Richmond as agent on the frontier on the 1st Nov. 1844, received Peshāwara Singh with civilities unusual under the circumstances, and proposed to assign him an allowance of a thousand rupees a month.

1844.

equally with the soldiers, and that the 'Khālsa' was a word which could be used to unite the high and low. He showed no respect even to sardars of ability and means. Lahna Singh Majīthīā quitted the Punjab, on pretence of a pilgrimage, in the month of March 1844,[1] and the only person who was raised to any distinction was the unworthy Lāl Singh, a Brāhman, and a follower of the Rājās of Jammu, but who was understood to have gained a disgraceful influence over the impure mind of Rānī Jindan. The Pandit again, in his arrogance, had ventured to use some expressions of impatience and disrespect towards the mother of the Mahārājā, and he had habitually treated Jawāhir Singh, her brother, with neglect and contempt. The impulsive soldiery was wrought upon by the incensed woman and ambitious man; the relict of the great Mahārājā appealed to the children of the Khālsa, already excited by the proscribed chiefs, and Hīra Singh and Pandit Jalla perceived that their rule was at an end. On the 21st December 1844 they endeavoured to avoid the wrath of the Sikh soldiery by a sudden flight from the capital, but they were overtaken and slain before they could reach Jammu, along with Sohan Singh, the cousin of the minister, and Labh Singh, so lately hailed as a victorious commander. The memory of Pandit Jalla continued to be execrated, but the fate of Hīra Singh excited some few regrets, for he had well avenged the death of his father, and he had borne his dignities with grace and modesty.[2]

Hīra Singh and Pandit Jalla fly, but are overtaken and put to death, 21st Dec. 1844.

Jawāhir Singh and Lāl Singh attain power.

The sudden breaking up of Hīra Singh's government caused some confusion for a time, and the state seemed to be without a responsible head; but it was gradually perceived that Jawāhir Singh, the brother, and Lāl Singh, the favourite of the Rānī, would form the most influential members of the administration.[2] Peshāwara Singh, indeed, escaped from the custody of the British authorities, by whom he had been placed under surveillance, when he fled across the Sutlej; but he made no attempt at the moment

[1] Lahna Singh went first to Hardwār and afterwards to Benares. He next visited Gayā and Jagannāth and Calcutta, and he was residing in the last-named place when hostilities broke out with the Sikhs.

[2] Cf. Major Broadfoot to Government, 24th and 28th Dec. 1844.

to become supreme, and he seemed to adhere to those who had so signally avenged him on Hīra Singh.[1] The services of the troops were rewarded by the addition of half a rupee a month to the pay of the common soldier, many fiefs were restored, and the cupidity of all parties in the state was excited by a renewal of the designs against Gulāb Singh.[2] The disturbances in the mountains of Kashmīr were put down, the insurgent Fateh Khān was taken into favour, Peshāwar was secure against the power of all the Afghāns, although it was known that Gulāb Singh encouraged the reduced Bārakzais with promises of support;[3] but it was essential to the government that the troops should be employed: it was pleasing to the men to be able to gratify their avarice or their vengeance, and they therefore marched against Jammu with alacrity.[4] 1844.

The Sikh army moves against Jammu.

Feb. to March 1845.

Gulāb Singh, who knew the relative inferiority of his soldiers, brought all his arts into play. He distributed his money freely among the Panchāyats of regiments, he gratified the members of these committees by his personal attentions, and he again inspired Peshāwara Singh with designs upon the sovereignty itself. He promised a gratuity to the army which had marched to urge upon him the propriety of submission, he agreed to surrender certain portions of the general possessions of the family, and to pay to the state a fine of 3,500,000 rupees.[5] But an altercation arose between the Lahore and Jammu followers when the promised donative was being removed, which ended in a fatal affray; and afterwards an old Sikh chief, Fateh Singh Mān, and one Bachna, who had deserted Gulāb Singh's service, were waylaid and slain.[6] The Rājā protested against the accusation of connivance or treachery; nor is it probable

[1] Cf. Major Broadfoot to Government, 28th Dec. 1844, and 4th Jan. 1845. As Major Broadfoot, however, points out, the prince seemed ready enough to grasp at power even so early as January.

[2] Cf. Major Broadfoot to Government, 28th Dec. 1844, and 2nd Jan. 1845.

[3] Major Broadfoot to Government, 16th Jan. 1845.

[4] The troops further rejected the terms to which the Lahore court seemed inclined to come with Gulāb Singh. (Major Broadfoot to Government, 22nd Jan. 1845.)

[5] Major Broadfoot to Government, 18th March 1845.

[6] Major Broadfoot to Government, 3rd March 1845.

1845.

that at the time he desired to take the life of any one except Bachna, who had been variously employed by him, and who knew the extent of his resources. The act nevertheless greatly excited the Sikh soldiery, and Gulāb Singh perceived that submission alone would save Jammu from being sacked. He succeeded in partially gaining over two brigades, he joined their camp, and he arrived at Lahore early in April 1845, half a prisoner, and yet not without a reasonable prospect of becoming the minister of the country; for the mass of the Sikh soldiery thought that one so great had been sufficiently humbled, the Panchāyats had been won by his money and his blandishments, and many of the old servants of Ranjīt Singh had confidence in his ability and in his good-will towards the state generally.[1] There yet, however, existed some remnants of the animosity which had proved fatal to Hīra Singh; the representatives of many expelled hill chiefs were ready to compass the death of their greatest enemy; and an Akāli fanatic could take the life of the 'Dogra' Rājā with applause and impunity. Jawāhir Singh plainly aimed at the office of Wazīr, and Lāl Singh's own ambition prompted him to use his influence with the mother of the Mahārājā to resist the growing feeling in favour of the chief whose capacity for affairs all envied and dreaded. Hence Gulāb Singh deemed it prudent to avoid a contest for power at that time, and to remove from Lahore to a place of greater safety. He agreed to pay in all a fine of 6,800,000 rupees, to yield up nearly all the districts which had been held by his family, excepting his own proper fiefs, and to renew his lease of the salt mines between the Indus and Jhelum, on terms which virtually deprived him of a large profit, and of the political superiority in the hills of Rohtās.[2] He was present at the installation of Jawāhir Singh as Wazīr on the 14th May,[3] and at the betrothal of the Mahārājā to a daughter of the Atāri chief Chattar Singh on the 10th July;[4] and towards the end of the following

Gulāb Singh submits and repairs to Lahore, April 1845.

Jawāhir Singh formally appointed Wazīr, May 14, 1845.

[1] Cf. Major Broadfoot to Government, 8th and 9th April and 5th May 1845.

[2] Major Broadfoot to Government, 5th May 1845.

[3] Major Broadfoot to Government, 24th May 1845.

[4] Major Broadfoot to Government, 14th July 1845.

month he retired to Jammu, shorn of much real power, but become acceptable to the troops by his humility, and to the final conviction of the English authorities, that the levies of the mountain Rājpūts were unequal to a contest even with the Sikh soldiery.[1] 1845.

Sāwan Mal, of Multān, assassinated, Sept. 1844.

The able Governor of Multān was assassinated in the month of September 1844 by a man accused of marauding, and yet imprudently allowed a considerable degree of liberty.[2] Mūlrāj, the son of the Dīwān, had been appointed or permitted to succeed his father by the declining government of Hīra Singh, and he showed more aptitude for affairs than was expected. He suppressed a mutiny among the provincial troops, partly composed of Sikhs, with vigour and success; and he was equally prompt in dealing with a younger brother, who desired to have half the province assigned to him as the equal heir of the deceased Dīwān. Mūlrāj put his brother in prison, and thus freed himself from all local dangers; but he had steadily evaded the demands of the Lahore court for an increased farm or contract, and he had likewise objected to the large 'Nazarāna', or relief, which was required as the usual condition of succession. As soon, therefore, as Gulāb Singh had been reduced to obedience, it was proposed to dispatch a force against Multān, and the 'Khālsa' approved of the measure through the assembled Panchāyats of regiments and brigades. This resolution induced the new governor to yield, and in September (1845) it was arranged that he should pay a fine of 1,800,000 rupees. He escaped an addition to his contract sum, but he was deprived of some petty districts to satisfy in a measure the letter of the original demand.[3]

Mūlrāj, his son, succeeds; and agrees to the terms of the Lahore court, 1845.

[1] Major Broadfoot confessed that 'late events had shown the Rājā's weakness in the hills', where he should have been strongest, had his followers been brave and trusty. (Major Broadfoot to Government, 5th May 1845.)

[2] Lieut.-Col. Richmond to Government, 10th Oct. 1844.

[3] In this paragraph the author has followed mainly his own notes of occurrences. The mutiny of the Multān troops took place in Nov. 1844. The Governor at once surrounded them, and demanded the ringleaders, and on their surrender being refused, he opened a fire upon their whole body, and killed, as was said, nearly 400 of them. Dīwān Mūlrāj seized and confined his brother in Aug. 1845, and in the following month the terms of his succession were settled with the

1845.

The rebellion of Peshāwara Singh;

The proceedings of Peshāwara Singh caused more disquietude to the new Wazīr personally than the hostility of Gulāb Singh, or the resistance of the Governor of Multān. The prince was vain and of slender capacity, but his relationship to Ranjīt Singh gave him some hold upon the minds of the Sikhs. He was encouraged by Gulāb Singh, then safe in the hills, and he was assured of support by the brigade of troops which had made Jawāhir Singh a prisoner, when that chief threatened to fly with the Mahārājā into the British territories. Jawāhir Singh had not heeded the value to the state of the prudence of the soldiers in restraining him ; he thought only of the personal indignity, and soon after his accession to power he barbarously mutilated the commander of the offending division, by depriving him of his nose and ears. Peshāwara Singh felt himself countenanced, and he endeavoured to rally a party around him at Siālkot, which he held in fief. But the Sikhs were not disposed to thus suddenly admit his pretensions ; he was reduced to straits ; and in the month of June he fled, and lived at large on the country, until towards the end of July, when he surprised the fort of Attock, proclaimed himself Mahārājā, and entered into a correspondence with Dost Muhammad Khān. Sardār Chattar Singh of Atāri was sent against the pretender, and troops were moved from Dera Ismail Khān to aid in reducing him. The prince was beleaguered in his fort, and became aware of his insignificance; he submitted on the 30th August, and was directed to be removed to Lahore, but he was secretly put to death at the instigation of Jawāhir Singh, and through the instrumentality, as understood, of Fateh Khān Tiwānā, who sought by rendering an important service to further ingratiate himself with that master for the time being who had restored him to favour, and who had appointed him to the management of the upper Derajāt of the Indus.[1]

March 1845;

who submits, but is put to death Aug.–Sept. 1845.

Lahore court. [Mūlrāj never paid his fine. In April 1848, when threatened with force, he resigned, and Kahn Singh was sent from Lahore to relieve him, accompanied by Mr. Vans Agnew and Lieut. Anderson. The murder of these officers on their arrival at Multān led to the second Sikh War and the final extinction of Sikh independence.—ED.]

[1] Cf. Major Broadfoot to Government, 14th and 26th July and 8th and 18th Sept. 1845.

This last triumph was fatal to Jawāhir Singh, and anger was added to the contempt in which he had always been held. He had sometimes displayed both energy and perseverance, but his vigour was the impulse of personal resentment, and it was never characterized by judgement or by superior intelligence. His original design of flying to the English had displeased the Sikhs, and rendered them suspicious of his good faith as a member of the Khālsa; and no sooner had his revenge been gratified by the expulsion of Hīra Singh and Pandit Jalla, than he found himself the mere sport and plaything of the army, which had only united with him for the attainment of a common object The soldiery began to talk of themselves as pre-eminently the 'Panth Khalsagi', or congregation of believers;[1] and Jawāhir Singh was overawed by the spirit which animated the armed host. In the midst of the successes against Jammu, he trembled for his fate, and he twice laid plans for escaping to the south of the Sutlej; but the troops were jealous of such a step on the part of their nominal master. He felt that he was watched, and he abandoned the hope of escape to seek relief in dissipation, in the levy of Muhammadan regiments, and in idle or desperate threats of war with his British allies.[2] Jawāhir Singh was thus despised and distrusted by the Sikhs themselves; their enmity to him was fomented by Lāl Singh, who aimed at the post of wazīr; and the murder of Peshāwara Singh added to the general exasperation, for the act was condemned as insulting to the people, and it was held up to reprobation by the chiefs as one which would compromise their own safety, if allowed to pass with impunity.[3] The Panchāyats of regiments met in council, and they resolved that Jawāhir Singh should die as a traitor to the commonwealth, for death is almost the only mode by which tumultuous, half-barbarous governments

1845.

The Sikh soldiery displeased and distrustful.

The perplexity of Jawāhir Singh.

The army condemns him and puts him to death, Sept. 21, 1845.

[1] Or, as the 'Sarbat Khālsa', the body of the elect. Major Broadfoot (letter of 2nd Feb. 1845) thought this title, which the soldiers arrogated to themselves, was new in correspondence; but Government pointed out, in reply, that it was an old term according to the Calcutta records.

[2] Cf. Major Broadfoot to Government, 23rd and 28th Feb., 5th April (a demi-official letter), and 15th and 18th Sept. 1845.

[3] Cf. Major Broadfoot to Government, 22nd Sept. 1845.

1845. can remove an obnoxious minister. He was accordingly required to appear on the 21st September before the assembled Khālsa to answer for his misdeeds. He went, seated upon an elephant; but fearing his fate, he took with him the young Mahārājā and a quantity of gold and jewels. On his arrival in front of the troops, he endeavoured to gain over some influential deputies and officers by present donatives and by lavish promises, but he was sternly desired to let the Mahārājā be removed from his side, and to be himself silent. The boy was placed in a tent near at hand, and a party of soldiers advanced and put the wazīr to death by a discharge of musketry.[1] Two other persons, the sycophants of the minister, were killed at the same time, but no pillage or massacre occurred; the act partook of the solemnity and moderation of a judicial process, ordained and witnessed by a whole people; and the body of Jawāhir Singh was allowed to be removed and burnt with the dreadful honours of the Satī sacrifice, among the last, perhaps, which will take place in India.

The army all-powerful.

For some time after the death of Jawāhir Singh, no one seemed willing to become the supreme administrative authority in the state, or to place himself at the head of that self-dependent army, which in a few months had led captive the formidable chief of Jammu, reduced to submission the powerful governor of Multān, put down the rebellion of one recognized as the brother of the Mahārājā, and pronounced and executed judgement on the highest functionary in the kingdom, and which had also without effort contrived to keep the famed Afghāns in check at Peshāwar and along the frontier. Rājā Gulāb Singh was urged to repair to the capital, but he and all others were overawed, and the Rānī Jindan held herself for a time a regular court, in the absence of a wazīr. The army was partly satisfied with this arrangement, for the committees considered that they could keep the provinces obedient, and they reposed confidence in the talents or the integrity of the accountant Dina Nath, of the paymaster Bhagat Rām,

[1] Cf. Major Broadfoot to Government, 26th Sept. 1845. It may be added that the Sikhs generally regarded Jawāhir Singh as one ready to bring in the English, and as faithless to the Khālsa.

and of Nur-ud-dīn, almost as familiar as his old and infirm brother Aziz-ud-dīn, with the particulars of the treaties and engagements with the English. The army had formerly required that these three men should be consulted by Jawāhir Singh; but the advantage of a responsible head was, nevertheless, apparent, and as the soldiers were by degrees wrought upon to wage war with their European neighbours, Rājā Lāl Singh was nominated wazīr, and Sardār Tej Singh was reconfirmed in his office of Commander-in-Chief. These appointments were made early in November 1845.[1]

1845.

Lāl Singh made wazīr, and Tej Singh Commander-in-Chief, in expectation of an English war.

[1] In this paragraph the author has followed mainly his own notes of occurrences.

CHAPTER IX

THE WAR WITH THE ENGLISH

1845–6

Causes leading to a war between the Sikhs and English—The English, being apprehensive of frontier disturbances, adopt defensive measures on a scale opposed to the spirit of the policy of 1809—The Sikhs, being prone to suspicion, consider themselves in danger of invasion—And are further moved by their want of confidence in the English representative—The Sikhs resolve to anticipate the English, and wage war by crossing the Sutlej—The tactics of the Sikhs—The views of the Sikh leaders—Ferozepore purposely spared—The Battle of Mudkī—The Battle of P'heeroo-shuhur, and retreat of the Sikhs—The effect of these barren victories upon the Indians and the English themselves—The Sikhs again cross the Sutlej—The Skirmish of Badowāl—The Battle of Alīwāl—Negotiations through Rājā Gulāb Singh—The Battle of Sobraon—The submission of the Sikh Chiefs, and the occupation of Lahore—The partition of the Punjab—The Treaty with Dalīp Singh—The Treaty with Gulāb Singh—Conclusion, relative to the position of the English in India.

1845–6.

The Indian public prepared for a war between the Sikhs and English.

THE English Government had long expected that it would be forced into a war with the overbearing soldiery of the Punjab: the Indian public, which considered only the fact of the progressive aggrandizement of the strangers, was prepared to hear of the annexation of another kingdom without minutely inquiring or caring about the causes which led to it; and the more selfish chiefs of the Sikhs had always desired that such a degree of interference should be exercised in the affairs of their country as would guarantee to them the easy enjoyment of their possessions. These wealthy and incapable men stood rebuked before the superior genius of Ranjīt Singh, and before the mysterious spirit which animated the people arrayed in arms, and they thus fondly hoped that a change would give them all they could desire; but it is doubtful whether the Sikh soldiery ever seriously thought, although they often vauntingly boasted, of fighting with the paramount power of Hindustān, until within two or three months of the first battles, and even then the rude and illiterate yeomen considered that they were about to enter upon a war purely defensive, although one in every way congenial to their feelings of youthful pride and national jealousy. 1845–6.

The apprehensions of the English.

From the moment the Sikh army became predominant in the state, the English authorities had been persuaded that the machinery of government would be broken up, that bands of plunderers would everywhere arise, and that the duty of a civilized people to society generally, and of a governing power to its own subjects, would all combine to bring on a collision; and thus measures which seemed sufficient were adopted for strengthening the frontier posts, and for having a force at hand which might prevent aggression, or which would at least exact retribution and vindicate the supremacy of the English name.[1] These were the fair and moderate objects of the British Government; but the Sikhs took a different view of the relative conditions of the two states; they feared the ambition of their great and growing neighbour, they did not understand why they should be dreaded when intestine commotions had reduced their comparative inferiority still lower; or why inefficiency of rule should be construed into hostility of purpose; defensive measures took in their eyes the form of aggressive preparations, and they came to the conclusion that their country was to be invaded. Nor does this conviction of the weaker and less intelligent power appear to be strange or unreasonable, although erroneous—for it is always to be borne in mind that India is far behind Europe in civilization, and that political morality or moderation is as little appreciated in the East in these days as it was in Christendom in the Middle Ages. Hindustān, moreover, from Kābul to the valley of Assam and the island of Ceylon, is regarded as one country, and dominion in it is associated in the minds of the people with the predominance of one monarch or of one race. The supremacy of Vikramājīt and Chandra Gupta, of the Turkomāns and Mughals, is familiar

The fears of the Sikhs.

[1] Cf. Minute by the Governor-General, of the 16th June 1845, and the Governor-General to the Secret Committee, 1st October 1845. (Parliamentary Paper, 1846.)

1845–6. to all, and thus on hearing of further acquisitions by the English, a Hindu or Muhammadan will simply observe that the destiny of the nation is great, or that its cannon is irresistible. A prince may chafe that he loses a province or is rendered tributary; but the public will never accuse the conquerors of unjust aggression, or at least of unrighteous and unprincipled ambition.

The English advance bodies of troops towards the Sutlej contrary to their policy of 1809.

To this general persuasion of the Sikhs, in common with other Indian nations, that the English were and are ever ready to extend their power, is to be added the particular bearing of the British Government towards the Punjab itself. In 1809, when the apprehensions of a French invasion of the East had subsided, when the resolution of making the Jumna a boundary was still approved, and when the policy of forming the province of Sirhind into a neutral or separating tract between two dissimilar powers had been wisely adopted, the English Viceroy had said that rather than irritate Ranjīt Singh, the detachment of troops which had been advanced to Ludhiāna might be withdrawn to Karnāl.[1] It was not indeed thought advisable to carry out the proposition; but up to the period of the Afghān war of 1838, the garrison of Ludhiāna formed the only body of armed men near the Sikh frontier, excepting the provincial regiment raised at Sabāthu for the police of the hills after the Gurkha war. The advanced post on the Sutlej was of little military or political use; but it served as the most conspicuous symbol of the compact with the Sikhs; and they, as the inferior power, were always disposed to lean upon old engagements as those which warranted the least degree of intimacy or dictation. In 1835 the petty chiefship of Ferozepore, seventy miles lower down the Sutlej than Ludhiāna, was occupied by the English as an escheat due to their protection of all Sikh lordships save that of Lahore. The advantages of the place in a military point of view had been perseveringly extolled, and its proximity to the capital of the Punjab made Ranjīt Singh, in his prophetic fear, claim it as a dependency of his own.[2] In 1838 the Mahārājā's apprehensions that the insignificant town

[1] Government to Sir David Ochterlony, 30th Jan. 1809.

[2] See chap. vii.

1845–6.

would become a cantonment were fully realized; for twelve thousand men assembled at Ferozepore to march to Khorasan; and as it was learnt, before the date fixed for the departure of the army, that the Persians had raised the siege of Herāt, it was determined that a small division should be left behind, until the success of the projected invasion rendered its presence no longer necessary.[1] But the succeeding warfare in Afghānistān and Sind gave the new cantonment a character of permanency, and in 1842 the remoteness from support of the *two* posts on the Sutlej was one of the arguments used for advancing a considerable body of troops to Ambāla as a reserve, and for placing European regiments in the hills still closer to the Sikh frontier.[2] The relations of 1809 were nevertheless cherished by the Sikhs, although they may have been little heeded by the English amid the multifarious considerations attendant on their changed position in India, and who, assured of the rectitude of their intentions, persuaded of the general advantage of their measures, and conscious of their overwhelming power, are naturally prone to disregard the less obvious feelings of their dependants, and to be careless of the light in which their acts may be viewed by those whose aims and apprehensions are totally different from their own.

The English views about Peshāwar, and their offer to

It had never been concealed from the Sikh authorities, that the helpless condition of the acknowledged government of the country was held to justify such additions to the

[1] This was the understanding at the time, but no document appears to have been drawn up to that effect. It was indeed expected that Shāh Shujā would be seated on his throne, and the British army withdrawn, all within a twelvemonth.

[2] The author cannot refer to any written record of these reasons, but he knows that they were used. When the step in advance was resolved on, it is only to be regretted that the cantonment was not formed at Sirhind, the advantages of which as a military post with reference to the Punjab, as being central to all the principal passages of the Sutlej, Sir David Ochterlony had long before pointed out. (Sir D. Ochterlony to Government, 3rd May 1810.) Some delicacy, however, was felt towards the Sikhs of Patiāla, to whom Sirhind belonged; although the more important and less defensible step of alarming the Sikhs of Lahore had been taken without heed or hesitation.

1845-6. support Sher Singh, all weigh with the Sikhs.

troops at Ludhiāna and Ferozepore as would give confidence to the inhabitants of these districts, and ensure the successful defence of the posts themselves against predatory bands.[1] Nor did the Sikhs deny the abstract right of the English to make what military arrangements they pleased for the security of their proper territories: but that any danger was to be apprehended from Lahore was not admitted by men conscious of their weakness; and thus by every process of reasoning employed, the Sikhs still came to the same conclusion that they were threatened. Many circumstances, unheeded or undervalued by the English, gave further strength to this conviction. It had not indeed been made known to the Sikhs that Sir William Macnaghten and others had proposed to dismember their kingdom by bestowing Peshāwar on Shāh Shujā, when Ranjīt Singh's line was held to end with the death of his grandson; but it would be idle to suppose the Lahore government ignorant of a scheme which was discussed in official correspondence, and doubtless in private society, or of the previous desire of Sir Alexander Burnes to bestow the same tract on Dost Muhammad Khān, which was equally a topic of conversation; and the Sikh authorities must at least have had a lively remembrance of the English offer of 1843, to march upon their capital, and to disperse their army. Again, in 1844 and 1845, the facts were whispered abroad and treasured up, that the English were preparing boats at Bombay to make bridges across the Sutlej, that troops in Sind were being equipped for a march on Multān,[2] and that the various garrisons of

[1] Cf. the Governor-General to the Secret Committee, 2nd Dec. 1845, (Parliamentary Papers, 1846); and also his dispatch of the 31st Dec. 1845 (Parliamentary Papers, p. 28).

[2] The collection of ordnance and ammunition at Sakhar for the equipment of a force of five thousand men, to march towards Multān, was a subject of ordinary official correspondence in 1844-5, as, for instance, between the Military Board in Calcutta and the officers of departments under its control. Sir Charles Napier assures the author that he, although Governor, had no cognizance of the correspondence in question, and made no preparations for equipping a force for service. Of the fact of the correspondence the author has no doubt; but the expression 'collection of the means', used in the first edition, can be held to imply too much, and the meaning is now correctly restored to 'ordnance and ammunition'. The object of the Supreme Government

1845–6.

the north-west provinces were being gradually reinforced, while some of them were being abundantly supplied with the munitions of war as well as with troops.[1] None of these things were communicated to the Sikh government, but they were nevertheless believed by all parties, and they were held to denote a campaign, not of defence, but of aggression.[2]

The Sikhs further moved by their estimate of the British Agent of the day.

The Sikhs thus considered that the fixed policy of the English was territorial aggrandizement, and that the immediate object of their ambition was the conquest of Lahore. This persuasion of the people was brought home to them by the acts of the British representative for the time, and by the opinion which they had preformed of his views. Mr. Clerk became Lieutenant-Governor of Agra in June 1843, and he was succeeded as Agent for the affairs of the Sikhs by Lieut.-Col. Richmond, whose place again was taken by Major Broadfoot, a man of undoubted energy and ability, in November of the following year. In India the views of the British Government are, by custom, made known to allies and dependants through one channel only, namely, that of an accredited English officer. The personal character of such a functionary gives a colour to all he does and says; the policy of the government is indeed judged of by the bearing of its representative, and it is certain that the Sikh authorities did not derive any assurance of an increasing desire for peace, from the nomination of an officer who, thirty

was not to march on Multān at that time, but to be prepared, at least in part, for future hostilities.

[1] The details of the preparations made by Lords Ellenborough and Hardinge may be seen in an article on the administration of the latter nobleman, in the *Calcutta Review*, which is understood to be the production of Lieut.-Col. Lawrence.

Up to 1838 the troops on the frontier amounted to one regiment at Sabāthu, and two at Ludhiāna, with six pieces of artillery, equalling in all little more than 2,500 men. Lord Auckland made the total about 8,000, by increasing Ludhiāna and creating Ferozepore. Lord Ellenborough formed further new stations at Ambāla, Kasaulī, and Simla, and placed in all about 14,000 men and 48 field guns on the frontier. Lord Hardinge increased the aggregate force to about 32,000 men, with 68 field guns, besides having 10,000 men with artillery at Meerut. After 1843, however, the station of Karnāl, on the Jumna, was abandoned, which in 1838 and preceding years may have mustered about 4,000 men.

[2] Cf. the Governor-General to the Secret Committee, Dec. 2, 1845.

1845–6. months before, had made so stormy a passage through their country.[1]

Major Broadfoot's views and overt acts equally displeasing to the Sikhs.

One of Major Broadfoot's [2] first acts was to declare the Cis-Sutlej possessions of Lahore to be under British protection equally with Patiāla and other chiefships, and also to be liable to escheat on the death or deposition of Mahārājā Dalīp Singh.[3] This view was not formally announced to the Sikh government, but it was notorious, and Major Broadfoot acted on it when he proceeded to interfere authoritatively, and by a display of force, in the affairs of the priest-like Sodhīs of Anandpur-Makhowāl, a fief to which some years before it had been declared to be expedient to waive all claim, especially as Ranjīt Singh could best deal with the privileged proprietors.[4] Again, a troop of horse had crossed the Sutlej near Ferozepore, to proceed to Kot Kapūra, a Lahore town, to relieve or strengthen the mounted police ordinarily stationed there ; but the party had crossed without the previous sanction of the British Agent having been obtained, agreeably to an understanding between the two governments, based on an article of the treaty of 1809, but which modified arrangement was scarcely applicable to so small a body of men proceeding for such a purpose. Major Broadfoot nevertheless required the horsemen to recross ;

[1] Sir Claude Wade, in his *Narrative of Services* (p. 19, note), well observes it to be essential to the preservation of the English system of alliances in India, that political representatives should be regarded as friends by the chiefs with whom they reside, rather than as the mere instruments of conveying the orders or of enforcing the policy of foreign masters.

[2] See p. 238, with regard to Major Broadfoot's passage of the Punjab in 1841.

[3] Major Broadfoot's letters to Government, of the 7th Dec. 1844, 30th Jan. and 28th Feb. 1845, may be referred to as explanatory of his views. In the last letter he distinctly says that if the young Mahārājā Dalīp Singh, who was then ill of the small-pox, should die, he would direct the reports regarding the Cis-Sutlej districts to be made to himself (through the Lahore vakīl or agent indeed), and not to any one in the Punjab.

[4] With regard to Anandpur, see chap. vii. About the particular dispute noticed in the text, Major Broadfoot's letter to Government of the 13th Sept. 1845 may be referred to. It labours in a halting way to justify his proceedings and his assumption of jurisdiction under ordinary circumstances.

1845–6.

and as he considered them dilatory in their obedience, he followed them with his escort, and overtook them as they were about to ford the river. A shot was fired by the English party, and the extreme desire of the Sikh commandant to avoid doing anything which might be held to compromise his government, alone prevented a collision.[1] Further, the bridge-boats which had been prepared at Bombay were dispatched towards Ferozepore in the autumn of 1845, and Major Broadfoot almost avowed that hostilities had broken out when he manifested an apprehension of danger to these armed vessels, by ordering strong guards of soldiers to escort them safely to their destination, and when he began to exercise their crews in the formation of bridges after their arrival at Ferozepore.[2]

Major Broadfoot's proceedings held to virtually denote war.

The views held by Major Broadfoot, and virtually adopted by the supreme government, with respect to the Cis-Sutlej districts, and also the measures followed in particular instances, may all be defended to a certain extent, as they indeed were, on specious grounds, as on the vague declarations of Sir David Ochterlony or on the deferential injunctions of Ranjīt Singh.[3] It is even believed that if the

[1] Cf. Major Broadfoot to Government, 27th March 1845. It is understood that the Government disapproved of these proceedings.

The *Calcutta Review* for June 1849 (p. 547) states that the Governor-General did not, as represented, disapprove, but, on the contrary, entirely approved, of Major Broadfoot's proceedings in this matter. The Reviewer writes like one possessed of official knowledge, but I am nevertheless unwilling to believe that the Governor-General could have been pleased with the violent and unbecoming act of his agent, although his lordship may have desired to see the irregular conduct of the Sikhs firmly checked.

[2] A detachment of troops under a European officer was required to be sent with each batch of boats, owing to the state of the Punjab. Nevertheless, small iron steamers were allowed to navigate the Sutlej at the time without guards, and one lay under the guns of Phillaur for several days without meeting aught except civility on the part of the Sikhs.

[3] Major Broadfoot is understood to have quoted to the Sikhs a letter of Sir David Ochterlony's, dated the 7th May 1809, to Mohkam Chand, Ranjīt Singh's representative, to the effect that the Cis-Sutlej Lahore states were equally under British protection with other states; and also an order of April 1824, from Ranjīt Singh, requiring his authorities south of the Sutlej to obey the English Agent, on pain of

1845–6. cession of the tracts in question had been desired, their relinquishment might have been effected without a resort to arms; but every act of Major Broadfoot was considered to denote a foregone resolution, and to be conceived in a spirit of enmity rather than of goodwill.[1] Nor did the Sikhs

having their noses slit. It is not improbable that Sir David Ochterlony may, at the early date quoted, have so understood the nature of the British connexion with reference to some particular case then before him, but that the Cis-Sutlej states of Lahore were held under feudal obligations to the English seems scarcely tenable, for the following reasons: (1) The protection extended by the English to the chiefs of Sirhind was declared to mean protection to *them* against Ranjīt Singh, and therefore not protection of the *whole* country between the Sutlej and Jumna, a portion of which belonged to Lahore. (See the Treaty of 1809, and Article I of the declaration of the 3rd May 1809; and also Government to Sir David Ochterlony, 10th April 1809.) Further, when convenient, the British Government could even maintain, that although the Treaty of 1809 was binding on Ranjīt Singh, with reference to Cis-Sutlej states, it was not binding on the English, whom it simply authorized to interfere at their discretion. (Government to Capt. Wade, 23rd April 1833.) This was indeed written with reference to Bahāwalpur, but the application was made general. (2) The protection accorded to the chiefs of Sirhind was afterwards extended so as to give them security in the plains, but not in the hills, against the Gurkhas as well as against Ranjīt Singh (Government to Sir David Ochterlony, 23rd Jan. 1810); while with regard to Ranjīt Singh's own Cis-Sutlej possessions, it was declared that he himself must defend them (against Nepāl), leaving it a question of policy as to whether he should or should not be aided in their defence. It was further added, that he might march through his Cis-Sutlej districts, to enable him to attack the Gurkhas in the hills near the Jumna, in defence of the districts in question, should he so wish. (Government to Sir David Ochterlony, 4th Oct. and 22nd Nov. 1811.) The opinion of Sir Charles Metcalfe, about the proceedings of the English with regard to Whadni (see *ante*, p. 163, note), may also be quoted as bearing on the case in a way adverse to Major Broadfoot.

[1] It was generally held by the English in India that Major Broadfoot's appointment greatly increased the probabilities of a war with the Sikhs; and the impression was equally strong that had Mr. Clerk, for instance, remained as Agent, there would have been no war. Had Mr. Clerk again, or Col. Wade, been the British representative in 1845, either would have gone to Lahore in person, and would have remonstrated against the selfish and unscrupulous proceedings of the managers of affairs as obviously tending to bring on a rupture. They would also have taken measures to show to the troops that the British Government would *not* be aggressors; they would have told the chiefs

seem to be menaced by their allies on one side only. In the summer of 1845 some horsemen from Multān crossed a few miles into the Sind territory in pursuit of certain marauders, and in seizing them, the Lahore soldiers were reported to 1845–6.

that a war would compromise them with the English, nor would they have come away until every personal risk had been run, and every exertion used to avert a resort to arms. That Major Broadfoot was regarded as hostile to the Sikhs may, perhaps, almost be gathered from his own letters. On the 19th March 1845 he wrote that the Governor of Multān had asked what course he, the Governor, should pursue, if the Lahore troops marched against him, to enforce obedience to demands made. The question does not seem one which a recusant servant would put under ordinary circumstances to the preserver of friendship between his master and the English. Major Broadfoot, however, would appear to have recurred to the virtual overtures of Dīwān Mūlrāj, for on the 20th Nov. 1845, when he wrote to all authorities in any way connected with the Punjab, that the British provinces were threatened with invasion, he told the Major-General at Sakhar that the Governor of Multān would defend *Sind* with *his* provincials against the Sikhs!—thus leading to the belief that he had succeeded in detaching the Governor from his allegiance to Lahore. When this note was originally written, the author thought that Major Broadfoot's warning in question had been addressed to Sir Charles Napier himself, but he has subsequently ascertained that the letter was sent to his Excellency's deputy in the upper portion of the country, and that Sir Charles Napier has no recollection of receiving a similar communication.

Some allusion may also be made to a falsified speech of Sir Charles Napier's, which ran the round of the papers at the time, about the British army being called on to move into the Punjab, especially as Major Broadfoot considered the Sikh leaders to be moved in a greater degree by the Indian newspapers than is implied in a passing attention to reiterated paragraphs about invasion. He thought, for instance, that Pandit Jalla understood the extent to which Government deferred to public opinion, and that the Brāhman himself designed to make use of the press as an instrument. (Major Broadfoot to Government, 30th Jan. 1845.)

In the first edition of this history the speech of Sir Charles Napier was referred to as if it had really been made in the terms reported, but the author has now learnt from his Excellency that nothing whatever was said about leading troops into the Punjab, or about engaging in war with the Sikhs. The author has likewise ascertained from Sir Charles Napier, that the mention made in the first edition about a proposal to station a considerable force at Kashmor having been disapproved by the Supreme Government is incorrect, and he offers his apologies to the distinguished leader misrepresented for giving original or additional currency to the errors in question.

1845–6.

have used needless violence, and perhaps to have committed other excesses. Nevertheless, the object of the troopers was evident; and the boundary of the two provinces between the Indus and the hills is nowhere defined, but the governor, Sir Charles Napier, immediately ordered the wing of a regiment to Kashmor, a few miles below Rojhan, to preserve the integrity of his frontier from violation. The Lahore authorities were thus indeed put upon their guard, but the motives of Sir Charles Napier were not appreciated, and the prompt measures of the conqueror of Sind were mistakenly looked upon as one more proof of a desire to bring about a war with the Punjab.

Sir Charles Napier's acts considered further proof of hostile views.

The Lahore chiefs make use of the persuasion of the people for their own ends,

The Sikh army, and the population generally, were convinced that war was inevitable; but the better informed members of the government knew that no interference was likely to be exercised without an overt act of hostility on their part.[1] When moved as much by jealousy of one another as by a common dread of the army, the chiefs of the Punjab had clung to wealth and ease rather than to honour and independence, and thus Mahārājā Sher Singh, the Sindhianwalas, and others, had been ready to become tributary, and to lean for support upon foreigners. As the authority of the army began to predominate, and to derive force from its system of committees, a new danger threatened the territorial chiefs and the adventurers in the employ of the government. They might successively fall before the cupidity of the organized body which none could control, or an able leader might arise who would absorb the power of all others, and gratify his followers by the sacrifice of the rich, the selfish, and the feeble. Even the Rājā of Jammu, always so reasonably averse to a close connexion with the English, began to despair of safety as a feudatory in the hills, or of

[1] Cf. Enclosure No. 6 of the Governor-General's letter to the Secret Committee of the 2nd Dec. 1845. (Parliamentary Papers, 26th Feb. 1846, p. 21.) Major Broadfoot, however, states of Gulāb Singh, what was doubtless true of many others, viz. that he believed the English had designs on the Punjab. (Major Broadfoot to Government, 5th May 1845.) It is indeed notorious that Sikhs and Afghāns commonly said the English abandoned Kābul because they did not hold Lahore, and that having once established themselves in the Punjab, they would soon set about the regular reduction of Khorasan.

1845–6.

authority as a minister at Lahore without the aid of the British name, and Lāl Singh, Tej Singh, and many others, all equally felt their incapacity to control the troops. These men considered that their only chance of retaining power was to have the army removed by inducing it to engage in a contest which they believed would end in its dispersion, and pave the way for their recognition as ministers more surely than if they did their duty by the people, and earnestly deprecated a war which must destroy the independence of the Punjab.[1] Had the shrewd committees of the armies observed no military preparations on the part of the English, they would not have heeded the insidious exhortations of such mercenary men as Lāl Singh and Tej Singh, although in former days they would have marched uninquiringly

and urge the army against the English, in order that it may be destroyed.

[1] Cf. Enclosures to the Governor-General's letter to the Secret Committee of the 31st Dec. 1845. (Parliamentary Papers, 26th Feb. 1846, p. 29.) It has not been thought necessary to refer to the intemperance of the desperate Jawāhir Singh, or to the amours of the Mahārānī, which, in the papers laid before the British Parliament, have been used to heighten the folly and worthlessness of the Lahore court. Jawāhir Singh may have sometimes been seen intoxicated, and the Mahārānī may have attempted little concealment of her debaucheries, but decency was seldom violated in public; and the essential forms of a court were preserved to the last, especially when strangers were present. The private life of princes may be scandalous enough, while the moral tone of the people is high, and is, moreover, applauded and upheld by the transgressors themselves, in their capacity of magistrates. Hence the domestic vices of the powerful have, comparatively, little influence on public affairs. Further, the proneness of newsmongers to enlarge upon such personal failings is sufficiently notorious; and the diplomatic service of India has been often reproached for dwelling pruriently or maliciously on such matters. Finally, it is well known that the native servants of the English in Hindustān, who in too many instances are hirelings of little education or respectability, think they best please their employers, or chime in with their notions, when they traduce all others, and especially those with whom there may be a rivalry or a collision. So inveterate is the habit of flattery, and so strong is the belief that Englishmen love to be themselves praised and to hear others slighted, that even petty local authorities scarcely refer to allied or dependent princes, their neighbours, in verbal or in written reports, without using some terms of disparagement towards them. Hence the scenes of debauchery described by the Lahore news-writer are partly due to his professional character, and partly to his belief that he was saying what the English wanted to hear.

1845–6. towards Delhi at the bidding of their great Mahārājā. But the views of the government functionaries coincided with the belief of the impulsive soldiery; and when the men were tauntingly asked whether they would quietly look on while the limits of the Khālsa dominion were being reduced, and the plains of Lahore occupied by the remote strangers of Europe, they answered that they would defend with their lives all belonging to the commonwealth of Gobind, and that they would march and give battle to the invaders on their own ground.[1] At the time in question, or early in November, two Sikh villages near Ludhiāna were placed under sequestration, on the plea that criminals concealed in them had not been surrendered.[2] The measure was an unusual one, even when the Sikhs and the English were equally at their ease with regard to one another; and the circumstance, added to the rapid approach of the Governor-General to the frontier, removed any doubts which may have lingered in the minds of the Panchāyats. The men would assemble in groups and talk of the great battle they must soon wage, and they would meet round the tomb of Ranjīt Singh and vow fidelity to the Khālsa.[3] Thus wrought upon, war with the English was virtually declared on the 17th November; a few days afterwards the troops began to move in detachments from Lahore; they commenced crossing the Sutlej between Hariki and Kasūr on the 11th December, and on the 14th of that month a portion of the army took up a position within a few miles of Ferozepore.[4]

The Sikhs cross the Sutlej, 11th Dec. 1845.

The initiative was thus taken by the Sikhs, who by an overt act broke a solemn treaty, and invaded the territories of their allies. It is further certain that the English people had all along been sincerely desirous of living at peace with the Punjab, and to a casual observer the aggression of the

[1] The ordinary private correspondence of the period contained many statements of the kind given in the text.

[2] Major Broadfoot's *official* correspondence seems to have ceased after the 21st Nov. 1845; and there is no report on this affair among his recorded letters.

[3] The Lahore news-letters of the 24th Nov. 1845, prepared for Government.

[4] Cf. the Governor-General to the Secret Committee, 2nd and 31st Dec. 1845, with enclosures. (Parliamentary Papers, 1846.)

Sikhs may thus appear as unaccountable as it was fatal; 1845-6.
yet further inquiry will show that the policy pursued by the English themselves for several years was not in reality well calculated to ensure a continuance of pacific relations, and that they cannot therefore be held wholly blameless for a war which they expected and deprecated, and which they knew could only tend to their own aggrandizement. The proceedings of the English, indeed, do not exhibit that punctilious adherence to the spirit of first relations which allows no change of circumstances to cause a departure from arrangements which had, in the progress of time, come to be regarded by a weaker power as essentially bound up with its independence. Neither do the acts of the English seem marked by that high wisdom and sure foresight, which should distinguish the career of intelligent rulers acquainted with actual life, and the examples of history. Treaties of commerce and navigation had been urged upon the Sikhs, notwithstanding their dislike to such bonds of unequal union; they were chafed that they had been withheld from Sind, from Afghānistān, and from Tibet, merely, they would argue, that these countries might be left open to the ambition of the English; and they were rendered suspicious by the formation of new military posts on their frontier contrary to prescriptive usage, and for reasons of which they did not perceive the force or admit the validity. The English looked upon these measures with reference to *their own* schemes of amelioration; and they did not heed the conclusions which the Sikhs might draw from them, although such conclusions, how erroneous soever, would necessarily become motives of action to a rude and warlike race. Thus, at the last, regard was mainly had to the chance of predatory inroads, or to the possibility that sovereign and nobles and people, all combined, would fatuitously court destruction by assailing their gigantic neighbour, and little thought was given to the selfish views of factious Sikh chiefs, or to the natural effects of the suspicions of the Sikh commonalty when wrought upon by base men for their own ends. Thus, too, the original agreement which left the province of Sirhind free of troops and of British subjects, and which provided a confederacy of dependent states to soften the mutual action of a half-

1845–6. barbarous military dominion and of a humane and civilized government, had been set aside by the English for objects which seemed urgent and expedient, but which were good in their motive rather than wise in their scope. The measure was misconstrued by the Sikhs to denote a gradual but settled plan of conquest; and hence the *subjective* mode of reasoning employed was not only vicious in logic, but, being met by arguments even more narrow and one-sided, became faulty in policy, and, in truth, tended to bring about that collision which it was so much desired to avoid.

A corresponding singleness of apprehension also led the confident English to persevere in despising or misunderstanding the spirit of the disciples of Gobind. The unity and depth of feeling, derived from a young and fervid faith, were hardly recognized, and no historical associations exalted Sikhs to the dignity of Rājpūts and Pathāns.

In 1842 they were held, as has been mentioned, to be unequal to cope with the Afghāns, and even to be inferior in martial qualities to the population of the Jammu hills. In 1845 the Lahore soldiery was called a 'rabble' in sober official dispatches, and although subsequent descriptions allowed the regiments to be composed of the yeomanry of the country, the army was still declared to be daily deteriorating as a military body.[1] It is, indeed, certain that English officers and Indian sepoys equally believed they were about to win battles by marching steadily and by the discharge of a few artillery shots, rather than by skilful dispositions, hard fighting, and a prolonged contest.[2]

[1] Major Broadfoot to Government, 18th and 25th Jan. 1845. A year before, Lieut.-Col. Lawrence (*Calcutta Review*, No. III, pp. 176, 177) considered the Sikh army as good as that of any other Indian power, and not inferior, indeed, to the Gwalior troops which fought at Mahārājpur. The Lahore artillery, however, he held to be very bad, although he was of opinion that in position the guns would be well served. In his *Adventurer in the Punjab* (p. 47, note *k*) he had previously given a decided preference to the Marāthā artillery.

[2] Major Smyth is, however, of opinion that the sepoys in the British service had a high opinion of the Sikh troops, although the English themselves talked of them as boasters and cowards. (Major Smyth, *Reigning Family of Lahore*, Introduction, pp. xxiv and xxv.) Cf. Dr. Macgregor, *History of the Sikhs*, ii. 89, 90.

1845–6.

The English unprepared for a campaign.

The English not only undervalued their enemy, but, as has been hinted, they likewise mistook the form which the long-expected aggressions of the Sikhs would assume.[1] It was scarcely thought that the ministry, or even that the army, would have the courage to cross the river in force, and to court an equal contest; the known treasonable views of the chiefs, and the unity and depth of feeling which possessed the troops, were not fully appreciated, and it continued to be believed that a desultory warfare would sooner or later ensue, which would indeed require the British to interfere,

[1] Cf. the Governor-General to the Secret Committee, 31st Dec. 1845 (Parliamentary Papers, 1846), and the *Calcutta Review*, No. XVI, p. 475. A few words may here be said on a subject which occasioned some discussion in India at the time, viz. Major Broadfoot's reputed persevering disbelief that the Sikhs would cross the Sutlej, although his assistant, Capt. Nicolson, stationed at Ferozepore, had repeatedly said they would. The matter was taken up by the Indian public as if Capt. Nicolson had for several months, or for a year and more, held that the British provinces would assuredly be invaded within a definite period; whereas, with regard to what the Sikh army might eventually do, Capt. Nicolson was as uncertain as others, up to within a week or so of the passage of the Sutlej in December 1845. The truth seems to be, that Major Broadfoot affected to disbelieve Capt. Nicolson's report of the actual march and near approach of the Lahore army, of its encampment on the Sutlej, and of its evident resolution to cross the river, giving the preference to intelligence of a contrary nature received direct from the Sikh capital, and which tallied with his own views of what the Sikhs would finally do. That such was the case, may indeed be gathered from the Governor-General's dispatch to the Secret Committee of the 31st Dec. 1845. (Parliamentary Papers, 1846, pp. 26, 27.)

The writer of the article in the *Calcutta Review*, No. XVI, endeavours to justify Major Broadfoot's views by showing that all the officers on the frontier held similar opinions. The point really at issue, however, is not whether, generally speaking, invasion were probable, but whether in the beginning of December 1845 Major Broadfoot should not have held that the Sutlej would be crossed. The Reviewer forgets to add that of the local officers Major Broadfoot alone knew at the time the extent of provocation which the Sikhs had received; and that the officers wrote with no later news before them than that of the 17th of November. Hence all, save Major Broadfoot himself, had very imperfect means of forming a judgement of what was likely to take place. With regard to what the English should have been prepared against, Lieut.-Col. Richmond's letter of the 3rd April 1844, to the address of the Commander-in-Chief, may be referred to as in favour of having stations strong if they were to be kept up at all.

1845–6.

but which would still enable them to do so at their own convenience. Thus boats for bridges, and regiments and guns, the natural and undesigned provocatives to a war, were sufficiently numerous; but food and ammunition, and carriage and hospital stores, such as were necessary for a campaign, were all behind at Delhi or Agra, or still remained to be collected; for the desire of the English was, it is said, peace, and they had hoped that an assemblage of troops would prevent predatory aggression, or deter the Sikhs from engaging in suicidal hostilities.[1]

The English hasten to oppose the Sikhs.

The Governor-General [2] joined the Commander-in-Chief at Ambāla early in December 1845, and as soon as it seemed certain that the Sikhs were marching in force towards the Sutlej, the English troops in the upper provinces were all put in motion. The nearest divisions were those of Ambāla, Ludhiāna, and Ferozepore, which numbered in all about 17,000 available men, with 69 field guns; and as the last-mentioned force was the most exposed, the Ambāla troops were moved straight to its support, and Lord Hardinge further prudently resolved to leave Ludhiāna with a mere garrison for its petty fort, and to give Lord Gough as large a force as possible, with which to meet the Sikhs, should they cross the Sutlej as they threatened.[3]

1 It was a common and a just remark at the time, that although the Indian Government was fortunate in having a practical and approved soldier like Lord Hardinge at its head, under the circumstances of a war in progress, yet that had Lord Ellenborough remained Governor-General, the army would have taken the field better equipped than it did.

[2 Sir Henry Hardinge had succeeded Lord Ellenborough as Governor-General in July 1844. The Commander-in-Chief was Sir Hugh Gough.—Ed.]

3 The effective force at Ferozeshāh was 17,727 men, according to the *Calcutta Review* (No. XVI, p. 472), and 16,700 according to Lord Hardinge's dispatch of the 31st Dec. 1845. This was the available force, out of 32,479 men in all, posted from Ambāla to the Sutlej. The author has learnt that Lord Gough is satisfied the number of the enemy at Ferozeshāh and the other battles of the campaign have been underestimated in this narrative. There cannot, indeed, be any statements of decisive authority referred to, but the settled conviction of the Commander-in-Chief is of primary consideration, and requires to be recorded in this new edition; especially as, with a characteristic singleness of heart, his lordship, in noticing the probable error, had

1845–6.

The numbers of the Sikhs.

The Lahore army of invasion may have equalled 35,000 or 40,000 men, with a hundred and fifty pieces of artillery, exclusive of a force detached towards Ludhiāna to act as circumstances might render advantageous. The numbers of the Sikhs were understood at the time to greatly exceed those given, but the strength of armies is usually exaggerated both by the victors and the vanquished; and there is no satisfactory proof that the regular troops of the Sikhs exceeded those of the English by more than a half, although numerous bodies of undisciplined horse swelled the army of the invaders to more than double that of their opponents.[1]

Ferozepore threatened, but purposely not attacked.

The Sikh leaders threatened Ferozepore, but no attack was made upon its seven thousand defenders, which with a proper spirit were led out by their commander, Sir John Littler, and showed a bold front to the overwhelming force of the enemy. The object, indeed, of Lāl Singh and Tej Singh was not to compromise themselves with the English by destroying an isolated division, but to get their own troops dispersed by the converging forces of their opponents. Their desire was to be upheld as the ministers of a dependent kingdom by grateful conquerors, and they thus deprecated an attack on Ferozepore, and assured the local British authorities of their secret and efficient goodwill. But these men had also to keep up an appearance of devotion to the interests of their country, and they urged the necessity of leaving the easy prey of a cantonment untouched, until the leaders of the English should be attacked, and the fame of the Khālsa exalted by the captivity or death of a Governor-General.[2] The Sikh army itself understood the necessity

The objects of Lāl Singh and Tej Singh.

regard rather to the reputation of the army he led than to his own fame.

[1] The Governor-General, in his dispatch of the 31st Dec. 1845, estimates the Sikhs at from 48,000 to 60,000 men; but with regard to efficient troops, it may be observed that the whole regular army of the country did not exceed 42,000 infantry, including the regiments at Lahore, Multān, Peshāwar, and Kashmīr, as well as those forming the main army of invasion. Perhaps an estimate of 30,000 *embodied* troops of all kinds would be nearer the truth than any other.

[2] It was sufficiently certain and notorious at the time that Lāl Singh was in communication with Capt. Nicolson, the British Agent at Ferozepore, but, owing to the untimely death of that officer, the details of the overtures made, and expectations held out, cannot now

1845–6.

The tactics of the Sikhs.

of unity of counsel in the affairs of war, and the power of the regimental and other committees was temporarily suspended by an agreement with the executive heads of the state, which enabled these unworthy men to effect their base objects with comparative ease.[1] Nevertheless, in the ordinary military arrangements of occupying positions and distributing infantry and cavalry, the generals and inferior commanders acted for themselves, and all had to pay some respect to the spirit which animated the private soldiers in their readiness to do battle for the commonwealth of Gobind. The effects of this enthusiastic unity of purpose in an army, headed by men not only ignorant of warfare, but studiously treacherous towards their followers, was conspicuously visible in the speediness with which numerous heavy guns and abundance of grain and ammunition were brought across a large river. Every Sikh considered the cause as his own, and he would work as a labourer as well as carry a musket; he would drag guns, drive bullocks, lead camels, and load and unload boats with a cheerful alacrity, which contrasted strongly with the inapt and sluggish obedience of mere mercenaries, drilled, indeed, and fed with skill and care, but unwarmed by one generous feeling for their country or their foreign employers. The youthful Khālsa was active and strong of heart, but the soldiers had never before met so great a foe, and their

be satisfactorily known. (Cf. Dr. Macgregor's *History of the Sikhs*, ii. 80.)

The *Calcutta Review* for June 1849 (p. 549), while doubting the fact, or at least the extent and importance, of Lāl Singh's and Tej Singh's treachery, admits that the former was not only in communication with Capt. Nicolson, as stated, but that on the 7th Feb. 1846 he was understood to have sent a plan of the Sikh position at Sobraon to Col. Lawrence, and that on the 19th Dec. 1845, the day after the battle of Mudkī, Lāl Singh's agent came to Major Broadfoot, and was dismissed with a rebuke. [As regards Tej Singh's treachery it may be stated that, according to a reliable tradition, that officer discovered early in the operations that his artillery ammunition had been tampered with and much of it rendered useless. Such treachery on the part of his own side doubtless had a considerable effect upon his subsequent conduct.—Ed.]

[1] Lāl Singh was appointed wazīr, and Tej Singh commander-in-chief of the army on or about the 8th Nov. 1845, according to the *Lahore News-Letter* of that date, prepared for Government.

tactics were modified by involuntary awe of the British army, renowned in the East for achievements in war. The river had been crossed, and the treaty broken; but the Sikhs were startled at their own audacity, and they partially entrenched one portion of their forces, while they timorously kept the other as a reserve out of danger's way. Thus the valiant Swedes, when they threw themselves into Germany under their king, the great Gustavus, revived the castrametation of Roman armies in the presence of the experienced commanders of Austria;[1] and thus the young Telemachus, tremulously bold, hurled his unaccustomed spear against the princes of Ithaca, and sprang for shelter behind the shield of his heroic father![2] 1845–6.

The battle of Mudkī, 18th Dec. 1845.

The Ambāla and Ludhiāna divisions of the British army arrived at Mudkī, twenty miles from Ferozepore, on the 18th December; and they had scarcely taken up their ground before they were attacked by a detachment of the Sikh army, believed at the time to be upwards of thirty thousand strong, but which really seems to have consisted of less than two thousand infantry, supported by about twenty-two pieces of artillery, and eight or ten thousand horsemen.[3] Lāl Singh headed the attack, but, in accordance

[1] As at Werben, before the battle of Leipzig. Col. Mitchell says Gustavus owed his success almost as much to the spade as to the sword. (*Life of Wallenstein*, p. 210.)

[2] *Odyssey*, xxii. The practice of the Sikhs would probably have resolved itself into the system of fortified camps of the Romans at night and during halts, and into the Greek custom of impenetrable phalanxes on the battle-field, while it almost anticipates the European tendencies of the day about future warfare—which are, to mass artillery, and make it overwhelming. The Sikhs would have moved with their infantry and guns together, while they swept the country with their cavalry; and it is clear that no troops in India or in Southern Asia, save the movable brigades of the English, could have successfully assailed them.

[3] See Lord Gough's dispatch of the 19th December 1845 for the estimate of 30,000 men, with 40 guns. Capt. Nicolson, in his private correspondence of the period, and writing from Ferozepore, gives the Sikh force at about 3,500 only, which is doubtless too low, although subsequent inquiries all tended to show that the infantry portion was weak, having been composed of small detachments from each of the regiments in position at Ferozeshāh. The *Calcutta Review*, No. XVI, p. 489, estimates the guns at 22 only, and, the estimate being moderate, it is probably correct.

1845–6. with his original design, he involved his followers in an engagement, and then left them to fight as their undirected valour might prompt. The Sikhs were repulsed with the loss of seventeen guns,[1] but the success of the English was not so complete as should have been achieved by the victors in so many battles ; and it was wisely determined to effect a junction with the division of Sir John Littler before assailing the advanced wing of the Sikh army, which was encamped in a deep horse-shoe form around the village of P'heerooshuhur, about ten miles both from Mudkī and from Ferozepore.[2] This position was strengthened by more than a hundred pieces of artillery, and its slight and imperfect entrenchments had, here and there, been raised almost waist high since the action at Mudkī. It was believed at the time to contain about fifty thousand men, but subsequent inquiries reduced the infantry to twelve regiments, and the cavalry to the eight or ten thousand which had before been engaged. The wing of the Sikh army attacked did not, therefore, greatly surpass its assailants, except in the number and size of its guns, the English artillery consisting almost wholly of six and nine pounders.[3] But the belief in the

[1] The British loss in the action was 215 killed and 657 wounded. (See Lord Gough's dispatch of the 19th Dec. 1845.) The force under Lord Gough at the time amounted to about 11,000 men. In this action the English may, in a military sense, be said to have been surprised. Their defective system of spies left them ignorant of the general position and probable objects of the enemy ; and the little use their commanders have usually made of cavalry left the near approach of the Sikhs unknown, and therefore unchecked. [Among the killed was Sir Robert Sale, the defender of Jalālābād.—Ed.]

[2] The correct name of the place, which has become identified with an important battle, is as given in the text :—' P'heeroo ' being the not uncommon name of a man, and ' shuhur ' an ordinary termination, signifying place or city. The name ' Ferozeshāh ' is erroneous, but it is one likely to be taken up on hearing ' P'heerooshuhur ' badly pronounced by peasants and others. The Sikhs call the battle ' P'heeroo ka larai ', or the fight of P'heeroo simply, without the addition of ' shuhur '.

[3] Both the Sikhs and the European officers in the Lahore service agree in saying that there were only twelve battalions in the lines of P'heerooshuhur, and such indeed seems to have been the truth. The Governor-General and Commander-in-Chief vaguely estimated the whole Sikh army on the left bank of the Sutlej at 60,000 strong, and

fortune of the British arms was strong, and the Sepoys would then have marched with alacrity against ten times their own numbers. 1845–6.

The battle of P'heerooshuhur, and retreat of the Sikhs, 21st and 22nd Dec. 1845.

A junction was effected with Sir John Littler's division about midday on the 21st December, and at a distance of four miles from the enemy's position. Considerable delay occurred in arranging the details of the assault, which was not commenced until within an hour of sunset. The confident English had at last got the field they wanted; they marched in even array, and their famed artillery opened its steady fire. But the guns of the Sikhs were served with rapidity and precision, and the foot-soldiers stood between and behind the batteries, firm in their order, and active with their muskets. The resistance met was wholly unexpected, and all started with astonishment. Guns were dismounted, and their ammunition was blown into the air; squadrons were checked in mid career; battalion after battalion was hurled back with shattered ranks, and it was not until after sunset that portions of the enemy's position were finally carried. Darkness, and the obstinacy of the contest, threw the English into confusion; men of all regiments and arms were mixed together; generals were doubtful of the fact or of the extent of their own success, and colonels knew not what had become of the regiments they commanded, or of the army of which they formed a part. Some portions of the enemy's line had not been broken, and the uncaptured guns were turned by the Sikhs upon masses of soldiers, oppressed with cold and thirst and fatigue, and who attracted the attention of the watchful enemy by lighting fires of brushwood to warm their stiffened limbs. The position of

Lord Gough makes Tej Singh bring 30,000 horse, *besides* fresh battalions, and a large park of artillery into action on the 22nd December, which would leave but a small remainder for the previous defence of P'heerooshuhur. (See the dispatches of the 22nd and 31st Dec. 1845.) The author has learnt that, after the war, Lord Gough ascertained, through the British authorities at Lahore, that the Sikhs estimated their numbers at P'heerooshuhur at 46,808 men, of all kinds, with 88 guns, 'including those brought up and taken away by Tej Singh'. This low estimate of the strength of the Sikhs in artillery is in favour of the credibility of the statement, and if Tej Singh's men are likewise included in the numbers given, the estimate may perhaps be fully trusted.

1845–6. the English was one of real danger and great perplexity; their mercenaries had proved themselves good soldiers in foreign countries as well as in India itself, when discipline was little known, or while success was continuous; but in a few hours the five thousand children of a distant land found that their art had been learnt, and that an emergency had arisen which would tax their energies to the utmost. On that memorable night the English were hardly masters of the ground on which they stood; they had no reserve at hand, while the enemy had fallen back upon a second army, and could renew the fight with increased numbers. The not imprudent thought occurred of retiring upon Ferozepore; but Lord Gough's dauntless spirit counselled otherwise, and his own and Lord Hardinge's personal intrepidity in storming batteries, at the head of troops of English gentlemen and bands of hardy yeomen, eventually achieved a partial success and a temporary repose. On the morning of the 22nd December, the last remnants of the Sikhs were driven from their camp; but as the day advanced the second wing of their army approached in battle-array, and the wearied and famished English saw before them a desperate and, perhaps, useless struggle. This reserve was commanded by Tej Singh; he had been urged by his zealous and sincere soldiery to fall upon the English at daybreak, but *his* object was to have the dreaded army of the Khālsa overcome and dispersed, and he delayed until Lāl Singh's force was everywhere put to flight, and until his opponents had again ranged themselves round their colours. Even at the last moment he rather skirmished and made feints than led his men to a resolute attack, and after a time he precipitately fled, leaving his subordinates without orders and without an object, at a moment when the artillery ammunition of the English had failed, when a portion of their force was retiring upon Ferozepore, and when no exertions could have prevented the remainder from retreating likewise, if the Sikhs had boldly pressed forward.[1]

[1] For the battle of P'heerooshuhur, see Lord Gough's dispatch of the 22nd, and Lord Hardinge's of the 31st Dec. 1845. The Governor-General notices in especial the exertions of the infantry soldiers; and one of the charges made by the 3rd Light Dragoons has been a

1845–6.

The difficulties and apprehensions of the English.

A battle had thus been won, and more than seventy pieces of artillery and some conquered or confiscated

theme of general admiration. The loss sustained was 694 killed, and 1,721 wounded. [The casualties among the officers were very heavy—103 in all. Among them was the political officer, Major Broadfoot, who has figured so prominently in previous pages.—Ed.]

After the war, Lord Gough learnt that the loss of the Sikhs in killed probably amounted to 2,000 in all, as the heirs of 1,782 men of the regular troops alone claimed balances of pay due to relatives slain. This argues a great slaughter; and yet it was a common remark at the time, that very few dead bodies were to be seen on the field after the action.

The statements of the *Quarterly Review* for June 1846, pp. 203–6, and of the *Calcutta Review* for Dec. 1847, p. 498, may be referred to about certain points still but imperfectly known, and which it is only necessary to allude to in a general way in this history. Two of the points are: (1) the proposal to fall back on Ferozepore during the night of the 21st December; and (2) the actual movement of a considerable portion of the British army towards that place on the forenoon of the following day.

Had the Sikhs been efficiently commanded, a retirement on Ferozepore would have been judicious in a military point of view, but as the enemy was led by traitors, it was best to fearlessly keep the field Perhaps neither the incapacity nor the treason of Lāl Singh and Tej Singh were fully perceived or credited by the English chiefs, and hence the anxiety of the one on whom the maintenance of the British dominion intact mainly depended.

At P'heerooshuhur the larger calibre and greater weight of metal of the mass of the Sikh artillery, and consequently the superiority of practice relatively to that of the field guns of the English, was markedly apparent in the condition of the two parks after the battle. The captured cannon showed scarcely any marks of round shot or shells, while nearly a third of the British guns were disabled in their carriages or tumbrils.

With regard to this battle it may be observed that the English had not that exact knowledge of the Sikh strength and position which might have been obtained even by means of reconnoitring; and it may also *perhaps* be said that the attack should have been made in column rather than in line, and after the long flanks of the enemy's position had been enfiladed by artillery. The extent, indeed, to which the English were unprepared for a campaign, and the manner in which their forces were commanded in most of the actions of the war, should be carefully borne in mind; for it was defective tactics and the absolute want of ammunition, as much as the native valour and aptitude of the Sikhs, which gave for a time a character of equality to the struggle, and which in this history seems to make a comparatively petty power dispute with the English supremacy in Northern India. Had the English been better led and better equipped, the

1845–6. territories graced the success; but the victors had lost a seventh of their numbers, they were paralysed after their prodigious exertions and intense excitement, and the Sikhs were allowed to cross the Sutlej at their leisure to prepare for fresh contests. The sepoy mercenaries had for the first time met an equal antagonist with their own weapons—even ranks and the fire of artillery. They loudly complained of the inferiority of their cannon; they magnified banks two and three feet high into formidable ramparts, and exploding tumbrils and stores of powder became, in their imaginations, designed and deadly mines. Nor was this feeling of respect and exaggeration confined to the Indians alone; the European soldiers partook of it; and the British public, as well as the dignitaries of the church and the heads of the state, became impressed with the immensity of the danger which had threatened the peace, and perhaps the safety, of their exotic dominion.[1] Regiments of men, and

fame of the Sikhs would not have been so great as it is, and the British chronicler would have been spared the ungracious task of declaring unpleasing truths. No one, however, can be insensible to the claims which the veteran chief of the army has established to his country's gratitude, by his cheering hardihood under every circumstance of danger, and by his great successes over all opponents. The robust character of Lord Gough has on many occasions stood England in good stead.

[1] The alarm of the English about the occupation of Delhi and the passage of the Jumna, may be likened to the nervous dread of Augustus, when he heard of the defeat of Varus and the destruction of his legions; and that one so astute, and so familiar with the sources of Roman power and the causes of Roman weakness, should have feared the consequences of a German invasion of Italy, at once palliates the apprehensions of the English in India and shows upon what slight foundations and undreamt-of chances the mightiest fabrics of dominion sometimes rest. Yet it is not clear that Augustus was not alarmed rather for himself than for Rome. He may have thought that a successful inroad of barbarians would encourage domestic enemies, and so lead to his own downfall, without sensibly affecting the real power of his country. Similarly, the apprehensions of the English after P'heerooshuhur may be said to have had a personal as much as a national reference, and there is no good reason for believing that one or two or even three defeats on the Sutlej would have shaken the stability of the British rule to the east and south of Delhi. All the chiefs of India, indeed, are willing enough to be independent, but no union for any such purpose yet exists among them, and only one or two are at any moment ready to take up arms; whereas the

numerous single officers variously employed, were summoned 1845–6.
from the most distant provinces to aid in vindicating the military renown of the English race, and the political supremacy of three generations. All longed for retribution, and all were cheered amid their difficulties by the genial temper and lofty bearing of one chief; and by the systematic industry and full knowledge of military requirements possessed by the other. But joy and gratitude were yet uppermost for the moment; the hope of revenge was disturbed by the remembrance of danger; and, unmindful of the rebuke of the wise Ulysses, a partial Divinity was praised by proclamation, for the deliverance *he* had vouchsafed to *his* votaries.

Unholy is the voice
Of loud thanksgiving over slaughtered men.[1]

---

resources of the English are vast, obedience among them is perfect, and victory would soon return to valour and unanimity. Still, an unsuccessful warfare on the part of the English of three or four consecutive years, might justly be regarded as the commencement of their decline; although it is very doubtful whether any combination of the present powers of India could drive them from Bengal, or from the coasts of the Deccan.

[1] *Odyssey*, xxii. The Governor-General's notification of the 25th December 1845 calls upon the troops to render acknowledgements to God, and the ecclesiastical authorities in Calcutta subsequently circulated a form of thanksgiving. The anxiety of the Governor-General may be further inferred from his proclamation, encouraging desertion from the Sikh ranks, with the assurance of present rewards and future pensions, *and the immediate decision of any lawsuits in which the deserters might be engaged in the British provinces!* (Major Smith, *Reigning Family of Lahore*, Introduction, p. xxvi *n.*)

The feeling which prompted the troops of Cromwell or Gustavus to kneel and return thanks to God on the field of victory must ever be admired and honoured; for it was genuine, and pervaded all ranks, from the leader downwards, and it would equally have moved the soldiers to reproaches and humiliation had they been beaten. But such tokens of reverence and abasement come coldly and without a vital meaning in the guise of a 'general order' or 'circular memorandum'; and perhaps a civilized and intelligent government might with advantage refrain from such tame and passionless assurances of devotion and gratitude, while it gave more attention to religious exercises in its regimental regulations. God should rather be kept ever present to the minds of the armed servants of the state by daily worship and instruction, than ostentatiously lauded on the rare occasion of a victory.

1845-6.

The Sikhs recross the Sutlej, and threaten Ludhiāna, Jan. 1846.

The British army was gradually reinforced, and it took up a position stretching from Ferozepore towards Hariki, and parallel to that held by the Sikhs on the right bank of the Sutlej. But the want of ammunition and heavy guns reduced the English to inactivity, and delay produced negligence on their part and emboldened the enemy to fresh acts of daring. The Cis-Sutlej feudatories kept aloof from their new masters, or they excited disturbances; and the Rājā of Lādwa, a petty prince dependent on the English, but who had been denounced as a traitor for a year past,[1] openly proceeded from the neighbourhood of Karnāl, and joined the division of the Sikh army under Ranjor Singh, which had crossed the Jullundur Doāb, to the neighbourhood of Ludhiāna. This important town had been denuded of its troops to swell the first army of defence, and it was but slowly and partially garrisoned by fresh regiments arriving from the eastward, although it covered the several lines of approach from the Jumna towards Ferozepore.[2] Early in January the Rājā of Lādwa returned to withdraw

[1] Major Broadfoot to Government, 13th Dec. 1844. This chief received the title of Rājā from Lord Auckland, partly as a compliment to Ranjīt Singh, to whom he was related, and partly in approbation of his liberality in providing the means of throwing a bridge across the classical Sarsuti, at Thānesar. He was a reckless, dissipated man, of moderate capacity; but he inherited the unsettled disposition of his father, Gurdut Singh, who once held Karnāl and some villages to the east of the Jumna, and who caused the English some trouble between 1803 and 1809.

[2] It is not clear why Ludhiāna was not adequately garrisoned, or rather covered, by the troops which marched from Meerut after the battle of P'heerooshuhur. The Governor-General's attention was, indeed, chiefly given to strengthening the main army in its unsupported position of Ferozepore—the real military disadvantage of which he had ample reason to deplore; while amidst his difficulties it may possibly have occurred to his Lordship, that the original policy of 1809—of being strong on the Jumna rather than on the Sutlej—was a truly wise one with reference to the *avoidance* of a war with the Sikhs.

The desire of being in force near the capitals of the Punjab and the main army of the Sikhs likewise induced Lord Hardinge to direct Sir Charles Napier to march from Sind, without heeding Multān, although, as his Lordship publicly acknowledged, that victorious commander had been sent for when it was thought the campaign might become a series of sieges.

1845–6.

his family from his fief of Badowāl near Ludhiāna, and he took the opportunity of burning a portion of the cantonment at the latter place, which the paucity of infantry and the want of cavalry on the spot enabled him to do with impunity. About the same time, the main army of the Sikhs, observing the supineness of their opponents, began to recross the Sutlej and to construct a bridge-head to secure the freedom of their passage. The English were unwillingly induced to let the Sikhs labour at this work, for it was feared that an attack would bring on a general engagement, and that the want of ammunition would prevent a battle being won or a victory being completed. The Sikhs naturally exulted, and they proclaimed that they would again fall upon the hated foreigners. Nor were their boasts altogether disbelieved; the disadvantages of Ferozepore as a frontier post became more and more apparent, and the English began to experience difficulty in obtaining supplies from the country they had annexed by the pen without having secured by the sword. The petty fort of Muktsar, where Gobind repulsed his Mughal pursuers after his flight from Chamkaur, was successfully defended for a time against some provincial companies and the auxiliaries of Bīkanír, which, like the legionaries themselves, were deficient in artillery ammunition. The equally petty fort of Dharmkōt was held, in defiance of the near presence of the right wing of the English army; and other defensible places towards Sirhind overawed the population, and interfered with the peaceful march of convoys and detachments.[1]

The skirmish of Badowāl, Jan. 21, 1846.

On the 17th January 1846, Major-General Sir Harry Smith[2] was sent with a brigade to capture Dharmkōt,

[1] The hill station of Simla, where many English families reside, and which is near the Sutlej, and the equally accessible posts of Kasaulī and Sabāthu, were at this time likewise threatened by the Lahore feudatory of Mandī, and some Sikh partisans; and as the regiments usually stationed at these places had been wholly withdrawn, it would not have been difficult to have destroyed them. But the local British authorities were active in collecting the quotas of the hill Rājputs, and judicious in making use of their means; and no actual incursion took place, although a turbulent sharer in the sequestered Anandpur-Makhowāl had to be called to account.

[[2] This distinguished officer, who fought through the Peninsular War, afterwards served in South Africa, where his memory is commemorated

1845–6. which was surrendered without bloodshed, and the transit of grain to the army was thus rendered more secure. The original object of Sir Harry Smith's diversion was to cover the march of the large convoy of guns, ammunition, and treasure in progress to Ferozepore, as well as to clear the country of partisan troops which restricted the freedom of traffic; but when it became known that Ranjor Singh had crossed the Sutlej in force and threatened Ludhiāna, the General was ordered to proceed to the relief of that place. On the 20th of January he encamped at the trading town of Jugrāon, within twenty-five miles of his destination, and the authorities of the son of Fateh Singh Ahluwalia, of the treaty of 1805, to whom the place belonged, readily allowed him to occupy its well-built fort. It was known on that day that Ranjor Singh was in position immediately to the westward of Ludhiāna, and that he had thrown a small garrison into Badowāl, which lay about eighteen miles distant on the direct road from Jugrāon. The British detachment, which had been swelled by reinforcements to four regiments of infantry, three regiments of cavalry, and eighteen guns, marched soon after midnight; and early on the morning of the 21st January it was learnt that the whole Sikh army, estimated at ten thousand men, had moved to Badowāl during the preceding day. That place was then distant eight miles from the head of the column, and Sir Harry Smith considered that if he made a détour to the right, so as to leave the Sikhs about three miles on his other flank, he would be able to effect his junction with the Ludhiāna brigade without molestation. A short halt took place to enable the baggage to get somewhat ahead, and it was arranged that the long strings of animals should move parallel to the troops and on the right flank, so as to be covered by the column. As Badowāl was approached, the Sikhs were seen to be in motion likewise, and apparently to be bent on intercepting the English; but as it was not wished to give them battle, Sir Harry Smith continued his

by the towns of Aliwal and Harrismith. His wife, a Spanish lady, who accompanied him through the Peninsular campaigns, also gave her name to a South African town, 'Ladysmith',—a place not without fame.—Ed.]

march, inclining however still more to his right, and making occasional halts with the cavalry to enable the infantry to close up, it having fallen behind owing to the heavy nature of the ground. But the Sikhs were resolved on fighting, and they commenced a fire of artillery on the British horse, which obtained a partial cover under sand-banks, while the guns of the detachment opened upon the Sikhs and served to keep their line in check. By the time that the British infantry and small rear-guard of cavalry had closed up, the fire of the Sikhs had begun to tell, and it was thought that a steady charge by the infantry would throw them into disorder, and would allow the baggage to pass on, and give time to the Ludhiāna troops to come to the aid of their comrades. A close contest was indeed the prompting of every one's heart at the moment; but as the regiments of foot were being formed into line, it was found that the active Sikhs had dragged guns, unperceived, behind sand hillocks to the rear of the column—or, as matters then stood, that they had turned their enemy's left flank. These guns threw their enfilading shot with great rapidity and precision, and whole sections of men were seen to fall at a time without an audible groan amid the hissing of the iron storm. The ground was heavy, the men were wearied with a march of nine hours and eighteen miles, and it became evident that a charge might prove fatal to the exhausted victors. The infantry once more resumed its march, and its retirement or retreat upon Ludhiāna was covered with skill and steadiness by the cavalry.[1] The Sikhs did not pursue, for they were without a leader, or without one who wished to see the English beaten. Ranjor Singh let his soldiers engage in battle, but that he accompanied them into the fight is more than doubtful, and it is certain that he did not essay the easy task of improving the success of his own men into the complete reverse of his enemy. The mass of the British baggage was at hand, and the temptation to plunder could not be resisted by men who were without orders to conquer. Every beast of burden which had not got within sight of Ludhiāna, or which had not, timorously but prudently, been taken back to Jugrāon, when the firing

1845–6.

[1 Under Col. Cureton.—ED.]

1845-6.

was heard, fell into the hands of the Sikhs, and they were enabled boastfully to exhibit artillery store carts as if they had captured British cannon.[1]

The Sikhs encouraged, and Gulāb Singh induced to repair to Lahore.

Ludhiāna was relieved, but an unsuccessful skirmish added to the belief so pleasing to the prostrate princes of India, that the dreaded army of their foreign masters had at last been foiled by the skill and valour of the disciples of Gobind, the kindred children of their own soil. The British sepoys glanced furtively at one another, or looked towards the east, their home; and the brows of Englishmen themselves grew darker as they thought of struggles rather than triumphs. The Governor-General and Commander-in-Chief trembled for the safety of that siege train and convoy of ammunition, so necessary to the efficiency of an army which they had launched in haste against aggressors and received back shattered by the shock of opposing arms. The leader of the beaten brigades saw before him a tarnished name after the labours of a life, nor was he met by many encouraging hopes of rapid retribution. The Sikhs on their side were correspondingly elated; the presence of European prisoners added to their triumph; Lāl Singh and Tej Singh shrank within themselves with fear, and Gulāb Singh, who had been spontaneously hailed as minister and leader, began to think that the Khālsa was really formidable to one greater far than himself, and he arrived at Lahore on the 27th of January, to give unity and vigour to the counsels of the Sikhs.[2] The army under Tej Singh had recrossed the Sutlej in force; it had enlarged the bridge-head before alluded to, and so entrenched a strong position in the face of the British divisions. The Sikhs seemed again to be about to carry the war into the country of their enemy; but Gulāb Singh came too late—their fame had reached its height, and defeat and subjection speedily overtook them.

[1] Cf. the Governor-General to the Secret Committee, 19th Jan. and 3rd Feb., and Lord Gough's dispatch of the 1st Feb. 1845. After the skirmish of the 21st January there were found to be sixty-nine killed, sixty-eight wounded, and seventy-seven missing; of which last, several were taken prisoners, while others rejoined their corps in a day or two. Of the prisoners, Mr. Barron, an assistant-surgeon, and some European soldiers were taken to Lahore.

[2] Cf. the Governor-General to the Secret Committee, 3rd Feb. 1846.

1845–6.

The battle of Alīwāl, 28th Jan. 1846.

During the night of the 22nd January, Ranjor Singh marched from Badowāl to a place on the Sutlej about fifteen miles below Ludhiāna, where he immediately collected a number of boats as if to secure the passage of the river. The object of this movement is not known ; but it may have been caused by a want of confidence on the part of the Sikhs themselves, as there were few regular regiments among them, until joined by a brigade of four battalions and some guns from the main army, which gave them a force of not less than fifteen thousand combatants. Sir Harry Smith immediately occupied the deserted position of the enemy, and he was himself reinforced simultaneously with the Sikhs by a brigade from the main army of the English. On the 28th January the General marched with his eleven thousand men, to give the enemy battle, or to reconnoitre his position and assail it in some degree of form, should circumstances render such a course the most prudent. The Sikhs were nearly ten miles distant, and midway it was learnt that they were about to move with the avowed object of proceeding with a part or the whole of their force to relieve the fort of Gūngrāna or to occupy the neighbouring town of Jugrāon, both of which posts were close to the line of the British communications with the Jumna. On reaching the edge of the table-land, bounding the sunken belt of many miles in breadth within which the narrower channel of the Sutlej proper winds irregularly, a portion of the Sikhs were observed to be in motion in a direction which would take them clear of the left of the British approach ; but as soon as they saw that they were liable to be attacked in flank, they faced towards their enemy, and occupied with their right the village of Būndrī, and with their left the little hamlet of Alīwāl, while with that activity necessary to their system, and characteristic of the spirit of the common soldiers, they immediately began to throw up banks of earth before their guns, where not otherwise protected, such as would afford some cover to themselves and offer some impediment to their assailants. An immediate collision was inevitable, and the British commander promptly gave the order for battle. The regiments of cavalry which headed the advance opened their glittering ranks to the right and left, and made

1845–6. apparent the serried battalions of infantry and the frowning batteries of cannon. The scene was magnificent and yet overawing: the eye included the whole field, and glanced approvingly from the steady order of one foe to the even array of the other; all bespoke gladness of mind and strength of heart; but beneath the elate looks of the advancing warriors there lurked that fierce desire for the death of his fellows which must ever impel the valiant soldier. When thus deployed, the lines of battle were not truly parallel. The Sikh line inclined towards and extended beyond the British right, while the other flanks were, for a time, comparatively distant. The English had scarcely halted during their march of eight miles, even to form their line; but the Sikhs nevertheless commenced the action. It was perceived by Sir Harry Smith that the capture of the village of Alīwāl was of the first importance, and the right of the infantry was led against it. A deadly struggle seemed impending; for the Sikh ranks were steady and the play of their guns incessant; but the holders of the post were battalions of hill-men, raised because their demeanour was sober, and their hearts indifferent to the Khālsa, and after firing a straggling volley, they fled in confusion, headed by Ranjor Singh, their immediate leader, and leaving the brave Sikh artillerymen to be slaughtered by the conquerors. The British cavalry of the right made at the same time a sweeping and successful charge, and one-half of the opposing army was fairly broken and dispersed; but the Sikhs on their own right seemed to be outflanking their opponents in spite of the exertions of the English infantry and artillery; for there the more regular battalions were in line, and the true Sikh was not easily cowed. A prompt and powerful effort was necessary, and a regiment of European lancers,[1] supported by one of Indian cavalry, was launched against the even ranks of the Lahore infantry. The Sikhs knelt to receive the orderly but impetuous charge of the English warriors, moved alike by noble recollections of their country, by military emulation, and by personal feelings of revenge; but at the critical moment, the unaccustomed discipline of many of Gobind's champions failed them. They rose, yet

[[1] H.M.'s 16th Lancers, under Col. Cureton.—Ed.]

they reserved their fire, and delivered it together at the distance of a spear's throw; nor was it until the mass had been three times ridden through that the Sikhs dispersed. The charge was timely and bold; but the ground was more thickly strewn with the bodies of victorious horsemen than of beaten infantry. An attempt was made to rally behind Bundrī; but all resistance was unavailing, the Sikhs were driven across the Sutlej, more than fifty pieces[1] of cannon were taken, and the General forgot his sorrows, and the soldiers their sufferings and indignities, in the fullness of their common triumph over a worthy enemy, in a well-planned and bravely fought battle.[2] 1845–6.

[[1] Sixty-seven is the official number given.—ED.]

[2] Cf. Sir Harry Smith's dispatch of the 30th January, and Lord Gough's dispatch of the 1st February 1846. (Parliamentary Papers, 1846.) The loss sustained was 151 killed, 413 wounded, and 25 missing.

The *Calcutta Review*, No. XVI, p. 499, states that Sir Harry Smith required some pressing before he would engage the Sikhs, after his reverse at Badowāl. That active leader, however, was in no need of such promptings, and had adequate reinforcements reached him sooner than they did, the battle of Alīwāl would have been sooner fought. It may likewise be here mentioned, that neither does the reviewer throughout his article do fair justice to Lord Gough, nor, in a particular instance, to the commissariat department of the army. Thus, with regard to the Commander-in-Chief, it is more than hinted (see p. 497), that Lord Hardinge was in no way to blame—that is, that Lord Gough *was* to blame—for the delay which occurred in attacking the Sikhs at P'heerooshuhur. It may be difficult to ascertain the causes, or to apportion the blame, but the Governor-General can proudly stand on his acknowledged merits and services, and wants no support at the expense of an ancient comrade-in-arms. Again, with regard to the commissariat, it is stated, at p. 488, that supplies, which the head of the department in the field asked six weeks to furnish, were procured by Major Broadfoot in six days. The commissariat department could only use money and effect purchases by contract, or in the open market; but Major Broadfoot could summarily require 'protected chiefs', on pain of confiscation, to meet all his demands; and the writer of the article might have learnt, or must have been aware, that the requisitions in question led to one chief being disgraced by the imposition of a fine, and had some share in the subsequent deposal of another. Had the British magistrates of Delhi, Sahāranpur, Bareilly, and other places, been similarly empowered to seize by force the grain and carriage within their limits, there would have been no occasion to disparage the commissariat department. Further, it is known to many, and it is in itself plain, that had the military authorities been required, or allowed, to prepare

1845–6.

The Sikh chiefs anxious to treat, and the English desirous of ending the war.

The victory was equally important and opportune, and the time-serving Gulāb Singh, whose skill and capacity might have protracted the war, first reproached the vanquished Sikhs for rashly engaging in hostilities with their colossal neighbour, and then entered into negotiations with the English leaders.[1] The Governor-General was not displeased that the Lahore authorities should be ready to yield; for he truly felt that to subjugate the Punjab in one season, to defeat an army as numerous as his own, to take two capitals, and to lay siege to Multān, and Jammu, and Peshāwar—all within a few months—was a task of difficult achievement and full of imminent risks. The dominion of the English in India hinges mainly upon the number and efficiency of the troops of their own race which they can bring into the field; and a campaign in the hot weather would have thinned the ranks of the European regiments under the most favourable circumstances, and the ordinary recurrence of an epidemic disease would have proved as fatal to the officers of every corps present as to the common soldiers. But besides this important consideration, it was felt that the minds of men throughout India were agitated, and that protracted hostilities would not only jeopardize the communications with the Jumna, but might disturb the whole of the north-western provinces, swarming with a military population which is ready to follow any standard affording pay or allowing plunder, and which already sighs for the end of a dull reign of peace. Bright visions of standing triumphant on the Indus and of numbering the remotest conquests of Alexander among the provinces of Britain, doubtless warmed the imagination of the Governor-

themselves as they wished, they as simple soldiers, who had no financial difficulties to consider, would have been amply prepared with all that an army of invasion or defence could have required, long before the Sikhs crossed the Sutlej. Lord Hardinge was chiefly responsible for the timely and adequate equipment of the army, in anticipation of a probable war; and with the Governor-General in the field, possessed of superior and anomalous powers, the Commander-in-Chief could only be held responsible—and that but to a limited extent—for the strategy of a campaign or the conduct of a battle.

[1] Cf. the Governor-General to the Secret Committee, of the 19th Feb. 1846.

1845–6.

General; but the first object was to drive the Sikhs across the Sutlej by force of arms, or to have them withdrawn to their own side of the river by the unconditional submission of the chiefs and the delegates of the army; for, until that were done, no progress could be said to have been made in the war, and every petty chief in Hindustān would have silently prepared for asserting his independence, or for enlarging his territory on the first opportunity. But the total dispersion of so large and so well equipped a body of brave men, as that which lay within sight of the available force of the British Government, could not be accomplished by one defeat, if the chiefs of the country were to be rendered desperate, and if all were to place their valour and unanimity under the direction of one able man. The English, therefore, intimated to Gulāb Singh their readiness to acknowledge a Sikh sovereignty in Lahore after the army should have been disbanded; but the Rājā declared his inability to deal with the troops, which still overawed him and other well-wishers to the family of Ranjīt Singh. This helplessness was partly exaggerated for selfish objects; but time pressed; the speedy dictation of a treaty under the walls of Lahore was essential to the British reputation; and the views of either party were in some sort met by an understanding that the Sikh army should be attacked by the English, and that when beaten it should be openly abandoned by its own government; and further, that the passage of the Sutlej should be unopposed and the road to the capital laid open to the victors. Under such circumstances of discreet policy and shameless treason was the battle of Sobraon fought.[1]

An understanding come to, that the Sikh army shall be attacked by the one and deserted by the other.

The defensive position of the Sikhs.

The Sikhs had gradually brought the greater part of their force into the entrenchment on the left bank of the Sutlej, which had been enlarged as impulse prompted or as opportunity seemed to offer. They placed sixty-seven pieces of

[1] Cf. the Governor-General's letter to the Secret Committee, of the 19th Feb. 1846; from which, however, those only who were mixed up with the negotiations can extract aught indicative of the understanding with Gulāb Singh which is alluded to in the text. It was for this note chiefly, if not entirely, that the author was removed from political employment by the East India Company. This was the author's own conviction, from careful inquiries made in India; and has been the result of equally careful inquiries made by me in England.

1845–6. artillery in battery, and their strength was estimated at thirty-five thousand fighting men; but it is probable that twenty thousand would exceed the truth; and of that reduced number, it is certain that all were not regular troops. The entrenchment likewise showed a fatal want of unity of command and of design; and at Sobraon, as in the other battles of the campaign, the soldiers did everything and the leaders nothing. Hearts to dare and hands to execute were numerous; but there was no mind to guide and animate the whole: each inferior commander defended his front according to his skill and his means, and the centre and left, where the disciplined battalions were mainly stationed, had batteries and salient points as high as the stature of a man, and ditches which an armed soldier could not leap without exertion; but a considerable part of the line exhibited at intervals the petty obstacles of a succession of such banks and trenches as would shelter a crouching marksman or help him to sleep in security when no longer a watcher. This was especially the case on the right flank, where the looseness of the river sand rendered it impossible to throw up parapets without art and labour, and where irregular troops, the least able to remedy such disadvantages, had been allowed or compelled to take up their position. The flank in question was mainly guarded by a line of two hundred 'zambūruks' or falconets[1]; but it derived some support from a salient battery, and from the heavy guns retained on the opposite bank of the river.[2] Tej Singh commanded in

[[1] These were light swivel guns—usually mounted on camels. In the muster-rolls of the Sikh army they are shown as organized into regular batteries like field artillery. Specimens of these guns may be seen in the Armoury in the Fort at Lahore.—ED.]

[2] The ordinary belief that the entrenchments of Sobraon were jointly planned and executed by a French and a Spanish colonel, is as devoid of foundation as that the Sikh army was rendered effective solely by the labours and skill of French and Italian generals. Hurbon the brave Spaniard, and Mouton the Frenchman, who were at Sobraon, doubtless exerted themselves where they could, but their authority or their influence did not extend beyond a regiment or a brigade, and the lines showed no trace whatever of scientific skill or of unity of design. [This note is typical of the author's belittling style. The works were really of an extremely strong nature. 'For some weeks the Sikhs under the direction of a Spanish officer named

this entrenchment, and Lāl Singh lay with his horse in loose order higher up the stream, watched by a body of British cavalry. The Sikhs, generally, were somewhat cast down by the defeat at Alīwāl, and by the sight of the unhonoured remains of their comrades floating down the Sutlej; but the self-confidence of a multitude soon returns: they had been cheered by the capture of a post of observation established by the English and left unoccupied at night, and they resumed their vaunting practice of performing their military exercises almost within hail of the British pickets. Yet the judgement of the old and experienced could not be deceived; the dangers which threatened the Sikh people pressed upon their minds; they saw no escape from domestic anarchy or from foreign subjection, and the grey-headed chief Shām Singh of Atarī made known his resolution to die in the first conflict with the enemies of his race, and so to offer himself up as a sacrifice of propitiation to the spirit of Gobind and to the genius of his mystic commonwealth. 1845–6.

In the British camp the confidence of the soldiery was likewise great, and none there despaired of the fortune of England. The spirits of the men had been raised by the victory of Alīwāl, and early in February a formidable siege train and ample stores of ammunition arrived from Delhi. The sepoys looked with delight upon the long array of stately elephants dragging the huge and heavy ordnance of their predilections, and the heart of the Englishman himself swelled with pride as he beheld these dread symbols of the wide dominion of his race. It was determined that the Sikh position should be attacked on the 10th February, and various plans were laid down for making victory sure, and for the speedy gratification of a burning resentment. The officers of artillery naturally desired that their guns, the

The English plan of attack.

Huerba had been employed in constructing a remarkably powerful *tête de pont* at the village of Sobraon to cover a bridge of boats which they had thrown across the river Sutlej . . . and it was now completed in a series of half-moon bastions, connected by curtains, and covered by a ditch in front, both flanks resting on the river. This great work, two and a half miles in length, was protected by batteries on the right bank of the river, so as to command the passage, and manned by 35,000 of the best of the Sikh troops with 67 guns.' (Meadows Taylor.)—Ed.]

1845–6. representatives of a high art, should be used agreeably to the established rules of the engineer, or that ramparts should be breached in front and swept in flank before they were stormed by defenceless battalions; but such deliberate tediousness of process did not satisfy the judgement or the impatience of the commanders, and it was arranged that the whole of the heavy ordnance should be planted in masses opposite particular points of the enemy's entrenchment, and that when the Sikhs had been shaken by a continuous storm of shot and shell, the right or weakest part of the position should be assaulted in line by the strongest of the three investing divisions, which together mustered nearly fifteen thousand men. A large body of British cavalry was likewise placed to watch the movements of Lāl Singh, and the two divisions which lay near Ferozepore were held ready to push across the Sutlej as soon as victory should declare itself. The precise mode of attack was not divulged, or indeed finally settled, until noon of the preceding day, for it was desired to surprise the commanding post of observation, which indifference or negligence had allowed to fall into the hands of the Sikhs a short time before. The evening and the early hours of darkness of the 9th February were thus occupied with busy preparations; the hitherto silent camp poured all its numbers abroad; soldiers stood in groups, talking of the task to be achieved by their valour; officers rode hastily along to receive or deliver orders; and on that night what Englishman passed battalion after battalion to seek a short repose, or a moment's solitary communion, and listened as he went to the hammering of shells and the piling of iron shot, or beheld the sentinel pacing silently along by the gleam of renewed fires, without recalling to mind his heroic king and the eve of Agincourt, rendered doubly immortal by the genius of Shakespeare?

The battle of Sobraon, 10th Feb. 1846.

The British divisions advanced in silence, amid the darkness of night and the additional gloom of a thick haze. The coveted post was found unoccupied; the Sikhs seemed everywhere taken by surprise, and they beat clamorously to arms when they saw themselves about to be assailed. The English batteries opened at sunrise, and for upwards of three hours an incessant play of artillery was kept up upon the general mass of the enemy. The round shot exploded tumbrils, or dashed heaps of sand into the air; the hollow shells cast their fatal contents fully before them, and the devious rockets sprang aloft with fury to fall hissing amid a flood of men; but all was in vain, the Sikhs stood unappalled, and 'flash for flash returned, and fire for fire'. The field was resplendent with embattled warriors, one moment umbered in volumes of sulphurous smoke, and another brightly apparent amid the splendour of beaming brass and the cold and piercing rays of polished steel. The roar and loud reverberation of the ponderous ordnance added to the impressive interest of the scene, and fell gratefully upon the ear of the intent and enduring soldier. But as the sun rose higher, it was felt that a distant and aimless cannonade would still leave the strife to be begun, and victory to be achieved by the valiant hearts of the close-fighting infantry. The guns ceased for a time, and each warrior addressed himself in silence to the coming conflict—a glimmering eye and a firmer grasp of his weapon alone telling of the mighty spirit which wrought within him. The left division of the British army advanced in even order and with a light step to the attack, but the original error of forming the regiments in line instead of in column rendered the contest more unequal than such assaults need necessarily be. Every shot from the enemy's lines told upon the expanse of men, and the greater part of the division was driven back by the deadly fire of muskets and swivels and enfilading artillery. On the extreme left, the regiments effected an entrance amid the advanced banks and trenches of petty outworks where possession could be of little avail; but their comrades on the right were animated by the partial success; they chafed under the disgrace of repulse, and forming themselves instinctively into wedges and masses, and headed by an old and fearless leader, they rushed forward in wrath.[1] With a shout they leaped the ditch, and upswarming, they mounted the rampart, and stood victorious amid captured cannon. But the effort was great; the Sikhs fought with steadiness 1845–6.

[1] Sir Robert Dick was mortally wounded close to the trenches while cheering on his ardent followers.

1845–6. and resolution ; guns in the interior were turned upon the exhausted assailants, and the line of trench alone was gained. Nor was this achievement the work of a moment. The repulse of the first assailants required that the central division should be brought forward, and these supporting regiments also moved in line against ramparts higher and more continuous than the barriers which had foiled the first efforts of their comrades. They too recoiled in confusion before the fire of the exulting Sikhs ; but at the distance of a furlong they showed both their innate valour and habitual discipline by rallying and returning to the charge. Their second assault was aided on the left by the presence, in the trenches of that flank, of the victorious first division ; and thus the regiments of the centre likewise became, after a fierce struggle on their own right, possessed of as many of the enemy's batteries as lay to their immediate front. The unlooked-for repulse of the second division, and the arduous contest in which the first was engaged, might have led a casual witness of the strife to ponder on the multitude of varying circumstances which determine success in war ; but the leaders were collected and prompt, and the battalions on the right, the victors of Alīwāl, were impelled against the opposite flank of the Sikhs ; but there, as on all other points attacked, destruction awaited brave men. They fell in heaps, and the first line was thrown back upon the second, which, nothing daunted, moved rapidly to the assault. The two lines mingled their ranks and rushed forward in masses, just as the second division had retrieved its fame, and as a body of cavalry had been poured into the camp from the left to form that line of advance which surpassed the strength of the exhausted infantry.

Openings were thus everywhere effected in the Sikh entrenchments, but single batteries still held out ; the interior was filled with courageous men, who took advantage of every obstacle, and fought fiercely for every spot of ground. The traitor, Tej Singh, indeed, instead of leading fresh men to sustain the failing strength of the troops on his right, fled on the first assault, and, either accidentally or by design, sank a boat in the middle of the bridge of communication. But the ancient Shām Singh remembered his vow ; he clothed himself in simple white attire, as one devoted to death, and calling on all around him to fight for the Guru, who had promised everlasting bliss to the brave, he repeatedly rallied his shattered ranks, and at last fell a martyr on a heap of his slain countrymen. Others might be seen standing on the ramparts amid showers of balls, waving defiance with their swords, or telling the gunners where the fair-haired English pressed thickest together. Along the stronger half of the battlements, and for the period of half an hour, the conflict raged sublime in all its terrors. The parapets were sprinkled with blood from end to end; the trenches were filled with the dead and the dying. Amid the deafening roar of cannon, and the multitudinous fire of musketry, the shouts of triumph or of scorn were yet heard, and the flashing of innumerable swords was yet visible; or from time to time exploding magazines of powder threw bursting shells and beams of wood and banks of earth high above the agitated sea of smoke and flame which enveloped the host of combatants, and for a moment arrested the attention amid all the din and tumult of the tremendous conflict. But gradually each defensible position was captured, and the enemy was pressed towards the scarcely fordable river; yet, although assailed on either side by squadrons of horse and battalions of foot, no Sikh offered to submit, and no disciple of Gobind asked for quarter. They everywhere showed a front to the victors, and stalked slowly and sullenly away, while many rushed singly forth to meet assured death by contending with a multitude. The victors looked with stolid wonderment upon the indomitable courage of the vanquished, and forbore to strike where the helpless and the dying frowned unavailing hatred. But the necessities of war pressed upon the commanders, and *they* had effectually to disperse that army which had so long scorned their power. The fire of batteries and battalions precipitated the flight of the Sikhs through the waters of the Sutlej, and the triumph of the English became full and manifest. The troops, defiled with dust and smoke and carnage, thus stood mute indeed for a moment, until the glory of their success rushing upon their minds, they gave expression to their feelings, and hailed their victorious

1845–6.

1845-6.

commanders with reiterated shouts of triumph and congratulation.[1]

The passage of the Sutlej, the submission of the Mahārājā, and the occupation of Lahore.

On the night of the victory some regiments were pushed across the Sutlej opposite Ferozepore; no enemy was visible; and on the 12th February the fort of Kasūr was occupied without opposition. On the following day the army encamped under the walls of that ancient town, and it was ascertained that the Sikhs still held together to the number of twenty thousand men in the direction of Amritsar. But the power of the armed representatives of the Khālsa was gone; the holders of treasure and food, and all the munitions of war, had first passively helped to defeat them, and then openly joined the enemy; and the soldiery readily assented to the requisition of the court that Gulāb

[1] Cf. Lord Gough's dispatch of the 13th Feb. 1846, and Macgregor, *History of the Sikhs*, ii. 154, &c. The casualties on the side of the British were 320 killed, and 2,083 wounded. The loss of the Sikhs, perhaps, exceeded 5,000, and possibly amounted to 8,000, the lower estimate of the English dispatches.

The Commander-in-Chief estimated the force of the Sikhs at 30,000 men, and it was frequently said they had 36 regiments in position; but it is nevertheless doubtful whether there were so many as 20,000 *armed* men in the trenches. The numbers of the actual assailants may be estimated at 15,000 effective soldiers. After the war, Lord Gough ascertained, through the British authorities at Lahore, that the Sikhs admitted their strength at Sobraon to have been 42,626 men. Perhaps, however, this estimate includes all the troops on the right bank of the river, as well as those in the entrenched position on the opposite side. If so, the statement seems in every way credible. Similarly, Lord Gough learnt that 3,125 heirs of soldiers killed claimed arrears of pay, from which fact and other circumstances which came to his knowledge, his Lordship thinks the Sikhs may have lost from 12,000 to 15,000 men in this decisive victory.

Sobraon, or correctly Subrāhān, the name by which the battle is known, is taken from that of a small village, or rather two small villages, in the neighbourhood. The villages in question were inhabited by the subdivision of a tribe called Subrah, or, in the plural, Subrāhān; and hence the name became applied to their place of residence, and has at last become identified with a great and important victory. This mode of designating villages by means of the plural form of a patronymic is common in India, and it was once frequent in our own country, as noticed by Mr. Kemble (*Saxons in England*, i. 59 *n.*, and Appendix A, p. 478) in 1,329 instances, such as Tooting in Surrey, Malling in Kent, &c., from the Totingas, Meallingas, and other families or clans.

1845–6.

Singh, their chosen minister, should have full powers to treat with the English on the already admitted basis of recognizing a Sikh government in Lahore. On the 15th of the month the Rājā and several other chiefs were received by the Governor-General at Kasūr, and they were told that Dalīp Singh would continue to be regarded as a friendly sovereign, but that the country between the Beās and Sutlej would be retained by the conquerors, and that a million and a half sterling must be paid as some indemnity for the expenses of the war, in order, it was said, that all might hear of the punishment which had overtaken aggressors, and become fully aware that inevitable loss followed vain hostilities with the unoffending English. After a long discussion the terms were reluctantly agreed to, the young Mahārājā came and tendered his submission in person, and on the 20th February the British army arrived at the Sikh capital. Two days afterwards a portion of the citadel was garrisoned by English regiments, to mark more plainly to the Indian world that a vaunting enemy had been effectually humbled; for throughout the breadth of the land the chiefs talked, in the bitterness of their hearts, of the approaching downfall of the stern unharmonizing foreigners.[1]

Negotiations.

The Governor-General desired not only to chastise the Sikhs for their past aggressions, but to overawe them for the future, and he had thus chosen the Beās, as offering more commanding positions with reference to Lahore than the old boundary of the Sutlej. With the same object in view, he had originally thought Rājā Gulāb Singh might advantageously be made independent in the hills of Jammu.[2] Such a recognition by the British Government had, indeed, always been one of the wishes of that ambitious family; but it was not, perhaps, remembered that Gulāb Singh was still more desirous of becoming the acknowledged minister of the dependent Punjab;[3] nor was it perhaps thought

Gulāb Singh.

[1] Cf. the Governor-General to the Secret Committee, under dates the 19th Feb. and 4th March 1846.

[2] Cf. the Governor-General to the Secret Committee, of 3rd and 19th Feb. 1846.

[3] This had been the aim of the family for many years; or, at least, from the time that Dhiān Singh exerted himself to remove Col. Wade, in the hope that a British representative might be appointed who

1845-6. that the overtures of the Rājā—after the battle of Alīwāl had foreboded the total rout of the Sikh army—were all made in the hope of assuring to himself a virtual viceroyalty over the whole dominion of Lahore. Gulāb Singh had been appointed Wazīr by the chiefs and people when danger pressed them, and he had been formally treated with as minister by the English when the Governor-General thought time was short, and his own resources distant;[1] but when Lāl Singh. Lāl Singh saw that after four pitched battles the English viceroy was content or compelled to leave Lahore a dependent ally, he rejoiced that his undiminished influence with the mother of the Mahārājā would soon enable him to supplant the obnoxious chief of Jammu. The base sycophant thus congratulated himself on the approaching success of all his treasons, which had simply for their object his own personal aggrandizement at the expense of Sikh independence. Gulāb Singh felt his inability to support himself without the countenance of the English; but they had offered no assurance of support as minister, and he suddenly perplexed the Governor-General by asking what *he* was to get for all he had done to bring about a speedy peace, and to render the army an easy prey. It was remembered that at Kasūr he had said the way to carry on a war with the English was to leave the sturdy infantry entrenched and watched, and to sweep the open country with cavalry

would be well disposed towards himself, which he thought Col. Wade was not. Mr. Clerk was aware of both schemes of the Lahore minister, although the greater prominence was naturally given to the project of rendering the Jammū chiefs independent, owing to the aversion with which they were regarded after Nau Nihāl Singh's death.

Had the English said that they desired to see Gulāb Singh remain minister, and had they been careless whether Lāl Singh lived or was put to death, it is highly probable that a fair and vigorous government would have been formed, and also that the occupation of Lahore, and perhaps the second treaty of 1846, need never have taken place.

[1] Cf. the Governor-General's letter to the Secret Committee, of the 3rd and 19th Feb. 1846. In both of these dispatches Lord Hardinge indicates that he intended to do something for Gulāb Singh, but he does not state that he designed to make him independent of Lahore, nor does he say that he told the Sikh chiefs the arrangements then on foot might include the separation of Jammū; and the truth would seem to be, that in the first joy of success the scheme of conciliating the powerful Rājā remained in a manner forgotten.

1845–6.

to the gates of Delhi; and while negotiations were still pending, and the season advancing, it was desired to conciliate one who might render himself formidable in a day, by joining the remains of the Sikh forces, and by opening his treasures and arsenals to a warlike population.

The partition of the Punjab, and independence of Gulāb Singh.

The low state of the Lahore treasury, and the anxiety of Lāl Singh to get a dreaded rival out of the way, enabled the Governor-General to appease Gulāb Singh in a manner sufficiently agreeable to the Rājā himself, and which still further reduced the importance of the successor of Ranjīt Singh. The Rājā of Jammu did not care to be simply the master of his native mountains; but as two-thirds of the pecuniary indemnity required from Lahore could not be made good, territory was taken instead of money, and Kashmīr and the hill states from the Beās to the Indus were cut off from the Punjab Proper, and transferred to Gulāb Singh as a separate sovereign for a million of pounds sterling. The arrangement was a dexterous one, if reference be only had to the policy of reducing the power of the Sikhs; but the transaction scarcely seems worthy of the British name and greatness, and the objections become stronger when it is considered that Gulāb Singh had agreed to pay sixty-eight lākhs of rupees (£680,000), as a fine to his paramount, before the war broke out,[1] and that the custom of the East as well as of the West requires the feudatory to aid his lord in foreign war and domestic strife. Gulāb Singh ought thus to have paid the deficient million of money as a Lahore subject, instead of being put in possession of Lahore provinces as an independent prince. The succession of the Rājā was displeasing to the Sikhs generally, and his separation was less in accordance with his own aspirations than the ministry of Ranjīt Singh's empire; but his rise to sovereign power excited nevertheless the ambition of others, and Tej Singh, who knew his own wealth, and was fully persuaded of the potency of gold, offered twenty-five lākhs of rupees for a princely crown and another dismembered province. He was chid for his presumptuous misinterpre-

[1] Major Broadfoot to Government, 5th May 1845. The author never heard, and does not believe, that this money was paid by Gulāb Singh.

1845–6.

tation of English principles of action ; the arrangement with Gulāb Singh was the only one of the kind which took place, and the new ally was formally invested with the title of Mahārājā at Amritsar on the 15th March 1846.[1] But a portion of the territory at first proposed to be made over to him was reserved by his masters, the payments required from him were reduced by a fourth, and they were rendered still more easy of liquidation by considering him to be the heir to the money which his brother Suchet Singh had buried in Ferozepore.[2]

Supplementary arrangements of 1846, placing Dalīp Singh under British tutelage during his minority.

Lāl Singh became minister once more ; but he and all the traitorous chiefs knew that they could not maintain themselves, even against the reduced army, when the English should have fairly left the country, and thus the separation of Gulāb Singh led to a further departure from the original scheme. It was agreed that a British force should remain at the capital until the last day of December 1846, to enable the chiefs to feel secure while they reorganized the army and introduced order and efficiency into the administration. The end of the year came ; but the chiefs were still helpless ; they clung to their foreign support, and gladly assented to an arrangement which leaves the English in immediate possession of the reduced dominion of Ranjīt Singh, until his reputed son and feeble successor shall attain the age of manhood.[3]

[1] On this occasion 'Mahārājā' Gulāb Singh stood up, and, with joined hands, expressed his gratitude to the British viceroy—adding, without however any ironical meaning, that he was indeed his 'Zurkharīd', or gold-boughten slave !

In the course of this history there has, more than once, been occasion to allude to the unscrupulous character of Rājā Gulāb Singh ; but it must not therefore be supposed that he is a man malevolently evil. He will, indeed, deceive an enemy and take his life without hesitation, and in the accumulation of money he will exercise many oppressions ; but he must be judged with reference to the morality of his age and race, and to the necessities of his own position. If these allowances be made, Gulāb Singh will be found an able and moderate man, who does little in an idle or wanton spirit, and who is not without some traits both of good humour and generosity of temper.

[2] See Appendices XXXIV, XXXV, and XXXVI, for the treaties with Lahore and Jammu.

[3] See Appendix XXXVII for the second treaty with Lahore.

1845–6.

The Sikhs not disheartened by their reverses.

While the Governor-General and Commander-in-Chief remained at Lahore at the head of twenty thousand men, portions of the Sikh army came to the capital to be paid up and disbanded. The soldiers showed neither the despondency of mutinous rebels nor the effrontery and indifference of mercenaries, and their manly deportment added lustre to that valour which the victors had dearly felt and generously extolled. The men talked of their defeat as the chance of war, or they would say that *they* were mere imitators of unapproachable masters. But, amid all their humiliation, they inwardly dwelt upon their future destiny with unabated confidence; and while gaily calling themselves inapt and youthful scholars, they would sometimes add, with a significant and sardonic smile, that the 'Khālsa' itself was yet a child, and that as the commonwealth of Sikhs grew in stature, Gobind would clothe his disciples with irresistible might and guide them with unequalled skill. Thus brave men sought consolation, and the spirit of progress which collectively animated them yielded with a murmur to the superior genius of England and civilization, to be chastened by the rough hand of power, and perhaps to be moulded to noblest purposes by the informing touch of knowledge and philosophy.[1]

Conclusion.—The position of the English in India.

The separate sway of the Sikhs and the independence of the Punjab have come to an end, and England reigns the undisputed mistress of the broad and classic land of India. Her political supremacy is more regular and systematic than the antique rule of the Brāhmans and Kshattriyas, and it is less assailable from without than the imperfect domination of the Muhammadans; for in disciplined power and vastness of resources, in unity of action and intelligence of design,

[1] In March 1846, or immediately after the war, the author visited the Sikh temples and establishments at Kīratpur and Anandpur-Makhowāl. At the latter place, the chosen seat of Gobind, reliance upon the future was likewise strong; and the grave priests or ministers said, by way of assurance, that the pure faith of the Khālsa was intended for all countries and times; and added, by way of compliment, that the disciples of Nānak would ever be grateful for the aid which the stranger English had rendered in subverting the empire of the intolerant and oppressive Muhammadans!

1845–6. her government surpasses the experience of the East, and emulates the magnificent prototype of Rome. But the Hindus made the country wholly their own, and from sea to sea, from the snowy mountains almost to the fabled bridge of Rāma, the language of the peasant is still that of the twice-born races; the speech of the wild foresters and mountaineers of the centre and south has been permanently tinged by the old predominance of the Kshattriyas, and the hopes and fears and daily habits of myriads of men still vividly represent the genial myths and deep philosophy of the Brāhmans, which more than two thousand years ago arrested the attention of the Greeks. The Muhammadans entered the country to destroy, but they remained to colonize, and swarms of the victorious races long continued to pour themselves over its rich plains, modifying the language and ideas of the vanquished, and becoming themselves altered by the contact, until, in the time of Akbar, the 'Islām' of India was a national system, and until, in the present day, the Hindu and Muhammadan do not practically differ more from one another than did the Brāhmans and Kshattriyas and Veisyas of the time of Manu and Alexander. They are different races with different religious systems, but harmonizing together in social life, and mutually understanding and respecting and taking a part in each other's modes and ways and doings. They are thus silently but surely removing one another's differences and peculiarities, so that a new element results from the common destruction, to become developed into a faith or a fact in future ages. The rise to power of contemned Sūdra tribes, in the persons of Marāthās, Gurkhas, and Sikhs, has brought about a further mixture of the rural population and of the lower orders in towns and cities, and has thus given another blow to the reverence for antiquity. The religious creed of the people seems to be even more indeterminate than their spoken dialects, and neither the religion of the Arabian prophet, nor the theology of the Vedas and Purāns, is to be found pure except among professed Mullas and educated Brāhmans, or among the rich and great of either persuasion. Over this seething and fusing mass, the power of England has been extended and her spirit sits brooding. Her pre-eminence in the modern world may well excite the envy of the nations; but it behoves her to ponder well upon the mighty task which her adventurous children have set her in the East, and to be certain that her sympathizing labours in the cause of humanity are guided by intelligence towards a true and attainable end. She rules supreme as the welcome composer of political troubles; but the thin superficies of her dominion rests tremblingly upon the convulsed ocean of social change and mental revolution. Her own high civilization and the circumstances of her intervention isolate her in all her greatness; she can appeal to the reason only of her subjects, and can never lean upon the enthusiasm of their gratitude or predilections.[1] To preserve her political ascendancy she must be ever prudent and circumspect; and to leave a lasting impress she must do more than erect palaces and temples, the mere material monuments of dominion. Like Greece and Rome, she may rear edifices of surpassing beauty, she may bridge gulfs and pierce mountains with the wand of wealth and science. Like these ancient peoples, she may even give birth in strange lands to such kings as Herod the Great and to such historians as Flavius Josephus; but, like imperial Rome, she may live to behold a Vortigern call in a Hengist, and a Syagrius yield 1845-6.

[1] Mr. Macaulay's comparison (*History of England*, i. 364, &c.) between the manners of the earlier Georges and Charles II, as bearing on the kingly office, is peculiarly applicable to the British rule in India. The English, like their own stranger sovereigns of the last century, govern in the East according to law, but they cannot give themselves a place in the hearts of their subjects, while those whom reason can convince are neither numerous nor influential in political affairs. Sir H. M. Elliot, in the Introduction (p. xxix) to his important and interesting volume on the Muhammadan Historians of India, admits 'the many defects inherent in a system of foreign administration, in which language, colour, religion, customs, and laws preclude all natural sympathy between sovereign and subject'; but he at the same time declares the English have, nevertheless, done more in fifty years for the substantial benefit of the people, at least of Upper India, than the Musalmāns did in ten times that period—an opinion that requires to be supported by a more extended comparison of material works than is given by the learned writer. [The author's gloomy prognostications have been rudely shaken by the events of 1914-15, and the spontaneous loyalty shown by all classes during the great European War.—Ed.]

1845–6. to a Clovis. She may teach another Cymbeline the amenities of civilized life, and she may move another Attalus to bequeath to her another Pergamus. These are tasks of easy achievement; but she must also endeavour to give her poets and her sages an immortality among nations unborn, to introduce laws which shall still be in force at the end of sixty generations, and to tinge the faith and the minds of the people with her sober science and just morality, as Christianity was affected by the adoptive policy of Rome and by the plastic philosophy of Greece. Of all these things England must sow the seeds and lay the foundations before she can hope to equal or surpass her great exemplars.[1]

But England can do nothing until she has rendered her dominion secure, and hitherto all her thoughts have been given to the extension of her supremacy. Up to this time she has been a rising power, the welcome supplanter of Mughals and Marāthās, and the ally which the remote weak sought against the neighbouring strong. But her greatness is at its height; it has come to *her* turn to be feared instead of courted, and the hopes of men are about to be built on her wished-for destruction. The princes of India can no longer acquire fame or territory by preying upon one another. Under the exact sway of their new paramount, they must divest themselves of ambition and of all the violent passions of their nature, and they must try to remain kings without exercising the most loved of the functions of rulers. The Indians, indeed, will themselves politely liken England and her dependent sovereigns to the benignant moon accompanied by hosts of rejoicing stars in her nightly progress, rather than to the fierce sun which rides the heavens in solitude scarcely visible amidst intolerable brightness; but men covet power as well as ease, and crave distinction as well as wealth; and thus it is with those who endeavour to jest with adversity. England has immediately to make her attendant princes feel, that while resistance is vain, they are themselves honoured, and hold a substantive position in the economy of the imperial government, instead of being merely tolerated as bad rulers or regarded with contempt and aversion as half-barbarous men. Her rule

[1] See Appendix XV.

has hitherto mainly tended to the benefit of the trading community; men of family name find no place in the society of their masters, and no employment in the service of the state; and while the peasants have been freed from occasional ruinous exaction, and from more rare personal torture, they are oppressed and impoverished by a well-meant but cumbrous and inefficient law,[1] and by an excessive and partial taxation, which looks almost wholly to the land for the necessary revenue of a government.[2] The husbandman is sullen and indifferent,[3] the gentleman nurses his wrath in secrecy, kings idly chafe and intrigue, and all are ready to hope for everything from a change of masters. The merchant alone sits partly happy in the reflection, that if he is not honoured with titles and office, the path to wealth has been made smooth, and its enjoyment rendered secure. 1845–6.

[[1] I have removed a footnote here inserted by the author in elaboration of this statement. The note is quite untrue under modern conditions and has ceased to have any practical value. The views of both the author and of Sleeman, whom he quotes (*Rambles and Recollections of an Indian Official*, Oxford Edition, p. 544), are typical of a point of view which has now happily passed away.—ED.]

[2] See Appendix XVI.

[3] Lieut.-Col. Sleeman considers (*Rambles and Recollections of an Indian Official*, p. 432) that neither have the English gained, nor did other rulers possess, the goodwill of the peasantry and landholders of the country.

In considering the position of the English, or of any ruling power, in India, it should always be borne in mind that no bodies of peasantry, excepting perhaps the Sikhs and, in a lesser degree, the Rājpūts of the West, and no classes of men, excepting perhaps the Muhammadans and, in a lesser degree, the Brāhmans, take any interest in the government of their country, or have collectively any wish to be dominant. The masses of the population, whether of towns or villages, are ready to submit to any master, native or foreign; and the multitudes of submissive subjects possessed by England contribute nothing to her strength except as tax-payers, and, during an insurrection or after a conquest, would at once give the 'government share of the produce' to the wielder of power for the time being, and would thereby consider themselves freed from all obligations and liabilities. England must be just and generous towards these tame myriads; but the men whom she has pre-eminently to keep employed, honoured, and overawed are the turbulent military classes, who are ever ready to rebel and ever desirous of acquiring power.

1845–6. Princes and nobles and yeomen can all be kept in obedience for generations by overwhelming means, and by a more complete military system than at present obtains. Numerous forts and citadels,[1] the occasional assemblage of armies, and the formation of regiments separately composed of different tribes and races,[2] will long serve to ensure supremacy and to crush the efforts of individuals; but

[1] The fewness of places of strength, and indeed of places of ordinary security, for magazines of arms and ammunition is a radical defect in the military system of the English in India. The want of extensive granaries is also much felt, both as a measure of the most ordinary prudence in case of insurrection or any military operation, and as some check upon prices on the common recurrence of droughts in a country in which capitalists do not yet go hand in hand with the government, and are but little amenable to public opinion beyond their order. Such was, and is, the custom of the native princes, and no practice exists without a reason. [The first defect was realized and remedied as one of the lessons of the Mutiny, while the question of the check on prices is one of the commonplaces of a modern administration.—Ed.]

[2] The English have not succeeded in making their well-ordered army a separate caste or section of the community, except very partially in the Madras presidency, where a sepoy's home is his regiment. It is, moreover, but too apparent that the active military spirit of the sepoys, when on service in India, is not now what it was when the system of the 'Company' was new and the fortune of the Strangers beginning. This is partly due to the general pacification of the country, partly to the practice of largely enlisting tame-spirited men of inferior caste because they are well behaved, or pliant intriguing Brāhmans because they can write and are intelligent; and partly because the system of central or rather single management has been carried too far. The Indian is eminently a partisan, and his predilection for his immediate superior should be encouraged, the more especially as there can be no doubt of the loyalty of the English commandant. The clannish, or feudal, or mercenary, attachments do not in India yield to rational conviction or political principle, and colonels of battalions should have very large powers. Regiments separately composed of men of one or other of the military classes might sometimes give trouble within themselves, and sometimes come into collision with other regiments; but a high warlike feeling would be engendered; and unless England chooses to identify herself with some of the inferior races, and to evoke a new spirit by becoming a religious reformer, she must keep the empire she has won by working upon the feelings she finds prevalent in the country. [The suggestion in the text has long since been dismissed as impracticable by modern military administrators.—Ed.]

England has carefully to watch the progress of that change in social relations and religious feelings of which Sikhism is the most marked exponent. Among all ranks of men there is a spirit at work which rejects as vain the ancient forms and ideas whether of Brāhmanism or Muhammadanism,[1] 1845–6.

[1] The following remark of the Hindus, regarding some of their most sacred persons, has now a wider application than smart sayings commonly possess. They describe Purs-Rām, Vyāsa, Rāma, and Krishna as 'Sirree, Siftee, Dāna, and Deewāna'—or *Purs-Rām* as hasty, heedless; because, for the fault of one ruler, he proceeded to slay a whole generation of men; *Vyāsa*, as wordy, or a flatterer, because he would make all to resemble gods; *Rāma*, alone, as wise, or politic, because all his actions denoted forethought; and *Krishna*, as eminently silly or trivial, because all he did was of that character. That names still revered are sometimes so treated denotes a readiness for change. [The most common phenomenon now apparent in both Hindu and Muhammadan worlds is somewhat akin to that which inspired the Reformation in Europe—a movement on the part of certain sections of the community in favour of the removal of accretions and the reversion to the more simple, patriarchal, and puritanical régime of an earlier epoch. To such a conception is due such a movement, in the Hindu world, as that of the Arya Somaj, which has so many supporters and so wide an influence in India to-day. This movement has for its primary object a return to the Vedas—as alone sufficient for the salvation of man—and to the simple existence of the earlier days. Space does not permit of a detailed examination of the whole history and progress of the Arya Somaj movement and of the life and teaching of its founder Swami Dayananda Saraswati. For a further study of the subject the reader is referred to the recently published history of the Arya Somaj by L. Lajpat Rai.

Another modern development has been that of the Brahmo Somaj —a body of Unitarian tendency and teaching. In the Muhammadan world the same tendency towards reform may be noticed. In modern times the most extensive reform movement within the borders of Islām has been the Senussi movement. But while this has become a distinct force among the Muhammadans of Africa it has had little or no effect upon India. Many intelligent Muhammadans in India have assured me that they consider the position of their Church in India to-day very analogous to that of the Church of England on the eve of the Reformation. The 'dead hand' of mediaeval England has in their judgement its counterpart in India to-day. Isolation and environment have both played their part in bringing about this state of affairs. As regards the first of these factors one may take the analogy a little farther back historically. It may be taken as an admitted fact that the Church in England anterior to the Norman Conquest suffered considerably from its isolation, and that one of the benefits of that conquest was the removal of that barrier. Cut off

1845–6. and which clings for present solace and future happiness to new intercessors and to another manifestation of divine power and mercy. This labouring spirit has developed itself most strongly on the confines of the two antagonist creeds; but the feeling pervades the Indian world, and the extension of Sikh arms would speedily lead to the recognition of Nānak and Gobind as the long-looked-for Comforters.[1] The Sikhs have now been struck by the petrific hand of material power, and the ascendancy of a third race has

from the religious life of the rest of the Continent, except in so far as the rather uncertain link of pilgrimage maintained the connexion, the Saxon Church became local, formalized, perhaps indifferent. And when we turn to Muhammadan India we find a similar state of things. The link of pilgrimage exists—made stronger by modern facilities for travel—but in the main the isolation exists. This isolation has resulted in the gradual growth of a host of local traditions and local cults. And here the second factor—environment—comes into play. Living in close association with Hinduism, drawing at an earlier period a number of converts from that religion, the followers of Islām in India have been profoundly affected. To take a single instance, caste. The Muhammadan of to-day of Rājpūt descent cannot, in many cases, forget his original caste. Despite the democratic nature of the religion to which he now belongs, his whole life is largely influenced by the traditions of the creed of his ancestors. One could give many instances of this from one's own experience. They are common phenomena of India to-day in the face of modern development. The intelligent Muhammadan of to-day views the state of his religion with the feelings of an Englishman just before the Reformation. He is fully conscious of imperfections, of accretions, of a departure from the pure tenets of his religion. Islām in modern India is looking for a Luther, but the desire for internal reform is not associated with any feeling of hostility towards other creeds. The idea is rather that it is because of its imperfections that Islām stands now where it does, and that reform is necessary to enable it to hold its place successfully amid other organized religions of to-day. A detailed description of the various reformed sects which do exist among the Punjabi Muhammadans to-day may be found in the Census Report of 1912.—Ed.]

[1] Widely spread notions, how erroneous soever they be, in one sense, always deserve attention, as based on some truth or conviction. Thus the Hindus quote an altered or spurious passage of the Bhāgavat, describing the successive rulers of India as follows: (1) the Yavvans (Greeks), eight kings; (2) the Tooshkurs (Turks or Muhammadans), fourteen kings; (3) the Gurand (the fair, i.e. the English), ten kings; and (4) the Mowna (or silent, i.e. the disciples of Nānak the Seer), eleven kings.

everywhere infused new ideas, and modified the aspirations of the people. The confusion has thus been increased for a time; but the pregnant fermentation of mind must eventually body itself forth in new shapes; and a prophet of name unknown may arise to diffuse a system which shall consign the Vedas and Korān to the oblivion of the Zendavest and the Sibylline Leaves, and which may not perhaps absorb one ray of light from the wisdom and morality of that faith which adorns the civilization of the Christian rulers of the country. But England must hope that she is not to exercise an unfruitful sway; and she will add fresh lustre to her renown, and derive an additional claim to the gratitude of posterity, if she can seize upon the essential principles of that element which disturbs her multitudes of Indian subjects, and imbue the mental agitation with new qualities of beneficent fertility, so as to give to it an impulse and a direction, which shall surely lead to the prevalence of a religion of truth and to the adoption of a government of freedom and progress. 1845–6.

APPENDIXES

APPENDIX I

THE JATS AND JĀTS OF UPPER INDIA

ACCORDING to the dictionaries *Jāt* means a race, a tribe, or a particular race so called, while *Jat* means manner, kind, and likewise matted hair. But throughout the Punjab *Jat* also implies a fleece, a fell of hair; and in Upper Sind *a Jat* now means a rearer of camels or of black cattle, or a shepherd in opposition to a husbandman. In the Punjab generally *a Jat* means still a villager, a rustic *par excellence*, as one of the race by far the most numerous, and as opposed to one engaged in trade or handicraft. This was observed by the author of the *Dabistān* nearly two centuries ago (*Dabistān*, ii. 252); but since the *Jats* of Lahore and the *Jāts* of the Jumna have acquired power, the term is becoming more restricted, and is occasionally employed to mean simply one of that particular race.

The Jāts merge on one side into the Rājpūts, and on the other into the Afghāns, the names of the Jāt subdivisions being the same with those of Rājpūts in the east, and again with those of Afghāns, and even Baluchīs, in the west, and many obscure tribes being able to show plausibly that at least they are as likely to be Rājpūts or Afghāns as to be Jāts. The Jāts are indeed enumerated among the arbitrary or conventional thirty-six royal races of the local bards of Rājputāna (Tod's *Rājasthān*, i. 106), and they themselves claim affinity with the Bhotiās, and aspire to a lunar origin, as is done by the Rājā of Patiāla. As instances of the narrow and confused state of our knowledge regarding the people of India, it may be mentioned that the Birks (or Virks), one of the most distinguished tribes of Jāts, is admitted among the Chaluk Rājputs by Tod (i. 100), and that there are *Kukker* and *Kākar* Jāts, *Kukker Kokur*, and *Kākar* Afghāns, besides Gakhars, not included in any of the three races. Further, the family of Umarkot in Sind is stated by Tod (*Rājasthān*, i. 92, 93) to be Pramār (or Powār), while the Emperor Humāyūn's chronicler talks of the followers (i.e. brethren) of that chief as being Jāts. (*Memoirs of Humāyūn*, p. 45). The editors of the *Journal of the Geographical Society* (xiv. 207 *n.*) derive *Jāt* from the Sanskrit

Jyest'ha, old, ancient, and so make the term equivalent to *aborigines* ; but this etymology perhaps too hastily sets aside the sufficiently established facts of Getae and Yuechi emigrations, and the circumstance of Taimūr's warfare with Jettehs in Central Asia.

Some of the most eminent of the Jāt subdivisions in the Punjab are named Sindhu, Chineh, Varaïtch, Chattheh, Sidhu, Kurrīal, Gondul, &c. For some notices of the Jāts of the Indus by early Muhammadan writers (about A.D. 977 and 1100) see Sir H. M. Elliot, *Historians of India*, pp. 69 and 270.

APPENDIX II

PROPORTIONS OF RACES AND FAITHS: POPULATION OF INDIA

OUT of 1,030 villages lying here and there between the Jumna and Sutlej, and which were under British management in 1844, there were found to be forty-one different tribes of *agriculturists*, in proportions as follows, after adding up fractions where any race composed a portion only of the whole community of any one village.

	Villages.
Jāts	443
Rājpūts	194
Gūjars	109
Saiyids	17
Shaikhs	25
Pathāns	8
Mughals	5
Brāhmans	28
Kshattriyas	6
Rains (or Arains)	47
Kambos	19
Mālīs	12
Rōrs	33
Dogrās (Muhammadans claiming Kshattriya origin)	28
Kalāls	5
Gusain religionists	3
Bairāgi religionists	2
24 miscellaneous tribes occupying equal to	46
Total	1,030

A classification of the tribes of India according to position, origin, and faith is much wanted, and is indeed necessary to a proper comprehension of the history of the country. The Revenue Survey, as conducted in the upper provinces of the Ganges, enumerates several castes, or at least the predominant ones, in each village, and the lists might easily be rendered more complete, and afterwards made available by publication for purposes of inquiry and deduction.

The Sikh population of the Punjab and adjoining districts has usually been estimated at 500,000 souls in all (cf. Burnes, *Travels*, i. 289; and Elphinstone, *History of India*, ii. 275 *n.*), but the number seems too small by a half or a third. There are, indeed, no exact data on which to found an opinion; but the Sikh armies have never been held to contain fewer than 70,000 fighting men; they have been given as high as 250,000, and there is no reason to doubt that between the Jhelum and Jumna they could muster nearly half the latter number of soldiers of their own faith, while it is certain that of an agricultural people no member of some families may engage in arms, and that one adult at least of other families will always remain behind to till the ground. The gross Sikh population may probably be considered to amount to a million and a quarter or a million and a half of souls, men, women, and children.

The proportion of Hindus to Muhammadans throughout India generally has been variously estimated. The Emperor Jahāngīr (*Memoirs*, p. 29) held them to be as five to one, which is perhaps more unequal than the present proportion in the valley of the Ganges. Mr. Elphinstone (*History of India*, ii. 238 and notes) takes the relative numbers for the whole country to be eight to one. From p. 169 of the *Statistics of the NW. Provinces*, printed in 1848 and published in 1849 by the Indian Government, it appears that out of a population of 23,199,668 dwelling between Ghāzīpur and Hardwār, and in the direct or active occupation of about 72,000 square miles of country, there are 19,452,646 Hindus and 3,747,022 Muhammadans, 'and others not Hindus'—the others forming, doubtless, a fraction so small that they may be here disregarded.

This gives somewhat more than five Hindus to one Muhammadan, and so differs but little from the estimate of the Emperor Jahāngīr above quoted, and which probably had reference to the same tract of country. The revenue of the Upper Provinces amounts to about £4,700,000, which gives a taxation of about five shillings a head. Throughout India the state of industry and the system of revenue is nearly the same; and taking the gross income of the whole country at forty millions sterling (22 British and 18 native princes), it will result that the population amounts to two hundred millions in all, or double what it is commonly believed to be. The calculation, however, is borne out by the analogous condition of affairs in Germany. In Prussia the taxation is about eleven shillings a head, and the proportion seems to hold good in the other component states of the empire.

[The Census of 1911 shows the population and proportion as follows. A total population of 23,807,750, distributed in the following proportions:

Muhammadans roughly one-half.
Hindus ,, three-eighths.
Sikhs ,, one-eighth.—ED.]

APPENDIX III

THE KSHATTRIYAS AND ARORAS OF THE PUNJAB

THE *Kshattriyas* of the Punjab maintain the purity of their descent, and the legend is that they represent those of the warrior race who yielded to Paras Rām and were spared by him. The tribe is numerous in the Upper Punjab and about Delhi and Hardwār. Kshattriyas are found in towns along the Ganges as far as Benares and Patna; but in Bengal, in Central India, and in the Deccan they seem to be strangers, or only to be represented by ruling families claiming a solar or lunar origin. In the Punjab the religious capital of the Kshattriyas seems to be the ancient Dīpālpur. The Kshattriyas divide themselves into three principal classes: (1) the Chārjātis, or the four clans; (2) the Bārajātis, or the twelve clans; and (3) the Bāwanjais, or fifty-two clans. The *Chārjātis* are, 1st, the Sēths; 2nd, the Merhōtas; 3rd, the Khannas; and 4th, the Kapūrs, who are again divided, the first into two, and the others into three classes. The principal of the *Bārajāti* subdivisions are Chopra, Tālwār, Tunnuhn, Seighul, Kākar, Mahta, &c. Some of the *Bāwanjais* are as follows: Bhandāri, Mahendro, Sethis, Sūri, Sāhni, Anand, Bhasin, Sodhi, Bedi, Tihan, Bhallah, &c.

The *Aroras* claim to be the offspring of Kshattriya fathers and of Vaisya or Sūdra mothers, and their legend is that they were settled in numbers about Uch, when the Kshattriyas, being expelled from Delhi, migrated to Tatta and other places in Sind, and subsequently to Multān. During their wars the Kshattriyas asked the aid of the Aroras, but they were refused assistance. The Kshattriyas in consequence induced the Brāhmans to debar the Aroras from the exercise of religious rites, and they thus remained proscribed for three hundred years, until Sidh Bhoja and Sidh

Siāma of Dīpālpur readmitted them within the pale of Hinduism. The Hindu bankers of Shikārpur are Aroras, and the Hindu shopkeepers of Khorasan and Bokhara are likewise held by the people of the Punjab to be of the same race. The Aroras divide themselves into two main classes: (1) *Utradi*, or of the north, and (2) *Dakhni*, or of the south, and the latter has likewise an important subdivision named *Duhuni*.

In the Lower Punjab and in Sind the whole Hindu trading population is included by the Muhammadans under the term 'Kirār'. In the Upper Punjab the word is used to denote a coward or one base and abject, and about Multān it is likewise expressive of contempt as well of a Hindu or a trafficker. In Central India the Kirārs form a tribe, but the term there literally means dalesmen or foresters, although it has become the name of a class or tribe in the lapse of centuries. Professor Wilson somewhere, I think, identifies them with the Chirrhadae of the ancients, and indeed *Kerāt* is one of the five *Prasthas* or regions of the Hindus, these being Chīn Prasth, Yavan Prasth, Indr Prasth, Dakshan Prasth, and Kerāt Prasth, which last is understood by the Indians to apply to the country between Ujjain and Orissa. (Cf. Wilson, *Vishnu Purān*, p. 175 *n.*, for the Kerātas of that book). Further, the Brāhmanical Gonds of the Nerbudda are styled 'Rāj Gonds', while those who have not adopted Hinduism continue to be called 'Kirrīa Gonds', a term which seems to have a relation to their unaltered condition.

APPENDIX IV

CASTE IN INDIA

THE system of *caste*, as it has become developed in India, as it obtained in Egypt and in Persia, as it was exemplified in an ancient 'Gens' with its separate religious rites and hereditary usages, as it partially obtained in Europe during the Middle Ages, and as it exists even now, is worthy of an essay distinguished by the ripest scholarship, and by the widest experience of life and knowledge of the human mind. In India it has evidently been an institution of gradual progress up to the pernicious perfection of later days, and in early times the bounds were less markedly defined, or less carefully observed, than during the last few hundred years. The instance of Viswāmitra's acquisition of Brāhmanhood is well known, as is Vikramājīt's almost successful desire of attaining to the same eminence. Vyāsa likewise raised a

Sūdra to an equality with the priestly class, and his descendants are still looked upon as Brāhmans, although inferior in degree. (Ward, *The Hindus*, i. 85; and see Manu, *Institutes*, chap. x, 42–72, &c., for admissions that merit could open the ranks of caste.) Even in the present generation some members of the Jāt Sikh family of Sindhianwala, related to that of Ranjīt Singh, made an attempt to be admitted to a participation in the social rites of Kshattriyas; and it may be assumed as certain that had the conquering Mughals and Pathāns been without a vivid belief and an organized priesthood, they would have adopted Vedism and have become enrolled among the Kshattriyas or ruling races.

Perhaps the reformer Rāmānand expressed the original principle of Indian sacerdotal caste when he said that Kabīr the weaver had become a Brāhman by knowing Brahm or God. (*The Dabistān*, ii. 188.)

The Muhammadans of India fancifully divide themselves into four classes, after the manner of the Hindus, viz. Saiyids, Shaikhs, Mughals, and Pathāns. All are noble, indeed, but the former two, as representing the tribe of Muhammad and the direct progeny of Alī his son-in-law, are pre-eminent. It is likewise a fact, at least in the northwest, that a Kshattriya convert from Hinduism, or any convert from Sikhism, is styled a Shaikh, and that converts of inferior races are classed as Mughals and Pathāns. Doubtless a Brāhman who should become a Muhammadan would at once be classed among the Saiyids.

Mr. Hodgson (*Aborigines of India*, p. 144) shows that the Koch princes of Assam were admitted to be Rājpūts on embracing Hinduism, although they are of the Tamil and not of the Arya race; but even the Jews were not altogether inflexible in former times, and Bossuet notices the conversion of the Idumaeans and Philistines, and sees their change of faith foretold by the prophets (*Universal History*, Translation of 1810, pp. 142 and 154).

[Possibly in his reference to Society in mediaeval Europe the author has not laid sufficient stress upon the rigid nature of what has been called the 'horizontal' division of Society during that period. The caste barrier that separated the knight from the merchant of his own country was a very real thing.—Ed.]

APPENDIX V

THE PHILOSOPHICAL SYSTEMS OF THE INDIANS

THE six orthodox schools will be found, among them, to partially represent the three great philosophic systems of the Greeks—the ethical, the logical, and the physical; or to be severally founded, in more modern language, on revelation or morality, reason, and sense. Thus the first and second Mīmāmsā, being based on the Vedas, correspond in a measure with the school of Pythagoras, which identified itself so closely with the belief and institutions of the age. The Nyāya and Vaiseshika systems of Gautama and Kanādia, which treat primarily of mind or reason, resemble the dialectics of Xenophanes, while the Sānkhya doctrines of Kapāl and Patanjali, which labour with the inertness and modifications of matter, correspond with the physical school of Thales, as taught by Anaxagoras. Mr. Elphinstone (*History of India*, i. 234) has some good observations on the marked correspondence of the Indian and Greek metaphysics, and Mr. Ward (*Hindus*, ii. 113) attempts a specific comparison with a series of individual reasoners, but too little is yet known, especially of Brāhmanical speculation, to render such parallels either exact or important.

The triple division of the schools which is adopted by the Indians themselves may here be given as some help to a better understanding of the doctrines of the modern reformers. They separate the systems into Arumbwād, Purnāmwād, and Vīvurtwād, or the simple atomic, the modified material, and the illusory. The 'Arumbwād' includes the first Mīmāmsā, the Nyāya, and the Vaiseshika, and it teaches the indestructibility of matter, while it leaves the atoms without any other inherent quality, and attributes their various shapes and developments to the exercise of God's will. The 'Purnāmwād' includes the Sānkhya and Yoga systems, and teaches that matter has not only a power of resistance, but a law of aggregation or development, or that it can only have forms given to it by God in accordance with its inherent nature. The modern Vaishnavas are mostly adherents of this doctrine, but they somewhat modify it, and say that the sensible world is God, so imbued with matter that he is himself manifest in all things, but under such varying forms and appearances as may suit his design. The 'Vīvurtwād', or the second Mīmāmsā, which is orthodox Vedantism, or the system of Shankar Achārj, teaches that God changes not his shape, but is himself at once both spirit and matter, although to the sense of man he is variously manifested by means of 'Māyā', his power or essence, his image or reflection—under the guise of the heavens and the earth, or as inorganic rocks and as sentient animals.

Another division of the schools is also made into 'Astik', and 'Nastik', or deist and atheist, so as to include doctrines not Brāhmanical. Thus the Astik comprehends all the six 'Dursuns', and some modern reasoners further admit Muhammadanism and Christianity, considered as speculative systems, into this theistic or partially orthodox pale. The Nastik comprehends primarily the Buddhist and Jain systems, with the addition sometimes of the Chārvāk, which has never been popularized; but Hindu zealots make it secondarily to include not only Muhammadanism and Christianity, but also the sects of Gorakh, Kabīr, and Nānak, as being irrespective of or repugnant to the Vedas, while similarly they place the Poorv and Utar Mīmāmsā above the mere deism of reason, as being the direct revelation of God.

The Buddhists are subdivided into four schools—the Sautrantik, the Waibhashik, the Yogachār, and the Madīamit. All agree in compounding animal existence of five essences or qualities: (1) independent consciousness, or soul, or self; (2) perception of form, or of external objects; (3) sensation, pleasure, or pain—the action of matter on mind; (4) understanding or comprehension, the reaction of mind on matter, or mind pervaded with the qualities of matter; (5) passion, volition, action, or mind, vital and motive. Scholars thus consider the present subjection of matter to mind as the greatest happiness of which man is capable, and they declare death to be the utter dissolution of the individual; while the Buddhas of vulgar adoration become simply revered memories or remembrances with the learned. The first section holds that intelligence, or the joint perception of the object and subject, is the soul or distinguishing characteristic of humanity; the second gives the preference to simple consciousness; the third prefers objective sensation, and the fourth teaches that the fact or the phenomenon of the assemblage of the component qualities is the only spirit; or, indeed, that there is naught permanent or characteristic save nonentity, or the void of non-being. This last evidently merges into the Chārvāk school, and it is also called the 'Shunyabad' system, or the doctrine of vacuity or non-existence, and an attempt was recently made to popularize it in Upper India, by one Bakhtāwar, and his patron, the Chief of Hattrass (Wilson, *As. Res.*, xvii. 305); nor is it difficult to perceive that practically it would resolve itself into the principle of self-reliance, or perhaps the 'know-thyself' of the Greek sage.

The Jains base human existence on the aggregation of nine phenomena, or principles, one of which, Jīv, vitality, may by merit become a Jin, or an immortal spirit. The two great divisions, 'Swetāmbar', the white clothed, and 'Digambar', the naked, seem to have few important metaphysical differences, except that the latter refuses emancipation to the Jīv, or vital power, in woman, or denies that woman has a soul capable of immortality.

The six heretical systems of Indian speculation thus comprise the four Buddhist and two Jain schools; or, if the Jain be held to be one, the sixth is obtained by including the Chārvāk.

The tendency of Indian speculation lies doubtless towards materialism, and the learned say the *mind* cannot grasp that which is without qualities, or which has force without form, and is irrespective of space. In how much does the philosophy of Humboldt differ from this, when he says he confidently expects what Socrates once desired, 'that Reason shall be the sole interpreter of Nature'? (*Kosmos*, Sabine's trans., i. 154.)

APPENDIX VI

ON THE MĀYĀ OF THE INDIANS

THE *Māyā* of the Hindus may be considered under a threefold aspect, or morally, poetically, and philosophically.

Morally, it means no more than the vanity of Solomon (Ecclesiastes i and ii), or the nothingness of this world; and thus Kabīr likens it to delusion or evil, or to moral error in the abstract. (*As. Res.*, xvi. 161.) The Indian reformers, indeed, made a use of *Māyā* corresponding with the use made by the Apostle Saint John of the Logos of Plato, as Mr. Milman very judiciously observes. (Note in Gibbon, *History*, iii. 312.) The one adapted *Māyā* to the Hindu notions of a sinful world, and the other explained to Greek and Roman understandings the nature of Christ's relation to God by representing the divine intelligence to be manifested in the Messiah.

Poetically, Māyā is used to denote a film before the eyes of gods and heroes, which limits their sight or sets bounds to their senses (Heereen, *Asiatic Nations*, iii. 203); and similarly Pallas dispels a mist from before the eyes of Diomed, and makes the ethereal forms of divinities apparent to a mortal. (*Iliad*, v.) The popular speech of all countries contains proof of the persuasion that the imperfect powers of men render them unable to appreciate the world around them.

Philosophically, the Māyā of the Vedant system (which corresponds to a certain extent with the Prākriti of the Sankhya school, and with the Cosmic substance of Xenophanes, or more exactly with the Play of the Infinite Being of Heraclitus), seems identical with the idealism of Berkeley. The doctrine seems also to have had the same origin as the 'Idola' system of Bacon; and thus, as an illusion or a false appearance, Māyā is the opposite of Plato's 'Idea' or the True. Ordinarily, Māyā is simply held to denote the apparent or sensible in opposition to the real, as when, according to the common illustration, a rope is taken for a snake, while in another point of view it is regarded as the Agent or Medium of God's manifestation in the universe, either as merely exhibiting images, or as really and actively mixed up with the production of worlds. It is curious that in England and in India the same material argument should have been used to confute Berkeley's theory of dreams and the Brāhmanical theory of illusion. An elephant was impelled against Shankar Achārj, who maintained the unreal nature of his own body and of all around him; and Dr. Johnson considered that he demolished the doctrine when, striking a stone with his foot, he showed that he recoiled from it. But Shankar Achārj had a readier wit than the supporters of the bishop, and *he* retorted upon his adversaries when they ridiculed his nimble steps to avoid the beast, that *all* was a fancy; there was no Shankar, no elephant, no flight—all was a delusion. (*Dabistān*, ii. 103.)

Māyā may also be said to be used in a fourth or political sense by the Indians, as in the Sāhit or Niti section of the 'Arth Shastra', or fourth 'Upved', which treats, among other things, of the duties of rulers, it is allowed as one of the modes of gaining an end. But Māyā, in the science in question, is used to signify rather secrecy, or strategy, or dexterous diplomacy, than gross deceit; for fraud and falsehood are among the prohibited ways. Māyā, it is said, may be employed to delude an enemy or to secure the obedience of subjects. Socrates admits that, under similar circumstances, such deceit would be fitting and proper, or that in his scheme it would come under the category of justice. (*Memorabilia*, book iv, chap. ii.)

APPENDIX VII

THE METAPHYSICS OF INDIAN REFORMERS

WHAT has been said in the text about the modern reformers relates chiefly to the popular theology. Some of them, however, likewise philosophized or speculated on the origin of things, and thus the 'Utar Mīmāmsā' school is sometimes subdivided into several branches, known (1) as the 'Adweit', or pure system of Shankar; and (2) as the 'Madhavadweit', the 'Vusisht-adweit', and the 'Shudadweit', or modified systems of Unity of Mādhav, Rāmānuj, and Vallabh respectively. Shankar Achārj taught that God is the original of all things, and is in reality unchangeable in form; wherefore, when oblivious (*aghīan*) of himself, he variously becomes manifest as vitality and matter, he does so as 'Māyā', or as Images, or as the mirror reflecting all things, yet remaining itself the same. Life and the Soul are one in this system, and salvation becomes absorption, while, as a proof that the same vitality may put on different shapes, he quotes the instance of the caterpillar, the chrysalis, and the butterfly. Mādhav holds Life to be distinct from Spirit, and with him the purified soul dwells with God without being absorbed, but he gives prominence to 'Māyā' as coexistent with God, or as the moving and brooding spirit which gives form to matter; and thus the followers of Rāmānuj extend Mādhav's notion, and talk of God, Māyā, and Life, as well as of Atoms. Vallabh and the Vishnuswamis or the Shudadweits likewise maintain the distinct nature of Life or of the human Soul, and make salvation a dwelling with God without liability to reappearance; but the doctrine of 'Māyā' is almost wholly rejected in favour of a Material Pantheism, as that the light which illumines a room is the same with the illuminating principle of the transmitting flame, and hence that what man perceives is actual and not illusory. For some partial notices of these reasonings see Wilson, *As. Res.*, xvi. 34, 89, and 104; and they may be perused at length in the Commentaries of the several speculators on the 'Bhagavadgītā', in the 'Urth Punchuk' of Rāmānuj, and in the 'Dusha Slōk' of Vishnuswami.

APPENDIX VIII

NĀNAK'S PHILOSOPHICAL ALLUSIONS POPULAR OR MORAL RATHER THAN SCIENTIFIC

Professor Wilson (*As. Res.*, xvii. 233, and continuation of Mill's *History of India,* vii. 101, 102) would appear to think slightingly of the doctrines of Nānak, as being mere metaphysical notions founded on the abstractions of Sufism and the Vedant philosophy ; but it is difficult for any one to write about the omnipotence of God and the hopes of man, without laying himself open to a charge of belonging to one speculative school or another. Milton, the poet and statesman, indeed, may have had a particular leaning, when he thought of 'body working up to spirit' (*Paradise Lost,* v) ; but is St. Paul, the reformer and enthusiast, to be contemned, or is he to be misunderstood when he says, 'It is sown a natural body, and is raised a spiritual body'? (1 Corinthians xv. 44). Similarly such expressions as 'Doth not the Lord fill heaven and earth?' (Jeremiah xxiii. 24), 'God, in whom we live and move and have our being' (Acts xvii. 28), and 'Of him, and to him, and through him are all things' (Romans xi. 36), might be used to declare the prophet and the apostle to be Pantheists or Materialists ; but it nevertheless seems plain that Jeremiah and Paul, and likewise Nānak, had another object in view than scholastic dogmatism, and that they simply desired to impress mankind with exalted notions of the greatness and goodness of God, by a vague employment of general language which they knew would never mislead the multitude.

Professor Wilson (*As. Res.*, xvii. 233, 237, 238) and Muhsin Fāni (*Dabistān*, ii. 269, 270, 285, 286) may be compared together, and the *Siar ul Mutakharin* (i. 110) may be compared with both, with reference to the contradictory views taken of the similarity or difference respectively between Sikhism and Brāhmanism. Each is right, the one with regard to the imperfect faith or the corrupt practices, especially of the Sikhs in the Gangetic provinces, and the other with regard to the admitted doctrines of Nānak, as they will always be explained by any qualified person.

It is to be remembered that the Sikhs regard the mission of Nānak and Gobind as the consummation of other dispensations, including that of Muhammad ; and their talk, therefore, of Brāhma and Vishnu and various heavenly powers is no more unreasonable than the deference of Christians to Moses and Abraham and to the archangels

Michael and Gabriel. Such allusions are perhaps, indeed, more excusable in the Sikhs than 'that singular polytheism' of our mediaeval divines, which they 'grafted on the language rather (indeed) than on the principles of Christianity'. (Hallam, *Middle Ages*, iii. 346.)

For an instance of the moral application which Nānak was wont to give to mythological stories see Ward, *Hindus*, iii. 465. Nānak, indeed, refers continually to Hindu notions, but he was not therefore an idolater; and it should further be borne in mind that as St. John could draw illustrations from Greek philosophy, so could St. Paul make an advantageous use of the Greek poets, as was long ago observed upon in a right spirit by Milton (Speech for the Liberty of unlicensed Printing). In the early ages of Christianity, moreover, the sibylline leaves were referred to as foretelling the mission of Jesus; but although the spuriousness of the passages is now admitted, the fathers are not accused of polytheism, or of holding Amalthaea, the nurse of Jupiter, to be a real type of the Virgin Mary! In truth, all religious systems not possessed of a body of literature or philosophy proper to themselves seek elsewhere for support in such matters. Thus the Chevalier Bunsen (*Egypt*, i. 194, &c.) observes that the early Christians were even desirous of reconciling Scripture with Greek *history*; and Ranke (*Hist. of the Popes*, ed. 1843, p. 125) says that the Church, so late as the sixteenth century, was willing to rest its dogmas and doctrines on the metaphysics of the Ancients.

APPENDIX IX

THE TERMS RAJ AND JŌG, DĒG AND TĒGH

THE warlike resistance of Har Gobind, or the arming of the Sikhs by that teacher, is mainly attributed by Malcolm (*Sketch*, pp. 34, 35) and Forster (*Travels*, i. 298, 299) to his personal feelings of revenge for the death of his father, although religious animosity against Muhammadans is allowed to have had some share in bringing about the change. The circumstance of the Gurū's military array does not appear to have struck Muhsin Fāni as strange or unusual, and his work, the *Dabistān*, does not therefore endeavour to account for it. The Sikhs themselves connect the modification of Nānak's system with the double nature of the mythological Janak of Mithilā, whose released soul, indeed, is held to have animated the body of their first teacher (*Dabistān*, ii. 268), and they have encumbered their *ideal* of a ruler with the following *personal* anecdote: The wife of

Arjūn was without children, and she began to despair of ever becoming a mother. She went to Bhai Buddha, the ancient and only surviving companion of Nānak, to beseech his blessing; but he, disliking the degree of state she assumed and her costly offerings, would not notice her. She afterwards went barefooted and alone to his presence, carrying on her head the ordinary food of peasants. The Bhai smiled benignly upon her, and said she should have a son, who would be master both of the *Dēg* and *Tēgh*; that is, simply of a vessel for food and a sword, but typically of grace and power, the terms corresponding in significance with the 'Raj' and 'Jōg' of Janak,[1] the 'Piri' and 'Miri' of Indian Muhammadans, and with the idea of the priesthood and kingship residing in Melchisedec and in the expected Messiah of the Jews. Thus Har Gobind is commonly said to have worn two swords, one to denote his spiritual, and the other his temporal power; or, as he may sometimes have chosen to express it, one to avenge his father, and the other to destroy Muhammadanism. (See Malcolm, *Sketch*, p. 35.)

The fate of Arjūn, and the personal character of his son, had doubtless some share in leading the Sikhs to take up arms; but the whole progress of the change is not yet apparent, nor perhaps do the means exist of tracing it. The same remark applies to the early Christian history, and we are left in ignorance of how that modification of feeling and principle was brought about, which made those who were so averse to the 'business of war and government' in the time of the [early] Caesars, fill the armies of the empire in the reign of Diocletian, and at last give a military master to the western world in the person of Constantine. (Cf. Gibbon, *History*, ed. 1838, ii. 325, 375.)

[1] 'Raj mēn jōg kumaio,' to attain immortal purity or virtue, or to dwell in grace while exercising earthly sway. It is an expression of not infrequent use, and which occurs in the *Adi Granth*, in the 'Sawayas', by certain Bhats. Thus one Bika says, Rām Dās (the fourth Gurū) got the 'Takht', or throne, of 'Raj' and 'Jōg', from Amar Dās. 'Dēg', as above stated, means simply a vessel for food, and thence, metaphorically, *abundance* on earth, and *grace* on the part of God. The two terms are clearly synonymous, and thus Thomson writes of the sun as the

> . . . 'great delegated source
> Of light, and life, and *grace*, and joy below.'
>
> THE SEASONS—*Summer*.

APPENDIX X

CASTE AMONG THE SIKHS

IT may nevertheless be justly observed that Gobind abolished *caste* rather by implication than by a direct enactment, and it may be justly objected that the Sikhs still uphold the principal distinctions at least of race. Thus the Gurūs nowhere say that Brāhmans and Sudras are to intermarry, or that they are daily to partake together of the same food; but that they laid a good foundation for the practical obliteration of all differences will be evident from the following quotations, always bearing in mind the vast pre-eminence which they assign to religious unity and truth over social sameness or political equality:

'Think not of caste: abase thyself, and attain to salvation.'—NĀNAK, *Sarang Rāg*.

'God will not ask man of what race he is; he will ask him what has he done?'—NĀNAK, *Parbhati Rāgni*.

'Of the impure among the noblest,
Heed not the injunction;
Of one pure among the most despised,
Nānak will become the footstool.'

NĀNAK, *Malhar Rāg*.

'All of the seed of Brahm (God) are Brāhmans:
They say there are four races,
But all are of the seed of Brahm.'

AMAR DĀS, *Bhairav*.

'Kshattriya, Brāhman, Sudra, Veisya, whoever remembers the name of God, who worships him always, &c., &c., shall attain to salvation.'—RĀM DĀS, *Bilāwal*.

'The four races shall be one,
All shall call on the Gurū.'

GOBIND, in the *Rahat Nama*
(not in the *Granth*).

Compare Malcolm (*Sketch*, p. 45 *n.*) for a saying attributed to Gobind, that the castes would become one when well mixed, as the four components of the 'Pān-Supari', or betel, of the Hindus, became of one colour when well chewed.

The Sikhs of course partake in common of the Prasād (vulg. Parshād) or consecrated food, which is ordinarily composed of flour, coarse sugar, and clarified butter. Several, perhaps all, Hindu sects, however, do the same. (See Wilson, *As. Res.*, xvi. 83 *n.*, and xvii. 239 *n.*)

APPENDIX XI

RITES OF INITIATION INTO SIKHISM

SIKHS are not ordinarily initiated until they reach the age of discrimination and remembrance, or not before they are seven years of age, or sometimes until they have attained to manhood. But there is no authoritative rule on the subject, nor is there any declaratory ceremonial of detail which can be followed. The essentials are that five Sikhs at least should be assembled, and it is generally arranged that one of the number is of some religious repute. Some sugar and water are stirred together in a vessel of any kind, commonly with a two-edged dagger, but any iron weapon will answer. The noviciate stands with his hands joined in an attitude of humility or supplication, and he repeats after the elder or minister the main articles of his faith. Some of the water is sprinkled on his face and person ; he drinks the remainder, and exclaims, Hail Gurū ! and the ceremony concludes with an injunction that he be true to God and to his duty as a Sikh. For details of particular modes followed, see Forster (*Travels*, i. 307), Malcolm (*Sketch*, p. 182), and Prinsep's edition of Murray's *Life of Ranjīt Singh* (p. 217), where an Indian compiler is quoted.

The original practice of using the water in which the feet of a Sikh had been washed was soon abandoned, and the subsequent custom of touching the water with the toe seems now almost wholly forgotten. The first rule was perhaps instituted to denote the humbleness of spirit of the disciples, or both it and the second practice may have originated in that feeling of the Hindus which attaches virtue to water in which the thumb of a Brāhman has been dipped. It seems in every way probable that Gobind substituted the dagger for the foot or the toe, thus giving further pre-eminence to his emblematic iron.

Women are not usually, but they are sometimes, initiated in form as professors of the Sikh faith. In mingling the sugar and water for women, a one-edged, and not a two-edged, dagger is used.

APPENDIX XII

THE EXCLAMATION WAH GURŪ AND THE EXPRESSION DĒG, TĒGH, FATH

THE proper exclamation of community of faith of the Sikhs as a sect is simply, 'Wah Gurū!' that is, O Gurū! or Hail Gurū! The lengthened exclamations of 'Wah! Gurū ki Fath!' and 'Wah! Gurū ka Khālsa!' (Hail! Virtue or power of the Gurū! or Hail! Gurū and Victory! and Hail to the state or church of the Gurū!) are not authoritative, although the former has become customary, and its use, as completing the idea embraced in 'Dēg' and 'Tēgh' (see *ante*, Appendix IX) naturally arose out of the notions diffused by Gobind, if he did not ordain it as the proper salutation of believers.

Many of the chapters or books into which the *Adi Granth* is divided, begin with the expression 'Eko Unkar, Sat Gurū Prasād', which may be interpreted to mean, 'The One God, and the grace of the blessed Gurū'. Some of the chapters of the *Daswen Padshah ka Granth* begin with 'Eko Unkar, Wah Gurū ki Fath', that is, 'The One God and the power of the Gurū'.

The Sikh author of the *Gur Ratnawali* gives the following fanciful and trivial origin of the salutation Wah Gurū!

Wasdev, the exclamation of the first age, or Satyug;
Har Har, the exclamation of the second age;
Gobind Gobind, the exclamation of the third age;
Rām Rām, the exclamation of the fourth age, or Kalyug; whence Wah Gurū in the fifth age, or under the new dispensation.

APPENDIX XIII

THE SIKH DEVOTION TO STEEL, AND THE TERM 'SACHCHA PĀDSHAH'

FOR allusions to this devotion to steel see Malcolm, *Sketch*, pp. 48, 117 *n.*, 182 *n.*

The meaning given in the text to the principle inculcated seems to be the true one. Throughout India the implements of any calling are in a manner worshipped, or, in Western moderation of phrase, they are blessed or consecrated. This is especially noticeable among merchants, who annually perform religious ceremonies before a heap of gold; among hereditary clerks or writers, who similarly idolize their ink-horn ; and among soldiers and military leaders, who on the festival of the Das-hara consecrate their banners and piled-up weapons. Gobind withdrew his followers from that undivided attention which their fathers had given to the plough, the loom, and the pen, and he urged them to regard the sword as *their* principal stay in this world. The sentiment of veneration for that which gives us power, or safety, or our daily bread, may be traced in all countries. In our own a sailor impersonates, or almost deifies, his ship, and in India the custom of hereditary callings has heightened that feeling, which, expressed in the language of philosophy, becomes the dogma admitting the soul to be increate indeed, but enveloped in the understanding, which again is designed for our use in human affairs, or until our bliss is perfect. It is this external or inferior spirit, so to speak, which must devote its energies to the service and contemplation of steel, while the increate soul contemplates God. [Compare also the mediaeval ceremony of 'watching his arms' regularly undergone by the candidate for knighthood.—Ed.]

The import of the term *Sachcha Pādshah*, or True King, seems to be explained in the same way. A spiritual king, or Gurū, rules the eternal soul, or guides it to salvation, while a temporal monarch controls our finite faculties only, or puts restraints upon the play of our passions and the enjoyment of our senses. The Muhammadans have the same idea and a corresponding term, viz. *Mālik Hakiki*.

APPENDIX XIV

DISTINCTIVE USAGES OF THE SIKHS

These and many other distinctions of Sikhs may be seen in the Rehet and Tankha Namas of Gobind, forming part of Appendix XX of this volume.

Unshorn locks and a blue dress, as the characteristics of a believer, do not appear as direct injunctions in any extant writing attributed to Gobind, and they seem chiefly to have derived their distinction as marks from custom or usage, while the propriety of wearing a blue dress is now regarded as less obligatory than formerly. Both usages appear to have originated in a spirit of opposition to Hinduism, for many Brāhmanical devotees keep their heads carefully shaved, and all Hindus are shaven when initiated into their religious duties or responsibilities, or on the death of a near relative. It is also curious, with regard to colour, that many religious, or indeed simply respectable Hindus, have still an aversion to blue, so much so indeed that a Rājpūt farmer will demur about sowing his fields with indigo. The Muhammadans, again, prefer blue dresses, and perhaps the dislike of the Hindus arose during the Musalmān conquest, as Krishna himself, among others, is described as blue clothed. Thus the Sikh author, Bhai Gurdas Bhalla, says of Nānak, 'Again he went to Mecca, blue clothing he had like Krishna'. Similarly, no Sikh will wear clothes of a 'sūhī' colour, i. e. dyed with safflower, such having long been the favourite colour with Hindu devotees, as it is gradually becoming with Muhammadan ascetics. As a distinction of race, if not of creed, the unshorn locks of the Sikhs have a parallel in the long hair of the Frankish nobles and freemen. The contrasting terms 'crinosus' and 'tonsoratus' arose in mediaeval Europe, and the virtue or privilege due to flowing hair was so great that Childebert talked of having his brother's children either *cropped* or *put to death*. (Hallam, *Middle Ages*, notes to Chap. II.)

The Sikhs continue to refrain from tobacco, nor do they smoke drugs of any kind, although tobacco itself seems to have been originally included as *snuff* only among proscribed things. Tobacco was first introduced into India about 1617. (M'Culloch, *Commercial Dictionary*, art. 'Tobacco'.) It was, I think, idly denounced in form by one of Akbar's successors, but its use is now universal among Indian Muhammadans.

Another point of difference which may be noticed is that the Sikhs wear a kind of breeches, or now many wear a sort of pantaloons, instead of girding up their loins after the manner of the Hindus. The adoption of the 'kachh', or breeches, is of as much importance to a Sikh boy as was the investiture with the 'toga virilis' to a Roman youth.

The Sikh women are distinguished from Hindus of their sex by some variety of dress, but chiefly by a higher topknot of hair.

APPENDIX XV

ON THE USE OF ARABIC AND SANSKRIT FOR THE PURPOSES OF EDUCATION IN INDIA

Up to the present time England has made no great and lasting impress on the Indians, except as the introducer of an improved and effective military system; although she has also done much to exalt her character as a governing power, by her generally scrupulous adherence to formal engagements.

The Indian mind has not yet been suffused or saturated by the genius of the English, nor can the light of European knowledge be spread over the country, until both the Sanskrit and Arabic (Persian) languages are made the vehicles of instructing the *learned*. These tongues should thus be assiduously cultivated, although not so much for what they contain as for what they may be made the means of conveying. The hierarchies of 'Gymnosophists' and 'Ulema' will the more readily assent to mathematical or logical deductions, if couched in words identified in their eyes with scientific research; and they in time must of necessity make known the truths learned to the mass of the people. The present system of endeavouring to diffuse knowledge by means of the rude and imperfect vernacular tongues can succeed but slowly, for it seems to be undertaken in a spirit of opposition to the influential classes; and it is not likely to succeed at all until expositions of the sciences, with ample proofs and illustrations, are rendered complete, instead of partial and elementary only, or indeed meagre and inaccurate in the extreme, as many of the authorized school-books are. If there were Sanskrit or Arabic counterparts to these much-required elaborate treatises, the predilections of the learned Indians would be overcome with comparative ease.

The fact that the astronomy of Ptolemy and the geometry of Euclid are recognized in their Sanskrit dress as text-books of science even among the Brāhmans, should not be lost upon the promoters of education in the present age. The philosophy of facts and the truths of physical science had to be made known by Copernicus and Galileo, Bacon and Newton, through the medium of the Latin tongue; and the first teachers and upholders of Christianity preferred the admired and widely spoken Roman and Greek, both to the antique Hebrew and to the imperfect dialects of Gaul and Syria, Africa, and Asia Minor. In either case the language recommended the doctrine, and added to the conviction of Origen and Irenaeus, Tertullian and Clement of Rome, as well as to the belief of the scholar of more modern times. Similarly in India the use of Sanskrit and Arabic and Persian would give weight to the most obvious principles and completeness to the most logical demonstrations.

That in Calcutta the study of the sciences is pursued with some success through the joint medium of the English language and local dialects, and that in especial the tact and perseverance of the professors of the Medical College have induced Indians of family or caste to dissect the human body, do not militate against the views expressed above, but rather serve as exceptions to prove their truth. In Calcutta Englishmen are numerous, and their wealth, intelligence, and political position render their influence overwhelming; but this mental predominance decreases so rapidly that it is unfelt in fair-sized towns within fifty miles of the capital, and is but faintly revived in the populous cities of Benares, Delhi, Puna, and Hyderābād.

APPENDIX XVI

ON THE LAND-TAX IN INDIA

THE proportions of the land-tax to the general revenues of British India are nearly as follows:

Bengal, $\frac{2}{5}$; Bombay, $\frac{2}{3}$; Madras, $\frac{3}{4}$; Agra, $\frac{4}{5}$.
Average = $\frac{3}{5}$ of the whole.

In some European states the proportions are nearly as below:

England, $\frac{1}{24}$; France, $\frac{1}{4}$; Spain, $\frac{1}{17}$ (perhaps some error); Belgium, $\frac{2}{11}$; Prussia, $\frac{2}{11}$; Naples, $\frac{1}{4}$; Austria, $\frac{1}{3}$.

In the United States of America the revenue is almost wholly derived from customs.

It is now idle to revert to the theory of the ancient laws of the Hindus, or of the more recent institutes of the Muhammadans, although much clearness of view has resulted from the learned researches or laborious inquiries of Briggs and Munro, of Sykes and Halhed and Galloway. It is also idle to dispute whether the Indian farmer pays a 'rent' or a 'tax' in a technical sense, since, practically, it is certain (1) that the government (or its assign, the jagīrdār or grantee) gets in nearly all instances almost the whole surplus produce of the land; and (2) that the state, if the owner, does not perform its duty by not furnishing from its capital wells and other things, which correspond in difficulty of provision with barns and drains in England. In India no one thinks of investing capital or of spending money on the improvement of the land, excepting, directly, a few patriarchal chiefs through love of their homes; and, indirectly, the wealthy speculators in opium, sugar, &c., through the love of gain. An ordinary village 'head-man', or the still poorer 'ryot', whether paying direct to government or through a revenue farmer, has just so much of the produce left as will enable him to provide the necessary seed, his own inferior food, and the most simple requisites of tillage; and as he has thus no means, he cannot incur the expense or run the risk of introducing improvements.

Hence it behoves England, if in doubt about Oriental 'socage' and 'freehold' tenures, to redistribute her taxation, to diminish her assessment on the soil, and to give her multitudes of subjects, who are practically 'copyholders', at least a permanent interest in the land, as she has done so largely by 'customary' leaseholders within her own proper dominion. There should likewise be a limit to which such estates might be divided, and this could be advantageously done, by allowing the owner of a petty holding to dispose as he pleased, not of the land itself, but of what it might bring when sold. .

For some just observations on the land tenures of India see Lieut.-Col. Sleeman's *Rambles and Recollections of an Indian Official* (Oxford, 1915), pp. 58, 561, 571; while, for a *fiscal* description of the transition system now in force in the North-Western Provinces, the present Lieut.-Governor's *Directions for Settlement Officers* and his *Remarks on the Revenue System* may be profitably consulted (1849).

APPENDIX XVII

THE *ADI GRANTH*, OR FIRST BOOK; OR, THE BOOK OF NĀNAK, THE FIRST GURŪ, OR TEACHER OF THE SIKHS

NOTE.—The first *Granth* is nowhere narrative or historical. It throws no light, by direct exposition, upon the political state of India during the sixteenth and seventeenth centuries, although it contains many allusions illustrative of the condition of society and of the religious feelings of the times. Its teaching is to the general purport that God is to be worshipped in spirit and in truth, with little reference to particular forms, and that salvation is unattainable without grace, faith, and good works.

The *Adi Granth* comprises, first, the writings attributed to Nānak, and the succeeding teachers of the Sikh faith up to the ninth Gurū, Tegh Bahādur, omitting the sixth, seventh, and eighth, but with perhaps some additions and emendations by Gobind; secondly, the compositions of certain 'Bhagats', or saints, mostly sectarian Hindus, and who are usually given as sixteen in number; and, thirdly, the verses of certain 'Bhāts', or rhapsodists, followers of Nānak and of some of his successors. The numbers, and even the names of the 'Bhagats', or saints, are not always the same in copies of the *Granth*; and thus modern compilers or copyists have assumed to themselves the power of rejecting or sanctioning particular writings. To the sixteen Bhagats are usually added two 'Dōms', or chanters, who recited before Arjūn, and who caught some of his spirit; and a 'Rabābi', or player upon a stringed instrument, who became similarly inspired.

The *Granth* sometimes includes an appendix, containing works the authenticity of which is doubtful, or the propriety of admitting which is disputed on other grounds.

The *Granth* was originally compiled by Arjūn, the fifth Gurū; but it subsequently received a few additions at the hands of his successors.

The *Granth* is written wholly in verse; but the forms of versification are numerous. The language used is rather the Hindi of Upper India generally, than the particular dialect of the Punjab; but some portions, especially of the last section, are composed in Sanskrit. The written character is nevertheless throughout the Punjābī, one of the several varieties of alphabets now current in India, and which, from its use by the Sikh Gurūs, is sometimes called 'Gurmukhī', a term likewise applied to the dialect of the Punjab. The language of the writings of Nānak is thought by modern Sikhs to abound with provincialisms of the country south-west of Lahore, and the dialect of Arjūn is held to be the most pure.

The *Granth* usually forms a quarto volume of about 1,232 pages, each page containing 24 lines, and each line containing about 35 letters. The extra books increase the pages to 1,240 only.

Contents of the Adi Granth

1st. The '*Japji*', or simply the '*Jap*', called also *Gurū Mantr*, or the special prayer of initiation of the Gurū. It occupies about 7 pages, and consists of 40 slōks, called *Pauri*, of irregular lengths, some of two, and some of several lines. It means, literally, the remembrancer or admonisher, from *jap*, to remember. It was written by Nānak, and is believed to have been appointed by him to be repeated each morning, as every pious Sikh now does. The mode of composition implies the presence of a questioner and an answerer, and the Sikhs believe the questioner to have been the disciple Angad.

2nd. '*Sudar Rah Rās*'—the evening prayer of the Sikhs. It occupies about $3\frac{1}{2}$ pages, and it was composed by Nānak, but has additions by Rām Dās and Arjūn, and some, it is said, by Gurū Gobind. The additions attributed to Gobind are, however, more frequently given when the Rah Rās forms a separate pamphlet or book. *Sudar* a particu ar kind of verse; *Rah*, admonisher; *Rās*, the expression used for the play or recitative of Krishna. It is sometimes corruptly called the 'Rowh Rās', from *Rowh*, the Punjābī for a road.

3rd. '*Kirit Sōhila*'—a prayer repeated before going to rest. It occupies a page and a line or two more. It was composed by Nānak, but has additions by Rām Dās and Arjūn, and one verse is attributed to Gobind. *Kirit*, from Sanskrit *Kirti*, to praise, to celebrate; and *Sōhila*, a marriage song, a song of rejoicing.

4th. The next portion of the *Granth* is divided into thirty-one sections, known by their distinguishing forms of verse, as follows:

1. Sri Rag.
2. Maj.
3. Gauri.
4. Asa.
5. Gujri.
6. Dev Gandhāri.
7. Bihāgra.
8. Wad Hans.
9. Sorath (or Sōrt).
10. Dhanāsri.
11. Jait Sri.
12. Todi.
13. Bairari.
14. Tailang.
15. Sudhi.
16. Bilāwal.
17. Gaund.
18. Rām Kali.
19. Nat Narayan.
20. Mali Gaura.
21. Maru.
22. Tukhari.
23. Kedāra.
24. Bhairon.
25. Basant.
26. Sarang.
27. Malhār.
28. Kānhra.
29. Kalian.
30. Parbhāti.
31. Jai Jaiwanti.

The whole occupies about 1,154 pages, or by far the greater portion of the entire *Granth*. Each subdivision is the composition of one or more Gurūs, or of one or more Bhagats or holy men, or of a Gurū with or without the aid of a Bhagat.

The contributors among the Gurūs were as follows:

1. Nānak.
2. Angad.
3. Amar Dās.
4. Rām Dās.
5. Arjūn.
6. Tegh Bahādur (with, perhaps, emendations by Gobind).

The Bhagats or saints, and others who contributed agreeably to the ordinary copies of the *Granth*, are enumerated below:

1. Kabīr (the well-known reformer).
2. Trilochan, a Brāhman.
3. Beni.
4. Rav Dās, a Chamār, or leather dresser.
5. Nāmdev, a Chhipa, or cloth printer.
6. Dhanna, a Jāt.
7. Shāh Farīd, a Muhammadan pīr, or saint.
8. Jaidev, a Brāhman.
9. Bhikan.
10. Sain, a barber.
11. Pipa (a Jogi ?).
12. Sadhna, a butcher.
13. Rāmānand Bairagi (a well-known reformer).
14. Parmanand.
15. Sur Dās (a blind man).
16. Mirān Bai, a Bhagatni, or holy woman.

17. Balwand, and
18. Satta, 'Dōms' or chanters who recited before Arjūn.
19. Sundar Dās, Rabābi, or player upon a stringed instrument. He is not properly one of the Bhagats.

5th. The '*Bhōg*'. In Sanskrit this word means to enjoy anything, but it is commonly used to denote the conclusion of any sacred writing, both by Hindus and Sikhs. The Bhōg occupies about 66 pages, and besides the writings of Nānak and Arjūn, of Kabīr, Shāh Farīd, and other reformers, it contains the compositions of nine Bhāts or rhapsodists who attached themselves to Amar Dās, Rām Dās, and Arjūn.

The Bhōg commences with 4 slōks in Sanskrit by Nānak, which are followed by 67 Sanskrit slōks in one metre by Arjūn, and then by 24 in another metre by the same Gurū. There are also 23 slōks in Punjābī or Hindi by Arjūn, which contain praises of Amritsar. These are soon followed by 243 slōks by Kabīr, and 130 by Shāh Farīd, and others, containing some sayings of Arjūn. Afterwards the writings of Kall and the other Bhāts follow, intermixed with portions by Arjūn, and so on to the end.

The nine Bhāts who contributed to the Bhōg are named as follows :

1. Bhikha, a follower of Amar Dās.
2. Kall, a follower of Rām Dās.
3. Kall Sahār.
4. Jālap, a follower of Arjūn.
5. Sall, a follower of Arjūn.
6. Nall.
7. Mathra.
8. Ball.
9. Kirit.

The names are evidently fanciful, and perhaps fictitious. In the book called the *Gurū Bilās* eight Bhāts only are enumerated, and all the names except Ball are different from those in the *Granth*.

Supplement to the Granth

6th. '*Bhōg ki Bani*', or Epilogue of the Conclusion. It comprises about 7 pages, and contains, first, some preliminary slōks, called 'Slōk Mahal Pahla', or Hymn of the first Woman or Slave ; secondly, Nānak's Admonition to Malhār Rājā ; thirdly, the 'Ratan Mala' of Nānak, i.e. the Rosary of Jewels, or string of (religious) worthies, which simply shows, however, what should be the true characteristics or qualities of religious devotees ; and, fourthly, the 'Hakikat', or Circumstances of Sivnāb, Rājā of Ceylon, with reference to a 'Pōthi' or sacred writing known as 'Pran Sangli'. This last is said to have been composed by one Bhai Bhannu in the time of Gobind.

The Ratan Mala is said to have been originally written in Turki, or to have been abstracted from a Turki original.

APPENDIX XVIII

THE *DASWIN PADSHAH KA GRANTH*, OR, BOOK OF THE TENTH KING, OR SOVEREIGN PONTIFF, THAT IS, OF GURŪ GOBIND SINGH

NOTE.—Like the *Adi Granth*, the book of Gobind is metrical throughout, but the versification frequently varies. It is written in the Hindu dialect, and in the Punjābī character, excepting the concluding portion, the language of which is Persian, while the alphabet continues the Gurmukhi. The Hindu of Gobind is almost such as is spoken in the Gangetic provinces, and has few peculiarities of the Punjābī dialect.

One chapter of the Book of the Tenth King may be considered to be narrative and historical, viz. the *Vichitr Nātak*, written by Gobind himself; but the Persian *Hikayats*, or stories, also partake of that character, from the circumstances attending their composition and the nature of some allusions made in them. The other portions of this *Granth* are more mythological than the first book, and it also partakes more of a worldly character throughout, although it contains many noble allusions to the unity of the Godhead, and to the greatness and goodness of the Ruler of the Universe.

Five chapters, or portions only, and the commencement of a sixth, are attributed to Gobind himself; the remainder, i.e. by far the larger portion, is said to have been composed by four scribes in the service of the Gurū; partly, perhaps, agreeably to his dictation. The names of Sham and Rām occur as two of the writers, but, in truth, little is known of the authorship of the portions in question.

The *Daswin Padshah ka Granth* forms a quarto volume of 1,066 pages, each page consisting of 23 lines, and each line of from 38 to 41 letters.

Contents of the Book of the Tenth King

1st. The '*Jāpji*', or simply the '*Jāp*', the supplement or complement of the *Japji* of Nānak—a prayer to be read or repeated in the morning, as it continues to be by pious

Sikhs. It comprises 198 distichs, and occupies about 7 pages, the termination of a verse and the end of a line not being the same. The *Jāpji* was composed by Gurū Gobind.

2nd. '*Akāl Stut*', or the Praises of the Almighty—a hymn commonly read in the morning. It occupies 23 pages, and the initiatory verse alone is the composition of Gobind.

3rd. The '*Vichitr Nātak*', i.e. the Wondrous Tale. This was written by Gobind himself, and it gives, first, the mythological history of his family or race; secondly, an account of his mission of reformation; and, thirdly, a description of his warfare with the Himālayan chiefs and the Imperial forces. It is divided into fourteen sections; but the first is devoted to the praises of the Almighty, and the last is of a similar tenor, with an addition to the effect that he would hereafter relate his visions of the past and his experience of the present world. The *Vichitr Nātak* occupies about 24 pages of the *Granth*.

4th. '*Chandi Charitr*', or the Wonders of Chandi or the Goddess. There are two portions called *Chandi Charitr*, of which this is considered the greater. It relates the destruction of eight *Titans* or Deityas by Chandi the Goddess. It occupies about 20 pages, and it is understood to be the translation of a Sanskrit legend, executed, some are willing to believe, by Gobind himself.

The names of the Deityas destroyed are as follows:

1. Madhu Kaitab.
2. Mah Khāsur.
3. Dhumar Lochan.
4 and 5. Chand and Mund.
6. Rakat Bij.
7. Nishumbh.
8. Shumbh.

5th. '*Chandi Charitr*' the lesser. The same legends as the greater Chandi, narrated in a different metre. It occupies about 14 pages.

6th. '*Chandi ki Var*.' A supplement to the legends of Chandi. It occupies about 6 pages.

7th. '*Gyan Prabodh*', or the Excellence of Wisdom. Praises of the Almighty, with allusions to ancient kings, taken mostly from the Mahabhārat. It occupies about 21 pages.

8th. '*Chaupayan Chaubis Avataran Kian*', or Quatrains relating to the Twenty-four Manifestations (Āvatārs). These 'Chaupays' occupy about 348 pages, and they are considered to be the work of one by name Sham.

The names of the incarnations are as follows:

1. The fish, or Machh.
2. The tortoise, or Kachh.
3. The lion, or Nar.
4. Narayan.
5. Mohani.
6. The boar, or Varāh.

7. The man-lion, or Nursingh.
8. The dwarf, or Bāwan.
9. Paras Rām.
10. Brahma.
11. Rudr.
12. Jalandhar.
13. Vishnu.
14. No name specified, but understood to be a manifestation of Vishnu.
15. Arhant Dev (considered to be the founder of the sect of Saraugis of the Jain persuasion, or, indeed, the great Jain prophet himself).
16. Man Rājā.
17. Dhanantar (the doctor, or physician).
18. The sun, or Suraj.
19. The moon, or Chandarma.
20. Rāma.
21. Krishna,
22. Nar (meaning Arjūn).
23. Bodh.
24. Kalki; to appear at the end of the Kalyug, or when the sins of men are at their height.

9th. No name entered, but known as '*Mihdi Mīr*'. A supplement to the Twenty-four Incarnations. Mihdi, it is said, will appear when the mission of Kalki is fulfilled. The name and the idea are borrowed from the Shia Muhammadans. It occupies somewhat less than a page.

10th. No name entered, but known as the '*Āvatārs of Brāhma*'. An account of seven incarnations of Brāhma, followed by some account of eight Rājās of bygone times. It occupies about 18 pages.

The names of the incarnations are as follows:

1. Valkmik.
2. Kashap.
3. Shukar.
4. Batchess.
5. Vyasi.
6. Khasht Rikhi (or the Six Sages).
7. Kaul Dās.

The kings are enumerated below:

1. Manu.
2. Prithu.
3. Sagar.
4. Bēn.
5. Māndhāt.
6. Dalīp.
7. Ragh.
8. Aj.

11th. No name entered, but known as the '*Āvatārs of Rudr or Siva*'. It comprises 56 pages; and two incarnations only are mentioned, namely, Dat and Pārasnāth.

12th. '*Shastr Nam Mala*', or the Name-string of Weapons. The names of the various weapons are recapitulated, the weapons are praised, and Gobind terms them collectively his Gurū or guide. The composition nevertheless is not attributed to Gobind. It occupies about 68 pages.

13th. '*Sri Mukh Vāk, Sawaya Battis*', or the Voice of the Gurū (Gobind) himself, in thirty-two verses. These verses were composed by Gobind as declared, and they are condemnatory of the Vedas, the Purāns, and the Kurān. They occupy about 3½ pages.

14th. '*Hazāra Shabd*', or the Thousand Verses of the Metre called Shabd. There are, however, but ten verses only in most *Granths*, occupying about 2 pages. Hazār is not understood in its literal sense of a thousand, but as implying invaluable or excellent. They are laudatory of the Creator and creation, and deprecate the adoration of saints and limitary divinities. They were written by Gurū Gobind.

15th. '*Istri Charitr*', or Tales of Women. There are 404 stories, illustrative of the character and disposition of women. A stepmother became enamoured of her stepson, the heir of a monarchy, who, however, would not gratify her desires, whereupon she represented to her husband that his first-born had made attempts upon her honour. The Rājā ordered his son to be put to death; but his ministers interfered, and procured a respite. They then enlarged in a series of stories upon the nature of women, and at length the Rājā became sensible of the guilt of his wife's mind, and of his own rashness. These stories occupy 446 pages, or nearly half of the *Granth*. The name of Sham also occurs as the writer of one or more of them.

16th. The '*Hikayats*', or Tales. These comprise twelve stories in 866 slōks of two lines each. They are written in the Persian language and Gurmukhi character, and they were composed by Gobind himself as admonitory of Aurangzeb, and were sent to the emperor by the hands of Daya Singh and four other Sikhs. The tales were accompanied by a letter written in a pointed manner, which, however, does not form a portion of the *Granth*.

These tales occupy about 30 pages, and conclude the *Granth* of Gurū Gobind.

APPENDIX XIX

SOME PRINCIPLES OF BELIEF AND PRACTICE, AS EXEMPLIFIED IN THE OPINIONS OF THE SIKH GURŪS OR TEACHERS

With an Addendum, showing the modes in which the missions of Nānak and Gobind are represented or regarded by the Sikhs.

1. *God—the Godhead*

THE True Name is God; without fear, without enmity; the Being without Death, the Giver of Salvation; the Gurū and Grace.

Remember the primal Truth ; Truth which was before the world began,
Truth which is, and Truth, O Nānak ! which will remain.
By reflection it cannot be understood, if times innumerable it be considered.
By meditation it cannot be attained, how much soever the attention be fixed.
A hundred wisdoms, even a hundred thousand, not one accompanies the dead.
How can Truth be told, how can falsehood be unravelled ?
O Nānak ! by following the will of God, as by Him ordained.

NĀNAK, *Adi Granth*, Japji (commencement of).

One, Self-existent, Himself the Creator.
O Nānak ! one continueth, another never was and never will be. NĀNAK, *Adi Granth*, Gauri Rāg.

Thou art in each thing, and in all places.
O God ! thou art the one Existent Being.

RĀM DĀS, *Adi Granth*, Asa Rāg.

My mind dwells upon One,
He who gave the Soul and the body.

ARJŪN, *Adi Granth*, Sri Rāg.

Time is the only God ; the First and the Last, the Endless Being ; the Creator, the Destroyer ; He who can make and unmake.
God who created Angels and Demons, who created the East and the West, the North and the South, how can He be expressed by words ?

GOBIND, *Hazāra Shabd.*

God is one image (or Being), how can He be conceived in another form ? GOBIND, *Vichitr Nātak.*

2. *Incarnations, Saints, and Prophets ; the Hindu Āvatārs, Muhammad, and Sidhs, and Pīrs*

Numerous Muhammads have there been, and multitudes of Brāhmas, Vishnus, and Sivas,
Thousands of Pīrs and Prophets, and tens of thousands of Saints and Holy men :
But the Chief of Lords is the One Lord, the true Name of God.
O Nānak ! of God, His qualities, without end, beyond reckoning, who can understand ?

NĀNAK, *Ratan Mala* (extra to the *Granth*).

Many Brāhmas wearied themselves with the study of the
Vēdas, but found not the value of an oil seed.
Holy men and Saints sought about anxiously, but they were
deceived by Māya.
There have been, and there have passed away, ten regent
Āvatārs and the wondrous Mahadev.
Even they, wearied with the application of ashes, could not
find Thee. ARJŪN, *Adi Granth*, Sūhi.

Surs and Sidhs and the Devtas of Siva; Shaikhs and Pīrs
and men of might,
Have come and have gone, and others are likewise passing
by. ARJŪN, *Adi Granth*, Sri Rāg.

Krishna indeed slew demons; he performed wonders, and he declared himself to be Brāhm; yet he should not be regarded as the Lord. He himself died; how can he save those who put faith in him? How can one sunk in the ocean sustain another above the waves? God alone is all-powerful: he can create, and he can destroy.

GOBIND, *Hazāra Shabd*.

God, without friends, without enemies,
Who heeds not praise, nor is moved by curses,
How could He become manifest as Krishna?
How could He, without parents, without offspring, become
born to a 'Devki'? GOBIND, *Hazāra Shabd*.

Rām and Rahim[1] (names repeated) cannot give salvation.
Brāhma, Vishnu and Siva, the Sun and the Moon, all are in
the power of Death. GOBIND, *Hazāra Shabd*.

3. *The Sikh Gurūs not to be worshipped*

He who speaks of me as the Lord,
Him will I sink into the pit of Hell!
Consider me as the slave of God:
Of that have no doubt in thy mind.
I am but the slave of the Lord,
Come to behold the wonders of Creation.

GOBIND, *Vichitr Nātak*.

4. *Images, and the Worship of Saints*

Worship not another (than God); bow not to the Dead.

NĀNAK, *Adi Granth*, Sorth Ragni.

[1] The Merciful, i.e. the God of the Muhammadans.

To worship an image, to make pilgrimages to a shrine, to remain in a desert and yet to have the mind impure, is all in vain, and thus thou canst not be accepted. To be saved thou must worship Truth (God).—Nānak, *Adi Granth*, Bhōg; in which, however, he professes to quote a learned Brāhman.

Man, who is a beast of the field, cannot comprehend Him whose power is of the Past, the Present, and the Future.

God is worshipped, that by worship salvation may be attained.
Fall at the feet of God; in senseless stone God is not.
Gobind, *Vichitr Nātak*.

5. *Miracles*

To possess the power of a Sidhi (or changer of shapes),
To be as a Ridhi (or giver away of never-ending stores),
And yet to be ignorant of God, I do not desire.
All such things are vain.
Nānak, *Adi Granth*, Sri Rāg.

Dwell thou in flames uninjured,
Remain unharmed amid ice eternal,
Make blocks of stone thy daily food,
Spurn the Earth before thee with thy foot,
Weigh the Heavens in a balance;
And then ask of me to perform miracles.
Nānak, to a challenger about miracles;
Adi Granth, Majh Var.

6. *Transmigration*

Life is like the wheel circling on its pivot,
O Nānak! of going and coming there is no end.
Nanak, *Adi Granth*, Asa. (Numerous other passages of a like kind might be quoted from Nānak and his successors.)

He who knows not the One God
Will be born again times innumerable.
Gobind, *Mihdi Mīr*.

7. *Faith*

Eat and clothe thyself, and thou may'st be happy;
But without fear and faith there is no salvation.
Nānak, *Adi Granth*, Sohila Maru Rāg.

8. *Grace*

O Nānak! he, on whom God looks, finds the Lord.
NĀNAK, *Adi Granth*, Asa Rāg.

O Nānak! he, on whom God looks, will fix his mind on the Lord.
AMAR DĀS, *Adi Granth*, Bilawal.

9. *Predestination*

According to the fate of each, dependent on his actions, are his coming and going determined.
NĀNAK, *Adi Granth*, Asa.

How can Truth be told? how can falsehood be unravelled?
O Nānak! by following the will of God, as by Him ordained.
NĀNAK, *Adi Granth*, Japji.

10. *The Vēdas, the Purāns, and the Korān.*

Pōthis, Simrats, Vēdas, Purāns,
Are all as nothing, if unleavened by God.
NĀNAK, *Adi Granth*, Gauri Rāg.

Give ear to Shastars and Vēdas, and Korāns,
And thou may'st reach 'Swarg and Nark'.
(i. e. to the necessity of coming back again.)
Without God, salvation is unattainable.
NĀNAK, *Ratan Mala* (an Extra book of the *Adi Granth*).

Since he fell at the feet of God, no one has appeared great in his eyes.
Rām and Rahim, the Purāns, and the Korān, have many votaries, but neither does he regard.
Simrats, Shastars, and Vēdas, differ in many things; not one does he heed.
O God! under Thy favour has all been done; naught is of myself.
GOBIND, *Rah Rās*.

11. *Asceticism*

A householder[1] who does no evil,
Who is ever intent upon good,
Who continually exerciseth charity,
Such a householder is pure as the Ganges.
NĀNAK, *Adi Granth*, Rām Kali Rāgni.

[1] i.e. in English idiom, one of the laity; one who fulfils the ordinary duties of life.

Householders and Hermits are equal, whoever calls on the name of the Lord.

NĀNAK, *Adi Granth*, Asa Rāgni.

Be 'Udās' (i.e. disinterested) in thy mind in the midst of householdership.

AMAR DĀS, *Adi Granth*, Sri Rāg.

12. *Caste*

Think not of race, abase thyself, and attain to salvation.

NĀNAK, *Adi Granth*, Sarang Rāg.

God will not ask man of his birth,
He will ask him what has he done.

NĀNAK, *Adi Granth*, Parbhāti Rāgni.

Of the impure among the noblest
Heed not the injunction;
Of one pure among the most despised
Nānak will become the footstool.

NĀNAK, *Adi Granth*, Malhār Rāg.

All say that there are four races,
But all are of the seed of Brāhm.
The world is but clay,
And of similar clay many pots are made.
Nānak says man will be judged by his actions,
And that without finding God there will be no salvation.
The body of man is composed of the five elements;
Who can say that one is high and another low?

AMAR DĀS, *Adi Granth*, Bhairav.

I will make the four races of one colour,
I will cause them to remember the words, 'Wah Gurū'.

GOBIND, in the *Rahat Nama*, which, however, is not included in the *Granth*.

13. *Food*

O Nānak! the right of strangers is the one the Ox, and the other the Swine.
Gurūs and Pīrs will bear witness to their disciples when they eat naught which had enjoyed life.

NĀNAK, *Adi Granth*, Māj.

An animal slain without cause cannot be proper food.
O Nānak! from evil doth evil ever come.

NĀNAK, *Adi Granth*, Māj.

14. *Brāhmans, Saints, &c.*

That Brāhman is a son of Brāhm,
Whose rules of action are devotion, prayer, and purity ;
Whose principles of faith are humility, and contentment.
Such a Brāhman may break prescribed rules, and yet find salvation. NĀNAK, *Adi Granth*, Bhog.

The cotton [1] should be mercy, the thread contentedness, and the seven knots virtue.
If there is such a ' Janeū ' of the heart, wear it ;
It will neither break, nor burn, nor decay, nor become impure.
O Nānak ! he who wears such a thread is to be numbered with the holy. NĀNAK, *Adi Granth*, Asa.

Devotion is not in the Kinta (or ragged garment), nor in the Danda (or staff), nor in Bhasm (or ashes), nor in the shaven head (Mundi), nor in the sounding of horns (Singheh weieh). NĀNAK, *Adi Granth*, Suhi.

In this age few Brāhmans are of Brāhm (i.e. are pure and holy). AMAR DĀS, *Adi Granth*, Bilāwal.

The Sanyāsi should consider his home the jungle.
His heart should not yearn after material forms :
Gyan (or Truth) should be his Gurū.
His Bhabut (or ashes) should be the name of God,
And he should neither be held to be ' Sat-juni ', nor ' Raj-juni ', nor ' Tamh-juni ' (that is, should neither seem good for his own profit only, nor good or bad as seemed expedient at the time, nor bad that he might thereby gain his ends). GOBIND, *Hazāra Shabd.*

15. *Infanticide*

—— With the slayers of daughters
Whoever has intercourse, him do I curse.

And again—

Whosoever takes food from the slayers of daughters,
Shall die unabsolved.
GOBIND, *Rahat Nāma*. (Extra to the *Granth.*)

16. *Satī*

They are not Satīs who perish in the flames.
O Nānak ! Satīs are those who die of a broken heart.

[1] Viz. the cotton of the Brāhmanical thread, or janeū.

And again—

The loving wife perishes with the body of her husband.
But were her thoughts bent upon God, her sorrows would be alleviated. AMAR DĀS, *Adi Granth*, Suhi.

ADDENDUM

Bhai Gurdās Bhalla's mode of representing the Mission of Nānak

There were four races and four creeds [1] in the world among Hindus and Muhammadans;
Selfishness, jealousy, and pride drew all of them strongly:
The Hindus dwelt on Benares and the Ganges, the Muhammadans on the Kaba;
The Muhammadans held by circumcision, the Hindus by strings and frontal marks.
They each called on Rām and Rahim, one name, and yet both forgot the road.
Forgetting the Vēdas and the Korān, they were inveigled in the snares of the world.
Truth remained on one side, while Mullas and Brāhmans disputed,
And Salvation was not attained.

. . . . .
. . . . .

God heard the complaint (of virtue or truth), and Nānak was sent into the world.
He established the custom that the disciple should wash the feet of his Gurū, and drink the water;
Pār Brāhm and Puran Brāhm, in this Kalyug, he showed were one,
The four Feet (of the animal sustaining the world) were made of Faith; the four castes were made one;
The high and the low became equal; the salutation of the feet (among disciples) he established in the world: [2]

[1] The four *races* of Saiyids, Shaikhs, Mughals, and Pathāns are here termed as of four creeds, and likened to the four castes or races of the Hindus. It is, indeed, a common saying that such a thing is 'harām-i-chār Mazhab', or forbidden among the four faiths or sects of Muhammadans. Originally the expression had reference to the four orthodox schools of Sunnīs, formed by the expounders Abu Hanifa, Hanbal, Shafei, and Mālik, and it still has such an application among the learned, but the commonalty of India understand it to apply to the four castes or races into which they have divided themselves.

[2] The Akālis still follow this custom.

Contrary to the nature of man, the feet were exalted above the head.
In the Kalyug he gave salvation : using the only true Name, he taught men to worship the Lord.
To give salvation in the Kalyug Gurū Nānak came.

NOTE.—The above extracts, and several others from the book of Bhai Gurdas, may be seen in Malcolm's *Sketch of the Sikhs*, p. 152, &c.; rendered, however, in a less literal manner than has here been attempted.

The book contains forty chapters, written in different kinds of verse, and it is the repository of many stories about Nānak which the Sikhs delight to repeat. One of these is as follows :

Nānak again went to Mecca ; blue clothing he wore, like Krishna ;
A staff in his hand, a book by his side ; the pot, the cup, and the mat, he also took :
He sat where the Pilgrims completed the final act of their pilgrimage,
And when he slept at night he lay with his feet towards the front.
Jīwan struck him with his foot, saying, 'Ho! what infidel sleeps here,
With his feet towards the Lord, like an evil doer?'
—Seizing him by the leg, he drew him aside; then Mecca also turned, and a miracle was declared.
All were astonished, &c., &c.

Gurū Gobind's mode of representing his Mission. (From the *Vichitr Nātak*, with an extract from the Twenty-four Incarnations, regarding the last Āvatār and the succeeding Mihdi Mīr.)

NOTE.—The first four chapters are occupied with a mythological account of the Sōdhi and Bedi subdivisions of the Kshattriya race, the rulers of the Punjab at Lahore and Kasūr, and the descendants of Lau and Kusu, the sons of Rām, who traced his descent through Dasrath, Raghu, Suraj, and others, to Kalsain, a primaeval monarch. So far as regards the present object, the contents may be summed up in the promise or prophecy, that in the Kalyug Nānak would bestow blessings on the Sōdhis, and would, on his fourth mortal appearance, become one of that tribe.[1]

[1] Cf. the translations given in Malcolm's *Sketch*, p. 174, &c.

Chapter V (abstract).—The Brāhmans began to follow the ways of Sudras, and Kshattriya of Vaisas, and, similarly, the Sudras did as Brāhmans, and the Vaisas as Kshattriyas. In the fullness of time Nānak came and established his own sect in the world. He died, but he was born again as Angad, and a third time as Amar Dās, and at last he appeared as Rām Dās, as had been declared, and the Gurūship became inherent in the Sōdhis. Nānak thus put on other habiliments, as one lamp is lighted at another. Apparently there were four Gurūs, but, in truth, in each body there was the soul of Gurū Nānak. When Rām Dās departed, his son Arjūn became Gurū, who was followed successively by Har Gobind, Har Rai, Har Kishan, and Tegh Bahādar, who gave his life for his faith in Delhi, having been put to death by the Muhammadans.

Chapter VI (abstract).—In the Bhim Khund, near the Seven Sring (or Peaks), where the Pandus exercised sovereignty (the unembodied soul of) Gurū Gobind Singh implored the Almighty, and became absorbed in the Divine essence (or obtained salvation without the necessity of again appearing on earth). Likewise the parents of the Gurū prayed to the Lord continually. God looked on them with favour, and (the soul of) Gobind was called from the Seven Peaks to become one of mankind.

Then my wish was not to reappear,
For my thoughts were bent upon the feet of the Almighty ;
But God made known to me his desires.

The Lord said, 'When mankind was created, the Daitayas were sent for the punishment of the wicked, but the Daitayas being strong, forgot me their God. Then the Devtas were sent, but they caused themselves to be worshipped by men as Siva, and Brāhma, and Vishnu. The Sidhs were afterwards born, but they, following different ways, established many sects. Afterwards Gorakhnāth appeared in the world, and he, making many kings his disciples, established the sect of Joghis. Rāmānand then came into the world, and he established the sect of Bairāgis after his own fashion. Muhadin (Muhammad) too was born, and became lord of Arabia. He established a sect, and required his followers to repeat his name. Thus, they who were sent to guide mankind, perversely adopted modes of their own, and misled the world. None taught the right way to the ignorant; wherefore thou, O Gobind! hast been called, that thou mayst propagate the worship of the One True God, and guide those who have lost the road.' Hence I, Gobind, have come into the world, and have established a sect, and have laid down its customs ; but whosoever regards me as the Lord shall be dashed into the pit of hell, for I am but as other men, a beholder of the wonders of creation.

[Gobind goes on to declare that he regarded the religions of the Hindus and Muhammadans as naught; that Jōgis, and the readers of Korāns and Purāns, were but deceivers; that no faith was to be put in the worship of images and stones. All religions, he says, had become corrupt; the Sannyasi and Bairāgi equally showed the wrong way, and the modes of worship of Brāhmans and Kshattriyas and others were idle and vain. 'All shall pass into hell, for God is not in books and scriptures, but in humility and truthfulness.'

The subsequent chapters, to the 13th inclusive, relate the wars in which Gobind was engaged with the Rājās of the hills and the imperial forces.]

Chapter XIV (abstract).—O God! thou who hast always preserved thy worshippers from evil, and hast inflicted punishment on the wicked; who hast regarded me as thy devoted slave and hast served me with thine own hand, now all that I have beheld, and all thy glories which I have witnessed, will I faithfully relate. What I beheld in the former world, by the blessing of God will I make known. In all my undertakings the goodness of the Lord hath been showered upon me. Loh (iron) has been my preserver. Through the goodness of God have I been strong, and all that I have seen during the various ages will I put in a book; everything shall be fully made known.

Extract from the Twenty-four Āvatārs

Kalki (conclusion of).—Kalki at last became strong and proud, and the Lord was displeased, and created another Being. Mihdi Mīr was created, great and powerful, who destroyed Kalki, and became master of the world. All is in the hands of God. In this manner passed away the twenty-four manifestations.

Mihdi Mīr.—In such manner was Kalki destroyed, but God manifests himself at all times, and at the end of the Kalyug, all will be his own.[1] When Mihdi Mīr had vanquished the world he became raised up in his mind. He assumed to himself the crown of greatness and power, and all bowed to him. He regarded himself as supreme. He taught not of God, but considered himself to be in all things and to exist everywhere. Then the Almighty seized the fool. God is One. He is without a second. He is everywhere, in the water and under the earth. He who knows not the One God, will be

[1] Nij jōt, jōt sumān.

born again times innumerable. In the end God took away the power of Mihdi Mīr, and destroyed him utterly.

A creeping worm did the Lord create;
By the ear of Mihdi it went and stayed:
The worm entered by his ear,
And he was wholly subdued.

APPENDIX XX

THE ADMONITORY LETTERS OF NĀNAK TO THE FABULOUS MONARCH KARUN; AND THE PRESCRIPTIVE LETTERS OF GOBIND FOR THE GUIDANCE OF THE SIKHS

NOTE.—Two letters to Karun are attributed to Nānak. The first is styled the 'Nasihat Nāma', or Letter of Admonition and Advice. The second is styled simply the 'Reply of Nānak', and professes to be spoken. Karun may possibly be a corruption of Harun, the 'Harun el Rashid' of European and Asiatic fame. Both compositions are of course fabulous as regards Nānak, and appear to be the compositions of the commencement or middle of the last century.

The two letters of Gobind are termed the 'Rahat Nāma' and the 'Tankha Nāma', or the Letter of Rules and the Letter of Fines respectively; and while they are adapted for general guidance, they profess to have been drawn up in reply to questions put by individuals, or for the satisfaction of particular inquirers. There is no evidence that they were composed by Gobind himself; but they may be held to represent his views and the principles of Sikhism.

1. *The Nasihat Nāma of Nānak, or the Letter to Karun, the Mighty Prince, possessing forty Capital Cities replenished with Treasure.* (Extracts from.)

Alone man comes, alone he goes.
When he departs naught will avail him (or bear him witness).
When the reckoning is taken, what answer will he give?
If then only he repents, he shall be punished.

. . . . .
. . . . .

Karun paid no devotions; he kept not faith:
The world exclaimed he ruled not justly.
He was called a Ruler, but he governed not well,

For the pleasures of the world ensnared him.
He plundered the earth : hell-fire shall torment him.

. . . . .
. . . . .

Man should do good, so that he be not ashamed.
Repent—and oppress not,
Otherwise hell-fire shall seize thee, even in the grave.

. . . . .

Holy men, Prophets, Shāhs, and Khāns,
The mark of not one remaineth in the world ;
For man is but as the passing shade of the flying bird.

. . . . .

Thou rejoicest in thy Forty Treasures,
See, oh people ! Karun utterly confounded.
O Nānak ! pray unto God, and seek God as thy refuge.

2. *The Reply of Nānak to Karun, the Lord of Medina*

First, Nānak went to Mecca ;
Medina he afterwards visited.
The lord of Mecca and Medina,
Karun, he made his disciple.
When Nānak was about to depart,
Karun, the fortunate, thus spoke :
Now thou art about to go,
But when wilt thou return ?
Then the Gurū thus answered :
When I put on my tenth dress
I shall be called Gobind Singh ;
Then shall all Singhs wear their hair ;
They shall accept the 'Pāhal' of the two-edged dagger :
Then shall the sect of the Khālsa be established ;
Then shall men exclaim, 'Victory, O Gurū !'
The four races shall become one and the same ;
The five weapons shall be worn by all.
In the Kalyug they shall array themselves in vestments of blue ;
The name of the Khālsa shall be everywhere.
In the time of Aurangzeb
The wondrous Khālsa shall arise.
Then shall battles be waged,
Endless war shall ensue,
And fighting shall follow year after year.
They shall place the name of Gobind Singh in their hearts ;
Many heads shall be rendered up,
And the empire of the Khālsa shall prevail.

First, the Punjab shall become the land of the Sikhs ;
Then other countries shall be theirs ;
Hindustan and the North shall be possessed by them ;
Then the West shall bow to them.
When they enter Khorasan,
Kābul and Kandahār shall lie low.
When Irān [1] has been laid prostrate,
Mecca shall be beheld,
And Medina shall be seized.
Mighty shall be the rejoicing,
And all shall exclaim, 'Hail, Gurū !'
Unbelievers shall everywhere be destroyed ;
The holy Khālsa shall be exalted ;
Beasts, and birds, and creeping things, shall tremble (in the presence of the Lord).
Men and women shall everywhere call on God.
The earth, the ocean, and the heavens, shall call on God.
By calling on the Gurū shall men be blessed.
Every faith shall become of the Khālsa ;
No other religion will remain.
'Wah Gurū' shall everywhere be repeated,
And Pain and Trouble shall depart.
In the Kalyug shall the Kingdom be established
Which Nānak received from the Lord.
Worthless, I fall before God ;
Nānak, the slave, cannot comprehend the ways of the Lord.

3. *The Rahat Nāma of Gurū Gobind.* (Extracts from, and abstracts of portions.)

Written for Dariyāī Udasi, and repeated to Prahlād Singh at Apchalnagar (Nader on the Godāvery).

The Gurū, being seated at Apchalnagar, spake to Prahlād Singh, saying, that through the favour of Nānak there was a sect or faith in the world for which rules (rahat) should be established.

A Sikh who puts a cap (topi) [2] on his head, shall die seven deaths of dropsy.

Whosoever wears a thread round his neck is on the way to damnation.

[1] Persia.

[2] Referring particularly to Hindu ascetics ; but, perhaps, also to the Muhammadans, who formerly wore skull-caps alone, and now generally wind their turbans round a covering of the kind. The Sikh contempt for either kind of 'topi' has been thrown into the shade by their repugnance, in common with all other Indians, to the English cap or hat.

[It is forbidden to take off the turban (pag) while eating, to have intercourse with Minas, Massandis, and Kurimars (children slayers), and to play at chess with women.

No prayers are to be offered up without using the name of the Gurū, and he who heeds not the Gurū, and serves not the disciples faithfully, is a Mlechh indeed.

A Sikh who does not acknowledge the Hukamnama (requisition for benevolences or contributions) of the Gurū shall fall under displeasure.]

First the Gurū (*Granth* or Book) and Khālsa, which I have placed in the world,
Whosoever denies or betrays either shall be driven forth and dashed into hell.

[It is forbidden to wear clothing dyed with safflower (i.e. of a 'Suhi' colour), to wear charms on the head, to break the fast without reciting the Jap (the prayer of Nānak), to neglect reading prayers in the morning, to take the evening meal without reciting the Rah Rās, to leave Akāl Purukh (the Timeless Being) and worship other Gods, to worship stones, to make obeisance to any not a Sikh, to forget the *Granth*, and to deceive the Khālsa.

All Hukamnamas (calls for tithes or contributions) given by the posterity of Nānak, of Angad, and of Amar Dās, shall be heeded as his own: whosoever disregards them shall perish.

The things which he had placed in the world (viz., the *Granth* and the Khālsa) are to be worshipped. Strange Gods are not to be heeded, and the Sikh who forsakes his faith shall be punished in the world to come.

He who worships graves and dead men ('gōr' and 'murri', referring to Muhammadans and Hindus), or he who worships temples (mosques) or stones (images), is not a Sikh.

The Sikh who makes obeisance or bows down to the wearer of a cap (topi) is a resident of hell.]

Consider the Khālsa as the Gurū, as the very embodiment of the Gurū:
He who wishes to see the Gurū will find him in the Khālsa.

[Trust not Jōgi or Turks. Remember the writings of the Gurū only. Regard not the six Darsans (or systems of faith or speculation). Without the Gurū, all Deities are as naught. The Image of the Almighty is the visible body (pragat deh) of the immortal Khālsa (Akal). The Khālsa is everything, other divinities are as sand, which slips through the fingers. By the order of God the Panth (or sect) of Sikhs has been established. All Sikhs must believe the Gurū and the *Granth*. They should bow to the *Granth* alone. All prayers save the prayers of the Gurū are idle and vain.

He who gives the 'Pāhal' to another shall reap innumerable blessings. He who instructs in the prayers and scriptures of the Gurūs shall attain salvation. Gobind will reverence the Sikh who chafes the hands and the feet of the wearied Sikh traveller. The Sikh who gives food to other Sikhs, on him will the Gurū look with favour.

Delivered on Thursday the 5th day of the dark phase of the Moon of Magh in the Sambat year 1752 (beginning of A.D. 1696). He who heeds these injunctions is a Sikh of Gurū Gobind Singh. The orders of the Gurū are as himself. Depend on God.]

4. *The Tankha Nāma, or Letter of Fines or Restrictions on Sikhs.* (Abstract of.)

Written in reply to the question of Bhai Nand Lāl, who had asked Gurū Gobind what it was proper for a Sikh to do, and what to refrain from.

Nand Lāl asked, &c.: and the Gurū replied that such were to be the acts of the Sikhs. A Sikh should set his heart on God, on charity, and on purity (Nām, Dān, Ishnan). He who in the morning does not repair to some temple, or visit some holy man, is greatly to blame. He who does not allow the poor a place (in his heart) is to blame. Without the favour of God nothing can be accomplished. He who bows his head (i.e. humbles himself) after having offered up prayers is a man of holiness. Charity (Karah Prasād, i.e. food) should be distributed in singleness of mind to all comers equally. Prasād should be prepared of equal parts of flour, sugar, and butter. The preparer should first bathe, and while cooking it he should repeat 'Wah Gurū' continually. When ready, the food should be put on a round place.

The Sikh who wears the (written) charms of the Turks, or who touches iron with his feet, is to be condemned. He who wears clothing dyed with safflower (of the colour called Suhi), and he who takes snuff (naswār), is to be condemned.[1]

He who looks lustfully upon the mother or sister of one of the brethren—he who does not bestow his daughter becomingly in marriage—he who takes to himself the property of a sister or daughter—he who wears not iron in some shape —he who robs or oppresses the poor, and he who makes obeisance to a Turk, is to be punished.

[1] This is the only recorded prohibition against tobacco, to refrain from which in every shape is now a rule. The Afghāns of Peshāwar and Kābul continue to take snuff, a practice but little known to the Indians.

A Sikh should comb his locks, and fold and unfold his turban twice a day. Twice also should he wash his mouth.

One tenth of all goods should be given (in charity) in the name of the Gurū.

Sikhs should bathe in cold water: they should not break their fast until they have repeated the Jap. In the morning Jap, in the evening, Rah Rās, and before retiring to rest, Sohila should always be repeated.

No Sikh should speak false of his neighbour. Promises should be carefully fulfilled.

No Sikh should eat flesh from the hands of the Turks.

A Sikh should not delight in women, nor give himself up to them.

The Sikh who calls himself a Sādh (or Holy man) should act in strict accordance with his professions.

A journey should not be undertaken, nor should business be set about, nor should food be eaten, without first remembering or calling on God.

A Sikh should enjoy the society of his own wife only. He should not desire other women.

He who sees a poor man and gives him not something, shall not behold the presence of God.

He who neglects to pray, or who abuses the holy, or who gambles, or who listens to those who speak evil of the Gurūs, is no Sikh.

Daily, some portion of what is gained is to be set aside in the name of the Lord, but all business must be carried on in sincerity and truth.

Flame should not be extinguished with the breath, nor should fire be put out with water, a portion of which has been drunk.

Before meals the name of the Gurū should be repeated. The society of prostitutes is to be avoided, nor is adultery to be committed with the wife of another. The Gurū is not to be forsaken, and others followed. No Sikh should expose his person; he should not bathe in a state of nudity, nor when distributing food should he be naked.[1] His head should always be covered.

He is of the Khālsa,
Who speaks evil to none,
Who combats in the van,
Who gives in charity,
Who slays a Khān,
Who subdues his passions,
Who burns the 'Karms',[2]

[1] The practices of many Hindu ascetics are mainly aimed at.

[2] i.e. who despises the ceremonial forms of the Brāhmans.

Who does not yield to superstitions,[1]
Who is awake day and night,
Who delights in the sayings of the Gurūs,
And who never fears, although often overcome.
Considering all as created by the Lord,
Give offence to none, otherwise the Lord will Himself be offended.

He is of the Khālsa,
Who protects the poor,
Who combats evil,
Who remembers God,
Who achieves greatness,[2]
Who is intent upon the Lord,
Who is wholly unfettered,
Who mounts the war horse,
Who is ever waging battle,
Who is continually armed,
Who slays the Turks,
Who extends the faith,
And who gives his head with what is upon it.
The name of God shall be proclaimed ;
No one shall speak against Him ;
The rivers and the mountains shall remember Him ;
All who call upon Him shall be saved.

O Nand Lāl ! attend to what is said ;
My own rule will I establish,
The four races shall be one,
I will cause all to repeat the prayer of 'Wah Guru'.
The Sikhs of Gobind shall bestride horses, and bear hawks upon their hands,
The Turks who behold them shall fly,
One shall combat a multitude,
And the Sikh who thus perishes shall be blessed for ever.
At the doorway of a Sikh shall wait elephants caparisoned,
And horsemen with spears, and there shall be music over his gateway.
When myriads of matches burn together,
Then shall the Khālsa conquer East and West.
The Khālsa shall rule ; none can resist :
The rebellious shall be destroyed, and the obedient shall have favours heaped upon them.

[1] Hindi Aān, said to correspond with the meaning of the Arabic Aār—one who does not affect to be in any way protected by saints or others. The same term is applied to the brotherhood or mutual dependence of a chief and his followers.

[2] Literally, who resides in state.

APPENDIX XXI

A LIST OF SOME SIKH SECTS OR DENOMINATIONS

(In which, however, some Names or Titles not properly distinctive o an Order are also inserted)

1st. *Udasi.*—Founded by Sri Chand, a son of Nānak. The Udasis were rejected by Amar Dās, as not being genuine Sikhs.

2nd. *Bedi.*—Founded by Lakshmi Dās, another son of Nānak.

3rd. *Tehun.*—Founded by Gurū Angad.

4th. *Bhalla.*—Founded by Gurū Amar Dās.

5th. *Sōdhi.*—Founded by Gurū Rām Dās.

NOTE.—The Bedis, Tihans, Bhallas, and Sōdhis are rather Sikhs of the subdivisions of Kshattriyas, so called (i.e. of the tribes of certain Gurūs), than distinct sects.

6th. *Ramraiya*, seceders who adhered to Rām Rai when Tegh Bahadur became Gurū. They have a considerable establishment in the Lower Himālayas, near Hardwār.

7th. *Banda-Panthi*, i.e. of the sect of Banda, who succeeded Gobind as a temporal leader.

8th. *Masandi.*—Masand is simply the name of a subdivision of the Kshattriya race; but it is also specially applied to the followers of those who resisted Gobind; some say as adherents of Rām Rai, and others as instigators of the Gurū's son to opposition. The more common story, however, is that the Masands were the hereditary stewards of the household of the several Gurūs, and that they became proud and dissipated, but nevertheless arrogated sanctity to themselves, and personally ill-used many Sikhs for not deferring to them; whereupon Gobind, regarding them as irreclaimable, expelled them all except two or three.

9th. *Rangrheta.*—Converts of the Sweeper and some other inferior castes are so called. (See note 4, p. 71, *ante.*)

10th. *Ramdāsi*, i.e. Rao or Rai Dāsi.—Sikhs of the class of Chamārs, or leather-dressers, and who trace to the Rao Dās, or Rai Dās, whose writings are inserted in the *Granth.*

11th. *Mazhabi.*—Converts from Muhammadanism are so called.

12th. *Akāli.*—Worshippers of Akal (God), the most eminent of the orders of Purists or Ascetics.

13th. *Nihang.*—The naked, or pure.

14th. *Nirmale.*—The sinless. One who has acquired this title usually administers the Pāhal to others.

15th. *Gyani*.—The wise, or perfect. A term sometimes applied to Sikhs who are at once learned and pious.

16th. *Suthra Shāhi*.—The true, or pure: said to have been founded by one Sucha, a Brāhman. (See *ante*, note 2, p. 62.)

17th. *Suchidari*.—Likewise the true, or pure: the founder not ascertained.

18th. *Bhai*.—Literally, brother. The ordinary title of all Sikhs who have acquired a name for holiness; and it is scarcely the distinctive title of a sect, or even of an order.

To these may perhaps be added bodies of men who attach themselves to particular temples, or who claim to have been founded by particular disciples of eminence, or by followers who obtained any distinctive title from a Gurū. Thus some claim to represent *Rām Dās*, the companion of Nānak, who lived till the time of Arjūn, and who obtained the title of 'Budha', or Ancient. Also many hereditary musicians call themselves *Rabābi Sikhs*, from the Rabāb, or particular instrument on which they play; and these affect to regard Mardāna, the companion of Nānak, as their founder. Others are called *Diwāne*, or the Simple or Mad, from one assiduous as a collector of the contributions of the faithful for the service of the Gurūs, and who, while so employed, placed a peacock's feather in his turban. Another class is called *Musaddi* (or, perhaps, Mutasaddi, i.e. the clerk or writer order), and it is stated to be composed of devotees of the Muhammadan religion, who have adopted the 'Jap' of Nānak as their rule of faith. The Musaddis are further said to have fixed abodes in the countries westward of the Indus.

APPENDIX XXII

GENEALOGICAL TABLE OF THE GURŪS.

NOTE.—The names of the Gurūs are included in rectangles of continuous lines; and the pretenders to apostolical succession to the present time are shown in rectangles of waved lines.

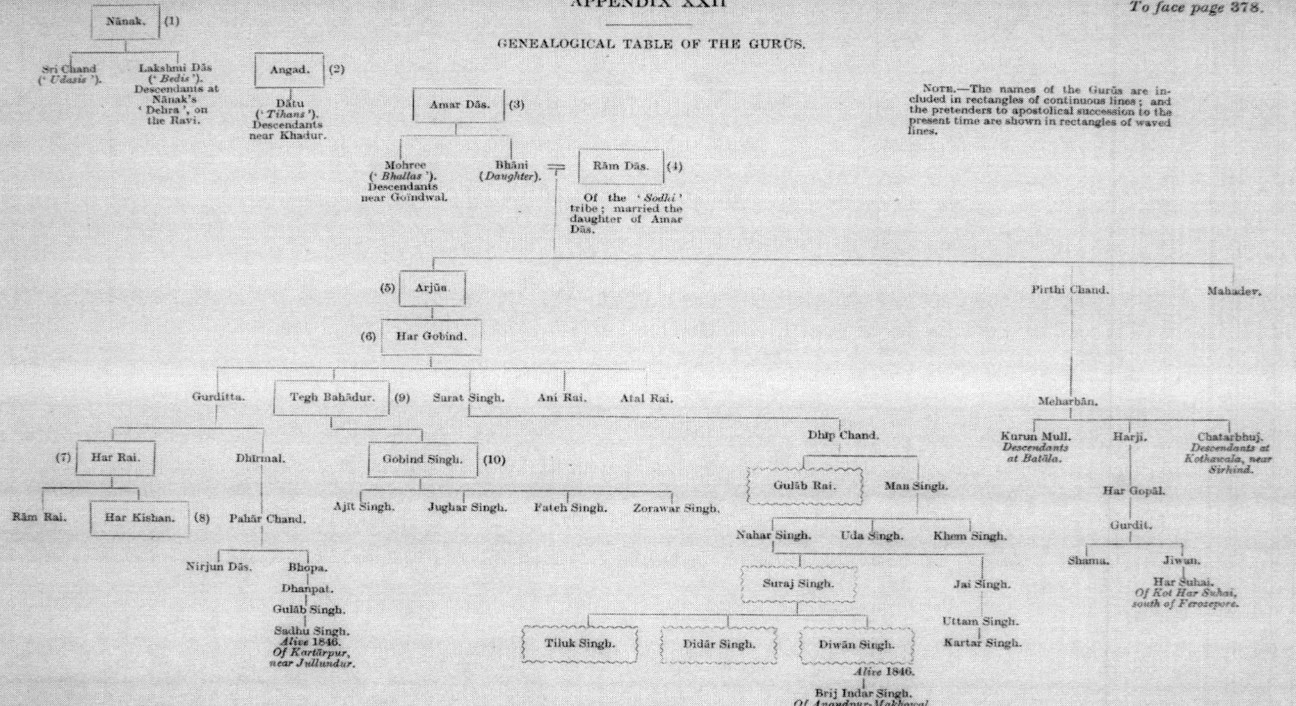

APPENDIX XXIII

THE TREATY WITH LAHORE OF 1806

Treaty of Friendship and Unity between the Honourable East India Company and the Sardars Ranjīt Singh and Fateh Singh. (1st January 1806.)

SARDAR Ranjīt Singh and Sardar Fateh Singh have consented to the following articles of agreement, concluded by Lieutenant-Colonel John Malcolm, under the special authority of the Right Honourable Lord Lake, himself duly authorized by the Honourable Sir George Hilaro Barlow, Bart., Governor-General, and Sardar Fateh Singh, as principal on the part of himself, and plenipotentiary on the part of Ranjīt Singh :

Article 1.—Sardar Ranjīt Singh and Sardar Fateh Singh Ahluwalia, hereby agree that they will cause Jaswant Rāo Holkar to remove with his army to the distance of thirty coss from Amritsar immediately, and will never hereafter hold any further connexion with him, or aid or assist him with troops, or in any other manner whatever ; and they further agree that they will not in any way molest such of Jaswant Rāo Holkar's followers or troops as are desirous of returning to their homes in the Deccan, but, on the contrary, will render them every assistance in their power for carrying such intention into execution.

Article 2.—The British Government hereby agrees, that in case a pacification should not be effected between that Government and Jaswant Rāo Holkar, the British army shall move from its present encampment, on the banks of the river Biah, as soon as Jaswant Rāo Holkar aforesaid shall have marched his army to the distance of thirty coss from Amritsar; and that, in any treaty which may hereafter be concluded between the British Government and Jaswant Rāo Holkar, it shall be stipulated that, immediately after the conclusion of the said treaty, Holkar shall evacuate the territories of the Sikhs, and march towards his own, and that he shall in no way whatever injure or destroy such parts of the Sikh country as may lie in his route. The British Government further agrees that, as long as the said Chieftains, Ranjīt Singh and Fateh Singh, abstain from holding any friendly connexion with the enemies of that Government, or from committing any act of hostility on their own parts against the said Government, the British armies shall never enter the territories of the said Chieftains, nor will the British Government form any plans for the seizure or sequestration of their possessions or property.

Dated 1st January 1806.

APPENDIX XXIV

SIR DAVID OCHTERLONY'S PROCLAMATION OF 1809

Precept or 'Ittila Nāma', under the Seal of General St. Leger, and under the Seal and Signature of Colonel Ochterlony; written the 9th of February 1809, corresponding to the 23rd Zī Hijeh, 1223, Hijri.

THE British army having encamped near the frontiers of the Mahārājā Ranjīt Singh, it has been thought proper to signify the pleasure of the British Government, by means of this precept, in order to make all the Chiefs of the Mahārājā acquainted with the sentiments of the British Government, which have solely for their object and aim to confirm the friendship with the Mahārājā, and to prevent any injury to his country, the preservation of friendship between the two States depending on particular conditions which are hereby detailed.

The Thānas in the fortress of Kharar, Khānpur, and other places on this side of the river Sutlej, which have been placed in the hands of the dependants of the Mahārājā, shall be razed, and the same places restored to their ancient possessors.

The force of cavalry and infantry which may have crossed to this side of the Sutlej must be recalled to the other side, to the country of the Mahārājā.

The troops stationed at the Ghat of Phillaur must march thence, and depart to the other side of the river as described, and in future the troops of the Mahārājā shall never advance into the country of the Chiefs situated on this side of the river, who have called in for their security and protection Thānas of the British Government; but if in the manner that the British have placed Thānas of moderate number on this side of the Sutlej, if in like manner a small force by way of Thāna be stationed at the Ghat of Phillaur, it will not be objected to.

If the Mahārājā persevere in the fulfilment of the above stipulations, which he so repeatedly professed to do in presence of Mr. Metcalfe, such fulfilment will confirm the mutual friendship. In case of non-compliance with these stipulations, then shall it be plain that the Mahārājā has no regard for the friendship of the British, but, on the contrary, resolves on enmity. In such case the victorious British army shall commence every mode of defence.

The communication of this precept is solely with the view of publishing the sentiments of the British, and to know those of the Mahārājā. The British are confident that the

Mahārājā will consider the contents of this precept as abounding to his real advantage, and as affording a conspicuous proof of their friendship; that with their capacity for war, they are also intent on peace.

NOTE.—The recorded translation of this document has been preserved, although somewhat defective in style.

APPENDIX XXV

THE TREATY WITH LAHORE OF 1809

Treaty between the British Government and the Rājā of Lahore. (Dated 25th April 1809.)

WHEREAS certain differences which had arisen between the British Government and the Rājā of Lahore have been happily and amicably adjusted; and both parties being anxious to maintain relations of perfect amity and concord, the following articles of treaty, which shall be binding on the heirs and successors of the two parties, have been concluded by the Rājā Ranjīt Singh in person, and by the agency of C. T. Metcalfe, Esquire, on the part of the British Government.

Article 1.—Perpetual friendship shall subsist between the British Government and the State of Lahore: the latter shall be considered, with respect to the former, to be on the footing of the most favoured powers, and the British Government will have no concern with the territories and subjects of the Rājā to the northward of the river Sutlej.

Article 2.—The Rājā will never maintain in the territory which he occupies on the left bank of the river Sutlej more troops than are necessary for the internal duties of that territory, nor commit or suffer any encroachments on the possessions or rights of the Chiefs in its vicinity.

Article 3.—In the event of a violation of any of the preceding articles, or of a departure from the rules of friendship, this treaty shall be considered null and void.

Article 4.—This treaty, consisting of four articles, having been settled and concluded at Amritsar, on the 25th day of April 1809, Mr. C. T. Metcalfe has delivered to the Rājā of Lahore a copy of the same in English and Persian, under his seal and signature; and the Rājā has delivered another copy of the same under his seal and signature, and Mr. C. T. Metcalfe engages to procure within the space of two months a copy of the same, duly ratified by the Right Honourable the Governor-General in Council, on the receipt of which by the Rājā, the present treaty shall be deemed complete and binding on both parties, and the copy of it now delivered to the Rājā shall be returned.

APPENDIX XXVI

PROCLAMATION OF PROTECTION TO CIS-SUTLEJ STATES AGAINST LAHORE. (Dated 1809)

Translation of an 'Ittila Nāma', addressed to the Chiefs of the Country of Mālwā and Sirhind, on this Side of the River Sutlej. (3rd May 1809.)

It is clearer than the sun, and better proved than the existence of yesterday, that the marching of a detachment of British troops to this side of the river Sutlej was entirely at the application and earnest entreaty of the several Chiefs, and originated solely from friendly considerations in the British Government, to preserve them in their possessions and independence. A treaty having been concluded, on the 25th of April 1809, between Mr. Metcalfe on the part of the British Government, and Mahārājā Ranjīt Singh, agreeably to the orders of the Right Honourable the Governor-General in Council, I have the pleasure of publishing, for the satisfaction of the Chiefs of the country of Mālwā and Sirhind, the pleasure and resolutions of the British Government, as contained in the seven following articles :

Article 1.—The country of the Chiefs of Mālwā and Sirhind having entered under the British protection, they shall in future be secured from the authority and influence of Mahārājā Ranjīt Singh, conformably to the terms of the treaty.

Article 2.—All the country of the Chiefs thus taken under protection shall be exempted from all pecuniary tribute to the British Government.

Article 3.—The Chiefs shall remain in the full exercise of the same rights and authority in their own possessions which they enjoyed before they were received under the British protection.

Article 4.—Should a British force, on purposes of general welfare, be required to march through the country of the said Chiefs, it is necessary and incumbent that every Chief shall, within his own possessions, assist and furnish, to the full of his power, such force with supplies of grain and other necessaries which may be demanded.

Article 5.—Should an enemy approach from any quarter, for the purpose of conquering this country, friendship and mutual interest require that the Chiefs join the British army with all their force, and, exerting themselves in expelling the enemy, act under discipline and proper obedience.

Article 6.—All European articles brought by merchants from the eastern districts, for the use of the army, shall be allowed to pass, by the Thanedars and Sardars of the several Chiefs, without molestation or the demand of duty.

Article 7.—All horses purchased for the use of cavalry regiments, whether in the district of Sirhind or elsewhere, the bringers of which being provided with sealed 'Rahdaris' from the Resident at Delhi, or officer commanding at Sirhind, shall be allowed to pass through the country of the said Chiefs without molestation or the demand of duty.

APPENDIX XXVII

PROCLAMATION OF PROTECTION TO CIS-SUTLEJ STATES AGAINST ONE ANOTHER. (Dated 1811)

For the Information and Assurance of the Protected Chiefs of the Plains between the Sutlej and Jumna. (22nd August, 1811.)

On the 3rd of May 1809 an 'Ittila Nāma' comprised of seven articles, was issued by the orders of the British Government, purporting that the country of the Sardars of Sirhind and Mālwā having come under their protection, Rājā Ranjīt Singh, agreeably to treaty, had no concern with the possessions of the above Sardars; That the British Government had no intention of claiming Peshkashs or Nazarana, and that they should continue in the full control and enjoyment of their respective possessions: The publication of the above 'Ittila Nāma' was intended to afford every confidence to the Sardars, that the protection of the country was the sole object, that they had no intention of control, and that those having possessions should remain in full and complete enjoyment thereof.

Whereas several Zamindars and other subjects of the Chiefs of this country have preferred complaints to the officers of the British Government, who, having in view the tenor of the above 'Ittila Nāma', have not attended, and will not in future pay attention to them; for instance, on the 15th of June 1811, Dilawar Alī Khān of Samana complained to the Resident of Delhi against the officers of Rājā Sahib Singh for jewels and other property said to have been seized by them, who, in reply, observed that the 'Kasba of Samana being in the Amaldari of Rājā Sahib Singh, his complaint should be made to him'; and also, on the 12th of July 1811, Dasaundha Singh and Gurmukh Singh complained to Colonel Ochterlony, Agent to the Governor-General, against Sardar Charat Singh, for their shares of property, &c.; and, in reply, it was written on the back of their arzī, 'that since, during the period of three years, no claim was preferred against Charat Singh by any of his brothers, nor even the name of any co-partner mentioned; and since it was advertised in the 'Ittila Nāma' delivered to the Sardars, that every Chief should remain in the quiet and full enjoyment of his domains, the petition could not be attended to,'—the insertion of these answers to complaints is intended as examples, and also that it may be impressed on the minds of every Zamindar and other subject, that the attainment of justice is to be expected from their respective Chiefs only, that they may not, in the smallest degree, swerve from the observation of subordination,—It is, therefore, highly incumbent upon the Rājās and other Sardars of this side of the river Sutlej, that they explain this to their respective subjects, and court their confidence, that it may be clear to them, that complaints to the officers of the British Government will be of no avail, and that they consider their respective Sardars as the source of justice, and that, of their free will and accord, they observe uniform obedience.

And whereas, according to the first proclamation, it is not the intention of the British Government to interfere in the possessions of the Sardars of this country, it is nevertheless, for the purpose of meliorating the condition of the community, particularly necessary to give general information, that several Sardars have, since the last incursion of Rājā Ranjīt Singh, wrested the estates of others, and deprived them of their lawful possessions, and that in the restoration, they have used delays until detachments of the British army have been sent to effect restitution, as in the case of the Rānī of Tirah, the Sikhs of Chulian, the Talukas of Karauli and Chehloundy, and the village of Chiba; and the reason of such delays and evasions can only be attributed to the temporary enjoyment of the revenues, and subjecting the owners to irremediable losses,—It is, therefore, by order of the British Government, hereby proclaimed that if any one of the Sardars or others has forcibly taken possession of the estates of others, or otherwise injured the lawful owners, it is necessary that, before the occurrence of any complaint, the proprietor should be satisfied, and by no means to defer the restoration of the property,—in which, however, should delays be made, and the interference of the British authority become requisite, the revenues of the estate from the date of ejection of the lawful proprietor, together with whatever other losses the inhabitants of that place may sustain from the march of troops, shall without scruple be demanded from the offending party; and for disobedience of the present orders, a penalty, according to the circumstances of the case and of the offender, shall be levied, agreeably to the decision of the British Government.

APPENDIX XXVIII

INDUS NAVIGATION TREATY OF 1832

Articles of a Convention established between the Honourable the East India Company, and his Highness the Mahārājā Ranjīt Singh, the Ruler of the Punjab, for the opening of the Navigation of the Rivers Indus and Sutlej. (Originally drafted 26th December 1832.)

By the grace of God, the relations of firm alliance and indissoluble ties of friendship existing between the Honourable the East India Company and his Highness the Mahārājā Ranjīt Singh, founded on the auspicious treaty formerly concluded by Sir T. C. Metcalfe, Bart., and since confirmed in the written pledge of sincere amity presented by the Right Honourable Lord W. G. Bentinck, G.C.B. and G.C.H., Governor-General of British India, at the meeting at Rūpar, are, like the sun, clear and manifest to the whole world, and will continue unimpaired, and increasing in strength from generation to generation:—By virtue of these firmly established bonds of friendship, since the opening of the navigation of the rivers Indus proper (i. e. Indus below the confluence of the Panjnad) and Sutlej (a measure deemed expedient by both States, with a view to promote the general interests of commerce),—has lately been effected through the agency of Captain C. M. Wade, Political Agent at Ludhiāna, deputed by the Right Honourable the Governor-General for that purpose. The following Articles, explanatory of the conditions by which the said navigation is to be regulated, as concerns the nomination of officers, the mode of collecting the duties, and the protection of the trade by that route, have been framed, in order that the officers of the two States employed in their execution may act accordingly:

Article 1.—The provisions of the existing treaty relative to the right bank of the river Sutlej and all its stipulations, together with the contents of the friendly pledge already mentioned, shall remain binding, and a strict regard to preserve the relations of friendship between the two States shall be the ruling principle of action. In accordance with that treaty, the Honourable Company has not, nor will have any concern with the right bank of the river Sutlej.

Article 2.—The tariff which is to be established for the line of navigation in question is intended to apply exclusively to the passage of merchandise by that route, and not to interfere with the transit duties levied on goods proceeding from one bank of the river to the other, nor with the places fixed for their collection : they are to remain as heretofore.

Article 3.—Merchants frequenting the same route, while within the limits of the Mahārājā's government, are required to show a due regard to his authority, as is done by merchants generally, and not to commit any acts offensive to the civil and religious institutions of the Sikhs.

Article 4.—Any one purposing to go the said route will intimate his intention to the agent of either State, and apply for a passport, agreeably to a form to be laid down ; having obtained which, he may proceed on his journey. The merchants coming from Amritsar, and other parts on the right bank of the river Sutlej, are to intimate their intentions to the agent of the Mahārājā, at Harike, or other appointed places, and obtain a passport through him ; and merchants coming from Hindustan, or other parts on the left bank of the river Sutlej, will intimate their intentions to the Honourable Company's agent, and obtain a passport through him. As foreigners, and Hindustanis, and Sardars of the protected Sikh States and elsewhere, are not in the habit of crossing the Sutlej without a passport from the Mahārājā's officers, it is expected that such persons will hereafter also conform to the same rule, and not cross without the usual passports.

Article 5.—A tariff shall be established exhibiting the rate of duties leviable on each description of merchandise, which, after having been approved by both Governments, is to be the standard by which the superintendents and collectors of customs are to be guided.

Article 6.—Merchants are invited to adopt the new route with perfect confidence : no one shall be suffered to molest them or unnecessarily impede their progress, care being taken that they are only detained for the collection of the duties, in the manner stipulated, at the established stations.

Article 7.—The officers who are to be entrusted with the collection of the duties and examination of the goods on the right bank of the river shall be stationed at Mithankot and Harike ; at no other places but these two shall boats in transit on the river be liable to examination or stoppage. When the persons in charge of boats stop of their own accord to take in or give out cargo, the goods will be liable to the local transit duty of the Mahārājā's government, previously to their being landed, as provided in Article 2. The superintendent stationed at Mithankot, having examined the cargo, will levy the established duty, and grant a passport, with a written account of the cargo and freight. On the arrival of the boat at Karike, the superintendent of that station will compare the passport with the cargo; and whatever goods are found in excess will be liable to the payment of the established duty, while the rest, having already paid duty at Mithankot, will pass on free. The same rule shall be observed in respect to merchandise conveyed from Harike by the way of the rivers towards Sind, that whatever may be fixed as the share of duties on the right bank of the river Sutlej, in right of the Mahārājā's own dominions and of those in allegiance to him, the Mahārājā's officers will collect it at the places appointed. With regard to the security and safety of merchants who may adopt this route, the Mahārājā's officers shall afford them every protection in their power; and merchants, on halting for the night on either bank of the Sutlej, are required, with reference to the treaty of friendship which exists between the two States, to give notice, and to show their passport to the Thanedar, or officers in authority at the place, and request protection for themselves: if, notwithstanding this precaution, loss should at any time occur, a strict inquiry will be made, and reclamation sought from those who are blameable. The articles of the present treaty for opening the navigation of the rivers above mentioned, having, agreeably to subsisting relations, been approved by the Right Honourable the Governor-General, shall be carried into execution accordingly.

Dated at Lahore the 26th of December 1832.

[Seal and signature at the top.]

APPENDIX XXIX

SUPPLEMENTARY INDUS NAVIGATION TREATY OF 1834

Draft of a Supplementary Treaty between the British Government and Mahārājā Ranjīt Singh for establishing a Toll on the Indus. (29th November 1834.)

In conformity with the subsisting relations of friendship, as established and confirmed by former treaties, between the Honourable the East India Company and his Highness Mahārājā Ranjīt Singh; and whereas in the 5th article of the treaty concluded at Lahore on the 26th day of December

1832, it was stipulated that a moderate scale of duties should be fixed by the two Governments in concert, to be levied on all merchandise on transit up and down the rivers Indus and Sutlej; the said Governments, being now of opinion that, owing to the inexperience of the people of these countries in such matters, the mode of levying duties then proposed (viz. on the value and quantity of goods) could not fail to give rise to mutual misunderstandings and reclamations, have, with a view to prevent these results, determined to substitute a toll, which shall be levied on all boats, with whatever merchandise laden. The following articles have therefore been adopted as supplementary to the former treaty; and, in conformity with them, each Government engages that the toll shall be levied, and its amount neither be increased nor diminished except by mutual consent.

Article 1.—A toll of 570 Rs. shall be levied on all boats laden with merchandise in transit on the rivers Indus and Sutlej between the sea and Rūpar, without reference to their size, or to the weight or value of their cargo; the above toll to be divided among the different States in proportion to the extent of territory which they possess on the banks of these rivers.

Article 2.—The portion of the above toll appertaining to the Lahore Chief in right of his territory on both banks of these rivers, as determined in the subjoined scale, shall be levied opposite to Mithankot on boats coming from the sea towards Rūpar, and in the vicinity of Harike-Pattan on boats going from Rūpar towards the sea, and at no other place:—

In right of territory on the right bank of the rivers Indus and Sutlej, 155 Rs. 4 ans.

In right of territory on the left bank of the rivers Indus and Sutlej, the Mahārājā's share, of 67 Rs. 15 ans. 9 pie.

Article 3.—In order to facilitate the realization of the toll due to the different States, as well as for the speedy and satisfactory adjustment of any disputes which may arise connected with the safety of the navigation and the welfare of the trade by the new route, a British officer will reside opposite to Mithankot, and a native agent on the part of the British Government opposite to Harike-Pattan. These officers will be subject to the orders of the British agent at Ludhiāna; and the agents who may be appointed to reside at those places on the part of the other States concerned in the navigation, viz. Bahāwalpur and Sind, together with those of Lahore, will co-operate with them in the execution of their duties.

Article 4.—In order to guard against imposition on the part of merchants in making false complaints of being plundered of property which formed no part of their cargoes, they are required, when taking out their passports, to produce an invoice of their cargo, which being duly authenticated, a copy of it will be annexed to their passports; and wherever their boats may be brought to for the night, they are required to give immediate notice to the Thanedars or officers of the place, and to request protection for themselves, at the same time showing the passports they may have received at Mithankot or Harike, as the case may be.

Article 5.—Such parts of the 5th, 7th, 9th, and 10th articles of the treaty of the 26th of December 1832 as have reference to the fixing a duty on the value and quantity of merchandise, and to the mode of its collection, are hereby rescinded, and the foregoing articles substituted in their place, agreeably to which and the conditions of the preamble the toll will be levied.

N.B.—A distribution of the shares due to the British protected States and the feudatories of the Mahārājā on the left bank of the Sutlej will be determined hereafter.

APPENDIX XXX

THE TRIPARTITE TREATY WITH RANJĪT SINGH AND SHĀH SHUJĀ OF 1838

Treaty of Alliance and Friendship between Mahārājā Ranjīt Singh and Shāh Shujā-ud-Mulk, with the approbation of and in concert with the British Government.

(Done at Lahore, 26th June 1838, signed at Simla, 25th June 1838.)

WHEREAS a treaty was formerly concluded between Mahārājā Ranjīt Singh and Shāh Shujā-ul-Mulk, consisting of fourteen articles, exclusive of the preamble and the conclusion: And whereas the execution of the provisions of the said treaty was suspended for certain reasons: And whereas at this time, Mr. W. H. Macnaghten having been deputed by the Right Honourable George, Lord Auckland, G.C.B., Governor-General of India, to the presence of Mahārājā Ranjīt Singh, and vested with full powers to form a treaty, in a manner consistent with the friendly engagements subsisting between the two States, the treaty aforesaid is revived, and concluded with certain modifications, and four new articles have been added thereto, with the approbation of and in concert with the British Government, the provisions whereof, ascertained in the following eighteen articles, will be duly and faithfully observed :

Article 1.—Shāh Shujā-ul-Mulk disclaims all title on the part of himself, his heirs and successors, and all the Saddozies, to all the territories lying on either bank of the river Indus, that may be possessed by the Mahārājā, viz. Kashmīr, including its limits, E., W., N., S., together with the fort of Attock, Chach-Hazāra, Khabal, Amb, with its dependencies, on the left bank of the aforesaid river, and on the right bank Peshāwar, with the Usufzais territory, the Khataks, Hashtnagar, Michni, Kohāt, Hanggu, and all places dependent on Peshāwar, as far as the Khaibar pass, Bannu, the Vaziri's territory, Daur-Tānk, Garang, Kalabagh, and Khushalgarh, with their dependent districts, Dera Ismail Khān, and its dependency, Kot Mithan, Umar Kot, and their dependent territory ; Sanghar, Harrand-Dajal, Hajipur, Rajanpur, and the three Kaches, as well as Mankehra, with its district, and the province of Multān, situated on the left bank. These countries and places are considered to be the property, and to form the estate, of the Mahārājā : the Shāh neither has nor will have any concern with them ; they belong to the Mahārājā and his posterity from generation to generation.

Article 2.—The people of the country on the other side of Khaibar will not be suffered to commit robberies, or aggressions, or any disturbances on this side. If any defaulter of either State, who has embezzled the revenue, take refuge in the territory of the other, each party engages to surrender him, and no person shall obstruct the passage of the stream which issues out of the Khaibar defile, and supplies the fort of Fatehgarh with water according to ancient usage.

Article 3.—As, agreeably to the treaty established between the British Government and the Mahārājā, no one can cross from the left to the right bank of the Sutlej without a passport from the Mahārājā, the same rule shall be observed regarding the passage of the Indus, whose waters join the Sutlej, and no one shall be allowed to cross the Indus without the Mahārājā's permission.

Article 4.—Regarding Shikarpur and the territory of Sind, on the right bank of the Indus, the Shāh will agree to abide by whatever may be settled as right and proper, in conformity with the happy relations of friendship subsisting between the British Government and the Mahārājā through Captain Wade.

Article 5.—When the Shāh shall have established his authority in Kābul and Kandāhar, he will annually send the Mahārājā the following articles, viz. 55 high-bred horses of approved colour, and pleasant paces ; 11 Persian scimetars ; 7 Persian poniards ; 25 good mules ; fruits of various kinds, both dry and fresh; and Sardas or Musk melons, of a sweet and delicate flavour (to be sent throughout the year by the way of the Kābul river to Peshāwar); grapes, pomegranates, apples, quinces, almonds, raisins, pistahs or chestnuts, an abundant supply of each; as well as pieces of satin of every colour; chogas of fur; kimkhabs wrought with gold and silver; and Persian carpets, altogether to the number of 101 pieces,—all these articles the Shāh will continue to send every year to the Mahārājā.

Article 6.—Each party shall address the other on terms of equality.

Article 7.—Merchants of Afghānistan who may be desirous of trading to Lahore, Amritsar, or any other parts of the Mahārājā's possessions, shall not be stopped or molested on their way; on the contrary, strict orders shall be issued to facilitate their intercourse, and the Mahārājā engages to observe the same line of conduct on his part, in respect to traders who may wish to proceed to Afghānistan.

Article 8.—The Mahārājā will yearly send to the Shāh the following articles in the way of friendship: 55 pieces of shawls; 25 pieces of muslin; 11 dupattas; 5 pieces of kamkhab; 5 scarfs; 5 turbans; 55 loads of Bara rice (peculiar to Peshāwar).

Article 9.—Any of the Mahārājā's officers, who may be deputed to Afghānistan to purchase horses, or on any other business, as well as those who may be sent by the Shāh into the Punjab, for the purpose of purchasing piece goods, or shawls, &c., to the amount of 11,000 rupees, will be treated by both sides with due attention, and every facility will be afforded to them in the execution of their commission.

Article 10.—Whenever the armies of the two States may happen to be assembled at the same place, on no account shall the slaughter of kine be permitted to take place.

Article 11.—In the event of the Shāh taking an auxiliary force from the Mahārājā, whatever booty may be acquired from the Bārakzais in jewels, horses, arms, great and small, shall be equally divided between the two contracting parties. If the Shāh should succeed in obtaining possession of their property, without the assistance of the Mahārājā's troops, the Shāh agrees to send a portion of it by his own agent to the Mahārājā in the way of friendship.

Article 12.—An exchange of missions charged with letters and presents shall constantly take place between the two parties.

Article 13.—Should the Mahārājā require the aid of any of the Shāh's troops in furtherance of the objects contemplated by this treaty, the Shah engages to send a force commanded by one of his principal officers: in like manner the Mahārājā will furnish the Shāh, when required, with an auxiliary force, composed of Muhammadans, and commanded by one of the principal officers, as far as Kābul, in furtherance of the objects contemplated by this treaty. When the Mahārājā may go to Peshāwar, the Shāh will depute a Shāhzada to visit him, on which occasions the Mahārājā will receive and dismiss him with the honour and consideration due to his rank and dignity.

Article 14.—The friends and enemies of each of the three high powers, that is to say, the British and Sikh Governments, and Shāh Shujā-ul-Mulk, shall be the friends and enemies of all.

Article 15.—Shāh Shujā-ul-Mulk engages, after the attainment of his object, to pay without fail to the Mahārājā the sum of two lacs of rupees, of the Nanakshahi or Kaldār currency, calculating from the date on which the Sikh troops may be dispatched for the purpose of reinstating his Majesty in Kābul, in consideration of the Mahārājā stationing a force of not less than 5,000 men, cavalry and infantry, of the Muhammadan persuasion, within the limits of the Peshāwar territory, for the support of the Shāh, and to be sent to the aid of his Majesty, whenever the British Government, in concert and counsel with the Mahārājā, shall deem their aid necessary; and when any matter of great importance may arise to the westward, such measures will be adopted with regard to it as may seem expedient and proper at the time to the British and Sikh Governments. In the event of the Mahārājā's requiring the aid of any of the Shāh's troops, a deduction shall be made from the subsidy proportioned to the period for which such aid may be afforded, and the British Government holds itself responsible for the punctual payment of the above sum annually to the Mahārājā, so long as the provisions of this treaty are duly observed.

Article 16.—Shāh Shujā-ul-Mulk agrees to relinquish for himself, his heirs, and successors, all claims of supremacy and arrears of tribute over the country now held by the Amīrs of Sind (which will continue to belong to the Amīrs and their successors in perpetuity), on condition of the payment to him by the Amīrs of such a sum as may be determined under the mediation of the British Government; 1,500,000 of rupees of such payment being made over by him to Mahārājā Ranjīt Singh. On these payments being completed, article 4th of the treaty of the 12th March 1833 [1] will be considered cancelled, and the customary interchange of letters and suitable presents between the Mahārājā and the Amīrs of Sind shall be maintained as heretofore.

Article 17.—When Shāh Shujā-ul-Mulk shall have succeeded in establishing his authority in Afghānistan, he shall not attack or molest his nephew, the ruler of Herāt, in the possession of the territories now subject to his Government.

[1] Between Shāh Shujā and Ranjīt Singh.

Article 18.—Shāh Shujā-ul-Mulk binds himself, his heirs, and successors, to refrain from entering into negotiations with any foreign State without the knowledge and consent of the British and Sikh Governments, and to oppose any power having the design to invade the British and Sikh territories by force of arms, to the utmost of his ability.

The three powers, parties to this treaty, namely, the British Government, Mahārājā Ranjīt Singh, and Shāh Shujā-ul-Mulk, cordially agree to the foregoing articles. There shall be no deviations from them, and in that case the present treaty shall be considered binding for ever, and this treaty shall come into operation from and after the date on which the seals and signatures of the three contracting parties shall have been affixed thereto.

Done at Lahore, this 26th day of June, in the year of our Lord 1838, corresponding with the 15th of the month of Asarh 1895, era of Bikarmajit.

Ratified by the Right Honourable the Governor-General at Simla, on the 23rd day of July, A. D. 1838.

(Signed) AUCKLAND.
RANJĪT SINGH.
SHUJĀ-UL-MULK.

APPENDIX XXXI

INDUS AND SUTLEJ TOLL AGREEMENT OF 1839

Agreement entered into with the Government of Lahore, regarding the Duties to be levied on the Transit of Merchandise by the Rivers Sutlej and Indus, in modification of the Supplementary Articles of the Treaty of 1832. (Dated 19th May 1839.)

OBJECTIONS having been urged against the levy of the same duty on a boat of a small as on one of a large size, and the merchants having solicited that the duties might be levied on the maundage, or measurement, of the boats, or on the value of the goods, it is therefore agreed, that hereafter the whole duty shall be paid at one place, and either at Ludhiāna, or Ferozepore, or at Mithankot ; and that the duty be levied on the merchandise, and not on the boats, as follows :—

Pashmīna	*per maund*	10 rupees.
Opium	,,	7½ rupees.
Indigo	,,	2½ rupees.
Dried fruits	,,	1 rupee.
Superior silks, muslins, broadcloth, &c.	,,	6 annas.
Inferior silks, cottons, chintzes	,,	4 annas.

On Exports from the Punjab

Sugar, ghi, oil, drugs, ginger, saffron, and cotton . . .	*per maund*	4 annas.
Madder	,,	8 annas.
Grain	,,	2 annas.

On Imports from Bombay

All imports whatever . .	*per maund*	4 annas.

APPENDIX XXXII

INDUS AND SUTLEJ TOLL AGREEMENT OF 1840

Treaty between the Lahore and British Governments, regarding the levy of Transit Duties on Boats navigating the Sutlej and Indus. (Dated 27th June 1840.)

FORMERLY a treaty was executed by the Right Honourable Lord W. Cavendish Bentinck, the Governor-General of India, on the 14th of Pūs Sambat 1889 (corresponding with A. D. 1832), through Colonel, then Captain, Wade, concerning the navigation of the Sutlej and the Sind rivers in the Khālsa territory, in concurrence with the wishes of both the friendly and allied Governments. Another treaty on the subject was subsequently executed, through the same officer, in Sambat 1891 (corresponding with A. D. 1834), fixing a duty on every mercantile boat, independent of the quantity of its freight and the nature of its merchandise. A third treaty was executed on this subject, in accordance with the wishes of both Governments, on the arrival of Mr. Clerk, Agent to the Governor-General at the Durbar, in May 1839, adjusting the rate of duties on merchandise according to quantity and kind; and it was also specified that no further reduction of those rates should be proposed between the two Governments. On the visit of that gentleman to the Khālsa Durbar at Amritsar, in Jith Sambat 1897 (corresponding with May 1840), the difficulties and inconveniences which seemed to result to trade under the system proposed last year, in consequence of the obstruction to boats for the purpose of search, and the ignorance of traders, and the difficulty of adjusting duties according to the different kinds of articles freighted in these boats, were all stated; and that gentleman proposed to revise that system, by fixing a scale of duties proportionate to the measurement of boats, and not on the kind of commodities, if this arrangement should be approved of by both Governments. Having reported to his Government the circumstance of the case, he now drew up a schedule of the rate of duties on the mercantile boats navigating the rivers Sind and Sutlej, and forwarded it for the consideration of this friendly Durbar; the Khālsa Government, therefore, with a due regard to the established alliance, having added a few sentences in accordance with the late treaties, and agreeably to what is already well understood, has signed and sealed the schedule; and it shall never be liable to any contradiction, difference, change, or alteration without the concurrence and consent of both Governments, in consideration of mutual advantages, upon condition it does not interfere with the established custom duties at Amritsar, Lahore, and other inland places, or the other rivers in the Khālsa territory.

Article 1.—Grain, wood, limestone, will be free from duty.

Article 2.—With exception of the above, every commodity to pay duty according to the measurement of the boat.

Article 3.—Duty on a boat not exceeding 50 maunds of freight proceeding from the foot of the Hills, Rupar, or Ludhiāna to Mithankot or Rojhān, or from Rojhān or Mithankot to the foot of the Hills, Rūpar, or Ludhiāna, will be 50 rupees; viz.

From the foot of the Hills to Ferozepore, or back	20	rupees.
From Ferozepore to Bahāwalpur, or back	15	,,
From Bahāwalpur to Mithankot or Rojhān, or back	15	,,
The whole trip, up or down	50	rupees.

Duty on a boat above 250 maunds, but not exceeding 500 maunds: from the foot of the Hills, Rūpar, or Ludhiāna to Mithankot or Rojhān, or from Rojhān or Mithankot to the foot of the Hills, Rūpar, or Ludhiāna, will be 100 rupees, viz.

From the foot of the Hills to Ferozepore or back	40	rupees.
From Ferozepore to Bahāwalpur or back	30	,,
From Bahāwalpur to Mithankot or Rojhān, or back	30	,,
The whole trip, up or down	100	,,

Duty on all boats above 500 maunds will be 150 rupees, viz.

From the foot of the Hills to Ferozepore, or back	60	rupees.
From Ferozepore to Bahāwalpur, or back	45	,,
From Bahāwalpur to Mithankot or Rojhān, or back	45	,,
The whole trip, up or down	150	rupees.

Article 4.—Boats to be classed 1, 2, or 3, and the same to be written on the boat, and every boat to be registered.

Article 5.—These duties on merchandise frequenting the Sutlej and Sind are not to interfere with the duties on the banks of other rivers, or with the established inland custom-houses throughout the Khālsa territory, which will remain on their usual footing.

Dated 13th Asar Sambat 1897, corresponding with 27th June 1840.

APPENDIX XXXIII

DECLARATION OF WAR OF 1845

Proclamation by the Governor-General of India.

Camp, Lashkari Khān ki Sarai,
December 13th, 1845.

THE British Government has ever been on terms of friendship with that of the Punjab.

In the year 1809, a treaty of amity and concord was concluded between the British Government and the late Mahārājā Ranjīt Singh, the conditions of which have always been faithfully observed by the British Government, and were scrupulously fulfilled by the late Mahārājā.

The same friendly relations have been maintained with the successors of Mahārājā Ranjīt Singh by the British Government up to the present time.

Since the death of the late Mahārājā Sher Singh, the disorganized state of the Lahore Government has made it incumbent on the Governor-General in Council to adopt precautionary measures for the protection of the British frontier: the nature of these measures, and the cause of their adoption, were, at the time, fully explained to the Lahore Durbar.

Notwithstanding the disorganized state of the Lahore Government during the last two years, and many most unfriendly proceedings on the part of the Durbar, the Governor-General in Council has continued to evince his desire to maintain the relations of amity and concord which had so long existed between the two States, for the mutual interests and happiness of both. He has shown, on every occasion, the utmost forbearance, from consideration to the helpless state of the infant Mahārājā Dalīp Singh, whom the British Government had recognized as the successor to the late Mahārājā Sher Singh.

The Governor-General in Council sincerely desired to see a strong Sikh Government re-established in the Punjab, able to control its army, and to protect its subjects; he had not, up to the present moment, abandoned the hope of seeing that important object effected by the patriotic efforts of the Chiefs and people of that country.

The Sikh army recently marched from Lahore towards the British frontier, as it was alleged, by the orders of the Durbar, for the purpose of invading the British territory.

The Governor-General's agent, by direction of the Governor-General, demanded an explanation of this movement, and no reply being returned within a reasonable time, the demand was repeated. The Governor-General, unwilling to believe in the hostile intentions of the Sikh Government, to which no provocation had been given, refrained from taking any measures which might have a tendency to embarrass the Government of the Mahārājā, or to induce collision between the two States.

When no reply was given to the repeated demand for explanation, while active military preparations were continued at Lahore, the Governor-General considered it necessary to order the advance of troops towards the frontier, to reinforce the frontier posts.

The Sikh army has now, without a shadow of provocation, invaded the British territories.

The Governor-General must therefore take measures for effectually protecting the British provinces, for vindicating the authority of the British Government, and for punishing the violators of treaties and the disturbers of the public peace.

The Governor-General hereby declares the possessions of Mahārājā Dalīp Singh, on the left or British bank of the Sutlej, confiscated and annexed to the British territories.

The Governor-General will respect the existing rights of all Jāgīrdārs, Zamīndārs, and tenants in the said possessions, who, by the course they now pursue, evince their fidelity to the British Government.

The Governor-General hereby calls upon all the Chiefs and Sardars in the protected territories to co-operate cordially with the British Government for the punishment of the common enemy, and for the maintenance of order in these States. Those of the Chiefs who show alacrity and fidelity in the discharge of this duty, which they owe to the protecting power, will find their interests promoted thereby; and those who take a contrary course will be treated as enemies to the British Government, and will be punished accordingly.

The inhabitants of all the territories on the left bank o the Sutlej are hereby directed to abide peaceably in their respective villages, where they will receive efficient protection by the British Government. All parties of men found in armed bands, who can give no satisfactory account of their proceedings, will be treated as disturbers of the public peace.

All subjects of the British Government, and those who possess estates on both sides the river Sutlej, who, by their faithful adherence to the British Government, may be liable to sustain loss, shall be indemnified and secured in all their just rights and privileges.

On the other hand, all subjects of the British Government who shall continue in the service of the Lahore State, and who disobey the proclamation by not immediately returning to their allegiance, will be liable to have their property on this side the Sutlej confiscated, and themselves declared to be aliens and enemies of the British Government.

APPENDIX XXXIV

FIRST TREATY WITH LAHORE OF 1846

Treaty between the British Government and the State of Lahore, concluded at Lahore, on March 9th, 1846.

Whereas the treaty of amity and concord, which was concluded between the British Government and the late Mahārājā Ranjīt Singh, the ruler of Lahore, in 1809, was broken by the unprovoked aggression on the British provinces of the Sikh army, in December last : And whereas, on that occasion, by the proclamation dated the 13th of December, the territories then in the occupation of the Mahārājā of Lahore, on the left or British bank of the river Sutlej, were confiscated and annexed to the British provinces ; and, since that time, hostile operations have been prosecuted by the two Governments, the one against the other, which have resulted in the occupation of Lahore by the British troops : And whereas it has been determined that, upon certain conditions, peace shall be re-established between the two Governments, the following treaty of peace between the Honourable English East India Company, and Mahārājā Dalīp Singh Bahādur, and his children, heirs, and successors, has been concluded, on the part of the Honourable Company, by Frederick Currie, Esq., and Brevet-Major Henry Montgomery Lawrence, by virtue of full powers to that effect vested in them by the Right Honourable Sir Henry Hardinge. G.C.B., one of Her Britannic Majesty's most Honourable Privy Council, Governor-General, appointed by the Honourable Company to direct and control all their affairs in the East Indies ; and, on the part of his Highness the Mahārājā

Dalīp Singh, by Bhai Rām Singh, Rājā Lāl Singh, Sardar Tej Singh, Sardar Chattar Singh Atariwala, Sardar Ranjor Singh Majithia, Dīwān Dīna Nath, and Fakīr Nūr-ud-dīn, vested with full powers and authority on the part of his Highness.

Article 1.—There shall be perpetual peace and friendship between the British Government, on the one part, and Mahārājā Dalīp Singh, his heirs and successors, on the other.

Article 2.—The Mahārājā of Lahore renounces for himself, his heirs and successors, all claim to, or connexion with, the territories lying to the south of the river Sutlej, and engages never to have any concern with those territories, or the inhabitants thereof.

Article 3.—The Mahārājā cedes to the Honourable Company, in perpetual sovereignty, all his forts, territories, and rights, in the Doāb, or country, hill and plain, situate between the rivers Beās and Sutlej.

Article 4.—The British Government having demanded from the Lahore State, as indemnification for the expenses of the war, in addition to the cession of territory described in Article 3, payment of one and a half crores of rupees; and the Lahore Government being unable to pay the whole of this sum at this time, or to give security satisfactory to the British Government for its eventual payment; the Mahārājā cedes to the Honourable Company, in perpetual sovereignty, as equivalent for one crore of rupees, all his forts, territories, rights, and interests, in the hill countries which are situate between the rivers Beās and Indus, including the provinces of Kashmīr and Hazāra.

Article 5.—The Mahārājā will pay to the British Government the sum of fifty lacs of rupees, on or before the ratification of this treaty.

Article 6.—The Mahārājā engages to disband the mutinous troops of the Lahore army, taking from them their arms; and his Highness agrees to reorganize the regular, or Āīn, regiments of infantry, upon the system, and according to the regulations as to pay and allowances, observed in the time of the late Mahārājā Ranjīt Singh. The Mahārājā further engages to pay up all arrears to the soldiers that are discharged under the provisions of this article.

Article 7.—The regular army of the Lahore State shall henceforth be limited to 25 battalions of infantry, consisting of 800 bayonets each, with 12,000 cavalry: this number at no time to be exceeded without the concurrence of the British Government. Should it be necessary at any time, for any special cause, that this force should be increased, the cause shall be fully explained to the British Government; and, when the special necessity shall have passed, the regular troops shall be again reduced to the standard specified in the former clause of this article.

Article 8.—The Mahārājā will surrender to the British Government all the guns, thirty-six in number, which have been pointed against the British troops, and which, having been placed on the right bank of the river Sutlej, were not captured at the battle of Sobraon.

Article 9.—The control of the rivers Beās and Sutlej, with the continuations of the latter river, commonly called the Ghara and Panjnad, to the confluence of the Indus at Mithankot, and the control of the Indus from Mithankot to the borders of Baluchistān, shall, in respect to tolls and ferries, rest with the British Government. The provisions of this article shall not interfere with the passage of boats belonging to the Lahore Government on the said rivers, for the purposes of traffic, or the conveyance of passengers up and down their course. Regarding the ferries between the two countries respectively, at the several ghāts of the said rivers, it is agreed that the British Government, after defraying all the expenses of management and establishments, shall account to the Lahore Government for one-half of the net profits of the ferry collections. The provisions of this article have no reference to the ferries on that part of the river Sutlej which forms the boundary of Bahāwalpur and Lahore respectively.

Article 10.—If the British Government should, at any time, desire to pass troops through the territories of his Highness the Mahārājā for the protection of the British territories, or those of their allies, the British troops shall, on such special occasions, due notice being given, be allowed to pass through the Lahore territories. In such case, the officers of the Lahore State will afford facilities in providing supplies and boats for the passage of rivers ; and the British Government will pay the full price of all such provisions and boats, and will make fair compensation for all private property that may be endamaged. The British Government will moreover observe all due consideration to the religious feelings of the inhabitants of those tracts through which the army may pass.

Article 11.—The Mahārājā engages never to take, or retain, in his service, any British subject, nor the subject of any European or American State, without the consent of the British Government.

Article 12.—In consideration of the services rendered by Rājā Gulāb Singh of Jammū to the Lahore State, towards procuring the restoration of the relations of amity between the Lahore and British Governments, the Mahārājā hereby agrees to recognize the independent sovereignty of Rājā Gulāb Singh, in such territories and districts in the hills as may be made over to the said Rājā Gulāb Singh by separate agreement between himself and the British Government, with the dependencies thereof, which may have been in the Rājā's possession since the time of the late Mahārājā Karak Singh : and the British Government, in consideration of the good conduct of Rājā Gulāb Singh, also agrees to recognize his independence in such territories, and to admit him to the privileges of a separate treaty with the British Government.

Article 13.—In the event of any dispute or difference arising between the Lahore State and Rājā Gulāb Singh, the same shall be referred to the arbitration of the British Government; and by its decision the Mahārājā engages to abide.

Article 14.—The limits of the Lahore territories shall not be, at any time, changed, without the concurrence of the British Government.

Article 15.—The British Government will not exercise any interference in the internal administration of the Lahore State; but in all cases or questions which may be referred to the British Government, the Governor-General will give the aid of his advice and good offices for the furtherance of the interests of the Lahore Government.

Article 16.—The subjects of either State shall, on visiting the territories of the other, be on the footing of the subjects of the most favoured nation.

This treaty, consisting of sixteen articles, has been this day settled by Frederick Currie, Esq., and Brevet-Major Henry Montgomery Lawrence, acting under the directions of the Right Honourable Sir Henry Hardinge, G.C.B., Governor-General, on the part of the British Government; and by Bhai Rām Singh, Rājā Lāl Singh, Sardar Tej Singh, Sardar Chattar Singh Atariwala, Sardar Ranjor Singh Majithia, Dīwān Dīna Nath, and Fakīr Nūr-ud-dīn, on the part of the Mahārājā Dalīp Singh; and the said treaty has been this day ratified by the seal of the Right Honourable Sir Henry Hardinge, G.C.B., Governor-General, and by that of his Highness Mahārājā Dālīp Singh.

Done at Lahore, this 9th day of March, in the year of our Lord 1846, corresponding with the 10th day of Rabi-ul-awal 1262, Hijri, and ratified on the same day.

APPENDIX XXXV

SUPPLEMENTARY ARTICLES TO FIRST TREATY WITH LAHORE OF 1846

Articles of Agreement concluded between the British Government and the Lahore Durbar, on the 11*th of March* 1846.

WHEREAS the Lahore Government has solicited the Governor-General to leave a British force at Lahore, for the protection of the Mahārājā's person and of the capital, till the reorganization of the Lahore army, according to the provisions of Article 6 of the treaty of Lahore, dated the 9th instant: And whereas the Governor-General has, on certain conditions, consented to the measure: And whereas it is expedient that certain matters concerning the territories ceded by Articles 3 and 4 of the aforesaid treaty should be specifically determined; the following eight articles of agreement have this day been concluded between the afore-mentioned contracting parties.

Article 1.—The British Government shall leave at Lahore, till the close of the current year, A. D. 1846, such force as shall seem to the Governor-General adequate for the purpose of protecting the person of the Mahārājā, and the inhabitants of the city of Lahore, during the reorganization of the Sikh army, in accordance with the provisions of Article 6 of the treaty of Lahore; that force to be withdrawn at any convenient time before the expiration of the year, if the object to be fulfilled shall, in the opinion of the Durbar, have been obtained; but the force shall not be detained at Lahore beyond the expiration of the current year.

Article 2.—The Lahore Government agrees that the force left at Lahore, for the purpose specified in the foregoing article, shall be placed in full possession of the fort and the city of Lahore, and that the Lahore troops shall be removed from within the city. The Lahore Government engages to furnish convenient quarters for the officers and men of the said force, and to pay to the British Government all the extra expenses, in regard to the said force, which may be incurred by the British Government, in consequence of their troops being employed away from their own cantonments, and in a foreign territory.

Article 3.—The Lahore Government engages to apply itself immediately and earnestly to the reorganization of its army, according to the prescribed conditions, and to communicate fully with the British authorities left at Lahore, as to the progress of such reorganization, and as to the location of the troops.

Article 4.—If the Lahore Government fails in the performance of the conditions of the foregoing article, the British Government shall be at liberty to withdraw the force from Lahore, at any time before the expiration of the period specified in Article 1.

Article 5.—The British Government agrees to respect the bona fide rights oft hose Jāgīrdārs within the territories ceded by Articles 3 and 4 of the treaty of Lahore, dated 9th instant, who were attached to the families of the late Mahārājā Ranjīt Singh, Kharak Singh, and Sher Singh; and the British Government will maintain those Jāgīrdārs in their bona fide possessions, during their lives.

Article 6.—The Lahore Government shall receive the assistance of the British local authorities in recovering the arrears of revenue justly due to the Lahore Government from their Kardars and managers in the territories ceded by the provisions of Articles 3 and 4 of the treaty of Lahore, to the close of the Kharīf harvest of the current year, viz 1902, of the Sambat Bikarmajit.

Article 7.—The Lahore Government shall be at liberty to remove from the forts in the territories specified in the foregoing article, all treasure and state property, with the exception of guns. Should, however, the British Government desire to retain any part of the said property, they shall be at liberty to do so, paying for the same at a fair valuation; and the British officers shall give their assistance to the Lahore Government, in disposing on the spot of such part of the aforesaid property as the Lahore Government may not wish to remove, and the British officers may not desire to retain.

Article 8.—Commissioners shall be immediately appointed by the two Governments, to settle and lay down the boundary between the two States, as defined by Article 4 of the treaty of Lahore, dated 9th March 1846.

APPENDIX XXXVI

TREATY WITH GULĀB SINGH OF 1846

Treaty between the British Government and Mahārājā Gulāb Singh, concluded at Amritsar, on 16th March 1846.

TREATY between the British Government on the one part, and Mahārājā Gulāb Singh of Jammū on the other, concluded, on the part of the British Government, by Frederick Currie, Esq., and Brevet-Major Henry Montgomery Lawrence, acting under the orders of the Right Honourable Sir Henry Hardinge, G.C.B., one of Her Britannic Majesty's most Honourable Privy Council, Governor-General, appointed by the Honourable Company to direct and control all their affairs in the East Indies, and by Mahārājā Gulāb Singh in person.

Article 1.—The British Government transfers and makes over, for ever, in independent possession, to Mahārājā Gulāb Singh, and the heirs male of his body, all the hilly or mountainous country, with its dependencies, situated to the eastward of the river Indus, and westward of the river Rāvi, including Chamba and excluding Lāhul, being part of the territory ceded to the British Government by the Lahore State, according to the provisions of Article 4 of the treaty of Lahore, dated 9th March 1846.

Article 2.—The eastern boundary of the tract transferred by the foregoing article to Mahārājā Gulāb Singh shall be laid down by commissioners appointed by the British Government and Mahārājā Gulāb Singh respectively, for that purpose, and shall be defined in a separate engagement, after survey.

Article 3.—In consideration of the transfer made to him and his heirs by the provisions of the foregoing articles, Mahārājā Gulāb Singh will pay to the British Government the sum of seventy-five lacs of rupees (Nānakshahi), fifty lacs to be paid on ratification of this treaty, and twenty-five lacs on or before the 1st of October of the current year, A. D. 1846.

Article 4.—The limits of the territories of Mahārājā Gulāb Singh shall not be at any time changed without the concurrence of the British Government.

Article 5.—Mahārājā Gulāb Singh will refer to the arbitration of the British Government any disputes or questions that may arise between himself and the Government of Lahore, or any other neighbouring State, and will abide by the decision of the British Government.

Article 6.—Mahārājā Gulāb Singh engages for himself and heirs, to join, with the whole of his military force, the British troops, when employed within the hills, or in the territories adjoining his possessions.

Article 7.—Mahārājā Gulāb Singh engages never to take, or retain, in his service any British subject, nor the subject of any European or American State, without the consent of the British Government.

Article 8.—Mahārājā Gulāb Singh engages to respect, in regard to the territory transferred to him, the provisions of Articles 5, 6, and 7, of the separate engagement between the British Government and the Lahore Durbar, dated 11th March 1846.

Article 9.—The British Government will give its aid to Mahārājā Gulāb Singh, in protecting his territories from external enemies.

Article 10.—Mahārājā Gulāb Singh acknowledges the supremacy of the British Government, and will, in token of such supremacy, present annually to the British Government one horse, twelve perfect shawl goats of approved breed (six male and six female), and three pairs of Kashmīr shawls.

This treaty, consisting of ten articles, has been this day settled by Frederick Currie, Esq., and Brevet-Major Henry Montgomery Lawrence, acting under the directions of the Right Honourable Sir Henry Hardinge, G.C.B., Governor-General, on the part of the British Government, and by Mahārājā Gulāb Singh in person ; and the said treaty has been this day ratified by the seal of the Right Honourable Sir Henry Hardinge, G.C.B., Governor-General.

Done at Amritsar, this 16th day of March, in the year of our Lord 1846, corresponding with the 17th day of Rabī-ul-awwal, 1262, Hijri.

APPENDIX XXXVII

SECOND TREATY WITH LAHORE OF 1846

Foreign Department, Camp, Bhyrowal Ghāt, on the left Bank of the Beās, the 22nd December 1846.

The late Governor of Kashmīr, on the part of the Lahore State, Shaikh Imām-ud-dīn, having resisted by force of arms the occupation of the province of Kashmīr by Mahārājā Gulāb Singh, the Lahore Government was called upon to coerce their subject, and to make over the province to the representative of the British Government, in fulfilment of the conditions of the treaty of Lahore, dated 9th March 1846.

A British force was employed to support and aid, if necessary, the combined forces of the Lahore State and Mahārājā Gulāb Singh in the above operations.

Shaikh Imām-ud-dīn intimated to the British Government that he was acting under orders received from the Lahore Durbar in the course he was pursuing ; and stated that the insurrection had been instigated by written instructions received by him from the Wazīr Rājā Lāl Singh.

Shaikh Imām-ud-dīn surrendered to the British agent on a guarantee from that officer, that if the Shaikh could, as he asserted, prove that his acts were in accordance with his instructions, and that the opposition was instigated by the Lahore minister, the Durbar should not be permitted to inflict upon him, either in his person or his property, any penalty on account of his conduct on this occasion. The

British agent pledged his Government to a full and impartial investigation of the matter.

A public inquiry was instituted into the facts adduced by Shaikh Imām-ud-dīn, and it was fully established that Rājā Lāl Singh did secretly instigate the Shaikh to oppose the occupation by Mahārājā Gulāb Singh of the province of Kashmīr.

The Governor-General immediately demanded that the Ministers and Chiefs of the Lahore State should depose and exile to the British provinces the Wazīr Rājā Lāl Singh.

His Lordship consented to accept the deposition of Rājā Lāl Singh as an atonement for the attempt to infringe the treaty by the secret intrigues and machinations of the Wazīr. It was not proved that the other members of the Durbar had cognizance of the Wazīr's proceedings; and the conduct of the Sardars, and of the Sikh army in the late operations for quelling the Kashmīr insurrection, and removing the obstacles to the fulfilment of the treaty, proved that the criminality of the Wazīr was not participated in by the Sikh nation.

The Ministers and Chiefs unanimously decreed, and carried into immediate effect, the deposition of the Wazīr.

After a few days' deliberations, relative to the means of forming a government at Lahore, the remaining members of the Durbar, in concert with all the Sardars and Chiefs of the State, solicited the interference and aid of the British Government for the maintenance of an administration, and the protection of the Mahārājā Dalīp Singh during the minority of his Highness.

This solicitation by the Durbar and Chiefs has led to the temporary modification of the relations between the British Government and that of Lahore, established by the treaty of the 9th March of the present year.

The terms and conditions of this modification are set forth in the following articles of agreement.

Articles of Agreement concluded between the British Government and the Lahore Durbar on 16th December 1846.

Whereas the Lahore Durbar and the principal Chiefs and Sardars of the State have, in express terms, communicated to the British Government their anxious desire that the Governor-General should give his aid and his assistance to maintain the administration of the Lahore State during the minority of Mahārājā Dalīp Singh, and have declared this measure to be indispensable for the maintenance of the government: And whereas the Governor-General has, under certain conditions, consented to give the aid and assistance solicited, the following articles of agreement, in modification of the articles of agreement executed at Lahore on the 11th March last, have been concluded, on the part of the British Government, by Frederick Currie, Esq., Secretary to the Government of India, and Lieutenant-Colonel Henry Montgomery Lawrence, C.B., Agent to the Governor-General, North-West Frontier, by virtue of full powers to that effect vested in them by the Right Honourable Viscount Hardinge, G.C.B., Governor-General, and on the part of his Highness Mahārājā Dalīp Singh, by Sardar Tej Singh, Sardar Sher Singh, Dīwān Dīna Nath, Fakīr Nūr-ud-dīn, Rai Kishan Chand, Sardar Ranjor Singh Majithia, Sardar Atar Singh Kaliwala, Bhai Nidhān Singh, Sardar Khān Singh Majithia, Sardar Shamsher Singh, Sardar Lāl Singh Muraria, Sardar Kehar Singh Sindhianwala, Sardar Arjūn Singh Rangranglia, acting with the unanimous consent and concurrence of the Chiefs and Sardars of the State assembled at Lahore.

Article 1.—All and every part of the treaty of peace between the British Government and the State of Lahore, bearing date the 9th day of March 1846, except in so far as it may be temporarily modified in respect to clause 15 of the said treaty by this engagement, shall remain binding upon the two Governments.

Article 2.—A British officer, with an efficient establishment of assistants, shall be appointed by the Governor-General to remain at Lahore, which officer shall have full authority to direct and control all matters in every department of the State.

Article 3.—Every attention shall be paid, in conducting the administration, to the feelings of the people, to preserving the national institutions and customs, and to maintain the just rights of all classes.

Article 4.—Changes in the mode and details of administration shall not be made, except when found necessary for effecting the objects set forth in the foregoing clause, and for securing the just dues of the Lahore Government. These details shall be conducted by native officers as at present, who shall be appointed and superintended by a Council of Regency, composed of leading Chiefs and Sardars, acting under the control and guidance of the British Resident.

Article 5.—The following persons shall in the first instance constitute the Council of Regency, viz., Sardar Tej Singh, Sardar Sher Singh Atariwala, Dīwān Dīna Nath, Fakīr Nūr-ud-dīn, Sardar Ranjor Singh Majithia, Bhai Nidhān Singh, Sardar Attar Singh Kaliwala, Sardar Shamsher Singh Sindhianwala ; and no change shall be made in the persons thus nominated, without the consent of the British Resident, acting under the orders of the Governor-General.

Article 6.—The administration of the country shall be

conducted by this Council of Regency in such manner as may be determined on by themselves in consultation with the British Resident, who shall have full authority to direct and control the duties of every department.

Article 7.—A British force, of such strength and numbers, and in such positions, as the Governor-General may think fit, shall remain at Lahore for the protection of the Mahārājā, and the preservation of the peace of the country.

Article 8.—The Governor-General shall be at liberty to occupy with British soldiers any fort or military post in the Lahore territories, the occupation of which may be deemed necessary by the British Government for the security of the capital, or for maintaining the peace of the country.

Article 9.—The Lahore State shall pay to the British Government twenty-two lacs of new Nānakshāhi rupees of full tale and weight per annum, for the maintenance of this force, and to meet the expenses incurred by the British Government; such sum to be paid by two instalments, or 13 lacs and 20,000 in May or June, and 8 lacs and 80,000 in November or December of each year.

Article 10.—Inasmuch as it is fitting that her Highness the Mahārāni, the mother of Mahārājā Dalīp Singh, should have a proper provision made for the maintenance of herself and dependents, the sum of 1 lac and 50,000 rupees shall be set apart annually for that purpose, and shall be at her Highness's disposal.

Article 11.—The provisions of this engagement shall have effect during the minority of his Highness Mahārājā Dalīp Singh, and shall cease and terminate on his Highness attaining the full age of 16 years, or on the 4th September of the year 1854; but it shall be competent to the Governor-General to cause the arrangement to cease, at any period prior to the coming of age of his Highness, at which the Governor-General and the Lahore Durbar may be satisfied that the interposition of the British Government is no longer necessary for maintaining the government of his Highness the Mahārājā.

This agreement, consisting of eleven articles, was settled and executed at Lahore, by the officers and Chiefs and Sardars above named, on the 16th day of December 1846.

APPENDIX XXXVIII

REVENUES OF THE PUNJAB, AS ESTIMATED IN 1844

TRIBUTARY STATES	*Rupees.*	*Rupees.*
Bilāspur. Tribute, 10,000. Under Lahna Singh	70,000	
Suket. Tribute, 25,000. Under Lahna Singh	70,000	
Chamba. Not known. Under Gulāb Singh	2,00,000	
Rajāuri. Not known. Under Gulāb Singh	1,00,000	
Ladākh. Tribute, 42,000. Under Gulāb Singh	1,00,000	
Iskardu. Tribute, 7,000. Under Gulāb Singh	25,000	
		5,65,000
NOTE.—All of these States, excepting Bilāspur, may be regarded rather as farms held by the Chiefs than as tributary principalities; and, ordinarily, all the resources of the Chiefs being at the disposal of the government representative, the probable revenues have therefore been entered in full, instead of the mere pecuniary payment.		
LAND REVENUE		
Farms.		
Mandī. Farm with the Rājā of Mandī, who was allowed one lac out of the four for his expenses	4,00,000	
Kullu. The members of the family had pensions	1,20,000	
Jaswan. The family had a Jāgīr	1,25,000	
Kāngra. The family had a Jāgīr, not included in the farm	6,00,000	
Kutlahar. The family had a Jāgīr	25,000	
Siba. The family may almost be regarded as Jāgīrdārs for the whole estate: they served with horse	20,000	
Nurpur. The family had a Jāgīr	3,00,000	
Harīpur. The family had a Jāgīr	1,00,000	
Datārpur. The family had a Jāgīr	50,000	
Katlah. The family had a Jāgīr	20,000	
NOTE.—The above were all under Lahna Singh Majithia.		

LAND REVENUE—*Farms* (*continued*)	*Rupees.*	*Rupees.*
Bisohli. Family at large: was held by Rājā Hīra Singh	75,000	
Kashmīr. Shaikh Ghulām Muhī-ud-dīn: Contract . . 21,00,000 Troops . . 5,00,000 Assignments . 4,00,000	30,00,000	
Muzaffarābād, &c. (Under Kashmīr.) The Muzaffarābād Chief a Jāgīrdār . .	1,00,000	
Chach-Hazāra and Pakhli Dhamtaur. { Rājā Gulāb Singh. The Gandghar and Tarnauli Chiefs have Jāgīrs; but they are almost independent freebooters }	1,50,000	
Rāwalpindi. Dīwān Hakim Rai . .	1,00,000	
Hasan Abdal, Khatir, and Ghipi. { Dīwān Mul Rāj: he lately held Chatch-Hazāra also }	1,00,000	
Dhanni, Katas, and Chakwal. } Rājā Gulāb Singh . .	1,00,000	
Peshāwar. Sardar Tej Singh. The Barakzais have Jāgīrs	10,00,000	
Tānk-Bannu. Dīwān Daulat Rai. The Chief fled; his brother a Jāgīr . .	2,50,000	
Dera Ismail Khān. Dīwān Daulat Rai. Chief a Jāgīr	4,50,000	
Multān, Dera Ghazi Khān, Mankera. } Dīwān Sawan Mal . Contract . . 36,00,000 Troops . . 7,00,000 Assignments, &c. 2,00,000	45,00,000	
Ramnagar, &c. Dīwān Sawan Mal . .	3,00,000	
Mitta Tuwana. The late Dhian Singh .	1,00,000	
Bhera Khushāb. Rājā Gulāb Singh. .	1,00,000	
Pind Dādan Khān. Rājā Gulāb Singh .	50,000	
Gujrāt. Rājā Gulāb Singh . . .	3,00,000	
Wazīrābād, &c. The late Suchet Singh .	9,00,000	
Siālkot. Rājā Gulab Singh . . .	50,000	
Jullundur Doāb. Shaikh Imām-ud-dīn .	22,00,000	
Shekhupura, &c. Shaikh Imām-ud-dīn .	2,50,000	
Cis-Sutlej farms	6,50,000	
Miscellaneous farms in the Punjab . .	15,00,000	
		1,79,85,000

LAND REVENUE (*continued*)	*Rupees.*	*Rupees.*
Religious Grants.		
Held by 'Sodhis'	5,00,000	
Held by 'Bedis'	4,00,000	
Miscellaneous; viz. Akalis, Fakīrs, Brāhmans, and the lands attached to Amritsar, &c. &c.	11,00,000	20,00,000
Hill Jāgīrs of the Jammū Rājās.		
Jesrota, &c. Hīra Singh. The Chief a Jāgīr	1,25,000	
Pader, and other districts of Chamba. Gulāb Singh	1,00,000	
Bhadarwa. Gulāb Singh (in Jāgīr with uncle of Chamba Rājā)	50,000	
Mankot. The late Suchet Singh. Family a Jāgīr	50,000	
Bhaddu. The late Suchet Singh. Family a Jāgīr	50,000	
Bandralta. The late Suchet Singh. Family a Jāgīr	1,25,000	
Chaninī (Ramnagar). Gulāb Singh. Family a Jāgīr	30,000	
Jammu and Riasi. Gulāb Singh. Family mostly refugees	4,00,000	
Samba. The late Suchet Singh. Family extinct or fled	40,000	
Kishtwār. Gulāb Singh. Family refugees	1,50,000	
Akhnur, including Chakkāna, with Kesri Singh's family. Gulāb Singh. Family a Jāgīr	50,000	
Bhimbar. The late Dhiān Singh. Some members of family Jāgīrs; others refugees	1,50,000	
The Chibh-Bhau tribes. The late Dhiān Singh. Family Jāgīrs	1,00,000	
Kotli. The late Dhiān Singh. Family Jāgīrs	30,000	
Sunach. The late Dhiān Singh. Family perhaps refugees	70,000	
Dangli, Khānpur, &c. Gulāb Singh. Some members of family Jāgīrs; others prisoners; others refugees	1,00,000	16,20,000
Jāgīrs.		
Various Jāgīrs held by the Jammu Rājās (in the plains)	5,00,000	
The Kāngra Rājās (Ranbir Chand, &c.)	1,00,000	

Land Revenue—*Jāgīrs* (*continued*).	*Rupees.*	*Rupees.*
Sardar Lahna Singh Majithia	3,50,000	
Sardar Nihal Singh Ahluwalia	9,00,000	
Sardar Kishan Singh (son of Jamadar Khushal Singh	1,20,000	
Sardar Tej Singh	60,000	
Sardars Sham Singh and Chattar Singh Atariwala	1,20,000	
Sardar Shamsher Singh Sindhianwala	15,000	
Sardar Arjūn Singh, and other sons of Harī Singh	15,000	
Kanwar Peshaura Singh	5,000	
Kanwar Tara Singh	20,000	
Sardar Jawahar Singh (uncle of Dalīp Singh)	50,000	
Sardar Mangal Singh	50,000	
Sardar Fateh Singh Man	50,000	
Sardar Attar Singh Kalanwala	50,000	
Sardar Hukam Singh Mulwai	50,000	
Sardar Bela Singh Mokal	50,000	
Sardars Sultān Muhammad, Saiyid Muhammad, and Pīr Muhammad Khāns	1,50,000	
Sardar Jamāl-ud-dīn Khān	1,10,000	
Shaikh Ghulām Muhī-ud-din	30,000	
Fakīr Aziz-ud-dīn and his brothers	1,00,000	
Dīwān Sāwan Mal	20,000	
Miscellaneous	50,00,000	
		79,15,000
CUSTOMS, &c.		
Salt Mines. Rājā Gulāb Singh	8,00,000	
Town Duties. Amritsar. The late Dhiān Singh	5,50,000	
Town Duties. Lahore. The late Dhiān Singh	1,50,000	
Miscellaneous Town Duties	1,00,000	
'Abkarī' (Excise), &c. &c. Lahore	50,000	
Transit Duties. Ludhiāna to Peshāwar	5,00,000	
'Mohurāna' (Stamps)	2,50,000	
		24,00,000
Total		3,24,75,000

Note.—As noted in the Preface, the whole of the papers of the administration of Ranjīt Singh now under examination and subsequent investigation may considerably modify some of these figures.—Ed.

RECAPITULATION

	Rupees.
LAND REVENUE:	
Tributary States	5,65,000
Farms	1,79,85,000
Eleemosynary	20,00,000
Jāgīrs	95,25,000
CUSTOMS, &c.	24,00,000
Total	3,24,75,000

APPENDIX XXXIX

THE ARMY OF LAHORE, AS RECORDED IN 1844

The Regular Army.		*Infantry Regiments.*	*Cavalry Regiments.*	*Light Artillery.*	*Heavy Guns.*	
Commandants of Corps.	*Description or Race of Men.*				*Field.*	*Garrison.*
Sardar Tej Singh	Sikhs	4	1	10	0	0
Gen. Pertab Singh Pattiwala	Sikhs	3	0	0	0	0
Gen. Jawala Singh	Inf. Sikhs; Art. Sikhs and Muhammadans	2	0	4	0	0
Shaikh Imām-ud-dīn	Muhammadans	3	0	4	0	0
Sardar Lahna Singh Majithia	Inf. Sikhs; Guns, chiefly Sikhs	2	0	10	3	2
Gen. Bishan Singh	Muhammadans; a few Sikhs	2	0	3	0	0
Gen. Gulāb Singh Puhuvindhia	3 Muhammadans; Guns, Sikhs & Muhammadans	3*	0	14	0	0
Gen. Mahtab Singh Majithia	Inf. Sikhs; Cav. mixed; Art. Sikhs and Muham.	4	1	12	0	0
Gen. Gurdut Singh Majithia	Inf. chiefly Sikhs; Guns, Sikhs & Muhammadans	3	0	0	0	0
Col. John Holmes	Formerly under General Court	1	0	10	0	0
Gen. Dhaukal Singh	Hindustanis; a few Sikhs.	2	0	0	0	0
Col. Cortlandt (discharged)	Inf. Sikhs & Hind.; Guns, Sikhs & Muhammadans	2	0	10	0	0
Shaikh Ghulām Muhī-ud-dīn	Inf. Sikhs? Guns, Sikhs and Muhammadans	1	0	6	8	0
	Carried forward	32	2	83	11	2

* Shaikh Imām-ud-dīn subsequently raised a fourth regiment.

THE ARMY OF LAHORE (*continued*)

The Regular Army.		Infantry Regiments.	Cavalry Regiments	Light Artillery.	Heavy Guns	
Commandants of Corps.	*Description or Race of Men.*				*Field*	*Garrison.*
	Brought forward .	32	2	83	11	2
Dīwān Adjudhia Parshad; Guns under Ilahi Bakhsh, General . . .	Inf. Sikhs; Art. Sikhs and Muhammadans (Gen. Ventura) . . .	4	2	12	22	0
Gen. Gulāb Singh Calcuttawala (deceased) . .	Sikhs	4	1	16	0	0
Dīwān Jodha Rām . .	Sikhs, Muham., Hill men (Gen. Avitabile) . .	4	1	12	3	0
Gen. Kanh Singh Man .	Sikhs & Muhammadans .	4	0	10	0	0
Sardar Nihal Singh Ahluwalia	Inf. Sikhs & Muham.; Art. chiefly Muhammadans .	1	0	4	11	0
Dīwān Sawan Mal . .	Muham. and some Sikhs .	3	0	6	0	40
Rājā Hīra Singh . .	Hill men, some Muham., &c.	2	1	0	3	5
Rājā Gulāb Singh . .	,, ,, ,,	3	0	15	0	40
Rājā Suchet Singh (dec.) .	,, ,, ,,	2	1	4	0	10
Capt. Kuldip Singh .	Gurkhas	1	0	0	0	0
Commandant Bhag Singh	Sikhs and Muhammadans .	0	0	6	0	0
Commandant Shev Parshad	,, ,, ,, .	0	0	8	0	0
Missar Lāl Singh . .	,, ,, ,, .	0	0	10	0	0
Sardar Kishan Singh .	Muham. and Hindustanis .	0	0	0	0	2
Gen. Kishan Singh .	Sikhs and Muhammadans .	0	0	22	0	0
Sardar Sham Singh Atariwala	,, ,, ,, .	0	0	0	10	0
Miān Pirthī Singh . .	Chiefly Muhammadans .	0	0	0	56	0
Gen. Mahwa Singh . .	Sikhs and Muhammadans .	0	0	10	10	0
Col. Amīr Chand . .	Chiefly Muhammadans .	0	0	0	10	0
Commandant Mazhar Alī .	Muham. and Hindustanis .	0	0	10	0	0
Jawāhir Mal Mistri (Lahore)	Muhammadans; a few Sikhs	0	0	0	20	12
Commandant Sukhu Singh (Amritsar)	Sikhs, and some Hindustanis	0	0	0	0	10
Miscellan. Garrison Guns .	. . . . . .	0	0	0	0	50
	Total .	60	8	228	156	171

Abstract of the whole Army.

Sixty Regiments Infantry, at 700 . .	42,000	
Ramghōls, Akalis	5,000	
Irreg. Levies, Garrison Companies, &c. .	45,000	
	——	92,000 Infantry.
Eight Regiments Cavalry, at 600 . .	4,800	
'Ghurcharhas' (Horse) . . .	12,000	
Jāgīrdāri Horse	15,000	
	——	31,800 Cavalry.
Field Artillery		384 Guns.

[By the courtesy of the Government of the Punjab I am enabled to add to this appendix the statement recently compiled by L. Sita Rām Kohly, M.A., who has been conducting some researches into the MS. records lying in the Punjab Secretariat. There are many hundreds of these records still to be examined, and further investigation will no doubt yield important results. In the meantime it may be of interest to the reader to compare the actual figures for 1844, as obtained from these records, with those given by the author.—Ed.]

YEAR COMMENCING WITH KATIK 1900 AND ENDING WITH HSUJ 1901 B.S. (A. D. 1844)

Commandant.	*Inf. batts.*	*Cav. regts.*	*Artillery.*	*Total strength.*	*Expenditure.* Rs.	A.	P.
Special Brigade: Gen. Ventura	4	3	Belonging to Illahi Baksh	4,415	83,609	8	0
Dīwān Jodha Rām	4	1	10 guns, 294 men	4,374	58,952	12	0
Gen. Gulāb Singh, acting for Gen. Court	4	1	392	3,882	54,751	4	0
Gen. Dhaukal Singh	2	0	0	1,763	23,159	15	0
Gen. Jawala Singh	2	0	0	1,811	22,285	12	0
Gen. S. Tej Singh	4	0	2 field guns, 293 men, light artillery	3,602	45,171	13	6
Gen. Kanh Singh Man	4	1	264	4,154	61,248	0	0
Gen. Mahtab Singh Majithia	4	1	366	3,879	59,582	1	0
Gen. Pertab Singh of Punach	3	0	250	2,690	32,743	1	0
Gen. Gurdit Singh Majithia	3	0	194	2,872	35,679	7	0
Gen. Courtlandt	2*	0	0	1,698	14,163	14	6
Gen. Gulāb Singh Puhuvindhia	4	0	360	3,467	43,273	6	0
Gen. Bishan Singh	2	0	0	1,581	19,191	8	0
Gen. Kishan Singh	1	1	467	1,381	20,782	1	0
Rājā Hīra Singh under Col. Jagat Singh	0	2	0	1,030	29,572	8	0
Rai Kesari Singh of Naulakha Cautt, formerly nr. Railway Station, Lahore	0	1	90	444	20,894	0	0
Sardar Lahna Singh Majithia	1	0	340	1,258	11,865	14	0
Missa Lāl Singh †	Different Companies			303	3,477	6	0
Miscellaneous Companies and soldiers	17 Companies			1,577	18,410	11	0

Total No. of Battalions: 45. Round No. 40,000 men.
" " " Regiments: 11. Approx. No. 6,000 men.
" " " Artillery: 104 + 126 = 230.

A number of mortars and Camel Swivels are not included in these computations.

* Plus 8th Company of Ramghoal Battalion.

† It seems that Lāl Singh had to pay these soldiers quartered on his farms. He farmed out certain districts.

YEAR COMMENCING WITH KATIK 1900 AND ENDING WITH HSUJ 1901 B.S. (A. D. 1814)

ARTILLERY CORPS

Commandant.		*Guns.*	*Strength.*	*Expenditure.*	*Jāgīr assignmen*
	Rs.			*Rs. A.*	*Rs. Per Yea*
Lāl Jawāhir Māl in charge of Mistrī Khānā.					620
1. M. Muzihr Ali Beg.	390	13			
2. B. Ishwar Singh, Col.	210	10			
3. Meva Singh, Gen.	100	12			
		—35	1,014	10,284 10	5,400
Sultan Muhd., Gen. Commanding heavy guns.					
1. Bakhtāwarkhan.	165	13*			9,000
2. Muhammad Baksh, Col.	205	12			1,980
3. ——					1,140
		—25*	622	6,673 0	
Illahi Baksh Khān, Gen.					
1. M. Illahi Baksh.	510	18*			4,120
2. Sikandar Khān, son of Illahi Baksh.					
3. Fateh Khān and Lahora Singh.	125 } 120 }	12			
		—30*	1,026	10,842 4	
Amīr Chand, Col.					
Amīr Chand, Col.	0	15			
		—15	400	3,436 0	3,040
Fateh Singh and Mubārak Khān.					
Fateh Singh. Mubārak Khān.	310 } 210 }	21			
		—21*	620	6,237 8	2,580 (made up smaller as signments
Total number of guns		126			

	Rs.	A.	P.
Infantry. Monthly expenditure	4,43,892	14	6
Cavalry. " "	1,62,811	5	0
Artillery. " "	67,030	10	0
GRAND TOTAL:			
(a) Annual land assignment to the military officers	2,02,439	4	0
(b) Cash disbursement	83,69,109	10	0
	85,71,448	14	0
Total number of men, 51,050	15,22,627	9	9
Total number of guns, 230, not including mortars and swivels.			
TOTAL FOR THE YEAR	1,00,94,076	7	9

* Plus one mortar.

APPENDIX XL

THE LAHORE FAMILY

- Nodha.
  - Budha Singh.
    - **Charat Singh.**
      - **Maha Singh.**
        - **Ranjit Singh.** *Dead.*
          - **Kharak Singh.** *Dead.* = **Chandkaur.**
            - Nau Nihāl Singh. *Dead.*
          - **Sher Singh.** *Dead.* *Reputed.*
            - Partap Singh. *Dead.*
            - Sahdev Singh.
            - Bakhshish Singh. *Adopted.*
          - Tāra Singh. *Reputed.*
            - Deva Singh.
          - Kashmira Singh. *Dead.* *Reputed or adopted.*
          - Peshaura Singh. *Dead.*
          - **Dalip Singh.** *Reputed.*
  - Chanda Singh.
    - Didār Singh.
      - Amir Singh. (The Sindhianwala Branch.)
        - Atar Singh. *Dead.*
          - Kehar Singh.
        - Budh Singh. *Dead.*
          - Shamsher Singh.
        - Basawa Singh. *Dead.*
          - Ajit Singh. *Dead.*
          - Ranjor Singh. *Illegitimate.*
        - Lahna Singh. *Dead.*
          - Partap Singh.
          - Thakur Singh.

APPENDIX XLI

THE JAMMU FAMILY

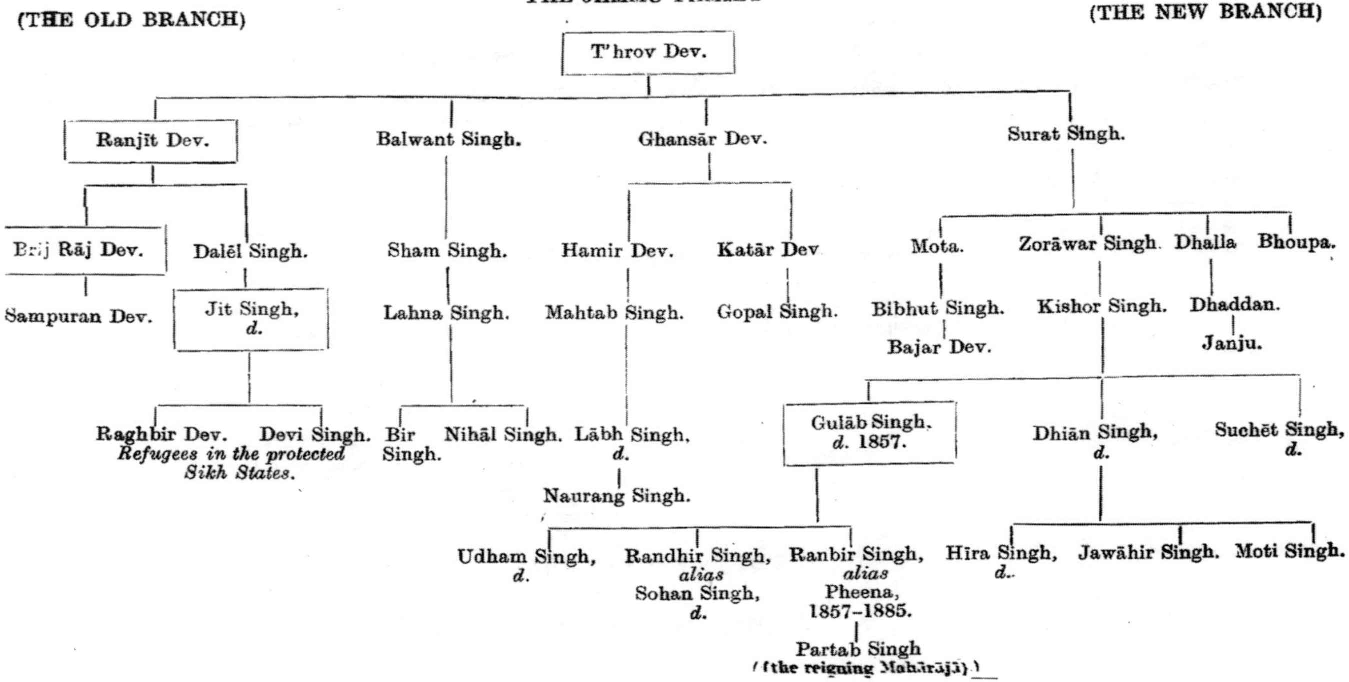

INDEX

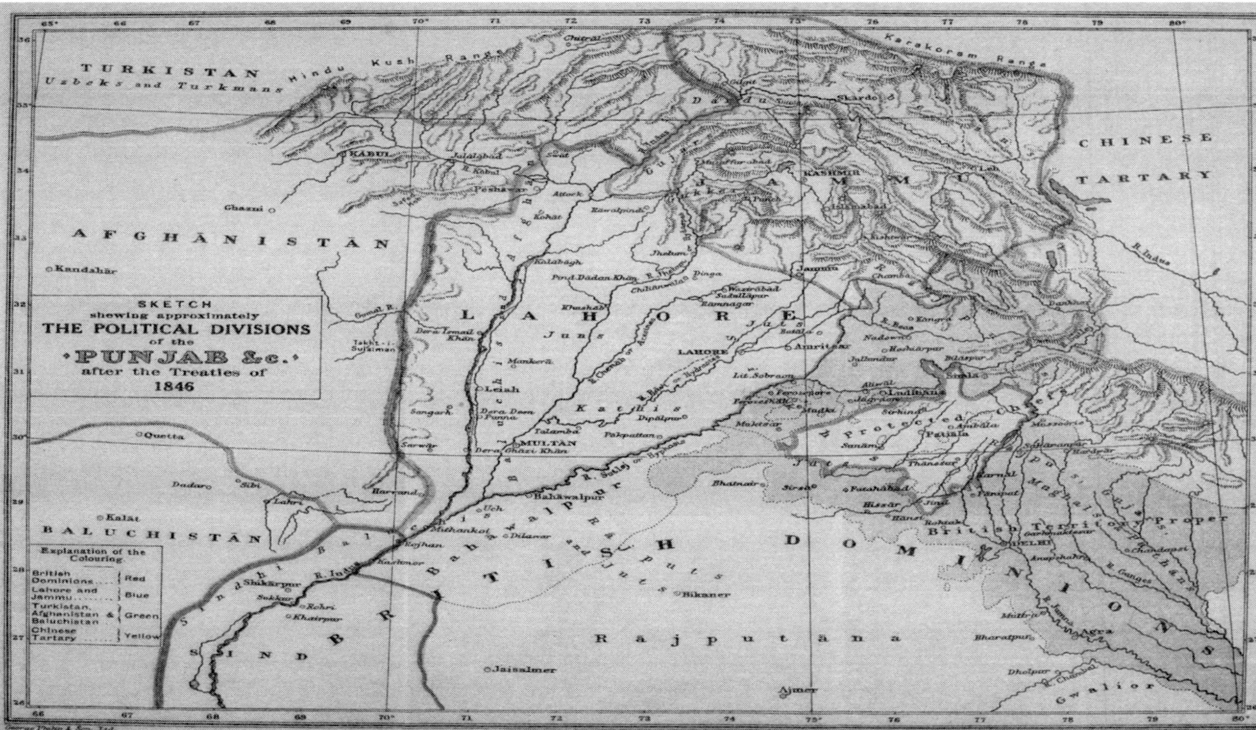
SKETCH
shewing approximately
THE POLITICAL DIVISIONS
of the
PUNJAB &c.
after the Treaties of
1846
Explanation of the Colouring.
British Dominions ... Red
Lahore and Jammu ... Blue
Turkistan, Afghanistan & Baluchistan ... Green
Chinese Tartary ... Yellow
TURKISTAN
Uzbeks and Turkmans
Hindu Kush Range
Karakoram Range
CHINESE
TARTARY
AFGHĀNISTĀN
BALUCHISTĀN
LAHORE
KASHMIR
Kabul
Peshawar
Kandahār
Ghazni
Quetta
Kalat
MULTAN
LAHORE
Amritsar
Jammu
Ludhiana
Ambala
Patiala
Simla
DELHI
Agra
Bahāwalpur
Bikaner
Jaisalmer
Ajmer
Rajputāna
BRITISH DOMINIONS
SIND
R. Indus
R. Sutlej
R. Ganges
R. Jumna
Gwalior
George Philip & Son, Ltd.
The London Geographical Institute